RAVES FOR JAMEY NEWE
THE NEWBERG REF

"Jamey Newberg is the consummate insider. He couples an advanced feel for the game with unparalleled passion and tremendous knowledge of the Texas Rangers' organization. With the Newberg Report, Jamey offers fans expert insight into the players who shape the current core of the Texas Rangers as well as those who will comprise future waves. Jamey's level of detail and accuracy rivals anything that I have ever read about another organization. The Newberg Report is an invaluable reference to baseball fans regardless of one's allegiance."

— Thad Levine, Assistant General Manager, Texas Rangers

"The Newberg Report has grown from being a luxury to a necessity for anyone who wants to follow the Rangers closely from top to bottom."

— Eric Nadel, Radio Play-by-Play Broadcaster, Texas Rangers

"To those of us who work in a world of East Coast and sometimes West Coast bias, Jamey Newberg provides a reminder that there is marvelous world of Rangers fans who are every bit the real baseball fans that grew up in Cohasset, Massachusetts or South Philly. The Newberg Report has become the eyes and ears of those fans."

— Peter Gammons, MLB Network

"Jamey's passion for Texas Rangers baseball is unparalleled, but it's his ability to share that passion, through his words, that makes him so special."

— Kevin Goldstein, Baseball Prospectus

"Over 10 years ago, my debut with the Texas Rangers coincided with my introduction to the Newberg Report. My career started with a pinch-run appearance in Oakland in 2000 and has recently taken me to my first ever post-season, culminating with a trip to the World Series in 2010. All throughout, I've felt support from my family and friends, my teammates, and the Texas Rangers fans—of the fans, none are more die-hard than the Newberg Report faithful. Looking forward to a memorable 2011 and beyond."

— Michael Young, third baseman, Texas Rangers

"After the Rangers' magical ride to the World Series this year, interest has never been higher in this organization. Win or lose, Jamey Newberg's information in his annual report has always been incredibly detailed, marvelous in its depth, solidly written, and a must-read for fans of the Rangers and baseball followers in general."

— Norm Hitzges, Sportsradio 1310 The Ticket

"Jamey Newberg is the Josh Hamilton of team bloggers—multi-tooled and most valuable."

— Jim Callis, Executive Editor, *Baseball America*

"Being a Rangers fan without also simultaneously experiencing the greatness of the Newberg Report is like watching your favorite band in concert while wearing sound-canceling headphones. It is the unspoken way that each Rangers fan returns volley on a claw or antler serve from the team. The Newberg Report is to Rangers baseball what the mustache is to Burt Reynolds, what the lightsaber is to a Jedi, and what Burt Reynolds's mustache would mean to a Jedi. If you're a Rangers fan and you're not following the comprehensive baseball offerings of my friend Jamey Newberg . . . quite simply, you are doing it wrong!"

— Ben Rogers, The Ben & Skin Show, ESPN 103.3 FM

"Obviously the Newberg Report is critical for any serious Rangers fan or DFW sports media folk, but it's Jamey's passion for everything Rangers that has Ben and myself constantly evaluating how we approach what we do. It's some ol' sure shot, #1 spot goodness."

— Jeff "Skin" Wade, The Ben & Skin Show, ESPN 103.3 FM

"From the days of the 'We Are Farm Animals' shirts to the book's annual 40-Man Conundrum, @newbergreport puts you right in the heart of the Rangers."

— C.J. Wilson, starting pitcher and mad tweeter, Texas Rangers

"If you're looking for the passion of a diehard Rangers fan embracing the incredible ride to that first World Series, it's in the Newberg Report. If you're looking for the knowledge of an insider who has worked the back fields at Surprise, Arizona, and seen the future of baseball's best farm system, it's all there in the Newberg Report, too."

— Tim Cowlishaw, Columnist, *Dallas Morning News;*
Panelist, ESPN "Around the Horn"

"Everything I learned about Rangers baseball I learned from Eric Nadel's voice, Charlie Hough's ashtray and Jamey Newberg's reports. They're as invaluable as a mid-season Cliff Lee acquisition. Robin Ventura will have to pry them from my cold, dead hands before I part with one of Jamey's books. And this I say even though in 1982 I'm pretty sure I traded him my George Brett rookie card for a Rollie Fingers double."

— Robert Wilonsky, *Dallas Observer*

"I highly recommend the Newberg Report's 2011 Bound Edition—to live through the great 2010 Rangers season all over again!"

— Jim Sundberg, Senior Executive Vice President, Texas Rangers

"The baseball season is long and the day to day of it is one of the many reasons we love the game . . . these games come quick . . . along the way, things get lost, and things that might seen insignificant at the time often come to hold greater significance, and vice versa. The Newberg Report Bound Edition is a repository for all of it, an invaluable looking glass for bringing into focus why a game, a series, a week, a month, a season turned out as it did . . . and on the heels of this most wonderful season of Rangers baseball, it is more must-have than ever."

— Mike Rhyner, Sportsradio 1310 The Ticket

"If you are a fan of the Texas Rangers, on any level, you will not find a more passionate or comprehensive look at the team than in this Bound Edition of the Newberg Report."

— Ken Rosenthal, Fox Sports

"We all saw the World Series run, and we saw where the core came from: the farm system. Some came via the draft. Others came via trade, but it was the Rangers' player development department that helped them hone their skills. And there are many more on the way who should enable the Rangers to compete for a long time to come. The Newberg Report let everyone know who these guys were before anyone else did and will continue to do so. If you really want to know the who, what, why, when and where of the Texas organization's success, this is a must-have manual."

— Jonathan Mayo, MLB.com

"Jamey Newberg's unique perspective combines informative insight with profound passion, making the 2011 Bound Edition of the Newberg Report the perfect look back at the most magical season in Texas Rangers history."

— Emily Jones, Fox Sports Southwest

"Jamey Newberg's book is an integral part of the information that any baseball fan, and all Rangers fans, need to begin the season. If content is king, Jamey's Texas Rangers information is the castle."

— Michael Durkin, lifelong Texas Rangers fan

"The Newberg Report isn't just indispensable for Rangers fans who want to follow everything about their favorite team, it's must-read content for everyone who needs to know about the rising power of the AL West."

— Christina Kahrl, Baseball Prospectus

"Simply, this is the Bible of of Texas Rangers baseball. It is my ultimate source. I guarantee you no one knows more about the Rangers organization than Jamey Newberg."

— Bob Nightengale, *USA Today*

"This book could be better only if it were about my favorite team."

— Rob Neyer, ESPN

"The Newberg Report is about as up-to-the-minute and personal as you can get if you sleep, eat and breath Rangers baseball. When I was with the club, I would read Jamey's reports and thought there must be six Jamey Newberg's living in each of our clubhouses. There is no one more passionate to let Rangers fans know what is going on, who is hot and who is not, and to provide insightful stories and information that keep you counting the hours to the next ballgame."

— Doug Melvin, General Manager, Milwaukee Brewers

"Jamey Newberg provides great insight from the ultimate fan's perspective."

— Gina Miller, TXA21

"The most powerful memory of my time with the Rangers was the special feeling of connection with the fans. Words inadequately describe the emotions that I still feel about my time in Texas. I applaud Jamey and his team for their amazing contribution to the Rangers community. The Newberg Report transcends the traditional media-based relationship between players and fans. Authenticity, passion and the pure joy of game radiate outward from the details, further instilling the deep grasp that baseball has on our hearts."

— Jeff Zimmerman, former closer, Texas Rangers

The Newberg Report
2011 Bound Edition

Covering the Texas Rangers from Top to Bottom

The Newberg Report
2011 Bound Edition

Covering the Texas Rangers from Top to Bottom

NEWBERGREPORT.COM

BROWN BOOKS
PUBLISHING GROUP

The Newberg Report
2011 Bound Edition

Covering the Texas Rangers from Top to Bottom

Brown Books Publishing Group
16200 North Dallas Parkway, Suite 170
Dallas, Texas 75248
brownbooks.com
(972) 381-0009

A New Era in Publishing.™

ISBN 978-1-934812-94-5
Library of Congress Control Number 2010917469

Printed in the United States of America
10 9 8 7 6 5 4 3 2 1

Cover design by Marty Yawnick (TypeADesign.com)
Book design and layout by Devin Pike (Hype Anvil Media)

Photographs courtesy of:
FRONT COVER: Jim Cowsert/Texas Rangers
BACK COVER: McCall Money (Lee, Feliz); Scott Lucas (Perez)

NewbergReport.com

For Mandy
This is your year

TABLE OF CONTENTS

Foreword by Chuck Greenberg

I spent much of the summer of 2009 hanging around the Metroplex, trying to get a feel for the community, their attitude towards the Rangers and a sense of what might be possible under new ownership. I spent hours upon hours speaking with waitresses, cab drivers, moms, dads, flight attendants, people in restaurants, bars, hotel lobbies . . . you name it, I tried to pick their brains. No one had any idea who I was or why I was asking all of these questions. I recall having a vague sense that there was something called the Newberg Report, but I wasn't sure what exactly it was, or who this Newberg character was anyway?

One day in September, near the end of a rainy, gloomy homestand, I was in the stands at Rangers Ballpark speaking with Machelle Noel, who works in the Rangers IT Department, and who, in an amazing coincidence, had been one of my favorite front office colleagues at my first minor league team in Altoona, Pennsylvania, when a video popped up on the roof of the homerun porch with a report from Jamey Newberg on the Rangers farm system. Machelle told me about Jamey and said his report was essential for Rangers fans. I signed up on the spot and was immediately hooked.

As our efforts to purchase the Rangers intensified throughout the fall, I eagerly read each of Jamey's reports every day. When Jamie Adams sent a welcome package to my wife a couple of months later, he included a copy of the Newberg Report's 2009 Bound Edition. Although by this time we were consumed round the clock in our efforts to try to complete the sale (of course, little did I know at the time that our "final push" would go on for another nine months), I read portions of the Bound Edition every chance I had.

From the moment I first read Jamey's reports, I was blown away by the passion and love that so clearly fueled his efforts. When combined with his uncommon intelligence, writing skills, energy, and apparent aversion to a good night's sleep, Jamey, along with his extraordinary team of dedicated collaborators, is a resource of immeasurable value and enjoyment for all who care about the Rangers.

After first being announced as the chosen purchaser of the Rangers on December 15, 2009, our group finally signed the actual agreement to purchase the franchise on January 23, 2010. A few days later, I made my first "public" appearance at a Newberg Report event at Sherlock's. I was anticipating an intimate little crowd where we all might sit around a few tables and enjoy some informal conversation. Instead, I walked into a packed house, with Ted Price set up to podcast the event, Chuck Morgan emceeing, Michael Young participating in a Q&A, and a rousing charity auction to benefit the Carson Leslie Foundation.

The excitement and sense of anticipation in the room was incredibly energizing, and reinforced what I had come to believe many months earlier—that the Rangers were a great success story just waiting to happen. That night, I said that I felt the Rangers were a sleeping giant, and that it would be fun for all of us to share in awakening the beast. I also said that I understood how long and patiently Rangers fans had been waiting for the level of success that had previously eluded the franchise, and that the wait would merely make the taste of champagne that much sweeter when we would all share it together.

I meant and believed every word of it. I also meant to tell everyone that night that Jon Daniels would outmaneuver the Yankees to acquire Cliff Lee, that Neftali Feliz would set a rookie save record, that Josh Hamilton would hit over .400 for months at a time, that C.J. Wilson would become a dominant starter, that the Rangers would not only win the division, but defeat Tampa in a decisive fifth game on the road in the ALDS, then beat up on the Yankees in the ALCS, then appear in their first World Series, that attendance would skyrocket to 2.5 million—including an average of nearly 40,000 per game after the All-Star Break, that players would make claw and antler gestures on the field and inspire fans to attend games with antlers glued to their heads, that we would finally acquire the franchise seven longs months later, but only after a no-holds-barred shootout in an auction in bankruptcy court of all places, and a bunch of other things too . . . but I forgot.

To say this has been an extraordinary year would be quite an understatement. The most meaningful thing for me is to know just how much this year has meant to millions of people, young and old, from all walks of life and backgrounds, who have awaited this day for so long. I receive hundreds of emails and letters every day from fans who want to share their suggestions and ideas for the franchise, which we invite and welcome, but also to share their emotions. I have heard from fans who rediscovered their love of baseball this year, who found baseball to be a source of comfort and joy following the loss of a loved one, who reconnected with a long-estranged parent through their mutual love of baseball, and on and on. It is inspiring and humbling to be a part of something that has resonated with so many people in so many ways.

Jamey Newberg embodies the passion and the hopes that Rangers fans had been waiting to realize, unfulfilled, for 39 years. As the season progressed so successfully, the pride and excitement when Jamey would write of his satisfaction at being able to focus at last on meaningful events at the Major League level late in the season was palpable. The fears he manifested upon temporary setbacks in the ALDS and ALCS accurately reflected the emotional scars formed from the years of disappointment. The pure joy in his writing following victory in Games Five and Six of the ALDS and ALCS, respectively, spoke for generations of Rangers fans, new and old.

Over the past year, Jamey has gone from an invaluable and enjoyable resource to a good friend and sounding board. Many among his legion of followers and subscribers have become advisors as well, enthusiastically and regularly sharing their opinions as to how we can best serve the true owners of the Rangers—our fans.

As I said that night back in January, the very best days for all of us who love the Rangers lie ahead. We have shared in a series of glorious moments in the year just passed, and everyone in the Rangers organization is committed to creating more wonderful memories in 2011 and beyond. No matter where the road takes us, Jamey Newberg and his team will be there to chronicle on a daily basis the ups, downs, and everything in between of our present and our future.

Oh and there is one other thing I forgot to mention back in January at Sherlock's . . . that the champagne would taste sweet . . . but the ginger ale would taste even sweeter.

— Chuck Greenberg
Managing Partner and CEO
Texas Rangers

Foreword by Brad Sham

It's not plagiarism if you have the same idea as someone else independently, at the same time. Is it?

I hope not, because I don't like the idea-stealing business. But obviously I'm not the first to think of "passion" and "Jamey Newberg" in the same sentence. (Besides his wife. Talk about outkicking your coverage.)

Here's how I was going to start this foreword:

There is no substitute for passion. If you have it, it fuels you. It defeats fatigue. It neutralizes boredom. It adds hours to the day. And if you do anything in public, you can't function without it. If you don't have it, your audience sees right through you, but if you do, it engenders trust.

Jamey Newberg and the Newberg Report are not primarily about baseball. They're about passion. A passion for baseball, and, just as important, a passion for the Texas Rangers.

That's where I was going. Then I went back and read the 20 forewords from the past 10 Bound Editions. Jamey's passion and commitment and connection with all the rest of you . . . us . . . Rangers fans . . . have been recognized by past writers, repeatedly.

So I can't claim original thought. But like the 2010 Rangers, I ain't backin' off either. As Wash might say, you write what the piece asks you to write.

In addition to everything else, Jamey Newberg is a generous and patient editor. When he asked me to do this in late August, he said he liked to have the foreword in by mid October. Sometime between Game Two and Cliff Lee of the ALDS with the Rays, I asked permission to wait until that series was over.

At 2-1 in the ALCS, I knew I was waiting until *that* was over. I didn't ask permission. I think he knew.

It is an honor almost beyond my vocabulary to be asked to contribute to this volume. While some of you are wondering why a longtime football announcer is taking up space in the most special Bound Edition after the most special Rangers season ever, Jamey knows that when you cut me, a baseball fan bleeds.

It would have been an honor just to write the second foreword with Chuck Greenberg, who with Nolan Ryan and Jon Daniels have given generations of Rangers fans something they've never had, and something many of them thought they'd never get.

But contributing to THIS book gives me a chance to be a fan, to reflect on what it means to have the Texas Rangers play in the World Series in Arlington, Texas.

There are a handful of us who were at Ted Williams's first news conference as Rangers manager, who got to talk baseball with broadcasters Bill Mercer and Don Drysdale at the first spring training in Pompano Beach, who remember the news conference where Bob Short fired Whitey Herzog to hire Billy Martin, who were at the David Clyde game, who hung out with rookies Jim Sundberg and Toby Harrah and Mike Hargrove, who covered Jeff Burroughs and Joe Lovitto and Fergie Jenkins and Rico Carty and Buddy Bell and Eddie Stanky's one day as manager, who remember Jim Panther and Piggy Suarez, Charlie Hough and the Emu, Tom Grieve as a home run hitter, Jim Bibby's no-hitter and Kenny Rogers's perfect game. There are a handful of us, but only that.

But the constant through all that, from Frank Howard's first Ranger home run to the '95 All-Star Game to the playoffs in the late '90s to this, to THE WORLD SERIES, is you. The constant is Ranger fans who for 38 years have bought tickets and T-shirts and jerseys, and who for these last years have been treated to one of us finding a way to pour emotion and passion and knowledge and a reporter's and attorney's mind into a daily recounting of the mini-lifetime that is a baseball season, day by day.

This is the most special Bound Edition because it only happens to be about baseball. This is more about hope and dreams and what's possible, success by pratfall. Someday when Max Newberg goes to his loving father and expresses worry and an absence of optimism about a class, a teacher, a relationship, a job, Dad can pull out this book and sit down with Max and go day by day. He can show Max how baseball is a metaphor for life, how if Wash and Josh and C.J. and Nolan and Chuck could overcome what they did to bring the TEXAS RANGERS TO THE WORLD SERIES, why, son, we can figure out a way through this, too.

There is nothing anywhere like the Newberg Report to chronicle every twist and turn, mostly because there is no one like Jamey Newberg.

No matter how many World Series the Rangers reach and win, none will be like the season and the postseason of 2010, ever. This is the first. This is where the mountain was climbed. Savor these pages, enjoy it forever, and thanks for letting me join you.

— Brad Sham
Dallas Cowboys Radio Network
Texas Rangers Radio 1995-97

PREFACE

A good friend gave me one of those "thought that counts" birthday gifts this year. He'd been in Vegas and came back at the end of February having purchased two pieces of paper, each about the size of a post-it note.

On one, just over the bar code, it said: "ODDS TO WIN 2010 WORLD SERIES—RANGERS—25/1." On the other: "ODDS TO WIN 2010 AL CHAMPION—RANGERS—15/1."

A pretty cool idea, I thought. Sort of like a lottery ticket. A pack of 1980 Topps that *just might* have a rookie Rickey inside. A box top promise of the biggest prize.

Still, baseball optimist that I am, I figured the vouchers were at least a year premature. My half-full-glass notion was that the 2010 Rangers could be the 1991 Cowboys, with 1992 coming into view over the horizon.

Packrat that I am, I didn't throw the two scraps into the trash.

As it turned out, Rangers fans got the 1991 Cowboys in 2010—and, for the most part, 1992.

We, as Rangers fans, are a loyal and resilient bunch, but admit it: The DNA has long included a defense mechanism (perhaps necessarily so) that had us expecting, somewhere along the line, that Lucy would pull the football back. It always happened. But we always lined back up for the next kick, because that's what we do. *That's the way being a Rangers fan goes.*

If I had to sit here, right now, and write a book (or, I'm here to confess, a preface) trying to capture the drama and the meaning and the emotion and the *implausibility* of the 2010 Texas Rangers season, I couldn't do it. Fortunately for me (and, my hope is, for you), I tried to convey those things day by day, week by week, thrill by gut punch, in the Newberg Report, and in these pages that organic, often surreal story is gathered and told.

The 2011 Bound Edition of the Newberg Report takes you from mid-October 2009, as plans for the 2010 season were underway in Arlington while eight other teams played on, through November 3, 2010, hours after the Major League Baseball season ended . . . on the field at Rangers Ballpark in Arlington. I could list a bunch of bullet points running down the highlights and key moments of those 12 and a half months, on the field and off of it, but that would add another five pages to this book (which, unlike any of the first 11 Bound Editions, already exceeds 400 pages).

There are the Bound Edition staples in this book, too. The Top 72 Prospects list, a rundown of the best tools in the system, the predictions on breakout minor leaguers for 2011, the 40-Man Roster Conundrum, and so on. But the main story line in this year's book was staged in Arlington.

There's never been a Texas Rangers season like this one. That much is obvious.

There will never be another one like it, either.

Whether this team goes on to win three titles in four years like the early 90s Cowboys did, or comes back to the pack like the 2005-06 Mavericks did, we as Rangers fans will never experience another baseball season like 2010, which was a culmination and validation of so many things, a surging dose of pain relief decades in the making, highlighted by the moment depicted on the front cover of this book, captured seconds after Alex Rodriguez, of all people, watched strike three sail by.

The final goal was not met, but the way this team has been built, and with the promise that its way of doing business is about to change as well, there's an exploding fan base that feels as good about the Rangers' future as it did about 2010.

Both Chuck Greenberg and Brad Sham used the words "hope" and "passion" in their forewords for this book. Those are two things a lot of us have invested in this franchise, some for months and others for decades, and in 2010 we started getting paid back.

I'm grateful to Chuck and to Brad for agreeing to write the forewords, and for what they said in them. I can't put into words how fortunate I think we are to have those two doing what they do in this market, but I think you all already know. Professionally, they're exactly what you want. On a personal level, they're every bit of that, too.

The list of people to thank in this space grows every year. Start with the book itself. Marty Yawnick (the cover) and Devin Pike (everything else) are Neftali Feliz. You just put the ball in their hands to seal the deal, and count on the win. But closers don't get it done alone, and the photography of Brad Newton, Jim Cowsert (the front cover shot: wow), Scott Lucas, McCall Money, Jason Cole, and Tracy Proffitt was integral to the result as well.

Scott's written work is not in this book, but it's in your e-mailbox every morning for six months and then some, and his coverage of everything—*everything*—that happens with this organization in player development helps us frame the big picture as far as the foundation for the Rangers' success is concerned. He's one helluva writer, and a friend.

The foundation of my friendship with Eleanor Czajka is Texas Rangers baseball, and I'm very happy for her that this season happened. Her vision for the Newberg Report, especially in the early years, was an inspiration that continues to push the project forward.

Ted Price can do anything. Jamie Adams, too.

I think Cynthia Stillar and Jessica Kinkel of Brown Books Publishing Group would probably admit they didn't expect our meeting 14 months ago to involve much more than cordial advice on how I could make the self-publishing process work better. I'm grateful that they saw enough potential in this project to want to be part of it, and like I said a year ago, that ISBN stamp on the back cover of the book is way up there on the list of things about the Newberg Report that I'm most proud of.

Thank you to Don Titus and Ed Coffin and Chris Barnes for another year of managing the website and the mailing list.

Steve Richardson (Arlington) and Marcus White (Dallas) and their crews at Sherlock's Baker St. Pub & Grill know how to throw a party. There's a reason we keep coming back. Thanks to Eleanor, Baseball Mom Toni, Devin, Ted, Scott, Norma Wolfson, Caroline Ryan, Sean Decker, and the Toys and Tots folks for helping, and Chuck Greenberg, Chuck Morgan, Ben Rogers, Jeff "Skin" Wade, Thad Levine, Jake Krug, Michael Young and Cristina Barbosa, Ian and Tess Kinsler, Rusty Greer, Tommy Hunter, Derek Holland, Scott Feldman, Chris Davis, and Annette Leslie for appearing at the four Sherlock's events we had in the last 12 months. We raised over $12,000 at the second book release party last year for Wipe Out Kids' Cancer, and you all should be proud of that.

Thanks to Mitch Moreland, Max Ramirez, Zach Phillips, Eric Hurley, Tanner Scheppers, Brandon Boggs, Kasey Kiker, Ben Snyder, Justin Smoak, and Blake Beavan for joining us at the Newberg Report set-up at Rangers Fan Fest last January.

Thanks to Jon Daniels, Kevin Goldstein, plus Eleanor, Cindy and Jeff Kuster, Luther Davis, Allen Cordrey, Pat Payton, Norma and George and Ryan Wolfson, Jim Hess of Leapfrog Executive Search, and John Demcher of OSAR Consulting for making this year's Newberg Report Night event at Rangers Ballpark the best one yet—not to mention every one of you who attended and helped us raise more than $12,000 on that night for Genesis Women's Shelter and the Hello Win Column Fund.

Along those lines, if it seems to you like Newberg Report Night gets to be a smoother operation each year (like it does to me), that's because of folks with the Rangers like Rob Matwick, Paige

Farragut, Paul Morrow, Chris Bielinski, Taunee Taylor, Heather King, Delia Willms, the great Chuck Morgan, and Sherry Flow.

The overwhelming support from everyone I've come across in the Rangers organization is something I'm super-grateful for. Aside from those I just mentioned, there's Nolan Ryan, Jon Daniels, Jim Sundberg, John Blake, Kellie Fischer, Rick George, and Jay Miller. Thad Levine, A.J. Preller, Don Welke, Scott Servais, Kipp Fagg, Josh Boyd, Jake Krug, Mike Daly, Bobby Crook, Matt Klotsche, Ron Hopkins, Danny Clark, Mike Boulanger, John Hart, Keith Boeck, Mike Grouse, Chris Lyngos, Hoggy Price, Mike LaCassa, and Joey Prebynski. Rich Rice, Angie Swint, Court Berry-Tripp, Brian SanFilippo, and Ashleigh Greathouse. Katie Crawford. Karin Morris, Kelly Calvert, Rush Olson, Hugo Carbajal, Kaylan Eastepp, and Diane Atkinson. Barbara Pappenfus, Karen Gallini, Courtney West, Leslie Dempsey, Gabrielle Stokes, Judy Southworth, and Jenny Martin Terrell. Terry Turner, Kate Jett, Brendan Marsh, and Kathy Price. Jamie Reed and Dr. Keith Meister. Grady Raskin, Rose Swenson, Mike Lentz, Breon Dennis, Troy King, Ryan Hoopes, and, as always, the inspiring Brad Newton. Tom Hicks, too, and Tommy, Alex, and Mack, Dale Petroskey, Andy Silverman, Chip Kisabeth, and the energizing Wayne Kirby.

I'm also indebted to Round Rock's Reid Ryan and Reese Ryan, George King, Mike Capps, Larry Little, and Tim Jackson. Reid and Reese's mother Ruth. Frisco's Aaron Goldsmith, Reese Gordon, and Jordan Roberts. Hickory's Mark Seaman and Andrew Buchbinder. Spokane's Joseph Siemandel. Michael Byrnes moves on from Frisco to Oklahoma City, and lots of folks with the RedHawks, and the Bakersfield Blaze, will be missed.

Scott and I look forward to working with Scotty Brown and the folks with the Myrtle Beach Pelicans.

Rick Weintraub, Harry Davis (who, with Craig Rothmeier, hosts the excellent "Sports Section" show on the Reading & Radio Resource network), and Gretchen Stark have capably led the Season Ticket Holder Advisory Board that I've been glad to be part of.

Thanks to Ryan Tatusko for two years of giving us a glimpse into the life of a minor leaguer, particularly one who turned himself from an organizational soldier into a prospect, in his "Back Field Diaries." Hope he gets the chance to pitch to Pudge Rodriguez in a game that counts in 2011.

Cliff Lee. Cliff Lee. Cliff Lee.

Cliff Lee.

Rally Minka.

Thanks to many in the local media for the support, starting with the great Eric Nadel and including Tom Grieve, Dave Barnett, T.R. Sullivan, Evan Grant, Jeff Wilson, Anthony Andro, Richard Durrett, Gil LeBreton, Jim Reeves, Tim Cowlishaw, Celia Barshop, Bryan Dolgin, Ted Nichols-Payne, Mike Disen, Chris Schneider, the aforementioned Ben & Skin, Mike Rhyner, Bob Sturm, Dan McDowell, Norm Hitzges, Sean Bass, Danny Balis, Corby Davidson, Mike Sirois, Dana Larson, Emily Jones, John Rhadigan, Ric Renner, Ben Rebstock, Newy Scruggs, Richie Whitt, Robert Wilonsky, Gina Miller, Joe Trahan, George Riba, Josh Harvey, and Eleno Ornelas. Josh Lewin was always a great help, and he'll be missed.

On a national level, the list includes Peter Gammons, Kevin Goldstein, Will Carroll, Joe Sheehan, Christina Kahrl, Jim Callis, John Manuel, Conor Glassey, Jonathan Mayo, Ken Davidoff, Rob Neyer, Ken Rosenthal, Jon Heyman, Bob Nightengale, Jayson Stark, John Sickels, Tim Dierkes, Bryan Curtis, and others.

I bounce things off Rangers bloggers Joey Matschulat, Jason Parks, Adam Morris, and Jason Cole from time to time, and off Mike Hindman and my brother Barry, too. All solid baseball brains.

So is LaDonna Sampsell, another of the longtime Rangers fans I first think of after a season like this.

Thanks to all the folks who provided the very flattering tip-in quotes at the front of this book.

I'll never be able to thank Judy Campos enough.

It took 11 years of the Newberg Report for the mailing list to grow to a subscriber base of 7,000. Then, in the last 13 months, it surged to 10,000. Appreciate that. A lot.

I don't delude myself into thinking that the flood of new readers had anything to do with my uber-keen baseball insights, good looks, or questionable grasp on the proper subject matter for a series of haiku. It was, obviously, the captivating, compelling, invigorating Rangers season that grabbed all of us, gave us moments with family and friends that we'll never forget and cost us sleep, and made one of those scraps of paper from Las Vegas pay off.

It was the year when, at long last, Lucy didn't pull the ball back. We—and yes, this felt like "*we*"—got the kick away. It had the distance. It hit the upright, granted, but we got the damn ball airborne.

There will be more kicks at this. Soon.

I can't wait for the first chance to go at it again, as Spring Training 2011 approaches. One reason, among plenty of others, is that baseball, Texas Rangers baseball, managed to become more important this year to the people most important to me. My wife Ginger and our kids Erica and Max and I never shared baseball season the way we did in 2010, an experience that I'm sure every one of you had with people close to you as well, and that's something I'm really thankful for, and looking forward to sharing again.

This is a team of character and resilience, mental toughness and heart, and as a baseball fan and as a parent, those things—along with a season that doesn't end until November—are pretty easy to get behind and share.

Thank you all for letting me share this one with you.

—J.D.N.

PROSPECT RANKINGS

I'm not going to lie to you. This section is shorter this year than it has been in the past. Part of the reason is that the six-week period between the end of the season and going to print was shortened, *gloriously*, to just two weeks this year.

Thematically, it makes some sense anyway, as this year's book primarily tells a story that was no longer about a top-ranked farm system and a carefully mapped-out five-step plan, but instead about a big league season that those things had been building toward, for years.

That's not to say that the farm system carries any less importance now than it did before. For one, you can look at last year's Top 72 list and find 15 players who contributed to the Rangers' World Series club, either as players or as components to trades that brought big league players in. The front office talks constantly about the pipeline and making sure there are waves of prospects coming, and as long as this management team is in place, that will always be at the foundation of how this club goes about its business of building and maintaining a contender.

We've talked frequently about how the nine franchises whose farm systems were ranked number one by *Baseball America* before the Rangers earned that nod in 2009 each made the playoffs in short order (within an average of two seasons, in fact). Texas made it 10 straight this year. It's the proper way to build a winner, and even in a season like this one, I'll never neglect the job that this organization is doing in the minor leagues.

Even though a number of the Rangers' 2010 prospects made it to the big leagues this year, and another 10 were traded in July, the farm system remains loaded. In *Baseball America*'s season-ending rankings of the top 20 prospects in each of the minor leagues, from rookie ball up to AAA and based on consultation with league managers and pro scouts, Texas had 18 players show up on at least one of the lists. No other organization had more than 15.

What follows is my assessment of the top 72 prospects in a system that remains among baseball's best, starting with a straight ranking of the players and followed by comments, by position, on all 72 of them.

As far as the measure for the ranking is concerned, what is it? Should it be based strictly on players' performance from the last season? Or purely on potential? Or on some amorphous combination of the two? How are you really supposed to judge Jorge Alfaro against Joe Wieland? Roman Mendez against Mike Olt? There's not an easily defined, objective measure. Which will drive a lawyer crazy.

So here's the test I'm applying in order to rank the Rangers' top 72 prospects:

Who would I least want to see in an Angels or A's uniform?

Posed another way: One of those teams suffers a teamwide outbreak of something really nasty and permanent, and the league orders the equivalent of an expansion draft to start restocking that club. Who is the first player (that still has rookie status) that I protect? The second? And so on.

Or: I'm on the doorstep of making a huge, legacy-defining trade with one of those teams, and I have to put one more prospect in the deal. Oakland tells me I can choose between two players: Pedro Strop or Miguel Velazquez. Craig Gentry or Jake Brigham. Zach Phillips or Teodoro Martinez. Which player would give me a bigger stomach ache to lose to a division rival? In answering that question I decide, unscientifically, how to slot these guys.

Here's the Top 72 list, followed by write-ups on every one of the ranked players.

Top 72 Texas Rangers Prospects

The primary criterion for this list is that the player goes into 2011 with rookie eligibility, which is why players like Mitch Moreland and Alexi Ogando don't show up, but Pedro Strop and Guillermo Moscoso do.

A player loses his rookie status one he reaches one of three thresholds: 130 big league at-bats, 50 big league innings pitched, or 45 days (not including September or October) on an active big league roster. Example: Ogando's 41.2 innings with Texas didn't meet the workload criterion, but he accumulated 80 pre-September days in the big leagues. So he's no longer a rookie, and he's not on this list.

Free agents at the time I went to print (such as Michael Schlact and Kevin Richardson) were not considered.

1. Martin Perez, LHP
2. Tanner Scheppers, RHP
3. Jurickson Profar, SS
4. Engel Beltre, OF
5. Robbie Erlin, LHP
6. Michael Kirkman, LHP
7. Luis Sardinas, SS
8. Robbie Ross, LHP
9. David Perez, RHP
10. Wilmer Font, RHP
11. Jake Skole, OF
12. Jorge Alfaro, C
13. Fabio Castillo, RHP
14. Joe Wieland, RHP
15. Matt Thompson, RHP
16. Luke Jackson, RHP
17. Christian Villanueva, 3B
18. Miguel De Los Santos, LHP
19. Mike Olt, 3B
20. Omar Beltre, RHP
21. Roman Mendez, RHP
22. Leury Garcia, SS
23. Miguel Velazquez, OF
24. Eric Hurley, RHP
25. Pedro Strop, RHP
26. Kellin Deglan, C
27. Jared Hoying, OF
28. Cody Buckel, RHP
29. Hanser Alberto, SS
30. Neil Ramirez, RHP
31. Tomas Telis, C
32. Zach Phillips, LHP
33. Justin Grimm, RHP
34. Teodoro Martinez, OF
35. Drew Robinson, IF-OF
36. Wilfredo Boscan, RHP
37. Odubel Herrera, 2B-SS
38. Jake Brigham, RHP
39. Craig Gentry, OF
40. Cody Eppley, RHP
41. Jose Felix, C
42. Chad Bell, LHP
43. Carlos Pimentel, RHP
44. Tommy Mendonca, 3B
45. Chris McGuiness, 1B
46. Kennil Gomez, RHP
47. Corey Young, LHP
48. Chad Tracy, 1B
49. Guillermo Moscoso, RHP
50. Kasey Kiker, LHP
51. Richard Alvarez, RHP
52. Josh Richmond, OF
53. Ovispo De Los Santos, RHP
54. Carlos Melo, RHP
55. Jordan Akins, OF
56. Trevor Hurley, RHP
57. Leonel De Los Santos, C
58. Danny Gutierrez, RHP
59. Geuris Grullon, LHP
60. Chris Hanna, LHP
61. Jimmy Reyes, LHP
62. Marcus Lemon, 2B-OF
63. Ruben Sierra Jr., OF
64. Randol Rojas, RHP
65. Ryan Strausborger, OF
66. Cristian Santana, OF
67. Shawn Blackwell, RHP
68. Mark Hamburger, RHP
69. David Paisano, OF
70. Joseph Ortiz, LHP
71. Tyler Tufts, RHP
72. Beau Jones, LHP

2010 Minor League Player of the Year
Mitch Moreland
2010 Minor League Pitcher of the Year
Michael Kirkman

Best Minor League Tools

Best Hitter for Average	Jurickson Profar, Jared Hoying, Drew Robinson
Best Raw Power	Mike Olt, Cristian Santana, Chad Tracy
Best Strike-Zone Discipline	Chris McGuiness, Johnny Whittleman
Best Plate Coverage	Chris McGuiness, Tomas Telis
Best Bat Control	Jurickson Profar, Luis Sardinas, Hanser Alberto
Best Bunter	Craig Gentry
Best Fastball	Tanner Scheppers, Wilmer Font, Luke Jackson, Fabio Castillo, Ovispo De Los Santos
Best Cutter	Robbie Ross, Geuris Grullon
Best Sinker	Richard Bleier, Omar Beltre, Robbie Ross
Best Curveball	Robbie Erlin, Tanner Scheppers, Martin Perez, Matt Thompson, Cody Buckel
Best Slider	Michael Kirkman, Robbie Ross, Pedro Strop
Best Changeup	Miguel De Los Santos, Martin Perez, Carlos Pimentel, Wilfredo Boscan
Best Control	Robbie Erlin, Richard Bleier
Best Command	Robbie Erlin, Wilfredo Boscan
Best Life	Roman Mendez, Geuris Grullon, Kennil Gomez, Guillermo Moscoso
Best Lefty Relief Specialist	Corey Young, Zach Phillips, Ben Snyder
Best Pickoff Move	Zach Phillips, Mike Ballard
Best Defensive Catcher	Jose Felix, Jorge Alfaro
Best Defensive 1B	Chris McGuiness
Best Defensive 2B	Santiago Chirino
Best Defensive SS	Luis Sardinas
Best Defensive 3B	Mike Olt, Christian Villanueva
Best Defensive Outfielder	Craig Gentry, David Paisano, Engel Beltre
Best Defensive Pitcher	Robbie Erlin, Pedro Strop, Mike Ballard
Best Catcher Arm	Leonel "Macumba" De Los Santos, Jorge Alfaro
Best Infield Arm	Leury Garcia
Best Infield Range	Leury Garcia
Best Outfield Arm	Craig Gentry, Guillermo Pimentel, David Paisano
Best Outfield Range	Engel Beltre, Craig Gentry
Fastest Baserunner	Leury Garcia, Luis Sardinas, Teodoro Martinez, Craig Gentry, Ryan Strausborger, Jordan Akins
Best Baserunner	Craig Gentry, Jared Hoying
Most Exciting Player	Jurickson Profar, Engel Beltre
Best Athlete	Jake Skole, Jared Hoying, Jordan Akins, Teodoro Martinez
Best Athlete (Pitcher)	Pedro Strop
Best Makeup (Position Player)	Jurickson Profar
Best Makeup (Pitcher)	Robbie Erlin
Best Manager Prospect	Steve Buechele, Jayce Tingler
Best Future Manager Prospect	Vin DiFazio, Jared Prince, Jhonny Gomez

Starting Pitchers

Martin Perez, LHP

The 5-8, 5.96 Frisco record was unimpressive, but Perez began the 2010 season as the youngest pitcher in the Texas League and finished it with a brilliant playoff effort, holding Midland to one run on two hits over six innings, fanning seven, reminding us what Texas has here. Although he issued an uncharacteristic 50 walks in 99.2 regular season innings, the lefthander struck out 101 and induced more outs on the ground than in the air. But he only went as much as five innings eight times all year, and for the first time in his career seemed to have a number of nights when he couldn't repeat his delivery and his stuff didn't play up. Strike one was huge for Perez, as he held opponents to a .167/.167/.229 slash line when ahead in the count, while he was tuned up at a .403/.576/.580 clip when down in the count. Despite Perez's struggles in 2010, it's important to remember that he's still only 19 years old, and his fastball-curve-change mix makes him one of baseball's top southpaw prospects (and in fact *Baseball America*'s number two pitching prospect in the Texas League based on season-ending input from league managers and scouts, despite the year's performance). He's sure to be the first player asked about by any club shopping a frontline starting pitcher to Texas over the next year.

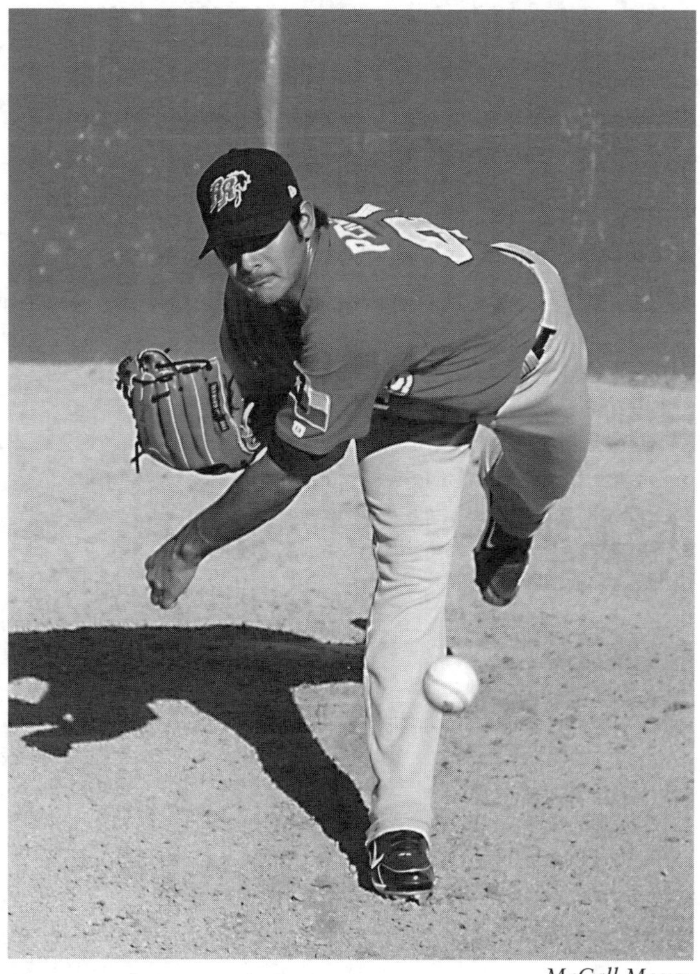

McCall Money

Robbie Erlin, LHP

In what was virtually his first pro action out of high school (he'd thrown four innings after signing as the Rangers' third-round pick in 2009), Erlin was sensational, challenged with an aggressive assignment to Low A Hickory (pitching all year at age 19) and dominating the South Atlantic League from start to finish. The short lefthander led the 14-team league in ERA (2.12—the third-lowest starters' ERA in the minor leagues in 2010) and hits plus walks per inning (0.92), and his opponents' average of .213 was second-stingiest in the circuit. Erlin, who works in the low 90s and adds a plus curve and solid change, struck out 125 while issuing only 17 walks in 114.2 innings, a ratio that's nearly Cliff Lee-esque in its awesomeness. Based on input from Sally League managers and scouts, *Baseball America* ranked Erlin as the circuit's number five prospect after the season, and the publication made him a Second-Team selection on its overall Minor League All-Star Team.

Michael Kirkman, LHP

After jumping back onto the radar in 2009, Kirkman took another huge step forward in 2010, ending the season pitching key innings out of the Rangers bullpen and landing on the club's World Series staff. As a AAA starter, the 23-year-old was leading the Pacific Coast League in strikeouts (130 in 131 innings) when he was summoned to Texas in mid-August, and he ended up second in the league in both ERA (3.09) and wins (13) and was first in opponents' batting average (.235), all of which led to PCL Pitcher of the Year honors. Kirkman projects as a big league starter, though he may continue to work in relief in the spring, depending on what else Texas does in the off-season to put its bullpen together. A key for him will be to harness control of the fastball, which eluded him at times late in the season. Locating that pitch would make his slider—ranked by *BA* as the best breaking pitch in the 16-team PCL in 2010—even more effective against big league hitters.

Robbie Ross, LHP

The diminutive lefty had a sensational season, winning eight games in the first half for Low A Hickory and earning a promotion to High A Bakersfield. Ross's ERA bulged from 2.59 to 5.37 and his opponents' batting average rose from .245 to .305 at the higher level, but his strikeouts also jumped from 5.9 per nine innings to 8.5 per nine, and his groundout-to-flyout rate, an outstanding 2.64 with the Crawdads, was an extraordinary 3.20 with the Blaze. Ross, who features a tremendous power sinker, possesses a unique ability to miss bats while keeping the ball on the ground, and he's been doing it against older competition.

David Perez, RHP

The 17-year-old Perez starred for the Rangers' dominant Dominican Summer League team this season, posting a 4-4, 1.41 record in 13 starts, striking out 62 and walking only eight in 64 innings, limiting opponents to a .202 batting average and keeping the ball on the ground (2.38 groundout-to-flyout rate, zero home runs allowed). Signed in July 2009 for a reported $425,000, Perez works in the low 90s but his lanky 6'5" frame projects for more, and he already shows a feel for spinning the ball. Remarkably, he allowed one run in his final 45 innings this summer (including six scoreless, two-hit innings in his one playoff start), scattering 20 hits and four walks in that stretch while punching out 42. Remember this name.

FULL-SEASON STARTING PITCHER OF THE YEAR FIVE YEARS AGO

1. Thomas Diamond
2. John Danks
3. Edinson Volquez
4. Eric Hurley
5. Juan Dominguez
6. C.J. Wilson
7. Josh Rupe
8. Michael Schlact
9. Ricardo Rodriguez
10. A.J. Murray

Wilmer Font, RHP

The big righthander had flashes of brilliance in 2010, a season during which he was promoted from Low A to High A before his 20th birthday. In the three starts he made for Bakersfield immediately after turning 20, he gave up one earned run on 13 hits and five walks in 19 innings in the hitter-friendly Cal League, punching out 19. Font struck out 85 hitters in 78.2 innings between his two stops, but he began to lose command at mid-season, and was shut down early in July with arm discomfort. Ultimately it was determined that the Venezuelan had a torn elbow ligament, and he'll miss the 2011 season due to Tommy John surgery.

Joe Wieland, RHP

Wieland made the same Low A/High A split that Ross and Font made in 2010, and while he was less effective after the promotion, he maintained an outstanding strikeout-to-walk ratio. After fanning 71 and walking only 15 in 89 Crawdad innings, the 20-year-old struck out 62 and issued only 10 walks in 59 innings for the Blaze. His promotion to the Cal League followed a standout June in which he was the organization's Minor League Pitcher of the Month, going 3-1, 1.67 in four starts (27 innings, 24 hits and five walks, no home runs, 20 strikeouts). A favorite of Nolan Ryan, Wieland will likely join Erlin and Ross atop what should be a standout rotation for the Rangers' inaugural High A Myrtle Beach club.

Matt Thompson, RHP

Thompson could be in the Pelicans' starting five as well, coming off a full season with Hickory that started strong before his results leveled off in the summer. A strike-thrower with a power curve that's a true swing-and-miss pitch, the Burleson native fanned 130 South Atlantic Leaguers (fifth-most in the circuit) over 129.1 innings, issuing only 22 unintentional walks all season. He'll need to prove his stamina in 2011, as his ERA's went up every month in 2010 (3.15, 3.24, 4.07, 5.40, 5.82, 18.90).

Luke Jackson, RHP

Texas signed Jackson in mid-August, convincing the supplemental first-rounder to forgo a commitment to the University of Miami. He'll make his official debut in 2011, likely with the Arizona League club once its short-season schedule kicks off in June. Thought in the days leading up to the draft to be a candidate to go to the Rangers as early as their first selection at number 15 overall, Jackson already sits in the low 90s with a fastball that touches 96. Texas is excited about the projectable righthander, who will pitch most of the 2011 season at age 19.

Omar Beltre, RHP

It was an extraordinary year for Beltre, who had been shut out of the United States for five years due to his unwitting involvement in a marriage/visa scam that robbed him of what should have been his prime pitching years. After being limited for years to competing against teenagers in the Dominican Republic, the 28-year-old was facing a league full of onetime big leaguers when Texas assigned him out of spring training to AAA Oklahoma City, and he was outstanding, especially once he was shifted from the RedHawks' bullpen into the rotation. The big righty induced tons of ground balls in relief but had trouble locating (11 walks in 16 innings), yet when he started taking the ball every fifth day he found his command. He continued to strike out a batter per inning but cut his walks down considerably (27 in 69 innings) and earned a two-start look with Texas. He'll return to AAA Round Rock in the spring, readying himself to help the big club again once the need arises.

Roman Mendez, RHP

Mendez was the key part of the return when Texas moved Jarrod Saltalamacchia to Boston at the end of

July. Acquired days after his 20th birthday, the hard-throwing righthander was brilliant in his Rangers debut, fanning eight in five scoreless innings for Spokane (three hits, one walk) before getting hit hard in his next two appearances (16 hits in 6.2 innings), after which Texas shut him down for remainder of the club's regular season and Northwest League playoff run. He has tremendous life on a fastball that sits in the mid-90s and projects for more, flashing a slider with plus potential, though his mechanics remain a work in progress. Mendez opened enough eyes that *Baseball America* ranked him as the number five prospect in this summer's New York-Penn League, based on his eight starts in that league as a Red Sox farmhand (.240 opponents' average, 35 strikeouts in 33 innings) in June and July.

Eric Hurley, RHP

Hurley spent 2010 rehabbing from shoulder surgery (also dealing with a non-throwing wrist injury), but his early work in the Arizona Fall League after the season was encouraging. After two inconsistent outings, the big righthander had his velocity back up to the mid-90s, commanding both it and a sharp slider, and he threw three consecutive scoreless five-inning stints, scattering seven hits and three walks while fanning nine. He goes into 2011 with a full complement of options, and could make a case with a solid showing at AAA Round Rock to get a handful of big league starts at some point in the season, just as he did in the summer of 2008. Big credit to Rangers instructors Brad Holman and Keith Comstock, both former big league pitchers themselves, for helping get Hurley back on a mound and back on the map.

Cody Buckel, RHP

Texas went well over slot to persuade Buckel to turn pro and forgo a commitment to Pepperdine, agreeing to pay the 18-year-old $590,000 in a second-round slot that called for nearly $100,000 less. His brief work in the Arizona League after signing (five innings, no runs on two hits and one walk, nine strikeouts) was nearly identical to the small sample that Erlin put up the year before, and the organization talks with the same excitement about Buckel as they did when Erlin got his career underway. The small righty works in the low 90s with an advanced curve that projects as a true out pitch.

Neil Ramirez, RHP

While the other four first-rounders taken by Texas in 2007 (Blake Beavan, Michael Main, Julio Borbon, Tommy Hunter) each contributed in varying degrees to the 2010 World Series club, Ramirez worked in Low Class A for the second straight season, but the progress he made in the second half of the summer for Hickory suggests he might be ready to break out. After posting a 5.21 ERA in the Crawdads' first half, he lowered his ERA to 3.74 thereafter, but more impressive was the ratio of 78 strikeouts to 17 walks in 74.2 innings over that second-half stretch. Ramirez's 142 strikeouts were tops in the Rangers' farm system in 2010 and second most in the South Atlantic League.

Justin Grimm, RHP

The Rangers said that the $350,000 that they got Boston to throw into the Jarrod Saltalamacchia trade would be used to help get a couple final draft picks signed in the two weeks that followed. Grimm was one of the players Texas got done in that window of time, as he agreed to sign for $825,000 in a $147,600 slot. The hard-throwing righthander from the University of Georgia gets his fastball up to the mid-90s and throws both a curve and a slider. He'll make his pro debut in 2011.

Wilfredo Boscan, RHP

Boscan had an inconsistent season with High A Bakersfield in 2010, getting off to a shaky start (5.33 ERA, .308 opponents' average over the first two months) before settling down at mid-season (3.08, .271), but he struggled late, posting a 6.18 ERA over seven starts in August and September—though he did post his best groundball rates of the year over that stretch. The 21-year-old did strike out 130 Cal Leaguers and walked only 40 in 163.2 innings, but was probably a longshot as the season ended to earn a winter spot on the 40-man roster, particularly given his lack of the kind of eye-opening stuff that makes a young pitcher a stronger Rule 5 candidate.

Jake Brigham, RHP

Brigham is another first-time draft-eligible this winter, and is probably more likely to sit on a team's Rule 5 radar, given his mid-90s velocity and hammer curve. But he had difficulty with his command in 2010, particularly early, prompting the Rangers to demote him from High A Bakersfield to Low A Hickory two months into the season. After posting a 6.93 ERA in the hitter-friendly Cal League (.333 opponents' average), he was much better with the Crawdads, going 6-5, 3.36 in 13 starts and a relief appearance, limiting opponents to a .214 average and coaxing 2.28 as many groundouts as flyouts. Take out a brutal 2.1-inning, 10-run effort on July 24, and Brigham's Hickory ERA would have been 2.34, and the batting average against would have been .192. The 22-year-old threw what might have been the most dominating game of the year in the Rangers system on August 10, when the first Greensboro hitter of the game grounded a single to center field, the second one dropped down a bunt single, and not another Grasshopper reached safely all night. Brigham struck out 12 in the near-perfect complete-game effort, getting another eight outs on the ground.

Chad Bell, LHP

Texas gave Bell second-round money ($450,000) as the club's 14th-round pick in 2009, but shut him down after he'd thrown 65 innings for Walters State Community College and another 45.2 frames for the Cotuit Kettleers in the post-draft Cape Cod League. He therefore made his official pro debut in 2010, and it was an outstanding year for the big lefty. Challenged with an April assignment to a full-season affiliate, Bell posted a 2.86 ERA in 18 relief appearances for Low A Hickory (27 strikeouts and 13 walks in 28.1 innings, .196 opponents' average, five inherited runners all stranded). Texas then transferred him to Short-Season A Spokane when that club's season opened in late June, in an effort to get the 21-year-old some rotation work. He went 2-0, 3.25 in eight starts (47 strikeouts and 12 walks in 44.1 innings, .213 opponents' average, 3.42 G/F), never allowing more than three runs in any one start, and he returned to Hickory, where he made four late-season starts (2.42 ERA) and four more relief appearances. Bell is quietly one of the real exciting lefthanders being developed by this organization.

Carlos Pimentel, RHP

One of the sole blemishes on Pimentel's 2009 season was the 15 home runs he allowed in 123 innings of work for Low A Hickory. He would replicate it in 2010, yielding the same number of longballs in virtually the same amount of innings (123.1) for High A Bakersfield, though it should be noted that the Cal League is far more cruel to pitchers' numbers than the South Atlantic League. Pimentel also saw his ERA jump two runs from 2009 (2.93) to 2010 (4.96), and his opponents' batting average soar from .256 to .292. Though he made one spot start for AA Frisco in August, a return to High A (Myrtle Beach this time) in April wouldn't be out of the question.

SHORT-SEASON STARTING PITCHER OF THE YEAR FIVE YEARS AGO

1. Zach Phillips
2. Doug Mathis
3. Michael Kirkman
4. Kea Kometani
5. Matt Nevarez
6. Omar Poveda
7. Broc Coffman
8. David Smith
9. Shane Funk
10. Kellan McConnell

Kennil Gomez, RHP

The 2010 season was one big struggle for Gomez, who returned to the Cal League for a second straight season and saw his numbers decline across the board. After going 8-10, 5.27 for Bakersfield in 2009 (.279 opponents' average, 126 strikeouts and 67 walks, 1.73 G/F), he went 5-9, 6.47 for the same club in 2010 (.321 opponents' average, 53 strikeouts and 48 walks, 1.36 G/F), falling out of the Blaze rotation and losing ground on the organization's depth chart as far as starting pitcher prospects are concerned. Along with the dip in groundout rate was a disturbing hike in home run frequency, as he went from a bomb every 12 innings in 2009 to one every seven frames in 2010.

Guillermo Moscoso, RHP

The shuttle between Oklahoma City and Arlington didn't run as often for Moscoso in 2010 as it did in 2009, due in part to what was a far less effective year in AAA for the 26-year-old. In 70 RedHawks innings last season, Moscoso posted a 2.31 ERA and held Pacific Coast Leaguers to a .218 batting average and just two home runs in 70 innings. This season, the league hit .281 off him and went deep 17 times in his 123.1 innings of work, and he limped home with a progressively inflating ERA that finished at 5.18. The righthander has one option left, and assuming he retains his roster spot it will surely be exercised in April with an assignment to the AAA Round Rock staff.

Kasey Kiker, LHP

The 2010 season was a miserable one for Kiker, who earned an invite to big league camp in February but never got his footing once the regular season got underway. Returning to AA Frisco for a second season, the 22-year-old—who was drafted two spots after Tim Lincecum in the 2006 draft, one spot ahead of Max Scherzer, and six spots ahead of Kyle Drabek—had a 5.73 ERA after seven RoughRider starts. The Texas League was hitting just .218 off the lefthander, but he'd issued 31 walks in 33 innings and drilled seven batters. Texas moved him into middle relief and the results were even worse (16.71 ERA in seven innings, 15 walks and 10 strikeouts). Kiker headed to Puerto Rico for winter ball to get a head start on erasing what has been a very disappointing season and restoring some confidence heading into 2011.

Richard Alvarez, RHP

Pitching most of the season at age 17, Alvarez was handled carefully, going five innings only once in eight Arizona League starts, and the surface results weren't great—0-3, 6.48 record, .308 opponents' average—but beneath those numbers it's easy to see why the Rangers are excited about the young righty from Venezuela, who signed in December 2008 for a reported bonus of $800,000. After fanning 35 and walking 19 in 41 AZL innings last summer, an impressive enough showing, Alvarez punched out 32 and issued only 12 free passes in 25 frames this summer with a solid fastball-curve-change repertoire and advanced idea on the mound.

Carlos Melo, RHP

Acquired from Detroit along with Moscoso for Gerald Laird in 2008, Melo made a huge leap forward in 2010. After posting a 7.09 Arizona League ERA in 2009, he showed an improved change and power curve to go along with low-90s velocity in 2010, posting a 3.83 ERA and finishing fifth in the league in strikeouts (65 in 51.2 innings) and second in opponents' average (.212, a dramatic improvement over the .317 clip he surrendered the year before). After allowing five home runs in 47 innings in 2009, Melo wasn't taken deep at all in 2010. The 19-year-old finished his season with an effective spot start (five innings, one run, one hit, four walks, three strikeouts) for Spokane, a club he'll probably pitch in rotation for when its 2011 season begins in June.

Danny Gutierrez, RHP

Coming off a standout showing in the Arizona Fall League, Gutierrez seemed poised to put himself on the big league doorstep in 2010. But instead, his season started with a 50-game suspension at the hands of Major League Baseball, the result of his failure to apply for a Therapeutic Use Exemption for the ADHD medication Adderall, which he tested positive for. Once he got back on the mound in June, the rest of the season was basically a ramp-up, as he was held back from going as many as five innings in an appearance until August. Acquired from Kansas City for prospects Manny Pina and Tim Smith at the end of the 2009 season, Gutierrez was widely judged to be among the Rangers' top 10 prospects a year ago, featuring mid-90s velocity and a swing-and-miss power curve, but after his fragmented 2010 season that resulted in just 51.1 innings of work, he'll need to reestablish himself in 2011.

Randol Rojas, RHP

Named the Co-Pitcher of the Year in the 33-team Dominican Summer League in 2009, Rojas made his stateside debut in 2010. Texas challenged him with an assignment to the Northwest League, where the 19-year-old faced mostly college draftees two and three years older, and he responded, finishing fifth in the league with 77.1 innings pitched, fourth with a 2.79 ERA, fourth with 2.33 walks per nine innings, and fourth in fewest baserunners per nine (11.52). Rojas didn't strike out many batters (40) but he did induce twice as many groundouts as flyouts and kept the ball in the park, allowing only two home runs all summer.

Shawn Blackwell, RHP

The exciting thing about a kid like Blackwell is that, while he projects to add to his low-90s velocity and has the makings of a plus curve, he's already proving himself as an exquisite strike-thrower. The 19-year-old from League City was taken in the 24th round in 2009 but commanded third-round money, and the Rangers delayed his pro debut until this summer. His ability to locate—he walked only nine Arizona Leaguers in 59.1 innings—enabled him to go at least five innings in nine of his 13 starts, and he went 6-3, 4.10, posting the circuit's second-highest win total.

Relief Pitchers

Tanner Scheppers, RHP

The way Scheppers's 2010 season began, the question of whether he'd reach Arlington this year wasn't even asked. It was merely a matter of when—and whether he was a future closer, or a future rotation horse. A rare talent who pitched big league spring training innings before he'd ever thrown a minor league pitch, Scheppers dazzled in the spring with command of a high-90s fastball with boring action that, in combination with a plus-plus sledgehammer curve, led scouts to invoke the names "Verlander" and "Wood" in their evaluations. His work out of the gate with AA Frisco was just silly, as he struck out 19 Texas Leaguers and walked zero in just 11 relief innings, giving up three base hits. Promoted to AAA Oklahoma City, he had a 1.89 ERA in his first month out of the RedHawks bullpen (19 innings, 13 hits, 10 walks, 27 strikeouts), at which time he was shut down for a little over a week (the first of multiple planned breaks in order to manage his workload) and transitioned to the rotation. That's when his season turned. In six starts he posted a 5.86 ERA (.328 opponents' average, 23 strikeouts and eight walks hits in 27.2 innings). Returned to the bullpen, he was not nearly the same pitcher, posting a 7.82 ERA, getting hit at a .327 clip, and fanning 25 while walking 12 in 25.1 innings. With Frankie Francisco's late-season unavailability, it's easy to imagine that Scheppers might have made a meaningful difference in the Rangers' playoff bullpen had he been able to maintain his early-season success on the farm, but his second-half ERA of 8.10 ultimately took him out of big league consideration as Texas neared the playoffs. Still, Pacific Coast League managers and pro scouts were high enough on him that *Baseball America* ranked him after the season as the circuit's number seven prospect, third among pitchers. Huge things are still expected out of the 23-year-old, however, and he'll be back in big league camp this spring trying to reestablish himself as part of the near-immediate plans.

Fabio Castillo, RHP

Once among the most exciting pitching prospects at the lower levels of the Rangers' farm system, Castillo had fallen off the radar after several ordinary seasons, but he broke out in relief in 2010 and is a near-lock to land a spot on the 40-man roster this winter. After two straight seasons at the Low Class A level, Castillo was assigned to High A Bakersfield out of spring training, and got rolling right away, yielding earned runs only twice in his first 12 appearances. Overall, in 36 Blaze games pitched, he held the offense-friendly Cal League to a .219 average, fanning 65 and walking 26 in 51.2 innings as he posted a 1.92 ERA (including 1.04 in the second half). He would finish the season with AA Frisco, unscored upon in four of five appearances (including two in the Texas League playoffs). The 21-year-old continued to open eyes in the Arizona Fall League with his mid-90s velocity and filthy slider, a combination we could see in Arlington sometime in 2012, if not late in 2011.

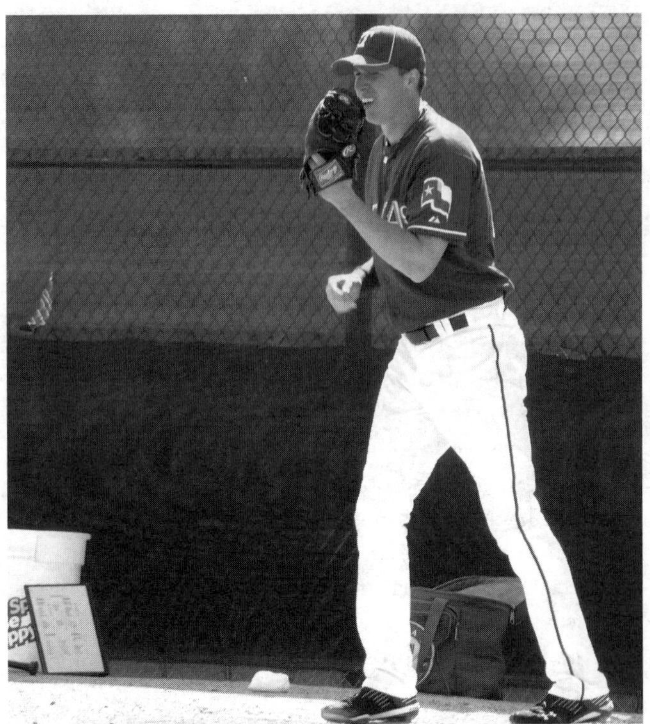

Jason Cole

Miguel De Los Santos, LHP

With his visa issues cleared up, De Los Santos was unleashed on the Low Class A South Atlantic League in 2010, and while his numbers were predictably not as gaudy as they'd been against Dominican Summer League teenagers in 2009, he was still a devastating weapon out of the Crawdads bullpen and projects as a late-inning power lefthander if he continues to progress. The 21-year-old made six relief appearances and six starts for Hickory, holding the league to a .199 average and striking out an extraordinary 62 batters in 38.1 innings, though he did issue 24 walks. Texas actually sent him down to Short Season-A Spokane in June to stretch him out as a starter before bringing him back up, and in seven starts at the lower level he posted a 1.69 ERA, fanning 50 batters and walking 20 in 32 innings while limiting the Northwest League to a helpless .116 batting average (helping to prompt *Baseball America* to name him the league's number 10 prospect). Righties actually fared worse against De Los Santos at both levels, the result of a dirty change that he pairs with low-90s velocity and a plus curve. This isn't a situational lefty that the Rangers are developing.

Pedro Strop, RHP

Strop had a tremendous AAA season that didn't translate to Arlington in 2010. Overlook the 12 runs on 17 hits and 11 walks in 10.2 ugly Texas innings for a minute. The converted infielder was brilliant in 42.1 frames for Oklahoma City, scattering 32 hits (.203 opponents' average, one home run) and just 14 walks while punching out 57 with a dirty fastball-splitter-slider mix. In 15 RedHawks appearances over July and August, the 25-year-old allowed zero earned runs on nine hits and four walks in 13.1 innings, striking out 24. He goes into 2011 with one remaining option, and a chance to show that he belongs in the big leagues and won't need any more minor league seasoning in 2012.

Zach Phillips, LHP

Phillips earned a spot on the 40-man roster last winter after posting a 1.39 ERA between High A Bakersfield and AA Frisco in 2009, and he picked up where he left off for the RoughRiders in 2010, giving up two runs (both coming in his 11th of 12 outings; 1.08 ERA overall) on nine hits (.155 opponents' average) and five walks in 16.2 innings, fanning an impressive 23 hitters over the season's first month (plus one appearance in late July). Promoted to AAA Oklahoma City in mid-May, the 23-year-old didn't allow a run until his seventh appearance, finishing with a 3.22 ERA in 50.1 RedHawks innings. After allowing just two home runs in 2009 (one to Buster Posey), Phillips was taken deep just one time in 2010 (by 28-year-old AAA outfielder Brad Snyder), and for the second straight season, only three baserunners even attempted to steal off him.

FULL-SEASON RELIEF PITCHER OF THE YEAR FIVE YEARS AGO

1. Scott Feldman
2. Jose Veras
3. Kelvin Jimenez
4. Marc Lamacchia
5. Chris Jalie
6. Johnny Luhan
7. Wes Littleton
8. Mark Roberts
9. Chris Cordeiro
10. Matt Roney

Cody Eppley, RHP

A 43rd-round pick in 2008, Eppley has rocketed through the Rangers system in short order, making himself a legitimate relief prospect who can offer a different look out of the bullpen. The 24-year-old sidewinder pitched at three levels in 2010, lasting one brilliant month with High A Bakersfield (18 scoreless innings, nine hits, one walk, 24 strikeouts, 5.00 G/F) before forcing his way to AA Frisco, where he was nearly as dominant (three runs in 22.2 innings, 12 hits, eight unintentional walks, 27 strikeouts, 5.67 G/F) for two months before a promotion to AAA Oklahoma City. Eppley proved to be human with the RedHawks, posting a 4.08 ERA, but he did fan 31 while issuing 13 walks in 28.2 innings, coaxing 2.38 as many groundouts as flyouts. Players drafted in the 43rd round aren't great bets to get to the Major Leagues, but remember that Darren O'Day wasn't drafted at all. If Eppley continues to throw strikes and generate ground balls at those rates, he's going to get a chance.

Corey Young, LHP

Young made the same Bakersfield-Frisco split in 2010 that he did in 2009. He was particularly tough on left-handed hitters in the Cal League, limiting them to a .176/.317/.206 slash line and yielding only two extra-base hits (both doubles) in 68 at-bats. He was twice as likely to get a groundout than a flyout in his 52.1 Blaze innings, getting stronger in that regard as the year wore on. The 23-year-old was scored on in two of his three AA appearances late in the season, though he get six of his 12 outs on strikes, and another five on the ground. Assigned to the Arizona Fall League after the season, the 2008 12th-rounder was unscored on in his first seven appearances (six hits and two walks in 7.2 innings, three strikeouts, 3.75 G/F). Chances are that we'll see Young in Frisco at the beginning of the season in 2011, rather than late in the year as in the last two seasons.

Ovispo De Los Santos, RHP

De Los Santos took a big step forward this year, increasing his strikeout rate from 6.9 per nine innings in the Arizona League in 2009 to 11.8 per nine between Short-Season A Spokane and Low A Hickory in 2010. The 22-year-old with a big fastball was difficult to hit all year, holding Northwest League opponents to a .118 average in his brief 5.1-inning stay in that circuit (two singles in 17 at-bats) before limiting South Atlantic Leaguers to a .213 clip over 20.2 innings. In 149.2 pro innings over five seasons, De Los Santos has surrendered only five home runs.

Trevor Hurley, RHP

The Tomball product, chosen by Texas in the 22nd round in 2008 out of Kansas State, had a tremendous 2010 season, punching out 84 and issuing 24 unintentional walks in 66 innings between Low A Hickory and High A Bakersfield. Hurley saved 15 games in 16 chances, holding the opposition to an anemic .151 batting average. Based on a survey of South Atlantic League managers and pro scouts, Baseball America judged Hurley to be the best reliever in the circuit in 2010, on the strength of his 1.43 ERA, 11 saves, 50 strikeouts and 10 walks in 37.2 innings, .136 opponents' average, and zero home runs allowed.

Geuris Grullon, LHP

Grullon is a fascinating pitching specimen, a lanky, 6'5" lefty with extraordinary life on everything he throws, and if he continues to harness his explosive stuff, he's unquestionably a prospect. In his four pro seasons, his walk rate has decreased each year (6.9 per nine innings, 6.5, 5.6, 5.2) while his strikeout rate has hovered between 10.3 and 11.1 per nine each season. Between the Arizona League, Short-Season A Spokane, and High A Bakersfield in 2010, the 20-year-old posted a composite 2.78 ERA, coaxed over four times as many groundouts as flyouts, and was never taken deep.

Chris Hanna, LHP

The Rangers' 11th-round pick had a phenomenal debut season, posting an ERA of 0.94 and setting 40 hitters down on strikes while issuing only four walks in 28.2 innings, all but one of which came in the Arizona League. He held the circuit to a .194 average and didn't allow a home run all season, and was actually more effective against right-handed hitters, limiting them to a .176/.195/.235 slash. Hanna's final two AZL appearances of the year were his most dominant, as he faced the Royals twice in six days, punching out 18 without issuing a walk in a combined nine innings. Texas rewarded the 18-year-old with a final-week promotion to Spokane—where he became the Northwest League's second-youngest pitcher, next to former Rangers farmhand Edwin Escobar—and in a one-inning assignment against the Tri-City Dust Devils on September 3, **he fanned two of the four batters he faced.**

SHORT-SEASON RELIEF PITCHER OF THE YEAR FIVE YEARS AGO

1. Jon Wilson
2. Nate Fogle
3. Tanner McElroy
4. Brandon James
5. Thomas Van Buskirk
6. Edwin Vera
7. Jose Marte
8. Jarrad Burcie
9. Cain Byrd
10. Warren Rosebrock

Jimmy Reyes, LHP

Taken in the seventh round in 2010, the stocky Reyes had a spectacular rookie season, posting a 2.36 ERA out of the Short-Season A Spokane bullpen while racking up 35 strikeouts against three walks in 26.2 innings of work. The Elon University product went just 10-4, 4.56 in the spring (96 strikeouts and 24 walks in 98.2 innings), but finished strong, going 3-0, 1.50 in three May starts (including a complete-game shutout in the first round of the Southern Conference Tournament) in which he averaged eight innings of work, earning conference Pitcher of the Month honors. He rode the hot streak into his pro debut, limiting the Northwest League to a meager .168 batting average and .263 slug. Reyes will turn 22 just before the 2011 season gets underway.

Mark Hamburger, RHP

The 23-year-old Hamburger, obtained in August 2008 from Minnesota for Eddie Guardado, had a bit of a breakout season in 2010. Assigned out of camp to High Class A for the first time, he posted a 3.38 ERA in April, a 2.70 ERA in May, a 1.86 ERA in June, and a 0.00 ERA in an extraordinary July, a month in which he saved nine games in nine opportunities, scattering nine hits and two walks in 14 innings while setting 21 down on strikes. A promotion to AA Frisco followed, and while Hamburger was not as dominant, he was effective, striking out 20 Texas Leaguers in 19.2 innings as he allowed seven runs (3.20 ERA) on 20 hits and eight walks. He ended up leading the Rangers' farm system with 21 saves.

Joseph Ortiz, LHP

There's no projection in the 5'7", 175-lb. Ortiz, but ever since joining the system in 2006, he's faced hitters several years older each season and continues to get them out. In 44.1 regular-season innings between Low A Hickory and High A Bakersfield in 2010, he fanned 63 and issued only five unintentional walks (including none to the final 59 batters he faced), holding opponents to a .198 batting average (with fairly consistent splits) and posting a 1.62 ERA. For his career, the 20-year-old from Venezuela strikes out 10.5 batters per nine innings and walks only 2.4 per nine.

Tyler Tufts, RHP

Tufts, taken in the 32nd round in 2008, generated more than twice as many groundouts as flyouts at three levels in 2010 (Low A Hickory, High A Bakersfield, AA Frisco), posting a 3.43 composite ERA. In 60.1 innings, he scattered 56 hits and only 15 walks (though he did drill eight hitters), striking out 44. In 165.2 pro innings, the Indiana University product has issued just 32 unintentional walks and allowed only three home runs, featuring a hard sinker-slider combination that has helped him generate more than twice as many groundouts as flyouts in each of his three pro seasons.

Beau Jones, LHP

The fifth player acquired in the 2007 Mark Teixeira trade, Jones had an interesting 2010 season with AA Frisco, posting a 1.90 ERA in 32 relief appearances (he was rocked in two starts), striking out 62 Texas Leaguers in 52.2 total innings and not giving up a home run all year. But the southpaw had extraordinary reverse splits, holding right-handed hitters to a .122/.221/.174 slash while lefties hit a healthy .315/.451/.425 off the 23-year-old. He had similar troubles with left-handed hitters in AA in 2009, after holding them to a .077/.111/.077 clip with High A Bakersfield in a mid-season stint. If he can regain anything close to that sort of effectiveness against same-siders, he's demonstrated enough of an ability to get righties out that he wouldn't need to be viewed strictly as a left-on-left candidate same-siders, he's demonstrated enough of an ability to get righties out that he wouldn't need to be viewed strictly as a left-on-left candidate.

CATCHERS

Jorge Alfaro

Much was made of the Rangers' relative inactivity internationally last summer, but those who ascribed it to the organization's financial handcuffs overlooked two factors: (1) Texas believed last year's July 2 crop was weaker than any in years; and (2) the club had already made a major splash six months earlier, when it paid a reported $1.3 million signing bonus to bring the 16-year-old Alfaro into the fold from Colombia. Blessed with tremendous tools across the board, Alfaro hit just .221/.278/.291 in the Dominican Summer League, but he caught the most innings on a club that went 42-23 on the strength of its pitching (2.02 team ERA, 9.0 strikeouts and 2.9 walks per nine innings) and gunned down 32 percent of would-be basestealers, the best mark of the five catchers on the squad. Alfaro is a physically mature 6'2", 185 and has tremendous raw power, though at his age it may take a few seasons to translate into results.

Scott Lucas

Kellin Deglan

Texas used its second first-round pick last June (22nd overall) on Deglan, whose British Columbia high school had no baseball program but who had extensive experience against international competition, having played for Canada's Junior National team. Big for a catcher at 6'2", 200, the 18-year-old is advanced defensively and shows enough potential with the bat that Arizona League managers and pro scouts convinced *Baseball America* to rank him 11th in the season-ending assessment of the 12-team circuit's top prospects. In 110 at-bats between the AZL and Northwest League, Deglan hit .191/.256/.255 but flashed a raw power tool that scouts expect to develop into double-digit home run totals. Behind the plate he's praised for his arm strength and footwork (he threw out 39 percent of runners trying to steal, including four of eight in the AZL), and he gets high marks for his makeup and coachability. Deglan finished the season as the NWL's second-youngest player (next to Spokane teammate Jurickson Profar), and he's a good bet to return to that club in 2011.

Tomas Telis

Telis had Tommy John surgery last winter and never put the shin guards on in 2010, but he was allowed to hit and, as always, he produced. Serving as the Arizona League squad's designated hitter, the 19-year-old got off to a slow start but caught fire in August, hitting .414/.434/.586 in 70 at-bats, striking out only two times in that stretch. His .326 average for the season ended up ninth best in the league, and he tied teammate Christian Villanueva for the circuit's second-highest RBI total, driving in 35 runs. The switch-hitter was getting in his defensive reps during Fall Instructs, and should be good to go as a two-way player when the 2011 short-season leagues get rolling. It's Telis's bat that will carry him as a prospect, but he's obviously tremendously more valuable if he can stay behind the plate on his way up the chain.

Jose Felix

Felix arrived well under the radar in 2008, signing not only out of Mexico (a far less fertile baseball region than the Dominican Republic or Venezuela) but also at the relatively advanced age of 19 (and in January rather than July). He has advanced quickly, however, and has a chance to get to the big leagues in the next season or two. The key to Felix's game is his defense, solid in all phases, including the intangibles involved in handling a staff. He had an outstanding year in the running game, erasing an extraordinary 63 percent of the 70 Cal League baserunners attempting to steal on him, and then 40 percent of the would-be basestealers who tested him in the Texas League after a promotion from Bakersfield to Frisco in July. The 22-year-old also had his finest year at the plate, hitting a combined .278/.311/.354 with only 31 strikeouts in 353 at-bats. Expect Felix to get a non-roster invite to big league camp, after which he'll likely start the season back in Frisco.

Leonel De Los Santos

"Macumba" took a huge step backward with the bat in 2010, hitting just .206/.223/.267 for Low A Hickory after compiling a .272/.299/.355 line for the same club in 2009. The 21-year-old is a defense-first catcher but if the bat's getting knocked out of his hands at age-appropriate levels, his opportunities to advance are going to be limited. De Los Santos can be special in limiting the running game—he gunned down 41 percent of baserunners attempting to steal—but he hit .182 or lower in three different months in 2010 and needs to refind an ability to contribute a little bit at the plate in order to sustain his prospect status, at least as a position player.

Corner Infielders

Jason Cole

Christian Villanueva, 3B

Vinny Castilla came up through the Braves system in the early 90s as a skinny, 6'1" shortstop without much of a hit tool and only flashes of power. Through his first three big league seasons, two with Atlanta and one with Colorado, the Mexico product hit .254 with nine home runs in 358 at-bats. Then he exploded, settling in as an everyday third baseman as he hit .300 five straight years and blasted 40 home runs in three of those seasons. Some think Villanueva, built like a young Castilla and like him from Mexico, could grow into a power hitter as well, but for now he's a lockdown defender at third with plenty to like in the bat. In his first stateside season, he was the Arizona League's second-best run producer, matching teammate Tomas Telis with 35 RBI (over 188 at-bats). The 19-year-old hit .261 in June, .310 in July (when he was also named the organization's Minor League Defender of the Month), and .333 in August, and was equally productive against left-handed and right-handed pitching. He was the AZL's Post-Season All-Star Third Baseman, and should start the 2011 season with Short-Season A Spokane.

Mike Olt, 3B

A month after Villanueva earned the organization's Minor League Defender of the Month honors, Olt was the recipient, and while there are aspects of his game's that differ from Villaneuva's, you'll get a spirited debate if you ask enough people who pay close attention which of the two they like as the top corner infielder in the system. Chosen with a supplemental first-round pick in June (compensation for the loss of free agent Ivan Rodriguez), Olt was advertised as bringing two plus aspects to his game: tremendous raw power (he passed former Rangers farmhand Jason Grabowski as UConn's all-time home run leader) and premium defense at third base. After hitting .318/.401/.659 with a school-record 23 homers in 264 Huskies at-bats in the spring, the 21-year-old hit .293/.390/.464 with nine more bombs in 263 at-bats for Short-Season A Spokane. He was fourth in the Northwest League with 40 walks (and also fourth with 77 strikeouts), and his 122 total bases were fifth most in the circuit. He displayed the plus range and arm at third base, along with good hands and footwork, that had led *Baseball America* to call him the third-best defensive player—at any position—in the 2010 draft. The publication also named him the NWL's number four prospect after the season. Olt should settle in somewhere in the middle of Low A Hickory's lineup when the 2011 season begins.

Tommy Mendonca, 3B

Then again, Texas could push Olt to High A Myrtle Beach, the same aggressive approach they took in 2010 with Mendonca, assigning him to High A Bakersfield in what was his first full pro season. After Mendonca's own productive Spokane debut last summer (.309/.361/.537), Texas rewarded him with a season-ending, two-level promotion to Bakersfield, 40 miles from his Turlock, California hometown. He hit just .209 in 43 at-bats for the Blaze and returned to that club this spring (with Matt West returning to Low A Hickory for a second season at third base at that level), and it was a tough year for him both at the plate and in the field, where he's generally considered to be a solid defender. Before a hot streak to finish the year (10 for 21 in September, with half his hits going for extra bases and only two strikeouts), Mendonca's batting average languished in the .230's, and he struck out every 3.3 at-bats for the season. Error totals are dangerous to read too much into in the minor leagues, but after the 22-year-old committed nine miscues in 60 games in 2009 (.941 fielding percentage), he made 28 errors (.904 fielding percentage) in 114 games at third in 2010.

Chris McGuiness, 1B

McGuiness is a different type of prospect than most Jon Daniels has traded for as Rangers GM, playing on a corner and not particularly projectable, but he has some unique, playable skills that add a dimension to the system that doesn't exist in heavy supply. Coming over from the Red Sox with righthanders Roman Mendez and Michael Thomas in the Jarrod Saltalamacchia trade, McGuiness should hit for average and already exhibits a tremendously patient approach at the plate. He has a .393 on-base percentage in his two pro seasons, including a .381 mark in 34 games with Bakersfield, in what was the first High Class A experience of his career. Boston's 13th-round pick in 2009, the 22-year-old hit a combined .284/.406/.488 this year between Low A Greenville (where he was in the South Atlantic League's top four in both slugging and reaching base) and the Blaze, piling up 23 doubles, 19 home runs, and 68 RBI in 402 at-bats, and drawing 77 walks in just 112 games. Some liken McGuiness to Mitch Moreland, which in scouting and player development circles is a serious compliment.

Chad Tracy, 1B

There was no hotter start offensively in the Rangers system than the one Tracy put together in April, his first month at the AAA level. Serving primarily as Oklahoma City's designated hitter that month (as Justin Smoak, Mitch Moreland, and Brandon Boggs held down first base and the outfield corners), the 24-year-old hit .342/.409/.658 in 79 at-bats for the month, briefly earning occasional mention as Texas developed a big league need for a right-handed corner bat off the bench. But he hit only .162 in May, striking out every fourth at-bat, and spent the middle of the summer pulling his numbers back up to a line of .263/.349/.502 when he suffered an oblique injury that ended his 2010 with two months to go. Despite missing nearly half the season, Tracy's 17 homers were one short of the most in the entire system.

FULL-SEASON PLAYER OF THE YEAR: FIVE YEARS AGO

1. Adrian Gonzalez
2. Gerald Laird
3. Jason Botts
4. Ian Kinsler
5. Joaquin Arias
6. Travis Metcalf
7. Kevin Mahar
8. Marshall McDougall
9. Drew Meyet
10. Ruddy Yan

Middle Infielders

Scott Lucas

Jurickson Profar, SS

At the end of the 2010 season, Baseball America's Jim Callis was asked to rank the top five prospects in baseball who had yet to reach a full-season league. One (Manny Machado) was the third overall pick in the 2010 draft. Two others (Zack Cox and Yasmani Grandal) were also 2010 first-rounders, and each 21 years old. Another (Gary Sanchez) received the third-largest signing bonus ever paid to a Dominican teenager—and fourth highest ever paid by the Yankees ($3 million). The other one was Profar, the youngest of the five and now the most experienced of them. The 17-year-old from Curacao is a dynamic athlete whom most interested teams wanted to put on a mound when his July 2 eligibility came up in 2009, but instead he made his pro debut as the youngest player in the Northwest League in 2010, serving as Spokane's everyday shortstop and more than holding his own. The switch-hitter put together a .250/.323/.373 line in 252 at-bats, striking out a manageable 46 times against pitchers four and five years older, and his 19 doubles were one short of the league lead. *BA* ranked him as the NWL's number one prospect after the season. Profar earns raves for his makeup and his instincts as much as for his plus tools across the board (the power lags the rest, though he did go deep on his seventh pro at-bat), and is validating the Rangers' decision to sign him not as a pitcher, but as a high-ceiling shortstop.

Luis Sardinas, SS

Sardinas signed at the same time as Profar and for virtually the same amount of money ($1.5 million vs. $1.55 million), but he didn't have Profar's Little League World Series legacy or his flashiness and thus made less of a splash on arrival. But he had a sensational debut season of his own, and would be attracting far more attention if he weren't in an organization that featured Profar and, of course, Elvis Andrus. The switch-hitting Sardinas got his average up to .364 as late as one week before the end of the Arizona League season, finishing at .311/.363/.350 in 103 at-bats, all but one of which came as the AZL club's number two hitter. He was *Baseball America*'s number eight AZL prospect at season's end. A plus runner, the 17-year-old from Venezuela is a premium defender who makes the game look easy. He's one of the Rangers' top minor league assets.

Leury Garcia, SS

Garcia made moderate strides in his second season with Low A Hickory, improving his offensive production (.262/.307/.323, up from .232/.288/.286) and cutting his errors down (30 in 89 games, after 42 in 83 games). His range and arm strength at shortstop and run tool are off the charts, giving rise (along with his diminutive physical stature) to the "Furcalito" nickname that has followed him since he signed out of the Dominican Republic in 2007. Based on a survey of South Atlantic League managers and pro scouts, *Baseball America* judged Garcia to be the best defensive shortstop in the circuit as well as its best baserunner. The switch-hitter was more productive from the right side, and stole a system-high 51 bases in 62 attempts between the Crawdads and the Arizona League squad, for whom he appeared six times.

Hanser Alberto, SS

Alberto had a remarkable season, not only winning the batting title in the 34-team Dominican Summer League with a .358 mark, but striking out only nine times in 179 at-bats. The 17-year-old fanned only two times through his first 34 games, and had separate stretches of 60 at-bats and 57 at-bats between strikeouts. And he did all of this in his first professional season, having signed without any fanfare out of the Dominican Republic in November 2009. Playing mostly shortstop with a little second base mixed in, he was solid defensively and gives Texas another intriguing prospect in the middle of the infield, an area that the franchise has upgraded dramatically in the past two years.

Drew Robinson, IF-OF

Robinson's a fascinating addition to the system. You look at the breakdown of his defensive splits and see time (in descending order of appearances) at shortstop, second base, left field, first base, third base, and right field—and not only did he not lead the Arizona League club in appearances at any one position, he didn't even log the second-most games at any spot on the field (though he played in more games than all but three teammates). You see that, despite a little slump at season's end (dropping his average, which sat above .300 most of the year, to .286), the 18-year-old still finished with a base-reaching clip of .406, fourth best in the league. *Baseball America* said before the draft that, next to Bryce Harper, scouts liked Robinson more than any hitter in the Nevada-Utah-Colorado-Arizona-New Mexico region. Signed away from a commitment to the University of Nebraska, he had one of the system's more interesting pro debuts, and after Texas experimented with the left-handed hitter all over the field this summer, it will be worth noting what the organization decides to do with him going forward. I'm trying to resist the idea that Texas might be developing its own Ben Zobrist here, but that's the obvious comp, and it's exciting.

Odubel Herrera, 2B-SS

Herrera was the Arizona League club's primary second baseman, occasionally sliding over to shortstop to give Sardinas a day off. Wherever the 18-year-old played, he raked. He hit .337/.394/.421 over 178 at-bats, racking up the second-most hits in the league while fanning only 27 times, and he had even splits across the board. The Venezuelan product made four late-season appearances at second base for Short-Season A Spokane, going 2 for 9 with one strikeout, and his composite .332 batting average was tops in the entire system among qualifying hitters.

Marcus Lemon, 2B-OF

Even if you can't quite put a finger on it, there's a certain makeup that the good utility players all have, and the effort to turn Lemon into a versatile asset for the bench began in earnest in 2010. There's no question he already has the intangibles. After playing nothing but shortstop his first three pro seasons and then splitting 2009 between second base and shortstop for AA Frisco, he returned to the RoughRiders in 2010 and worked at all three outfield spots as well as at second, while turning an offensive line (.271/.325/.355) that was almost identical to the previous year's output. He's likely to be left off the roster this winter and could attract some team as a Rule 5 flyer for the bench, but otherwise will likely be assigned to AAA Round Rock (five years after the Rangers lured the Florida native away from a commitment to the University of Texas) and will continue his development as a role player.

OUTFIELDERS

Scott Lucas

Engel Beltre

Beltre turned a corner in 2010, as his considerable raw skills began to translate into real results. He's similar to the player Ruben Mateo was 10 years ago, a dynamic athlete with the range to play center field and the arm to play right, and every offensive tool. Part of the return from Boston for Eric Gagné in July 2007 (along with David Murphy and Kason Gabbard), Beltre dazzled the organization with his potential before breaking through last spring with a .331/.376/.460 run with High A Bakersfield. Texas had tried to force plate patience on Beltre by leading him off for much of his time since arriving from the Red Sox, but that experiment hit a low when he reached base at a meager .281 clip for the Blaze in 2009. Moved into the three hole with the same club this spring, he suddenly put together a .405 on-base percentage in that slot, and it was game on. Beltre had hit .233 in April, .347 in May, and .406 in June, prompting a promotion to AA Frisco (days after which Texas reportedly refused to include him in the Cliff Lee trade with Seattle). He hit mostly third and fifth for the RoughRiders en route to a line of .254/.301/.337. The Texas League slash line didn't jump off the page, but this was a 20-year-old playing against competition several years older and showing managers and scouts enough to earn *Baseball America*'s ranking as the circuit's number 18 prospect (he was number five in the Cal League rankings). The lefthander has plus bat speed, and though he can't yet be called selective at the plate, he did a much better job in 2010 of laying off pitches he can't do much with. There's still work to be done, but the walks were up this year, the strikeouts were down, the on-base and slug were career full-season highs, and the picture is starting to come into full focus.

Jake Skole

Given that Skole played so little as a high school senior in 2010 due to a high ankle sprain, it would have fully made sense for the Rangers to have given him a one-way ticket to Surprise after he quickly signed (forgoing an opportunity to play baseball and football at Georgia Tech), with the message that he'd spend two-and-a-half months in the Arizona League playing against other teenagers, after which the organization would convene there for Fall Instructs. But as the club is so often with its top prospects, Texas was aggressive with the 18-year-old, getting him acclimated in the AZL for about a week and a half (.286/.394/.357) before reassigning him to Short-Season A Spokane, where he'd spend the remaining two months of the season facing players mostly three years older, hitting a respectable .254/.327/.348 (.288/.350/.405 against righthanders). *Baseball America* ranked the left-handed hitter as the Northwest League's number 13 prospect (despite being the circuit's third-youngest position player), noting that he stood out physically among his college-aged competition. Skole played center field for the Indians and hit all over the order, holding his own to such an extent that a 2011 assignment to Low A Hickory out of the chute wouldn't come as a surprise.

Miguel Velazquez

After a sputtering start to his career due to off-field issues, Velazquez has had his development accelerated the last two years, and while he has progressed well, there is more in terms of offensive potential that he has yet to tap into. Texas had the Puerto Rico native split the 2009 season between the short-season Arizona League and Northwest League (composite .296/.363/.514) and the 2010 season between the next two levels up, Low A Hickory (.270/.342/.449) and High A Bakersfield (.270/.333/.392). He played all three outfield spots with the Crawdads and Blaze, and though he saw most of his time in center field, he projects to end up on a corner, where his power should eventually play. The 22-year-old hit 23 doubles and 15 homers in 2010, driving in 78 runs (most in the system next to Chris Davis) in 119 games, but the ever greater power potential exists for him to develop into a Carlos Lee type of hitter, if not a Nelson Cruz profile, as some suggest.

Jared Hoying

Hoying signed quickly after Texas chose him in the 10th round in June, and Northwest League pitchers exploited his funky, Kirk Gibson-like swing out of the gate, limiting him to six hits in his first 40 at-bats (.150), culminating with a golden sombrero in the fourth game of a five-game set against Everett. The 21-year-old got the AquaSox in the series finale, however, putting up a single and double and three runs scored in five trips, and he never stopped hitting. Starting with that June 30 effort, the left fielder would hit .360/.416/.601 over his remaining 52 games with Spokane, earning league MVP honors as he finished among the leaders in hitting (.325, fifth), slugging (.543, third), total bases (132, third), extra-base hits (28, third), triples (5, third), RBI (51, third), stolen bases (20, fourth), and runs (47, fourth). Rangers coaches widened Hoying's hitting base, bent him a bit at the waist, and raised his hands, but the left-handed hitter took the instruction and ran with it, and put together a fantastic rookie season.

SHORT-SEASON PLAYER OF THE YEAR: FIVE YEARS AGO

1. Taylor Teagarden
2. Steve Murphy
3. Johnny Whittleman
4. Freddie Thon
5. John Mayberry, Jr.
6. Lizahio Baez
7. Truan Mehr
8. K.C. Herren
9. German Duran
10. R.J. Anderson

Teodoro Martinez

"Café" may be the smallest prospect in the Rangers system, standing a generously listed 5'11" and weighing 160 pounds at best, but considering the fact that his late father Carlos, a corner infielder with the White Sox and Indians in the late '80s and early '90s, and his brother Jose (a White Sox outfield prospect) checked in at a lanky 6'5", there's hope that the 18-year-old center field prospect has some growing left to do—he's already filled out some from the 5'6", 125-lb. frame he carried when he signed in 2008. Martinez was very productive out of the leadoff spot for the Arizona League squad in 2010, his first season stateside, hitting .313/.357/.422 with a league-leading 66 hits in 53 games (striking out only 25 times in 211 at-bats), adding 20 steals (third most in the league) in 27 attempts and 43 runs scored (second most). His 89 total bases ranked fourth in the AZL, and *Baseball America* ranked him as the circuit's number 19 prospect after the season.

Craig Gentry

Gentry's breakout season in 2009 was followed by one in 2010 that was even better in some respects, and if it weren't for a broken hand in mid-August, the 26-year-old would undoubtedly have been back in Texas in September and a legitimate candidate for the post-season roster. After hitting .303/.378/.418 for AA Frisco in 2009, Gentry basically replicated it at a higher level with a .309/.393/.413 campaign for AAA Oklahoma City this year, and his outfield defense and baserunning ability have always been premium tools. He goes into 2011 with two remaining options, and should be roaming center field for AAA Round Rock when that club's season begins.

Josh Richmond

Richmond was considered by some to be a third-round talent who fell to the 12th round only because of a 2009 hand surgery that didn't heal well and a February reinjury to the hand that cost him 41 of Louisville's 64 games in the spring and suppressed his junior year numbers (.262/.343/.369) when he was able to play. The 21-year-old didn't sign until mid-July but contributed right away, driving in runs in his first four games for Short-Season A Spokane, and six of eight. Because of the late start he got, Richmond appeared in just under half of the Indians' games, but in 118 at-bats he put together a solid .297/.417/.458 line, playing primarily in right field.

Jordan Akins

The Rangers' third-round pick in June, Akins chose the club's $350,000 offer to sign over a chance to play both baseball and football for the University of Central Florida (or just football for Georgia, Georgia Tech, Maryland, or Ole Miss). He has a tremendous ceiling but will take time to develop, as everything's raw. Judged by some to be the best prep athlete in Georgia this year, the 18-year-old struggled against Arizona League pitching, hitting a punchless .187/.241/.252 from the bottom of the order with 35 strikeouts in 107 at-bats. He's a strapping 6'3", 192 pounds, runs a 6.4 60, throws well, and has considerable raw power, but patience will be called for. The same was true for Nelson Cruz.

Ruben Sierra Jr.

Texas started Sierra off in the Dominican Summer League, after he'd struggled in his 2009 pro debut in the Arizona League (.202/.229/.254) as the club's sixth-round draft pick. The 19-year-old was somewhat more productive this summer, hitting .244/.305/.337 in 86 DSL at-bats, and it paved the way for a solid, if brief, return to the AZL. The son of the former Rangers great spent only five weeks in Surprise, but he flourished, hitting .302, reaching base at a .362 clip, and slugging .535 in 43 at-bats.

Ryan Strausborger

Signed as an Indiana State senior out of the 16th round in June, Strausborger offers plus speed and a strong outfield arm, generating Gentry comps. He struggled out of the gate for Short-Season A Spokane, hitting .143/.268/.171 in June, but lifted his numbers to .241/.302/.399 in July and an impressive .330/.405/.505 slash line in August, all primarily out of the leadoff spot and at all three outfield spots. The right-handed hitter beat up on left-handed pitching (.327/.375/.519), and in 64 games he stole 21 bases in 25 tries, a total that was two swipes short of the Northwest League lead.

Cristian Santana

Hopes were extremely high when Texas signed Santana as a 16-year-old catcher out of the Dominican Republic in 2005, but he's now a left fielder/DH with a career batting average of .246 and a strikeout for every third at-bat. There are still few in the system with as much raw power as the 21-year-old, but he's now played three straight seasons at the Low Class A level, and a probable assignment to High A Myrtle Beach in the spring could provide his final real chance to prove that the Rangers' trust and patience has been worth maintaining.

David Paisano

With the unceremonious departure of Brandon McCarthy after the season to free agency, Paisano is all that remains from the disappointing 2006 trade that sent John Danks, Nick Masset, and Jake Rasner to the White Sox. While the Venezuelan product is among the Rangers system's top defensive outfielders, the bat hasn't developed and the clock is ticking. He'll be 23 when the 2011 season begins, without having played above the Class A level yet, and he's basically been the same .700-OPS hitter the last three years, flashing very little power and moderate production on the bases, with too many strikeouts and not enough walks. As the organization's depth in position players increases at the lower levels, players like Paisano will soon be in jeopardy of losing their places in the system.

POISED

Ten Position Players Who Could Break Out in 2011

You can count on several position players each year in any given system taking a major step forward in their development. This season, Mitch Moreland and Engel Beltre convinced us to view them in a different light, just as Craig Gentry (2009), Jose Vallejo (2008), Chris Davis (2007), Nate Gold (2006), Kevin Mahar (2005), and Ian Kinsler (2004) had done in recent years. When a player escapes the pack into prospecthood, or goes from prospect to blue-chipper, what's the cause? Reps and experience? Responsiveness to coaching? Physical maturity? Focus on a weakness until it dissolves? The answer is probably that there are as many explanations as there are players who have breakout seasons.

Here are my top 10 picks among position players in the Rangers system to redefine themselves in 2011.

Scott Lucas

Luis Sardinas, SS

Christian Villanueva, 3B
Jake Skole, OF
Mike Olt, 3B
Drew Robinson, IF-OF
Tomas Telis, C
Hanser Alberto, SS
Teodoro Martinez, OF
Josh Richmond, OF
Kellin Deglan, C

FIVE YEARS AGO

1. Johnny Whittleman
2. John Mayberry Jr.
3. Drew Meyer
4. Brandon Boggs
5. R.J. Anderson
6. Manuel Pina
7. Johan Yan
8. Cristian Santana
9. Jim Fasano
10. Andrew Wishy

POISED

Ten Pitchers Who Could Break Out in 2011

Minor league pitchers are probably more susceptible than position players to coming virtually out of nowhere, at least to those who don't actually see them on the field. Why? Statistics are more suggestive of a hitter's abilities than a pitcher's on the farm. Pitchers are often trained in different roles from what they'll eventually be expected to fill, and sometimes objectives change from year to year with pitchers; for example, a new pitch might be added to the repertoire or a key mechanical adjustment might be introduced while the games count. In 2010, Tanner Scheppers and Fabio Castillo had breakout seasons on the mound, just as Martin Perez (2009), Derek Holland (2008), Luis Mendoza (2007), Wes Littleton (2006), Edinson Volquez (2005), and Chris Young (2004) had done before them.

Which pitchers are set to break out in 2011? Here are my top 10 candidates.

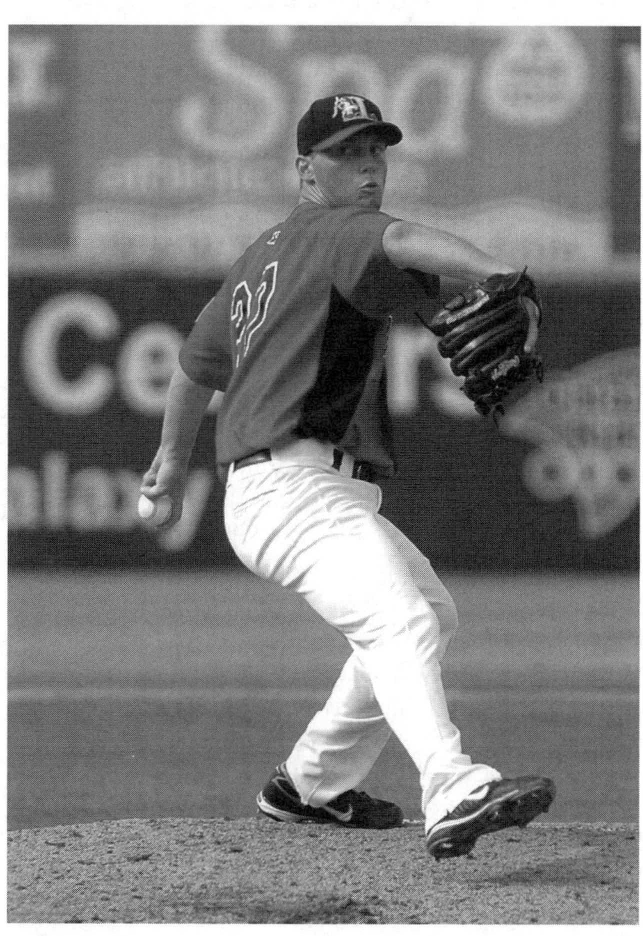

Tracy Proffitt

Robbie Erlin, LHP

David Perez, RHP
Miguel De Los Santos, LHP
Cody Buckel, RHP
Joe Wieland, RHP
Justin Grimm, RHP
Matt Thompson, RHP
Neil Ramirez, RHP
Richard Alvarez, RHP
Shawn Blackwell, RHP

FIVE YEARS AGO

1. Michael Schlact
2. Omar Poveda
3. Jesse Carlson
4. Matt Nevarez
5. Kelvin Jimenez
6. Brandon James
7. Fabio Castillo
8. Kyle Rogers
9. Shane Funk
10. Jake Rasner

The 40-Man Roster Conundrum 2011

The Newberg Report's annual look at the Rule 5 Draft and the long-range implications of the Rangers' off-season 40-man roster decisions

Mechanics of the Rule 5 Draft

Every December during the Winter Meetings, Major League Baseball conducts the Rule 5 Draft, a procedure that affords minor leaguers on the periphery of their organizations' plans an opportunity to find new homes and, occasionally, gives teams the chance to steal legitimate prospects for next to no cost. Any player is eligible to be selected in the major league phase of the draft if he meets two criteria: (1) he must not be on his organization's 40-man roster; and (2) assuming the player has never been released, the draft in question must be the fifth one conducted since he signed his first professional contract if he was 18 years old or younger on the June 5 immediately preceding his signing date, or the fourth one since his signing date if he was at least 19 on the June 5 immediately before he signed—though the signing date is not applicable in either instance if it occurred after the minor league regular season concluded, in which case the trigger date is the beginning of the following season. Getting traded doesn't affect a player's Rule 5 timetable.

A club can only make a selection if it has an opening on its 40-man roster. Teams select in reverse order of the previous season's finish.

In the draft's major league phase, the drafting club must pay $50,000 to the player's original team, and the player must remain on the drafting club's active major league roster (or major league disabled list) for the entire ensuing season or be placed on waivers. If the player is placed on waivers by the drafting club, another team can claim him but then has the same constraints as the original drafting club and must keep the player in the majors for the whole season. If the player instead clears waivers, he must be offered back to his original team for $25,000. Occasionally, a trade is worked out between the drafting club and the original team so that the drafting club, even if it decides it can't hide the player in the majors all season, can keep the player in its farm system rather than giving him back.

Rule 5 also provides for a minor league phase. Teams place their players who fit the same service criteria as above on Class AAA, Class AA, or Class A rosters in the fall if they aren't on the 40-man roster. Any player on a Class AA roster and with enough service can be selected by another organization in the AAA phase of the draft for $12,000, and any player on a Class A roster can be taken in the AA phase for $4,000. The minor league phase is not nearly as strict as the major league phase, however—a player isn't required to be assigned to a level higher than the roster he was drafted from. Examples of players the Rangers have acquired recently in the minor league phase of the draft are Alexi Ogando, Guilder Rodriguez, and James Tomlin. Beau Vaughan and Andy Cavazos are probably the most prominent players Texas has lost via the minor league phase in recent years.

The Rule 5 Draft in Rangers History

The Rangers have been involved in the Rule 5 Draft as shown in the table on the next page.

Some footnotes:

1. The Rangers' involvement in the 2002 Rule 5 Draft was practically a primer on how the draft works. Texas drafted 23-year-old Cleveland infielder Marshall McDougall and 22-year-old Cincinnati lefthander John Koronka and lost two players that it hadn't protected on the 40-man roster, 23-year-old shortstop Jose Morban (who had been in the organization for six years) and 26-year-old outfielder Rontrez Johnson (who had been in the organization for one month), but neither stuck with his drafting club. Journeyman Chris Gomez won the Minnesota bench spot that Morban was fighting for, and Chris Singleton outplayed Johnson and landed a job with Oakland. Before Texas had the chance to buy those two back, however, they were claimed by other clubs off waivers, Morban by Baltimore and Johnson by Kansas City. Morban spent all of 2003 with the Orioles, hitting .141 in 71 at-bats and succeeding in all eight stolen base attempts. He then spent all of 2004 in the Baltimore farm system. Johnson lasted almost three weeks with the Royals, singling in one of his three at-bats and striking out in the other two, but he was cut when Carlos Beltran came off the disabled list to start his season. The Rangers repurchased Johnson for $25,000 and assigned him to AAA Oklahoma, where he hit .224/.296/.353 in 241

Year	Player	Original Team	Drafting Club	Result
1972	Ken Esposito, RHP	Mets	Rangers	Returned to Mets
1975	Tom Robson, 1B	Rangers	Yankees	Retired
1982	Odell Jones, RHP	Padres	Rangers	Made Ranger team
1983	Pat Underwood, LHP	Padres	Rangers	Released
1984	Mitch Williams, LHP	Padres	Rangers	Returned to Padres, reacquired by trade
1985	Scott Patterson, RHP	Yankees	Rangers	Returned to Yankees
1986	Cecil Espy, OF	Pirates	Rangers	Returned to Pirates, reacquired by trade
1988	Darrel Akerfelds, RHP	Indians	Rangers	Returned to Indians, reacquired for cash
1989	Ramon Manon, RHP	Yankees	Rangers	Made Ranger team, returned to Yankees April 30
1994	Francisco Saneaux, RHP	Orioles	Rangers	Returned to Orioles
1995	Mark Mimbs, LHP	Dodgers	Rangers	Returned to Dodgers
1995	Tim Rumer, LHP	Yankees	Rangers	Returned to Yankees
1997	Melvin Brazoban, RHP	Rangers	Pirates	Returned to Rangers
1998	Ricky Williams, OF	Phillies	Expos/Rangers	Placed on "restricted list" by Rangers
2002	Jose Morban, SS	Rangers	Twins	Waived, claimed by Orioles, made team
2002	Rontrez Johnson, OF	Rangers	Oakland	Waived, claimed by Royals, made team, waived, returned to Rangers April 18
2002	Marshall McDougall, IF	Indians	Rangers	Returned to Indians, reacquired by trade
2002	John Koronka, LHP	Reds	Rangers	Returned to Reds
2004	Chris Mabeus, RHP	Athletics	Rangers	Returned to Athletics
2004	Andy Fox, IF	Rangers	Expos	Made team
2006	Fabio Castro, LHP	White Sox	Royals/Rangers	Made team, traded to Phillies June 29
2007	Alfredo Simon, RHP	Rangers	Orioles/Phillies	Returned to Rangers
2009	Ben Snyder, LHP	Giants	Orioles/Rangers	Returned to Giants, reacquired by trade

at-bats before being released in July of 2003 and hooking on with the Braves. Texas decided in mid-March 2003 that McDougall was not going to make the active roster, but John Hart, after getting McDougall through waivers, worked out a deal with his former club to keep McDougall in the Ranger farm system, agreeing to send lefthander Derrick Van Dusen to the Indians. McDougall eventually worked his way up until making his big league debut in 2005. Koronka was the one player taken or lost by the Rangers who took the customary Rule 5 path: he failed to make the Ranger club and was returned to the Reds right as camp concluded. He was traded, however, from Cincinnati to the Cubs late in August of 2003 and reached the big leagues with Chicago in 2005, before Texas reacquired him at the end of spring training in 2006 in the three-team deal that sent Juan Dominguez to Oakland and netted Texas lefthanders Koronka and John Rheinecker.

2. Texas drafted 20-year-old lefthander Mitch Williams from San Diego in 1984—he hadn't pitched above Class A and had walked 127 in 164 innings that season—and when the Rangers decided in April that they couldn't hide him in their bullpen (even though the lone lefty reliever on that 99-loss team was the immortal Chris Welsh), they offered the Padres their top third base prospect, Randy Asadoor, for the right to be able to keep Williams in the minor leagues. San Diego agreed, accepting Asadoor rather than paying Texas $25,000 to get Williams back. (Texas still had Buddy Bell at third, and when Asadoor was traded to the Padres just after Opening Day, the Rangers moved AAA second baseman Steve Buechele to third base. Three months later, Bell was traded to the Reds, and Buechele was brought up to play third for Texas, which he would do for the next seven seasons.) Asadoor made it up briefly with the Padres in 1986, appearing in 15 games and hitting .364 in that limited look; he would never see the big leagues again. Williams spent the 1985 season in the Texas farm system and was wilder than ever, walking an unfathomable 165 batters in 132 innings as a starting pitcher between Class A Salem and Class AA Tulsa, but allowing just 84 hits and fanning 175. The following season Williams made one of the most improbable ascensions in recent history when he led the American League in appearances (80) and went 8-6, 3.58 with eight saves. It was the lowest ERA he had ever posted in five years as a pro—by more than a full run—and he held the AL to a .202 batting average and led all big league left-handed relievers with 90 strikeouts. Two years later, he had cemented his value enough to be the linchpin in the deal that brought Rafael Palmeiro and Jamie Moyer to Texas.

3. Texas worked out a deal to keep Cecil Espy in April of 1987 by sending catcher Mike Dotzler to the Pirates. Espy had a four-year stint with Texas and spent another three years in the majors thereafter. Dotzler never made it to the big leagues.

4. Texas had Baltimore draft left-on-left specialist Ben Snyder with the third overall pick in the 2009 draft, after which the Orioles sent the 24-year-old to the Rangers to complete the trade that had sent them righthander Chris Ray in exchange for righthander Kevin Millwood and cash. Snyder didn't pitch particularly well in spring training but the Rangers wanted to keep him in the system. They were able to get Snyder through waivers last April and traded 17-year-old lefthander Edwin Escobar to San Francisco on April 1, 2010 for the right to keep Snyder in the minor leagues.

5. Phillies outfield prospect Ricky Williams was taken by Montreal in the 1998 Rule 5 Draft, evidently at the Rangers' request. Texas, not wanting another club higher in the draft order to snag the University of Texas product, had Montreal draft him and pay Philadelphia the requisite $50,000 draft price, after which the Rangers paid the Expos $100,000 and assumed the rights to the Heisman Trophy winner. The Rangers put Williams on the restricted list once he gave baseball up and was drafted by the Saints, and accordingly Texas was not required to place him on its Opening Day roster or even its 40-man roster. Had he ever returned to professional baseball, the Rule 5 guidelines would have revived and he would have had to make the Rangers' major league roster, or be placed on waivers and then, after clearing, be offered back to the Phillies for $25,000.

6. Tom Robson hit 41 home runs in 1974, which remains a Ranger minor league record. He later became the Rangers' big league hitting coach during the Bobby Valentine regime.

7. The Mets made the wise decision to pluck righthander Darren O'Day from the Angels in the 2008 draft after he'd been outrighted off the Los Angeles roster two months earlier. New York then made the awful decision—after O'Day made the 2009 Mets squad with a solid showing in camp (2.57 ERA in a team-leading 13 appearances, 12 hits and three walks in 14 innings) and gave up two unearned runs in four regular season appearances over three innings—to designate him for assignment two weeks into the season, in order to make room for 34-year-old righthander Nelson Figueroa to make a spot start. Two days after that, the Mets designated Figueroa for assignment himself, a day after which Texas claimed O'Day off waivers, assuming not only O'Day's contract but his Rule 5 constraints. That is, the Rangers were required to keep O'Day in the big leagues all season or else run him through waivers and (if unclaimed) offer him back to the Angels. Of course, that was never an issue, as O'Day was brilliant out of the Texas bullpen all year (.188/.265/.260 opponents' slash line, 1.94 ERA, 30 of 42 inherited runners stranded), proving to be not only the greatest waiver claim to date in Jon Daniels's tenure as Rangers GM, but unquestionably one of the best in franchise history.

8. Among the players acquired in the Rule 5 Draft over the years have been Roberto Clemente, Johan Santana, Josh Hamilton, George Bell, Bobby Bonilla, Dan Uggla, Joakim Soria, and Kelly Gruber. Detroit drafted John Wetteland, coming off a full season in Class A, from the Dodgers in 1987, but returned him to Los Angeles at the end of spring training.

Current Rangers 40-Man Roster

Here is the current Texas 40-man roster (as of mid-November), with the contract status of each player:

PITCHERS (20)

Beltre, Omar	Pre-arbitration
Feldman, Scott	Under contract
Feliz, Neftali	Pre-arbitration
Harrison, Matt	Pre-arbitration
Holland, Derek	Pre-arbitration
Hunter, Tommy	Pre-arbitration
Hurley, Eric	Pre-arbitration
Kirkman, Michael	Pre-arbitration
Lewis, Colby	Under contract
Lowe, Mark	Arbitration-eligible
Moscoso, Guillermo	Pre-arbitration
Nippert, Dustin	Arbitration-eligible
O'Day, Darren	Arbitration-eligible
Ogando, Alexi	Pre-arbitration
Oliver, Darren	Under contract
Phillips, Zach	Pre-arbitration
Rapada, Clay	Pre-arbitration
Strop, Pedro	Pre-arbitration
Tucker, Ryan	Pre-arbitration
Wilson, C.J.	Arbitration-eligible

CATCHERS (2)

Ramirez, Max	Pre-arbitration
Teagarden, Taylor	Pre-arbitration

INFIELDERS (6)

Andrus, Elvis	Pre-arbitration
Blanco, Andres	Pre-arbitration
Davis, Chris	Pre-arbitration
Kinsler, Ian	Under contract
Moreland, Mitch	Pre-arbitration
Young, Michael	Under contract

OUTFIELDERS (5)

Borbon, Julio	Pre-arbitration
Cruz, Nelson	Arbitration-eligible
Gentry, Craig	Pre-arbitration

Hamilton, Josh	Arbitration-eligible
Murphy, David	Arbitration-eligible

FREE AGENTS (7)

Jorge Cantu, Frankie Francisco, Vladimir Guerrero, Cristian Guzman, Cliff Lee, Bengie Molina, Matt Treanor

Paring the Roster Down

Cantu, Francisco, Guzman, Lee, Molina, and Treanor declared free agency days after the World Series ended. Texas declined the mutual option in Guerrero's contract, making him a free agent as well. In addition, righthanders Doug Mathis and Brandon McCarthy, infielder Esteban German, and outfielder Jeff Francoeur declined outright assignments and declared free agency. Beltre, Hurley, and Moscoso were reinstated to the roster from the 60-day disabled list. All told, the moves put the roster at 33 players.

Texas could clear additional roster space in November if needed. Nippert (who is arbitration-eligible), Ramirez, and Tucker are out of options and, while each could get a chance to earn a job in camp, none is a strong bet to make the Opening Day roster, and as a result, depending on other roster opportunities that could present themselves in the off-season, any of the three could be candidates for removal.

For the sake of this exercise, let's assume two of the three are dropped from the roster in November—which doesn't necessarily mean they'll be lost to another club. Nippert, having been outrighted once before (by Texas in May 2008), can refuse a minor league assignment and take his free agency if the Rangers designate him for assignment, but as for Ramirez and Tucker, if they are designated for assignment and aren't claimed by another organization on waivers, Texas can outright them to the farm without either player having any recourse.

In any event, let's say two of the three are taken off the roster. Now we're at 31 players.

The above sets aside for now the possibility that November trades could alter the makeup of the roster, and this front office has demonstrated a willingness to shake things up. There's always the chance that the Rangers could package two or three players in a deal, and those types of trades, even if prospects are included, typically involve players on the 40. The most likely exception would be a player like Martin Perez or Tanner Scheppers or Engel Beltre, that is, one with significant trade value but who doesn't yet have enough service time to require inclusion on the 40-man roster. The obvious point is that fall trades could trim the roster even further. But for this exercise, we'll assume the roster is at 31.

Building the Roster Back Up: The Candidates

Obviously, we can't get carried away and start to pick off anything close to nine names from the farm system to fill out the 40-man roster. We have to account for space the club will hold for veteran free agents to fill several of the vacant spots (conceivably including a returning free agent like Lee or Molina or Guerrero). But those signings could be after early December, so for argument's sake we'll concentrate on the minor leaguers Texas must consider in November to protect from the Rule 5 Draft by adding them to the 40. (Also recognize, however, that the Rangers will have the April roster in mind when making these decisions, because there is no sense putting a guy on the roster and then having to designate him for assignment to make room for players acquired to address Opening Day roster needs. Third baseman Jason Grabowski was lost in that manner in December 2000.)

To be conservative, let's speculate that the Rangers will try and fill five spots with veterans over the winter—for instance, Lee (or a new staff ace), Francisco or another eighth-inning option, a starting catcher, a designated hitter, and a right-handed corner bat—and assume that any trades that are made to bring veterans aboard will remove as many roster occupants as they add. That would bring the roster up to 36 members, giving us four spots to fill with minor leaguers who would otherwise be exposed to the Rule 5 Draft.

Like John Hart before him, Daniels has averaged three to four November roster additions from the minor league ranks. This exercise, however, is obviously player-specific and based on roster makeup—only Kirkman and Phillips were added a year ago—and this year, unless more room is created by way of trades, it's hard to imagine that the Rangers could add any more than four minor leaguers to the roster, and it could be fewer. But make no mistake: This is the deepest crop of legitimate draft-eligibles the Rangers have had in many years, if ever. Texas hasn't lost a true prospect in the Rule 5 Draft in a long time. This could be the year.

Let's examine the dozens of non-roster players in the Ranger farm system who will be eligible for this winter's Rule 5 Draft if not protected. We'll put them in three categories:

1. *Newly eligible players who signed at age 18 or younger in 2006:* Pitchers Wilfredo Boscan, Jake Brigham, Miguel De Los Santos, Ovispo De Los Santos, Wilmer Font, Kennil Gomez, Geuris Grullon, Danny Gutierrez, Kasey Kiker, Yoon-Hee Nam, Joseph Ortiz, and Carlos Pimentel; catcher Leonel De Los Santos; infielders Andres James and Alejandro Selen; and outfielders Engel Beltre, Marcus Lemon, Junior Payano, and Cody Podraza

2. *Newly eligible players who signed at age 19 or older in 2007:* Pitchers Mark Hamburger and Hector Nelo; catcher Chris Gradoville; and infielders Jonathan Greene, Jacob Kaase, and Davis Stoneburner

3. *Repeat eligibles:* Pitchers Michael Ballard, Fabio Castillo, Brennan Garr, Beau Jones, Ben Snyder, and Johan Yan;

catchers Kevin Cash and Alberto Puello; infielders Mitch Hilligoss, Renny Osuna, Chad Tracy, and Johnny Whittleman; and outfielders David Paisano and Cristian Santana

Two notes on the third category: First, I didn't include players like Brandon Boggs, Kevin Richardson, Warner Madrigal, Gregorio Petit, Hernan Iribarren, Emerson Frostad, Matt Brown, Michael Schlact, or a number of others who had enough service time to declare themselves as six-year minor league free agents and are not under Rangers control at the moment. Second, the above is not meant to represent a complete list of the Rangers' minor leaguers who will be eligible for the Rule 5 Draft this winter; it's merely a list of those who might be considered prospects of some measure (though as Montreal's selection of Andy Fox evidenced a few winters ago, you can't rule out veterans that some team would conceivably have an eye on).

It's probably also worth noting that Mitch Moreland would have been up for roster consideration for the first time this winter had he not already been added to the roster during the season and, more pertinent to the discussion, that Josh Lueke, Matt Lawson, Evan Reed, and Ryan Tatukso would have been first-time eligibles here as well had they not been traded for veterans in July. As deep as the Rangers' crop of draft-eligibles is right now, the risk of losing legitimate prospects in December would have been even greater had the club not moved some of them in the summer.

Protecting Our Own: Minor Leaguers Who Might Be Added to the 40-Man Roster

In my opinion, there are two virtual locks to be added to the roster in November from the minor league ranks, righthander Fabio Castillo and outfielder Engel Beltre. After that is a second tier that might include righthanders Wilmer Font, Jake Brigham, and Ovispo De Los Santos and lefthander Miguel De Los Santos, and then another group that includes righthanders Wilfredo Boscan, Mark Hamburger, Carlos Pimentel, Kennil Gomez, and Danny Gutierrez; lefthanders Geuris Grullon, Beau Jones, Kasey Kiker, and Joseph Ortiz; catcher Kevin Cash; infielders Chad Tracy and Davis Stoneburner; and outfielders Marcus Lemon and David Paisano.

There's also the possibility that the Rangers could acquire someone else's minor leaguer close to the deadline to freeze rosters, as they did in 2004 when they signed six-year free agent Agustin Montero on November 19 and put him on the 40-man roster two days later. Texas traded for Cubs righthander Jon Leicester days before the November 2005 freeze date. The November 2008 trade that moved John Mayberry Jr. to Philadelphia for Greg Golson deal was made in conjunction with the deadline to finalize the roster before the draft as well.

Castillo had a breakout season between Bakersfield and Frisco, one in which he struck out 11 batters for every nine innings and gave up three earned runs in his final 20 Class A appearances, and then threw four scoreless appearances out of five in Class AA before an impressive run in the Arizona Fall League. Beltre exploded at the same time that the organization decided to stop trying to make a leadoff hitter out of him and moved him to the middle of the lineup, and he made the same High A/AA split that Castillo did.

Neither 21-year-old is ready for the big leagues, but they're getting close, close enough that the promise of their near-futures would be worth carrying for a year in the big leagues and used in spots. They won't be exposed to the draft, because the risk of losing them would be too great.

The four pitchers I placed on the next tier have varied profiles. Font would be a roster lock if he hadn't gotten hurt. There's risk, however, in letting another team take on the rehab process and work him back to health. Brigham, in his second season after his own elbow surgery, struggled in High A but was brilliant in Low A, and has explosive stuff. The two De Los Santos's are raw and have been old for their leagues.

And there are names in the third grouping who, at one recent time or another, were viewed as legitimate major league prospects, and it just takes one team who believes in the player enough to give him a spring training look. Some other team that believed enough in Castillo a year ago could have stolen him for $50,000 and spent six weeks of camp deciding if they could hide him for a year in the big leagues.

Keep in mind that when assessing who to protect, it's not simply a measure of who has big league potential. As precious as roster spots are for flexibility purposes, organizations evaluate Rule 5 candidates primarily from the standpoint of how likely they are to be drafted and, if drafted, what the odds are that they would stick on an active roster and not be returned. The Rangers have exposed players like Travis Hafner, Craig Monroe, Frankie Francisco, and Pedro Strop—and Castillo—in past years and weren't punished for it. There's probably someone in the system right now that we'll look back at years from now and wonder how the Rangers left them unprotected without losing them in the draft.

Taking a Stab at It

Within the constraints of our hypothetical, under which we have four spots we can fill, my prediction is that Fabio Castillo, Engel Beltre, Wilmer Font, and Miguel De Los Santos will be added to the 40-man roster in November.

[Nov. 19, 2010 update: The Rangers in fact added Fabio Castillo, Engel Beltre, Wilmer Font, and Miguel De Los Santos to the 40-man roster.]

The Newberg Report 2010 Season

OCTOBER 2009

40-MAN ROSTER (40)

PITCHERS (19)

Willie Eyre, Scott Feldman, Neftali Feliz, Frankie Francisco, Jason Grilli, Eddie Guardado, Derek Holland, Tommy Hunter, Warner Madrigal, Doug Mathis, Brandon McCarthy, Luis Mendoza, Kevin Millwood, Guillermo Moscoso, Dustin Nippert, Darren O'Day, Omar Poveda, Pedro Strop, C.J. Wilson

CATCHERS (5)

Max Ramirez, Kevin Richardson, Ivan Rodriguez, Jarrod Saltalamacchia, Taylor Teagarden

INFIELDERS (8)

Elvis Andrus, Joaquin Arias, Hank Blalock, Chris Davis, Esteban German, Ian Kinsler, Omar Vizquel, Michael Young

OUTFIELDERS (8)

Julio Borbon, Marlon Byrd, Nelson Cruz, Craig Gentry, Greg Golson, Josh Hamilton, Andruw Jones, David Murphy

60-DAY DISABLED LIST (4)

Joaquin Benoit, Brandon Boggs, Matt Harrison, Eric Hurley

RESTRICTED LIST (2)

Omar Beltre, Alexi Ogando

October 14, 2009

Two years, four months, and six days ago, in my recap of Day One of the Rangers' landmark 2007 draft, I wrote this:

Rounds six through 50 take place today. And then we can start to envision how the Rangers might staff the Arizona League and Spokane rotations, with [Blake] Beavan and [Michael] Main and [Neil] Ramirez (should they sign) joining a promising collection of arms that includes pitchers like Fabio Castillo, Jake Brigham, Wilmer Font, Geuris Grullon, and Carlos Pimentel.

And that brings up a point that must be made. For yesterday and today to pay off the way they need to, it's not necessary that all, or even most, of those pitchers are wearing Rangers caps four years from now.

In fact, it's not conceivable.

At least a couple won't be able to get AA hitters out. Another one or two might get hurt, as much as we don't want to think about it. And who knows, maybe three years from now, Rangers general manager Jon Daniels . . . trades Main and third baseman Emmanuel Solis, both of whom are starring in Frisco, and big league left fielder Chad Tracy to Colorado for free-agent-to-be outfielder Brad Hawpe, who helps Texas separate itself from the Angels on the way to a playoff berth.

It's not quite three years later yet, but all four players in my silly little hypothetical were in my notes over the past few days.

A couple stories this week suggest the Rockies may shop the Fort Worth native Hawpe, coming off a solid .285/.384/.519 season, right in line with the .288/.384/.518 slash line that the right fielder sports over the last four seasons in Colorado (with his road numbers [.284/.381/.508] only slightly lagging his Coors Field production [.292/.387/.528]). Cons: he hits left-handed, he turned 30 this year, he'll make $7.5 million in 2010 (with a $10 million club option in 2011 [and $500,000 buyout] that he can void if traded), and he's not a better defender than any of the outfielders in the current Texas mix. But he's a base-reacher, and the Rangers are likely looking at players who can inject some of that skill into the lineup. What he might be, particularly if Marlon Byrd departs, is a potential bridge at DH to Justin Smoak.

(Colorado will also continue to look to move 29-year-old arbitration-eligible corner infielder Garrett Atkins, coming off a $7.05 million contract and a third straight season of offensive decline. A right-handed hitter, he's better against lefties and could fill the backup first baseman role, but at his compensation level he's a possible non-tender candidate. It's probably more likely that the Rangers, if at all interested, would wait to see if the Rockies cut him loose, as opposed to trading for his arbitration case.)

Main told Lone Star Dugout's Jason Cole that the mysterious illness that crippled his 2009 season was an unidentified viral infection of the liver whose onset may have been as early as last January. He's healthy again, and Main, my top 2009 breakout candidate, will probably be near the top of that list in the 2010 Bound Edition as well.

Solis, who signed for a reported $525,000 out of the Dominican Republic in July 2006, hasn't hit much in his four pro seasons (.212/.284/.332), and the Rangers are experimenting at Fall Instructs with a shift of the third baseman to the mound. Early reports on his velocity are encouraging—he's reportedly touching 94 (but righthander Tanner Scheppers is sitting 95-96 and touching 98, with a plus breaking ball).

Tracy has played 160 games in AA over the last two years and has hit .288/.341/.490 with 35 Frisco doubles, 30 home runs, and 122 RBI in that span, prompting roving minor league hitting instructor Mike Boulanger recently to call him the most overlooked hitter in the system. Said Boulanger: "This guy can flat-out hit."

Chris Ruddick of The Sports Network is one of dozens of writers suggesting in the past couple days that Boston could shop closer Jonathan Papelbon this winter, but he's the first to predict that Papelbon will be shipped to Texas for Smoak, and converted back into a starting pitcher.

Jon Daniels and Nolan Ryan have both hinted that Neftali Feliz will go to spring training as a candidate to win a spot in the Rangers' rotation.

Feliz will be eligible for Rookie of the Year votes in 2010, having not reached 50 big league innings or 45 pre-September days of active service. Julio Borbon's 157 at-bats exceeded the 130-at-bat threshold and thus his rookie eligibility was exhausted in 2009. (Why the league measures by at-bats rather than plate appearances makes no sense, not that it would change Borbon's status.)

For all his flaws, Nelson Cruz—in what was his first full big league season—was ninth among American League outfielders in OPS in 2009. Among those behind him: Ichiro Suzuki, Bobby Abreu, Byrd, Nick Markakis, Grady Sizemore, Curtis Granderson.

In Baseball Prospectus's season-ending "Hit List" power rankings, the website had the Rangers as baseball's 10th-best team in 2009, based on win-loss records and run differentials, actual and adjusted. Minnesota was 12th.

Contrary to popular belief, Texas didn't exactly change Scott Feldman's slot in 2008. The club changed Feldman's slot *back*. When the righthander went 25-2, 1.26 in two seasons with the College of San Mateo, he did so with a three-quarters slot not unlike the one he featured in 2009. It was only after the Rangers drafted him the 30th round in 2003 that he began to drop down sidearm.

Texas will draft 15th and 22nd in the June 2010 draft. The earlier pick is compensation for the failure to sign high school lefthander Matt Purke with the 14th choice in 2009. The latter pick is subject to forfeiture should the Rangers sign a Type A free agent this winter who was offered arbitration by his 2009 club.

Texas has let longtime equipment manager Zack Minasian and veteran scouts Jay Robertson and Mel Didier go. Minasian (whose son Calvin, a clubhouse assistant, won't return either) had been with the Rangers in some capacity for 22 years. Robertson had been a special assistant to the GM in Texas for both John Hart (with whom he'd also spent 11 years in the Indians organization) and Daniels. The 83-year-old Didier, who has spent more than 60 years in the game, was a Rangers senior advisor out of Arizona for seven seasons.

Toronto promoted Minasian's son Perry from pro scout to director of pro scouting, and named former Rangers catcher Doug Davis minor league field coordinator.

Phil Rogers of the *Chicago Tribune* suggests that the Cubs, who dismissed Von Joshua as the club's hitting coach, ought to wait until Rudy Jaramillo's contract expires at the end of this month and money-whip him, not unlike the move the Rangers made last winter to lure pitching coach Mike Maddux away from the Brewers once his contract expired. Said Rogers of the Jaramillo-to-Chicago idea: "This marriage should be a slam dunk, even if the Cubs offend other teams by paying Jaramillo at a premium." Rogers notes that Cub disappointments Alfonso Soriano and Milton Bradley were far more productive in Texas under the tutelage of Jaramillo, who is already the highest-paid hitting coach in baseball.

A Jaramillo hiring would qualify as an instant splash by the new Cubs ownership group.

Houston got infielder German Duran through waivers and outrighted his contract to AAA. The 25-year-old hit .136/.250/.159 for the Astros' AA affiliate in Corpus Christi after Houston claimed him from Texas off release waivers in July.

Former Rangers farmhand Johnny Washington is the hitting coach for the rookie-level Ogden Raptors in the Dodgers system.

The Fort Worth Cats of the independent American Association released outfielder Wally Backman Jr. The Pensacola Pelicans of the same league exercised their 2010 option on infielder Marshall McDougall.

Arizona Fall League play has gotten underway. The Surprise Rafters, whose roster includes lefthander Matt Harrison, righthanders Scheppers, Danny Gutierrez, Evan Reed, and Brennan Garr, catcher Doug Hogan, infielder Marcus Lemon, and outfielder-first baseman Mitch Moreland (as well as hitting coach Brant Brown), won their opener yesterday, 17-4. Lemon, Hogan, and Garr each appeared late without distinction.

The Fall Instructional League schedule concludes today, and my work on the 2010 Bound Edition is underway.

October 14, 2009

The Rangers have announced that hitting coach Rudy Jaramillo has declined a contract offer and will not return to the coaching staff next year. The remainder of the big league coaching staff has been invited to return for the 2010 season.

October 15, 2009

According to at least one local report, the Rangers are moving scouting director Ron Hopkins, who had been in charge of the club's amateur drafts the last five years, into a position as Special Assistant to the GM (a post opened up when Jay Robertson was let go earlier this week), and significantly expanding the responsibilities of A.J. Preller, who will now assume the role that Hopkins vacates while continuing to oversee pro and international scouting.

According to the story, reporting to Preller will be Kip Fagg, who moves from National Crosschecker to Director of Amateur Scouting, and Josh Boyd, who moves from Manager of Pro Scouting to Pro Scouting Director.

October 15, 2009

A clarification of my characterization (and some others') of today's baseball operations moves: A.J. Preller is not assuming Ron Hopkins's draft-related duties as part of Preller's newly created position as the Rangers' Senior Director of Player Personnel. Kip Fagg will take over Hopkins's role as Amateur Scouting Director.

Preller, as I noted before, will be in charge of all scouting, with Fagg reporting to him on the amateur side and new Pro Scouting Director Josh Boyd reporting to him on pro scout coverage and player evaluation. Preller will also continue to oversee international scouting, an arena in which his impact since joining the Rangers in 2004 has been most visible.

October 16, 2009

According to Carrie Muskat of MLB.com, the Cubs have asked the Rangers for permission to interview hitting coach Rudy Jaramillo, whose Rangers contract doesn't expire until October 31. Bruce Miles of the *Chicago Daily Herald* expects the Cubs to hire Jaramillo.

October 17, 2009

Here's what I know. Texas has had some great, MVP-level hitters over the last 15 years. Through both decent seasons and bad ones, the offense here has generally boasted production and swagger levels that the pitching and defense rarely could. Rangers hitters swear by Rudy Jaramillo, and he by them.

I know that the lineup struggled in 2009. A lot. This team might still be playing if the offense did what a Rangers offense usually does.

And that's the thing about a hitting coach. His job may be the most difficult on a coaching staff to measure, as a fan. We see the third base coach sending runners or holding them, and the results are basically black and white. The impact that a baserunning coach has is somewhat quantifiable. The pitching coach gets credit for the adjustments a pitcher makes in his slot or his delivery or the confidence that he has in his stuff, things that, as subtle as they might be, we notice.

But does the hitting coach or the hitter get credit for Juan Gonzalez? For Ivan Rodriguez? For Rusty Greer? For Michael Young? Obviously there's plenty of credit to be shared, but for hitters like those whose big league careers either began in Texas or soared to a new level here, every one of them is going to heap praise on Jaramillo, and they should. Like Eric Chavez's Gold Glove inscription to Ron Washington—"Wash, not without you"—a hitter who came into his own in Texas is always going to have Jaramillo's back, rightfully so.

And Marlon Byrd, Mark DeRosa, Gary Matthews Jr., Ramon Vazquez? Whole different story. If Jaramillo helped finish off Gonzalez, Rodriguez, Greer, and Young—each a hitting star, each a different type—he basically remade the careers of Byrd, DeRosa, Matthews, and Vazquez, examples of players who have come here and reinvented themselves. To speculate whether those guys are indebted to Jaramillo would be a waste of time. "Rudy, not without you."

The point? I don't know whether Jaramillo's departure is a crushing blow, or a good thing. Would Greer have become the same hitter without him? Would Byrd have bloomed late under a different hitting coach? Did Jaramillo get the benefit of having transcendent hitters like Alex Rodriguez and Mark Teixeira and Rafael Palmeiro cross paths with him in Texas, or they him? Matthews wasn't the same before Jaramillo and hasn't been the same since moving on. DeRosa came into his own here and sustained it after leaving. Milton Bradley, though he'd had good years elsewhere, was never better than in his Rangers season. But why did Brad Wilkerson regress? Hank Blalock?

More immediately, there are the cases of Ian Kinsler, Josh Hamilton, and Chris Davis, who weren't the only Rangers hitters to regress in 2009 but were the most significant. Jaramillo said in a radio interview, the day after his decision to turn down a Rangers contract was announced, that he thought Kinsler was trying to overdo things this year, especially once Hamilton and then Young were injured. Kinsler didn't take the right approach to the plate, Jaramillo said, opening up too quickly and not figuring out a way to fix it. Jaramillo's remarks were just short of throwing Kinsler under the bus, considering his job as hitting coach was to give the player the means to fix things. In any event, he said Kinsler will rebound, no doubt—but for more than four months in 2009 (30-30 notwithstanding) he wasn't able to do it.

As for Hamilton, Jaramillo pointed to the massive pressure the slugger was dealing with coming into the season—harboring the January slip in an Arizona bar; entering off-season, long-term contract talks but coming out of them without a deal; trying to meet the expectations of a repeat of 2008 (when he drove in his 54th run in the first inning on May 27, reaching in 53 games the RBI total he'd end up with in 89 games in 2009)—and, said Jaramillo, Hamilton didn't deal with the pressure very well. Out of sync early, and unable to find a rhythm due to multiple injuries, Hamilton lost his approach so badly that, at one point, Jaramillo pointed out, he saw only six pitches one game, swinging at five of them, and when Jaramillo asked him what was going on, Hamilton responded: "I can't help myself." In that case, Jaramillo seemed to suggest, in spite of the message being delivered, it wasn't being heard. Leads you to wonder whether it was an epidemic issue that went further than just Hamilton.

Much has been made of Davis's monumental struggles over the first three months of the 2009 season (.202/.256/.415 with 114 strikeouts in 258 at-bats, after hitting .285/.331/.549 with 88 strikeouts in 295 at-bats in 2008), followed by a terrific seven-week run at Oklahoma City under the tutelage of RedHawks hitting coach Scott Coolbaugh (.327/.418/.521 with 39 strikeouts in 165 at-bats), and then an impressive six-week finish with Texas (.308/.338/.496 with 36 strikeouts in 133 at-bats) that featured a much better approach. According to a local report, Davis said he and Jaramillo "had a tough time staying on the same page" in the first half but he was quick to say Jaramillo did everything he could to help him, and that his early season difficulties were not Jaramillo's fault.

As a whole? The club was near the bottom of the league in batting average and reaching base, swung at pitch one at an extraordinary rate (something opponents quickly began exploiting), seemed at times to lose any semblance of pitch recognition and to routinely make inadequate adjustments according to the count, and scored nearly three-fourths of a run per game fewer in 2009 than in 2008, a massive decline. In a season that featured better pitching and defense than this club has had in a long time, the lineup struggles were blamed for potentially keeping Texas from reaching the playoffs for the first time in a decade.

Jaramillo suggested that as the offense's strikeout totals began to mount, Rangers hitters—especially the young ones—lost trust in themselves. Needing to tap into more patience at the plate, Jaramillo intimated, they instead began to put more pressure on themselves and made things worse. There were a number of Jaramillo comments during the radio interview along the lines of "You'll have to ask him why he couldn't find his rhythm" or "They tell me one thing, but how am I supposed to know what's really going on in their heads?," but Jaramillo wasn't denying accountability. He said, straight up: "I felt personally responsible. I take great pride in my job."

Again, I can't decide whether I'm disappointed or optimistic about a change at hitting coach, though I have faith in this working out. The Cowboys, to the surprise (if not chagrin) of many, were better off once Tom Landry moved on. I thought "Bellybutton" was the best CD I'd ever heard until listening to "Spilt Milk." For months, maybe years, there was always a jar of Archer Farms salsa in the fridge—until we discovered Clint's. Jay Novacek? Jason Witten.

Maybe whoever comes here next will get more out of the Rangers lineup than Jaramillo was able to in 2009.

Or maybe Texas will go through three new hitting coaches in the next 12 months, not unlike what Milwaukee will have done when it fills its currently vacant pitching coach post for the third time since losing Mike Maddux to Texas last winter.

We don't know who Jaramillo's replacement will be (local reports speculate that Coolbaugh, Don Baylor, Thad Bosley, Carney Lansford, and Clint Hurdle could be candidates—and Gary Pettis was thought to be a possibility back when Jaramillo was flirting with the Mets as a managerial candidate), and even when we learn the name we won't know how much of an impact to expect him to make—just as I'm not exactly sure how much to credit Jaramillo for Gonzalez and Young and Byrd and DeRosa, or how much to blame him for what happened this season with Kinsler and Hamilton and Davis and Blalock. We do know this much: the Rangers need to find ways to get on base a lot more often, particularly now that the offense has become far more dangerous on the basepaths.

We know that Jaramillo is going to have a new job before long, and that's what he wanted. He acknowledged that it was his decision to leave Texas, that both Jon Daniels and Nolan Ryan told him they wanted him back, and that the club offered him a one-year deal—something he'd said publicly he'd be willing to take—that reportedly contained a $45,000 raise from his 2009 salary of $500,000, which was already baseball's highest for a hitting coach. Jaramillo suggested that, at age 59, the time was right for him to look around for a different job, for more multi-year security, and he pointed out that there are certain jobs presently open that a year from now probably won't be (the Cubs, who have already requested permission to talk to him before his contract expires in two weeks, seem to be at the top of that list). "This was my choice," Jaramillo said. "It's on me."

Hitting coach isn't as visible a post as manager or pitching coach or general manager or president, but Jaramillo was an institution here, a model of integrity, toughness, loyalty, and, for almost all of his time in Arlington, results. He'll be missed, but that doesn't mean—like Landry, or Joe Torre—that his departure will result in an automatic setback.

Nobody who has ever said "I've been fortunate enough to learn from two great coaches" or teachers or bosses or mentors wanted to see the first one go. And it's not as if Rangers hitters won't continue to employ what Jaramillo taught, and what he reinforced.

Still, bringing in a different hitter or two could make a difference, and so might a different voice. Compare the arrival of Maddux a year ago.

The important thing for Texas, going forward without Jaramillo, is that no comparison is drawn to the *departure* of Maddux a year ago, a mess that the Brewers are still trying to recover from.

October 19, 2009

The Rangers are expected to visit with 18-year-old Japanese lefthander Yusei Kikuchi and his adviser in Japan today, joining the Red Sox, Dodgers, and Giants as teams with Monday meetings scheduled. The Yankees, Mariners, Mets, and Indians will reportedly meet with the pitcher tomorrow.

Kikuchi, who boasts a fastball that touches 96 miles per hour, faces a Wednesday deadline to declare for Japan's October 29 amateur draft, in which he's certain to be the top selection.

If drafted by a Japanese club, he can still sign with a major league franchise but, if he does so, he'd be banned from pitching in Japan for three years if he were ever to seek re-eligibility. (Non-issue.)

But if he signs to pitch in Japan, the only way he could pitch in the United States in the next nine years would be for his club to choose sooner than that to post him for MLB negotiating rights.

Kikuchi conducted meetings with each of the 12 Japanese clubs on Friday and Saturday, which might seem unusual for a consensus number one overall pick if not for the crazy Nippon Professional Baseball rule that a player may be drafted by more than one team. In the event that Kikuchi submits to the NPB draft and multiple clubs select him—Patrick Newman of NPB Tracker speculates that as many as 10 clubs could use their first-round pick on the lefthander—there will be a drawing to determine which of those clubs has the right to negotiate with him.

It's worth noting that players are restricted to a maximum signing bonus in Japan of $1 million, plus salary and incentives that could bring a total package to about $1.65 million, an amount that is expected to be dwarfed by the Kikuchi offers coming from the interested major league clubs. The noted former big league scout Ray Poitevint compares Kikuchi's stuff to Clayton Kershaw's and suggested he'd be a top-five pick if eligible for the MLB draft.

The $5.1 million deal (including a $1.3 million bonus) that Boston gave 22-year-old righthander Junichi Tazawa in November—which was short of the $7 million offer the Rangers reportedly made—could be a baseline for what Kikuchi seeks.

Texas has been in on Kikuchi for many months and, for what it's worth, was characterized earlier this season as the possible frontrunner to sign him.

October 19, 2009

According to *Sports Illustrated*'s Jon Heyman, Rudy Jaramillo is in "serious talks" with the Cubs and "it appears likely that the sides will reach an agreement for Jaramillo to join the Cubs soon."

Heyman reports that Jaramillo is expected to receive a multi-year contract in the range of $800,000 per year. He was already baseball's highest-paid hitting coach with the Rangers, earning more than $500,000 annually on the contract that is set to expire.

October 21, 2009

According to Bruce Levine of ESPNChicago.com, the Cubs will announce at a press conference this afternoon that they have signed Rudy Jaramillo to a three-year, $2.42 million contract to serve as Chicago's hitting coach.

As for where Texas goes to replace Jaramillo, a number of names have been tossed out by the local press, but no candidates have been confirmed by the club. An interesting quote from Jon Daniels (published in a local beat writer's blog) on the profile he's looking for in the team's next hitting coach: "Watching the playoffs, it's obvious that regardless of personnel type, managerial style, etc., the one thing winning clubs do is consistently make pitchers earn every out. That's an area we can improve in. It's a combination of everything—situational hitting, forcing the pitcher to make a pitch, playing as a team rather than at-bat to at-bat."

The quote is interesting not because it's provocative or peculiar; anyone watching this club in 2009 would agree that the Rangers were extraordinarily easy to pitch to. It's interesting because it may shed light on an organizational mindset that the vacancy left by Jaramillo's departure may actually be an opportunity to get better. Notice that Daniels doesn't point a finger at the hitting coach—his comments could just as easily be pointed at the players whose job is to execute the at-bats—but the expectation is obviously that, between coach and hitters, there is a concrete philosophy that the club is focused on adhering to in order to reverse the widespread backward step that the lineup took in 2009.

According to one local report, Jaramillo's departure could push Ivan Rodriguez toward not re-signing with Texas.

The Rangers were among eight big league clubs to meet with 18-year-old Japanese pitching phenom Yusei Kikuchi in Japan earlier this week, sending not only Senior Director of Player Personnel A.J. Preller and Director of Pacific Rim Operations Jim Colborn, but also lefthander Derek Holland. According to reports from the Japanese site Yakyubaka.com, Kikuchi "had fun talking to" Holland as he picked his brain on life in the minor leagues.

Texas came armed with a message from Nolan Ryan and a visual presentation comparing the young lefthander's opportunity to that of 18-year-old pro golfer Ryo Ishikawa, who the Rangers happened to know is Kikuchi's favorite athlete. The Rangers hope to separate themselves by appealing to Kikuchi's desire to be a pioneer like his hero Ishikawa, who has broken onto the PGA scene—and by sending Holland, whose quick path to the big leagues might be one that he feels he can follow in an organization committed to developing young pitching.

A photo of Holland toting the Ishikawa prop:

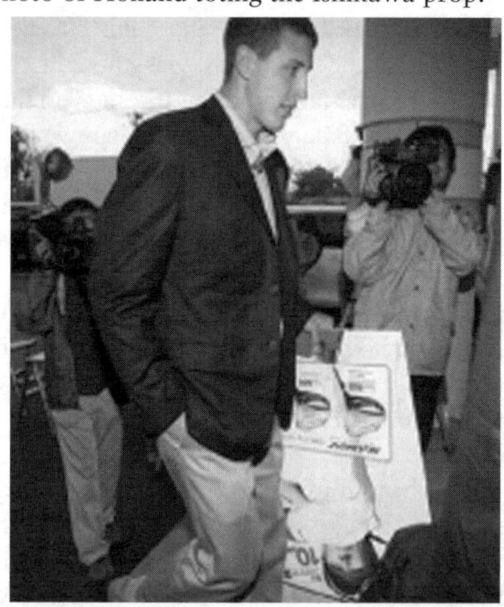

Righthander Tanner Scheppers is sitting 95-97 in the Arizona Fall League and has touched 99. In two relief outings, he's permitted one hit and one walk in three innings, punching out four and picking off a runner. Righthander Danny Gutierrez—sitting 93-95—fired three no-hit innings in his AFL debut, walking two, fanning two (both looking), and coaxing two infield pop-ups. Both Scheppers and Gutierrez are flashing plus curves.

Infielder Marcus Lemon is seeing AFL time in center field.

Baseball America named Neftali Feliz the number two prospect in the Pacific Coast League (though he "drew strong consideration for the number one ranking," which instead went to Giants catcher Buster Posey) and Justin Smoak the number nine prospect in the league.

According to Yakyubaka.com, the Nippon Ham Fighters have released Jason Botts (and Ryan Wing), and according to Sanspo.com, the Hanshin Tigers are planning to release Kevin Mench.

Catcher Kenji Johjima's decision to opt out of the final two years of his Mariners contract is bad news, as Seattle paid Johjima no buyout and now has $16 million of found money as a result of Johjima's departure.

Unsigned Rangers draftees identified by *Baseball America* in its rundown of the top 25 college recruiting classes:

4. TCU (LHP Matt Purke, Rangers' 1st-round pick)
5. Cal State Fullerton (OF Anthony Hutting, 38th)
8. Mississippi State (LHP/OF C.C. Watson, 29th)
17. Miami (LHP Jared Grundy, 46th)

Renowned infield coach Perry Hill declined the Pirates' offer to return as the club's first base coach and infield instructor.

The Rangers are putting on an instructional youth baseball camp on Saturday, November 14, headlined by Josh Hamilton. The camp, which will be held at Rangers Ballpark from 9:00 a.m. until 2:00 p.m., is for ages 10 to 18. Campers will receive instruction from former Rangers players like Dave Hostetler, Mike Jeffcoat, Mike Simms, and Todd Van Poppel on hitting, fielding, throwing, baserunning, weight training, flexibility, and team offense and defense. Guest speakers will include Jim Sundberg and David Murphy, and each camper will have the opportunity to meet Hamilton and receive an autographed photo and cap.

Spots in the camp are available for $150, and lunch will be provided.

More details and registration information can be found at texasrangers.com/youthballpark or by calling 817-273-5297.

October 21, 2009

The Rangers have gotten righthander Jason Grilli and catcher Kevin Richardson through outright waivers and assigned them to AAA Oklahoma City. Grilli is expected to decline the assignment and opt for free agency. Richardson, like Grilli, had been outrighted before and so he has the right to take free agency as well if he chooses.

The moves reduce the Rangers' 40-man roster to 38 players.

October 23, 2009

For no good reason (but maybe inspired subliminally by the Rangers' flirtation with Yusei Kikuchi), today I'm launching a new Newberg Report feature, which will recur (1) every Friday or (2) not. We'll see.

Rangers haiku.

The maiden voyage (hopefully not in the Titanic sense) follows.

Ninety-eight, plus curve
Can't believe the Angels passed
See you soon, Tanner

October 24, 2009

According to *Kyodo News*, Japanese high school lefthander Yusei Kikuchi announced within the last hour that he will play in Japan next year rather than sign with a major league organization. The Rangers, who scouted Kikuchi since the spring and sent a contingent including A.J. Preller, Jim Colborn, and Derek Holland to Japan for a recruiting interview this week, were reported to have significant interest in the 18-year-old.

Should Kikuchi sign with a Japanese club following Thursday's draft, he won't be eligible for free agency for nine years, unless his club decides to post his negotiating rights beforehand.

October 27, 2009

A few Arizona Fall League notes:

Righthander Daniel Gutierrez was named co-pitcher of the week after firing 6.2 scoreless Surprise Rafters innings over two appearances, scattering two hits and four walks while fanning three. Left-handed hitters are 0 for 17 (three walks and three strikeouts) off Gutierrez.

Gutierrez's teammate Tanner Scheppers (five scoreless innings, one hit, one walk, six strikeouts) continues to be the talk of the league, pairing a fastball that sits 95-98 with a mid-80s power curve. Very Verlander.

Scheppers gets some *Baseball America* love in the publication's "Draft Report Card" for the Rangers' 2009 crop, published yesterday for subscribers only.

Lefthander Matt Harrison, coming back from thoracic outlet syndrome, threw a scoreless AFL inning on Friday, permitting a hit and setting one Phoenix Desert Dog down on strikes, hitting another.

Outfielder Mitch Moreland, whose breakout season was cut short in mid-August when he fouled a ball off his right foot and broke a bone in it, has picked up in Arizona where he left off. After hitting .341/.421/.594 for Bakersfield and .326/.373/.488 for Frisco (and leading all of minor league baseball with 156 hits at the time of his injury), the 24-year-old sits at .348/.444/.652 through 23 Surprise at-bats.

Catcher Taylor Teagarden is reportedly headed to the AFL. No word yet on when he's expected to get into games.

There are various unofficial reports circulating that the cutoff for Super Two arbitration eligibility this winter will be two years and 141 days of big league service. If true, Jarrod Saltalamacchia (2.137) and Dustin Nippert (2.140) will have to wait until after the 2010 season to take advantage of the arbitration process. As it stands, I believe the Rangers' arbitration-eligibles are Scott Feldman, Josh Hamilton, Frankie Francisco, C.J. Wilson, Brandon McCarthy, and Esteban German.

T.R. Sullivan reported in an MLB.com mailbag feature that the Rangers met with Wilson at the end of the season to discuss the possibility of converting him back to a starting pitcher.

Toronto has hired Mel Didier to serve as senior advisor to new GM Alex Anthopoulos, a role not unlike the one that the 82-year-old Didier held in Texas the last seven years.

When the Nippon Ham Fighters took Game One of the best-of-seven Japanese Pacific League championship series on Wednesday from the Rakuten Eagles, 9-8, they did so on a walkoff grand slam by outfielder Terrmel Sledge, who was Texas Rangers property for a month in the 2005-2006 off-season (acquired in the Alfonso Soriano trade with Washington and sent to San Diego in the Adrian Gonzalez deal). Sledge hit the bomb off of momentary Rangers reliever Kaz Fukumori.

Houston claimed utility player Jason Bourgeois off waivers from Milwaukee. The Astros will be the sixth organization for Bourgeois, who was the Rangers' second-round pick in 2000.

Former Rangers farmhand Jeff Smith, who caught for Frisco in its inaugural 2003 season, was the Florida State League manager of the year this season, leading the Fort Myers Miracle to a 80-58 record in his second season at the helm of the club, and his third managing in the Twins system. He's been promoted to manage Minnesota's AA affiliate at New Britain of the Eastern League.

Outfielder-second baseman Garrett Nash, who turned down above-slot money as the Rangers' fourth-round pick in 2007 and instead enrolled at Oregon State, took the 2009 season off and will miss 2010 as well. He's in the midst of a two-year Mormon mission and plans to return to the Beavers in 2011.

Nash, a Utah native, became the highest-drafted player in the history of the state when Texas selected him with the 140th pick in a draft that also produced Julio Borbon, Tommy Hunter, Blake Beavan, Michael Main, Moreland, Tim Smith (who was traded along with Manny Pina to get Gutierrez), Neil Ramirez, Evan Reed, and a number of other Rangers farmhands who have progressed. That 2007 draft crop stands as one of the club's strongest in years, and that's without not only Nash but also righthander Anthony Ranaudo, lefthander Drew Pomeranz, and outfielder Kevin Keyes, the first two of whom in particular are likely first-rounders next summer.

October 28, 2009

According to local reports, the Rangers have begun interviewing candidates to replace Rudy Jaramillo as Rangers hitting coach, and among those whom the club has talked to is Rusty Greer.

Others characterized as "potential candidates" (among a field that could include as many as eight) are Oklahoma City hitting coach Scott Coolbaugh and former big league hitting instructors Thad Bosley, Gerald Perry, Rick Down, and Carney Lansford.

Bill Mitchell wrote an excellent feature for *Baseball America* on AFL teammates Tanner Scheppers and Aaron Crow, whose paths to pro ball share some similarities. Check it out.

Mitchell adds that Taylor Teagarden's arrival on the Surprise Rafters roster was brought about by an injury to Yankees catcher prospect Austin Romine. ESPN's Jason Grey reports that New York had the right to send a catcher to replace Romine but declined, leaving the door open for Texas to delegate Teagarden. According to Grey, the Rangers wanted Teagarden to play winter ball in an effort to get more at-bats, but he jumped at the opportunity to play in the AFL, which he'd done after his breakout 2007 season. The 25-year-old acknowledges the need to work offensively on his timing, bat path, plate coverage, and pitch recognition.

Matt Harrison threw two innings for the Rafters yesterday, permitting two runs on two hits, a walk, and a hit batsman, fanning two. Among the pitchers who relieved Harrison were Danny Gutierrez (two runs in two innings, four strikeouts), Tanner Scheppers (three runs in two innings, two strikeouts and three groundouts), and Evan Reed (one perfect frame, two groundouts and a strikeout), each of whom threw roughly two-thirds of his pitches for strikes.

Starting for Phoenix was Stephen Strasburg, who limited Surprise to a run on one hit and two walks (including one earned by Mitch Moreland) in 4.1 innings, setting five down on strikes.

Washington named Jay Robertson special assistant to general manager Mike Rizzo.

New San Diego general manager Jed Hoyer's first move was to dismiss vice president of scouting and player development Grady Fuson. Fuson, who had been with the Padres for five years, was under contract through the 2010 season.

The Royals promoted Kyle Turner from minor league medical coordinator to assistant big league trainer. He's been with Kansas City for three seasons, after a seven-year run in the Rangers system.

Fourth outfielder Gary Matthews Jr., three years and $27 million into a five-year, $50 million Angels contract, would like to be traded. His plate appearances in Los Angeles have gone from 579 to 477 to 360 in his three

Angels seasons, over which he's a .248/.325/.383 hitter, which is almost exactly what he was over the five seasons (.242/.324/.371) he played before coming to Texas, where he hit .285/.349/.468 from 2004 through 2006 and hit the free agency jackpot, leaving the Rangers righthanders Michael Main and Neil Ramirez as compensatory parting gifts.

A crusty, crotchety baseball writer from the mainstream media told me, almost a decade ago, that you can never put any stock in the work of a baseball writer not from the mainstream media. (I think he was referring to me, qualifying the one-way conversation as trash talk.)

Yesterday that conversation came to mind when a number of you were quick to point out that Garrett Nash was not only not the highest-drafted player in the history of the state of Utah, but (according to one of you) he actually sits at 41st on that list.

I'm embarrassed about the mistake, having foolishly trusted this article: http://www.collegebaseballprospects.net/2008/01/prospect-watch-garrett-nash.html. Maybe, before rolling with the Nash note, I should have given weight to the fact that that website hasn't published an article since May of 2008.

Maybe (for once), Crusty McCrotchety was right.

October 29, 2009

According to local reports, the Rangers have narrowed the field of candidates for their vacant hitting coach position to Rusty Greer, Thad Bosley, Gerald Perry, and Clint Hurdle, all four of whom will meet with Jon Daniels, Thad Levine, Ron Washington, and Scott Servais on Monday.

Club officials have previously indicated that they'd like to have Rudy Jaramillo's successor in place by the end of next week.

October 30, 2009

The Rangers have re-signed catcher Kevin Richardson to a minor league contract with an invite to big league camp. The club had outrighted Richardson last week.

This week's Friday haiku:

Feliz/Smoak/Perez
Best farm trio, says BA
— With Scheppers: best four?

November 2009

40-MAN ROSTER (40)

Pitchers (18)

Willie Eyre, Scott Feldman, Neftali Feliz, Frankie Francisco, Eddie Guardado, Derek Holland, Tommy Hunter, Warner Madrigal, Doug Mathis, Brandon McCarthy, Luis Mendoza, Kevin Millwood, Guillermo Moscoso, Dustin Nippert, Darren O'Day, Omar Poveda, Pedro Strop, C.J. Wilson

Catchers (4)

Max Ramirez, Ivan Rodriguez, Jarrod Saltalamacchia, Taylor Teagarden

Infielders (8)

Elvis Andrus, Joaquin Arias, Hank Blalock, Chris Davis, Esteban German, Ian Kinsler, Omar Vizquel, Michael Young

Outfielders (8)

Julio Borbon, Marlon Byrd, Nelson Cruz, Craig Gentry, Greg Golson, Josh Hamilton, Andruw Jones, David Murphy

60-Day Disabled List (4)

Joaquin Benoit, Brandon Boggs, Matt Harrison, Eric Hurley

Restricted List (2)

Omar Beltre, Alexi Ogando

November 3, 2009

According to local reports, "chances are good" that the Rangers will name their new hitting coach today. Each of the four finalists—Rusty Greer, Thad Bosley, Gerald Perry, and Clint Hurdle—interviewed for two hours yesterday with Jon Daniels, Nolan Ryan, Ron Washington, Thad Levine, and Scott Servais. Daniels told the local press that the club was "going to sleep on it [and] discuss it internally, and there's a decent chance we'll make an offer Tuesday."

Another thing that Texas is discussing internally, according to a local story, is the possibility of trading for Cubs hitter Milton Bradley, though the club doesn't expect to make a deal. The same writer reported three weeks ago that the Rangers had no interest in reacquiring Bradley.

Set your DVR's. Righthanders Tanner Scheppers and Danny Gutierrez were selected to play in the Arizona Fall League "Rising Stars" All-Star Game, which will be televised at 7:15 p.m. Central time this Saturday by MLB Network and streamed online via MLB.com.

Baseball America, in a look back at the 2009 draft, ranked Scheppers's fastball as second only to Stephen Strasburg's (just as BA had done before the draft), and had lefthander Matt Purke atop the "One Who Got Away" list of high school draft picks who didn't sign. Outfielder Jabari Blash, the Rangers' unsigned ninth-rounder, was fourth on the equivalent list of unsigned college draftees.

Rangers Vice President of In-Park Entertainment Chuck Morgan will be honored with a tribute at VideoFest 22 this Friday night at 7:00 at the Angelika Film Center at Mockingbird Station. As part of the event, Morgan will show and discuss several of his early Rangers video compilations.

Jim Reeves is retiring from the *Fort Worth Star-Telegram*. Nobody in this market did the human interest story any better.

Mike Brumley is Seattle manager Don Wakamatsu's new third base coach. Brumley was the Rangers' minor league field coordinator from 2005 to 2007, during which time Wakamatsu was on the Rangers' big league coaching staff, and the two also crossed paths in the Angels organization in 2001 and 2002. Brumley joins pitching coach Rick Adair, bullpen coach John Wetteland, and performance coach Steve Hecht as former members of the Rangers organization now on Wakamatsu's staff.

According to Kiley McDaniel of Baseball Prospectus, the Rangers are among a number of teams in on 20-year-old Cuban lefthander Noel Arguelles.

The Traverse City Beach Bums of the independent Frontier League released lefthander Jared Locke. The Sioux Falls Canaries of the independent American Association released righthander Pat Mahomes.

You guys set a record for day-one Bound Edition sales. Thanks a ton.

November 5, 2009

The Rangers have announced the hiring of Clint Hurdle as the club's new hitting coach.

November 6, 2009

I've been warding off a cold for a few days and have some things to say about Clint Hurdle, the Rangers' new hitting coach whose presence at his Thursday press conference reminded me of Mike Maddux during his own introduction to the media almost exactly one year ago; about the free agency filings of a number of Rangers veterans; about this Jermaine Dye idea; about a few fall and winter ball developments. Bear with me. I'll get to those things in a day or two.

I'll have nothing to say, however, about the Yankees' World Series win and the national media's sympathy card to the team and its fans for having to fight through nine grueling years to reclaim what apparently belonged to them. I had no idea how punishing that must have been. I now realize what a crummy, insensitive baseball fan I've been. Thank you, national media.

In the meantime, this week's Friday haiku:

Hearing Hurdle talk
Makes me want to grab a bat
(Umm, in a good way)

November 7, 2009

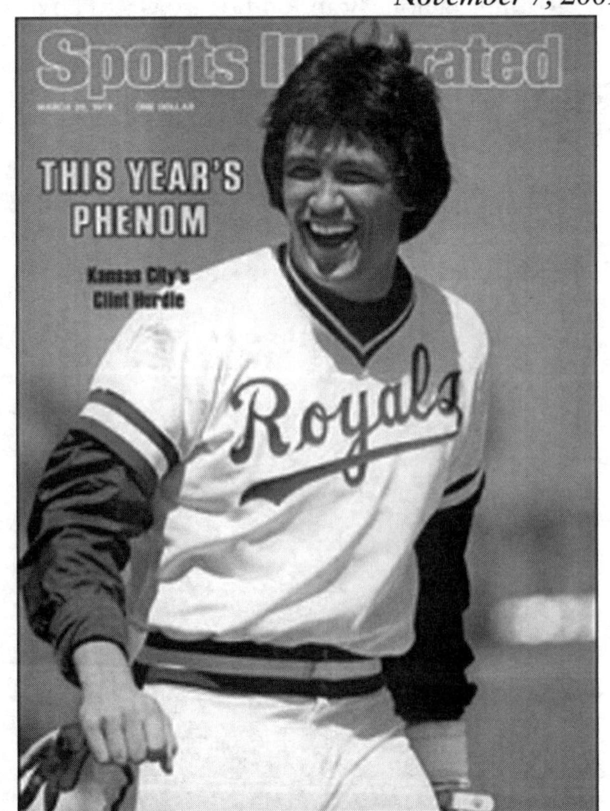

There are probably fewer than 10 *Sports Illustrated* covers that, for whatever reason, branded themselves for life on my brain. The March 20, 1978 issue had one of those. I can't swear that, at age nine, I read the feature story on Clint Hurdle. But I always remembered the cover photo.

I'm not sure why. Hurdle didn't have a baseball card yet so it's unlikely I had any idea, in the pre-SportsCenter days, who he was. (I doubt at age 20 he'd been invited yet to steal the Superstars Competition crown from Kyle Rote Jr. or Wayne Grimditch on Wide World of Sports.) I don't think in third grade I was quite yet a subscriber to The Sporting News, though if I was I certainly would have learned about Hurdle from Joe Falls or Peter Gammons.

We were about to move that spring from Farmers Branch to Dallas, where I'd be in a new school with all new friends, and I'm sure there was some anxiety about that. Maybe I was unusually in tune with the things that stirred my imagination, opting without realizing it to avoid thinking about the more scary realities laid out in front of me.

Maybe it was that, apprehensive or not, by mid-March in 1978, like every year since, the onset of spring training (and then, of the Little League season, which for me was about to be my first with Coach Prager's vaunted Henry S. Miller squad, having graduated from the Metropolitan Mets) had me fired up for baseball of any kind, and the smile on that player's face, and that Ian Kinsler mop (not a whole lot unlike what I was sporting back then), and those batting gloves, one on and one off, captivated my attention and stuck with me.

The Rangers were training in Pompano Beach that month, coming off a 94-win season in which they finished second in the AL West to the 102-win Royals. Hurdle had debuted in September 1977, hitting .308/.357/.538 in nine games, but none against Texas. But again, no SportsCenter, and Hurdle didn't make Kansas City's playoff roster, so there's no chance I'd seen him play. Still, he belonged to the team Texas was chasing, and that likely grabbed my attention, too.

If I did flip to the story itself, it was probably to look at photos, maybe of George Brett or John Mayberry or Whitey Herzog. I doubt this Hurdle quote from the Larry Keith story jumped out:

"I'm not getting any younger. My career has been like a book and this is the climax. I'm just going out and deal. I've got my chance and if I don't make it I won't have anybody to blame but myself."

But it does now. Hurdle made that comment as a 20-year-old, less than two years after turning down both an academic scholarship to Harvard and a football scholarship to play quarterback for the University of Miami, 26 at-bats into a major league career (with fewer than 1,100 pro at-bats, including the minors) that seemed destined for greatness. He wasn't a Yankee or a Dodger or a Red, but to *SI* he was still worthy of the label "This Year's Phenom."

More than 30 years later, and a couple days after listening to Hurdle's press conference announcing his arrival as the Rangers' new hitting coach, those very words he uttered as a kid who was a year younger than Elvis Andrus—or Tommy Mendonca—resonate as something that might be part of the message he has for the hitters, phenoms and veterans and longshots alike, whose offensive game he's being entrusted to get more out of.

When I wrote about the hiring of Mike Maddux as pitching coach a year and four days ago, I said this:

" . . . I had the chance to listen to Mike Maddux for about 20 minutes tonight, talking about the job he just accepted, the challenges he's eager to take on and how he plans to confront them, the things that made this organization and this opportunity so appealing for him. And man, my day has come and gone, but I want to pitch for that guy. . . ."

I came away with a similar feeling during Hurdle's Thursday press conference. He talked about helping players "get to a place they've never been" yet keeping things as simple as possible. He talked about his duty, as he sees it, not to overhaul anything, not to ask players to adapt to his methods, but instead for him to adapt to his players' strengths. He doesn't impose a "my way or the highway" mentality, as he puts it: he'll challenge his hitters "to paint a picture of themselves, and we'll go from there." To come to a two-man consensus about what the player is, and is not, and figure out, through trust, what the next step is to be better.

"I've got my chance and if I don't make it I won't have anybody to blame but myself."

Talk is cheap? Maybe so (though I'd argue otherwise when talking about coaching big league hitters or pitchers or baserunners, where the instructor's role includes serving as a mind coach), but there's a track record here, too. Yes, the Rockies were always markedly better hitters at Coors Field than on the road, but you had to admire the way they performed late in the season, especially in recent years, under Hurdle, who was the Rockies' minor league hitting instructor from 1994 through 1996, big league hitting coach from 1997 through late April 2002, and manager from that point until his dismissal in May of this year.

There were a number of factors—struggles—to which Hurdle's disappointing career as a player gets attributed. A 10-year career that was celebrated before it really ever got started produced 32 home runs, a .259 batting average, and just two seasons with as many as 80 games played.

The "All-American boy," so dubbed by venerable Royals scout Art Stewart, responded to the celebrity pedestal, by all accounts, by living the life of a rock star. There were late nights. At some point there was evidently a battle with alcoholism.

There was a serious, lengthy back injury.

There was a conclusion that he'd been rushed to the big leagues.

There were the pressures of failing to meet boundless expectations, to live up to the hype thrust upon him that he'd embraced himself.

Each of those experiences that Hurdle lived through as a player ought to resonate, in some cases more than others, with a number of the Rangers hitters whose productivity in this game, to some extent, now lies in Hurdle's hands.

"We're prepared for our future through our paths," Hurdle has said. "I've been given a lot of preparation for different situations."

Hurdle admitted he has no direct past relationships with any Rangers hitters, other than from across the field. He does have ties to Jon Daniels (2001) and Thad Levine (2000-2005), who were in the Rockies baseball operations department while Hurdle was there, and to Rangers director of player development Scott Servais, who played for the Rockies in 2000 and scouted for the club in 2005. Hurdle was on Don Baylor's Colorado coaching staff with Jackie Moore in 1997 and 1998. (He's never teamed up with Nolan Ryan, though he did single, double, and triple in nine at-bats against Ryan, adding a sac fly.)

And although Hurdle and Ron Washington were both Kansas City minor leaguers in 1975 and 1976, they never wore the same uniform. That wouldn't happen until 1992, when the 40-year-old Washington served as a coach on the 34-year-old Hurdle's AAA Tidewater staff in the Mets system.

Ron Washington's managerial career began the following year, in 1993, when he skippered the Mets' Low A club, the Capital City Bombers. But not really.

It was just before the 1992 Tidewater season ended that the Mets decided that Washington would manage the Bombers in 1993. Hurdle let Washington manage the final two games of the Tides' season, to get a little head start. It's something Washington never forgot.

Hurdle is apparently fond of saying, "It takes courage to have patience" (one in a series of self-help-esque Hurdle aphorisms that includes "They never care how much you know until they know how much you care"). While he's probably talking about a larger message, those words also tie in to the ideas of pitch recognition and command of the strike zone that Texas hopes Hurdle (here on a one-year contract with a club option for a second) can help instill in the Rangers offense.

More than once during his press conference, his job as hitting coach was rebranded as "offensive coordinator." Hurdle reduced strikeouts as Rockies hitting coach, increased walk totals, and brought the team's road batting average up (though it remained below the league median). All of those things would be quite welcome here. Hurdle talks about utilizing all 27 outs, about taking this club's "usable speed and power" and improving its "hittability," at-bat to at-bat.

Among the things Texas raved about when Maddux arrived was his proficiency as a communicator and motivator, as important if not more so than his abilities as a technician. The same goes for Hurdle, who calls this career decision (which he apparently chose over an offer to return to the Rockies in a front office position) "the right move at the right time with the right people for all the right reasons."

The Rangers believe it, too. They feel they've got the right guy to coordinate this offense, to make a team-first concept and lengthier at-bats and lengthier innings as contagious as last season's lineup malaise was.

Hurdle's way of doing that will vary from player to player, as he tries to make Rangers hitters better at what they do, rather than better at what he wants. If you heard him talk on Thursday, the former star prospect who never became a star player, you know how motivated he is to motivate again. As a player and as a coach, he's seen what works, and what doesn't.

Eager to get his tenure as Rangers hitting coach underway, Hurdle is gathering video and scouting reports and data, preparing to get a job done here, which will start with the 52-year-old connecting with Michael Young, with Ian Kinsler and Josh Hamilton, with Chris Davis, and, season to season, with whoever this year's phenom happens to be.

November 8, 2009

Hope you caught the visitor halves of innings five and seven from last night's Arizona Fall League Rising Stars Showcase game. Righthander Tanner Scheppers did what he does, sitting 96-99 in his perfect inning of work and spinning a couple big curves. But righthander Danny Gutierrez? Wow. He gave up a single and issued a walk, but struck out the side—with all three strike threes coming on devastating 12-6 hammer curves—while sitting 93-95, and touching 97.

Outfielder Jermaine Dye, whose 2010 option was bought out on Friday by the White Sox, is getting some mention as a veteran right-handed bat the Rangers might be interested in bringing in. I'd rather have Mike Cameron, a free agent whose job in Milwaukee has already been taken, as the Brewers have traded shortstop J.J. Hardy to Minnesota for center fielder Carlos Gomez, whose shockingly bad throwing ability I'm sorry to see departing the American League.

Rangers veterans Marlon Byrd, Hank Blalock, Ivan Rodriguez, Eddie Guardado, and Joaquin Benoit have filed for free agency, and Omar Vizquel and Andruw Jones will soon follow. Texas has made it clear it wants Vizquel back, and the interest is reportedly mutual. Byrd, too, but he's understandably going to explore the open market once the exclusive negotiating period expires on November 19. There's interest in re-signing Rodriguez but that one's a little trickier, given the club's depth at catcher.

Blalock will be somewhere else in 2010, as will Jones. Guardado is expected to retire. Benoit is going to have to take a non-roster deal somewhere, and I suppose it can't be ruled out that it could happen here.

Byrd and Rodriguez are Type B free agents. If they sign with another club this month, or if Texas offers them arbitration (a safe bet with Byrd) and they sign elsewhere after that, the Rangers would get a supplemental first-round pick as compensation. (The supplemental first round is where Texas has drafted Tommy Hunter, Julio Borbon, and Scheppers the last few years.)

Ben Sheets? Back on the market, after his deal with the Rangers in late January was killed by a failed physical. Texas remains interested. But with Neftali Feliz and maybe even C.J. Wilson in line for rotation looks, Sheets might be less of a target than he was a year ago.

As far as possible trades are concerned, there will probably be some around the league this week, as the General Manager Meetings are set to take place in Chicago tomorrow through Wednesday. And there will be groundwork laid for trades that will come down later in the off-season.

In February, San Diego general manager Kevin Towers denied the Rangers' request for permission to interview Padres national crosschecker Scott Littlefield, telling the *San Diego Union-Tribune* at the time that he "didn't think that (the Rangers') job description for him was a promotion—it looked to be a lateral move, and we valued him too much on the amateur side to grant it."

Towers is gone from the Padres, Jed Hoyer is in, and according to *USA Today*, the Rangers have hired Littlefield to become a special assistant—a week after *Baseball America*'s Jim Callis had speculated that Hoyer might promote Littlefield to the Padres' scouting director position.

I'm gonna be honest here. I'd be very happy if you ordered the 2010 Bound Edition in the next couple days. I've got a publishing house interested in my book for the first time, and have a real chance at a book deal. It won't mean much extra money, if any, but I'd really like the deal. I need to decide on this in next few days, and if I'm gonna do it, I owe the publisher a huge production cost check that will be doable if I get a lot of preorders in the next day or two.

So if you're a fan of Peter Gammons forewords, of a back cover featuring Tanner Scheppers and Justin Smoak and Martin Perez, of doing your part to boost the national economy and cementing your reputation as a Great American, and of me possibly getting my first book deal—and if you're interested in the Bound Edition—I'd be really fired up if you ordered books today or tomorrow.

Thanks.

November 10, 2009: TROT COFFEY

- There are "rumblings" that the Rangers and Braves have had discussions about righthander Javier Vazquez, whose three-year contract has one year left on it, an $11.5 million deal for 2010 (Buster Olney, ESPN, who speculates that Chris Davis and Nelson Cruz and possibly even Josh Hamilton could be persons of interest to Atlanta)
- The Braves, however, are exploring the possibility of negotiating a contract extension with Vazquez (David O'Brien, *Atlanta Journal-Constitution*)
- Florida is exploring long-term contract possibilities with righthander Josh Johnson, and I have an intense desire to see those talks fall apart
- The Rangers could also reengage Toronto about Roy Halladay (who reportedly would have vetoed a deal to Texas in July), and are probably a good fit for John Lackey, but with the ownership issue unresolved, the timing to sign Lackey might not be right (Olney; Jon Heyman, *Sports Illustrated*)
- The Rangers "are looking to sell high [on Cruz] because they feel he had a career year" (John Perrotto, Baseball Prospectus)
- Jarrod Saltalamacchia is one of several catchers around the league whose names are "floating as trade possibilities" (Perrotto)
- Reiterating a note that circulated locally last week, the Rangers reportedly have some interest in acquiring Milton Bradley "if the Cubs will pay a hefty chunk of [the two years and $20 million remaining on his] contract," and Chicago has apparently contacted Texas about a trade (local report)
- Texas is one of a number of teams linked to 30-year-old Japanese reliever Ryota Igarashi, a free agent who is interested in pitching in the Major Leagues in 2010 (local reports)
- Brandon McCarthy could be available given the Rangers' depth in the back half of the rotation (local reports)
- Not really a Coffey note, but the Royals got righthander John Bannister through waivers and outrighted his contract to AAA Omaha
- How do you think McCarthy and Kevin Millwood compared in opponents' slash line in 2009? Scott Lucas has your answer: http://www.rangers.scottlucas.com/archives/2009/11/texas_pitchers.html
- Among those categorized by Elias as Type B free agents are Mike Cameron, Mark DeRosa, Vladimir

Guerrero, and Justin Duchscherer, which means the Rangers would forfeit no draft picks to sign them; Jermaine Dye is a Type A and (assuming Chicago were to offer him arbitration, which may be unlikely) it would therefore cost Texas its second first-round pick (22nd overall) to sign him

Finally, thanks for the rush of Bound Edition orders yesterday. I'm getting close to hooking up on this book deal.

To answer a question I got several times yesterday—yes, if you preorder now, you can pick your books up at the book release party in mid-December. Don't have an exact date yet, but if you'd prefer not to wait for the mail, I'm happy to set your order aside for you at the party.

November 11, 2009

The GM Meetings wrap up today, and the Rangers have been a hot topic nationally, showing up on both sides of various starting pitcher trade scenarios. The latest circulating rumor involves Kevin Millwood going to the Cubs in a deal for Milton Bradley, with the possibility that cash (and maybe prospects) could be infused to bring one side or the other closer to an agreement. It's a fascinating idea, potentially setting up some domino play with the rest of the Rangers' roster if it were to come down.

Cubs GM Jim Hendry has said he'd like to resolve the Bradley situation before the December 7-10 Winter Meetings. (Ya think?) There's also growing speculation that he'd like to extend Marlon Byrd's relationship with Rudy Jaramillo by bringing the free agent Byrd in to play center field in Wrigley.

Speaking of which, I've been meaning to get to this for a few weeks but it slipped my mind. When teams submit final 40-man rosters in a week and a half (I believe by November 20) in preparation for the December 10 Rule 5 Draft, Texas might add anywhere from two to four draft-eligible minor leaguers to the roster, but I think there's only one lock, and he was a longshot at best when the 2009 season started. Lefthander Michael Kirkman, whose career seemed to be in jeopardy in 2006 and 2007 when he couldn't find the strike zone, went 9-8, 3.48 between Bakersfield and Frisco in 2009 (118 strikeouts and 61 walks in 144.2 innings) and kicked his velocity up to the point at which he was sitting 91-94. The 23-year-old threw quality starts six of his final seven times out for the RoughRiders.

Among the others who could be under serious consideration for roster spots are relievers Fabio Castillo, Beau Jones, and Zach Phillips, first baseman-outfielder Chad Tracy, and outfielder David Paisano. But I wouldn't be surprised if Kirkman is the only consensus addition.

Rockies corner infielder Garrett Atkins has resurfaced as a possible player of interest should Colorado non-tender the third-year arbitration-eligible as expected. New hitting coach Clint Hurdle would obviously have some important input on the wisdom of bringing in Atkins (who made $7.05 million in 2009) as a right-handed bat for the bench (and possibly a DH platoon).

Derek Jeter won the AL shortstop Gold Glove yesterday. Such an inspired choice. My tribute: http://www.bobanddan.com/contact/corbylaughs.mp3

Scott Feldman is the Rangers' 2009 Pitcher of the Year.

In addition to the hiring of Padres national crosschecker Scott Littlefield as a special assistant with a focus on scouting, which we discussed on Sunday, the Rangers announced a number of other hires and promotions. John Booher, who had been an area scout for Boston, moves into a pro scout role here. Former big league infielder Greg Smith was last a pro scout for Cleveland and will serve as a major league scout with Texas. New Director of Baseball Operations Matt Vinnola spent 12 years in baseball operations with the Rockies.

Jake Krug, who moved internally from Manager of Baseball Operations to East Coast Crosschecker last December, is the new Assistant Director of Player Development. Replacing Krug as East Coast Crosschecker will be Phil Geisler, a onetime Phillies outfield prospect who had last been an area scout with Seattle. Todd Walther moves from Assistant in Player Development and Scouting to pro scout. Matt Klotsche moves from pro scouting assistant to Assistant in Baseball Operations.

Richard "Hoggy" Price is the new Equipment and Home Clubhouse Manager. He's been with the Rangers for 34 seasons, the last 22 as umpire room manager.

Finally, we've gotten a few exciting commitments and near-commitments from Rangers players to sign autographs at this year's Newberg Report Book Release Party, which will probably be sometime during the week of December 14. More details on that very soon.

In the meantime, here's an excerpt from the Bound Edition's prospect rankings section—one of the 72 prospect features that appear in the front of the book:

Tanner Scheppers, RHP

The Padres made one of the worst top overall picks in recent draft history when they chose local high school shortstop Matt Bush in 2004 rather than Old Dominion righthander Justin Verlander.

San Diego would pay Bush $3.15 million to sign, which was $30,000 more than Detroit, who had the second pick, would pay Verlander (though to be fair, his Tigers deal included another $1.3 million guaranteed over the following five years).

There will be a lot more than just one team regretting the decision to pass on Tanner Scheppers in the 2009 draft. The 22-year-old hasn't yet thrown a professional pitch that counts, so to start up the Verlander comparisons would be hasty. Overly ambitious. Irresponsible.

Guilty.

It apparently wasn't money that veered clubs away from calling Scheppers's name with any of the first 43 picks in June. It was his history of shoulder problems, issues that caused him to fall to the second round (48th overall) as a Fresno State junior in 2008 and, despite a healthy spring in the independent Northern League and a clean bill of health from renowned physician Dr. Lewis Yocum, pushed him in 2009 to the supplemental first round (44th overall), where Texas called his name. Dr. Yocum's employer, the Angels, had picks at 24, 25, 40, and 42, but chose to go in a different direction each time, taking two high school outfielders, a high school lefthander, and Oklahoma University senior righthander Garrett Richards and leaving Scheppers for the Rangers.

Having used their first pick on high school lefthander Matt Purke, considered a signability risk, the Rangers could have gone conservative with pick number 44, and nobody would have blamed them. But Texas, who had Scheppers in for a pre-draft physical and MRI, jumped on the big righthander. It took until mid-September to get a deal done—Scheppers, having voided his college eligibility by pitching in the indie leagues, wasn't subject to the August 17 signing deadline—and it's fair to say that coming to terms took on added importance once the club's negotiations with Purke broke off short of a deal.

The most prominent national sources—*Baseball America*, Baseball Prospectus's Kevin Goldstein, ESPN's Keith Law, and John Sickels—all had Scheppers ranked not only as one of the top nine prospects going into the draft, but also ahead of Purke. His fastball was considered second only to Stephen Strasburg's, his power curve a true out-pitch—a combination giving rise to the Verlander comps. He'd proven in four spring starts with the independent St. Paul Saints (1-1, 3.32) and in a number of side sessions—all of which Texas was present at—that he was not only throwing well but also pitching healthy, convincing the Rangers that his previous shoulder issue, while a risk, was not enough of one to push the club away from investing seven figures in him. Scheppers signed for $1.25 million, the most of any supplemental first-rounder and nearly double his slot.

There were teams who passed on Tim Lincecum in 2006 (taken 10th overall) out of fear that his unorthodox delivery would lead to arm troubles, even though he'd never had any. There were obviously teams who didn't take Scheppers in June because of his shoulder history, even though he pitched in full health in the spring and passed pre-draft physicals and claimed his arm never felt better. All pitchers have some level of injury risk. Scheppers may carry one bigger red flag than the average first-year pro, but he unquestionably promises a greater reward than most as well.

The big righthander was the talk of the Arizona Fall League, sitting in the mid-to-upper-90s and flashing a devastating curve to go along with a slider and a change. Baseball people remarked about how easy the ball came out of Scheppers's hand, and he showed no lingering effects of a tweaked hamstring he suffered early at Fall Instructs. Though he was working in relief in the AFL, the Rangers plan to prepare him in spring training to pitch out of the rotation when the 2010 season gets underway, possibly in Bakersfield or even Frisco.

It would be premature to predict that Scheppers will reach Arlington in his first pro season, but it can't be ruled out, and while it's not as common for a pitcher to arrive in the big leagues that quickly as it is for a hitter, it's not as if there's no precedent for it. Especially with Verlander as the Scheppers prototype.

November 11, 2009: TROT COFFEY

- The Rangers are not interested in pursuing a trade involving Kevin Millwood and Cubs outfielder Milton Bradley (local report)
- Omar Vizquel is not likely to be back with Texas in 2010 (local report) (*this saddens me*)
- The Rangers are among at least eight clubs who have contacted free agent Mark DeRosa (Jon Heyman of *Sports Illustrated*) (*this makes me very happy . . . but I'm not optimistic that the fit is good for the player*)
- Detroit will listen to trade offers for Curtis Granderson, Edwin Jackson, and Gerald Laird (numerous reports)
- "No one has heard from Ben Sheets or his agent, according to Brewers GM Doug Melvin" (Bob Nightengale of *USA Today*)
- Contrary to reports last month that the cutoff for Super Two arbitration eligibility would be two years and 141 days of big league service, the cutoff is actually two years and 139 days, according to Arizona GM Josh Byrnes (Nightengale) (*if true, righthander Dustin Nippert—with two years and 140 days of service—will be arbitration-eligible after all, but Jarrod Saltalamacchia [two years, 137 days] still won't*)
- Bo Porter is Arizona's new third base coach

Don't mark any of this down in Sharpie yet, but here are some <u>tentative</u> details for the Newberg Report Book Release Party:

WHERE: Sherlock's Baker Street Pub & Grill, 254 Lincoln Square Center, Arlington (same spot as last year)

WHEN: 6:00—9:00 p.m, Monday, December 14 . . . or Wednesday, December 16 . . . or Thursday, December 17

GUESTS: Some are definite, some are tentative . . . alphabetically: Chris Davis, Scott Feldman, Rusty Greer, Derek Holland, Tommy Hunter, Justin Smoak

ADMISSION: Free—but the "cost" for getting autographs from our guests is the purchase of a 2010 Bound Edition, which you can buy now or at the event.

(If you pay ahead of time, I can bring your order to the party and you can avoid the line to buy books. As we get closer to the event, I'll find out from those of you who have preordered whether you want your order shipped or if you'd prefer to pick your books up at the party.)

The where, the when, and the guests are all tentative, but now you know where things stand at the moment.

November 12, 2009: TROT COFFEY

- The Rangers are reportedly looking at Vladimir Guerrero, a lifetime .394/.471/.705 hitter in Rangers Ballpark; at age 34 and with declining numbers (falling from .324/.403/.547 to .303/.365/.521 to .295/.334/.460 the last three seasons), he might not be able to command more than a one-year deal with a $3-5 million base (Ken Rosenthal and Jon Paul Morosi, Fox Sports)
- Texas officials met with John Lackey's agent yesterday, but it's difficult to imagine under any scenario that he would fit the Rangers' budget (Jon Heyman, *Sports Illustrated*)

I met John Wetteland once. He came to Newberg Report Night in 2005, thanking those of you who were there for participating in the "Toys for Summer" drive that he and his wife Michele spearheaded. Wetteland spoke eloquently, as he has every time I've seen him in front of a crowd, seemingly a man at peace and appreciative of the chance to share some words with a room full of Rangers fans. I admired the guy, and liked him.

The latest word tonight is that—despite earlier reports that the midday call to the police department from Wetteland's home, possibly from Michele, was because he was complaining of depression and contemplating suicide—the actual reason he told reporting officers that he "needed help" was high blood pressure and an elevated heart rate. Wetteland is out of the hospital and back home.

I'm happy nobody got hurt.

November 13, 2009

Kicking Vlad's tires
Careful not to kick too hard —
Don't want a blowout.

November 13, 2009: TROT COFFEY

- The Rangers have discussed center fielder B.J. Upton with Tampa Bay since the season ended, but there are no ongoing talks—the Rays "would need [a] big return," even after Upton's disappointing 2009 (Buster Olney, ESPN)

A few other things:

Texas reinstated pitchers Matt Harrison and Eric Hurley and outfielder Brandon Boggs from the 60-day disabled list to the 40-man roster. Reports out of the Arizona Fall League have Harrison sitting 94-97 with his fastball. He fired three hitless innings this afternoon (a leadoff walk followed by nine straight outs), needing just 33 pitches.

The roster sits at 35 players. A week from today is the deadline to add minor leaguers to the roster in advance of the Rule 5 Draft. Expect two or three additions, with lefthander Michael Kirkman the safest bet to be among them.

The Rangers also announced that they're bringing three free agents back on new minor league deals: righthanders Jumbo Diaz and Adalberto Flores and infielder Guilder Rodriguez.

Rangers vice president of community development Norm Lyons has retired.

Toronto has hired Gary Rajsich away from the Rangers to serve in a pro scouting role. Rajsich spent the last three seasons as a pro scout for Texas.

The Bound Edition early discount expires Sunday. This weekend, preorders are still $23. After Sunday, the price goes back to $25.

November 15, 2009

JD, please make a trade.

Max Ramirez and Wilfredo Boscan for Ryan Tucker. Tim Smith and Manny Pina for Danny Duffy (maybe the Royals won't notice). Randy Galloway for Ben Shpigel. The guy who does the Rangers Ballpark video board prospect features for a couple Carl's cheesesteaks from Yankee Stadium. It doesn't matter.

Just please make a trade. In fact, tonight would be much appreciated.

While I'm sitting here at the computer waiting for a breaking news bulletin, let me punch up my Cowboys macro. . . . OK, here we go . . . <ALT-b.s.> . . . *overmatched, unprepared, undisciplined, pathetic, sloppy, embarrassing, nauseating*. This football team plays predictably stupid football, and I'm stupid for caring.

It all flows down from the head coach, who is so obviously ill-equipped that it would shock me if there were one person aside from the owner who would even attempt to argue the point. Force me to sum up the Wade Phillips Cowboys in one play from tonight?

Ten defensive men on the field—coming out of a timeout—ought to do the job.

While Aaron Rodgers still looks like Ellen DeGeneres, my football team plays with the tenacity and focus of Gallagher. Ten more penalties (and who knows how many more that were declined), countless mental errors and concentration lapses, an inability (indifference?) to color within the lines. Demoralizing. The "coach" will surely blame this one on injuries, because the franchise embodies a culture of unaccountability—so why not keep the theme rolling?

Two good friends who know exponentially more football than I do will tell me I'm overreacting, and one will go so far as to try and talk me off the ledge. Save it. Marc Colombo's season ended tonight, and so did mine.

Come on, JD. Do me a solid. Trade Jorge Carrion and Bucky Buckles for Stubby Clapp. Distract me.

November 16, 2009

Oakland reliever Andrew Bailey is the American League Rookie of the Year. He received 13 of 28 first-place votes and finished with 88 points. Rangers shortstop Elvis Andrus was the runner-up with 65 points, one more than Detroit righthander Rick Porcello.

November 18, 2009: TROT COFFEY

- While the Rangers are trying to stay in contact with the agents for righthanders John Lackey and Ben Sheets and outfielders Vladimir Guerrero and Jermaine Dye, they "are likely to improve their team through trades rather than free agency this winter" (T.R. Sullivan, MLB.com)
- The Rangers "might be willing to chase" Tigers center fielder Curtis Granderson, who is probably going to fetch a huge return in trade from someone this winter (Lynn Henning, *Detroit News*)
- The Nationals are "drawing strong trade interest" in outfielder Josh Willingham—*now we're talking* (Ken Rosenthal and Jon Paul Morosi, Fox Sports)
- There is "major interest" around the league in arbitration-eligible Marlins righthander Ricky Nolasco (as well as corner infielder Jorge Cantu) (Buster Olney, ESPN)
- Texas is among the clubs that has expressed interest in free agent righthander John Smoltz (Rosenthal and Morosi)
- Texas is among a number of clubs who have reached out to free agent reliever Billy Wagner—the problem is he's a Type A free agent and Boston can probably afford to risk an arbitration offer to the veteran lefthander, meaning if the Rangers were to sign him, they'd forfeit the 22nd overall pick in June's draft to the Red Sox (Rosenthal and Morosi)
- In at least one Chicago reporter's opinion, the Rangers and Rays remain the most likely trade partners with the Cubs for Milton Bradley, and "[i]t appears Kevin Millwood would be coming back from Texas" (Bruce Levine, ESPN Chicago)

Finally, a few notes: Elvis Andrus plans to play winter ball in the Dominican Republic from November 24 through December 23 . . . the Florence Freedom of the independent Frontier League exercised its 2010 contract option on Andrus's brother Erold . . . Pittsburgh traded reliever Jesse Chavez to Tampa Bay (to get second baseman Akinori Iwamura) . . . John Lombardo, who finished the 2009 season scouting for Boston, has been hired to scout for Toronto . . . Cleveland named Steve Smith infield and third base coach . . . Cleveland named Sandy Alomar Jr. first base coach . . . Houston named Jamie Quirk bullpen coach . . . Boston has interviewed Red Sox minor league outfield/baserunning coach Tom Goodwin for a possible big league coaching position . . . St. Louis named Bryan Eversgerd pitching coach for High A Palm Beach . . . the Yankees outrighted outfielder Freddy Guzman, who declined the assignment and opted for free agency . . . the Rangers' minor league free agents are righthanders Bryan Corey, Brian Gordon, Jailen Peguero, Corey Ragsdale, Elizardo Ramirez, Josh Rupe, and Mike Wood; lefthanders Mike Hinckley and A.J. Murray; infielders Casey Benjamin, Adam Fox, Ian Gac, Mauro Gomez, Royce Huffman, Justin Leone, and Travis Metcalf; and outfielders Ryan Freel (sorta, I guess), Dustin Majewski, and Kevin Thompson (catcher Emerson Frostad wasn't listed but it seems like he should have six-year free agency rights as well)

November 19, 2009

The Rangers' 40-man roster has only 35 players on it at the moment, but that's about to change, as one window is about to shut and another is on the verge of opening.

The deadline to add non-roster players to the 40 is tomorrow, and the surest bet for Texas is 23-year-old lefthander Michael Kirkman, who went 9-8, 3.48 between Bakersfield and Frisco this year, finishing strong. For what it's worth, in the Bound Edition (which is a few weeks from coming off the presses) my prediction for roster protection is Kirkman and fellow southpaw Zach Phillips, who posted a 1.39 ERA between the Blaze and RoughRiders in 2009, pitching primarily in relief and doing an outstanding job harnessing left-handed hitters, keeping the ball in the park and on the ground, and killing the running game.

Among the other candidates for roster protection are corner hitter Chad Tracy, righthander Fabio Castillo, lefthander Beau Jones, outfielder David Paisano, and third baseman Johnny Whittleman. The Rangers also have a recent history of acquiring a minor leaguer just before the deadline to finalize the roster, so don't rule that possibility out.

At 11 p.m. tonight, teams can begin signing free agents who finished the 2009 season with other clubs. Local reports suggested on Wednesday that the chances of Marlon Byrd returning to Texas are "growing dim," as talks during with Byrd's agent at last week's GM Meetings in Chicago reportedly left the club less than optimistic that he's willing to take what the Rangers are willing to offer.

Faced with the possible loss of Byrd (who would net a supplemental first-round pick as compensation), the

Rangers seem more intent on replacing his right-handed production than his center field defense, apparently comfortable with the depth at the position that Julio Borbon and Josh Hamilton provide. It still wouldn't surprise me to see Texas look into a short-term center field option, with Mike Cameron sitting at the top of my list, at least.

With a Friday deadline looming for the submission of proposals from potential suitors interested in the sale of the Rangers, an interesting wrinkle developed yesterday, as Tom Hicks acknowledged that he's received commitments from Nolan Ryan and Roger Staubach to join "a number of local prominent families" in a group of potential investors headed by Hicks himself.

I haven't weighed in much on the ownership issue—mainly because we know very little about what's really going on with the process and any commentary on it would be pure guesswork—but I'll say this: Staubach has always occupied a well-earned reputation in this market and community that Ryan and very few others have. The two of them have always been all about tenacity on the field and unassailable integrity off of it, and just as Ryan has infused a tremendous amount of added credibility to this franchise, Staubach would push that needle even further. Those are two guys who have always done things right, and are all about winning.

I didn't know much about Hicks before he bought the Stars and then the Rangers, or about Jerry Jones or Mark Cuban before they came to Dallas to own sports franchises. I'm not about to suggest I know anything about the various candidates reported to have interest in the sale of the Rangers, or what kind of owners they'd make, but I'd be lying if I said the idea of Staubach being involved, even in a minority role, didn't excite me a bit.

Ron Washington finished fifth in the American League Manager of the Year vote, tied with fourth-place finisher Don Wakamatsu in points but trailing the Seattle skipper in first-place votes, two to one.

Clint Hurdle and Rudy Jaramillo shared an employer in 1994, the year before Jaramillo joined the Rangers' big league coaching staff. That season, Hurdle was in his first year as the Rockies' minor league hitting instructor and Jaramillo managed Colorado's short-season Northwest League affiliate in Bend, Oregon.

Kansas City reassigned Darryl Kennedy from the High A Wilmington Blue Rocks, a club he managed the last two seasons, to the Royals' Arizona League squad, which he'll manage for the first time. Kennedy's interesting managerial history includes four stops in the Rangers system—a three-year assignment followed by three two-year stints—and now three gigs with Kansas City, the first of which was a one-year assignment followed by the last two in Wilmington.

The leaders in most inherited big league runners allowed to score in 2009: Jamey Wright and Ron Mahay, with 22 each (out of 46 inherited for Wright, and 45 for Mahay).

Stay tuned for news flashes whenever the Rangers' roster begins to build back up toward 40, a process that will begin tomorrow, if not today.

November 19, 2009

After a couple years of missing on my 40-man roster predictions by a player or two, I got it right this time around. As I speculated in this morning's report, the Rangers have announced that lefthanders Michael Kirkman and Zach Phillips have been added to the 40-man roster, protecting them from exposure to next month's Rule 5 Draft.

November 20, 2009: TROT COFFEY

- The Rangers (as well as the Giants) got "pretty hot and heavy" in trade talks with Florida at last week's GM Meetings, possibly regarding right-handed hitter Dan Uggla, though the Marlins are also considering trading arbitration-eligibles like righthander Ricky Nolasco, corner infielder Jorge Cantu, outfielder Cody Ross, and utility player Alfredo Amezaga (Jayson Stark, ESPN)
- Colorado continues attempts to trade corner infielder Garrett Atkins; Texas and Baltimore are among the clubs reluctant to deal for Atkins because they believe the Rockies will ultimately non-tender him by the December 12 deadline (Troy Renck, *Denver Post*)
- ESPN makes the really odd suggestion that Texas should consider forfeiting the 21st pick in next June's draft (actually, the club picks at 22) in order to sign catcher Bengie Molina, a Type A free agent
- The Arizona Fall League season is over for the Surprise Rafters. While Mitch Moreland's AFL season (.300/.398/.457) simply continued to cement his legitimacy as a big league hitting prospect, what Marcus Lemon did in the prospect league (.343/.389/.627—which included four home runs after just one all year at Frisco—plus a transition from middle infielder to middle infielder-center fielder) makes him a far more interesting asset and potential bench candidate going forward. Taylor Teagarden struggled to find a rhythm after his late arrival (.212/.268/.423, 18 strikeouts in 52 at-bats) but finished the season with a bang, blasting a three-run walkoff bomb in yesterday's season finale.
- Matt Harrison gave up five runs in his nine AFL innings and predictably had some command issues (six walks) on his return from thoracic outlet syndrome surgery, but he allowed only five hits and was routinely in the mid-90s. I still think he probably starts the season on option to Oklahoma City, but his Fall League work was encouraging. Tanner Scheppers (.573 ERA) and Danny Gutierrez (4.08 ERA) saw their ERA's rise late

in the season but both struck out around eight hitters per nine innings with big stuff, fanning more than twice as many hitters as they walked. Scheppers held the league to a .214 average and Gutierrez was just as stingy, allowing opponents to hit just .209.

Check out Scott Lucas's analysis of the Rangers' 40-man roster additions, lefthanders Michael Kirkman and Zach Phillips, and the organization's top candidates for loss in next month's Rule 5 Draft.

Free agents now freed
So will first Rangers headline
Be "Bye Bye Byrdie"?

November 20, 2009: TROT COFFEY

- According to Phil Rogers of the *Chicago Tribune*, in a story posted in the last half hour, the Cubs and Mets and Rangers are reportedly engaged in talks regarding a three-way trade that would send righthander Kevin Millwood to the Mets, second baseman Luis Castillo to the Cubs, and hitter Milton Bradley to Texas. A Cubs source told Rogers that "there's a deal to be made there," but the Rangers have yet to commit to the idea of bringing Bradley back to Texas and would also insist that Chicago and perhaps New York kick some cash into the deal.

Take this one with a huge grain of salt. Seems unlikely.

November 20, 2009: TROT COFFEY

- The Rangers have summarily dismissed the Mets-Cubs-Rangers rumor that Phil Rogers ran in this morning's *Chicago Tribune*, telling MLB.com's T.R. Sullivan: "Not happening."
- Infielder Omar Vizquel is reportedly close to signing with the White Sox; as the 42-year-old is a no-compensation free agent, the Rangers would not receive a draft pick for his loss (Ken Rosenthal, FoxSports)

November 20, 2009: TROT COFFEY

- Long-term extension talks have apparently broken off between Florida and one of my favorite pitchers in the game, 25-year-old righthander Josh Johnson; Johnson is two years away from free agency and was seeking a four-year contract, while the Marlins would only discuss a three-year commitment; Johnson's agent Matt Sosnick says he "made it clear [to the Marlins] that it was going to be this year or it wasn't going to happen—it was now or never" if the club wanted to lock him up into his free agent years (Jerry Crasnick, ESPN.com) (*I suggested Justin Smoak and Matt Harrison for Johnson in May, and would give up even more now*)
- The Rangers, Phillies, and possibly the Giants are clubs for whom free agent infielder Miguel Tejada could "make some sense" (Jon Heyman, *Sports Illustrated*)
- Cincinnati got outfielder Laynce Nix through waivers and outrighted his contract to AAA, but the 29-year-old declined the assignment and is now a free agent

November 24, 2009: TROT COFFEY

- Though a number of teams have called Texas asking about right fielder Nelson Cruz, the Rangers are "not motivated" to deal him, according to a major league source (Ken Rosenthal, Fox Sports)
- According to Matt Sosnick, the agent for Florida righthander Josh Johnson, the Marlins offered Johnson (over whom they still have two years of control) a three-year contract with a club option for a fourth year, while Johnson wanted the fourth season guaranteed and a total deal at least matching the $38 million that Kansas City paid righthander Zack Greinke (multiple sources)
- The White Sox join the Rangers among the teams reportedly indicating interest in trading for Tampa Bay center fielder B.J. Upton (Rosenthal; Joe Smith, *St. Petersburg Times*)
- Texas is among the clubs reportedly interested in 34-year-old Japanese left-handed starter Hisanori Takahashi, a screwball specialist who went 10-6, 2.94 with a 4:1 strikeout-to-walk ratio in 2009 (Patrick Newman, NPB Tracker)
- The Mets are showing interest in righthander Ben Sheets (Bart Hubbuch, *New York Post*)
- Righthander Jason Grilli announced via Twitter that he is signing with his seventh team, though he declined to say which club it is—but we can deduce that it's not San Francisco, Florida, the White Sox, Detroit, Colorado, or Texas
- Baltimore could be in on Hank Blalock as a potential short-term option at first base (Jeff Zrebiec and Dan Connolly, *Baltimore Sun*)
- Infielder Omar Vizquel is signing a big league deal with the White Sox for a reported $1.375 million; he played for $1 million in Texas last year and didn't meet any of his workload incentives, which could have boosted his deal to as much as $2.35 million if he'd reached 600 plate appearances
- Not surprisingly, a couple minor leaguers recently traded by Texas were added by their new clubs to the 40-man roster to protect them from the Rule 5 Draft: Houston purchased righthander Matt Nevarez's contract and Kansas City added catcher Manny Pina to its roster (designating infielder Tug Hulett for assignment to help make room)
- The Astros also added righthander Jose Valdez, a 26-year-old that the club just signed away from the Yankees organization, to their 40-man roster; nearly six years ago, Valdez was made available to the Rangers as the player to be named later in the Alex Rodriguez

trade, along with second baseman Robinson Cano, outfielder Rudy Guillen, catcher Bronson Sardinha, and the player Texas selected, infielder Joaquin Arias

- Boston promoted DeMarlo Hale from third base coach to bench coach
- Seattle hired Todd Greene to serve as a pro scout
- Elvis Andrus played his first game of the off-season on Sunday, starting at shortstop for Magallanes in the Venezuelan Winter League and going 4 for 4 with a double and two RBI
- Michael Young finished 16th in the AL MVP vote (one 7th-place vote, one 8th, two 9th, two 10th); Ian Kinsler finished tied for 26th (one 10th)
- It turns out catcher Emerson Frostad isn't a six-year free agent even though his first pro season was 2004 (since his first renewal was for 2005), but infielder-outfielder Adam Fox is, and he has signed a minor league deal with Washington; Fox was the epitome of an organizational soldier here, and in 2009 had his breakout year offensively (.286/.344/.517 with 18 home runs in just 294 Frisco at-bats) while playing all over the field; the 2003 10th-rounder, who turned 28 yesterday, will coach one day if he wants to

November 25, 2009

There are a number of likely reasons that the free agent and trade markets have been slow to get rolling this winter, but one impediment goes away a week from now, as the deadline for clubs to offer arbitration to their free agents—in order to get compensation if they sign elsewhere—is on Tuesday the 1st.

Type A free agents are the only ones that cost teams their own draft picks to sign, but until it's known which Type A's around the league will be available without draft pick forfeiture tied to them, it would stand to reason that clubs are going to hold off in some cases on adding Type B's and no-compensation players whom they might see as lesser fits.

Texas has no Type A's among its free agents. Marlon Byrd and Ivan Rodriguez are Type B's. If either signs elsewhere before December 1, the Rangers will get a supplemental first-round pick as compensation. If they don't sign by the 1st, Texas will have to make arbitration offers in order to get the supplemental first (a round which in recent years has produced Tommy Hunter, Julio Borbon, and Tanner Scheppers for Texas).

An arbitration offer to Byrd is a lock; Texas would be happy to get him back on a one-year contract if he were to accept arbitration . . . and he's not going to accept it anyway, so the offer has no downside.

As for Rodriguez, that's trickier. It's not that his one-year, arbitration-produced deal would bust payroll if he were to accept the offer, but instead a situation where the club may decide it wants Jarrod Saltalamacchia and Taylor Teagarden splitting the catcher at-bats in 2010 and would be more comfortable having a veteran backup stashed away at Oklahoma City to protect against injury—in which case Rodriguez wouldn't make sense.

But with this winter's unusually flexible roster (not to mention the fact that the young catchers have options remaining), and the lure of that extra first-round pick if Rodriguez were to sign elsewhere, I'd lean toward guessing that we see the Rangers offer him arbitration by Tuesday as well.

There's no potential draft pick compensation tied to Hank Blalock, Eddie Guardado, Joaquin Benoit, or Andruw Jones (nor was there any tied to new White Sox infielder Omar Vizquel). Texas won't offer any of them arbitration.

Baseball America crunched the Pitch F/X data from this fall's Arizona Fall League season and determined that Scheppers clocked fourth-highest in the league with a fastball that touched 98.2 mph. Danny Gutierrez (96.2), Evan Reed (95.5), Matt Harrison (95.4), and Brennan Garr (94.0) were all in the league's top 50 as well. Scheppers was third in the league in average velocity (95.93 mph), and Gutierrez, Reed, and Harrison each sat between 92.5 and 93.31.

Baltimore signed 27-year-old lefthander Mike Hinckley to a minor league deal with an invite to big league camp. After the Nationals designated Hinckley for assignment in May, the Rangers picked him up and assigned him to Oklahoma City, where he pitched reasonably well in relief for four months, posting a 3.26 ERA, holding the Pacific Coast League to a .276 batting average, fanning 32 and issuing 22 unintentional walks in 49.2 innings, and allowing four home runs. He was slightly more effective against lefties.

The Mets named Jack Voigt hitting coach for AAA Buffalo, promoting him from their Short-Season A affiliate, the Brooklyn Cyclones.

November 25, 2009

Righthander Josh Rupe has signed a non-roster deal with Kansas City. Acquired by Texas from the White Sox in July 2003, along with righthander Frankie Francisco and outfielder Anthony Webster for outfielder Carl Everett, Rupe had been outrighted off the Rangers roster in April and spent the balance of the season pitching for Oklahoma City.

November 25, 2009

The White Sox have reportedly signed designated hitter Andruw Jones to a one-year contract worth $500,000, with another $1 million in incentives.

November 25, 2009

It's official—the book release party for the 2010 Bound Edition will be on **Thursday, December 17**, from 6:00-9:00 p.m. at Sherlock's Baker Street Pub & Grill (254

Lincoln Square, a few blocks west of Rangers Ballpark). The private party will be non-smoking—definitely kid-friendly.

Autograph / Q&A guests will be Rusty Greer, Ian & Tess Kinsler, Scott Feldman (probably), Tommy Hunter, Derek Holland, and Chris Davis.

Admission is free—but the "cost" for getting autographs from our guests is the purchase of a 2010 Bound Edition, which you can pay for now (via PayPal) or at the event. (The guys will sign your baseballs, bats, cards, etc., too—but you have to have the book to get autographs.) Limit three autographs per player.

Representatives from the U.S. Marine Corps Reserve will also be at the gathering to collect new, unwrapped toys for the Rangers/Toys for Tots program—which the Kinslers are the team spokespeople for. Please consider supporting the effort to help needy children in North Texas experience the joy of the holidays.

Follow-up reminders on Bound Edition orders:

Free shipping on November orders.

Starting December 1, a shipping and handling fee (the publisher's, not mine) of $4.95 per order will be applied.

No shipping fee, of course, if you pick your order up at the party. **If you've already ordered your books or plan to before the party, I need to know from you in advance whether you plan to pick your book(s) up at the party.** Otherwise your order will ship to you a few days before that and may not arrive in time for you to bring it to the party for autographs.

So if you plan to come to the December 17 party and haven't told me yet, please do that. Thanks.

November 27, 2009: TROT COFFEY

- The Marlins, according to MLB.com's Joe Frisaro, may buck conventional wisdom and let righthander Josh Johnson play out his final two arbitration seasons and then take the draft picks when he leaves for a massive multi-year contract, rather than trade him sometime in the next two years (*what Frisaro doesn't point out is that Florida would have to shell out at least $2.5 million to sign the 2012 first-round pick and the supplemental first-rounder they'd get as compensation for Johnson leaving as a free agent—if the Marlins believe they can win in 2010 or 2011, that's one thing, but otherwise they would do far better to trade Johnson, even if they wait until July 2011, both in terms of the players they'd get and the $2.5 million they'd save*)
- Pittsburgh has contacted Scott Boras, proposing a short-term deal for Hank Blalock to play first base (Dejan Kovacevic, *Pittsburgh Post-Gazette*)

Black Friday note: If you're going to do any of your holiday shopping at Amazon.com, here's a way to help us out a bit at zero cost to you. If you click the Amazon link on the top of any page on www.NewbergReport.com first, any purchases you then make at Amazon will kick a small referral fee to the Newberg Report (at no cost to you), which we'll use to help upgrade our website features.

Hope you had a great Thanksgiving and have a great weekend.

Aggies quarterback
Was great, but another J.
Johnson's on my mind.

Hook 'em.

November 28, 2009: TROT COFFEY

- Florida is "very willing to trade Josh Johnson right now for the right package" (John Perrotto, Baseball Prospectus, via Twitter)
- At least two executives from rival teams said on Thursday night that the Marlins had not yet told them that Johnson is available (Buster Olney, ESPN)
- Florida should be able to land "two [Major League]-ready guys, plus two solid prospects at the Double-A level" for Johnson (Keith Law, ESPN)
- The Rangers could view Jermaine Dye, who would "like to go 'west,'" as a "decent alternative to [Milton Bradley] or [Vlad Guerrero] as [a] righty bat" (Jon Heyman, *Sports Illustrated*, via Twitter)
- Roy Halladay wouldn't waive his no-trade clause to come to Texas (or Minnesota), but hey, he's willing to do so to go to the Yankees! Whoopee!! (Bob Elliott, *Toronto Sun* and *Slam!*)
- Halladay's preferred destinations are the Yankees, Red Sox, Angels, and Phillies (Olney)
- Oklahoma City catcher Max Ramirez, who goes into 2010 with one option remaining, hit .230/.318/.334 (including a four-game rehab stint in Surprise) in 2009, with five home runs in 287 at-bats; in half as many at-bats (142) in the Venezuelan Winter League, Ramirez has a league-leading nine homers, though he's hitting just .246/.358/.479 (he also leads the league in strikeouts, hit-by-pitches, and sac flies)
- Jonathan Mayo of MLB.com names first baseman-outfielder Mitch Moreland his Player of the Year and lefthanders Martin Perez and Zach Phillips his co-Pitchers of the Year in the Rangers system (very close to my selections in the 2010 Bound Edition)—it's an excellent article, very much worth reading
- Boston traded a player to be named later or cash considerations to Kansas City for infielder-outfielder-basereacher Tug Hulett, whom the Royals had designated for assignment
- Bud Selig plans to step down after the 2012 season (*Chicago Tribune*, *Boston Herald*, *Sporting News*, and others)

November 28, 2009: TROT COFFEY

- As reported by Geoff Baker of the *Seattle Times* and Jordan Bastian of MLB.com, based on a story written by Augusto Cardenas of *Diario Panorama*, Type A free agent shortstop Marco Scutaro says he's been approached by Boston, the Dodgers, Seattle, and Texas, noting that teams are interested in him as a shortstop (where he started for Toronto in 2009), as a second baseman (where he started for Oakland in 2004), and as a third baseman (he's been a utility infielder otherwise since his rookie season in 2002). Rumored Rangers interest in the 34-year-old (coming off a .282/.379/.409 career year) seems odd.

Let me be more direct: That one doesn't even need a grain of salt. Can't be accurate. Not sure whether it's a matter of something getting lost in the translation from the Venezuelan newspaper or just faulty reporting, but there's no way the Rangers would have an interest in Scutaro as a backup infielder—costing millions of dollars plus the forfeiture of a first-round pick—and he's obviously not a player who would start at second, shortstop, or third here.

Peter Gammons via Twitter (@pgammo): "Tis the season when agents try to spin news. So here is reality: Josh Johnson isn't going anywhere. 2010 @ $4M is good business for Phish."

November 29, 2009: TROT COFFEY

- Florida doesn't plan to trade righthander Josh Johnson this winter, according to several sources, including Johnson's agent Matt Sosnick (Ken Rosenthal, Fox Sports)
- Jarrod Saltalamacchia is headed to the Dominican Winter League, where he plans to play for about two weeks to test his shoulder (Nick Cafardo, *Boston Globe*)
- For what it's worth, both Jordan Bastian of MLB.com and Geoff Baker of the *Seattle Times* have updated their Saturday stories, backing off their initial interpretations of Augusto Cardenas's *Diario Panorama* article regarding the Rangers and Marco Scutaro. Bastian now suggests Texas contacted Scutaro but not about playing third base, and Baker says the same thing, adding that he'd read between the lines of the Cardenas story and assumed that Texas was interested in Scutaro as a third baseman when in actuality (according to Cardenas) there were more teams than just the Red Sox, Dodgers, Mariners, and Rangers interested in Scutaro, and it's possible that some team among those unidentified (along with Seattle) liked Scutaro at the hot corner (Baker: "I'll take the blame for this one, for not assuming there were more teams than what he mentioned in the story"). Cardenas adds via Twitter (@ACardenas13): "By the way, never mentioned that Scutaro said that Texas wanted him as a 3B"—which is true . . . if you run a translation of Cardenas's Friday story, it has these two quotes from Scutaro, in different parts of the article: (1) "Boston is interested, like the Dodgers, Seattle and Texas," and (2) "The Dodgers want me to play second base, shortstop in Boston, and there are other teams who have called to play third, although not [to] close doors, I would rather be between short and second." It appears those two quotes led to yesterday's since-retracted reports by Bastian and Baker, which led Evan Grant of the *Dallas Morning News* to ask Jon Daniels about the rumor, prompting this Daniels response: "We haven't inquired about anyone for 3B and have no plans to. End of story."

End of TROTTING on all that speculation, too. This seems like a "move along, there's nothing to see here" thing.

I watched a Florida Gators game from start to finish for the first time this season yesterday, and was blown away by Riley Cooper, just as much by his downfield blocking as his ability to separate and make the big catch; he's not going to be any fun for the catcher in a home plate collision

November 29, 2009: TROT COFFEY

- Milwaukee has "made a few inquiries" about righthander Kevin Millwood, though the Rangers aren't presently inclined to move him (Nick Cafardo, *Boston Globe*, who posits that trading Millwood could facilitate a Texas offer to John Lackey)
- Maybe so, but Jon Daniels says he hasn't spoken to Brewers GM Doug Melvin in weeks (Adam McCalvy, MLB.com, who: (1) points out that Texas and Milwaukee discussed Millwood [who has a limited no-trade clause] a year ago, when the Brewers lost C.C. Sabathia; (2) speculates that the Rangers are one of the few clubs with starting pitching to trade, though they would probably prefer to trade Brandon McCarthy rather than Tommy Hunter or Derek Holland; and (3) adds that Brewers outfielder Corey Hart is a conceivable fit for Texas, particularly if Marlon Byrd signs elsewhere)
- Miguel Tejada is on the radar of the Rangers (obviously in a backup role), Giants, Orioles, and possibly Mariners (Cafardo)
- Nelson Cruz "could be" a Braves target (Cafardo)

December 2009

40-MAN ROSTER (37)

Pitchers (21)

Willie Eyre, Scott Feldman, Neftali Feliz, Frankie Francisco, Matt Harrison, Derek Holland, Tommy Hunter, Eric Hurley, Michael Kirkman, Warner Madrigal, Doug Mathis, Brandon McCarthy, Luis Mendoza, Kevin Millwood, Guillermo Moscoso, Dustin Nippert, Darren O'Day, Zach Phillips, Omar Poveda, Pedro Strop, C.J. Wilson

Catchers (3)

Max Ramirez, Jarrod Saltalamacchia, Taylor Teagarden

Infielders (6)

Elvis Andrus, Joaquin Arias, Chris Davis, Esteban German, Ian Kinsler, Michael Young

Outfielders (7)

Brandon Boggs, Julio Borbon, Nelson Cruz, Craig Gentry, Greg Golson, Josh Hamilton, David Murphy

Restricted List (2)

Omar Beltre, Alexi Ogando

December 1, 2009

The Rangers have offered arbitration to outfielder Marlon Byrd and catcher Ivan Rodriguez, who now have until Monday night at 11 pm to accept or decline.

December 2, 2009

The Rangers' offer of salary arbitration to Ivan Rodriguez isn't all that surprising. Here are the possible outcomes:

1. Rodriguez accepts the offer by Monday night's deadline and is considered a signed player for 2010 (with salary to be determined just before spring training at the latest)
2. Rodriguez declines the offer and continues to negotiate with Texas, ultimately signing
3. Rodriguez declines the offer and signs with another team, which would net the Rangers a compensatory draft pick in the supplemental first round (which in the past three seasons has produced Tommy Hunter, Julio Borbon, and Tanner Scheppers)

Rodriguez, whose 2009 salary was $1.5 million, isn't going to command a huge contract (whether via free agency or arbitration), certainly one that's less than the average big league salary of about $3 million. Could Texas find a suitable backup catcher—maybe even one arguably a better fit than Rodriguez—for less than what Rodriguez may earn in 2010? Maybe. But there are potential question marks surrounding both Jarrod Saltalamacchia (health) and Taylor Teagarden (wisdom of having him play just twice a week), meaning you want someone with the ability to catch every day in a pinch if needed (*i.e.*, probably not an Adam Melhuse/B.J. Waszgis type), and the prospect of the bonus draft pick as protection against Rodriguez choosing a different home is significant.

I'd bet on Rodriguez accepting the offer. Even with Rudy Jaramillo's departure, he wants to be in Texas, and the arbitration-driven salary range is likely going to pay him as much as any club would offer him on the open market.

The arbitration offer to Marlon Byrd was a lock. He's not going to accept (because he knows he can get more than a one-year deal on the open market), and so he'll either sign with Texas at a mutually acceptable number or sign elsewhere, entitling the Rangers (who already have two first-round picks in June) to the added pick.

The decisions not to offer arbitration to Hank Blalock, Eddie Guardado, and Joaquin Benoit (none of whom would have netted Texas a compensatory pick) were equally unsurprising.

Only 10 Type A free agents around the league were offered arbitration: starter John Lackey; relievers Billy Wagner (who is reportedly signing with Atlanta), Jose Valverde, Mike Gonzalez, Rafael Soriano, and Rafael Betancourt; infielders Chone Figgins and Marco Scutaro; and outfielders Matt Holliday and Jason Bay. Signing any of them would cost the Rangers their second first-round pick (22nd overall), but with the possible exception of a couple of the relief pitchers, none of those players were going to be in play for Texas this winter, whether a draft pick was on the line or not.

Among the Type A's not offered arbitration who have been media-linked at some point to Texas: relievers Darren Oliver and Octavio Dotel; infielder Miguel Tejada; and outfielder Jermaine Dye, who has reportedly made it known he's willing to play a little first base if needed. San Francisco is also apparently in on Dye, and it wouldn't bother me if the Giants prevailed, given that Dye (who, according to Joe Cowley of the *Chicago Sun-Times*, isn't crazy about DH'ing, which Texas would want him to do) will be 36 and hit .179/.293/.297 after a strong first half last year. Atlanta, St. Louis, Boston, and the Yankees are also among the eight clubs that have been attached to Dye.

Thirteen Type B's were offered arbitration (including Byrd and Rodriguez), but signing them doesn't cost a draft pick, as a team losing a Type B it offered arbitration to simply gets a manufactured pick in the supplemental first round (not a pick forfeited by any club). For what it's worth, the Angels didn't offer arbitration to outfielder Vlad Guerrero, so Los Angeles won't get a supplemental first when Guerrero signs elsewhere.

The Winter Meetings kick off in Indianapolis on Monday, with the Rangers probably less likely to be in the mix for the top tier or two of free agents than to get together with another club on a trade—or at least lay the groundwork for one. There are more than 200 arbitration-eligibles (Super Two's through those short of six years of service), and many will be non-tendered on December 12, flooding the market with a new wave of free agents—including many players that clubs are trying to trade right now.

The Rangers' arbitration-eligibles are Scott Feldman, Josh Hamilton, Frankie Francisco, C.J. Wilson, Dustin Nippert, Brandon McCarthy, and Esteban German.

The key roster pieces needed appear to be a utility infielder, a right-handed bat for the middle of the order, and probably one dependable arm—which could be a starter or reliever because of the club's flexibility with pitchers like Neftali Feliz, Derek Holland, Wilson, Matt Harrison, McCarthy, Doug Mathis, and Guillermo Moscoso (and Nippert, if retained) each possibilities for work out of either the rotation or the bullpen.

Baltimore has reportedly asked Texas about Kevin Millwood, according to Ken Rosenthal and Jon Paul Morosi of Fox Sports, though talks were characterized as "not serious."

According to a local reporter, free agent reliever J.J. Putz (coming off July non-Tommy John elbow surgery) is on the Rangers' radar, free agent starter Ben Sheets remains of interest, free agent infielder Bobby Crosby is a possible target, and Marlins second baseman Dan Uggla isn't—and never was—of interest to Texas. The same reporter writes that Texas asked Florida about righthander Josh Johnson and "other pitching" but "didn't get anywhere."

Marlins GM Michael Hill (a Harvard product who played outfield and first base in the Rangers farm system in the early 1990s) told a Florida radio station "with certainty" that Johnson will open the 2010 season as a Marlin.

Jerry Crasnick of ESPN reports that Texas and Houston are interested in free agent righthander Brett Myers if he'd consider a short-term deal heavy on incentives.

The Padres named Doug Dascenzo manager of their AA Texas League affiliate in San Antonio.

According to NPB Tracker, the Hanshin Tigers will fire scout Tom O'Malley.

December 2, 2009

A few things:

1. Scott Feldman confirmed today that he'll be at the Newberg Report Book Release Party on December 17 (6-9 p.m.) at Sherlock's in Arlington. He rounds out the guest list that also includes Rusty Greer, Ian & Tess Kinsler, Tommy Hunter, Derek Holland, and Chris Davis. (The price of autographs is the purchase of the book, either in advance or at the party.)
2. If you've pre-ordered a book and plan to pick it up at the party (since shipments won't arrive at your home until after the 17th), I need you to let me know that tonight if you haven't already.
3. I will be Brady Tinker's guest on DFW Sports Beat tomorrow night. The show will be televised at 6:30 p.m. on Fox Sports Southwest and again at midnight.
4. Online fan voting to choose the 2010 Ford C. Frick Award for broadcasting excellence is underway. Fans are allowed to cast votes every day for the entire month of December. Among the candidates are Mark Holtz, Eric Nadel, Josh Lewin, and Tom Grieve.
5. A few TROT COFFEY notes:

- Jarrod Saltalamacchia made his 2009 Dominican Winter League debut yesterday, singling in five trips as the Toros del Este designated hitter—but was reportedly removed after an at-bat today with numbness and tingling down his throwing arm, symptoms that can't be dismissed as he rehabilitates following September surgery for thoracic outlet syndrome
- The Giants, Mets, and Royals are among the teams interested in catcher Ivan Rodriguez, who has until Monday night to accept or decline the Rangers' arbitration offer (Jon Heyman, *Sports Illustrated*); Texas would get a supplemental first-round pick as compensation if he signs with another club—but the Saltalamacchia development probably intensifies the Rangers' interest in retaining the veteran
- Outfielder-first baseman Chad Tracy (the Rangers farmhand, not the Diamondbacks free agent) is among 10 players *Baseball America* features as potential picks in next Thursday's Rule 5 Draft, and righthander Brennan Garr is among the publication's second set of 10 draft-eligible players to watch
- The Pirates, Dodgers, Braves, and A's are interested in righthander Kameron Loe, who posted a 6.33 ERA in limited action for the Fukuoka SoftBank Hawks in Japan last season (Dejan Kovacevic, *Pittsburgh Post-Gazette*)
- Righthander Jason Grilli signed a minor league deal with Cleveland
- According to Jorge Arangure on Twitter (@ jorgearangure), MLB owners are "strongly in favor" of a worldwide draft, and the Players Association reportedly won't oppose it—not especially good news for the Rangers, who are among the most aggressive teams in Latin America in particular and would lose a competitive advantage if that open market becomes subject to the draft

December 4, 2009: TROT COFFEY

Indy shopping list:
Reliever, bat, infielder—
And now catcher too?

- According to various local reports, Texas is interested in oft-injured, high-ceiling righthanders Ben Sheets, Rich Harden, and Brett Myers, particularly if they'd be willing to take one-year deals heavy on incentives
- Also according to local reports, other free agents who could be on the Rangers' radar as the Winter Meetings get set to kick off in Indianapolis on Monday: right-handed relievers J.J. Putz and LaTroy Hawkins; left-handed relievers Darren Oliver and Will Ohman; catchers Ivan Rodriguez (who is expected to decline the club's arbitration offer by Monday night's deadline) and Yorvit Torrealba; right-handed bats Marlon Byrd (a certainty to decline arbitration), Jermaine Dye, and Vladimir Guerrero; and infielders Bobby Crosby, Craig Counsell, and Jamey Carroll
- Carroll has also drawn interest from the Red Sox, Angels, Dodgers, A's, Pirates, Reds, Indians, and Marlins (Ed Price, AOL FanHouse)
- Should Byrd depart, center field apparently belongs to Julio Borbon the way the roster looks right now (said Jon Daniels in a local chat session)—Borbon is playing center field exclusively in the Dominican Republic
- Joaquin Arias's shoulder has held up well in winter ball and he's in the mix for the utility infielder spot (Daniels)

- Infielder Esteban German may be non-tendered by the December 12 deadline, as he could be in line for an arbitration-driven contract close to the $1 million that Omar Vizquel made last year (local report)
- Justin Smoak, Mitch Moreland, and Chad Tracy will each see time behind Chris Davis at first base when spring training opens (local report)
- Internal left-handed bullpen candidates include C.J. Wilson, Derek Holland, and Matt Harrison (each of whom will get a shot at the rotation as well), plus Zach Phillips, Michael Kirkman, Kasey Kiker, and Mike Ballard (Daniels)
- Righthander Eric Hurley is working out in Arlington and will be in big league camp, though he'll be behind others as he continues to rehab his shoulder (Daniels)
- Texas, Minnesota, Milwaukee, and Seattle are interested in free agent lefthander Jarrod Washburn (Tim Brown, Yahoo! Sports)
- The Cardinals and Cubs are frontrunners for free agent righthander Vicente Padilla (*La Prensa*, a news outlet out of Managua, Nicaragua)
- Seattle has emerged as the frontrunner to sign Chone Figgins (Jon Paul Morosi, Fox Sports)
- Manager Steve Buechele was promoted from Bakersfield to Frisco, headlining a slew of minor league coaching moves; Mike Micucci was promoted from the RoughRiders' helm to minor league field coordinator, a position that the Rangers didn't fill last year after 2008 field coordinator Dave Anderson was promoted to Ron Washington's coaching staff; the Bakersfield managerial post remains vacant
- Rusty Greer will have a role with the organization during spring training and then in a community relations capacity after that; the club has discussed minor league jobs with Greer "a few times" but the fit for Greer and his family hasn't been right yet (Daniels)
- Lefthander Martin Perez will start the season back in Frisco and is expected to spend most of 2010 there (Daniels)
- Sixteen-year-old shortstop Jurickson Profar will get the chance to compete for a full-season assignment in camp (Daniels)
- *Baseball America* editor in chief John Manuel has only one of several votes for the publication's annual winter ranking of baseball's farm systems, but he revealed yesterday that he will have the Texas system ("still bursting with impact talent") number one for the second straight season, even though Elvis Andrus, Tommy Hunter, Borbon, Holland, and Taylor Teagarden have graduated to the big leagues
- The Windy City Thunderbolts exercised a 2010 contract option on first baseman-outfielder J.T. Restko

December 4, 2009

Texas has claimed veteran utility infielder Joe Inglett, age 31, off waivers from Toronto. His addition brings the club's 40-man roster total to 38 players.

December 6, 2009

If my pro football team (whose lack of character and lack of intensity and lack of pride and lack of discipline get exploited by well-coached teams) is going to lose to the Giants, it might as well be on the day before the Winter Meetings, when (1) I can take my mind fully off of pro football and (2) my baseball team's general manager can go into Monday with a little extra boost. What an embarrassing "effort" by a mentally weak football team.

There are four to six teams kicking the tires on first-time arbitration-eligible Marlins reliever Matt Lindstrom, including Texas and Tampa Bay, with a trade described as "virtually certain" by one source and "imminent" by another (Ken Rosenthal, Fox Sports; Buster Olney, ESPN; Jon Heyman, *Sports Illustrated*)

Tampa Bay and Cincinnati are among the clubs that have asked about outfielder Nelson Cruz, but Texas remains reluctant to move him (Jon Paul Morosi, Fox Sports)

Chicago and Tampa Bay will probably consummate a Milton Bradley/Pat Burrell deal during the Winter Meetings, and Marlon Byrd could sign a deal with someone other than Texas this week as well (Peter Gammons, ESPN)

Atlanta has a "strong interest" in Byrd, according to his agent Seth Levinson (Mark Bowman, MLB.com)

A Texas official says the club would take outfielder Bradley back but the Rangers are "not sure they want to deal with 'that headache' again" (Carrie Muskat, MLB.com)

Tomorrow night at 11 p.m. Central is the deadline for Byrd and Ivan Rodriguez to accept or decline the Rangers' arbitration offers, though a decline (a certainty for Byrd and a likelihood for Rodriguez) doesn't prevent Texas from continuing efforts to re-sign them

Doctors say that the discomfort in Jarrod Saltalamacchia's right arm is not unusual following thoracic outlet syndrome surgery; he'll be shut down for about a month and is expected to be ready for spring training

Infielder-outfielder Joe Inglett, claimed off waivers from Toronto on Friday, is not yet eligible for arbitration

Ian and Tess Kinsler, the Rangers' ambassadors for the Toys for Tots program for the fourth straight season, kicked things off on Thursday with a shopping spree for kids along with teammates Chris Davis and Craig Gentry; to participate between now and this Thursday, December 10, you can drop off new, unwrapped toys at either the Grand Slam Gift Shop at Rangers Ballpark in Arlington, the Rangers' Dallas Team Shop at 2222 McKinney Avenue (at Pearl), or the Rangers' Fort Worth Team Shop at 316 Main Street, between 9:00 a.m. and 5:00 p.m.—I'd also encourage you to bring new, unwrapped toys to the December 17 Newberg Report Book Release Party, where Ian and Tess will be among our guests

Nolan Ryan's seventh no-hitter is airing in its entirety right now on MLB Network (Channel 213 on DirecTV) (wow, does anyone remember that "Shout!" used to play on home runs in the pre-"Theme from the Natural" days at Arlington Stadium?)

December 7, 2009: TROT COFFEY

Early rumors from Indianapolis:

- Texas is "perhaps the most serious among teams in discussion for" Florida reliever Matt Lindstrom; two interested teams have dropped out of talks, leaving two others besides the Rangers in the mix (Buster Olney, ESPN)
- Marlon Byrd is drawing interest from Atlanta, Seattle, the Cubs, and the Yankees, whose priority is to bring Johnny Damon back (Jon Heyman, *Sports Illustrated*)
- One reporter for another club claims to have heard Sunday night that "the Rangers are looking to move righthander Kevin Millwood because of their continuing financial dilemma" (La Velle E. Neal, *Minneapolis Star Tribune*)
- Seattle hired Andy Fox as a minor league instructor
- Roy Halladay is now "said to be open to listen to all possibilities, including the Angels, despite [the fact that] they hold spring training [in Arizona]" (Olney)
- The Rangers have talked to the agent for righthander Brett Myers about a one-year contract, but Myers is still hunting for a multi-year deal (Jerry Crasnick, ESPN)
- All the talk about Lindstrom and Myers and J.J. Putz as right-handed set-up options seems to support the idea that the Rangers are trying to free Neftali Feliz up to compete for a rotation spot (various local reports)
- One of the potential bidders for the Rangers apparently said Sunday that "he had 'no interest' at all in acquiring [outfielder Milton] Bradley if his group gets the club, even if the Cubs pay the entire amount of the contract" (Paul Sullivan, *Chicago Tribune*)

December 7, 2009

The Rangers made a trade with Detroit on the first day of the Winter Meetings last year, shipping Gerald Laird to the Tigers for minor league righthanders Guillermo Moscoso and Carlos Melo. The two teams have gotten together on Day One again this year, as the Rangers have acquired 28-year-old left-handed reliever Clay Rapada for a player to be named or cash considerations.

Rapada, as far as I can tell, is a 40-man roster member and out of options, making this deal not unlike the one a couple years ago in which Texas acquired right-handed reliever Jon Leicester from the Cubs (for player to be named Clint Brannon), a low-risk move to give Leicester a shot to win a bullpen job in camp (which he failed to do).

Rapada, who stands 6'5" and pitches from a low slot, split each of the last three seasons between AAA and Detroit, compiling a big league ERA of 4.94 in that span. He's been especially tough against left-handed hitters.

In AAA last season, he fanned 47 and issued 14 unintentional walks in 45.2 innings, allowing one home run.

Texas also outrighted righthander Willie Eyre to AAA—keeping the roster at 38 members—and Eyre has accepted the assignment.

December 7, 2009: TROT COFFEY

According to various local reports:

- The Rangers have expressly acknowledged, for what I believe is the first time, that they plan to go forward with Julio Borbon as the everyday center fielder (and leadoff hitter) going into camp, flanked by Josh Hamilton in left field and Nelson Cruz in right, with David Murphy slated to get his at-bats both at designated hitter and as the fourth outfielder; credit was given to the progress Borbon has made patrolling center field in the Dominican Winter League; the offensive plan is to follow Borbon in the lineup with Ian Kinsler, Michael Young, and Hamilton, with Elvis Andrus continuing to hit ninth so that he and Borbon are back to back in the order
- Texas has inquired about San Diego closer Heath Bell, a longtime favorite of mine, though the Padres' wish list that includes help at catcher, center field (right-handed hitter, preferably), and middle infielder doesn't match up well with what the Rangers can offer
- One local reporter, citing "sources" (plural), says the Rangers are "still talking about dealing [Kevin] Millwood" and that "[Milton] Bradley [is] not off [the] table"
- Oakland righthander Justin Duchscherer has reportedly declined the club's offer of arbitration (Jerry Crasnick, ESPN)

December 7, 2009: TROT COFFEY

- The Orioles, "quite interested" in Kevin Millwood, met with Texas about the veteran pitcher today (Peter Schmuck, *Baltimore Sun*, and various local reports)
- The Diamondbacks "would like nothing more than to get their hands on Derek Holland or Neftali Feliz," but that ain't happening (local report)
- Boston gave a major league contract to lefthander Fabio Castro, who was the first pick in the Rule 5 Draft

that concluded the 2005 Winter Meetings in Dallas (Kansas City selected him and traded him to Texas for infielder Esteban German), and signed lefthander Kason Gabbard to a minor league deal

- The number of clubs interested in Marlins reliever Matt Lindstrom evidently totals as many as 10 (Jerry Crasnick, ESPN)
- The deadline for Marlon Byrd and Ivan Rodriguez to accept or decline arbitration is in half an hour; both are expected to decline

December 7, 2009

According to local reports, as expected, Marlon Byrd and Ivan Rodriguez have declined the Rangers' arbitration offers. They are free to sign with any team—including Texas—but if either signs with another club, the Rangers will get a supplemental first-round pick as compensation.

And there's a breaking report, from Tim Brown of Yahoo! Sports, that Rodriguez has signed with the Nationals for two years and $6 million. We'll see if that report bears out.

December 8, 2009: TROT COFFEY

- Washington apparently did give Ivan Rodriguez two years and $6 million last night, which is sort of amazing; Texas gets a supplemental first-round pick as compensation for the loss of the 38-year-old catcher
- Baltimore "may be getting closer to acquiring [Kevin Millwood] for one of the Orioles' second-level pitching prospects," with Texas possibly subsidizing some of Millwood's $12 million 2010 salary depending on the quality of the prospect (Peter Schmuck, *Baltimore Sun*)
- The Mets have talked to Texas about Millwood as well, but "executives involved in talks say other suitors are better positioned on Millwood than the Mets" (Joel Sherman, *New York Post*)
- The Orioles not only spoke to Texas about Millwood but also obtained Erik Bedard's medical records, though their interest in Bedard is contingent on 100 percent health (Jeff Zrebiec, *Baltimore Sun*)
- The Rangers' interest in Marlins reliever Matt Lindstrom is apparently "not as strong as some reports have led to believe" (Clark Spencer, *Miami Herald*)
- Righthander Brandon McCarthy "is drawing trade interest from other clubs," according to a major league source (Jon Paul Morosi, Fox Sports)
- Baltimore is still looking at Hank Blalock as a first base option (Zrebiec)
- Texas has asked Pittsburgh about right-handed reliever Matt Capps, as has Tampa Bay; the arbitration-eligible Capps, who closed for the Pirates the last three seasons, is a candidate to be non-tendered by Saturday's deadline to do so (Dejan Kovacevic, *Pittsburgh Post-Gazette*)
- The Rangers (and possibly the Blue Jays, Mariners, and Giants) have shown interest in switch-hitting, arbitration-eligible Pirates catcher Ryan Doumit (Kovacevic; Morosi)
- The list of clubs interested in reliever J.J. Putz includes the Rangers, Cubs, White Sox, Diamondbacks, Nationals, and Tigers (Morosi)
- Texas, according to sources, is interested in Dodgers outfielder Juan Pierre, set to make $10 million in 2010 and $8.5 million in 2011 (Danny Knobler, CBS Sports)
- The Pirates were "known to be interested" in Texas reliever Willie Eyre and were reportedly preparing to place a waiver claim on him on Monday (Kovacevic) (*yet the Rangers were able to get him through league-wide waivers in order to outright him*)
- Contrary to reports yesterday that Boston had signed lefthander Fabio Castro to a major league contract, word this morning is that it was a minor league deal, which makes far more sense (Peter Abraham, *Boston Globe*)

Stay tuned.

December 8, 2009: TROT COFFEY

- Arizona unsuccessfully offered catcher Chris Snyder to Texas for lefthander C.J. Wilson (local report)
- Texas is "actively talking to other clubs" about Kevin Millwood (though one club source says the club has not "tried to move him"); the Orioles are "quite serious in their interest" in Millwood, and the Diamondbacks, Mets, Cardinals, and Nationals "could" have interest as well; Texas would want young pitching or a right-handed bat in return (local report)
- The Mets are NOT interested in Millwood, having explored the idea weeks ago but concluding they couldn't make it work financially (Ken Rosenthal, Fox Sports)
- If Texas moves Millwood, the ripple effect could be the signing of a veteran bat, with Vlad Guerrero and Jermaine Dye as possibilities (local report)
- Buster Olney of ESPN suggests the two-year deal Ivan Rodriguez got from Washington is for $5 million rather than $6 million
- Pirates GM Neal Huntington confirmed that teams have called him regarding catcher Ryan Doumit, but Texas is actually "not a serious suitor" and has no interest in trading for him (Jenifer Langosch, MLB.com)

December 8, 2009: TROT COFFEY

- Baltimore was the "hottest" of the teams interested in Kevin Millwood but may have cooled off some; Texas was interested in righthander Chris Tillman (good grief—that would have been a spectacular deal) but the Orioles instead offered righthanders David Hernandez and Brandon Erbe (not a terrible offer by any means), though both have physical issues (local report)

- There's a "reasonable" amount of interest in Millwood from other teams (including the Mets and Diamondbacks) and that interest is increasing; Texas wants young pitching in return (same local report)
- The Rangers could take the savings if Millwood is dealt to pursue other free agent pitchers such as Ben Sheets or Rich Harden, or a right-handed bat like Vlad Guerrero (who seeks a two-year deal) or Jermaine Dye (same local report)
- Baltimore offered outfielder Felix Pie to Texas for Millwood (John Perrotto, Baseball Prospectus)
- John Lackey is drawing interest from the Rangers, Mariners, Angels, Red Sox, Yankees, Nationals, and others (Jon Heyman, *Sports Illustrated*)
- Brett Myers, courted by Texas and Houston, is "definitely gone from the Phillies" (Heyman)

The requisite grains of salt, friends.

December 8, 2009: TROT COFFEY

- Get this: according to multiple local reports this afternoon, a baseball official says Texas offered Neftali Feliz and Justin Smoak to Florida for righthander Josh Johnson at some point, and the Marlins said no
- With Ivan Rodriguez having departed and Jarrod Saltalamacchia's health a potential uncertainty, Texas is considering Rod Barajas, Jason Kendall, Yorvit Torrealba, Jose Molina and Henry Blanco in an effort to bring in a veteran catcher (local report)
- The Rangers plan to meet with Casey Close, the agent for Ben Sheets, before the Winter Meetings end on Thursday (local report)
- According to one National League source, Brandon McCarthy could interest San Francisco, who lost Brad Penny to St. Louis and doesn't want to rush top prospect Madison Bumgarner (Eli Greenspan, MLB Daily Dish)
- The Nationals talked to Texas about both McCarthy and Kevin Millwood; the Millwood talks went nowhere and "it is still too early" as far as the McCarthy talks are concerned
- The Cubs are reportedly close to dealing Milton Bradley to a "surprise AL team" (Gordon Wittenmyer, *Chicago Sun Times*)
- What was Arizona thinking? Love what the Tigers did, like what the Yankees got, can't understand why the Diamondbacks did it
- And the White Sox—three years and $14 million for Mark Teahen? Really?
- I'm happy for Peter Gammons, but sad for me.

December 8, 2009: TROT COFFEY

- Texas is expected to meet with the agent for lefthander Darren Oliver tonight; the Angels did not offer arbitration to the Type A reliever so he won't cost a draft pick to sign (local report)
- The Rangers are no longer interested in Milton Bradley (Joel Sherman, *New York Post*)
- Seattle could be the mystery team on the verge of trading for Bradley, possibly for righthander Carlos Silva (Tim Brown, Yahoo! Sports)
- Casey Close, the agent for Ben Sheets, is not yet making his client's medical records available or letting teams watch him throw (local report)
- The 2011 Winter Meetings will be back in Dallas, on December 5-8 at the Hilton Anatole

December 8, 2009: TROT COFFEY

- Texas reportedly asked Baltimore for righthander David Hernandez and a lower-level prospect in exchange for Kevin Millwood, offering also to send the Orioles $3 million to help pay Millwood's $12 million 2010 contract; the two clubs have exchanged other proposals as well, and Baltimore remains "one of the frontrunners" for Millwood (Jeff Zrebiec, *Baltimore Sun*)
- The Rangers are "very interested" in 27-year-old Marlins corner infielder Jorge Cantu, who has destroyed lefthanders the last two years; Texas is apparently dangling pitching (Jon Paul Morosi, Fox Sports)
- Foremost among the catchers that Texas is keying on—possibly to start—are Rod Barajas, Jason Kendall, and Jose Molina, and the club has also talked with Tampa Bay about Dioner Navarro and could ask the Rays about Kelly Shoppach and Kansas City (who is also interested in Barajas and Kendall) about John Buck (various local reports)
- Another starting pitcher name to add to Ben Sheets and Rich Harden is that of Joel Pineiro (local report)
- Texas talked to Cincinnati about left-handed reliever Arthur Rhodes "but didn't get far" (local report) (*the fact that Rhodes and Darren Oliver are in the Rangers' sights makes me think the club is trying to replace Eddie Guardado not only on the field but also as a veteran bullpen influence*)
- The Rangers' search for a right-handed power reliever includes not only Brett Myers, Matt Lindstrom, and J.J. Putz, but also Ramon Ramirez and Chris Ray (local report)
- Let me take this opportunity to say something I should say more often. The beat writers from this market have done a fantastic job in Indianapolis this week. We're lucky to have them. You might have noticed that I credit national writers by name in these reports, but not the individual reporters from this market, instead referring generally to "local reports"—I do that not by choice but at the request of those guys. It's by no

means meant to be a slight—quite the opposite. Those guys are solid writers, tireless reporters, and good dudes. Props.

- I couldn't be happier about this news: Peter Gammons's departure from ESPN has him on the verge of joining MLB Network, which I devoted at least 10 times more of my time to than ESPN since I added it in February
- Houston is inviting eight non-roster players to big league camp, including Drew Meyer, Chris Shelton, and Casey Daigle
- You can still buy the Bound Edition for shipping in time for the holidays or for pickup at the December 17 Book Release Party at Sherlock's in Arlington (ordering details: http://www.newbergreport.com/buythebook.asp), and I should point out that all these TROT COFFEY reports, heaviest in November and December and late July and late August, while they don't appear on the website, are all in the book—looking back at the trade rumors that Texas was involved in a year ago is fascinating

December 9, 2009: TROT COFFEY

- Baltimore has ex-Oriole Erik Bedard higher than Kevin Millwood and Ben Sheets on its priority list, primarily because they "know who he is" (Will Carroll, Baseball Prospectus)
- While Texas may not be pushing a Millwood trade, the club recognizes that he's "more highly regarded within the industry than the free agent starters likely to sign for one year, such as Vicente Padilla, Brett Myers and Braden Looper" and could appeal to "clubs wary of investing multi-year deals for Joel Pineiro and others," and thus the Rangers are exploring opportunities to get a strong return for the righthander, who turns 35 later this month (Jon Paul Morosi, Fox Sports)
- Millwood and Boston third baseman Mike Lowell will each earn $12 million in 2010, and the Red Sox would probably welcome a one-for-one trade, but the Rangers—despite needing a right-handed bat who can fill in at first base and DH—consider Lowell (who is coming off hip surgery and has actually never played first in the big leagues) "not as attractive as the alternatives" (Morosi)
- Before Ivan Rodriguez signed with Washington for two years and $6 million, Texas offered him a one-year deal worth $1-1.5 million with a club option for 2011 (local report)
- Bakersfield Blaze owner D.G. Elmore tells *Baseball America* that the club has made no progress in its efforts to find a new ballpark or new home, as there are no public funds available, which killed a potential arrangement with Cal State Bakersfield; California League president Charlie Blaney is now in charge of finding a workable solution for the Blaze
- The Yankees' trade of reliever Brian Bruney to the Nationals earlier this week will reportedly be completed with Washington conveying the first overall pick in tomorrow's Rule 5 Draft to New York
- *BA* editor in chief John Manuel said in a *Dallas Morning News* chat session yesterday that Martin Perez is among baseball's top 15 prospects in his opinion, and may be the best lefthander in the minor leagues

December 9, 2009: TROT COFFEY

- One local reporter suggests that, based on talking with others, yesterday's report of a Justin Smoak/Neftali Feliz for Josh Johnson offer "might be most unfounded rumor of meetings" (idle thought: might the Marlins have actually been the ones to make the ultimately declined offer?)
- The Rangers reportedly asked Baltimore for righthander David Hernandez and a low-level prospect for Kevin Millwood, offering to send $3 million to the Orioles (Jeff Zrebiec, *Baltimore Sun*), and there's also a version that would involve Chris Ray coming to Texas in which the Rangers—or the Orioles (I know, I know: there are conflicting reports on this aspect of the Ray scenario)—would pay most of Millwood's $12 million salary (Peter Schmuck, *Baltimore Sun*, who says this morning that "it seems like Orioles officials are getting more confident that they can complete a deal" for Millwood)
- The Rangers met with the agent for Ben Sheets yesterday and are reviewing the righthander's medical records; Sheets might decide to wait things out to see if his market value improves as other pitchers find teams (local report)
- The Royals "want [outfielder Felix] Pie more than the Orioles want to trade him" (Kevin Goldstein, Baseball Prospectus) (I don't suppose Kansas City wants Pie so badly that they'd be interested in taking him in a prospect-heavy package for Zack Greinke, huh? Surely not, but hey, let a dude dream)
- Many of the same clubs (including the Braves, Angels, Cubs, Yankees, Mariners, Mets, and Giants) are interested alternatively in both Mike Cameron and Marlon Byrd, some looking to patch up center field but others viewing them as corner outfielders (Jon Paul Morosi, Fox Sports)
- The Diamondbacks denied a Tuesday report that they had offered catcher Chris Snyder to Texas for C.J. Wilson (Nick Piecoro, *Arizona Republic*)
- The Yankees are shopping the top overall pick in tomorrow's Rule 5 Draft, which they obtained from the Nationals for reliever Brian Bruney (Jayson Stark, ESPN)

December 9, 2009

According to Jeff Zrebiec of the *Baltimore Sun*, the Orioles and Rangers are "nearing an agreement on a trade" that would send former O's closer Chris Ray to Texas for Kevin Millwood and "some cash," according to multiple Orioles team sources. Zrebiec writes that "[m]any of the particulars have been agreed upon, but the there are still a few details to work out, including a review of medical records."

Ray, a righthander, had Tommy John surgery on his elbow in August 2007.

Stay tuned.

December 9, 2009: TROT COFFEY

- A Rangers official says the club hasn't yet signed off on the Kevin Millwood-Chris Ray deal with Baltimore (Jayson Stark, ESPN); Scott Boras, who represents Millwood, acknowledges club discussions but says that nothing has been completed (Jerry Crasnick, ESPN); it's likely that the deal hasn't been confirmed because medical reports are still being reviewed (local reports)
- Jon Heyman of *Sports Illustrated* and MLB Network, however, is calling it a done deal
- Should the deal go through, Texas is expected to pay $3 million of Millwood's $12 million salary for 2010 (Ken Rosenthal, Fox Sports)
- The Rangers and Angels are Darren Oliver's most aggressive suitors (Rosenthal)
- Ben Sheets, who is throwing now at 60 feet—though just off flat ground—and claims he will be ready to go in spring training, evidently seeks a contract similar annually to the $12 million he earned in 2008 (local reports)
- The Rangers have expressed interest in Arizona utility infielder Augie Ojeda, though the Diamondbacks are reluctant to upset their middle infield depth (local reports)
- Rich Harden is willing to take a one-year deal from someone to prove himself to the league before reentering free agency a year from now; most interest in Harden has come from the American League, with the Yankees, Red Sox, and Mariners as the most serious suitors—the Angels are not in on Harden (Jon Paul Morosi, Fox Sports)
- Texas is "said to be shopping Josh Hamilton but clubs aren't biting" (George A. King III, *New York Post*—in a story published on Monday, with no traction since)
- San Diego will non-tender righthander Kevin Correia by Saturday's deadline, making him a free agent (Crasnick)
- The Rangers' interest in catcher Rod Barajas has diminished some due to his contract demands (local report)
- Florida is on the verge of trading reliever Matt Lindstrom to Houston (multiple reports)

December 9, 2009

According to a local report:

"The Rangers are close to signing Rich Harden, who was 9-9 with a 4.09 ERA in 26 games for the Cubs. He would replace Kevin Millwood in the rotation. A highly-placed source said it's close."

Craig Calcaterra of NBC Sports says it will be a one-year deal worth $7.5 million, with an $11.5 million option for 2011.

I'm excited.

December 9, 2009: TROT COFFEY

- According to local reports, Texas will in fact trade Kevin Millwood to Baltimore for Chris Ray, with the Orioles paying all but $3 million of Millwood's 2010 salary; with the $9 million saved, the Rangers will be able to pay both Ray's salary and the $7.5 million commitment they have made to Rich Harden for 2010 (there's also a club option for 2011 at $11.5 million, which is a fantastic aspect of this deal); the Harden signing is not yet official
- The club has just issued a press release, indicating that Texas will get not only Ray but also a player to be named later from the Orioles (maybe a non-roster draft-eligible that the Rangers first want to be sure isn't drafted tomorrow morning?) According to another local report, Texas is working on a deal with Boston that would send catcher Max Ramirez to the Red Sox for Mike Lowell (and presumably a meaningful amount of cash), giving the Rangers the right-handed bat they've been seeking this off-season

December 9, 2009

According to a local report, the player to be named later in the Kevin Millwood for Chris Ray deal will be the player Baltimore selects with the third pick in tomorrow morning's Rule 5 Draft. Washington selects first (making the pick for the Yankees), followed by Pittsburgh, and then the Orioles, who will choose a player for Texas.

That player will go onto the Rangers' 40-man roster (which presently stands at 38 players) and will have to remain on the active major league roster (or major league disabled list) for all of 2010 or be placed on waivers (and, if he clears, must be offered back to his 2009 team for $25,000).

Only a few Rule 5 picks each year pan out at all, but there are two recent draftees who have made huge impacts in Texas: Josh Hamilton, whom Tampa Bay failed to protect in 2006 (he was the third overall pick in that Rule 5 Draft and was also part of a trade, incidentally—the Cubs drafted him and immediately shipped him to the Reds), and Darren O'Day, the 15th overall pick in last year's draft by the Mets, after the Angels left him unprotected.

Last year's third pick was shortstop Everth Cabrera, chosen by San Diego.

It's been a solid day of Rangers maneuvering.

December 9, 2009: TROT COFFEY

- The Rangers' deal with Rich Harden, which reportedly pends a Thursday physical in Arlington, will pay the 28-year-old $6.5 million in 2010 (with $3.5 million in additional innings pitched incentives) and an $11 million *mutual* option for 2011 with a $1 million buyout if either side declines (Ed Price, AOL FanHouse) (the buyout clause is what guarantees a total of $7.5 million; the mutual option, if accurate, is a different story from the early reports of 2011 being a club option)
- Seattle, a club that Harden had expressed interest in joining since it's close to his British Columbia hometown, apparently balked at some feature of the contract, possibly that mutual option (Geoff Baker, *Seattle Times*)
- While Texas and Boston are evidently discussing Mike Lowell, it's in the "kicking of tires" stage and "not very far along" (Ken Rosenthal, Fox Sports)
- Other power bats being considered by Texas are Marlon Byrd, Vladimir Guerrero, and Jermaine Dye, all right-handed hitters, and lefty Jim Thome; the Rangers haven't ruled out Milton Bradley, but the Cubs would have to chip in "significantly more salary" than they have offered to thus far (local report)
- Kansas City has offered catcher Jason Kendall two years (Bob Dutton, *Kansas City Star*), but Texas continues to talk to him (Price)
- Detroit insists it's not in fire sale mode, but in addition to Curtis Granderson and Edwin Jackson, whom the Tigers have traded, the club is also open to discussing Miguel Cabrera and Gerald Laird (John Perrotto, Baseball Prospectus)

December 9, 2009

According to Ken Rosenthal of Fox Sports, Texas and Boston have a preliminary agreement on a trade that will send Max Ramirez to the Red Sox for Mike Lowell, though Boston ownership still must approve the deal—which would evidently involve the Sox "eating nearly all" of Lowell's $12 million salary for 2010.

December 10, 2009

When news broke on Wednesday that Texas and Baltimore were zeroing in on a trade that would move Kevin Millwood for Chris Ray, I got emails from nearly 100 of you, more than half of which delivered a message fitting into one of these categories:

1. How could we trade our ace for a middle reliever?
2. How does it make sense to trade our one established starter if 2010 is supposed to be "the year"??
3. This is nothing but a salary dump! Rarr!

In nearly every instance, partly because I don't have much time during the day to respond to non-work emails, I replied by saying, simply: "Let's wait and see what we do with the saved money."

Didn't have to wait long.

Wednesday was the busiest day of the Winter Meetings for Texas, and a busy day for me at the office, and so you'll have to forgive me if today's report—on the Millwood-Ray trade and the imminent signing of Rich Harden and reportedly imminent trade of Max Ramirez for Mike Lowell—doesn't go all nine. I know it's the stretch run, but I'm a little gassed.

In fact, you know what? I'm scratched today.

Tomorrow I'll get to the heavy slate of moves, and in the meantime I'll throw you a flash with news of the player Texas has Baltimore select with the third overall pick in this morning's Rule 5 Draft, which, as always, closes the Meetings.

Thanks for your patience.

December 10, 2009

With the third overall pick in the Rule 5 Draft, Baltimore has selected 24-year-old AA lefthander Ben Snyder from the San Francisco system, and will reportedly convey him to Texas to complete yesterday's Kevin Millwood trade.

December 10, 2009

No word from the Rangers yet, but according to Jon Paul Morosi of Fox Sports, Rich Harden has passed his physical and his free agent deal is set to be made official.

December 10, 2009: TROT COFFEY

- Rich Harden's deal has a $6.5 million base for 2010 and a mutual $11 million option (with $1 million buyout) for 2011, as reported yesterday, but the 2010 incentives apparently amount to an extra $2.5 million, not $3.5 million (local report)
- St. Louis considered Harden before signing Brad Penny, reportedly backing off of Harden after seeing his medical records (Phil Rogers, *Chicago Tribune*)
- Texas and Boston are still evaluating the rumored deal that would send Max Ramirez to the Red Sox for Mike Lowell and as much as $9 million; financial and medical issues (particularly Lowell's hip) are still being looked at, and "Lowell himself has to address a few undisclosed issues" as well (multiple reports, local and otherwise)
- The two clubs are "considering" the deal, whose parameters are basically set, but are also "looking at alternatives," according to Jon Daniels (Jayson Stark, ESPN; Daniel Barbarisi and Joe McDonald, *Providence Journal*)
- The trade is "roughly 75 percent done," what-ever that means (Barbarisi and McDonald) The trade is "better

than 50-50 to happen" (Jon Hey-man, *Sports Illustrated*)

- According to a "baseball source," Commissioner Bud Selig is likely to approve the trade, though he'll do so "with some reservations" since it would reportedly raise the Rangers' payroll by $3 million (Gordon Edes, ESPN Boston)
- Should the Lowell trade get completed, "it looks like Marlon Byrd is definitely done in Texas," because payroll would basically be exhausted until the ownership situation is resolved; "we haven't eliminated it," said Daniels of the possibility of re-signing Byrd, "but it's very unlikely" (local reports)
- Texas met with Darren Oliver a second time this morning, competing with the Angels and Red Sox for his services, which could cost as much as $3.5 million for 2010 (local report)
- The Royals have offered catcher Jason Kendall two years, possibly for more than $4 million (Jon Paul Morosi, Fox Sports)
- Accordingly, Kansas City is expected to non-tender catcher John Buck by Saturday's deadline, making him a free agent; a Rangers target last summer before Texas traded for Ivan Rodriguez, Buck could become the "latest . . . frontrunner" in the club's search for a veteran catcher to bring in (local report)
- Tampa Bay traded well-traveled reliever (and original Rangers draftee) Jesse Chavez to Atlanta for reliever Rafael Soriano
- Phil Nevin will manage Detroit's AA club in 2010 (Bob Nightengale, *USA Today*)
- If you want to make a trade that gets lots and lots of media coverage, even before it's finalized, get the Red Sox involved

December 10, 2009

Quoting a report from Rob Bradford of WEEI.com (Boston), published 45 minutes ago:

According to a source familiar with the negotiations, the Rangers and Red Sox have agreed upon the terms of a deal that would send Mike Lowell to the Rangers in exchange for catcher/first baseman Max Ramirez, with multiple outlets reporting that the Sox will pay $9 million of Lowell's $12 million 2010 salary. It still figures to be 2-3 days before the trade is finalized, with both teams having to look at each player's medical situation.

For Lowell, the Rangers will be focusing in on the progress of his surgically-repaired right hip, while the Red Sox figure to prioritize the health of both of Ramirez' wrists, which he injured at different times in 2009.

Boston.com was first to report that the teams had agreed to terms, Thursday night. WEEI.com published the initial report that the Red Sox and Rangers were negotiation [sic] *the trade, Wednesday.*

December 11, 2009

I still remember standing outside my mother-in-law's home in Seabrook, Texas, the day after Christmas 2005, watching our five- and one-year-old play in the snow—one of the first our kids had seen, and I think also the first snow in the Houston area in something like 30 years—when I got the call on my cell phone that prompted me to run upstairs and hammer out this Newberg Report News Flash:

I want to take this opportunity to say Merry Christmas, Happy Chanukah, and best wishes for a happy, healthy, and prosperous 2006, 2007, 2008, 2009, and a vesting option for 2010.

Kevin Millwood has agreed to terms with the Texas Rangers.

Reeling from the four-year Chan Ho Park disaster that had been euthanized five months earlier, I was desperate for Kevin Millwood to come in here and be a true ace for this club, something he probably wasn't cut out to be, if only in terms of stuff and ability to dominate. Tenacity, yes. Example-setter, no doubt. Leader and tremendous teammate, you bet. "A presence in the clubhouse, on the field, in the community," said Jon Daniels in a press briefing yesterday, "an all-world human being."

An ace? Only in comparison to Park.

I was seduced by a couple 18-win seasons Millwood had under his belt (ignoring the seven, the two nines, and the 10), and by the ERA title he'd just won in his first run at American League hitters.

Millwood was solid here. He answered the bell. Never backed down. Led this staff. But there's a difference between being a team's number one starter and being a Number One.

Put it this way: Millwood had a very good season in 2005. Though he won only nine Cleveland games (losing 11), he led the American League with a 2.86 ERA. At age 30, and in that market, he'd probably warranted the five-year, $60 million contract that Texas agreed to pay him, beating Boston out to land the righthander.

But that same 2005 season, Rich Harden was more dominant. At age 23. In what was his second full season in the big leagues, he went 10-5, 2.53 in his 19 starts and three relief appearances, and was less hittable than Millwood, less homer-prone, nearly as stingy with free passes, and more likely to strike out a batter.

Both Millwood and Harden averaged just over 6.1 innings per start that year. Since then, Millwood hasn't matched his hits per nine or strikeout rate (each of which was inferior to Harden's to begin with), while Harden's hittability has fluctuated around the same rate and his strikeout rate has been higher every year since.

Millwood's ERA title and sixth-place Cy Young finish merited the big contract. But it was Harden who was the budding Number One.

The 2009 season started so well for Millwood, who through June 26 had gone 8-5, 2.64 over 16 starts, holding opponents to a .237/.306/.390 slash line and helping keep Texas in first place 52 straight days.

But over Millwood's next 12 starts, he went 4-8, 6.29. Opponents hit .303/.380/.512. At the end of that two-and-a-half-month stretch, the Rangers were 5.5 games back in the West. Yes, the offense had run into a wall, but had Millwood managed to reverse his win-loss record over those 10 weeks, Texas would have still been squarely in the race.

Millwood made three starts after that awful stretch, locking in his 2010 contract (by reaching a workload threshold) with the first. He won all three games, giving up four earned runs in 23 innings (1.57 ERA) and serving at least some notice that the staff leader was still in there somewhere, even if he was no longer as reliable as Scott Feldman.

That three-game effort was Simon and Garfunkel performing "Sound of Silence," "The Boxer," and "Bridge Over Troubled Water" a month ago at the Rock and Roll Hall of Fame Concert. It was brilliant, powerful, adrenalizing. But *nostalgic.*

This team might be ready to win in 2010. We'd all like to think that to be the case. I'm pretty sure most of us believe that even if 2010 isn't the year, we're on the doorstep of a run of contending seasons. Was Millwood going to contribute to that? Conceivably in 2010, when he'll pitch at age 35. Almost surely not beyond that.

But back to 2010. What can be expected? Even with his very good first half and burst of effectiveness at season's end, Millwood struck batters out in 2009 at the lowest rate of his career. His strikeout-to-walk rate was a career worst. His flyball rate and home run rate were the highest since his first year as an arbitration-eligible (2001). What's he going to be going forward?

A $12 million pitcher?

Or even a $9 million pitcher, which is what he'll be for Baltimore with the Rangers' $3 million subsidy?

The only way Harden will earn as much as the Orioles alone will pay Millwood in 2010 (let alone what Millwood will earn all told) is if he hits every incentive. Harden's 2010 base is only $6.5 million. Another $2.5 million in workload bonuses (half a million each for reaching 155, 165, 175, 185, and 195 innings) could lift the deal to the $9 million Baltimore will pay Millwood regardless of how he performs, or how often.

In exchange for Millwood, Texas comes away with Harden, plus 27-year-old former closer Chris Ray (entering his second season after Tommy John surgery, which often stages a big spike in performance), plus Rule 5 draftee Ben Snyder (a candidate to win a job as a left-on-left bullpen specialist).

Even counting the $3 million the Rangers are sending to Baltimore to help pay Millwood, the Harden-Ray-Snyder trio will cost Texas less than it would have cost to keep Millwood.

Imagine what Jon Daniels and his industrious, resourceful crew could have accomplished this week *without* a charge to keep payroll level.

Yes, there's the matter of Harden's chronic injury issues. But as has been pointed out several times the last couple days, he's made as many starts the last two years (51) as John Lackey, who could be on the verge of a $100 million contract from someone. And when he's on the mound, he's legit.

No starting pitcher in baseball had a better strikeout rate than Harden's 10.9 per nine innings in 2009, or than his 11.0 per nine in 2008. Not Tim Lincecum. Not Justin Verlander. Not Zack Greinke, not Jon Lester. Harden has been the best in baseball each of the last two years. His 9.4 strikeouts per nine innings for his seven-year career is the game's best among pitchers with at least 125 starts. His .220 opponents' average over that span is second only to Johan Santana's .219.

Not only was Harden's contact rate (total percentage of contact made when swinging) of 67.3 percent baseball's best in 2009—and his rate of 69.6 percent in 2008 also best in the game—but no other starting pitcher has had a season below 70 percent since Francisco Liriano's 2006 season with Minnesota.

And Harden achieved that mark in 2009 even though his fastball velocity hovered around 90 at times, rather than 95-97 where it often sits. His command of a splitter and change are good enough that even a dip in velocity doesn't prevent him from missing bats *better than any starter in baseball.* (He's also one of only 40 pitchers in the last 120 years to have a nine-pitch, three-strikeout inning.)

No Texas Rangers starting pitcher has had stuff like Rich Harden since Kevin Brown. It's Ace stuff. The kind you throw out there in Game One of a best-of-seven.

Harden, who turned 28 after the season, is 50-29, 3.39 over seven years, owning the eighth-lowest ERA among all big league pitchers with at least 125 starts in that span. He went 9-9, 4.09 in 26 starts last year, with increased home run numbers. Underwhelming? Disappointing? On the surface, probably. But he struck out 171 batters in 141 innings, and had an opponents' slash line of .234/.327/.407. In his first three 2009 starts, he fanned 26 batters in 15 innings—no pitcher since 1900 had ever logged that many strikeouts in so few innings over a three-start span in a single season. Still, it wasn't a brilliant year in the overall results, and maybe if it had been we'd be talking today about the Yankees or Red Sox—both of whom were reportedly finalists for him in Indianapolis this week—giving him a massive four-year deal that Texas couldn't have competed with.

In what ballpark does Harden have his worst career numbers? Among the parks where he's pitched more than a couple times, it's Rangers Ballpark (7.66 ERA, .330/.417/.404 slash line). If you want to fill your glass half full with me, maybe assume it was the Texas lineup that he had trouble with, not the yard itself. And for what it's worth, he's fared well in Anaheim and really, really well in Seattle, and of course in Oakland.

A teammate of Ian Kinsler at Central Arizona Community College in 2001, Harden signed with Oakland as a draft-and-follow that May (having been chosen in the 17th round in 2000) and reached the big leagues just over two years later, exploding on the league with four straight quality starts (3-0, 1.33). His six seasons with the A's (the first four of which Ron Washington was on the coaching staff) were marred by frequent injuries and disabled list stints: a shoulder strain and oblique strain in 2005, a back strain and elbow sprain in 2006, and shoulder strains in 2007 and early 2008. His run with the Cubs the last year and a half were relatively healthy, spoiled only by a four-week stay on the DL last spring with a lower back strain.

Of course, without the significant medical history, Harden (who has never logged 190 innings and hasn't reached 150 innings since 2004, calling into question how reachable those incentive levels are going to be) is never available on a one-year deal with an option.

This business of the $11.5 million mutual option in 2011 is interesting. If Harden has a career year, he'll opt out (and take the $1 million buyout). If he struggles or can't stay healthy, Texas will opt out. Under what scenario do both sides allow the option to kick in? Maybe if his 2010 season isn't quite the type that he thinks would fetch $11.5 million on the open market but the Rangers want him back anyway. Realistically, that second year isn't going to come into play. But should Harden pitch well enough this year to get a big contract from someone next winter, Texas will still be able to offer him arbitration and net a first-round pick as compensation.

There's certainly a much better chance of that than with Millwood (whom Texas would almost certainly never offer arbitration to).

For what it's worth, Harden was a Type B free agent this winter and wouldn't have cost Texas a draft pick even if the Cubs had offered him arbitration—which they didn't. Had they offered it, they would have received a supplemental first-round pick once he signed elsewhere.

Harden's medicals may have scared off teams such as St. Louis, but he passed a Rangers physical yesterday and will be introduced at a press conference this morning. There will always be a health cloud over Harden, but ESPN's Keith Law made what I thought was a solid point on that subject: "[I]f the Rangers can make sure they have a backup starter available for his inevitable month stay on the DL, they've got value. If you think about it, adding 20-25 good starts to that rotation could very well help push them closer to the top of the division." The Rangers have starter depth, unquestionably.

I'd be upset if the Angels or Mariners landed Harden. And that's usually my test.

As for Ray, I'm not going to go into too much depth, but suffice it to say that he's probably a good risk to be a lot better in 2010 than he was in 2009 (0-4, 7.27), which was his first full season back on a mound since August 2007 Tommy John surgery, because that's what the empirical evidence on TJ cases says. Not long ago, he was one of the bright young closers in the league, racking up 33 saves in 38 tries for Baltimore in 2006 (2.73 ERA, .193/.275/.352 slash line), which was just his third full pro season after being drafted out of the College of William and Mary. Over his first two seasons (2005-06), the league hit just .205 off of him, the sixth-lowest opposing batting average among all big league pitchers with at least 100 appearances.

A max-effort righthander with a heavy mid-90s fastball and hard slider, Ray was unable to harness his stuff on his return from surgery, but that's not atypical. Command almost always lags health by as much as a year after Tommy John, and he showed signs late last year of rounding into form. Through June 28, his ERA was 10.24 and opponents hit .379/.450/.586. Thereafter—before struggling over his final 1.2 innings of work—his ERA was 3.22 and opponents hit .291/.344/.465.

Though the 27-year-old debuted in the big leagues in 2005, I believe he still has two options, and so unlike a pitcher like Luis Mendoza or Clay Rapada or the Rule 5 pick Snyder, Ray isn't a "use it or [potentially] lose it" case. There's plenty of upside here, and particularly given the plan to provide Neftali Feliz and C.J. Wilson opportunities to win rotation jobs, adding another high-ceiling arm like Ray builds the staff's depth and flexibility even further.

Snyder, left off the 40-man roster last month by San Francisco, was the player Texas had the Orioles choose with the third pick in yesterday's Rule 5 Draft. The 24-year-old, in his third full pro season out of Ball State (taken in the fourth round in 2006, two spots before the Rangers selected Marcus Lemon), was transitioned from starter to reliever by the Giants in 2009, and the move paid off. Snyder posted a 2.04 ERA out of the AA Connecticut bullpen, holding Eastern League hitters to a .210 average while fanning 70 in 70.2 innings. Commanding an average fastball and a deadly slider, Snyder destroyed left-handed AA hitters, limiting them to an anemic .146/.198/.197 slash line and just one home run in 157 at-bats, and posting a 5.7 K/BB rate.

Scott Lucas dug up the interesting note that in 2008, Snyder made four of his 14 High A San Jose starts against

Bakersfield, and in those games he went 2-0, 0.70, holding the Blaze scoreless three times and fanning 19 while issuing seven walks in 25.2 innings.

Will Snyder make the team out of camp? He'll have a shot, likely competing for one of two spots with Rapada and whichever lefties among Wilson, Derek Holland, and Matt Harrison don't win spots in the rotation—and maybe a veteran southpaw like Darren Oliver or Arthur Rhodes. Will Zach Phillips and Michael Kirkman and possibly even Kasey Kiker and Michael Ballard have a chance to win a job? Not much of one, since several like Snyder can't be sent to the minor leagues without clearing waivers first. They'll get their opportunities, but probably not in April.

Ray may struggle in camp and start the season in Oklahoma City. Snyder may fail to prove his readiness and find himself back with the Giants before the end of March. But they may also trot out of the home dugout on April 5, lining up along the first base line in Rangers uniforms, introduced in front of a sellout Arlington crowd.

Whether Ray and Snyder are there to take their places on the baseline for those introductions, chances are good that Rich Harden might be 300 feet to the south, getting loose in the home bullpen as he prepares to take on the Blue Jays, not only as the Rangers' number one starter but, for the first time since Rangers Ballpark's inaugural 1994 season, as a true Rangers Number One.

Texas got things done
At Meetings; first and foremost
Was staff Hardening.

December 12, 2009

The Rangers signed arbitration-eligible infielder Esteban German to a 2010 contract today, making him the fourth player under contract for the upcoming season (along with Michael Young, Ian Kinsler, and Rich Harden).

The club tendered contracts to all of the other 36 players on the roster, including arb-eligibles Josh Hamilton, Scott Feldman, Frankie Francisco, C.J. Wilson, Chris Ray, Brandon McCarthy, and Dustin Nippert.

Keep an eye on the rest of the league tonight, as there will be a number of established, useful players non-tendered and made free agents.

December 13, 2009

Baseball Prospectus's Will Carroll, the national media's foremost expert on baseball injuries and sports medicine, emailed me after reading Friday morning's Newberg Report, and had this to say:

"Did you really just go 1000 words on Rich Harden without using the word "Meister" to explain why Texas can do this and other teams couldn't/wouldn't? Meister's starting to develop the reputation as 'the next James Andrews.'"

Later that day, Carroll threw this out there via Twitter:

"Any injured pitcher should consider White Sox, Cards, Rangers, Brewers—med staffs and pitching coaches give them better chance."

There are several areas in which the Rangers get praised for sitting on the cutting edge, primarily in scouting and player development, but the medical and training programs here are also recognized in the industry as state of the art, and that's a huge thing when it comes to attracting pitchers here, particularly ones with past arm health issues. You take Carroll's comments and it gives more texture to Harden's own remarks:

"I really feel this is a good fit for me. Everybody I've heard from has said this is a good organization. I feel like it's a good spot for me to go out there and make all my starts and pitch 200 innings."

And:

"I want to have a great season here and be here for more than one year."

Harden's 2011 option is almost surely not going to come into play, but that's not only a pitcher whose career could end up like Ben McDonald's or Mark Prior's but also one who acknowledges it head-on, and when I read what Carroll had to say, I started to think that the Meister-Maddux-Reed-Harmon-Vazquez team might turn out to be a reason that Harden may really want to be here past 2010, and that those weren't just empty words that get said the day a player signs with a new team.

An interesting note from Harden's history: After splitting 2002, his first full pro season, between High A Visalia (4-3, 2.93) and AA Midland (8-3, 2.95), racking up 11 strikeouts per nine innings and holding opponents to a .210 batting average, Harden was reassigned to Midland for some reason to start the 2003 season. That assignment was brief. The RockHounds opened in Round Rock on April 3 and Harden got the Opening Day nod.

He fired six perfect innings, punching out nine.

Series in the minor leagues often last nearly a week, to keep travel costs down. Midland stayed in Round Rock for six days, meaning Harden's turn would come around a second time before the RockHounds left town.

On April 8, Harden fired seven perfect innings, setting eight Express hitters down on strikes.

He wouldn't make it back to West Texas for the RockHounds' home opener, earning a promotion to AAA Sacramento, an assignment that would last 16 games (9-4, 3.15) before Harden would move on to Oakland in mid-July.

The Round Rock manager who watched Harden face 39 of his hitters over two games, not letting one of them reach base and piling up 17 strikeouts?

Rangers bench coach Jackie Moore.

(And it's probably safe to assume that Express owner Nolan Ryan was on hand at least for the first Harden effort, since it was Opening Day.)

Harden with the Cubs (2008-2009): 4.33 ERA in day games, 2.44 ERA at night. Batters didn't fare particularly well against Harden during the day: .235/.328/.439. But they were carved up at night: .185/.279/.293.

Texas plays far more night games than the Cubs.

Texas non-tendered nobody yesterday, but around the league there were some interesting names thrust onto the free agent market: righthanders Chien-Ming Wang, Matt Capps, Mike MacDougal, Jose Arredondo (scheduled for Tommy John surgery), Seth McClung, and Adam Miller; lefthander Scott Olsen; catcher John Buck (who played for Moore at Round Rock and probably rises to the pole position as Texas continues to look for veteran catcher insurance); corner infielders Ryan Garko, Garrett Atkins, and Jonny Gomes; utility infielder-outfielder Alfredo Amezaga; and DH Jack Cust. Another couple notable players who seem not to fit the Rangers' needs are second baseman Kelly Johnson and left-handed-hitting outfielder Ryan Church.

Carroll thinks Wang would be a "great fit" in Texas "because of its medical team and his sinkerball."

According to Peter Abraham of the *Boston Globe*, the Rangers are satisfied with the condition of Mike Lowell's surgically repaired right hip, but continue to look at the medicals on his right thumb, which hampered him late in the season. Interestingly, Red Sox assistant general manager Ben Cherington, noting that there remain things for the clubs to go over, said on Saturday regarding the rumored trade of Lowell (and $9 million) for Max Ramirez: "It would not be a complete surprise if it didn't happen."

Baseball Prospectus's Kevin Goldstein on lefthander Ben Snyder, whom the Rangers had Baltimore take for them with the third overall pick in Thursday's Rule 5 Draft to complete the Kevin Millwood trade:

In discussions with a scout (who's not with the Orioles, Giants, or Rangers) last week about the list, Snyder was his number one target, as he already has one definite big-league skill. A beefy lefty with good fastball and an even better breaker, Snyder is absolute murder [on] lefties, limiting them to a .146/.198/.197 mark during the regular season. He would have been my Giants sleeper for their Top 11, now he just might be the Rangers' version. This is my number-one choice to stay with his new team. Odds to Stick: 2-1.

Texas lost nobody in the major league phase of the Draft and just one player in the minor league phase: 28-year-old reliever Beau Vaughan, who had been acquired from Boston a year ago for Wes Littleton. Oakland drafted Vaughan.

The Rangers added three players in the minor league phase: lefthander Winston Marquez (Minnesota), catcher Andrew Jenkins (Florida), and outfielder James Tomlin (Dodgers). Marquez, just 22, has big stuff but has had trouble staying healthy.

The Mets drafted righthander Johnny Lujan from the White Sox in the minor league phase.

Tom Verducci thinks Philadelphia is emerging as the favorite to acquire Roy Halladay. Excellent.

In less flashy Phillies news, the club signed lefthander Bill White to a minor league deal with a big league invite.

Righthander Tanner Scheppers made the Arizona Fall League's All-Prospect Team, notable in that only four pitchers from the entire league were so honored.

Josh Lewin will be back in the Rangers TV booth, having agreed to a one-year deal with an option for 2011. He'll be permitted to miss no more than three September games to do NFL work.

We'll record the next episode of Rangers Podcast in Arlington tomorrow night, and we're planning to take questions. Submit yours now by sending them to *rangerspodcast@gmail.com*.

I've got a computer that's about to die, and I need a new one. Any suggestions? Needs to be a desktop PC. I don't need a monitor. A fast processor is key. At least 320 GB of hard drive space, 64-bit. Would rather not spend a ton, but needs to be reliable. Let me know if you have some advice. Thanks.

Finally, up-to-date details on Thursday's Book Release Party for the 2010 Bound Edition:

WHEN: 6:00-9:00 pm, Thursday, December 17, 2009 (though you can arrive at 5:00 and probably even earlier)

WHERE: Sherlock's Baker Street Pub & Grill, 254 Lincoln Square Center in Arlington (few blocks west of the Ballpark, just south of I-30 and west of Collins; ample parking, and a huge party room that we have sole access to)—phone number is 817-226-2300

GUESTS: Rusty Greer, Ian & Tess Kinsler, Scott Feldman, Tommy Hunter, Derek Holland, and Chris Davis

FOOD:

http://www.sherlockspubco.com/Images/Final_Food_Menu.pdf (the party is during Sherlock's Happy Hour, by the way)

ADMISSION: Free—but the "cost" for getting autographs from our guests is the purchase of a 2010 Bound Edition, which you can pay for now (via PayPal) or at the event. (The guys will sign your baseballs, bats, cards, etc., too—but you have to have the book to get autographs.) Limit three autographs per player.

BOOK ORDERING DETAILS: http://www.newbergreport.com/buythebook.asp (there will be copies for sale at the event; if you prepay or have already done so, I'll have your order prepackaged for you to pick up when you arrive)

Q&A: Will follow the autograph session.

TOYS: Representatives from the U.S. Marine Corps Reserve will also be at the gathering to collect new, unwrapped toys for the Rangers/Toys for Tots program—which the Kinslers are the team spokespeople for. Please consider supporting the effort to help needy children in North Texas experience the joy of the holidays.

Our private party will be non-smoking. Kids definitely welcome.

Let me know if you have questions (or computer advice).

December 14, 2009

Couple quick things today:

Peter Gammons reports via Twitter (@pgammo) that Mike Lowell might need thumb surgery. He's expected, according to Ken Rosenthal of Fox Sports, to undergo a physical in Texas sometime this week.

Toronto signed catcher John Buck over the weekend (one year, $2 million). In addition to the free agent catchers who remain on the market, Tampa Bay catcher Dioner Navarro could be a trade target for Texas. He re-signed last week with the Rays (who also have Kelly Shoppach), a one-year deal for $2.1 million.

Jon Daniels will do a live chat with fans at 10:30 a.m. this morning at ESPN Dallas. You can head there now and submit questions in advance.

Righthander Luis Mendoza continues to establish himself as whatever the equivalent is to a "4-A" for a player who dominates in the winter but struggles to put it all together in the big leagues. The Dominican Winter League strikeout leader (70 in 78.1 innings) is 6-3, 2.76 in a dozen Yaquis de Obregon starts, holding opponents to a .243 batting average, walking only 22, and inducing 2.02 as many groundouts as flyouts. The 26-year-old is out of options.

Six-year minor league free agents who have signed elsewhere this winter: lefthander A.J. Murray (Milwaukee), first baseman Mauro Gomez (Atlanta), and outfielder Ramon Nivar (staying with the Dodgers). First baseman Ian Gac might have signed with the White Sox.

Righthander Colby Lewis has announced his intention to return to the States after two dominant seasons (26-17, 2.83) in Japan. Pitching for the Hiroshima Carp, Lewis (now 30) has led the league in strikeouts two straight years while issuing just a tenth as many walks.

December 14, 2009

Jon Heyman of *Sports Illustrated* reports that Roy Halladay is headed to Philadelphia and Cliff Lee is headed to Seattle in what has to be one of the biggest three-team deals in recent memory. No further details yet, though the Mariners are certainly going to be parting with some serious young talent.

That's a wow.

December 15, 2009

While continuing to honor my self-imposed embargo against commenting on the ownership situation until there is news to report, multiple local mainstream media outlets are indicating tonight that the group steered by Chuck Greenberg and including Nolan Ryan and a number of local investors will be Tom Hicks's choice to purchase the franchise.

Nothing official has been announced—and we must keep in mind that this is only an early step in the process, as MLB must approve any proposed deal, which could take weeks or months—but there are at least two reputable local sources reporting this development, so I'm comfortable at least passing it along to you.

December 15, 2009

Additional details emerging:

The Greenberg-Ryan group, which includes Tom Hicks's family among the local investors, will have a 45-day exclusive negotiation period with Hicks to hammer out a deal, after which approval from 75 percent of MLB's 30 owners will be required to finalize it.

Greenberg's group reportedly increased its offer today, in response to a new bid in the last couple days from Houston businessman Jim Crane that was reported to have made Crane the momentary frontrunner as today's league-imposed deadline approached.

December 15, 2009

The Rangers have officially announced that Tom Hicks has decided to grant exclusive negotiating rights with regard to the sale of the club to an investment group that includes Chuck Greenberg and Nolan Ryan, and will ask MLB to approve that decision.

According to the organization, a 30-day window now opens, during which the principals of Hicks Sports Group will need to negotiate a final purchase agreement with the Greenberg-Ryan group, obtain approval from HSG's lenders, and seek approval from MLB owners.

Greenberg's group consists primarily of Dallas-Fort Worth investors, including the Hicks family. Ryan will remain President of the club.

Hicks and Greenberg and Ryan each recognized the importance of maintaining the stability and long-term position of the franchise, and "doing whatever is necessary to build upon the team's tradition and bring home a World Series championship."

December 16, 2009

The Rangers have gotten infielder Esteban German and left-handed reliever Clay Rapada (who was acquired from Detroit on December 7) through league-wide waivers and have outrighted both to AAA Oklahoma City. Both have been invited to big league spring training.

The two removals reduce the Rangers' 40-man roster to 38 members.

In addition, Texas has signed right-handed reliever Geoff Geary and infielder Ray Olmedo to minor league contracts, giving them non-roster invites to big league camp as well. German, Rapada, Geary, and Olmedo join righthander Willie Eyre and catcher Kevin Richardson as non-roster players invited to camp. There will be more.

Geary has spent parts of the last seven years pitching out of the Philadelphia and Houston bullpens. The 33-year-old has a career 3.92 ERA but that includes an 8.10 mark in 20 Astros innings in 2009 (after he'd posted a 2.53 ERA for Houston in 2008).

Olmedo is a career .228/.276/.293 hitter in five big league seasons (2003-07) with Cincinnati and Toronto. The 28-year-old switch-hitter hit .250/.290/.335 last year for Tampa Bay's AAA affiliate, playing mostly third base but also seeing time at shortstop and second base as well as left field.

Finally, according to an unconfirmed report, Jason Botts is back from Japan, having been signed to a minor league deal by the White Sox. He'll have an invite to big league camp as well, presumably to get a look as a candidate for the DH role that Andruw Jones was signed by Chicago to fill.

December 17, 2009

Some Chuck Greenberg remarks you might enjoy:

"The goal is simple: Win. Win the division, get through the LCS, get to the World Series and win. Our intention is to make smart decisions that achieve those goals. You can't just throw money out there at things. But you also can't win without having the resources to add pieces when you need to. If there are additional moves that need to be made, we want to be smart about it but we'll make the moves. We want to win a championship."

"If we have a chance to improve the ballclub during the season leading up to the trade deadline, we will be able to make those moves. Money will not stop us from doing it."

"In this area, there is a tremendous amount of pent-up enthusiasm for the Rangers that is just waiting to explode. They may not have a history of World Series championships, but there is a great deal of hope and passion. With a little help and tender love and care, it can be pushed over the top, and hopefully our group can push it over the top."

"With all the things the Rangers have done the last few years on the baseball side, the club is poised to have a great future. . . . Hopefully our group can build off that foundation that is already in place."

"I think it could be one of the great success stories in professional baseball and all of sports. It's the perfect opportunity. The vitality and the quality of life in the DFW area and surrounding communities are tremendous. It's a wonderful place to live and do business."

"To have the judgment and wisdom and personal touch of Nolan Ryan, and the tremendous group that JD has assembled, I think the Rangers on the baseball side are the envy of every franchise in baseball in terms of talent."

"If they had a Mount Rushmore of baseball in Texas, [Nolan would] be the first face chiseled out. . . . If he had affiliated with any other group, I would have dropped out immediately. There are 29 other teams out there. But the Rangers and Ryan belong together."

"My role is to have great people in positions of authority and to create an environment that enables them and encourages them to be their best, then to let them do their job. I think on the baseball side, this team is the envy of the baseball world right now. I won't inject myself in a way that would interfere with anything."

"There are certain things I'd like to do give [Rangers Ballpark] a little bit of a facelift. I think the Ballpark as it is is terrific, but there are things we can do to make it the absolute best. The absence of a giant video board, with the advent of those amenities in other facilities is one aspect I would really like to look into. Those things can really help. That's something that really jumps to mind."

"Our job is to make Texas Rangers baseball a compelling, memorable experience. It starts with having a great team on the field that relates to the community off the field. We want an organization that is connected to the fans and that is completely obsessed to do everything possible to service our fans' needs and do everything they want."

"My colleagues and I have a very similar approach. We take what we do very seriously, but we don't take ourselves seriously at all. We're going to do whatever it takes to make this work for fans."

"In this organization, there will be no walls between us and the fans. One of our most important skills is to be good listeners, and we're going to do a lot of listening during the season. We're going to be adjusting on the fly in 2010, but we're going to be flying out of the gate in the fall of 2010 going into the offseason and the next season. Whatever it takes, we will do it."

Ready for a Michael Young comment about his new teammate, Rich Harden?

"I think he has the best stuff in the league. I didn't say some of the best stuff. I mean the best stuff I've seen. I think the biggest compliment a hitter can give a pitcher is that he can get you out with a fastball at 90 or 91, just like he can at 97. That's Rich. His fastball has so much life that he can beat you even when the velocity isn't there. . . . He's got great ability."

According to Steven Henson of Yahoo! Sports, Dennis Gilbert, who at one time was considered the frontrunner for the ownership transfer, "wasn't thrilled" by the signing of Harden or the trade of Kevin Millwood.

Even if the rumored deal with the Red Sox to bring Mike Lowell here is completed (apparently pending a Lowell physical, which is supposed to take place sometime this week in Arlington), there are reports that Texas might still be interested in free agents Vlad Guerrero, Jim Thome, or Jermaine Dye.

Right-handed-hitting corner infielder Garrett Atkins, considered by some a possible fallback to Lowell given his lengthy history with Rangers hitting coach Clint Hurdle, is reportedly signing with Baltimore.

The Rangers are reported to be among the dozen or more clubs interested in right-handed reliever Matt Capps, non-tendered Saturday by the Pirates.

The Cubs, though they haven't yet been able to trade Milton Bradley, are reportedly stepping up efforts to sign Marlon Byrd now that Mike Cameron has signed with Boston.

ESPN's Jorge Arangure reports that Texas was among the 14 teams on hand for 21-year-old Cuban defector Aroldis Chapman's 10-minute throwing session in Houston on Tuesday.

Righthander Josh Johnson's agent, Matt Sosnick, told Joe Capozzi of the *Palm Beach Post* that he expects Florida to trade Johnson before the 2011 season starts. Marlins general manager Michael Hill has already told reporters that he will not trade Johnson before the 2010 season.

Daniels shot down (1) the local reports that emanated from the Winter Meetings suggesting Texas offered Neftali Feliz and Justin Smoak to Florida for Johnson ("this rumor is completely inaccurate") and (2) George King's recent *New York Post* assertion that Texas has been shopping Josh Hamilton, saying that the Rangers "haven't had a single [trade] conversation about Josh this winter."

Daniels added that righthander Tanner Scheppers is penciled in for a season-opening assignment to Frisco, though things could change that plan in camp.

Kevin Goldstein of Baseball Prospectus wrote a feature called "The Top 20 of the New Decade," and though no Rangers made his list of the top 20 players of the next 10 years, Elvis Andrus and Feliz made the "just missed" list, as did LSU righthander Anthony Ranaudo, whom the Rangers drafted in the 11th round in 2007 out of a New Jersey high school but couldn't persuade not to honor his LSU commitment.

The great MLB Network is in the midst of a two-month series called "30 Clubs 30 Recaps," in which it covers a different team each episode and discusses what they need to do to succeed in 2010. The Rangers segment airs December 22 during the "Hot Stove Live" program from 5:00 until 6:00 p.m. Central.

Philadelphia named Mark Parent manager for Low A Lakewood and Donnie Sadler hitting coach for the organization's rookie-level Gulf Coast League entry. Arizona named Gil Heredia pitching coach for the rookie-level Missoula Osprey.

December 18, 2009

I'm not easily awed.

In the nearly 12 years of this project, there haven't been too many moments that knocked me speechless. But last night was one of them.

I'm still stunned at how many of you packed the room (well, rooms) at Sherlock's for the book release party. I'd sit here and thank everyone again, but since I think everyone who's ever heard of the Newberg Report was there when I did so last night, what's the point?

But I do want to give repeat thanks to Steve, Rosco, Jason, Amber, and April for making Sherlock's the perfect place for our gathering once again, and to Eleanor and Toni and Devin and Norma for working so hard to make the party great. There are many others.

We're seriously thinking about having a second party, probably at the Sherlock's in Dallas (near Northpark Mall) sometime in January. We'll work on a new player lineup for the next one, for those of you who might want to come again. Stay tuned.

When I asked Rusty Greer, Ian and Tess Kinsler, Scott Feldman, Tommy Hunter, Derek Holland, and Chris Davis a month ago if they could join us last night, without exception they responded not with an "I'll get back to you" or "Check back with me if you can't find someone else." In every case it was "What time do you need me there?"

I told them 6:00 until 9:00. But it took until 9:30 to get through the entire autograph line (the manager was thrilled with last year's crowd of a little bit over 400 Rangers fans—last night we approached 600).

And then we Q&A'd until 10:00.

Those four tall boxes built to hold Toys for Tots donations weren't enough. The Marines on hand had to empty the boxes in their vans more than once to make sure there was always something for you all to put your toys in. Awesome.

Speaking of boxes, I said half-jokingly on Twitter yesterday that I was lugging 500 copies of the 2010 Bound Edition to the party and was hoping to come home with only about one-fifth of those.

Turns out I did.

Tack on the 400 copies that shipped out earlier this week, and we're off to our best start ever with book sales.

A number of you vowed to pass along photos from the party. We'll get those put up on one page once they start to come in, and I know there will be a blogged writeup or two. I'll share the links to those as well.

I had a great time last night. Thank you all.

Owners from Pittsburgh
There's precedent for those here
To contend yearly

December 19, 2009

According to multiple reports, Mike Lowell is set to undergo a physical in Arlington today, which could lead to a final resolution this weekend, one way or the other, of the conditional trade that would send catcher Max Ramirez to Boston for Lowell and a $9 million subsidy toward the veteran's $12 million 2010 contract.

Lowell would reportedly be expected to back up Chris Davis at first base, share DH duties primarily with David Murphy, and serve as insurance at third base in case of injury to Michael Young.

Another couple quick notes:

Milwaukee signed righthander Kameron Loe, who comes back from Japan, to a non-roster deal that will pay $650,000 if he makes the Brewers' staff, with another $200,000 in workload incentives.

Meanwhile, righthander Bryan Corey heads in the opposite direction, having signed with the Chiba Lotte Marines.

Stay tunes for more Lowell news as it becomes available.

December 19, 2009

According to multiple sources, a torn ligament was discovered in Mike Lowell's thumb during his Arlington physical today, prompting Texas to kill the trade that would have sent Max Ramirez to Boston for the veteran. Lowell is slated to have surgery later this month, with an expected recovery time of 6-8 weeks.

December 20, 2009: TROT COFFEY

According to ESPN.com's Jerry Crasnick, Texas is in "serious discussions" with left-handed free agent reliever Darren Oliver, and "[i]t's believed an agreement could be in place early this week." The 39-year-old, heading toward his 17th big league season, went 5-1, 2.71 in one start and 62 relief appearances for the Angels in 2009. Los Angeles chose not to offer Oliver arbitration earlier this month, meaning the Rangers would not forfeit their first-round pick for signing the Type A free agent.

Whether this means Texas is roughly reallocating the $3 million that it had earmarked for Mike Lowell (meaning there will be a significantly cheaper right-handed bat targeted) or if instead the payroll budget is higher than has been speculated—either all along or perhaps by virtue of where the process stands as far as the ownership transfer is concerned—the addition of a middle reliever at what stands to be a pretty significant cost is interesting.

December 22, 2009

The Rangers have announced that lefthander Darren Oliver has signed a one-year contract with a vesting option for 2011. The 39-year-old passed a club physical earlier today.

December 23, 2009

Yesterday's Yankees acquisition of Javier Vazquez from Atlanta suggests that the quality of the free agent starting pitcher class has thinned out to the point at which the remaining alternatives are largely either health risks (Ben Sheets, Erik Bedard), age risks (Pedro Martinez, Jose Contreras), or both (Randy Johnson, John Smoltz), or simply not good enough risks to perform to the level at which they're seeking to be paid as they continue to shop themselves on the notion that demand still exceeds supply.

MLB Network suggested last night that the cream of the crop still on the market consists of righthanders Joel Pineiro, Vicente Padilla, Jon Garland, Martinez, and Smoltz. Fair enough (maybe throw in lefthander Jarrod Washburn), but outside of Pineiro, is any really worth committing multiple years to? There's a reason New York was willing to give up a serviceable, affordable outfield bat and two legitimate prospects to get one year of Vazquez (and unremarkable reliever Boone Logan) from the Braves, rather than spend on a free agent.

Yesterday's Rangers signing of reliever Darren Oliver to a one-year contract (with a club option that vests if he pitches 59 times in 2010—he averaged 59.33 appearances the past three seasons with the Angels) brings to 23 the number of pitchers on the Rangers' 40-man roster. That doesn't count relievers Willie Eyre and Clay Rapada, who were each outrighted off the roster earlier this month.

In the Bound Edition, I head every month of reports from the preceding year with a snapshot of the Rangers' 40-man roster as it stood on the 1st of that particular month. The last month that started with as many as 23 pitchers on the roster?

March.

Of *2007*.

The Rangers won't say it, but I can't help but wonder if the club's stockpiling of arms—when there remain obvious holes to fill on the rest of the roster—could signal an effort to use some of its pitching depth to address other needs. Just as the Braves did yesterday.

Rotation candidates now include Scott Feldman, Rich Harden, Tommy Hunter, Derek Holland, Brandon McCarthy, Matt Harrison, Neftali Feliz, C.J. Wilson, Dustin Nippert, Doug Mathis, Guillermo Moscoso, and Luis Mendoza, and Jon Daniels has at least suggested the club may add one more veteran reinforcement candidate. A number of those 12 will compete for bullpen spots if they don't land in the rotation, but with the additions of Oliver, Chris Ray, and Rule 5 pick Ben Snyder, plus Rapada, there's depth in relief, too.

At some point in this market, might a team decide it would be better off taking a flier on McCarthy, who is under affordable control for two more years, than paying Braden Looper or Tim Redding or Todd Wellemeyer, or than rolling the dice that Chien-Ming Wang is past his issues, or that Justin Duchscherer is past his?

Could the addition of Oliver be the prelude to a deal including C.J. Wilson for an impact bat? This was a solid, deep bullpen even before Texas guaranteed at least $3.5 million to Oliver.

Nippert and Mendoza are out of options. McCarthy and Ray are not, but given their service time it would be unlikely Texas could get them to AAA. The 23 pitchers currently on the Texas roster won't all be there Opening Day, and some may be gone within a month. The Rangers' pitching depth may start to attract increasing interest from clubs unable (or unwilling) to fill their needs through what's left via free agency.

Crazy Oliver splits: Against left-handed hitters in 2009, he struck out 37 and walked only four (a 9.25 K/BB rate), but they hit .263 and slugged .412. Right-handed hitters hit only .217 with just a .294 slug—but they drew 18 walks and fanned 28 times (a 1.56 K/BB rate).

The organization notes that Oliver joins Kenny Rogers and Bill Haselman as three-tour Rangers. Seems Ruben Sierra should be counted as well.

Interesting stories coming out of Boston in the aftermath of the Mike Lowell non-trade. The veteran told Boston reporters that his right thumb injury, which is what killed the deal to Texas after a physical revealed a torn ligament last week, wasn't filmed by the Red Sox—despite his repeated complaints—until December 7. According to Lowell, he injured the thumb on October 2, told the club in early November his symptoms hadn't subsided, said something again in mid-November, had it splinted by the Red Sox's assistant trainer in late November, and finally, two weeks ago, during the Winter Meetings, was asked by Boston to submit to an MRI.

Whether Red Sox personnel misdiagnosed their MRI, or didn't share the results with Texas, it wasn't until his Arlington MRI last week that the Rangers found the ligament tear and backed out of a trade for Lowell. Had Boston discovered the tear nearly two months ago, it's conceivable that he could have had surgery right away—which he's told reporters was what he wanted—and been pronounced healthy by now.

Now the Red Sox have an injured $12 million player that they don't want to go forward with and that they're going to have trouble moving. Nonetheless, Ken Rosenthal of Fox Sports and others are convinced that Lowell has played his last game for Boston.

John Perrotto of Baseball Prospectus suggests that Vladimir Guerrero now tops the Rangers' wish list for the right-handed DH role that Lowell was being targeted to fill.

Anyone a little surprised that the Cubs, having succeeded in moving Milton Bradley, haven't yet nailed down a deal with Marlon Byrd? Is this a Mark DeRosa situation, where Byrd is drawing plenty of league interest but is going to have to set his dollar sights lower? Or is Byrd instead waiting things out to see what other clubs join the mix as they alter their rosters?

It sounds like DeRosa could soon be a Yankee. Hate that. Hate to see a player I like as much as that guy ending up in that place.

Man, if the dollars worked (and if DeRosa weren't able to command an everyday defensive position on the open market), he'd be the absolutely perfect answer for what Texas had pinpointed Lowell to do. Perfect.

Texas, according to Jon Heyman of *Sports Illustrated*, was in on Yakult Swallows reliever Ryota Igarashi before the 30-year-old righthander signed a two-year, $3 million deal with the Mets.

Washington is close to signing lefthander Eddie Guardado, who had hinted at retirement as the 2009 season ended. Cincinnati re-signed outfielder Laynce Nix, but only to a minor league contract. San Diego signed catcher Chris Stewart to a minor league deal. The Mets plan to sign righthander R.A. Dickey to a minor league deal.

(Gotta love the *New York Times* headline: "Mets Near Deal With Pitcher Missing an Elbow Ligament." Maybe if the Yankees sign Jermaine Dye, who is evidently a candidate along with DeRosa for left field, the *Times* will report: "Yankees Sign Former Pitcher.")

The Rangers gave minor league contracts to catchers John Otness (a 27-year-old who spent six seasons in the Boston system, briefly reaching AAA for the first time in 2009) and Robbie Alcombrack (a 21-year-old who spent 2009 with Michigan's own Traverse City Beach Bums of the independent Frontier League after three seasons in the Cleveland chain).

Otness—who caught Tim Lincecum at the University of Washington—played in 2006, 2007, and 2008 for AA Portland, which was managed by former Rangers farm skipper Arnie Beyeler, re-hired by Boston earlier this month to stay on at the helm of the Eastern League affiliate.

As of this moment, the Rangers will draft 15th, 22nd, and 41st in June, though that third pick will probably move down another eight spots or so once the remaining Type A and Type B free agents find new homes, and they'll also add a fourth first-rounder in the 50 range if Byrd signs elsewhere.

Update on links to stories and blogs recapping last week's Newberg Report Book Release Party:

T.R. Sullivan, MLB.com (preview): *http://trsullivan.mlblogs.com/archives/2009/12/of_the_bound_edition_sherlocks.html*

T.R. Sullivan, MLB.com (recap): *http://trsullivan.mlblogs.com/archives/2009/12/one_night_in_arlington_and_it.html*

Tim Cowlishaw, *Dallas Morning News*: *http://www.dallasnews.com/sharedcontent/dws/spt/baseball/rangers/stories/121809dnsporangerscowlishaw.365da1f29.html*

Grant Schiller, Texas Rangers Trades: *http://texasrangerstrades.blogspot.com/2009/12/newberg-bound-edition-release-party.html*

Katie Brownfield (with photos):

http://iheartrangersbaseball.blogspot.com/2009/12/newberg-book-signing-aka-meeting-tr.html

Scott Lucas (photos):

http://s408.photobucket.com/albums/pp170/slucas66/NewbergBook09/?action=view¤t=9a393600.pbw

Susan Minatrea (photo): http://www.facebook.com/photo.php?pid=30513900&op=1&view=all&subj=831393986&id=1007720841#/photo.php?pid=30513900&op=1&o=global&view=global&subj=831393986&id=1007720841

Still working on details to have a second party in January, somewhere in Dallas. Stay tuned.

December 24, 2009

Among the annual exercises undertaken by *Baseball America* this time of the year is the ranking of the game's top 100 prospects, a three-headed effort by co-editors-in-chief Will Lingo and John Manuel and executive editor Jim Callis, each of whom submits a personal top 50 list that gets published in the *BA* Prospect Handbook, which has apparently been finalized and sent off to the printer for production. Tonight Manuel has revealed the first 20 of his own top 50 prospects list.

Of Manuel's top 20 prospects in baseball, 13 players are the lone representatives of their organizations.

Two are Rays (OF Desmond Jennings [number 4] and RHP Jeremy Hellickson [number 15]). Two are Giants (C Buster Posey [number 9] and LHP Madison Bumgarner [number 10]).

Three are Rangers:

8. Neftali Feliz, rhp, Rangers

WHY HE'S HERE: Feliz has one of baseball's quickest, most electric arms, and showed it off when he first was called up to the major leagues last August.

WHAT HE'LL BE: The big question with Feliz is his ultimate role. Before tiring down the stretch last year, Feliz showed he could be an impact relief arm, and his feel for his secondary stuff comes and goes. The Rangers see that easy upper-90s gas, though, and see a starter.

WHEN HE ARRIVES: Feliz is expected to break camp in 2010 in Texas' rotation. It might take a while for him to truly arrive as a starter, as was the case for flamethrowers such as Edwin Jackson and A.J. Burnett.

12. Justin Smoak, 1b, Rangers

WHY HE'S HERE: A switch-hitter from the South, Smoak looks a bit like Chipper Jones at the plate with his stance and mannerisms. He has a chance to hit like Jones, too, with consistency, polish and power.

WHAT HE'LL BE: Smoak doesn't quite have Mark Teixeira's explosive power, but he's a similar-caliber hitter and defender. He just needs to add a bit of polish and figure out how to turn on inside pitches.

WHEN HE ARRIVES: With Hank Blalock out of the picture, the first-base job is open in Texas. While Smoak has competition (especially if the Rangers add Mike Lowell from the Red Sox to play first), he should become the full-time first sacker by 2011.

20. Martin Perez, lhp, Rangers

WHY HE'S HERE: The third Ranger on the list, Perez has a delivery and repertoire that draw comparisons to Johan Santana. That may not be fair to Perez, but as an 18-year-old, he was the best pitcher in the South Atlantic League, and his compact delivery is a near-duplicate of Santana's.

WHAT HE'LL BE: Well, have we mentioned Santana? There's just a long way for Perez to go from A-ball to the majors, and his workload has been handled very carefully so far.

WHEN HE ARRIVES: Let's give Perez a couple of years to let his low-90s fastball that touches 96, plus changeup and plus curveball time to incubate. He should be on this list at least two more times.

Happy Holidays, Rangers fans.

December 25, 2009

In lieu of a Friday haiku, Max and Snowlan Ryan and Erica issue this winter advisory:

"*Snowdibbe McDowell, Buck Snowalter, Snowby Harrah, Emerson Frosty, Kameron Snow, Doug Dascenzsnow, Akinori Snowtsuka (*Snowsshaa!!*), Snowgelio Moret, Pete Snow'Brien, Alfonsnow Snowriano, snow monkeys, and Ian Gac love the 2010 Bound Edition of the Newberg Report!*

Get snow-Bound today!!"

December 27, 2009: TROT COFFEY

According to Nick Cafardo of the *Boston Globe*, "[a] market is beginning to develop [for free agent righthander Jon Garland], and Texas appears to be the early leader" (*the 30-year-old Garland has won in double digits in each of his eight big league seasons but profiles at best as an inning-eating, middle-to-back-of-the-rotation pitcher these days—sort of a veteran version of Tommy Hunter; not that there's anything wrong with that*)

Cafardo adds that the Rangers might have more interest in Jermaine Dye than Vladimir Guerrero since Dye can still play the outfield (*hmm; not a real significant factor if you asked me, and I'm still hopeful, if the choice is between those two, that Guerrero prevails*)

Cafardo also thinks that free agent infielder Miguel Tejada could be a fit for Texas "in a modified [Mike] Lowell role"

It's now being reported that the deal lefthander Eddie Guardado signed with Washington was of the non-roster variety—that makes more sense

I'll get into this in greater depth in a future report, but the Angels' winter ledger card, so far, has Hideki Matsui and Fernando Rodney heading the add column and John Lackey, Chone Figgins, and Darren Oliver in the subtract column; I don't believe Los Angeles is really done, but for the moment? Winner: American League

December 29, 2009

Reports on imminent acquisition activity around the league have slowed to a relative crawl with the holidays—suggesting that either front offices or those who typically report on the Hot Stove have taken their foot off the gas a bit until the New Year—but while two key Rangers roles (right-handed middle-of-order bat and rotation addition) seem poised for eventual movement once the market continues to shake out, two spots at the bottom of the 40-man roster, which currently accommodates 39 players, may be worthy of a bit of attention.

With two days left in the Mexican Pacific League regular season, Obregon righthander Luis Mendoza leads the eight-team circuit in strikeouts (82; nobody else in the league has more than 54), strikeout rate (8.17 per nine innings; next best is 5.70), and opponents' batting average by a starter (.249), and is second in ERA (2.89), WHIP (1.229), and wins (seven).

Mendoza is pitching into the seventh inning *on average*. He's walking under three batters per nine innings. And he continues to generate ground balls at a sparkling rate (2.10 groundouts for every flyout).

We've talked regularly about how big (and relatively uncommon) it is to combine a high strikeout rate and a high groundball rate. Is Mendoza, at age 26 the prototypical 4-A, possibly turning a corner?

Here's the thing: Mendoza is out of options. With his repertoire, and certainly the winter he's having, chances are he wouldn't clear waivers in March. And even if he were to clear, he's been outrighted before (by Boston in 2005), which means he'd have the right to decline a Rangers outright and take immediate free agency.

By virtue of his options/outright status and his difficulty getting big leaguers out the last two years, if Mendoza is not the last of the 23 pitchers currently on the 40-man roster, he's close to it. Same goes for the roster security of infielder Joaquin Arias, who is also out of options and has the type of skill set that would probably lead at least one club to put in a waiver claim if he fails to make the Rangers' Opening Day roster.

Arias has had a solid Dominican Winter League season, hitting .296/.345/.327 in the regular season for Escogido with six stolen bases in eight attempts and more walks (seven) than strikeouts (five), and more notably playing shortstop for the most part (his last 24 starts have been at shortstop, after alternating between second base and shortstop during his first week of play). If the shoulder is back, Arias's candidacy for the Rangers' utility infield spot becomes more legitimate.

Three weeks ago, there was a report out of Arizona that Texas had expressed interest in veteran utility infielder Augie Ojeda but that the Diamondbacks were hesitant to impair their middle infield depth. Now comes a report from MLB.com's Steve Gilbert that Arizona has an offer on the table to free agent infielder Kelly Johnson, the addition of whom would relegate Tony Abreu to a bench role and make Ojeda expendable. Worth keeping an eye on, maybe.

A couple other things:

Mark DeRosa has agreed to terms with the Giants on a two-year, $12 million contract, and that's a lot better as far as I'm concerned than if he'd signed with the Yankees—not only because I didn't want to see DeRosa in pinstripes, but also because it makes it more likely that New York turns to Jermaine Dye. Wouldn't mind seeing that happen.

Baseball Prospectus writer Russell A. Carleton points out that Rangers hitters were last in the big leagues in 2009 at making contact, hitting the ball on only 77.1 percent of their swings. The second-worst, third-worst, fourth-worst, fifth-worst, and sixth-worst clubs were National League teams, for an obvious reason, which accentuates the embarrassing point that all 16 NL teams, whose percentage of pitcher plate appearances was 15 times greater than their AL counterparts, swung and missed at a lesser rate than the Rangers.

This sorta surprised me: Dye (82.0 percent) and Guerrero (81.0 percent) fared better in 2009 than Michael Young (80.6 percent) or Marlon Byrd (79.8 percent). (The top two Texas regulars were Ian Kinsler [87.7 percent] and Elvis Andrus [87.3 percent].)

Back to the top. Mendoza's dominant winter and the utility infield situation aren't front page developments—and won't be even when things fully shake out—but they are *developments* nonetheless, which made me think this morning about two points I wanted to make:

1. Last year at this time, Texas had not yet come to terms with Ben Sheets or signed Omar Vizquel or Eddie Guardado (or Jason Jennings or Andruw Jones or Kris Benson, each of whom was at least envisioned to hold down a key role) or claimed Darren O'Day off waivers. The winter work is far from over.
2. 51 sleeps.

JANUARY 2010

40-MAN ROSTER (39)

PITCHERS (23)

Scott Feldman, Neftali Feliz, Frankie Francisco, Rich Harden, Matt Harrison, Derek Holland, Tommy Hunter, Eric Hurley, Michael Kirkman, Warner Madrigal, Doug Mathis, Brandon McCarthy, Luis Mendoza, Guillermo Moscoso, Dustin Nippert, Darren O'Day, Darren Oliver, Zach Phillips, Omar Poveda, Chris Ray, Ben Snyder, Pedro Strop, C.J. Wilson

CATCHERS (3)

Max Ramirez, Jarrod Saltalamacchia, Taylor Teagarden

INFIELDERS (6)

Elvis Andrus, Joaquin Arias, Chris Davis, Joe Inglett, Ian Kinsler, Michael Young

OUTFIELDERS (7)

Brandon Boggs, Julio Borbon, Nelson Cruz, Craig Gentry, Greg Golson, Josh Hamilton, David Murphy

RESTRICTED LIST (2)

Omar Beltre, Alexi Ogando

January 1, 2010

So of the three principals at *Baseball America* who collaborate on the publication's ranking of the game's top 100 prospects, two (editor-in-chief John Manuel and executive editor Jim Callis) have now said in the last month that they have the Rangers repeating as the number one farm system in baseball, and each has Neftali Feliz, Justin Smoak, and Martin Perez among baseball's top 25 prospects.

But let's shift to something more immediate.

Texas finished second in the West in 2009 for the second straight year, winning 87 games despite 14 losses over its final 21 games. Can 2010 be better?

Is it reasonable to expect a lot more out of Josh Hamilton? He doesn't need to repeat 2008 (.304/.371/.530), even though he hinted at a return to form over his final 32 games in 2009 (.346/.391/.512). It's the 57 games that preceded that stretch (.220/.269/.373) that Hamilton can't give this club in 2010.

Two years ago, new Rangers hitting coach Clint Hurdle said this:

"One of the best things I was ever told as a young player that I never understood until I was an older player: There's two kinds of people that play this game, those that are humble and those that are about to be. At the age of 18 I laughed, yeah, that's cute. Well, by the age of 38 I was wearing it."

And this:

"Early in my career, I was in a hurry. I've had to learn patience through challenging times. That's been good. It's proved to be an asset, especially in this profession."

Hamilton is Hurdle's most important project. A return to health is obviously important. So is rhythm at the plate. And confidence. Hamilton needs to have all those things come back together. If he can figure out (as he did in August) how to give his teammates a reliable plate presence once again—not necessarily MVP-level production but just a consistent threat in the middle of the order—it will make a huge difference. Imagine what this 87-team club would have done with any consistency from Hamilton last year.

Ian Kinsler's first 35 games in 2009: .318/.380/.622.

His remaining 109 games: .230/.308/.440.

We all know the 27-year-old should be a lot closer to the first guy in 2010 than the second guy. Is there any reason to believe he can't at least be the .319/.375/.517 hitter he was in 2008 again?

We can expect more production from first base in 2010. There won't be a repeat of last year's .226/.272/.411. One way or the other, there just won't.

Rangers catchers hit .234/.286/.379 in 2009. Fair to expect better?

Can Elvis Andrus avoid a sophomore setback, and settle in as the hitter he was in the second half (.280/.342/.395, after a .253/.315/.350 first half)?

Julio Borbon hit .320/.386/.467 in his first 23 big league games, .305/.367/.366 over his remaining 23. Nothing wrong with the second set of numbers. Even if he doesn't replicate either slash line, just having a full year of Borbon atop the order, batting after Andrus and allowing Kinsler to move into a run-producing slot permanently, should help the offense.

A full year of Feliz is an upgrade, no matter how he's used.

Tommy Hunter and Derek Holland went a combined 15-18, 5.19 in 40 starts. I'd bet against those numbers getting worse.

Frankie Francisco and C.J. Wilson had more great stretches in 2009 than the not-so-great runs. Aren't they about what they are? Francisco, for what it's worth, is essentially in a contract year, as he'll be a free agent next winter for the first time. Wilson is a year behind him in service time.

Is it overly optimistic to hope for repeats of the spike years that Scott Feldman (17-8, 4.08), Michael Young (.322/.374/.518), and Darren O'Day (1.94 ERA, .188/.265/.260 slash, 3.18 K/BB) had?

Losing Marlon Byrd isn't a positive. Defensively, Borbon's improvement in center field will be important. As for Byrd's bat (.283/.329/.479, including .282/.336/.538 at home), let's see what the club does about adding another right-handed run producer.

Put it this way: Moving Kevin Millwood for two bullpen candidates couldn't be counted a positive as far as 2010 is concerned.

Until Texas signed Rich Harden two days later.

Give me Darren Oliver over Eddie Guardado.

And give me an impact addition or two in July, which, as long as the team is hanging around in playoff contention, I think we can expect this season more than we could last year.

Another thing we can expect, at least on paper, is that the Angels (having lost John Lackey, Chone Figgins, Oliver, and eventually Vlad Guerrrero, and having added Hideki Matsui and Fernando Rodney) aren't going to be as strong in 2010 as their 97-win team was in 2009.

If the Rangers do repeat atop *Baseball America*'s organizational talent rankings, they'll be just the third franchise to do so in the last 20 years (Atlanta 1994-95, Tampa Bay 2007-08). There are plenty of players in the Texas system who will contribute eventually to winning clubs.

But think about last year's 87-win Rangers club, about the Angels' winter, about having players like Feliz and Borbon and Hunter for a full season, about the odds of getting more out of Hamilton and Kinsler, and about Harden.

And about this July.

Could 2010 be The Year, after all?

To kick our 2010 off, a Newberg Report New Year's Day custom: My top 72 Rangers prospects, as laid out (with detailed commentary on each player) in the 2010 Bound Edition—which was released less than three weeks ago but has already had more copies sold than any of the previous 10 books, thanks to you all:

1. Neftali Feliz, RHP
2. Justin Smoak, 1B
3. Martin Perez, LHP
4. Tanner Scheppers, RHP
5. Wilmer Font, RHP
6. Jurickson Profar, SS
7. Michael Main, RHP
8. Danny Gutierrez, RHP
9. Robbie Ross, LHP
10. Engel Beltre, OF
11. Mitch Moreland, 1B-OF
12. Blake Beavan, RHP
13. Pedro Strop, RHP
14. Kasey Kiker, LHP
15. Michael Kirkman, LHP
16. Wilfredo Boscan, RHP
17. Max Ramirez, C
18. Joe Wieland, RHP
19. Guillermo Moscoso, RHP
20. Tomas Telis, C
21. Tommy Mendonca, 3B
22. Luis Sardinas, SS
23. Omar Poveda, RHP
24. Eric Hurley, RHP
25. Miguel Velazquez, OF
26. Carlos Pimentel, RHP
27. Leury Garcia, SS
28. Mike Bianucci, OF
29. Neil Ramirez, RHP
30. Kennil Gomez, RHP
31. Craig Gentry, OF
32. Zach Phillips, LHP
33. Corey Young, LHP
34. Jake Brigham, RHP
35. Braden Tullis, RHP
36. Richard Bleier, LHP
37. Richard Alvarez, RHP
38. Evan Reed, RHP
39. Alexi Ogando, RHP
40. Miguel De Los Santos, LHP
41. Fabio Castillo, RHP
42. Tim Murphy, LHP
43. Edwin Escobar, LHP
44. Matt Thompson, RHP
45. Marcus Lemon, 2B
46. Chad Tracy, 1B
47. Leonel De Los Santos, C
48. Robbie Erlin, LHP
49. Geuris Grullon, LHP
50. Johnny Whittleman, 3B
51. Greg Golson, OF
52. Jose Felix, C
53. David Paisano, OF
54. Shawn Blackwell, RHP
55. Cristian Santana, OF
56. Carlos Melo, RHP
57. Beau Jones, LHP
58. Tanner Roark, RHP
59. Chad Bell, LHP
60. Randol Rojas, RHP
61. Guillermo Pimentel, OF
62. Yoon-Hee Nam, LHP
63. Joseph Ortiz, LHP
64. Vin DiFazio, C
65. Clark Murphy, 1B
66. Paul Strong, LHP
67. Brennan Garr, RHP
68. David Perez, RHP
69. Jose Monegro, RHP
70. Andrew Doyle, RHP
71. Nick McBride, RHP
72. Ryan Tatusko, RHP

Best wishes for a happy, healthy, and prosperous New Year to you, your family, and your baseball team.

January 4, 2010: TROT COFFEY

- Boston has reportedly signed third baseman Adrian Beltre to a $9 million contract for 2010, with a $5 million *player* option for 2011 (and a $1 buyout)—good on two fronts: (1) if Texas remains interested in Mike Lowell and he proves to be healthy when camps open in a month and a half, the presence of Beltre impairs Boston's leverage and ought to mean the Red Sox will have to accept less than Max Ramirez, toss in more than $9 million toward's Lowell's $12 million obligation for 2010, or both; and (2) Oakland was rumored to be the runner-up for Beltre—glad to see he won't be in green and gold, which would have primed the A's to add two first-round picks in June 2011 if not a couple blue-chip prospects this coming July
- During last week's surgical procedure, it was discovered that Lowell's right thumb ligament had a *95 percent* tear; the Mets are apparently kicking around the idea of taking Lowell for second baseman Luis Castillo
- Texas is reportedly interested in 30-year-old righthander Colby Lewis, who plans to return to the United States after two strong seasons pitching for the Hiroshima Carp in Japan (15-8, 2.68 and 11-9, 2.96, leading the league in strikeouts both seasons with a combined 369 in 354.1 innings—and issuing

only 46 walks, a smooth one per nine innings); don't view this as an organization trying to justify a past decision—very few decision-makers who were around when Lewis was lost on waivers to Detroit in 2004 are still here now . . . though current scouting director Kip Fagg was the area scout who signed the big righty as the Rangers' top pick in the 1999 draft

- Vladimir Guerrero? Jermaine Dye? Which one will first decide he's willing to sign for just one guaranteed year? (between the two, hopefully Vlad—though Jim Thome could apparently figure in as well; one local reporter adds the names Gary Sheffield, Xavier Nady, Carlos Delgado, Garret Anderson, Melvin Mora, Mike Sweeney, and Aubrey Huff as bat candidates, one of whom stands out for me as a very intriguing name and one of whom stands out as a "please, no"; the reporter also mentions Craig Monroe, Ryan Garko, Marcus Thames, Austin Kearns, Jonny Gomes, Randy Winn, Fernando Tatis, Rocco Baldelli, and Emil Brown)
- Marlon Byrd's Cubs deal: $3 million in 2010, $5.5 million in 2011, $6.5 million in 2012
- University of Florida wide receiver Riley Cooper told reporters (according to a *Gainesville Sun* article with conspicuous typographical errors and sloppy quotes) that he's now considering the NFL rather than beginning his minor league career with the Rangers, and plans to play in the January 30 Senior Bowl and attend the NFL Combine (receivers work out on February 22); he acknowledges that he'll have to return his $250,000 bonus to Texas should he opt for football—Cooper is slated to report to minor league camp at the beginning of March, more than seven weeks before the NFL Draft
- Catcher Miguel Olivo signed with Colorado today for one year and a club option for a second—a possible sign that the veteran catcher market is no longer commanding two-year deals; Jarrod Saltalamacchia will reportedly have his shoulder re-examined next week, the results of which (plus a club-friendly shift in the market) could accelerate the Rangers' efforts to add a veteran, though Saltalamacchia told reporters today his shoulder feels good
- Seattle is rumored to be mulling over the idea of pitching a trade for Minnesota lefthander Francisco Liriano, a buy-low effort that would upset me as a Mariners rival
- We are fortunate to have Scott Lucas writing about our team

Tardy Friday haiku:

Gerald, Brandon Laird
Arrested after bar brawl
Hmm; two men, two tools?

January 5, 2010

According to a December 30 report by Melissa Segura of *Sports Illustrated*, the Rangers have apparently signed highly touted Dominican lefthander Victor Payano, a 16-year-old who had agreed to sign with Boston for $900,000 in July before reportedly failing a physical due to shoulder concerns, which prompted the Red Sox to void the deal.

A lanky 6'4", 175, Payano was reportedly touching 90 in the spring and, with that build, obviously projects for more. Here's 12 seconds of video from Baseball Prospectus writer Kiley McDaniel: http://vimeo.com/5055849

No word on terms.

January 6, 2010

According to a report posted by Evan Grant of the *Dallas Morning News*, Texas has hired former Rangers catcher Bill Haselman—long considered a future big league manager prospect—to manage Class A Bakersfield. No official announcement has been made.

January 7, 2010

Anyone else expect one of these local weathermen to break into a Deion end zone dance talking about this McFarland Signature junk?

Speaking of football, I'm not sure if Lonnie Maclin is Jeremy Maclin's disclaimed biological father (they were both born in Missouri, 21 years apart), but at the moment I'd say Lonnie can hold his head up higher about his 13-at-bat big league career (with the Cardinals in September and October 1993) than Jeremy can after the Eagles' final snap on Sunday, when he 100 percent gave up on Donovan McNabb's pass, taking his eyes off the ball and turning them—not just peripherally—toward an approaching Ken Hamlin. Sorry play.

Jimmy would have taken him off the playoff roster.

A final football note, and then some Rangers content:

AP

Can't wait for tonight.

One local reporter suggests that of the right-handed bat alternatives that remain on the free agent market, Vladimir Guerrero and Xavier Nady make the most sense for Texas. Agree.

Peter Gammons of MLB Network believes the Mets are the frontrunners to sign righthander Jon Garland, whom some have reported Texas to be squarely in the mix for.

Baseball Prospectus (January 11) and *Baseball America* (January 25) haven't yet revealed their Rangers prospect rankings, but John Sickels did so yesterday:

1. Neftali Feliz, RHP, Grade A
2. Justin Smoak, 1B, Grade A-
3. Martin Perez, LHP, Grade A- ("Could be a left-handed version of Feliz if all goes well")
4. Tanner Scheppers, RHP, Grade B+
5. Wilmer Font, RHP, Grade B
6. Michael Main, RHP, Grade B
7. Mitch Moreland, 1B-OF, Grade B-
8. Kasey Kiker, LHP, Grade B-
9. Robbie Ross, LHP, Grade B-
10. Danny Gutierrez, RHP, Grade C+
11. Engel Beltre, OF, Grade C+
12. Guillermo Moscoso, RHP, Grade C+
13. Max Ramirez, C, Grade C+
14. Miguel Velazquez, OF, Grade C+
15. Omar Poveda, RHP, Grade C+
16. Blake Beavan, RHP, Grade C+
17. Carlos Pimentel, RHP, Grade C+
18. Robbie Erlin, LHP, Grade C+
19. Tommy Mendonca, 3B, Grade C+
20. Vin DiFazio, C, Grade C+

OTHERS (Grade C): Richard Alvarez, RHP; Mike Bianucci, OF; Richard Bleier, LHP; Wilfredo Boscan, RHP; Andrew Doyle, RHP; Edwin Escobar, LHP; Craig Gentry, OF; Kennil Gomez, RHP; Michael Kirkman, LHP; Marcus Lemon, INF; Zach Phillips, LHP; Jurickson Profar, SS; Neil Ramirez, RHP; Luis Sardinas, SS; Ben Snyder, LHP; Pedro Strop, RHP; Tomas Telis, C; Matt Thompson, RHP; Braden Tullis, RHP; Joe Wieland, RHP

Asked to put together a starting lineup of the best prospects in baseball, *BA*'s Jim Callis included no Rangers position players (though he singled Smoak out as one of three players he "couldn't find room for," as he cagily moved Dustin Ackley in from the outfield to first base), but Feliz was his closer and, though he didn't crack the rotation, Perez was identified as one of three starting pitchers who just missed the cut.

Callis also made outfielder Ruben Mateo the number four player on his All-Bust Team from the last decade. (Another football note: Drew Henson was number seven.) And in naming the biggest bust of the decade at each of the first 10 slots in the draft, Drew Meyer was Callis's pick for the worst number 10 pick.

Frisco righthander Blake Beavan will appear with Cowboys defensive lineman Marcus Spears and wide receiver Jesse Holley from 7-8 p.m. on January 12 at the Coppell location of Mooyah Burgers & Fries (104 N. Denton Tap Road) to support the great Allen Cordrey's Cards2Care gift card drive. Come on out and get your Bound Edition signed.

The Joliet Jackhammers of the independent Northern League signed first baseman Freddie Thon.

Pittsburgh named Anthony Telford minor league personal development coordinator. Colorado named Joey Eischen pitching coach for Low A Tri-City. Milwaukee named Bob Miscik manager at High A Brevard County, after he managed AA Huntsville last year, and hired Ross Sapp to serve as a major league scout. Boston promoted Mike Cather to major league advance scout.

One of the cool things about having a book deal for the first time is that the Bound Edition is now available on Amazon and Borders.com, and should be soon on BN.com. If you feel like it, you can go to the Amazon link and post a Customer Review.

January 7, 2010

The Rangers have announced that lefthander Martin Perez is the organization's 2009 Nolan Ryan Minor League Pitcher of the Year, first baseman/outfielder Mitch Moreland is the Tom Grieve Minor League Player of the Year, and outfielder Craig Gentry is the Minor League Defender of the Year. (I sure would like to see that last award named for Jim Sundberg, for what it's worth.)

Perez, Moreland, and Gentry will be honored, along with many other Rangers players, at the 2010 Dr Pepper Texas Rangers Mid-Winter Awards Banquet on Friday, January 29, at the Omni Fort Worth Hotel.

Also, Texas has signed infielder Matt Brown to a minor league contract with an invitation to big league camp. The 27-year-old has spent his entire nine-year career in the Angels organization, routinely with solid power numbers over the last six seasons. Primarily a third baseman, the right-handed-hitting Brown has seen at least limited time all over the infield. He got brief looks in Anaheim in 2007 and 2008, getting into 15 games and going 1 for 24.

Brown joins righthanders Willie Eyre and Geoff Geary, lefthander Clay Rapada, catcher Kevin Richardson, and infielders Esteban German and Ray Olmedo as Texas non-roster invites to date.

January 7, 2010: TROT COFFEY

- According to ESPN's Enrique Rojas, as passed along minutes ago via Twitter by ESPN'S Jorge Arangure,

Texas has reportedly offered free agent hitter Vladimir Guerrero a one-year, $7 million deal; Arangure adds that Rojas says "it's not certain whether Vlad would accept" the Texas offer

January 7, 2010: TROT COFFEY

- According to Jerry Crasnick of ESPN, a source says that the Rangers are unlikely to offer Vlad Guerrero more than the one-year, $5 million deal that Bobby Abreu got last winter from the Angels . . . contrary to Crasnick's Bristol cohort Enrique Rojas's report of a $7 million offer earlier today.
- Granulated sodium chloride, gang.
- I found this fairly interesting. Check out Matt Brown's left-right splits since reaching AA in 2006:

In 2006 (AA), Brown hit .293/.362/.495 overall—but .339/.388/.589 against lefthanders.

In 2007 (AAA), Brown hit .276/.358/.509 overall—but .302/.386/.603 against lefthanders.

In 2008 (AAA), Brown hit .320/.373/.580 overall—but .339/.397/.653 against lefthanders.

In 2009 (AAA), Brown hit .245/.333/.415 overall—but .330/.404/.532 against lefthanders.

Is Brown, whom Texas signed to a non-roster deal today, the league-minimum right-handed-hitting DH stopgap we were hoping a year ago that Max Ramirez would be?

Viewed another way, is he the type of player—a no-risk corner infield acquisition—who might serve as a placeholder while the Rangers monitor the Mike Lowell's condition in Boston camp?

As far as I can tell, Brown is out of options, so the first time he's activated in Texas, if ever, he won't be able to return to the farm without clearing waivers first.

January 8, 2010

Friday haiku:

I stinkin' love sports.
No need for a second line.
No need for a third.

January 8, 2010

- According to former big league GM Jim Bowden, who I believe now works for XM Radio's MLB channel, via Twitter in the last half-hour: "Source close to Vladimir Guerrero says Vlad and Texas Rangers finalizing one-year contract pending physical"
- Salt, friends.

January 9, 2010

Read the blog entry T.R. Sullivan posted overnight. It's cryptic in places, turbo-cryptic in others, but it struck a nerve with me, and I think it's worth your time.

The reason I created the "Trot Coffey" emails a year and a half ago (around the 2008 trade deadline) was less to drive up mailing list numbers than to separate rumor from news. I used to include all of it together, but with the advent and explosive growth of Twitter and MLB Trade Rumors and beat writers maintaining blogs (responsibly so in most cases), it's easier now to send messages out several times a day than to wait for the papers when the alarm clock sounds each morning.

Easier, and exponentially more dangerous.

For many, the objective is, as it always has been, to be right.

For others, the sole objective, substantiation be damned, is to be first.

I'll admit to that urge from time to time, but it's always been my policy not to break news (or, to be more fair to the discussion, to *attempt* to break news). I have my opportunities. Hey, here's an email from a fan who is buddies with a bigtime free agent who told him at the gym an hour ago that he's signing either with Texas or that other team! There's one from a reporter in another market who is about to break news of a trade—here are the specifics!—but not until he gets confirmation from one of the teams. And there's that text from a player who just found out he's getting The Call to the big leagues.

I could send those things out, but I choose not to. There are reasons those things don't go public before they do—even if they're true, which they aren't always—and my purpose isn't to be the one whose name or website might somehow get attached to the story. I usually won't be first, even if I always try to be prompt.

That's why, even in the Trot Coffey's, the rumors come from what I count on as established sources. You can't always tell if the rumor is reliable—but you can try (successfully most of the time, you hope) to stick to the sources who generally are.

And you (well, I) put your (my) trust in the likelihood that, despite the allure of the social networking race, they did their homework, and that they ran down their normal traps before tweeting.

As T.R. wrote: "It's just a matter of knowing the right URL and how to get there. There are certain boulevards that all play on, but make sure they arrive from multiple cross-streets."

Anyway, I have nothing (as of now) to report today. Just wanted to remind you that the Trot Coffey's are there for a reason. I used to crave getting my *Sporting News* in the mail as a kid, tearing through it to find the Peter Gammons column first because I knew it would be full of trade rumors that nobody else had. Now we all get blasts all day long, and I do my best to pass along only those coming from dependable places. The Trot Coffey's have been a popular feature, and I'll keep sending them, but they're sent out in a different format by design.

There's nothing wrong with Twitter or MLBTR—I'm a believer in both—as long as the underlying source is reliable.

But even then, the Trot Coffey's—which I send to the mailing list but don't post on the website for real reasons—always end with that salt shaker capsized under its own weight.

January 9, 2010

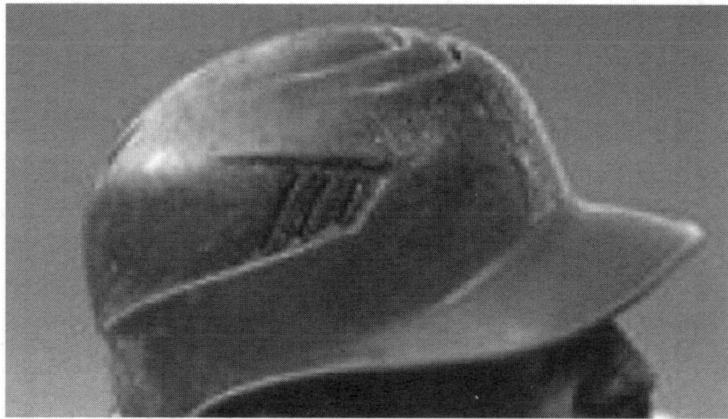

One-year deal, a club option for a second year. Apparently a $5 million base, with some reports of maybe another $500,000-600,000 in reachable appearance incentives. The option evidently has a $1 million buyout attached to it, which would mean $6 million is guaranteed.

Like it.

January 9, 2010

According to at least one local report, Texas has signed infielder Khalil Greene, who has experience not only at shortstop but third base as well, to a one-year contract worth $750,000, pending a physical.

If this is a big league contract, one player is going to need to be removed from the 40-man roster to make room for both Greene and Vladimir Guerrero. Wouldn't surprise me, particularly given Greene's addition, if this is where Joaquin Arias, who is out of options, sees his Rangers career end.

January 10, 2010

I'm working up a report on the signings of Vladimir Guerrero and Khalil Greene, but in the meantime the great Kevin Goldstein has just posted his Top 11 Rangers Prospects feature on the Baseball Prospectus website. It's among BP's wealth of subscriber-only content that I'd encourage you to add to your plate, but I can share this much with you—Kevin's top 11 (which happen to be the same 11 players as mine, though not in the same order), although you'll have to check the website to get his provocative commentary:

Five-Star Prospects
1. Neftali Feliz, RHP
2. Martin Perez, LHP
3. Justin Smoak, 1B

Four-Star Prospects
4. Tanner Scheppers, RHP

Three-Star Prospects
5. Jurickson Profar, SS
6. Danny Gutierrez, RHP
7. Mitch Moreland, RF
8. Michael Main, RHP
9. Engel Beltre, CF
10. Wilmer Font, RHP
11. Robbie Ross, LHP

Four More:
12. Miguel Velasquez, OF
13. Kasey Kiker, LHP
14. Max Ramirez, C
15. Guillermo Moscoso, RHP

The Sleeper:
Shawn Blackwell, RHP

I hope you're a subscriber if for no other reason than to read what Goldstein wrote about Profar.

January 10, 2010

Maybe you play fantasy league baseball. Maybe you're really, really good at it.

It's the off-season and your perennially contending roster has just a few holes. You need, among a couple other things, a DH and a utility infielder. Frustratingly, you might have to part with a few prospects you love in order to get the big bat (unless your son also owns a team in the league and you can foist your second-tier minor leaguers on him), but you bite the bullet and give something up to get Adam Lind. For the utility spot, you make it a priority and outbid everyone at the spring auction, landing Mark DeRosa, whose versatility (not to mention his production) is exactly what you need to make another run at a title.

One of the really helpful things about running the Stiff Pocorobas in your bad-ass keeper league is that Lind and DeRosa have no say in the matter.

The big leagues aren't fantasy leagues.

In the real thing, you not only have to find the right guy. You also have to convince that guy (at least in free agency, and sometimes in trades) that you're the right team.

Would Ron Washington have liked to have Marco Scutaro, tied by several reputable media outlets to Texas six weeks ago, on his bench? Sure. But that speculation was just goofy, because Scutaro was never going to accept a reserve role (or get paid like a starter to fill one).

Jamey Carroll? Miguel Tejada? Both believe they can start. Carroll just might with the Dodgers. Tejada may land with the Cardinals, as the everyday third baseman.

Bobby Crosby and Alfredo Amezaga? Different backgrounds, but both utility players at this point, with a chance to start for a bad team. Crosby signed with the Pirates because there's a chance he ends up playing every day. Amezaga has been sorting through what his agent has suggested is interest from close to half the league. He's probably going to end up with a deal not a whole lot unlike what Crosby got from Pittsburgh ($1 million with another $500,000 in incentives), and will likely choose his team based on opportunity to play.

The utility infielder in Texas faces a different lot. He's injury insurance. The job behind Michael Young, Ian Kinsler, and Elvis Andrus may be one of the worst in the game, in terms of opportunity to play. How many games will those three rest? Twenty total? There doesn't stand to be a whole lot of days those three will slide over to DH. They won't ever be pinch-hit for. They don't need late-inning defensive replacements.

You can add DeRosa to your keeper league roster, but you're not going to get him or Scutaro or Carroll or Amezaga to choose Texas. Omar Vizquel said he wanted to play in a bigger metropolitan market, but backing up Gordon Beckham, Alexei Ramirez, and Mark Teahen is also a better gig than he would have had here, especially with Andrus no longer the kid that the club was merely counting on being ready for the big leagues.

What did Texas have to offer Khalil Greene, besides a contract that's less than double the league minimum (after he'd made $11 million the last two years)? It's not playing time. The brand new environment for the career National Leaguer was probably appealing, and if he does end up getting significant at-bats due to injury to someone else, he can hope for an offensive resurgence in a ballpark that has historically offered that possibility.

It's not as obvious a selling point as the Rangers were able to put in front of Vladimir Guerrero, a career .394/.471/.705 hitter in Rangers Ballpark, where interestingly he's amassed more plate appearances than anywhere else other than his home parks in Montreal and Anaheim—and where he's done the most damage among all parks where he has at least 100 plate appearances. (Was it just the stadium? Or was it Rangers pitching? Guerrero hit .398/.452/.628 against Texas in Angel Stadium, but an OPS-ier .394/.471/.705 in Arlington. Site matters.) But I'd be surprised if the DeRosa-Byrd-Matthews-Bradley evidence over the last handful of seasons wasn't something that factored into Greene's decision.

What was the biggest factor for Guerrero? Probably a loss of leverage. Even if this is the team he wanted to join (and we don't necessarily know that to be the case), he certainly didn't get the contract he wanted, in length or in dollars. But, Guerrero's options were limited by virtue of his demise as an everyday defender, and, as one local beat reporter cleanly laid out on Thursday, of the 14 American League clubs, the only other ones not locked in at designated hitter were Detroit, Kansas City, Toronto, Baltimore, and maybe the White Sox. None of the lavish spenders.

The Rangers waited on this one, pretty much knowing he was going to have to lower his sights more than they'd have to push in more chips. We'll never know for sure how serious Texas was about Jermaine Dye, but my pet theory is that, while he might have been a fallback consideration had Guerrero chosen some other team, it didn't hurt the club's negotiation posture with Guerrero by maintaining the appearance that they had choices (Dye) just as Guerrero did.

Bobby Abreu is a year older than Guerrero. He was, then, the same age last winter that Guerrero is now. The Angels waited until last February, when Abreu had few choices left, and signed him for $5 million with incentives. His year went well, of course, and he parlayed it two months ago into a new two-year, $19 million contract with a club option that could convert (via club option) to a three-year, $27 million deal.

Texas would be thrilled if Guerrero has the kind of resurgent year that makes him a 2/18 or 3/27 guy a year from now. The odds aren't in favor of it, but after a run of Richard Hidalgo, Phil Nevin, Sammy Sosa, and Andruw Jones, I'm more than ready for an experiment with Guerrero in which he has a *chance* to revive his pinball numbers by playing half his games in his favorite arcade.

Another thought: Guerrero's physical profile being what it is (though it should be noted that his last disabled list stint before 2009's torn pectoral muscle and strained knee issues was in 2005), his addition may end up effectively paving the way for Justin Smoak to get his feet big league-wet with a brief stint or two during the season.

Let's be realistic and assume Guerrero doesn't return to the form that, in every year but one between 2002 and 2007, made him a Silver Slugger, a top 10 hitter, a top 10 slugger, a top 10 base-reacher, a top 10 run producer, and a top 10 MVP finalist. A year that fits that profile would be huge, but even something a little short of it would be quite welcome, and after 14 seasons in which his salary increased every single year, culminating with last year's $15 million contract, he's probably motivated to prove that the $5 million base he's playing for in 2010 will have been a league-wide mistake.

Consider the lineup that Texas figures to run out there most days:

1. Julio Borbon, CF
2. Michael Young, 3B
3. Josh Hamilton, LF
4. Vladimir Guerrero, DH
5. Ian Kinsler, 2B
6. Nelson Cruz, RF

7. Chris Davis, 1B
8. Jarrod Saltalamacchia, C
9. Elvis Andrus, SS

Which third of that lineup doesn't at least have the *potential* to do as much damage as any in the league?

And couldn't you say that just about every slot, for various reasons (a full year, better health, mechanical fixes, a better lineup fit, a new player), could reasonably be expected to be more productive in 2010 than it was in 2009?

Greene's productivity demise has been less traditional and far less predictable than Guerrero's. A reliable shortstop and standout hitter over his first five seasons with the Padres (.280/.335/.515 away from San Diego), he enjoyed a run of productivity that was routinely referenced in Texas as Drew Meyer (who played collegiately 130 miles away at South Carolina and was Grady Fuson's first-ever choice as Rangers scouting director at the number 10 slot, before Clemson's Greene went 13th overall to the Padres) failed to pan out. Greene signed his big two-year deal after the 2007 season, struggled in 2008 (.213/.260/.339), a year that ended two months early when he broke his glove hand punching a dugout wall in frustration, and was traded to St. Louis after that season.

It appeared that the change of scenery might have set the stage for a big rebound. In spring training with the Cardinals last year, Greene hit .408/.436/.535 over 71 at-bats, leading the club in exhibition hits and walking more times (five) than he struck out (four). But once the season got underway, his 2008 troubles resurfaced, both on and off the field.

Two months into the season, Greene spent three weeks on the disabled list with a "social anxiety disorder," admitting to having fought through diminished concentration and energy, an inability to relax and avoid overthinking, and what amounted to "an extreme version of what you might call 'butterflies.'" When he returned to action he dealt with a left foot bruise and a right ankle injury his first few days back before returning to the DL 11 days after he'd come off of it, again for the emotional disorder that would end up shelving him for the entire second half. He finished with a miserable .200/.272/.347 slash line.

(Interestingly, when Greene returned from his first DL stint with the Cardinals last year, he was moved to third base for the first time in the big leagues, after playing nothing but shortstop for seven seasons. In his first start, he homered, doubled, and walked. The next day, again at third base, he homered again. The day after that? Another home run. But he got hurt in that third game, derailing his momentum.)

Though he didn't turn 30 until after the season, Greene's no longer the player he was as a young Padres shortstop—in 2008 and 2009 he reached base at a .265 clip, the lowest in baseball over that time, and his defensive range was said to have diminished as well—but Texas isn't paying for the old Khalil Greene. The Rangers are buying low, and Greene is buying into the opportunity to change his scenery again and capitalize on it. For what it's worth, Greene's former college coach, Tim Corbin, has been working with him this winter and is raving about how hard his ex-All-American ("the best third baseman I have seen in college baseball") has been getting after it, both in the cages and in the infield.

It may not happen for him here, or ever, and the Rangers can win in 2010 without Greene being a key factor.

But winning teams regularly succeed rolling the dice somewhere on the roster, as Texas is attempting to do with Greene and Guerrero, for example, and Rich Harden as well.

The key to those signings is not only that the Rangers targeted three players with recent success who they believe can contribute to a winning club in 2010, but also that they presented opportunities that, for one reason or another, fit what the player, at the moment, was looking for.

There was plenty of timing and opportunity involved, both in career terms and on the winter calendar, for Texas to get signatures done with these three veterans. It takes two sides to make an acquisition happen when there's more than a bottle of Yoo-Hoo at stake.

January 11, 2010

Vladimir Guerrero has passed his physical and his deal is being made official today. Interesting: the 2011 option is not a club option as originally reported, but rather a mutual option (not unlike what was tacked onto Rich Harden's one-year deal) that either side can decline. The buyout, like Harden's, is rumored to be $1 million.

Here's what I wrote about Harden's mutual option a month ago today:

This business of the $11.5 million mutual option in 2011 is interesting. If Harden has a career year, he'll opt out (and take the $1 million buyout). If he struggles or can't stay healthy, Texas will opt out. Under what scenario do both sides allow the option to kick in? Maybe if his 2010 season isn't quite the type that he thinks would fetch $11.5 million on the open market but the Rangers want him back anyway. Realistically, that second year isn't going to come into play. But should Harden pitch well enough this year to get a big contract from someone next winter, Texas will still be able to offer him arbitration and net a first-round pick as compensation.

Guerrero's situation differs in that he's not going to land a mega-deal on the open market next winter, at this stage of his career, and so there's probably a slightly better chance of Guerrero and the Rangers mutually exercising the 2011 contract (the dollar amount has not been disclosed) than in Harden's case. But the fact that the option is mutual does lessen the likelihood that the second year will kick in. At its foundation, this is a creative way to guarantee the player more money while deferring part of the obligation past 2010.

January 11, 2010

When you watch the 10:00 local sportscasts tonight, if the Rangers manage to elbow in for 30 seconds between Cowboys and Mark McGwire, you'll probably see one of two automatic shots from a day like this: Vladimir Guerrero trying on number 27 in his home whites, or Guerrero shaking the hand of his new manager, or general manager.

Those aren't the shots I hope you get to see.

Guerrero, conducting himself with what has to be the least swagger of any sports bad-ass you've ever seen, was polite, reserved, seemingly almost ashamed of his greatness throughout today's press conference. His keel was totally even.

Until the press conference ended, when he stepped down from the head table and got bear hugs from three new teammates who'd been standing in the back of the room during the whole presser, along with one old teammate. From the look on Vlad's face as he hugged it out with Josh Hamilton, then Michael Young, then Ian Kinsler, and then Darren Oliver, you'd think these were his old frat brothers, not longtime rivals. It wasn't an exchange of respect as much as it was a "welcome aboard / damn glad to be here" thing, with a bigger smile frozen on Guerrero's face than you'll probably ever see from him between the lines. It was very cool.

It's what I choose to imagine we'll see a year from now when Josh Beckett is introduced to the local press.

Brad Newton

The great Brad Newton was there today, and I'm only disappointed that his vantage point during that impromptu moment, as luck would have it, was behind Guerrero rather than in front.

If we're fortunate, at least one of the many TV cameras on hand was trained on Guerrero's face and captured the moment, and their producers will decide tonight to run that footage in place of the clichéd handshake or shirt fitting.

January 14, 2010

I heard on one talk show yesterday that because there's been media speculation but next to no news filtering out of the negotiations to transfer ownership of the Rangers from Hicks Sports Group to the Greenberg-Ryan Group, the deal therefore must be in trouble and we ought to brace ourselves for some bad news.

Really?

This is not a Texas walkoff win over Boston, or a trade between the Rangers and Reds, or the hiring of a new hitting coach, where the principals have some level of responsibility to bring the press up to date, and maybe even talk about the process that led to the result. This is a complicated transaction, with large moving parts, time-sensitive and issue-sensitive. To expect the parties to spend any time updating the media on negotiations is crazy.

Think about what Jon Daniels and nearly every other general manager in sports will say when asked by a reporter for a remark or two about rumored trade discussions or free agent negotiations: "Not going to comment on that." There are plenty of reasons that should be the only response.

Why would anyone demand any comment, any public progress reports, any news regarding a process that's a similarly unfinished work in progress, only on a much larger, more complex, more consequential level? Don't blame the press for the absence of concrete developments to report so far.

Maybe we'll hear some news today, maybe we won't. (Actually, we don't really know for sure if the 30-day window that was triggered on December 15 shuts today or tomorrow. Reports differ.) And if we don't hear anything, it's not necessarily catastrophic. It's been reported in a number of places that the 30-day window isn't inflexible—it may turn out that the deadline gets extended for some period of time.

Hang in there.

Khalil Greene passed his club physical and his acquisition should be made official soon. When it is, someone (the optionless Joaquin Arias?) will have to come off the 40-man roster to make room.

Greene played nothing but shortstop in the big leagues until last June, when he slid over to third base for St. Louis, but he's expected to prepare himself in Rangers camp to play all four infield spots.

What do these players have in common: Roy Halladay, John Lackey, Javier Vazquez, Edwin Jackson, Aroldis Chapman, Chone Figgins, Jason Bay, and Curtis Granderson?

The Angels were reportedly interested in every one of those players this off-season, and in each case on a short list of the leading contenders to get them.

Not one will go to camp with Los Angeles.

Speaking of the Angels, here's something I wrote almost 10 years ago (in the August 26, 2000 Newberg Report):

The cover story in the current issue of Baseball Weekly *is on the coming of age of Vladimir Guerrero. After discussing the fact that the Dodgers signed his brother Wilton but passed on Vlad, then age 16, despite scouting him for eight months, the article has the following to say:*

"The same year, 1992, the Rangers gave him a tryout. Their scouts agreed with the Dodgers: He wasn't big-league material. 'Hector Acevedo of the Rangers saw me and said I was a tigrazo. That I had una cara de tigre (face of a tiger),' Guerrero says. In the Dominican Republic, the word tigre can mean a streetwise kid, but it also can mean an undisciplined young boy, a thug, a hood. To call him a tigrazo was an insult. 'I didn't say anything back to him,' Guerrero says, and smiles. 'If someone does not know you, they should not put a label on you. But, thanks to God, I'm here in the big leagues with another team. And now (the Rangers) wish I was playing with them.'"

Acevedo spent about ten years in the Ranger organization as an international scout, leaving last season.

Some more detail on Guerrero's Rangers contract: He's reportedly set to make $5.5 million in 2010, with an added $900,000 in incentives for days spent on the active roster. The mutual option for 2011 is apparently for $9 million, with the $1 million buyout payable if either side opts out.

At the moment, Texas will draft 15th, 22nd, 43rd, and 47th in June. I believe the third pick will fall to number 45 (once Type A free agent Jose Valverde and Type B Rod Barajas sign with new teams), and the fourth pick to 49 (not 50 since Type B Brian Shouse signed a minor league contract with Boston rather than a roster deal).

(Think Shouse is second-guessing his decision to turn down Tampa Bay's arbitration offer?)

Something to tuck away:

Oklahoma City's player development contract with the Rangers expires after the 2010 season. So does Round Rock's PDC with the Astros. Nolan Ryan, of course, owns the Express.

Bakersfield's PDC with Texas expires after 2010 as well . . . and so does Atlanta's PDC with the Myrtle Beach Pelicans—a High A franchise that Chuck Greenberg owns.

How about this note from Kevin Goldstein in his Rangers Top 11 Prospects feature: 16-year-old shortstop Jurickson Profar drew 26 walks while striking out only eight times over 91 at-bats in a secondary Dominican League this summer.

MLB has reportedly chastised the Marlins for bending the rules of the Basic Agreement by pocketing too much of the revenue-sharing dollars they receive each year rather than allocating the money toward player salaries. If forced to boost payroll by another $10 million or so, the two most likely beneficiaries could be second baseman Dan Uggla, who is set to land something in the range of $8 million in arbitration, or righthander Josh Johnson, with whom the club has been unable to come to terms on a multi-year extension. (Of course, the sticking point in those negotiations was reportedly a fourth guaranteed year, not the level of commitment for the 2010 season.)

Do you doubt the sweeping influence of the weekly Newberg Report haiku? Yahoo! Sports just kicked off its off-season series of team features with a Jeff Passan story that ended this way:

ROYALS IN HAIKU
One hundred losses
A Kansas City birthright
Futility lives

John Sickels, in reviewing the Astros' farm system earlier this week, named righthander Matt Nevarez that organization's number 11 prospect.

If Nevarez (traded with infielder Jose Vallejo for Ivan Rodriguez last summer) were still in the Rangers system, he'd have fallen somewhere in the 40s for me.

Judging all 30 clubs' drafts over the last four years, only two teams (San Francisco and Tampa Bay) are in the midst of a stronger three-year run than Texas, according to *Baseball America*. (The Rangers and Dodgers were tied for third.) In the four-year study, only Houston ranked lower overall than Seattle and the Angels.

University of Alabama quarterback Greg McElroy Jr. is not only the son of the former Rangers marketing director, but was apparently also a Rangers batboy himself.

Righthander Derrick Turnbow is expected to throw for 16 teams tomorrow in Phoenix.

Houston, making room for newly signed righthander Brett Myers, designated infielder/outfielder Jason Bourgeois for assignment. The Astros also signed first baseman Chris Shelton to a minor league deal.

Lefthander Scott Eyre retired.

The Grand Prairie Airhogs of the independent American Association named Curtis Wilkerson bench coach (for manager Pete Incaviglia). The Airhogs also resigned infielder David Espinosa, who would have become a Rangers prospect had Kenny Rogers not vetoed a trade to Cincinnati in 2002.

Doug Harris is the new director of player development for the Nationals.

Jon Daniels will be the keynote speaker at the Hickory Crawdads' "2010 Hot Stove" event next Wednesday.

Stay tuned for news on the Rangers' ownership transfer. But not on the edge of your seat.

January 14, 2010: TROT COFFEY

- According to a local report, Texas will be among as many as 10 teams who will attend righthander Ben Sheets's throwing session Tuesday at the University of Louisiana-Monroe; the Cubs and Mariners are thought to be in the mix as well
- Jon Paul Morosi of Fox Sports reports that the Mets' expected deal with catcher Bengie Molina could lead to an intensified market for veteran catcher Yorvit Torrealba; Morosi notes that the Rangers are "keeping tabs on Torrealba [but] probably won't make an aggressive offer ... unless they get bad news on the condition of Jarrod Saltalamacchia" in his recovery from shoulder surgery; according to Troy E. Renck of the *Denver Post*, Texas has already expressed some level of interest in the 31-year-old
- Lefthander Sam Narron and Coppell product Jason Stokes have gotten minor league deals with the Tigers

January 14, 2010: TROT COFFEY

- More from Jon Paul Morosi of Fox Sports: according to a source of his, the Rangers are "close to signing Colby Lewis to a two-year deal"

January 15, 2010

As the league's December 15 deadline for a potential Rangers buyer to be identified and granted exclusive negotiating rights approached, we were prepped for that to be the Chuck Greenberg/Nolan Ryan group. Then, on December 2, according to some reports, the Dennis Gilbert group seemed to break from the pack and settle into the lead. Then, Greenberg/Ryan again. Jim Crane then emerged on the 15th as the new frontrunner. Then, late in the day, Greenberg/Ryan got the nod.

Those of you who negotiate or mediate as part of your day-to-day know that, no matter how much progress is made early on, no matter how things seem to be going, and most notably no matter how much time has been set aside for the negotiations, the 10th and 11th hours are almost always the most productive.

Just as I refrained from commenting on the ownership story before the December 15 announcement that the Greenberg/Ryan group had secured the 30-day negotiating rights, I'm not going to fire off status updates on whether the two sides look like they're going to get this done. I'll let you know when there's actual news. As we talked about yesterday, that may be today. But it might not.

Righthander Colby Lewis's two-year deal, according to Jon Paul Morosi of Fox Sports, will apparently pay $5 million with another $1 million in incentives. It's less guaranteed money than Jason Kendall, Danys Baez, and John Grabow are getting this winter on their two-year contracts. Based on what Lewis has done in Japan the last two years (15-8, 2.68 and 11-9, 2.96, leading the league in strikeouts both seasons with a combined 369 in 354.1 innings—while issuing only 46 walks), and recognizing that Texas has had Jim Colborn in place scouting the Pacific Rim that whole time (that is, it's not as if the Rangers are just reading stat lines and relying on second-hand accounts), I feel good about this Lewis move, particularly with its relatively modest financial commitment.

The competition for rotation spots in camp is going to be interesting.

Once the Lewis and Khalil Greene signings are made official, two players will come off the 40-man roster. Candidates would seem to include Joaquin Arias, Luis Mendoza, and Joe Inglett, none of whom have options, and maybe Greg Golson and Brandon Boggs.

Yes, it was disappointing (though not surprising) to see Florida and Josh Johnson to come to terms on a four-year ($39 million) extension yesterday, but I'm not fully discouraged. It might turn out that it's easier to trade for Johnson (who did not receive a no-trade clause) a couple years from now than to battle the usual suspects at free agency time. Especially with the deal being heavily backloaded (to replicate Johnson's arbitration years up front), expect the Marlins to try to move him during the last two years of the contract, which call for $13.75 million each. A trade would cost Texas several important young players rather than just a forfeited first-round draft pick, but Johnson, as long as he stays healthy, will be worth it.

I'll let you know if there's any ownership news, whenever any of it comes down.

Peek in that window
Hurry! Before it slams shut!
Or, you know, doesn't.

January 15, 2010

Texas has agreed to terms with righthanders Brandon McCarthy and Dustin Nippert on one-year contracts, avoiding arbitration with each and leaving righthanders Scott Feldman, Frankie Francisco, and Chris Ray, lefthander C.J. Wilson, and outfielder Josh Hamilton as the club's remaining arbitration-eligibles.

The Rangers also announced non-roster invitations to big league camp for the following six minor leaguers: righthander Tanner Scheppers, lefthander Kasey Kiker, catcher Emerson Frostad, first baseman Justin Smoak, and first basemen-outfielders Mitch Moreland and Chad Tracy. They join righthanders Willie Eyre and Geoff Geary, lefthander Clay Rapada, catcher Kevin Richardson, and infielders Matt Brown, Esteban German, and Ray Olmedo as non-roster invites.

Also, Eric Nadel received the 2009 National Sportscasters and Sportswriters Association Texas Sportscaster of the Year Award, the fifth time since 1999 that he's been selected for the award.

January 17, 2010

32 sleeps.

January 18, 2010

According to Jesse Sanchez of MLB.com, the Rangers have signed catcher Jorge Alfaro, a highly touted 16-year-old from Colombia, for a reported $1.3 million.

January 18, 2010

Out of the corner of my eye, I could see Max, next to me on the couch, checking me out from the corner of his eye, either startled by how steamed I was that Terence Newman left Gerald Sensabaugh hung out to dry or, more likely, measuring how steamed I was as a way of figuring out how steamed it was OK for him to be. License to fume.

But this isn't about Minnesota 34, Dallas 3, which, along with Alabama 37, UT 21, I think, has been Max's Pittsburgh 21, Dallas 17 entry into Sports Matterdom.

I didn't have it in mind that Sunday's playoff game or the BCS Championship would be bonding moments for me and Max. I did think about how cool it was to have him care that much, at about a year younger than I was for Super Bowl X. I'm not great company when there's a game on that I care a lot about—unless it's with someone else who cares that much. Max is growing into that role. Good.

I didn't think of those as bonding moments any more so than a week ago when Erica's frustration at not grasping the new improper fraction exercises gave way to mastery, proven by the huge smile on her face.

But they could have been bonding moments for them.

There are things we're lucky to be able to share with our kids. Not enough, maybe. But they're there. Sometimes the simple ones are the most lasting.

Nothing's guaranteed. Not playoff wins, math making sense, time with your kids.

I'm not sure why a couple moments late in Super Bowl X have never faded from my memory, even after 34 years to the day. Maybe it was the first time I felt gut-punched by Sports Matterdom, and saw that Dad was experiencing the same thing, giving me all the approval I needed at age six, without even knowing he was doing it. His disgust authorized mine, empowered it. It was a bond, early on.

Ballgames don't really matter, of course. The outcomes don't, at least not to most people. But there are many reasons sports are super-important to me, and I think to Max, and I know they were to Carson Leslie, too. Maybe in the moment it's about the final score or the play-calling or the execution on the 6-4-3. Ultimately, though, there's character being forged. Focus. Competitive spirit, leadership, professionalism. Learning to handle adversity and use it to your advantage. Persistence, resilience, and heart.

Three things that struck home today, not unrelated to each other: I'm over Minnesota 34, Dallas 3. I wish I knew Carson Leslie a lot longer than I did. And I've never looked forward to a baseball season more, or to the next set of decimal coefficients to tackle, together.

January 21, 2010

The Rangers, needing to clear a roster spot for recently signed infielder Khalil Greene, have designated outfielder Greg Golson for assignment. Texas now has 10 days to trade or release Golson, or outright his contract to the minor leagues if the club is able to get him through waivers.

No word yet on the roster move to clear a spot for righthander Colby Lewis.

January 22, 2010

The Rangers' top eight starters in 2005, in order of games started, were Chris Young, Kenny Rogers, Chan Ho Park, Pedro Astacio, Ryan Drese, Ricardo Rodriguez, Juan Dominguez, and Joaquin Benoit. Despite the club's middle-of-the-road 79-win finish, the rotation was bad, compiling a composite 5.04 ERA.

Jon Daniels was promoted to general manager at the end of that season. To suggest that overhauling the rotation was among his priorities would be grossly understating things. Astonishingly, the top eight Texas starters in 2006 had not one name in common with the previous season's eight: Kevin Millwood, Vicente Padilla, John Koronka, Kameron Loe, Robinson Tejeda, Adam Eaton, John Rheinecker, and Edinson Volquez made the club's most 2006 starts.

Still, lots of journeymen.

The top eight starters in 2007: Millwood, Padilla, Loe, Brandon McCarthy, Tejeda, Jamey Wright, Kason Gabbard, and Rheinecker.

McCarthy, Wright, and Gabbard in place of Koronka, Eaton, and Volquez (whose 2006 ERA was 7.29, after a

14.21 debut in 12.2 innings in 2005). Without hindsight, it was probably a slight upgrade going into 2007.

The top eight starters in 2008: Millwood, Padilla, Feldman, Matt Harrison, Gabbard, Luis Mendoza, Sidney Ponson, and Jason Jennings.

Feldman, Harrison, Mendoza, Ponson, and Jennings in place of Loe, McCarthy, Tejeda, Wright, and Rheinecker. Push at best.

Big changes going into 2009: a commitment to youth over journeymen, an improved defense, and the arrival of Mike Maddux.

The top eight starters in 2009: Feldman, Millwood, Derek Holland, Tommy Hunter, Padilla, McCarthy, Harrison, and Dustin Nippert. And they were the top eight of just 10 starters overall (Doug Mathis and Kris Benson started two times each). That's after Texas averaged 14 starters a year from 2005 through 2008.

Better. Much, much better.

Going into 2010, the probable top eight at the moment: Feldman, Rich Harden, Colby Lewis, Hunter, Holland, Harrison, McCarthy, and Neftali Feliz.

Maybe even C.J. Wilson, but he's going to be either top five or not on the list at all (hard to imagine him joining the rotation mid-season). Bet on him returning to the bullpen. Eric Hurley won't be ready Opening Day, but he should be before the All-Star Break.

Compare the 2010 group to 2009.

Can Feldman repeat? Don't know, but he's a far better bet going into 2010 than he was going into 2009.

Holland and Hunter and McCarthy and Harrison: Probably fair to expect more out of the first three with 2009 under their belts.

Harden instead of Millwood: Works for me.

Lewis instead of Padilla: As much of an unknown as Lewis might be this second time around, there's no question which of those two you'd take.

Feliz instead of Nippert: There's a reason that, though both are still around, the 21-year-old is the one getting the rotation shot.

I'm not sure I'd be able to argue that the 2009 starter crop, at least in advance of the season, was in better shape than the 2010 group.

Assuming Feldman, Harden, and Lewis are locks, the competition for the final two spots coming out of camp will leave four of Hunter, Holland, Harrison, McCarthy, Feliz, and Wilson to evaluate for bullpen roles alongside Frankie Francisco, Darren O'Day, Darren Oliver, Chris Ray, Mathis, and Nippert.

And that doesn't even account for Rule 5 selection Ben Snyder, or Guillermo Moscoso and Pedro Strop, who showed flashes in 2009, or Warner Madrigal, who did so in 2008. Big depth.

While Texas is probably done for the winter (with the exception of adding a backup catcher—probably of the non-roster variety—and possibly another non-roster starting pitcher willing to take a AAA assignment), there the Rangers were on Tuesday, among at least eight teams attending Ben Sheets's two-inning simulated game in Monroe, Louisiana. Maddux and Don Welke were on hand to evaluate Sheets, who had agreed in principle to a two-year contract with the Rangers last year before a failed physical scuttled the deal.

One unidentified scout in attendance suggested the Rangers, Mets, and Cubs were the leading candidates to sign Sheets. Other stories have the Mariners and A's in the mix. I have my doubts that he'll end up here.

Yes, Texas is looking to Lewis to replace Millwood's innings and production (an average the last three years of 11 wins and a 4.58 ERA over 180 innings) at a dramatically lower cost. But that overlooks the addition of Harden. Look at it this way: The Rangers were on the hook to pay Millwood $12 million in 2010 once his contract vested last summer. Instead, they will pay Lewis $1.75 million this year, will send $3 million to the Orioles to help pay Millwood, and will owe Harden a guaranteed $7.5 million (including the buyout). Lewis and Harden are here at virtually the same cost to the club as Millwood would have been himself.

Another point to clarify: Yes, McCarthy and Ray both have options (I believe each has two, despite what you might have read elsewhere) but would have to clear waivers in order to be optioned, because they reached the active big league roster more than three years ago. However, the waivers are revocable, and thus teams generally don't block waivers of that kind. (Also, neither has the requisite five years of big league service needed to decline an option.)

Outfielder Greg Golson, designated for assignment yesterday to make room for infielder Khalil Greene on the 40-man roster, after having been acquired last winter from Philadelphia for outfielder John Mayberry Jr., has a plus arm and plus speed, can play all three outfield spots well, and has the type of raw power that completes a package that has had scouts waiting for the reincarnation of Ron Gant for years. But he hasn't hit, regressing from .282/.333/.434 with 13 home runs in AA in 2008 to .258/.299/.344 with two homers in AAA in 2009, and not only did Julio Borbon predictably race past him on the club's depth chart, but fellow speed/defense type Craig Gentry got the September nod rather than Golson, notable in that Gentry's addition cost Texas an extra roster move (the loss of Thomas Diamond on waivers).

Golson has two options remaining and would seem to be a strong candidate to be claimed off waivers. If Texas perceives that to be the likely result, the club could look to trade the 24-year-old for a non-roster prospect during this 10-day window before running him out on the waiver wire in hopes of keeping him.

The Rangers settled on one-year deals with Josh Hamilton ($3.25 million, with several award-based incentives), Wilson ($3.1 million), and Ray ($975,000), and two arbitration-eligibles remain: Feldman (seeking $2.9 million, club offering $2.05 million) and Francisco ($3.6 million vs. $3 million).

John Perrotto of Baseball Prospectus recently reported that Texas and San Francisco could be the leading contenders to sign catcher Yorvit Torrealba, since which time the Giants signed Bengie Molina. Perrotto suggests San Diego and Seattle could also be in on Torrealba.

Rest in peace, Bobby Bragan.

The early buzz on Colombian 16-year-old catcher Jorge Alfaro has been considerable. He flashes tools at the plate and behind it.

Texas named Joe Furukawa coordinator of Pacific Rim operations.

Padilla signed a one-year deal to stay with the Dodgers. It will pay $4.025 million, with a deferred $1 million signing bonus.

Seattle locking Felix Hernandez up through 2014 isn't great news for Texas, but something about that guy makes me think a Carlos Zambrano path isn't out of the question.

I've always been a Joel Pineiro fan. The Angels did well to land him for two years and $16 million.

Milwaukee and Todd Coffey avoided arbitration. I mention that as much for the reason that the contract settlement is for the unusual figure of $2,025,002 as for his pseudo-cousinhood to the Newberg Report.

ESPN's Buster Olney wrote that "[a] numbers-oriented friend recently ran a 1,000-season simulation of the AL West, and in most cases, the Rangers won the division, and in most cases, the last-place team was the Mariners."

Outfielder Engel Beltre is one of 11 players on *Baseball America*'s "All-Non-Top 10 All-Stars," comprised of prospects who missed their clubs' *BA* top 10 lists. ANTTAS alums include Josh Hamilton, Chris Davis, and Howie Kendrick.

The Rangers released minor league righthanders Dustin Brader, Jake Geglein, and Brock Piper.

Boston signed righthander Edwin Moreno. Houston got utility man Jason Bourgeois through waivers and outrighted him to AAA Round Rock.

The Kansas City T-Bones of the independent Northern League re-signed first baseman Jim Fasano.

Does anyone have a iPod of 40 GB or more you want to sell? I've got a 20 GB iPod I'd put into the deal and would pay you the difference.

We'll be set up at Fan Fest at Rangers Ballpark on January 30, hosting autograph guests this year in the Cuervo Club rather than the Diamond Club. We'll have the player list at some point as we get closer to the event. (Last year, we had Michael Young, Michael Ballard, Holland, Kasey Kiker, Tim Murphy, Blake Beavan, Andrew Laughter, Feliz, Michael Main, and Kevin Richardson.)

Overall, more than 50 current and former Rangers players and coaches will be at Fan Fest to sign autographs. There will also be the standard activities, including Q&A sessions with players, club officials, and announcers; opportunities to run the bases, catch pop-ups, and hit in the indoor batting cages; pitching, hitting, and catching clinics led by Rangers coaches and alumni; silent auction and memorabilia sales; and season ticket and mini-plan Select-A-Seat sales. Admission is $10 for adults and $5 for children 13 and under. Parking is free.

It's confirmed: The second book release party will be on Tuesday, February 2, at Sherlock's in Dallas (9100 N. Central Expressway, at the northeast corner of Central and Park Lane). Time to be determined, but most likely starting at 6:00 or 7:00 p.m. We'll have the 2010 Bound Edition for sale, as well as Carson Leslie's book, "Carry Me." Michael Young will appear for a Q&A session, and we might have another Q&A guest or two as well.

This will not be an autograph event, but I think we're going to have Michael sign five of my books and five of Carson's and make the signed books available to the 10 highest bidders. We might even bring a professional live auctioneer out to liven things up. All winning bid proceeds will benefit Wipe Out Kids' Cancer.

Yes, I know "Lost" premieres that night. TiVo is your friend.

Harden & Lewis
Both for no more than Millwood
Does that work for you?

January 22, 2010

The Rangers have apparently found their veteran catcher insurance. Texas has signed 34-year-old Toby Hall, a career .262/.297/.374 hitter with nine years of big league experience, most prominently with Tampa Bay from 2000 through the first part of 2006, a stretch that included five straight Opening Day starts (which remains a Rays record). Hall gets a minor league contract with an invite to big league camp.

Hall is expected to be fully healthy this spring, after missing the 2009 season due to right shoulder surgery. His 28 percent kill rate behind the plate is fourth highest among American League catchers with at least 600 games played from 2000-09, behind Ivan Rodriguez, Joe Mauer, and Bengie Molina.

Hall is likely a fallback in case Jarrod Saltalamacchia proves not to be ready to go physically when the season begins.

January 22, 2010

In addition to Michael Young, we'll have Rangers assistant director of player development Jake Krug with us for

Q&A at the Book Release Party II on Tuesday, February 2, at Sherlock's in Dallas (9100 N. Central Expressway, at the northeast corner of Central and Park Lane). Time to be determined, but most likely starting at 6:00 or 7:00 p.m.

Krug is a rising star in the Rangers' baseball operations department, having been promoted the last two years from manager of baseball operations to East Coast crosschecker and now to assistant director of player development, where he works with Scott Servais in overseeing the development of prospects in the Rangers' highly acclaimed minor league system.

January 23, 2010

Deal.

January 25, 2010

It's basketball season. It's hockey season. College football is finished, and so is pro football for most in these parts, although this was the ultimate weekend each year on the NFL schedule.

At halftime of Colts-Jets, I threw a red cap on backwards and drove to Tom Thumb to pick up a couple things.

As I got to the front of the checkout line, the checker—late teens, maybe early 20s—looked up and said, "Rangers cap?"

Me: "Yep."

Checker: "All *RIGHT*. . . . You know, the Angels are tough to beat, but they had a rough winter. This could be our year."

I smiled, and said I thought he was right.

The thing that struck me was not so much the kid's optimism, but instead that he saw a the back of a red ballcap, assumed it had a "T" on the other side, and wanted to talk Rangers baseball with a complete stranger.

I'm not sure I remember that happening during the summer, let along Conference Championship weekend in January.

This is good. I've mentioned how there seem to be more Texas caps and T-shirts and bumper stickers around town over the last year, and while I get hit with plenty of Rangers small talk around the office and the kids' soccer games and dinner with friends, it's different when one stranger brings it up to another.

It feels like there's a difference these days, maybe subtle, but noticeable.

There are those phrases that seem to turn up whenever Chuck Greenberg is interviewed. This fan base is a "sleeping giant." It's time "to awaken the beast." And in the press release issued by the Rangers on Saturday night, his comment:

"We are fortunate to be assuming the stewardship of a franchise poised for greatness. The tremendous foundation of talent that has been assembled on both the major and minor league levels, combined with our passionate commitment to achieve excellence in every facet of the organization's operation, and the pent-up thirst for success we observe from our fans every day, creates the opportunity for the Rangers to become one of the great franchises in baseball."

The fans' *pent-up thirst for success*.

I think there's more of that, and less baseball cynicism, than there's been around here in a long time, no matter what your favorite columnist is telling you. Rangers Baseball Express, LLC isn't the reason for the growing buzz—this groundswell has been developing for a while—but the Chuck Greenberg/Nolan Ryan investment group, funded primarily by Co-Chairmen of the Board Ray Davis and Bob Simpson and a number of other local investors, comes in at a time when there's a barrage of arrows flying in the right direction, and the group seems motivated to push this thing forward, not derail the momentum by giving in to an urge to shake things up just because it can. Ryan's continued presence is key in that regard.

This is an exciting time.

There's really not a lot I can add about the latest hurdle cleared in the sale of the team—it's all been said by people closer to the situation than I am (and unlike the games played on the field, we don't get to see what the writers are privy to)—but I will refer back to something I wrote back in May:

Word broke yesterday that Tom Hicks is open to selling a majority stake in the Rangers. I don't have much to say about that other than (1) I hope Nolan Ryan chooses to be a big player in this (it's clear that Hicks wants him to be) and (2) it's crucial that, whatever transition takes place, the baseball operations crew is allowed to stay on the course that it laid out two years ago and has this franchise poised to be where we all want it be.

Hicks gets far too much criticism from the mainstream media, who choose not to recognize the guts and foresight it took to make Jon Daniels, who at the time had less than five years in baseball, his general manager, and the patience and lack of ego it took to authorize the plan that Daniels presented to him in May 2007 to trade Mark Teixeira and shift focus and resources to scouting and player development and a wholesale effort to load up on young talent through the draft and international market and trades, a philosophy that's a lot less flashy and far more gradual than many owners would have signed off on.

Baseball America's Jim Callis in an ESPN chat session yesterday:

Q: Bedard trade for Orioles . . . best trade in baseball in 10 years?

Callis: Check out the Mark Teixeira trade to the Braves.

The Herschel Walker trade wasn't the Herschel Walker <u>Trade</u> until the Cowboys turned the Minnesota draft picks into Emmitt Smith and Darren Woodson and Russell

Maryland and Kevin Smith and three Lombardi Trophies. The Teixeira trade is no Herschel Walker Trade—yet. But there's no question that without it, this franchise wouldn't be in nearly as good a position as everyone agrees that it is. Hicks should get some credit for believing in, and consenting to, the plan that Jon Daniels and his crew proposed and have now been executing for two very good years.

Don't count on the general columnists recognizing Hicks's role in that, however.

Or acknowledging in print the millions of Hicks dollars that may not have gone to player payroll (a favorite topic of the media, rarely mentioning Ben Sheets or Torii Hunter or Daisuke Matsuzaka or Barry Zito or Carlos Delgado as free agent acquisitions he has consistently greenlighted even though they'd have busted the budget) but did go to annual decisions to pay out of slot to pave the way for the drafting and signing of the right high school and college players (Teixeira, Derek Holland, Justin Smoak, Taylor Teagarden, Julio Borbon, Jake Brigham, Neil Ramirez, Marcus Lemon, Robbie Ross, Clark Murphy, Johnny Whittleman, Kyle Ocampo, Matt Thompson, and others), to outspend the competition in Latin America (examples: Martin Perez, Fabio Castillo, Cristian Santana, and Richard Alvarez, plus the aggregate of a Preller/Welke/Batista class like 2006's Wilmer Font/ Wilfredo Boscan/Kennil Gomez/Carlos Pimentel/Geuris Grullon/Macumba haul), to pay top dollar to make sure we had the hitting coach and pitching coach we'd zeroed in on, and to hire Nolan Ryan.

The Ryan hiring was, of course, an inspired one that has paid off in many ways and will continue to do so, and though the media has been wholly supportive of Ryan's arrival and impact, rarely is Hicks credited for bringing him in at what had to be a significant financial investment.

Hicks wants to win, and though some with newspaper space will continue to disparage the team payroll (for a roster that today maintains the best record in the American League) and ignore all else, if Hicks wasn't interested in spending to win, would we have Holland and Smoak and Perez and Mike Maddux . . . and Ryan?

What I'm hoping for, if Hicks does indeed sell controlling interest in the Rangers, is continuity. I would have faith in a Ryan-led ownership to insist on that and to make it happen. So might someone coming in from the outside, but if that's where this is headed, I sure hope that stability is a priority for whoever that might be.

I guarantee you that the Angels and A's and Mariners would be thrilled to see someone come in here and push massive changes.

I get the sense that the Greenberg-Ryan group is all about continuity and stability, in building rather than rebuilding, and I'm confident that the progress of the last couple years is about to be boosted, that is, on the field, just like the checker at Tom Thumb sees it, and not only without the interference of a new ownership group dying to make widespread changes, but instead with that group's full support of what's happening here and the contributions it's positioned to make to help this team take the next step, and the one after that.

January 25, 2010

Texas has designated infielder Joe Inglett for assignment to make room on the 40-man roster for righthander Colby Lewis. The Rangers had claimed Inglett off waivers from Toronto on December 4, but his candidacy for utility work took a hit when Texas signed Khalil Greene. Having never been outrighted, the 31-year-old Inglett could end up on the Oklahoma City roster should he clear league-wide waivers.

January 26, 2010

The Rangers have traded outfielder Greg Golson, who had been designated for assignment on Thursday (to make roster room for infielder Khalil Greene), to the Yankees for minor league infielder Mitch Hilligoss and cash.

Hilligoss, a 24-year-old left-handed hitter, has a career .275/.323/.352 slash line in four minor league seasons, all at the Class A level, playing mostly third base and shortstop with a little first base and outfield mixed in. His career highlight has been a 38-game hit streak he had for Low A Charleston in 2007, which at the time was the longest minor league hit streak since 1961.

Golson goes onto New York's 40-man roster.

Additionally, righthander Ben Sheets has signed a one-year deal with Oakland, reportedly for a $10 million base with incentives to earn more.

January 26, 2010

Well, this oughtta be cool.

One week from tonight, Tuesday, February 2, Chuck Greenberg is going to make a public appearance.

At the second Newberg Report Book Release Party.

Michael Young and Rangers assistant director of player development Jake Krug have already committed to do Q&A sessions with us that night, and now Mr. Greenberg has agreed to do the same. He'll have a microphone in hand and will take your questions, too.

The party will begin at 6:00 p.m. at Sherlock's Baker St. Pub (9100 N. Central Expressway, at the northeast corner of Central and Park Lane). We'll plan to go until 8:30 or so.

We'll have the 2010 Bound Edition for sale, as well as Carson Leslie's book, "Carry Me." This won't be an autograph event, but Michael will sign five of my books and five of Carson's and we'll auction the signed books off live to the 10 highest bidders. Professional auctioneer Luther Davis will help us get the job done, and there's a strong chance we'll also have some baseballs, bats, batting gloves, and other good stuff donated by a number of Rangers players up for auction.

All winning bid proceeds will benefit Wipe Out Kids' Cancer.

I'll get back to you with more details.

Make plans to join us Tuesday night.

January 27, 2010

Milwaukee has claimed infielder Joe Inglett off waivers from the Rangers, after Texas had designated the 31-year-old for assignment on Monday to make roster space for righthander Colby Lewis.

January 28, 2010

"My expectation is that we will be extremely competitive, and if we don't win our division, I will be disappointed, because I think we've positioned ourselves to be right there with everybody else."

So says Nolan Ryan. Quite a bit different from the front office message of "managed expectations" delivered to us after an 89-win season five years ago.

"JD made some very smart moves at the winter meetings. . . . [Then] we were able to get Vlad. . . . The signings we had before that were exciting, but to be able to get Vlad, it just got us all excited. We realize that this is our year. It's all up to us now."

That's from Ian Kinsler, one of this team's leaders.

JD agrees that the expectations should now be ratcheted up—not managed:

"As a group, we expect to win, and now that we've put a plan in place to do so, we hold ourselves to that standard."

Chuck Greenberg has arrived on the battlefront late—and of course has yet to officially join the ranks—but his eyes are already getting big:

"If we succeed on the business side and continue on path on the baseball side and combine it with a dynamic market like this is, we can be and should be one of the powerhouse franchises in baseball... [I]n a community as wonderful and dynamic as Metroplex with a franchise and fans who waited patiently to have their moment, to have a chance to try to deliver on that promise is awfully exciting."

Josh Hamilton thinks that delivery could be imminent: "We've got so much talent it's crazy. The key is staying healthy. . . . If we can stay healthy as a team, we've got such a great lineup from 1-to-9, and then the pitching obviously stepped up big time last year with Nolan Ryan coming in and Mike Maddux. It was such a dramatic difference from '08 to '09, and even if we can improve just a little bit on that going into '10, it will be a great year."

And Michael Young, whose character and mental toughness and tenacity have always set a tone, has been unusually effusive with reporters as far as his immediate outlook is concerned:

"You look at every great baseball town, whether it's New York or Boston or Chicago or St. Louis, and there's always this great relationship between the team and the fans. The fans are supportive and they come to see winning baseball and that's where we're heading to right now. . . . I've served time for about nine years now. I'm ready to kind of bust out a little bit and be a part of something that's going to be memorable and fun. This [organization] is going to be one of those jewels of baseball."

Finally, consider another Daniels remark:

"I feel a tremendous obligation to the owner to deliver. He's given me and our group an opportunity to mold the franchise, spend resources against our vision. It's more pride than pressure, if that makes sense."

It's an interesting comment, since his words and Ryan's and Young's unquestionably create—invite—a certain degree of pressure with regard to the job to be done between the lines. Pressure is something everyone on this club has played through at every level, from Darren Oliver on down to Michael Kirkman. But the pride part, which Ryan and Young always exhibited as much of as any of their playing peers, if an extra concentration of that starts to rub off and take hold up and down the roster, then, yes, it will be important to stay healthy and catch a break or two, but there's no reason 2010 can't be the kind of season the players and the front office and the prospective owner expect it to be.

Greenberg said on a radio talk show yesterday, specifically asked about cash infusion into the roster, that the business models that the Rangers look to as the paradigm belong to the Angels and Phillies. The answer is more textured than looking strictly at player payroll (Greenberg told Richie Whitt of the *Dallas Observer*: Los Angeles and Philadelphia "are smart, clever, have resources and use them wisely—those are types we can emulate"), but just for grins, *USA Today* had those two clubs' 2009 Opening Day payrolls ($113,709,000 and $113,004,046) as sixth and seventh highest in baseball, while Texas ($68,178,798) sat at 22nd.

Something else to tuck away about zeroing in on Philadelphia and Los Angeles as models: both clubs were aggressive in the second half last year, adding Cliff Lee and Scott Kazmir to their rotations, respectively, to provide a pennant race boost.

It brings to mind a point that Tom Verducci made on MLB Network last night: The Rangers' ownership situation could very well position Texas to make an impact splash at the trade deadline, armed not only with a tremendously deep farm system (that is, trade ammunition) but also an ability (and motivation, if the club is in the race) to increase payroll that hasn't existed this winter.

That depth of prospects led ESPN's Keith Law to judge the Rangers' system, for the second straight year, as baseball's best. Law summarized yesterday: "The AL West has suddenly become very competitive, with four well-run organizations all trying to balance immediate contention with long-term building goals, but Texas remains the best-positioned team there for long-term success."

MLB Network ran a Top 50 Prospects special last night, featuring Jonathan Mayo and John Hart as the lead analysts, and the Rangers were among the most dominant clubs featured, placing Neftali Feliz (number 7), Justin Smoak (9), Martin Perez (18), and Tanner Scheppers (39) on the list.

Baseball America's top 10 Rangers prospects:

1. Neftali Feliz, RHP
2. Justin Smoak, 1B
3. Martin Perez, LHP
4. Tanner Scheppers, RHP
5. Jurickson Profar, SS
6. Kasey Kiker, LHP
7. Robbie Ross, LHP
8. Mitch Moreland, OF/1B
9. Danny Gutierrez, RHP
10. Wilmer Font, RHP

The Rangers agreed to terms on a one-year deal with closer Frankie Francisco, avoiding arbitration. Francisco will be eligible for free agency next winter. Righthander Scott Feldman is the lone remaining arbitration case on the club, but count on him settling as well.

Texas will attend lefthander Noah Lowry's throwing session on Tuesday. The 29-year-old, who hasn't pitched since 2007 due to shoulder problems (stemming from thoracic outlet syndrome), was the Rangers' 19th-round pick in 1999 but didn't sign.

Baltimore designated righthander Dennis Sarfate for assignment. Texas took Sarfate in the 15th round of that same 1999 draft, a stellar crop even without Lowry and Sarfate coming to terms. Among the Rangers' picks were eventual big leaguers Colby Lewis, Aaron Harang, Hank Blalock, Kevin Mench, Jason Botts, Nick Regilio, Andy Cavazos, and Jason Jones, plus Justin Echols, who would go to Montreal in the 2004 trade for Chris Young.

Officials from two other big league clubs told ESPN's Jayson Stark that the Rangers' signing of Lewis to a two-year, $5 million deal was among the best under-the-radar moves of the winter.

Veteran corner infielder Chad Tracy's non-roster deal with the Cubs is not good news for Blalock.

Ben Sheets at a surprising $10 million (and as much as $12 million if he reaches several workload incentives, all short of 200 innings)—given what a number of healthy, reasonably effective starting pitchers have pulled in on the open market this winter—is a pretty clear indication that the league gave Oakland the same dictate that it gave Florida: Spend your revenue-sharing money on the roster. If he pitches well, the A's can trade off a third of that commitment in July for prospects (or at least recoup a pair of first-round picks when he signs elsewhere next winter).

Seventeen-year-old Dominican righthander Rafael DePaula, coming off a one-year suspension by MLB for lying about his age, is drawing interest from the Yankees and Red Sox, and ESPN's Jorge Arangure suggests Texas is in the mix, too.

University of Florida wide receiver Riley Cooper reportedly no-showed his Rangers physical a week and a half ago, an appearance that would have netted him half of his $250,000 signing bonus. Cooper has apparently decided to pursue an NFL career instead of playing minor league baseball. He'll presumably land on the Rangers' restricted list, which currently houses Alexi Ogando and Omar Beltre and for years included Ricky Williams.

A "friend and business associate of Ryan" told the *Austin American-Statesman* that he expects the Round Rock Express to replace the Oklahoma City RedHawks as the Rangers' AAA affiliate after the 2010 season.

The Florence Freedom of the independent Frontier League signed righthander Ryan Schlecht. The New Jersey Jackals of the independent Can-Am League signed infielder Myron Leslie.

Chuck Morgan has offered to emcee Tuesday's Newberg Report Book Release Party at Sherlock's in Dallas, which will include Q&A sessions with Chuck Greenberg, Jake Krug, and Michael Young as well as a live auction of various Rangers players' equipment plus Young-autographed copies of Carson Leslie's book, "Carry Me," and of the 2010 Bound Edition. (Copies of Carson's and my book will be on sale as well.) Winning bid proceeds will benefit Wipe Out Kids' Cancer.

Hope to see you there, and maybe at the awards dinner tomorrow night and Fan Fest on Saturday. Once the Rangers release the autograph schedule for Saturday, I'll let you know.

January 28, 2010

No wonder ESPN's Keith Law had the Texas farm system ranked number one. He has three Rangers among his top 13 prospects in baseball, including a super-heady ranking for the first one:

7. Martin Perez, LHP ("Perez is already the best left-handed prospect in baseball even though he probably would still be finishing high school if he had been born in the United States. . . . The Johan comparison works on a more important level—Perez projects to be one of the best left-handed starters in the majors when he arrives, perhaps as soon as this September.")

9. Justin Smoak, 1B ("His upside . . . remains untarnished, as he remains an impact bat from both sides of the plate with a plus glove at first base.")

13. Neftali Feliz, RHP ("I'd give him a chance to start while recognizing all along that his future could very well be in the 'pen, where I would expect him to be dominant.")

Righthander Tanner Scheppers is number 78 ("He's 23, has some sort of damage in his shoulder and can miss big league bats now. Texas should push him as aggressively as possible through their system with an eye toward a mid-2010 debut, not only because of the injury issue but also because he's not far from ready, even if it's just in a relief apprenticeship a la Neftali Feliz in 2009."), and righthander Danny Gutierrez is number 110 ("...ended up dumped off on Texas for two fringe prospects. If the Rangers can help Gutierrez keep his nose clean, they'll have a steal, but he needs to stay healthy and out of trouble before he's a top 100 guy.").

Law's Rangers top 10:

1. Perez
2. Smoak
3. Feliz
4. Scheppers
5. Gutierrez
6. Jurickson Profar, SS
7. Wilmer Font, RHP
8. Mitch Moreland, 3B/1B (obviously he meant OF/1B)
9. Michael Main, RHP
10. Wilfredo Boscan, RHP

January 28, 2010

The Rangers have revealed that *Baseball America* will rank the Texas farm system as baseball's second best in this winter's Prospect Handbook, behind Tampa Bay.

The Rangers will be one of only four organizations over the last 10 years to finish first or second in back-to-back seasons. The others were the Cubs (second in 2001 and first in 2002), the Dodgers (second in 2004, 2005, and 2006), and the Rays (first in 2007 and 2008). All three clubs made playoff appearances either during or shortly after those rankings.

Checking in after Tampa Bay and Texas are Cleveland, San Francisco, and Philadelphia.

Seattle is 11th, Oakland is 12th, and the Angels are 25th out of 30.

Also, briefly, there is speculation that Texas is considering free agents Ryan Garko and Rocco Baldelli (according to Jerry Crasnick of ESPN) and has "fringe interest" in Melvin Mora (according to Ken Rosenthal of Fox Sports) to fill one final spot on the bench, namely, the one that Mike Lowell had been earmarked for (versatile right-handed bat off the bench). Peter Gammons suggests today that Lowell is no longer a Rangers option.

January 29, 2010

You can listen to a Rangers-centric radio segment I did with Ben & Skin on ESPN Dallas last night by clicking this link:

http://www.zshare.net/audio/71823071fe489e0a/

I'll send out an email later today once the Rangers announce the autograph lineup for tomorrow's Fan Fest. We'll have a Newberg Report set-up with a bunch of players in the Cuervo Club (which used to be the Gold Club).

BA*'s number two*
Good and all, but rank that counts
Is now AL West

Two more things:

1. That audio file from last night's Ben & Skin Show contains the first-ever Newberg Report theme song/intro. Props to the great Ben Rogers . . . I think. You can shake his hand—or dog-cuss him—at Tuesday night's book launch party at Sherlock's.

2. Alongside our set-up tomorrow in the Cuervo Club will be the Texas Rangers Baseball Foundation, conducting its annual sale of bats, jerseys (including autographed and game-used), prints, media guides, yearbooks, and player banners. Along with the 2010 Bound Edition, which I'll also have on hand, they'd make great options for you to have the players sign, and all proceeds go to the Foundation to help the Rangers continue to give back to area kids in need.

January 29, 2010

In reverse chronological order:

1. These items have been added to the live auction we'll have this at Tuesday night's Book Release Party at Sherlock's in Dallas (9100 N. Central Expressway, at Park Lane):

Signed bats: Josh Hamilton, Ian Kinsler, Michael Young

Signed baseball glove: Michael Young

Signed batting gloves: Michael Young

Signed baseballs: Josh Hamilton, Ian Kinsler, Michael Young, Scott Feldman, Neftali Feliz, Derek Holland

We will auction off those 11 items, plus the 10 books (five of Carson Leslie's and five of mine, each autographed by Michael Young), separately.

2. The autograph schedule for tomorrow's Fan Fest has been released:

Note: Lines may form up to two hours in advance.

Diamond Club—Line A

* *Lines form on the Main Concourse behind Sections 3-9*

9:30 a.m.	Josh Hamilton
11:00a.m.	Michael Young
Noon	Chris Davis and Craig Gentry
1:00 p.m.	Ian Kinsler

2:00 p.m. Neftali Feliz
3:00 p.m. Scott Feldman and Brandon McCarthy

Diamond Club—Line B

** Lines form near the Third Base Gate*

9:30 a.m. Elvis Andrus
11:00 a.m. Ron Washington
Noon Derek Holland
1:00 p.m. Rich Harden
2:00 p.m. Tommy Hunter and Darren Oliver
3:00 p.m. David Murphy and Jarrod Saltalamacchia

The Newberg Report in the Cuervo Club

** Lines form near Home Plate Gate*

10:00 a.m. Brandon Boggs and Kasey Kiker
11:00 a.m. Zach Phillips and Tanner Scheppers
Noon Justin Smoak and Ben Snyder
1:00 p.m. Blake Beavan and Mitch Moreland
2:00 p.m. Eric Hurley and Max Ramirez

Majestic Grand Slam Gift Shop

** Lines form in Center Field Sports Park area*

10:00 a.m. Scott Coolbaugh, Claude Osteen, Pete O'Brien, Luis Ortiz, Curtis Wilkerson
11:00 a.m. Tim Crabtree, Bill Fahey, Jim Kern, Ken Suarez, Ellis Valentine
Noon Tom Grieve, Jose Guzman, Larry Hardy, Dan Smith
1:00 p.m. Rich Billings, Dave Chalk, Rusty Greer, Dave Hostetler
2:00 p.m. Frank Lucchesi, Bill Stein, Jim Sundberg
3:00 p.m. Steve Buechele, Ray Burris, Benji Gil, Mike Jeffcoat

NOTE FROM RANGERS: One autograph per person is allowed. Personalizations and posing for photographs with players are not permitted. Autograph schedule is subject to change without notice.

Q&A Schedule

All Q&A Sessions are in the Rangers Ballpark Theater. Entrance to the Theater is in Lower Home Run Porch in right field.

10:00-10:30 a.m. Manager Ron Washington
10:30-11:00 a.m. President Nolan Ryan
11:00-11:30 a.m. Outfielder Josh Hamilton
Noon-12:30 p.m. Third Baseman Michael Young
1:15-1:45 p.m. Pitcher Darren Oliver
2:30-3:00 p.m. General Manager Jon Daniels

Texas Rangers Coaches and Alumni Clinics

Clinics are located in the Media Interview Room. Entrance is in the tunnel area of Rangers Ballpark.

12:15-12:45 p.m. Hitting with Rangers Hitting Coach Clint Hurdle
1:00-1:30 p.m. Catching with All-Star Catcher and Rangers Hall of Famer Jim Sundberg
2:30-3:00 p.m. Pitching with Alumni Mike Jeffcoat and Ray Burris

Texas Rangers Weight Room

The Weight Room will be open from 11:30 a.m.-2:30 p.m. Entrance is in the tunnel area of Rangers Ballpark.

11:30 a.m.-12:30 p.m. Head Athletic Trainer Jamie Reed
12:30-1:30 p.m. Strength and Conditioning Coach Jose Vazquez
1:30-2:30 p.m. Assistant Athletic Trainer Kevin Harmon

FEBRUARY 2010

40-MAN ROSTER (40)

PITCHERS (24)

Scott Feldman, Neftali Feliz, Frankie Francisco, Rich Harden, Matt Harrison, Derek Holland, Tommy Hunter, Eric Hurley, Michael Kirkman, Colby Lewis, Warner Madrigal, Doug Mathis, Brandon McCarthy, Luis Mendoza, Guillermo Moscoso, Dustin Nippert, Darren O'Day, Darren Oliver, Zach Phillips, Omar Poveda, Chris Ray, Ben Snyder, Pedro Strop, C.J. Wilson

CATCHERS (3)

Max Ramirez, Jarrod Saltalamacchia, Taylor Teagarden

INFIELDERS (6)

Elvis Andrus, Joaquin Arias, Chris Davis, Khalil Greene, Ian Kinsler, Michael Young

OUTFIELDERS (7)

Brandon Boggs, Julio Borbon, Nelson Cruz, Craig Gentry, Vladimir Guerrero, Josh Hamilton, David Murphy

RESTRICTED LIST (2)

Omar Beltre, Alexi Ogando

February 1, 2010

Oh, somewhere in this favored land the sun is shining bright;

The band is playing somewhere, and somewhere hearts are light,

And somewhere men are laughing, and somewhere children shout;

But there is no joy in Mudville migh—

Not so fast.

According to multiple local reports, the U.S. State Department has notified the Rangers that Dominican righthanders Alexi Ogando and Omar Beltre have been provided waivers to permit them to apply for work visas, and all immigration restraints to their entry into the United States have been removed. Their five-year eviction for participation in a marriage fraud scam looks like it's coming to an end, and it appears they should be admitted to the country. Rangers assistant GM Thad Levine reportedly played a significant role in the process from the organization's side.

Ogando and Beltre were unquestionably top-tier prospects, and it obviously remains to be seen whether, at age 26 and 28, respectively, pitching dominantly for five years against largely overmatched Dominican Summer League competition will translate stateside. But there's a reason Texas kept both on the restricted list for three years (adding Ogando to the 40-man roster before doing so in his case) rather than moving on, as all other clubs have long since done with the other 30 Dominican players around the league caught up in the scandal. (Apparently, the players were promised and in some cases not even paid $5,000 by a Dominican crime syndicate to agree to sham marriages to women they didn't know, after which the women would gain entry into the United States with their newly acquired visas, obtain divorces shortly after arriving, and in some instances sell their visas on the black market.)

The two prospects reportedly spent the last year making public service speeches to educate Dominican citizens about these human trafficking scams, an effort apparently not overlooked by the State Department. Charisse Espinosa, agent for the two, gets credit for coming up with and helping execute the concept and the plan.

Beltre, whom Texas signed for a hefty $650,000 in 2000, and Ogando, purchased by the Rangers from Oakland for $12,000 in the minor league phase of the 2005 Rule Draft and promptly converted from outfield to pitcher, both offer nasty stuff on the mound, touching the upper 90s with remarkable strikeout-to-walk numbers (though those can be skewed in the DSL, as we know). Just to get a sense of things: last year, in 18.1 DSL innings, Ogando struck out 31 and issued one walk, with a typographical 10 groundouts for every flyout. Beltre, in 7.1 DSL innings, allowed no earned runs and fanned 10 while walking three. Flip to the back of any Bound Edition from the last few years those numbers weren't aberrations.

Jon Daniels suggests the two will probably begin the season in Frisco or Oklahoma City.

It will be interesting to see what the roster implications are. In order to participate in camp, both righthanders will need to be reinstated from the restricted list, and since both are already on the 40-man roster (and would never be exposed to waivers at this point far too risky), two players are going to need to come off the roster to make room for them. Righthander Luis Mendoza and infielder Joaquin Arias's lack of options (and longshot chances to make the Opening Day roster) could make them the primary candidates.

Few doubt Ogando and Beltre would have been big leaguers several years ago had they not been denied stateside entry in 2005 and ever since. Now it appears that they're going to get their chance.

February 1, 2010

The Awards Dinner/Fan Fest weekend is always a predictable rush, a 24-hour marathon that hammers home that it's time for baseball season. You go into it knowing you'll see and hear things that get you fired up, and sometimes choked up, but you can't always predict what those will be.

I still laugh every time I think about that lousy Elvis Presley impersonator (not hired to perform just a fan walking around in that get-up) asking during the 2001 Fan Fest (I think it was called something different then) for broadcaster Bill Jones's autograph . . . on Jim Sundberg's baseball card.

In 2002, prospects Hank Blalock and Justin Duchscherer putting their artistic touches on each other's promotional photos . . . Craig Monroe showing up for his Newberg Report autograph time slot even though he'd been claimed off waivers by Detroit the day before . . . and Jeff Zimmerman, both his remarkable Awards Dinner introduction of the recently retired John Wetteland and his moment the next day when he accidentally smudged his own signature on a fan's 8 x 10 glossy photo and promised to mail him a new one (a promise he kept).

In 2003, hearing what had just happened to Space Shuttle Columbia as I arrived at the Ballpark.

Juan Marichal's 2004 Awards Dinner speech just ended.

Juan Dominguez's demeanor that same night was shockingly strange. Almost emotionless, but not in a shocked or petrified way. More like the Nolan Ryan Pitcher of the Year was brooding.

Last year: I won't forget T.R. Sullivan's moving award presentation to Josh Hamilton, or Vernon Wells showing up to present Michael Young (and his wife Cristina) the Marvin Miller Man of the Year Award.

I may or may not remember that the 2010 Awards Dinner/Fan Fest weekend was also when Erica scored her first basket in a league game or when my law firm, having outgrown our space, moved to a new building, but I will remember that there were what had to be twice as many fans in the Omni Fort Worth Hotel banquet room as the event has had in years, that the highlights of the night were at the beginning (a spectacular, up-tempo season preview highlight montage that I'm sure was a Chuck Morgan, Rush Olson, and Hugo Carbajal creation) and the middle (Dale Hansen's wheelhouse roast of Jim Reeves and Nolan Ryan's rebuttal on Revo's behalf) and the end (Annette Leslie's spot-on remarks about Young, and Young's perfect words right afterwards to close the evening).

I also appreciated the idea whoever in the organization gets the credit for seating Clayton Kershaw next to Young at the head table. Was there a subtle design at work (other than putting a childhood Rangers fan next to a childhood Dodgers fan)? Who knows? I liked it.

Every one of us knows all about Martin Perez the player by now. Let me tell you this:

He's going to be the Elvis Andrus of the pitching staff when he gets here.

And I don't just mean between the lines.

The star quality (magnetic, but not pretentious) is unmistakable. You noticed it Friday night if you were there.

Every year there's one minor leaguer at the Newberg Report set-up at Fan Fest who I gain a whole new appreciation of. This year's winner of the Chad Hawkins/ Ben Kozlowski/Justin Hatcher Award goes to Mitch Moreland. That man is Big League.

Until you spend an hour with guys like Justin Smoak and Tanner Scheppers, you'd never imagine that they're just a couple of normal dudes. Normal dudes who are very good at baseball. Rock-solid, regular guys.

The crowds were huge wonder how much bigger they'd have been if it weren't 27 degrees (which felt at times like 27 below).

A few of Eleanor Czajka's photos from our set-up:

http://picasaweb.google.com/EleanorCzajka/FanFest2010NewbergReportBooth#

Grant Schiller's writeup from the weekend: http://texasrangerstrades.blogspot.com/2010/01/fan-fest-review.html

Memorable moments aside, the significance of the weekend was, like it is every year, its place on the calendar and its clarion call to the baseball fan to get geared up. Michael Young nailed it:

"When you get to this point with FanFest and the banquet, that's when it starts to hit. It's baseball season. It's about time to get ready. . . . This is a great time to be a Ranger. I see great times ahead for the organization. As players, we feel this organization is set up to be good this year and it's set up to be good for the future. This organization is ready to take off and I'm excited to be a part of it."

Seventeen sleeps.

February 2, 2010

Join us tonight from 6:00 until 8:30 at Sherlock's Baker St. Pub (9100 N. Central Expressway, at the northeast corner of Central and Park Lane) for the off-season's second Newberg Report Book Release Party. Come early if you'd like and get something to eat and drink.

The evening, emceed by the great Chuck Morgan, will kick off with Q&A sessions with Rangers assistant director of player development Jake Krug and prospective managing general partner Chuck Greenberg, followed by a live auction and then a Q&A session with Michael Young. These won't be scripted sessions. Your questions, their answers.

We'll have the 2010 Bound Edition for sale, as well as Carson Leslie's book, "Carry Me." Carson, as most of you know, passed away three weeks ago at age 17, after a courageous, dignified three-year battle with cancer. To hear from Carson himself and learn more about his book, take a look at this four-minute YouTube video: http://www.youtube.com/watch?v=rYJ7zgJISpM

Carson's family will be on hand for tonight's event. All proceeds from the winning auction bids will benefit Wipe Out Kids' Cancer, the charity through which Carson and Michael met and became friends.

The auction, presided over by local auctioneer Luther Davis, will include five copies of Carson's book and five copies of mine, each signed by Young; bats signed by Young, Ian Kinsler, and Josh Hamilton; baseballs signed by Young, Kinsler, Hamilton, Scott Feldman, Neftali Feliz, and Derek Holland; a glove signed by Young; and a batting glove signed by Young. We'll auction off the 21 items separately.

Young and his wife Cristina Barbosa have committed to make a contribution to Wipe Out Kids' Cancer that matches the total of the 21 winning bids.

See you tonight.

February 2, 2010

The great Ted Price tells me that he will have equipment at tonight's event at Sherlock's that will permit us to live-stream the Q&A with Jake Krug, Chuck Greenberg, and Michael Young. You can check it out starting at 6:00 p.m. at this link:

http://www.ustream.tv/channel/newberg-report-book-release-party

February 3, 2010

In 1999, Rangers assistant director of player development Jake Krug was playing third base behind Grayson County Community College teammate John Lackey on the way to the Vikings' Junior College World Series title.

Chuck Morgan was holding court before 2.8 million fans in what was the Rangers' third playoff season out of four.

That year, Michael Young was playing his final full season in the Toronto system, splitting time between second base and shortstop for High A Dunedin.

Also in 1999, Chuck Greenberg helped Mario Lemieux save the NHL's Pittsburgh Penguins from bankruptcy.

Eleven years later, they all converged in a packed room at Sherlock's Baker St. Pub in North Dallas, each talking about what it will take to get the Rangers back to where they haven't been since that 1999 season.

I have a lot to say about last night's event, but I'm a bit tired this morning and think I'll put it off for a day or two.

Between your generosity during the live auction, and Michael & Cristina's matching contribution, Wipe Out Kids' Cancer has $10,470 more to do good things with. Inspiring.

When I write next, I'll have links to others' write-ups and photos from the party. In the meantime, you can watch Ted Price's live video stream of the entire event at http://www.ustream.tv/recorded/4405103. (Not sure how many days it will remain up, but I think it will be there all day today.)

That was a blast. Thanks to everyone who was there.

February 5, 2010

Well, I made a mistake. It happens.

I made a mistake about how much you all contributed Tuesday night at our Sherlock's event to support Wipe Out Kids' Cancer. When I told you it was $10,470, that was wrong.

It was actually $12,170.

That's pretty great.

There's a video on Sherlock's Facebook of Annette Leslie's meaningful comments about her son Carson, about Michael Young, and about Wipe Out Kids' Cancer.

I was motivated to sit down and write up a recap of the event, but I'm having some computer issues, on top of which it's really not necessary for me to summarize things. You can watch the entire Q&A portions with Jake Krug, Chuck Greenberg, and Michael Young, moderated by Chuck Morgan, courtesy of Ted Price's video footage, at www.newbergreport.com. Click "Media/Video" on the top menu.

Plenty of recaps out there, too:

Eleanor Czajka: http://emcmlb.blogspot.com/2010/02/newberg-report-wipe-out-kids-cancer.html

ESPN's Richard Durrett: http://espn.go.com/blog/dallastexas-rangers/post/_/id/4843769/newberg-report-party-is-online

A handful of Tweets from the *Fort Worth Star-Telegram*'s Jeff Wilson: http://twitter.com/JeffWilson_FWST

The Dallas Observer's Richie Whitt: http://blogs.dallasobserver.com/sportatorium/2010/02/chuck_greenberg_is_dare_i_say.php

The Fan's Sybil Summers (video interview with Chuck Greenberg from the event): http://www.1053thefan.com/ (under "Fan Tube")

Home on the Rangers' Brandon Wilson: http://homeontherangers.com/2010/02/03/newberg-book-night-and-qa/

Texas Summer Heat's Roger Busby: http://tsheat.mlblogs.com/archives/2010/02/newberg-night-attended-short-hops.html

Lone Star Ball message board: http://www.lonestarball.com/2010/2/2/1288723/final-details-for-tonights

We were sold out of Carson's book minutes after the event got underway. If you weren't one of the five who bid on and won a copy signed by Michael Young (those went for $500, $375, $375, $375, and $275), you can get a copy of "Carry Me" at www.carrymecarson.com, at under $18.

According to ESPN's Tim Kurkjian, 12 or 13 teams showed interest in righthander Colby Lewis (including at least two, Oakland and Minnesota, who offered two-year contracts) before he agreed to his two-year deal with Texas.

Catcher Jarrod Saltalamacchia is reportedly up to 200 feet in his long-toss throwing program as he rehabilitates his shoulder.

I mentioned back when Oakland signed righthander Ben Sheets that I expect the A's to trade him in July or recoup a couple first-round draft picks next winter when he departs for a multi-year deal. What I didn't know at the time was that Sheets's contract prohibits Oakland from offering him arbitration in the event that he's so good in 2010 that he earns Type A status so forget the two firsts, and turn up the likelihood of that summer trade.

Catcher Tomas Telis, an 18-year-old switch-hitter who hit .330/.340/.498 between the Arizona League and Spokane in 2009, will miss the 2010 season due to Tommy John elbow surgery. Telis was number 20 on my Top 72 Rangers Prospects list this winter, after checking in at number 40 a year ago.

As T.R. Sullivan points out, Nolan Ryan is fourth best in baseball in the last 60 years (minimum 125 starts) with a career rate of 9.55 strikeouts per nine innings. Fifth best? Rich Harden, at 9.35.

Texas signed shortstop Travis Adair, son of Mariners pitching coach and former Rangers minor league pitching coordinator Rick Adair. The 22-year-old, who has worked out with the Rangers in the past during Fall Instructional League, was Atlanta's 13th-round pick in 2008 and spent the last two summers playing short-season ball in the Braves system.

The Rangers also signed third baseman Lee Soto, a huge disappointment in the Toronto system after signing for $600,000 out of the Dominican Republic in 2005. Soto is a .201/.248/.293 hitter in four pro seasons.

Lots of agate to cover:

Minor league deals: outfielder Frank Catalanotto (Mets), outfielder Kevin Mench (Washington), outfielder Freddy Guzman (Philadelphia), lefthander John Koronka (Dodgers), and lefthander Jimmy Gobble (Colorado).

San Diego named Jeff Pickler a pro scout. The Mets named Mark Brewer pitching coach at AA Binghamton.

The Gary Southshore Railcats of the independent Northern League signed righthander Bear Bay. The Kalamazoo Kings of the independent Frontier League signed shortstop Kyle Higgins. The Sioux City Explorers of the independent American Association signed lefthander Jared Locke.

Righthander Doug Brocail retired.

Righthander Akinori Otsuka, according to NPB Tracker's Patrick Newman, could miss the 2010 season after undergoing his third elbow surgery.

The Rangers' four first-round and supplemental first-round picks in July sit at 15, 22, 44, and 48. The final two picks will drop one spot each if Rod Barajas signs a big league deal with a club other than Toronto.

Joe Siegler is looking for your obscure Rangers photos for his uniform number project: http://www.rangerfans.com/archives/2010/02/uniform_numbers.html

Finally, I really encourage you to check out the video on the website from Tuesday's event. If you want to see this team win, I guarantee you there are a handful of moments from the event that will give you chills.

And if that's not enough to get you fired up?

The truck leaves today.

It's February
Month for those three Hallmark words:
"Pitchers & Catchers"

February 7, 2010

There are moments of cool, like the complicated things you've been looking forward to (the return of "Lost") and the simple things that you never expected (Max drawing box-and-one treatment yesterday after scoring two-thirds of his team's [six] points). And then there's the math.

Whether the objectivity of it appeals to you or turns your stomach, there's lift in the numbers. You see it in your daughter's eyes when that new, intimidating formula clicks. You (or maybe just I) get a little rush when the checkbook balances perfectly. You feel the bang when the numbers mount, like at Tuesday night's WOKC auction, and sometimes when they whittle away.

As the final moments of Colts-Saints tick down to zero tonight, another countdown takes center stage, feeding my numbers buzz. As Peyton or Drew tells us he's going to Disney World, football will be headed for dry dock for me, fully stepping aside to make room for the hourglass full of rosin.

Eleven sleeps.

February 10, 2010

Last year the Rangers went to camp knowing that a handful of non-roster invitees were near-locks to make the Opening Day roster, even if they didn't anticipate in mid-February that Elvis Andrus, Omar Vizquel, Andruw Jones, Eddie Guardado, Jason Jennings, and Kris Benson would all make the club.

For several reasons, the 2010 non-roster crew coming to camp pitchers Willie Eyre, Geoff Geary, Kasey Kiker, Clay Rapada, and Tanner Scheppers; catchers Emerson Frostad, Toby Hall, and Kevin Richardson; infielders Matt Brown, Esteban German, Ray Olmedo, and Justin Smoak; and first basemen-outfielders Mitch Moreland and Chad Tracy is not likely to claim any more than one roster spot, if that, and so it's not necessary to spend much time picking apart the current 40-man roster to see who is on thin ice between now and the season opener. Even if another non-roster player or two were to be added (a right-handed hitter? a catcher? one more 4-A swingman?) at this time last year, Guardado had just been signed and the club had yet to bring Benson or Brendan Donnelly aboard there still won't have to be as heavy a roster adjustment made at the end of camp as there was in 2009.

(Last year's roster casualties, for what it's worth: Frank Catalanotto [released]; Kason Gabbard, Travis Metcalf, and Joe Koshansky [designated for assignment, the latter two lost on waivers]; and Eric Hurley and Joaquin Benoit [shifted to the 60-day disabled list].)

There's been much speculation about the tenuous hold that righthander Luis Mendoza and infielder Joaquin Arias might have on their roster spots, given their lack of minor league options and the unlikelihood that either will make the Opening Day roster, but we learned from the Rangers this week, via MLB.com's T.R. Sullivan, that decisions on those two won't have to come as soon as many of us (myself included) had thought: Though righthanders Omar Beltre and Alexi Ogando are expected to be in camp when it opens next week, they won't need to be reinstated to the 40-man roster from the restricted list until the end of spring training.

That's good news for Mendoza and Arias (or bad news, depending on how you look at it), and definitely good for Texas, who essentially goes to camp with a protected roster of 42.

By the way, credit Assistant GM Thad Levine, Senior Director of Player Personnel A.J. Preller, and Director of International Scouting Mike Daly for taking lead on behalf of the Rangers in the ultimately successful effort to free Beltre and Ogando back up for a return to the States.

According to Roch Kubatko of MASN Sports, Baltimore would consider trading right-handed-hitting corner infielder Ty Wigginton during camp, with the Orioles having signed Garrett Atkins and Miguel Tejada. Interested? Prior to 2009 he'd been a consistent lefty-killer (and very comfortable hitting in Rangers Ballpark), but I think at his salary ($3.5 million), I'd just as soon wait to see if Mike Lowell (at an adjusted $3 million) is healthy and would definitely prefer outfielder (and perhaps first baseman) Rocco Baldelli, who is sure to command less than either on the free agent market.

Jon Paul Morosi of Fox Sports suggests that the Rangers "could benefit from signing free agent catcher Rod Barajas" but are "either (A) at their payroll limit or (B) unable to increase payroll in an ownership transition without approval from both the selling and buying groups." Yorvit Torrealba, another rumored catcher target earlier this winter, signed yesterday with San Diego.

Morosi also passes along that one amateur scout tells him that super-turbo-uber-LeBron-o-prospect Bryce Harper may not go any higher than fifth overall in June's draft and that LSU righthander Anthony Ranaudo should go before the 17-year-old Harper. Ranaudo was the Rangers' unsigned 11th-round pick in their productive 2007 draft.

Also unsigned in that draft was Mississippi lefthander Drew Pomeranz (12th round), who, along with Ranaudo, earned First-Team Pre-Season All-America recognition from *Baseball America*, based on voting by big league scouting directors. The Rangers' unsigned 36th-round pick in 2008, Vanderbilt righthander Jack Armstrong Jr., was a Third-Team selection.

ESPN's Jorge Arangure reports that Texas is among a handful of teams interested in Cuban first baseman Jose Julio Ruiz, a left-handed-hitting 25-year-old who defected last summer.

Cleveland signed righthander Jamey Wright to a non-roster deal, and according to Ken Rosenthal of Fox Sports, the Indians are also kicking the tires on Hank Blalock (and Russell Branyan and Jermaine Dye). Florida signed righthanders Derrick Turnbow and Jose Veras to non-roster deals. Seattle signed catcher Guillermo Quiroz to a non-roster deal.

According to multiple reports, Houston infielder Jose Vallejo severed tendons in the fourth and fifth fingers of his right hand while slicing meat at his Dominican Republic home in December. He could miss the entire 2010 season.

Former Rangers third base coach Steve Smith is a contestant in the new season of The Amazing Race. Seriously.

For those of you planning to order the 2010 Bound Edition by check, please note my new office address (we moved to a new building last week):

Jamey Newberg
Vincent Lopez Serafino Jenevein, P.C.
Thanksgiving Tower
1601 Elm Street
Suite 4100
Dallas, TX 75201

One week from today is the final day of the off-season. I'd guess that Omar Beltre and Alexi Ogando are more eager for the 18th to arrive than I am, but probably not by a whole lot. I'm ready.

February 12, 2010

As I sat at work yesterday and watched powdered-donut-sized snowflakes swirling upward outside my window, my thoughts wandered to the last time we were hit with a mid-February blast anything like it.

We had two dogs, and one child.

Though that was about to be reversed. We would lose Sneaker a little over a week after that Valentine's Day snowstorm. And six months later, to the day, Max was born.

Photo courtesy of the great Brad Newton

On Valentine's Day 2004, on Erica's bedroom wall was this:

Once Max was born, I changed it:

Other changes:

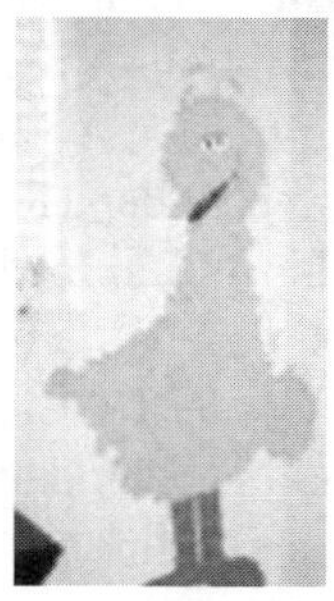

But the baseballing up of the nursery couldn't make up for the humiliating baseball blow that had been dealt six months earlier. On the day the snow covered everything back on Valentine's Day 2004, practically (and laughably) immobilizing the city, the news of the day was this:

The New York Yankees and Texas Rangers have agreed in principle on a trade that will send American League MVP Alex Rodriguez to New York for Alfonso Soriano and a minor league player to be named later.

It was a cold day in Rangers history, a day on which a landmark decision was made not to make the club better but to make it more financially flexible. The 89-win season that followed a third-place finish after A-Rod's three seasons each produced fourth-place records felt like a bit of a mirage, something the front office and manager not only accepted but also drilled into the fan base with the "managed expectations" catchphrase assault that next winter.

It's different now. The diffidence the apologetic mission statement following 2004's 89 wins bears no resemblance to the confidence and accountability that the Rangers, to a man, from the President to the General Manager to the players to the prospective owner, are preaching after last season's 87 victories. They believe it's time to win, aren't willing to accept anything less in 2010, and invite all of us to demand the same.

So much has changed since the day A-Rod was traded six years ago. The health of the Rangers has improved in many ways dramatically so in almost every facet, but that doesn't necessarily mean 2010 will be The Year. That's the plan, but things don't always work out the way they're supposed to.

Case in point: Look back at that final A-Rod club in 2003. One of the club's biggest disappointments was 23-year-old righthander Colby Lewis, having posted a 7.30 ERA in 26 starts. Today he finds himself penciled in as the club's number three starter, after a two-year-run in Japan that resuscitated his flagging career. And perhaps the 2003 club's greatest young hope, 22-year-old third baseman Hank Blalock (.300/.350/.522 in his first full big league season), sits here five days before some clubs' pitchers and catchers will report and doesn't yet know whether he'll need to fly west or east to for the start of his own spring training.

The idea that Lewis would go into 2010 with a multi-year contract, and Blalock would be facing the real possibility of having to accept a minor league deal, would have made no more sense five years ago than the way Alex Rodriguez engineered his way out of Texas.

On the subject of making sense, it's too soon to comment on Danny Gutierrez's 50-game suspension at the hands of Major League Baseball, but giving the righthander every benefit of the doubt, it's at the very least a hugely disappointing instance of carelessness, if not bad judgment. If the substance he tested positive for was in fact the ADHD medication Adderall, and if he does have a prescription for it, and if none of this would have happened had he properly applied to the league for a Therapeutic Use Exemption, then bad on him.

Would I take back the trade that sent catcher Manny Pina and outfielder Tim Smith to the Royals for Gutierrez (number eight on my Bound Edition list of the system's top 72 prospects, and number nine in the system according to *Baseball America*) in September? Absolutely not. But it's too bad that his regular season, which was set to start in the Frisco rotation, isn't going to get rolling until the end of May. He's eligible to participate fully in camp, but his Surprise program just changed. The organization will ask him to help educate his teammates about the TUE process, and to set an example by working his tail off on the field.

It will be another abbreviated season for Gutierrez, who will be eligible for the Rule 5 Draft next winter if not added to the 40-man roster. Texas will have to make roster decisions on a class that includes Mitch Moreland, Kasey Kiker, Wilmer Font, Engel Beltre, Wilfredo Boscan, Carlos Pimentel, and several others who stand as much of a chance today to break through in 2010 as Michael Kirkman had at this time a year ago. Texas will still have four months to figure out whether Gutierrez needs to be protected and at least this isn't an injury issue but it's disappointing.

It couldn't look any more like winter today, but in a week the Rangers will have gotten camp underway in Surprise, where highs are already in the 70s without a lick of a chance of anything falling out of the sky. Hopes are going to be high, as they are in every team's camp in February, but for Texas it feels like the first year in many that even a slight improvement would be viewed as a disappointment. It's time to win.

Nothing's guaranteed. We don't know who 2010's Scott Feldman will be, nor who will take a huge step back like Josh Hamilton did last year. This could be The Year, but Texas thought that in 2001 too, and in 2002, and in 2003, when they had the best player in baseball and never finished anything other than last in the division. You never know. And that's one of the greatnesses of sports.

There will be surprises this season that we can't anticipate any more than close to a foot of Metroplex snow in one mid-February day, and it's all that awesome uncertainty that I pretty much can't wait any longer for.

A Surprise party
Snowballs are great, but enough —
Could use some baseball.

February 13, 2010

Guy Edmonds was born on March 16, 1993, two years before lefthander Mike Venafro was drafted by the Rangers out of James Madison University. News came down yesterday that each had signed minor league contracts.

Venafro, who last pitched professionally in 2007 (splitting the season between St. Louis's, Toronto's, and Minnesota's AAA clubs), has signed a non-roster deal with the Nationals, in whose camp he might get a chance to pitch to Ivan Rodriguez, his teammate during his entire 1999-2001 tenure in the Rangers bullpen. It appears that Venafro's deal does not include an invite to big league camp, but at age 36 he's sure to get a look with the big club at some point in March if he shows anything at all on the back fields.

As for Edmonds, the 16-year-old catcher joins pitchers Tim Stanford (2008) and Aaron Thompson (2009) as players signed by Texas out of Australia since Director of Pacific Rim Operations Jim Colborn joined the Rangers organization. A right-handed hitter, Edmonds starred in the 2009 IBAF World Youth Baseball Championship held in August in Taiwan, putting up a slash line of .464/.484/.893 and driving in 15 runs (third most in the 12-team tournament) as he started all seven games for Team Australia. He struck out just two times in 28 at-bats and was named the catcher on the Tournament All-Star Team.

Last month at the National Youth Championships in Australia, Edmonds (whose signing bonus is reportedly in the $150,000 range) hit .378/.453/.733 in 45 at-bats for New South Wales, champions of the Under-18 bracket.

Edmonds is currently catching Stanford on the Canterbury Bankstown Vikings baseball club, which sits in third place in the 1st Grade Division of the Sydney Major League, 4.5 games behind the hated Blacktown Workers. In 104 at-bats, Edmonds is hitting .317/.357/.471. The Vikings' regular season concludes on March 7, after which Edmonds (whose father and uncle were professional rugby players) is expected to travel to Surprise to join Rangers minor league camp.

Other news:

As expected, righthanders Omar Beltre and Alexi Ogando received their work visas without a problem, and both are expected to be in Surprise next week.

Texas signed 26-year-old righthander Jae-Kuk Ryu, a onetime Cubs prospect who last pitched in the Tampa Bay system in 2008. He was claimed off waivers by San Diego last January and then by Cleveland in March, but the latter claim was voided by MLB (because Ryu was injured) on April 1, after which the Padres released him. Ryu's Rangers deal does not include an invite to big league camp.

Ryu, whose lifetime minor league record is 39-29, 3.35 (7.9 strikeouts and 3.1 walks per nine innings) and who has a 7.49 ERA in 39.2 big league innings, is perhaps best known for throwing a baseball at an osprey in its perch in his home ballpark with High A Daytona in 2003, striking the bird (an endangered species) with a blow that eventually killed it.

Other minor league deals (with invites): infielder Mike Lamb (Florida) and righthander Kip Wells (Cincinnati).

Washington is reportedly in discussions with righthander Kris Benson apparently with the thought that the former number one overall draft pick could serve as a mentor (and cautionary tale) for Nationals righty Stephen Strasburg.

Texas, according to Melissa Segura of *Sports Illustrated*, is among at least seven teams interested in highly touted 17-year-old Dominican righthander Rafael DePaula, who is reportedly also considering Japan.

Doug Brocail, who retired last week, was named a front office advisor by the Astros, who also offered him a minor league pitching coach position.

The Lake County Fielders of the independent Northern League signed infielder Kyle Higgins.

February 16, 2010

Monday's signing of outfielder Endy Chavez doesn't belong in the same discussion as Vladimir Guerrero or Rich Harden. This isn't a Caron Butler or Brendan Haywood pickup, or Kari Lehtonen.

But Chavez isn't necessarily Jason Ellison or Ryan Christenson, either.

Consider the thoughts of the great Dave Cameron, co-force behind the great U.S.S. Mariner website, via his Twitter account:

Endy Chavez to Texas. Another good move for a club that is making a habit of making them. AL West, best run group of teams in baseball.

Texas signed Chavez, who is rehabbing from major knee surgery, to a minor league contract that (according to Jon Heyman of *Sports Illustrated*) will reportedly pay $1 million (half of what he earned last year) while he's in the big leagues and includes a $1.25 million option for 2011. After Chavez tore the ACL in his right knee in a mid-June collision with Seattle teammate Yuniesky Betancourt, some expected his 2010 season to be jeopardized as he recovered from surgery. But there are reports that Chavez is dramatically ahead of schedule and could be ready for action as soon as a month into the season.

Cameron, a Mariners expert, saw Chavez firsthand in 2009, when he broke camp as part of Seattle's everyday lineup. Starting each of the club's first 13 games (10 in left field, two in right, one in center), and hitting first (while Ichiro Suzuki recovered from a bleeding ulcer) or second in the lineup, Chavez sat at a healthy .392/.446/.471 in 51 at-bats. While it was out of character for the career .270/.312/.367 hitter (he managed to hit only .171/.234/.186 in his next 80 at-bats), it wasn't completely a fluke, according to Cameron.

"He's been wildly underrated for years," Cameron suggests. "A completely healthy Endy Chavez was probably [one of the] two or three best defensive outfielders in baseball, and the bat is just below average, not terrible. Good contact skills, good bunter, good runner, great glove he's an average-ish major league player at full strength. . . . [I]f he recovers, he's a high quality role player, and good enough to start in the outfield for a lot of teams."

For what it's worth, Chavez was a procedural grab bag early in his career, signing with the Mets out of Venezuela at age 18, getting selected by Kansas City in the 2000 Rule 5 Draft; clearing waivers at the end of 2001 spring training but remaining in the Royals system when they traded minor league outfielder (and future Frisco RoughRider) Michael Curry to the Mets for the right to keep him; making it to the big leagues with Kansas City later that 2001 season, after which he landed with Detroit on a December waiver claim; ending up back with the Mets on another waiver claim in February 2002; hitting the waiver wire again just three weeks later and getting snapped up by Montreal; spending three seasons with Montreal/Washington and a month into his fourth when he was traded to Philadelphia in May 2005 straight up for Marlon Byrd; getting non-tendered after the season and returning to the Mets as a free agent; establishing himself with New York in 2006 and earning $1.725 million for the 2007 season and then a two-year, $3.85 million deal for 2008-09; and getting traded to Seattle midway through that contract in the three-team, 12-player deal highlighted by reliever J.J. Putz going from the Mariners to the Mets and outfielder Franklin Gutierrez going from the Indians to the Mariners. Chavez missed the second half of the 2009 season with the torn ACL and was a free agent this winter.

In a way, Chavez and Byrd have something else in common. Texas signed Byrd as center field depth in December 2006, as insurance behind Kenny Lofton. Chavez and Byrd are very different offensive players, of course, but Byrd was no more of an impact signing three years ago than Chavez is now.

The Rangers were set to feature Craig Gentry, Brandon Boggs (returning from a shoulder injury), and likely Mitch Moreland in the AAA outfield, but since the loss of Greg Golson when he was designated for assignment last month (and traded to the Yankees), the club decided to go out to add another outfielder to the mix, targeting the versatile 32-year-old. An insurance policy in the event that Borbon struggles to hold center field down all season, Chavez can also serve as a mentor to the three young outfield prospects bound for Oklahoma City.

Chavez gets the 15th non-roster invite to Rangers camp (and there will probably be at least one more there are reports that Texas is interested in veteran catcher Jose Molina, for instance). Toss in restricted list occupants

Omar Beltre and Alexi Ogando and a full 40-man roster complement, and Texas is bringing at least 57 players to camp, which officially opens in two days.

The 57:

40-MAN ROSTER

PITCHERS (24): Scott Feldman, Neftali Feliz, Frankie Francisco, Rich Harden, Matt Harrison, Derek Holland, Tommy Hunter, Eric Hurley, Michael Kirkman, Colby Lewis, Warner Madrigal, Doug Mathis, Brandon McCarthy, Luis Mendoza, Guillermo Moscoso, Dustin Nippert, Darren O'Day, Darren Oliver, Zach Phillips, Omar Poveda, Chris Ray, Ben Snyder, Pedro Strop, C.J. Wilson

CATCHERS (3): Max Ramirez, Jarrod Saltalamacchia, Taylor Teagarden

INFIELDERS (6): Elvis Andrus, Joaquin Arias, Chris Davis, Khalil Greene, Ian Kinsler, Michael Young

OUTFIELDERS (7): Brandon Boggs, Julio Borbon, Nelson Cruz, Craig Gentry, Vladimir Guerrero, Josh Hamilton, David Murphy

RESTRICTED LIST (2): Omar Beltre, Alexi Ogando

NON-ROSTER INVITEES

PITCHERS (5): Willie Eyre, Geoff Geary, Kasey Kiker, Clay Rapada, Tanner Scheppers

CATCHERS (3): Emerson Frostad, Toby Hall, Kevin Richardson

INFIELDERS (4): Matt Brown, Esteban German, Ray Olmedo, Justin Smoak

OUTFIELDERS (3): Endy Chavez, Mitch Moreland, Chad Tracy

Setting aside the inevitable injury or two going into the season, here are the near-locks to break camp on the active roster:

PITCHERS (9): Scott Feldman, Neftali Feliz, Frankie Francisco, Rich Harden, Tommy Hunter, Colby Lewis, Darren O'Day, Darren Oliver, C.J. Wilson

CATCHERS (1): Jarrod Saltalamacchia

INFIELDERS (4): Elvis Andrus, Chris Davis, Ian Kinsler, Michael Young

OUTFIELDERS (5): Julio Borbon, Nelson Cruz, Vladimir Guerrero, Josh Hamilton, David Murphy

That leaves, in all likelihood, spots for three pitchers, one catcher, one infielder who can play shortstop, and one right-handed hitter who ideally can play first base and somewhere in the outfield.

As for the three pitchers, if Feliz and Wilson end up in relief (Jon Daniels has suggested, at least in Feliz's case, that the starter vs. reliever determination should be made by March 15-20), the open spots will be the number five starter, one middle reliever, and the long man. Of the 20 remaining pitchers in camp, you can safely pencil in options for Kirkman, Phillips, Poveda, Beltre, and Ogando, and minor league assignments for Geary, Kiker, Rapada, and Scheppers. Expect Hurley to begin the season on option, if not the 60-day disabled list.

Let's categorize the rest further.

Fifth starter candidates: Harrison, Holland, McCarthy

Middle relief candidates: Madrigal, Mendoza, Ray, Snyder, Strop, Eyre

Long man candidates: Mathis, Moscoso, Nippert

Do McCarthy and Ray have an edge in their categories since they'd have to be exposed to waivers in order to be sent to the farm? Not really, as we've discussed before. The type of service-time-related waivers involved for the two righthanders, each of whom still has two options, would be revocable and is rarely blocked. Still, assuming health for each, they might be the pitchers to beat for the number five and middle relief roles. But not because of their procedural status.

Holland has three options and (depending on what he shows in March) could benefit from some extra minor league seasoning. (Cameron on Holland in a piece he wrote yesterday for FanGraphs.com: "In an organization with a lot of good young arms, in a division with a lot of good young arms, Holland gets overlooked, but he may be the single most important player in the AL West in 2010. If he's as good as I think he is, Texas has a legitimate shot at winning 90 games. This kid can really pitch. . . . There should be way more excitement about a kid with these tools . . . . Forget the ERA Holland can pitch, and could easily emerge as the ace of the Rangers rotation.") Harrison, returning from thoracic outlet syndrome, has two options.

In the bullpen, Madrigal has an option, and Strop has two. Mendoza is out of options, Snyder would need to clear waivers and be offered back to San Francisco for $25,000 if he doesn't make the active Opening Day roster, and Eyre is off the roster to begin with. (For what it's worth, this is as good a place as any to let you know that righthander Joaquin Benoit signed a minor league deal with Tampa Bay yesterday.)

The only procedural issue with regard to the three long relievers belongs to Nippert, who is out of options and would surely be lost on waivers if he doesn't make the club. Mathis has three options left, Moscoso two.

So is the prediction here that McCarthy, Ray, and Nippert round out the Opening Day staff? If they're healthy, and if they pitch satisfactorily in Surprise, I'd at least give them the pole position.

At catcher, Teagarden (two options) is the favorite to stick, while Ramirez (one option) is a certainty not to and he could even be dealt to Boston if Mike Lowell proves to be healthy and the two clubs revisit those trade talks. But a Molina arrival could push both Teagarden and Ramirez to the RedHawks, where there's already an interesting logjam of capable backstops.

The utility infielder is likely to be Greene, with Arias a good bet to be traded. (Jon Daniels hinted at it last week, acknowledging that Arias proved enough with his shoulder this winter that he probably wouldn't clear waivers.)

The right-handed hitter? Ramirez figures in there, but probably lags behind Brown, and maybe even Gentry. (Boggs may not be ready physically.) Don't rule out the Lowell idea, or someone like Rocco Baldelli. But don't count on Smoak, even if he destroys Cactus League pitching from the right side. With Guerrero at designated hitter, the role we're talking about is likely to get sporadic work, and that's not a good idea for Smoak.

Let's say one non-roster player (Brown?) makes the club. Will finding a 40-man roster spot for him be difficult? Not at all. Mendoza is likely to be off the roster by Opening Day. Arias, too, unless he wins a job, in which case Greene would probably be dropped from the roster. The way things shape up, Snyder is probably more likely to relinquish his roster spot than to win a left-on-left job in the bullpen. Hurley could be placed on the 60-day disabled list, too.

If Mathis or Moscoso (or one of the two among Harrison, Holland, and McCarthy who don't win a rotation spot) were to beat Nippert out for the long relief role, Nippert's lack of options means he'd come off the 40-man roster as well.

(There would be no need to create room for Lowell, as he'd just take Ramirez's roster spot.)

A pitcher like Madrigal could conceivably pitch his way into a designation for assignment with an awful camp.

Yes, two more spots will need to be created so that Beltre and Ogando can be reinstated from the restricted list and optioned to minor league clubs to start the season, but the way the roster is set up right now, it's simply not going to be much of a problem.

Now, if the club decides a month into the season that Chavez would help? If Smoak forces his way to Arlington during the season? Scheppers (whose fastball is top five in the minor leagues, along with Feliz's, says *Baseball America*'s Jim Callis), same thing? Then it gets a little trickier, not to mention in November, when the club has to figure out whether (and how) to find room on the roster for Moreland, Kiker, Wilmer Font, Danny Gutierrez, Engel Beltre, Wilfredo Boscan, and Carlos Pimentel, among others. That's going to be difficult, and is one reason (among several) that I think a major trade in July (several prospects for an impact veteran) makes a huge amount of sense.

Of course, everything you just read is grossly premature and sort of worthless, since before the roster is set at the end of March there will be injuries and there could be another non-roster veteran or two added and there could even be trades.

It's also the exercise of a crazy baseball fan who pretty much can't wait any longer for spring training to get rolling.

February 18, 2010

A handful of things:

1. Texas reportedly offered minor league contracts recently to veteran catchers Jose Molina and Rod Barajas, each of whom turned the offers down. (Barajas seems poised to accept the Mets' minor league deal, one that reportedly has a million-dollar big league split [similar to what Texas gave Endy Chavez] and that's a situation in which he could easily break camp as New York's big league starter.) The defensively advanced Molina is reportedly the Rangers' top choice. Molina's agent is Alan Nero, who evidently also represents Toby Hall, the journeyman catcher who signed a minor league deal with Texas last month. (Potential conflict of interest for Nero?)

2. A couple more details on Chavez's non-roster contract: He reportedly has an out clause that allows him to opt for instant free agency sometime in July should he not be in Arlington at the time. There's a $50,000 buyout on the $1.25 million club option for 2011, which increases to $100,000 if he spends at least 30 days in the big leagues in 2010. He can earn almost $500,000 extra this year if he maxes out on certain plate appearance and service time incentives.

3. Do you have a pitching machine for sale? Need to buy one for Max's Little League team.

4. I made a mistake two days ago when I wrote that Texas signed Marlon Byrd as insurance behind Kenny Lofton in December 2006. Byrd actually signed four days before Lofton did. But the point remains unchanged.

5. We need someone at our office to wall-mount and hook up a couple HD TV's. If you do that sort of thing, let me know.

6. MLB.com ran a story Tuesday about the 2010 season projections of some of the more prominent sabermetric systems. All three highlighted systems PECOTA, CHONE, and CAIRO project Texas to win the AL West (with between 82 and 87 wins).

7. Foot cramps suck.

8. Mike Lowell will head to Red Sox camp believing he'll end spring training in someone else's uniform. But his uncertainty pays him $12 million, which is a far more comfortable situation than the one Hank Blalock finds himself in.

9. Righthander Dustin Brader caught on with the Southern Illinois Miners of the independent Frontier League, lefthander Broc Coffman hooked up with the Fargo-Moorhead Redhawks of the independent Northern League, righthander Josh Giles agreed to terms with the Northern League's Schaumburg Flyers, and lefthander Michael Tejera is now with Japan's Chiba Lotte Marines.

10. Happy Holidays.

February 19, 2010

The winter can be long, and it's with that caveat that I measure the words of folks who have been champing at the bit not only to put a uniform back on and to get back on the freshly cut Bermuda, or to get back on a director's chair in front of a live camera, but also to talk baseball again.

Does it mean anything when Bobby Valentine says on ESPN on February 18 that Ron Washington is on the hottest seat of any manager in the league? Does it mean anything when C.J. Wilson tells a reporter in so many words that his stuff is better than Rich Harden's and that he has too many weapons to be assigned to the eighth inning?

We've all been waiting months and months for baseball. Part of that for Valentine and Wilson has been preparing to make bold comments that will show up the next day in newspapers and on blogs and around water coolers, and that's fine. What they said wasn't as carefully scripted as whatever it is that Tiger Woods will say later this morning, but that's two guys who have never shied away from the provocative, and whether it's issuing a proclamation before clubs have even fully reported to camp — as to which manager has the least job security or announcing that you disagree with the role your team has given you, that sort of talk basically generates more talk. Things will sort themselves out on the field.

Matt Harrison losing 30 pounds is a bigger *story* than what C.J. Wilson thinks his job should be.

Look, I hope that a stretched-out Wilson is so dominant in camp that the club has to decide how to sort out having too many quality starting pitchers. And truthfully, I want every player on this team believing he's capable of doing more than he's ever done, or filling a more highly leveraged role. My guess is that Wilson ends up reassigned to the eighth inning, but there's nothing wrong with him getting the opportunity to go out and prove he should be entrusted with more.

Speaking of words, and things playing out between the lines, this focus in the press this week on how the situation behind the plate may be the camp's most spirited battle is interesting. This isn't Taylor Teagarden declaring that he should be the starter, or Toby Hall scoffing at the thought that Texas continues to hunt for a veteran to compete for a roster spot. It's coming from the manager and the general manager, whose thoughts on such a subject mean something. The job isn't being taken away from Jarrod Saltalamacchia, but it's been made clear the last couple days that it's not being handed to him, either.

Everyone who is supposed to be in camp in time for today's first workout is there, and a few who didn't have to be there yet are, too. Time to roll.

Changing batteries?
Is there more competition
At C than at P?

February 19, 2010: TROT COFFEY

- According to Ken Rosenthal of Fox Sports, catcher Rod Barajas is weighing minor league offers from the Mets and the Rangers, with the Texas offer reportedly higher. Earlier today, Jose Molina (supposedly a Rangers target) signed a major league deal with Toronto. Something to consider as far as Barajas is concerned: While the Rangers may be offering more money than New York, he would arguably stand a better chance to win a starting job with the Mets.
- Left-handed slugger Russell Branyan signed with Cleveland. Had he opted to sign with Tampa Bay, the Indians reportedly would have turned to Hank Blalock.

February 20, 2010: TROT COFFEY

- Ken Rosenthal of Fox Sports has updated his story on catcher Rod Barajas, reporting now that the Mets have upgraded their offer to the veteran so that it's now a guaranteed major league deal. Last night Rosenthal had reported that the Mets and Rangers had both offered Barajas non-roster deals, with Texas coming in at a higher number. The updated story suggests that the Texas minor league offer was for $1.5 million if Barajas were to make the big club, while the New York split was for $1 million if he were to win a job. Now, writes Rosenthal, the Mets offer remains at $1 million but is a major league deal.

February 20, 2010

According to Ken Rosenthal of Fox Sports, the Mets have signed catcher Rod Barajas to a one-year, $1 million contract (*Sports Illustrated*'s Jon Heyman reports that the base is "a bit less than $1 million") that includes another $1 million in "easily attainable" incentives.

There's almost no question that any remaining catchers on the free agent market would only be able to command a minor league contract at this point, with the possible exception, I suppose, of Paul Bako. Should Texas feel it needs a more reliable competitor in camp for one of its two big league catching jobs, the club might have to resort to a trade.

The major league signing awards Toronto (Barajas's 2009 club) with the 41st pick in this June's draft, pushing the Rangers' two supplemental first-rounders down to 45th and 49th overall. Texas picks 15th and 22nd in the first round as well.

Also, lefthander Derek Holland tweaked his right knee during agility drills this morning in Surprise, and will have a precautionary MRI on Monday. Holland and the club have each told reporters they don't believe the injury is serious.

February 21, 2010

The weather is still lousy. I woke up not feeling great today. Our first C League baseball practice looks like it might get postponed for the second straight week. I haven't even thought about getting our taxes started. Wade Phillips still coaches the Cowboys.

But I got a little lift when I stopped by our neighborhood Barnes & Noble this morning and slid over to the sports shelves.

That was a pretty cool, unexpected surprise.

February 21, 2010

I've got about seven or eight ideas in mind for my next report, but to some degree they've all been touched on (if not beaten to death) by at least one of the many mainstream media outlets and solid Rangers blogs out there.

So I ask for your input: What would you like to see me write about this week? Looking for more big-picture ideas than something like Derek Holland's knee or C.J. Wilson's comments. You guys always come through.

In the meantime, I'd had all I could take of Rascal Flatts long before now, but they're threatening to ruin the Olympics for me. Two Flattsy thoughts:

1. They're the new Nickelback.
2. Drew Meyer.

Hit me up with your report ideas.

February 22, 2010

According to Ken Rosenthal of Fox Sports, infielder Khalil Greene will not report with the rest of the Rangers' position players Tuesday and "could miss significant time, according to major-league sources," apparently due to the anxiety issues that limited him in 2009.

The Rangers have not issued comment.

February 22, 2010

It's a delicate situation, both given the circumstances of Khalil Greene's history and the attendant HIPAA considerations, so I'll just post the club's official statement, released this morning:

KHALIL GREENE WILL NOT REPORT TO SPRING TRAINING WITH TEXAS RANGERS

Surprise, Arizona—The Texas Rangers this morning announced that infielder Khahil Greene will not be joining the team and will not report to spring training camp.

Rangers General Manager Jon Daniels issued the following statement this morning:

"The Rangers fully support Khalil's decision to address this private matter. Per club policy, we will not comment on his medical situation. We have agreed to leave the door open for a continued relationship, if both Khalil and the team desire that in the future.

"We have not put a timetable on a possible return to the club with the sole focus right now on doing what we can to assist him. The Rangers will continue to work with Khalil and his representatives to monitor his situation and interest in rejoining our organization.

"Over the next few days, we expect that Khalil's status will be more clearly defined. We will also communicate the impact on the 40-man roster once we've walked through our administrative options."

February 23, 2010

You all came up with a ton of great suggestions for report topics. Can't get to nearly all of them, but let's hit on a few.

What happens to the bench now that Khalil Greene is out of the picture? Can't be answered yet. But the Rangers have said the utility infield job will be won internally (Felipe Lopez? Really? Why would he ever sign here, when the job of backing up Elvis Andrus, Michael Young, and Ian Kinsler promises so little opportunity?), and Esteban German isn't a very good shortstop, so that means the competition at this point features Joaquin Arias and Ray Olmedo. If Arias's shoulder can hold up on the left side of the infield, the job should be his. As for the other infield spot, preferably a right-handed bat that can play both corners? I give Matt Brown a one-in-three shot, Mike Lowell twice that. Another possibility: either infield spot on the bench could be manned by a player in someone else's camp a month from now. Such as Arizona's Augie Ojeda.

In the age of video scouting and league adjustments, can Scott Feldman do it again? As long as he commands that filthy cutter, a true out pitch, you bet. It's not the kind of pitch a hitter can sit on and punish when it's working. Remember, Feldman's 17-8, 4.08 mark 17-8, 3.79 as a starter came in just 31 starts. Given a full year in the rotation, can he win 17 again? Of course. Can he maintain the peripherals? Don't see why not.

Compare the 40-man roster to that of the last Rangers playoff team. Good one.

Going into 1999, 19 pitchers were on the roster: starters Rick Helling, Aaron Sele, John Burkett, Esteban Loaiza, and Mark Clark; relievers John Wetteland, Tim Crabtree, Eric Gunderson, Danny Patterson, and Al Levine; minor league starters Doug Davis, Ryan Glynn, Danny Kolb, Corey Lee, Jonathan Johnson, Brandon Knight, Derrick Cook, and Matt Perisho; and reliever Mike Venafro.

The current roster has 24 pitchers 26 if you count Omar Beltre and Alexi Ogando including starters Feldman, Rich Harden, Colby Lewis, Tommy Hunter, and we'll say Brandon McCarthy; relievers Frankie Francisco, Neftali Feliz, C.J. Wilson, Darren O'Day, Darren Oliver, Chris Ray, and Dustin Nippert; staff contenders Derek Holland, Matt Harrison, Doug Mathis, and Ben Snyder; minor league starters Eric Hurley, Michael Kirkman, Guillermo Moscoso, and Omar Poveda; and minor league relievers Beltre, Ogando, Pedro Strop, Warner Madrigal, Luis Mendoza, and Zach Phillips.

Call Sele and Feldman a wash. Burkett was coming off a 5.68 ERA season; I'll take Lewis. Loaiza had a 5.90 ERA after his summer arrival in Texas; Hunter is just as good a bet today as Loaiza was going into his first full season as a Ranger. Clark or McCarthy? Clark or Holland? Clark or Harrison? C'mon.

Helling or Harden? Tough call. Lunchpail consistency vs. risk/reward. Depends on what you're looking for.

The bullpens aren't close. Wetteland beats Francisco but every other matchup favors the current group.

The minor league pitching groups are close, but there's greater upside today.

To be fair, there was one non-roster invite at this time in 1999 who promised to make an impact during the season, but there's one today, too. This isn't a hindsight exercise, though, and anyone who says he expected Jeff Zimmerman (whom *Baseball America* judged that winter to be the Rangers' number 10 prospect) to be anything close to a rookie All-Star in middle relief is lying, and there's just as much buzz about 23-year-old Tanner Scheppers as Camp 2010 gets rolling as there was in February 1999 about the 26-year-old Zimmerman.

Catchers? The red-shoed '99ers (Ivan Rodriguez and Gregg Zaun) have the obvious advantage.

The Lee Stevens/Mark McLemore/Royce Clayton/ Todd Zeile infield? Texas is measurably stronger now at second, shortstop, and third, and similar at first offensively. But Chris Davis has a better chance of outproducing Stevens than McLemore had to put together a Kinsler-type year (not to mention Davis's massive edge defensively), and nobody would take the 29-year-old Clayton over Andrus. I'd take Young over Todd Zeile, even discounting the off-the-field factors. Luis Alicea and Jon Shave probably make a stronger bench case than Greene or Arias plus a non-roster type like Brown or Esteban German, but Lowell would tilt things the other way.

Outfield and DH: Juan Gonzalez, Rusty Greer, Tom Goodwin, and Rafael Palmeiro vs. Nelson Cruz, Josh Hamilton, Julio Borbon, and Vladimir Guerrero. There are scenarios in which you can imagine the current group outplaying the 1999 group, both offensively and defensively, but you have to give the old guys the edge. Roberto Kelly and David Murphy as fourth outfielders make a pretty good match. Other big leaguers: Ruben Mateo and Mike Simms in 1999; Brandon Boggs and Craig Gentry today. You had to give the older crew the decided edge because of pre-injury Mateo and the 1998 that Simms was coming off of.

Minor league position players: catcher Cesar King, infielders Kelly Dransfeldt, Shawn Gallagher, and Rob Sasser, and outfielders Mike Zywica and Ricky Williams (yes, that Ricky Williams) in 1999. Today: Catcher Max Ramirez and no infielders or outfielders. Off the roster but in camp, the club now has Justin Smoak, Mitch Moreland, and Chad Tracy, but in 1999 had Carlos Pena and Mike Lamb. Strong in both cases.

Overall? Better pitching staff today, better catcher and outfield then, better infield today.

And Martin Perez's on the way: 2010 one, 1999 zero.

What Rangers player has the biggest 2010 beta? I'm not sure which I'd say is more likely: Scheppers starting and finishing the year with Frisco (remember, he logged only 19 innings last summer), or closing games in Arlington in September. Surely it will be something between the two extremes, but the possibilities are all over the map.

You nailed it coming up with realistic trade ideas for Zack Greinke and Josh Johnson a year before each of them really broke through. Do it again. OK, in time. I will say this: The odds of making an impact July trade go up this year, for two reasons: (1) the ownership transition and (2) tougher 40-man roster decisions this coming November than in any off-season in memory.

Among those who will need to be added to the roster to avoid exposure to next December's Rule 5 Draft: Moreland, Wilmer Font, Kasey Kiker, Danny Gutierrez, Engel Beltre, Wilfredo Boscan, and Carlos Pimentel.

I'll go ahead and say this: If (when) Kansas City is 20 games out in mid-July, despite a second straight Cy Young-quality season from Greinke, I'd call the Royals and offer them Holland, Font, Ogando, Moreland, and Engel Beltre for Greinke and a middle reliever or veteran bench piece (whichever makes more roster sense at that point).

But that's just off the top of my head. I'll work on this idea and expand it to other trade targets soon.

OK, one more: Smoak, Font, and Kiker for Brandon Webb.

Twist my arm: Poveda and Engel Beltre for (righthander) Chris Young, or if the decision is made to move Feliz into the rotation Harrison, Font, and Engel Beltre for Heath Bell, who is under control through 2011 (a year longer than Frankie Francisco is).

Can Texas commit to Neftali Feliz in the bullpen again without scuttling the idea of making him a starter eventually? Of course. See what the Dodgers did with Pedro Martinez at age 21 in 1993 (after his brief 1992 debut). One difference to think about, though: Los Angeles was coming off a terrible 1992 season (63-99) and managed to play only .500 ball in 1993. They were arguably better able to blueprint Martinez's development, with little heed paid to the team's chances to win, than the Rangers can now. Texas expects to win, and for that reason the decision on Feliz may have more than just his own development to factor in.

In other words, even if the Dodgers thought Martinez was one of their five best rotation options coming out of camp in 1993, they probably didn't expect to win and could focus on what was best for the young Martinez's development (managing his workload in a bullpen role). If, on March 15, Texas believes Feliz gives it a better chance to win than the pitchers against whom he's competing for the fourth or fifth rotation spot? Trickier.

For those of us who didn't get to go to Sherlock's to meet Chuck Greenberg, is he going to be another Arte Moreno? Who does he remind you of? Roger Staubach. (Apologies to Chuck, a Steelers guy, if he's reading this.) Same inspiring mix of humility and command.

Has Chris Davis ever tried to catch? He has the footwork and arm to do it. That's super-interesting. A little too late in the game to consider that kind of transition (Davis did catch a little in high school), but wow, that would have been an inspired experiment years ago. Like Justin Morneau and Carlos Delgado and Dale Murphy and Mike Sweeney and a bunch of other power hitters, Davis might not have lasted long behind the plate (to preserve his career as a run producer), but imagine how valuable he'd have been as a catcher if it all came together, even for a few years.

After the Rangers are successful this year, do you fear that we could lose Thad Levine or A.J. Preller or Scott Servais to other organizations raiding our system? Damn right I do. Cost of being good.

Jarrod Saltalamacchia seems to be the biggest wild card in the lineup. What do you see happening with him this year? How great would an Anthony Spencer/ Mike Jenkins breakout be? Even if Saltalamacchia doesn't quite pull that off, he could still be Clint Hurdle's greatest Year One accomplishment.

With Marlon Byrd gone, who steps up as the vocal leader in the clubhouse? Michael Young is more of a quiet leader, and Vladdy doesn't seem to be a rah-rah type, either. Young isn't as quiet as you think. Yes, he leads primarily by example, but one offshoot of being more selective with your words is that whenever you speak, it counts. A lot.

Who are you most looking forward to seeing in Surprise? Righthanders Beltre and Ogando, outfielder Miguel Velazquez, and catcher Jorge Alfaro.

And outfield/baserunning coordinator Wayne Kirby. That's when I'll know it's baseball season.

February 23, 2010

According to a local report, the MRI on Derek Holland's right knee revealed a mild sprain. He's expected to resume non-throwing baseball activities right away, and could resume his throwing program in the next few days.

Baseball America's Top 100 Prospects list just came out, with the following Rangers on it:

9. Neftali Feliz (Best Tool: Fastball; *BA* Grade: 80)
13. Justin Smoak (Best Tool: Bat; *BA* Grade: 70)
17. Martin Perez (Best Tool: Curveball; *BA* Grade: 65)
42. Tanner Scheppers (Best Tool: Fastball; *BA* Grade: 70)

BA will name Texas the number two farm system in baseball (behind Tampa Bay), though at least one *BA* exec (Jim Callis) had the Rangers number one for the second straight year.

February 24, 2010

The first full camp workout for Texas is hours away. Everyone's in camp, other than Khalil Greene, who won't be.

Jarrod Saltalamacchia, Derek Holland, Doug Mathis, Brandon Boggs, Eric Hurley, and Omar Beltre are each further along physically than it seemed a couple weeks ago they might be.

To say Matt Harrison is further along physically would totally miss the point, if this AP shot isn't showing an imposter on the right side of the photo.

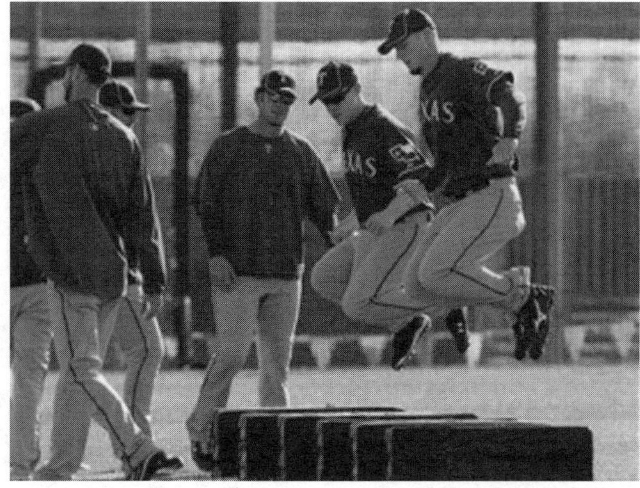

Good grief.

It's also the first full workout today in Red Sox camp, where Mike Lowell will begin to show where he is physically. Lowell celebrates birthday number 36 today. What's he got left? And where does he want to be to prove it?

Given the events of the last few days involving Greene, Lowell's comments to a pool of Boston reporters yesterday take on a greater significance 2,300 miles west of Fort Myers in Surprise, Arizona.

Asked about his state of mind after his failed physical in Arlington two months ago killed a trade to Texas, Lowell said: "I was like, 'All right, it didn't go through.' [But] I'm pretty confident I'm going to be in the big leagues this year somewhere. And I still view that as a privilege. . . . No one needs to feel sorry for me."

Two weeks after the near-trade, the Red Sox signed Adrian Beltre to play third base. After seeing his trade to the Rangers taken away, the Beltre signing once and for all took his Red Sox job away.

Less than a week after that, Texas signed Vladimir Guerrero and Khalil Greene. Did that slam the door shut on the possibility of the trade to the Rangers reviving during camp? Seemingly so. Until Greene fell out of the plans this week, perhaps.

It's fair to say it might be an opportunity Lowell would like to see come back together. "I looked at the Texas thing as a pretty good challenge," he said. "I thought that the team did a lot of good things last year [when] they were in it basically 'til the end.

"I didn't see that as a bad situation. I thought that was a place I could fit in the lineup . . . and put up the numbers on a team that was going to be competitive. I wasn't ashamed of going over there. I wasn't disappointed that it might be a possibility where I landed."

Lowell's thumb and hip? He's not swinging a bat yet but thinks he'll be ready to play when Boston opens exhibition play a week from today. And when he proves that he's healthy, he's ready for whatever that may bring:

"If I was on the trading block before, I can't imagine all of a sudden I'm not now. My health is something that I obviously need to show to the Red Sox and every other team. If that opens the door to something else, I'll go wherever I go or stay wherever I stay."

Red Sox GM Theo Epstein met with Lowell yesterday to discuss his situation. Coming out of that meeting, Epstein told reporters that if Lowell is "really impressive and impressive to other clubs, then maybe something can be worked out" so that he's traded before Opening Day. Lowell said: "I don't think it hurts to show the fact I can play another position, whether that means I'm more versatile here in Boston *or somewhere else.*"

"I'm highly motivated to show I can play," Lowell added. "Where that takes me, I don't know. We'll see."

Yes, we will.

On an unrelated note: When Texas landed three prospects among the first 17 players ranked on *Baseball America*'s Top 100 Prospects list, revealed yesterday, it was the sixth time in 12 years that a club had done so. But there's something interesting about the other five:

Seattle (2001): Ryan Anderson (8), Ichiro Suzuki (9), Antonio Perez (16)

Minnesota (2003): Joe Mauer (4), Justin Morneau (14), Michael Cuddyer (17)

Arizona (2006): Justin Upton (2), Stephen Drew (5), Conor Jackson (17)

Tampa Bay (2007): Delmon Young (3), Evan Longoria (7), Reid Brignac (17)

Tampa Bay (2008): Evan Longoria (2), David Price (10), Jake McGee (15), Wade Davis (17)

Seattle's group included a world-class international free agent (Suzuki) and a mid-first-rounder (Anderson). Minnesota's included two premium first-rounders (Mauer first overall pick, Cuddyer ninth overall). Arizona's also included a first overall pick (Upton) plus two mid-firsts. Tampa Bay's two groups each included a first overall pick (Young and Price) and a third overall pick (Longoria both times).

Overall, four of those five groups included a player who was the first pick in the nation. The fifth included Ichiro. Those teams were *supposed* to hit big on those players.

That's not to denigrate the terrific job that the Mariners, Twins, Diamondbacks, and Rays did drafting and developing their players, but when you look at the Texas trio (Neftali Feliz, Justin Smoak, and Martin Perez), the two pitchers were not nearly sure things when the Rangers acquired them, and while Smoak was the closest thing to a lock, the 10 teams that drafted ahead of Texas in 2008 didn't all think they were passing on a sure thing. (For what it's worth, not that it's apples to apples, Smoak was chosen later than Mauer and Cuddyer and Upton and Young and Longoria and Price were in their drafts.)

Not sure what any of that means, but I thought it was pretty impressive that the Rangers put three in the top 17 without a Mauer or Upton or Mark Teixeira "birthright prospect" in the bunch.

February 24, 2010

Photographic artistry courtesy of the great Ron Jenkins/*Fort Worth Star-Telegram*

February 24, 2010

According to at least one local reporter, righthander Omar Poveda will have Tommy John surgery on his right elbow, which would wipe out his 2010 season, at least.

Not good news at all. It does conceivably create a 40-man roster spot, as Poveda is an obvious candidate for the 60-day disabled list, but I believe that would require that he's paid his major league split (as opposed to an option, which would trigger the minor league split). Not a meaningful expense, however, if the club encounters a roster crunch at some point this season, if not at the end of camp (plus it saves an option).

Those are side issues, though (particularly since 40-man roster spots aren't so problematic right now). Crummy blow for the Rangers and Poveda, who isn't on the organization's top tier of pitching prospects but who spent nearly the entire 2009 season as a 21-year-old pitching in AA, going 11-5, 4.14 in 22 Frisco starts and who has certain big league potential. The big Venezuelan was likely slated for a rotation spot with Oklahoma City.

There are other camp developments, some positive, some negative, some neither, but nothing that can't wait until the next Newberg Report.

February 25, 2010

The Rangers have voided the contract of infielder Khalil Greene.

February 26, 2010

Hambone dings shoulder
Blast the breaking news sounder!
With Josh: So much ink.

Josh Hamilton is a physical specimen, a powerful, graceful, seven-skills ballplayer who could have pitched or played wide receiver or dominated on a hockey rink.

He's also assaulted his body, on the field and off of it, and given his history, and the recent stack of evidence, his durability will always be part of the profile. With Michael Young, you never ask about durability. With Hamilton, you never don't.

So when Hamilton bruised his left (throwing) shoulder during Wednesday's first full-squad workout of camp reportedly losing his balance while stretching for a pop-up and falling to the ground in what he described as an "embarrassing" moment it was news. Had it happened to David Murphy (and who's to say it hasn't?), we probably wouldn't even know about it.

But this is Josh Hamilton, who in three big league seasons has had documented in-season instances of a rib cage strain, abdominal muscle tear, right wrist sprain, right hamstring strain and left hamstring strain, left knee inflammation, right hand bruise, right foot bruise, groin strain, lower back pinched nerve, gastroenteritis, viral infection, dizziness, and tooth abscess. This is apparently nothing more than a shoulder bruise (with a muscle spasm near his neck), calling for a couple days off the field and some ice, but there's a reason that a minor Milton Bradley injury would get more attention than a Marlon Byrd tweak, that a bark in Brandon McCarthy's throwing arm would have been a bigger story than if it were Matt Harrison.

X-rays on Hamilton's shoulder were happily negative, and he's day-to-day. Not perpetually so, like they used to say about Bradley, but he is for now. Hopefully this story goes away in a week or two and is forgotten by time the games count.

The voiding of Khalil Greene's contract reduces the roster to 41 players (Omar Beltre and Alexi Ogando don't procedurally count against the limit of 40 until camp ends), but don't expect the addition of another veteran infielder until much later in camp, if at all.

For the time being, middle infielder Marcus Lemon has been given a non-roster invite, meaning he will train with the big league squad for at least a couple weeks before returning to minor league camp in preparation for a likely season-opening assignment to Oklahoma City. Nice recognition for Lemon, an all-world character kid whose ceiling is probably on a big league bench but who is solid across the board.

Derek Holland (knee sprain) is hoping to be back on a mound this weekend.

According to Rangers assistant GM Thad Levine, the MRI on righthander Omar Poveda's elbow was "fairly conclusive" in its indication of a tear in the ulnar collateral ligament, but the club awaits a second opinion from Dr. Lewis Yocum before scheduling season-ending Tommy John surgery for the 22-year-old.

Max Ramirez is working out at first base, according to a local report. Meanwhile, Taylor Teagarden is said to be impressing early. As they did in 2009, he and Jarrod Saltalamacchia will alternate starts once exhibition play begins March 6.

There are good things being said about McCarthy's work and first baseman-outfielder Mitch Moreland's bat speed.

Speaking of first base and rave reviews, according to one local report Justin Smoak is defending "significantly better" than he did last spring but Ron Washington is quick to note that Chris Davis is the best defensive first baseman in the American League.

The Rangers signed Plano East product Wes Bankston to a minor league deal. The 26-year-old corner infielder spent the first six years of his pro career in the Rays system, followed by one season with the Athletics (including a 59-at-bat look in Oakland) and one with the Reds. He's a lifetime .277/.341/.467 hitter in the minor leagues.

Word emerges from *Baseball America* assistant editor Ben Badler that the signing bonus Texas gave 16-year-old lefthander Victor Payano late in 2009 months after his $900,000 deal with Boston was voided due to a failed physical was $75,000.

Boston righthander Josh Beckett, set to become a free agent after the season, told reporters last night that he doesn't plan to negotiate an extension with the Red Sox during the season.

Florida and Tampa Bay are reportedly considering Hank Blalock.

The Yankees signed righthander Chan Ho Park. Philadelphia signed outfielder Brad Wilkerson to a minor league deal without an invite to big league camp. Same with Colorado and lefthander Nick Bierbrodt.

Boston released righthander Edwin Moreno after having signed him to a minor league contract last month. The 29-year-old has decided to pitch in Mexico in 2010.

The Fort Worth Cats of the independent American Association re-signed catcher Kelley Gulledge, son of Chuck Morgan. The New Jersey Jackals of the independent Can-Am League signed infielder Enrique Cruz. The Kansas City T-Bones of the independent Northern League signed lefthander Ryan Knippschild.

LSU righthander Anthony Ranaudo, expected by many to be the first pitcher drafted this June, has been scratched for tonight's start with discomfort in his throwing elbow. Team officials are saying it's not a ligament issue. Texas drafted Ranaudo out of a New Jersey high school in the 11th round in 2007 but couldn't persuade him to sign.

The Rangers promoted Mike Daly from Assistant Director of International Scouting, removing "Assistant" from his title.

Oakland has rehired Grady Fuson, naming him special advisor to the baseball operations department. Upon rehiring Fuson, A's GM Billy Beane promptly threw a chair through a wall.

The Rangers' "30 Clubs in 30 Days" feature on MLB Network is set to air on March 25 at 6:00 p.m.

Here's hoping there's no mention in the hour-long program of Josh Hamilton's shoulder.

February 26, 2010

According to more than one local report, right-handed reliever Warner Madrigal had to cut his throwing session short this morning due to tightness in his right elbow. Madrigal has one option remaining, and even without this development the Rangers were likely to exercise it, given the current makeup of the bullpen.

ADDENDUM: The Rangers have clarified some of the media reports regarding Warner Madrigal's arm discomfort it's tightness in Madrigal's forearm, rather than his elbow. Potentially a big difference, and less foreboding.

February 27, 2010

When I was finishing up law school 16 springs ago, the market was much better and I was fortunate to have a job lined up for the fall. It made it pretty easy to occasionally choose Disch-Falk Field over Secured Credit, or a three-hour lunch on the patio at Z'Tejas instead of working on getting the next issue of the journal out. Coasting a bit was priority one. Because I had that job waiting.

That's what seeped into my mind when I read yesterday that Joaquin Arias was not out there doing "voluntary" early infield work with Ron Washington, that veteran Ray Olmedo and first-time invitee Marcus Lemon were, and that Washington said to reporters, on that subject, "We're not babysitting these guys."

Arias shouldn't be coasting. He may be the only infielder on the roster other than the four starters, and he may be out of options, but he doesn't have a job. Yet.

Glad to hear Arias was apparently out there this morning, doing early work.

Rich Harden will pitch in Thursday's exhibition opener, followed by Scott Feldman on Friday. It doesn't lock them in, in that order, as far as the season-opening series in Arlington is concerned, but it's a good indication that things might be headed that way.

Harden should go two innings on Thursday, likely followed by Colby Lewis, Doug Mathis, Ben Snyder, and Pedro Strop. After Feldman's two innings on Friday, C.J. Wilson, Dustin Nippert, Neftali Feliz, and Kasey Kiker are slated to pitch.

According to at least one local report, Warner Madrigal will rest his forearm for a couple days before testing it again, and Omar Poveda will in fact have Tommy John elbow reconstruction surgery this Wednesday. Derek Holland (knee) is throwing a side today for the first time in one week.

February 27, 2010

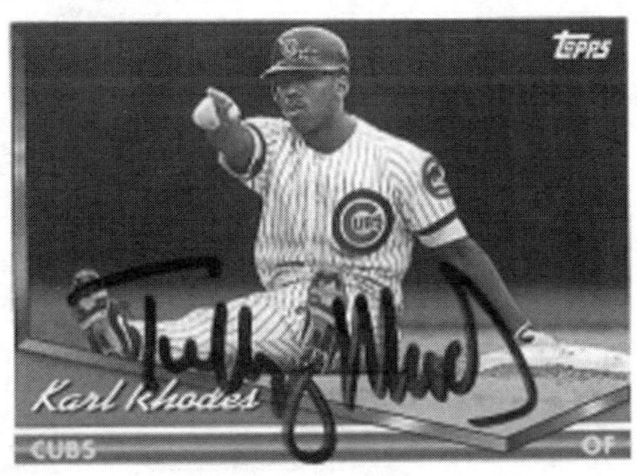

That's my tribute to Max and his first Wildcats game of the season, just completed.

Max's amateur soccer career may end up being no more distinguished than Rhodes's Major League career, but he got this season started off in Tuffy fashion.

Incidentally: The Cubs lost their game, too.

Trivia: Of the eight pitchers to take the hill for the Cubs and Mets in that 1994 opener (NYM 12, CHC 8) that made Tuffy Rhodes famous, the most effective was New York middle reliever Mike Maddux, whose perfect eighth featured a swinging strikeout of former Ranger Steve Buechele (who had singled twice off Dwight Gooden), a groundout from former Ranger farmhand Rey Sanchez, and a swinging strikeout of pinch-hitter Willie Wilson.

February 28, 2010

Robin Yount and Paul Molitor made me want to be a baseball player.

— September 13, 2004 Newberg Report

When I was growing up, the Rangers were so predictably terrible every year, and seemingly comfortable being so uncompetitive, that I cheated a bit by mid-summer and began scanning for a second box score every day before rummaging through the rest of the sports page. By the mid-'80s, it was the Reds . . . . But before that, it was the Yount-Molitor Brewers, with Coop and Simba and Gumby and Vuke and Rollie and Stormin' Gorman. I think there were even years that I had a fitted Milwaukee cap, with its genius logo, and didn't have a Ranger lid. Although Texas was always my team first and foremost, the Brewers were a big deal to me, and remained so, at least marginally, until the Reds pushed them aside.

— March 3, 2003 Newberg Report

According to Scott Miller of SportsLine.com, during a roundtable discussion in Cooperstown in the course of the weekend's Hall of Fame festivities, several Hall of Famers were asked to identify the young player they'd trade their futures for. Johnny Bench chose Albert Pujols. Lou Brock picked Miguel Cabrera. And Paul Molitor selected Young.

— July 29, 2004 Newberg Report

[Young is] going to change positions at some point. It may be this year, it may be next year, it may be after that. It's going to happen, and I suspect he knows it, and understands it. There's some merit to the Paul Molitor comp.

— November 7, 2008 Newberg Report

I want to ask all five of you [Michael Young, Chuck Greenberg, Jake Krug, Chuck Morgan, and Jamey Newberg] who your favorite Rangers player is. We all get emails from Jamey every couple days that are kind of like love letters to Michael Young, so Jamey, you can tell us who your second favorite is.

— a fan at the February 2, 2010 Newberg Report Q&A event at Sherlock's

The Young-Molitor comps have resurfaced this week, this time trained on the idea that it wouldn't be unprecedented for Young, like Molitor, to be even better after turning 33 than he was before. (Molitor hit .298/.361/.432 in his career until that age, and .316/.378/.466 thereafter in nearly as many games, sealing his Hall of Fame credentials.) Young's numbers through age 32 (.302/.349/.449) are actually a shade better than Molitor's were, but it's more about what Molitor did in the second half of his career that Young is focused on.

"The guy is a huge motivator for me," Young told Evan Grant of the *Dallas Morning News*. "He had a lot of success, including winning a World Series, from the mid-point in his career until the end. He was a guy who always seemed to raise the bar. He was an animal for the last eight years of his career. I know he's the exception to the rule, but it can be done. You have to trust your approach to the game and . . . keep yourself prepared, physically and mentally."

Where I hope the comparison breaks down is that while Molitor was a Brewer for the first half of his career before splitting the second half split evenly between Milwaukee, Toronto, and Minnesota, I'm hopeful that Young accomplishes everything Molitor did, including winning a World Series (in 1993, when he was the MVP runner-up in his age 36-37 season), but would just assume it all happens here.

Young on Molitor: "I love talking hitting with him and would talk it all day long with him, if I could. I think we are kind of the same way in the way we approach hitting. And I hope I can keep raising the bar for myself, too."

The young player that Molitor singled out six years ago is now the veteran player who looks to Molitor as motivation for the back half of his career. Not so much the Cooperstown bullet point as the sustained productivity. The approach and the preparation and the adjustments. The World Series title.

The player who made me want to be a baseball player, and the player who makes Max want to be a baseball player.

So endeth this love letter.

MARCH 2010

40-MAN ROSTER (41*)

PITCHERS (21)

Omar Beltre, Scott Feldman, Neftali Feliz, Frankie Francisco, Rich Harden, Matt Harrison, Derek Holland, Tommy Hunter, Eric Hurley, Michael Kirkman, Colby Lewis, Warner Madrigal, Doug Mathis, Brandon McCarthy, Luis Mendoza, Guillermo Moscoso, Dustin Nippert, Darren O'Day, Alexi Ogando, Darren Oliver, Zach Phillips, Omar Poveda, Chris Ray, Ben Snyder, Pedro Strop, C.J. Wilson

CATCHERS (3)

Max Ramirez, Jarrod Saltalamacchia, Taylor Teagarden

INFIELDERS (5)

Elvis Andrus, Joaquin Arias, Chris Davis, Ian Kinsler, Michael Young

OUTFIELDERS (7)

Brandon Boggs, Julio Borbon, Nelson Cruz, Craig Gentry, Vladimir Guerrero, Josh Hamilton, David Murphy

** Per MLB rules, righthanders Beltre and Ogando were permitted to participate in spring training without counting against the 40-man roster.*

March 1, 2010

Two days of intrasquad games kick off today, and with them will be natural overreaction, melodrama over a AA pitcher's perfect inning of work against the starting lineup or a three-run shot by Matt Brown or Chad Tracy or Toby Hall off a veteran reliever.

Some of us will probably take the time to think about, and maybe even write about, how many pitches it took Rich Harden to get his three outs and how many of those pitches found the strike zone. Some reliever the team is counting on to hold down a key role will put up a 0.2-3-3-3-2-0 line, and it will generate message board threads and maybe even a blog entry or Tweet from a veteran beat writer that he couldn't even complete his allotted inning of work. If Vladimir Guerrero goes deep off Luis Mendoza and Ben Snyder, it will be reported one way. If Brandon McCarthy surrenders a Rey Olmedo homer and issues a Joaquin Arias walk, it will be written up another.

I'll apologize in advance for any overreacting with which I might assault you on the heels of these two scrimmages that don't even amount to official exhibition games, whose stats and results are subject to wasted hyperbole themselves.

I'll apologize, but that doesn't mean I won't go there. It's been 148 days since a Texas Rangers baseball game of any sort, and when Ron Washington says, regarding today's and tomorrow's intrasquad games, "We'll get the adrenaline going a little bit," he's talking about you and me, too.

Rain wiped out yesterday's Rangers-Royals Home Run Derby, and will wipe out my kid's first Little League machine pitch practice for the third straight week today, but it better not get in the way of Rangers vs. Rangers this afternoon, at 12:00 Surprise time. Not acceptable.

March 2, 2010

I shouldn't overreact to what Julio Borbon, Engel Beltre, Matt Brown, and Mitch Moreland did in yesterday's intrasquad game, or what Rich Harden, Pedro Strop, Tanner Scheppers, or Alexi Ogando did (especially given, in the case of the latter two, who was in the game offensively for the opposition by that time), and I won't. (Got that out of my system yesterday in my shadow-Twittering of Evan Grant's play-by-play.) But I will say one thing.

If the early reports out of Surprise, not just yesterday afternoon but in the days leading up to it as well, about Moreland are a fair indication of what's going on, this could be a very, very, very good thing for the Rangers. This year.

March 3, 2010

As a reminder to myself that it's pretty much all downhill from here, that all good things going forward may turn out to be flukes, if not mirages . . . on this, the day I turn 41, I throw down a photo of the lefthander who was the greatest flop in Newberg Report projection history:

Watch Out for Juan Carlos Vegas Moreno. Number 41.
He might be creepin' up on ya.
Now get off my lawn.

March 4, 2010

Since arriving in camp, outfielder Brandon Boggs, recovering from a shoulder injury, has been allowed to do everything but slide.

For the last week or so, I've pretty much allowed myself to do *nothing* but slide.

Sorry for the half-baked-ness the last few days. I should have time for a full-length report tomorrow morning.

Tune into The Fan (105.3 FM) for today's first Cactus League pitch, at 2:05 p.m. Rich Harden takes the ball to open the bottom of the first, and Colby Lewis, Doug Mathis, Ben Snyder, and Pedro Strop are slated to follow.

March 5, 2010

Rites of spring training
Nadel calls a Jimmy Jack
The season's begun

Fun to do bad things
Borbon creating havoc
Makes the offense go

Harden and Scheppers
Seven groundouts, and no flies
Present and future

Prospect bats pitch in
Moreland, Brown, Tracy, Gentry
Is this '86??

Thirteen Ranger runs
But was pitching the real story?
Seven hits, one walk

A ton of interesting things to touch on from Texas 13, Kansas City 3, from Rich Harden's efficiency despite working in the upper 80s, to Matt Brown's sizzling day at the plate (and clunky one at third base), to Tanner Scheppers and Alexi Ogando tripping efficient upper-90s, to Hit Dog Mitch Moreland, to an offense that racked up more walks (five) than strikeouts (four), and a pitching staff that fanned just five itself but issued only one walk, to a Jarrod Saltalamacchia cannon blast that came on a two-strike count, to an attack that put 20 runners in scoring position—and converted on eight of them, to Julio being Julio.

Still, a 10-run win to open Cactus League play is no more indicative of what this team is going to achieve in 2010 than a left fielder's prediction of 96 wins, or a team president's forecast of 92.

What to make of the win total guesses? Not much. You don't go into a game in late May and say, "Hey, we're a 91-win team, so we ought to beat those guys tonight," or, riding a three-game win streak, "We're supposed to be a .500 club, so no big deal if we give a couple games back this weekend."

It's about winning the next game on the schedule, no matter what the pre-season predictions say, and doing it more times over the course of the season than at least 10 other teams in the league.

A 10-run win counts the same as a one-run win, and neither counts at all when it happens in March. But, yeah, as meaningless as yesterday's game was, that sure was some meaningless greatness.

(Want some video highlights from the game? Check out www.foxsportssouthwest.com, where I'm also providing spring training notes most days this month. Scroll down the "Latest Headlines" on the right side for the Newberg Report entries.)

There was nothing more exhilarating yesterday than listening to Scheppers and Ogando make what amounted to their pro debuts on the mound. Despite both being converted position players, the two couldn't have more different backgrounds, with Scheppers closer to pro ball in a sense than any fellow draftee last summer (having pitched in the independent leagues) and Ogando arguably further away from the minor leagues than any prospect in baseball, having been banished from stateside entry due to his getting caught up in a visa fraud scandal five years ago just as his transition from hitter to pitcher was about to kick off.

Scheppers retired the Royals in order in the sixth, needing just seven pitches to get three ground ball outs, five of which were fastballs that registered between 96 and 98, all for strikes, mostly low in the zone. Ogando worked at 95-99 in the eighth, and his one strikeout came on an 89-mph change.

Saltalamacchia's majestic three-run blast in the second inning, which nearly cleared the berm in right center field, came off Royals righthander Kyle Davies, whom Saltalamacchia caught twice in 2006 with AA Mississippi (on August 1, when he went 2 for 2 with two walks, and caught two no-hit innings from Davies and five no-hit innings from Matt Harrison; and again on August 11) and twice in 2007 with Atlanta (on May 27, when he hit his first big league home run [off Cole Hamels]; and on June 6).

Ron Washington told reporters this week that Saltalamacchia and Taylor Teagarden are "dead even" in the battle to win the starting catcher job. Teagarden should get today's start at catcher, with Scott Feldman, Dustin Nippert, C.J. Wilson, Neftali Feliz, and Kasey Kiker among those slated to pitch. Zack Greinke gets the Kansas City nod.

Despite getting a considerable amount of work in camp at first base, Max Ramirez came off the bench to relieve Saltalamacchia behind the plate yesterday. Ramirez caught Scheppers, Ben Snyder, Ogando, and Pedro Strop, who combined to allow one unearned run on three hits and no walks in four innings, fanning three.

More scheduled pitching assignments: Tommy Hunter and Harrison tomorrow. Brandon McCarthy, Guillermo Moscoso, and Luis Mendoza on Sunday. Colby Lewis (one perfect 11-pitch frame yesterday) and Derek Holland (whose knee sprain is evidently no longer an issue) on Monday. Harden and Mathis on Tuesday, when Darren Oliver is set to make his spring debut. Today's foursome then gets split, with Wilson and Feliz going on Wednesday and Feldman and Nippert pitching Thursday.

One beat writer suggests that Feliz "has not yet started throwing well," which may stall his rotation candidacy enough that it never really materializes in camp.

Righthanders Chris Ray and Warner Madrigal have thrown bullpens, and Holland and righthander Omar Beltre have thrown live batting practice. Progress for each of them. Righthander Eric Hurley threw a side but isn't expected to see any exhibition game action this spring. Righthander Omar Poveda had Tommy John surgery Wednesday and will miss the 2010 season.

Josh Hamilton didn't play Thursday, still nursing his bruised left shoulder. He's resumed conditioning drills, hit off a tee yesterday, and is apparently shooting for game action early next week. He says throwing is causing more pain than swinging a bat right now.

I'm not sure I'd seen this reported anywhere a year ago, but according to a note this week from Jon Heyman of *Sports Illustrated*, Hamilton turned down a four-year, $24 million contract offer from the Rangers last year, one that would have covered him through his arbitration seasons.

For now, Nelson Cruz is hitting sixth, one spot ahead of Chris Davis, but the plan, assuming Davis earns it, is to have the two flip spots before the season begins, allowing Washington to break up the trio of Vladimir Guerrero, Ian Kinsler, and Cruz with a left-handed hitter to force more late-inning bullpen moves.

When Rangers officials (including Jon Daniels, Washington, and A.J. Preller) flew down to the organization's Dominican Republic Academy last month, they had Cruz, Elvis Andrus, Borbon, Feliz, and Strop address a group of Rangers minor leaguers. An offshoot of that program was, according to ESPN's Jorge Arangure, a meeting between Washington and Cruz in which the manager challenged his right fielder to take on a greater leadership role in Arlington this season.

The stories about Andrus's level of focus in camp lasted one news cycle. I sort of like that it became a story. Probably good for him.

Two local reporters have suggested this week that the Rangers would like to keep Snyder (who retired the two left-handed hitters he faced yesterday) even if the Rule 5 pick doesn't make the Opening Day staff (there may not be a job open if Wilson and Oliver both start the season in the bullpen) and could approach San Francisco with a trade offer to allow them to option the lefthander to the minors, but both reports are missing a key fact: Snyder would first have to clear league-wide waivers before Texas could negotiate such a trade.

Speaking of March trades: (1) one local report suggests Texas remains interested in Arizona utility infielder Augie Ojeda; (2) there's also some sentiment that St. Louis could make middle infielder Julio Lugo available and that the Rangers could be interested; and (3) Nick Cafardo of the *Boston Globe* believes Minnesota could get in on Mike Lowell if he proves in Red Sox camp that he's healthy. Lowell took batting practice on Monday, without incident.

Tim Marchman of *Sports Illustrated* ranked baseball's general managers on Thursday. Daniels was number eight. Said Marchman:

General managers are always going on about the virtues of building a strong farm system, and what they generally mean is that they want to win major league games so they can keep their jobs. Daniels has actually built a preposterously good system (Justin Smoak, Neftali Feliz, Derek Holland) over the last few years, bringing in talent every way you can, and now has his team positioned to contend for the next several years. That he has kept the major league team perfectly respectable on modest payrolls while overseeing this rebuilding project is really very impressive, and with a good run over the next couple of years he could well move up on this list.

Kevin Goldstein of Baseball Prospectus released his Top 101 Prospects list this week. Feliz checked in at number three (behind Nationals righthander Stephen Strasburg and Braves outfielder Jason Heyward), Martin Perez was number 15 (the top lefthander next to number 10 Aroldis Chapman), Justin Smoak was number 17 (the top first baseman next to number 11 Chris Carter), and Scheppers was number 68.

Andy Silverman (Executive Vice President, Sales) and Dale Petroskey (Executive Vice President, Marketing and Community Development) are leaving the Rangers organization. Silverman will join the Marlins, who are opening a new ballpark in 2012, as their Vice President for Sales and Service. Both have been good friends to the Newberg Report, and are true professionals.

I'm happy for Victor Rojas but saddened that he's leaving MLB Network for the Angels television booth, where he'll handle play-by-play duties.

The Marlins and Rays have each reportedly made offers to Hank Blalock, but in each case they are apparently minor league deals.

Minor league deals: righthander Jason Jennings (Oakland), righthander Wes Littleton (Seattle), and third baseman Travis Metcalf (Colorado).

Outfielder Rocco Baldelli, rumored over the winter to be a potential Rangers target, is taking a special assistant's position in the Tampa Bay front office. He's not ruling out an eventual return as a player but is limited at the moment by a shoulder injury.

Seattle outfielder Milton Bradley on his miserable 2009 season with the Cubs: "Two years ago, I played, and I was good. I go to Chicago, not good. I've been good my whole career. So, obviously, it was something with Chicago, not me."

The Rangers are wearing a patch on their uniform sleeves this spring to honor the late Bobby Bragan.

We need to have a bunch of framing done at our law firm (paintings, diplomas, etc.). If that's something you do and you're interested in the job, let me know.

No broadcast of today's game (a rarity this spring). No big deal, right, since these games don't count?

Can't wait for a box score.

March 7, 2010

This time of year there's one email I get twice as much as any other: "Got any tips for a first-time trip to Surprise?" My answer every time is generally the same. "Get yourself to the back fields at 10 a.m. every day."

If you're at Rangers camp now, and you're taking that advice, you're going to have some company today.

Josh Hamilton is reportedly pushing for a spot in the Rangers lineup in the 10 a.m. "B" game (weather permitting) against the Royals, as the majority of the starting lineup prepares to travel half an hour south to Goodyear to take on Cleveland in the club's regularly scheduled game.

And slated to get the Texas start in that "B" game: Tanner Scheppers.

Not that there won't be interest in seeing how righthanders Brandon McCarthy, Guillermo Moscoso, and Luis Mendoza fare against the Indians, but after Scheppers, who has yet to throw a pitch that counts since signing as the Rangers' supplemental first-round pick last summer, sat 96-98 in a perfect seven-pitch inning against Kansas City on Thursday, not even showing his plus curve, his follow-up effort should be a stopdown for lots of folks this morning—even if Hamilton (who took batting practice against Omar Beltre and Warner Madrigal on Saturday and went yard to the opposite field off each) weren't possibly slated to lead off each of six innings as the Texas DH.

Lefthanders Michael Kirkman and Zach Phillips are scheduled to follow Scheppers in the "B" game.

The quiet surprise of camp so far? Maybe Matt Harrison, who reportedly sat 93-95 with a plus cutter yesterday, firing two perfect innings and getting all six of his outs on the ground.

If Harrison—don't forget, younger than Moscoso, Madrigal, and Doug Mathis—takes the next step this year, and if Jarrod Saltalamacchia builds off what's been a solid early camp, and both move toward establishing themselves as core players, think about what the discussion about the Mark Teixeira trade will sound like.

Rangers pitchers through three games: 1.73 ERA, 15 strikeouts and two walks (over 26 innings), 43 groundouts and 15 flyouts, no home runs.

In those 26 innings, Texas pitchers have permitted five earned runs.

Which is one fewer than Kevin Millwood gave up in just two-thirds of an inning yesterday. Ten Detroit hitters: one home run (leadoff hitter Clete Thomas), one double, five singles, one walk, two flyouts (and a balk tossed in as well). Doesn't mean a lot, but that's a pretty ugly Orioles debut.

Julio Borbon was held out of action on Saturday with a sore right forearm muscle, suffered while diving for a ball on Friday. Not expected to be serious.

Isolated moments in spring training may not mean a whole lot, but it's fair to assume that Matt Brown's second throwing error in three half-games at third base (each, as I recall, leading to an unearned run) isn't going to be written off by Ron Washington. Leury Garcia's error yesterday was as costly, but not as critical in the bigger picture.

Check out Scott Lucas's lengthy essay on Michael Young's chances to reach 3,000 hits.

Tampa Bay is reportedly on the verge of signing Hank Blalock to a non-roster contract, making him a candidate to back up Carlos Pena at first base, Evan Longoria at third base, and Pat Burrell at DH. Not a lot of opportunity there defensively, but Burrell is someone Blalock could conceivably start to take more than just platoon at-bats away from.

Righthander Jason Grilli, in camp with Cleveland on a non-roster deal, tore his right quadriceps while running sprints and could miss the season.

The forecast for Cactus League rain is stronger today than it is for North Texas, but if the weather holds up, you can tune into Texas-Cleveland on KRLD 1080-AM at 2:05 Central time.

March 8, 2010: TROT COFFEY

- Nick Cafardo of the *Boston Globe* dropped this note on Sunday: *Josh Hamilton, RF, Rangers—Scouts are watching him in Arizona in case the Rangers entertain thoughts of dealing him before the end of spring training. Said a National League scout, "Everybody in Texas denies it, and I don't know what to base it on, but there's a feeling the Rangers may do something, and teams want to be ready."*

Well, nobody's untouchable.

But it doesn't make a lot of sense to deal an affordable player who's under control for the next three seasons, and who's a difference-maker when healthy, unless you're blown away by a trade offer, and given what Hamilton went through in 2009, and the fact that he's not healthy at the moment, you're not only not going to get blown away—you're going to get offers of 25 cents on the dollar. Teams sell low when there's an overriding reason to desperately want to rid themselves of a player.

Plus, this is a scout talking to a beat writer in another market—neither of whom is "close to the situation"—and he admits he "[doesn't] know what to base it on." Move along, folks. There's *almost surely* nothing to see here.

A few more things:

1. Outfielder Brandon Boggs (left biceps tendinitis) and first baseman Justin Smoak (left hip flexor) were held out of baseball activities yesterday and will be evaluated today.

2. The Texas Rangers Women's Club is seeking new members for its volunteer organization. If you are at least age 18 and interested in helping hand out promotional items at the gates before home games, e-mail Martha Meyer (Vice President-Membership) at marthakm1@gmail.com, or check out www.trwc.net. Members can work as many or as few games as they wish, and can park at no cost, buy half-price food at the concession

stands, and attend the games for free after finishing their work at the gates. Annual dues are only $22 per year plus a one-time $7 badge fee, and dues go toward various group outings and monthly charitable efforts.

3. Apropos of nothing, T.R. Sullivan posted this excerpt yesterday by my favorite author, Michael Chabon, from his newest book *Manhood for Amateurs*:

What's important was that baseball, after all these years of artificial turf and expansion and the designated hitter and drugs and free agency and thousand-dollar bubble-gum cards, is still a gift given by fathers to sons.

4. Kevin Goldstein of Baseball Prospectus jumps on ESPN Radio in Dallas with Ben & Skin at 11:40 this morning to discuss why he doesn't think as highly of Elvis Andrus as most others do.

March 9, 2010

The moment that stuck out for me last night as we recorded the latest edition of Rangers Podcast in Arlington was when our guest Eric Nadel recounted something Fergie Jenkins told him in Pompano Beach in 1979, Nadel's first spring with the Rangers. It went something like this: "All this stuff you're seeing in these spring training games? Ignore it. It's *spring training*."

It's good advice, but when the results belong to players clearly competing for a job, they probably can't be discounted completely.

In other words, when you view the work put in so far by Matt Harrison (outstanding), Brandon McCarthy (inconsistent), and Derek Holland (sputtering), the three primary candidates for the number five spot in the rotation, it's hard not to view Harrison as the leader at this point. There's nearly a month to go, and things can change, but Harrison is off to an encouraging start.

And this isn't just about a couple innings of work. Harrison came to camp 30 pounds more fit, fully recovered from thoracic outlet syndrome, toting an extra three ticks on the radar gun (now touching 97). As Nadel points out in the Podcast, results aren't as important in a competition like this one as consistency, stuff, command, and efficiency, and right now Harrison appears to be ahead of McCarthy and Holland in all four categories.

Josh Hamilton had two singles in three trips yesterday, his first game action of camp, and made two uneventful plays in left field.

Tanner Scheppers wowed onlookers on Thursday, pumping upper-90s heat in a swift, perfect seven-pitch inning against the Royals, keeping his power curve in his pocket. He unleashed the curve in a "B" game yesterday, throwing three of them, all for strikes, two of them going for strike three.

The Scheppers fastball gets lots of attention (ranked by *Baseball America* among the top five in minor league baseball), but *BA* also says that, in a system with a number of plus curves (Martin Perez, Danny Gutierrez, Jake Brigham), it's Scheppers whose bender is the best.

BA also projects Scheppers to be the Rangers closer in 2013. Don't bet against him figuring in somewhere near the top of the rotation instead.

Lots more from *BA*'s Prospect Handbook—here's the publication's top 30 Rangers prospects:

1. Neftali Feliz, RHP
2. Justin Smoak, 1B
3. Martin Perez, LHP
4. Tanner Scheppers, RHP
5. Jurickson Profar, SS
6. Kasey Kiker, LHP
7. Robbie Ross, LHP
8. Mitch Moreland, 1B-OF
9. Danny Gutierrez, RHP
10. Wilmer Font, RHP
11. Max Ramirez, C
12. Joe Wieland, RHP
13. Luis Sardinas, SS
14. Engel Beltre, OF
15. Leury Garcia, SS
16. Michael Kirkman, LHP
17. Blake Beavan, RHP
18. Tommy Mendonca, 3B
19. Guillermo Moscoso, RHP
20. Omar Poveda, RHP
21. Michael Main, RHP
22. Miguel Velazquez, OF
23. Pedro Strop, RHP
24. Neil Ramirez, RHP
25. Jake Brigham, RHP
26. Tomas Telis, C
27. Wilfredo Boscan, RHP
28. Craig Gentry, OF
29. Andrew Doyle, RHP
30. Richard Alvarez, RHP

BA's assessment of the organization's best tools:

Best Hitter for Average	Justin Smoak
Best Power Hitter	Justin Smoak
Best Strike-Zone Discipline	Justin Smoak
Fastest Baserunner	Leury Garcia
Best Athlete	Greg Golson
(published, obviously, before he was traded to the Yankees)	
Best Fastball	Neftali Feliz
Best Curveball	Tanner Scheppers
Best Slider	Robbie Ross
Best Changeup	Kasey Kiker
Best Control	Blake Beavan
Best Defensive Catcher	Leonel De Los Santos
Best Defensive Infielder	Leury Garcia
Best Infield Arm	Leury Garcia

Best Defensive Outfielder Craig Gentry
Best Outfield Arm Greg Golson

It's interesting how Perez, considered by most experts to be one of the two best lefthander prospects in baseball, isn't even listed atop any of the "best pitch" categories.

The depth of this standout system is unquestionably on the mound.

BA's projected 2013 lineup:

Catcher	Taylor Teagarden (same as last year's 2012 projection)
First Base	Justin Smoak (same)
Second Base	Ian Kinsler (same)
Third Base	Michael Young (same)
Shortstop	Elvis Andrus (same)
Left Field	Josh Hamilton (last year: Julio Borbon)
Center Field	Julio Borbon (last year: Engel Beltre)
Right Field	Nelson Cruz (last year: Hamilton)
Designated Hitter	Chris Davis (same)
No. 1 Starter	Neftali Feliz (same)
No. 2 Starter	Martin Perez (last year: Derek Holland)
No. 3 Starter	Derek Holland (last year: Perez)
No. 4 Starter	Scott Feldman (last year: Michael Main)
No. 5 Starter	Tommy Hunter (last year: Matt Harrison)
Closer	Tanner Scheppers (last year: Blake Beavan)

After several years of multiple changes in the projected lineup, there's some stability now in terms of how the position players project three years down the road.

BA ranks 88 Rangers prospects position by position, and while I won't run all of those down (I'd encourage you to buy the book, whose Rangers chapter was written by Aaron Fitt), I'll tell you for example that, after the left-handed starters who show up in the top 30 (Perez at 3, Kiker at 6, Ross at 7, Kirkman at 16), *BA* ranks further southpaw starters this way: Robbie Erlin, Chad Bell, Richard Bleier, Tim Murphy, Paul Strong, and Edwin Escobar.

According to *BA*, righthander Matt Nevarez is the number 15 prospect and infielder Jose Vallejo is not among the top 30 in the Astros system, which is ranked last overall among the 30 organizations.

Neither catcher Manny Pina nor outfielder Tim Smith is among Kansas City's top 30 prospects. Gutierrez, obtained by Texas for those two, is the number nine Rangers prospect, though he'll start the season under a 50-game league suspension after testing positive for a prescribed ADHD medication called Adderall that he didn't obtain a Therapeutic Use Exemption for in advance. The Royals are ranked 17th overall, while the Rangers are number two.

Outfielder John Mayberry Jr. was eligible but not ranked among the Phillies' top 30 prospects.

Righthander Thomas Diamond is not listed among the Cubs' top 86 prospects.

Righthander Graham Stoneburner, the younger brother of Rangers minor league infielder Davis Stoneburner, is the Yankees' number 21 prospect. Not sure where Golson would have fit; he was still with Texas at the time the book was printed, and not among the top 30 Rangers.

BA revealed yesterday that the 17-year-old Profar, who has yet to play a professional inning, got Top 100 Prospect votes on three of the four ballots (each of which included 150 players) though he failed to crack the overall top 100. He was number 74 on one voter's ballot. Ross was also listed on three ballots, getting a high vote of number 96. Font was number 57 on one voter's ballot—and not listed among the top 150 on the other three. Also listed on one ballot: Kiker (number 112) and Moreland (130).

Smoak got treatment for his sort left hip flexor yesterday and hopes to play today.

Hank Blalock is back in Port Charlotte, where he first made noise a decade ago as an uber-prospect on the verge of becoming a perennial contender for batting titles. The 29-year-old has signed a minor league deal with Tampa Bay for $925,000, with an extra $350,000 based on plate appearance incentives. Those bonuses may be hard to come by unless Carlos Pena or Evan Longoria gets hurt, or unless Blalock is able to take at-bats away from Pat Burrell.

While it's not confirmed, there's speculation that Blalock has an out clause if he's not added to the active Rays roster at some point late in camp. Makes sense.

March 9, 2010

He's not Erasmo Ramirez, and he's not Elizardo Ramirez. He's Edwar Ramirez, and the Rangers have acquired him from the Yankees for cash considerations.

New York designated the 28-year-old righthander for assignment nine days ago. After posting a 3.55 ERA with 63 strikeouts in 55.1 innings out of the Yankees bullpen in 2008 (.215 opponents' batting average), Ramirez posted a 5.73 ERA with 22 strikeouts in 22 innings in 2009, spending most of the year in AAA.

Texas adds Ramirez to the 40-man roster, which is now full. Out of options, he may be this year's Joe Koshansky, a player the club claims in hopes that it can get him through waivers itself closer to Opening Day. The other possibility is that the added depth that he provides could create trade opportunities involving another right-handed reliever. Decent arm to take a flier on.

In less uplifting news, Jarrod Saltalamacchia was scratched from today's game with soreness in the area where he had a rib surgically removed last year to improve circulation. Team physician Dr. Keith Meister is optimistic that the soreness is merely a result of the breaking up of scar tissue. Saltalamacchia will be re-evaluated tomorrow.

CORRECTION: Ramirez does have an option remaining. Changes things a bit, though when the time comes to pare down the 40-man roster to make room for Omar Beltre and Alexi Ogando (and an infielder, and possibly two), Ramirez could be a candidate for a second designation for assignment in a month. But if the 40-man roster crunch doesn't cost Ramirez a spot, Texas can option him to the farm without having to get him through waivers first (which distinguishes him, for instance, from Luis Mendoza).

March 10, 2010

I checked this morning on newly acquired righthander Edwar Ramirez's career splits, just for grins. The samples are all small, given that the reliever pitched just one full season for the Yankees and parts of two others, but facing nine batters in Rangers Ballpark, he got seven of them out, allowing two singles and no walks while fanning three in those 2.1 innings of work.

He's been pretty good against the Mariners and Athletics (at least those who suited up between 2007 and 2009), firing 10 scoreless innings (three hits [all singles] and 13 strikeouts, though an unsightly seven walks).

But keep the changeup artist off the mound against the Angels: 6.2 innings, 14 earned runs (18.90 ERA) on 16 hits and six walks (.485/.548/.909), eight strikeouts.

In the bigger picture, the key objective with Ramirez will be to cut his walk rate (5.13 per nine innings) so that the club can feel confident taking advantage of his extraordinary strikeout rate (10.62 per nine) in high-leverage situations. Or any situations at all.

Randy Galloway said on his radio show yesterday that he asked five Rangers officials who the club's first baseman will be in 2012: Chris Davis or Justin Smoak?

According to Galloway, the leading answer: Mitch Moreland.

I have some thoughts on that, but without going into much detail today, the half-baked scenario cooking in my head is that Davis or Smoak gets traded this July, maybe with Derek Holland or Matt Harrison, plus Wilmer Font or Engel Beltre, to the Giants for righthander Matt Cain (who has a $4.25 million salary plus a $6.25 million club option for 2011 that could escalate to $8.15 million) and right-handed corner bat Mark DeRosa (set to earn $12 million in 2010-2011).

Nolan Ryan was on Galloway's show yesterday and singled out righthanders Joe Wieland and Matt Thompson as back field arms who have impressed him this week. Wieland was an instant favorite of Ryan's when the sturdy 20-year-old arrived two summers ago.

Kevin Goldstein of Baseball Prospectus ranked baseball's farm systems, with the Mariners coming in at number 23, the Angels at 20, the A's at seven (after last year's number one nod), and the Rangers at two, behind Tampa Bay. Goldstein on the Texas system, which he ranked number two last year as well:

Why They Are Here: *No system in baseball can match a left/right pitching prospect combination like Neftali Feliz and Martin Perez, and there's just an embarrassment of riches after than when it comes to young arms. The system is actually below average when it comes to hitting prospects, but Justin Smoak is a future three-hole hitter, and Jurickson Profar could explode.*

Where They Will Be Next Year: *It will be tough to repeat this high of a ranking, as Feliz will be gone, while Smoak could be as well. Two first-round picks will certainly help, but overall, we're looking at a net loss 12 months from now, albeit not the kind anyone should be complaining about.*

Four spring games for Matt Brown, three throwing errors from third base.

Hank Blalock's out clause with Tampa Bay allows him to ask for his release if he's not on the roster as of April 1. The Rays would have a defined period of days at that point to add him to the roster or let him go.

Richard Durrett turned in a solid, lengthy feature on Jon Daniels at the ESPN Dallas website. Check it out.

March 12, 2010

Fewest walks in league,
Best batting clip in AZ
Who cares about wins?

About time for me to get myself out to Surprise, but before that to share with you this year's version of the annual "32 things I'm looking forward to seeing" list:

1. Tanner Scheppers. Huge. Quickly.
2. Alexi Ogando. Omar Beltre, too. But Ogando has a better chance to make me come away from Surprise with the same feeling I got after seeing Ian Kinsler, Derek Holland, and Scheppers for the first time in camp.
3. Outfielder Miguel Velazquez, who was limited physically when I saw him at Fall Instructs. I'll squint a little to see if he's a young Nelson Cruz for me, as he is for many others.
4. In 2007, I was eager to see the trio of Summer 2006 Latin American bonus babies (Wilmer Font, Carlos Pimentel, and Geuris Grullon) so I could begin

to differentiate them. This year's group: Chad Bell, Paul Strong, Shawn Blackwell, Nick McBride, and Andrew Doyle. (Robbie Erlin has already separated himself for me—can he do in his first full season what Robbie Ross did in his?)

5. Sixteen-year-old catcher Jorge Alfaro. Macumba, too, primarily to see where the bat is.

6. For some pitching phenom to get absolutely spanked—then to see how he responds in the following inning.

7. Vladimir Guerrero and Chris Davis batting practice sessions.

8. When I saw 16-year-old Jurickson Profar at Fall Instructs, he was a man among boys playing with and against kids a couple years older. Will he stand out in camp, too? Bet on it.

9. If I make it to any big league games, Mitch Moreland against someone with a vested pension. Justin Smoak, too, but Moreland is the gotta-see-this-guy right now.

10. That 0 percent chance of rain that weather.com is promising.

11. The new Matt Harrison.

12. The new Wilfredo Boscan and the new Johnny Whittleman and the new Neil Ramirez.

13. Elvis, of course. Hopefully not a new one.

14. Is there a newness that Blake Beavan's ready to unleash? If so, that could be big.

15. Ron Washington's interaction with Joaquin Arias. Clint Hurdle's interaction with everyone.

16. Nolan Ryan's watchful back-fields gaze: Where is it trained?

17. Lefthander Miguel De Los Santos, assuming he's in camp. Is it real?

18. I want to see how Danny Gutierrez is handling his challenge.

19. Matt Brown taking infield.

20. Colby Lewis, v.2.

21. Matt Thompson, a serious breakout candidate.

22. Take a look at the service time of the Rangers' various late-inning relief options. Chris Ray could be an important piece of the bigger puzzle. (Aside: Kevin Millwood pitched for the second time last night, and got drilled again: five earned runs on nine hits and a walk over 2.2 innings.)

23. Tommy Mendonca, in drills and in games. Engel Beltre, in games. At the plate. Julio Borbon, on defense.

24. Michael Main. It's time.

25. The very different comic stylings of Wayne Kirby and Don Welke.

26. Max Ramirez. It's obviously a massively huge time for him.

27. I still have a little interest in seeing if Cristian Santana can take the next step. A little.

28. Whatever it is that holds Max's attention this year. And some cool memory with the kids that comes anywhere close to Erica's interview of Josh Hamilton last year or Ron Washington's fungo to 3-year-old Max two years ago.

29. How C.J. Wilson and Neftali Feliz respond if and when their rotation auditions end.

30. How Derek Holland responds if he's reassigned to minor league camp while I'm there, not as a punishment but in an effort to get him stretched out as a starter while the remaining rotation candidates begin to fall into their usage routines.

31. Writing. Lots and lots of writing. (Now's a good time to tell your pals who make you forward reports to them from time to time to go ahead and sign up themselves. Free, and easy, like Feliz cheese: Just go to the website and click "Mailing List.")

32. Martin Perez. There are a handful of young blue-chip arms in this organization, some with big league experience and some without it, who are locks to figure in over the next few years while the core of the Rangers lineup is still intact. None, however, has as clearly visualized a role as Perez.

See you from sunny Surprise.

March 13, 2010

The Rangers have reportedly claimed 25-year-old infielder Hernan Iribarren off waivers, according to a report out of Milwaukee. Iribarren, out of options, had been designated for assignment last week by the Brewers.

Primarily a second baseman, Iribarren has big league experience at third base and in the outfield as well. The lack of shortstop duty is interesting, given the Rangers' roster needs.

No word yet on who Texas is removing from the 40-man roster to make room for Iribarren.

UPDATE: Texas has reportedly placed righthander Eric Hurley on the 60-day disabled list to make room for Iribarren on the roster.

One possible reason Hurley was the choice rather than, say, Omar Poveda is that the DL assignment results in major league pay. Poveda could still end up on the 60 once room on the roster is needed for righthanders Alexi Ogando and Omar Beltre. Iribarren could end up off the roster too, as he's out of options.

March 14, 2010: From Surprise, AZ

It's a game of inches.

I'm not sure what would have happened had we not left the house at 5:45 a.m., had we not arrived at the airport at 6:20, had we not checked in and arrived at the security check line at 6:30, nearly an hour before our 7:25 a.m. flight.

They Know Why We Fly, but they must not know when Spring Break is, because they had only one guy in place to check boarding passes and ID's for the hundreds of us lined up for security checks. He deserves a merit badge for moving the line as fast as he did, but it still took us 30 minutes to get through the line.

But that was OK, because it was just 7:00, our gate was 50 feet away, and departure wasn't until 7:25. No sweat.

Except that as we walked over to the gate, we heard: ". . . Last call before we give your seats away to standby passengers. Last call for Smith, Newberg, . . . "

Really? Really?? When you check in, at the airport, an hour before your flight, if you don't show up at the gate (because of backed up security checks) until 25 minutes before departure, they'll give your seats away?

It takes a lot to torque me off on a trip to Surprise, but if we'd shown up at the airport an hour before our break-of-dawn flight instead of 65 minutes early, and had our seats taken away from us, then the 3-14-10 Newberg Report would have put this particular airline on a short list that includes Todd Zeile, Dish Network, Luis Alicea, Flip Boone, and Nickelback.

Instead, it all worked out—barely—and instead of a bunch of vitriol you're subjected only to seven wasted paragraphs that you didn't sign up for.

I was pretty tired yesterday so there's a 10 percent chance I'm wrong about these things:

1. I think I saw Reds third baseman Scott Rolen hanging out with his kids at the pool at our hotel.

2. I think I saw Indians AAA pitching coach (and 129-game winner) Charles Nagy at dinner (bemoaning Cleveland's 5-0 loss to Texas earlier in the day).

3. I think I saw Johnny Whittleman wearing a Whittleman 49 jersey during afternoon BP on the back fields.

I've been to more than 20 spring trainings. There are a handful of moments I still remember as being the very first thing I saw on a particular trip. Donald Harris bloodying his own lip on a foul ball in BP in 1990 in Port Charlotte. Dodgers rookie Raul Mondesi making a throw to the plate that you could have hung clothes on in 1994 in a game against the Astros in Kissimmee. John Bannister blowing Royals uberprospect Billy Butler away on three fastballs in 2005.

And five years later, on that same field where I saw Bannister-Butler, the southeast of the four surrounding the Eagle's Nest on the back fields in Surprise, I saw a guy who I've been expecting for several years now to have that breakout season take another dazzling round of BP. I don't know if Johnny Whittleman is going to have a big summer, but there's no question he had a big winter. The 23-year-old put on what had to be 20 extra pounds of good weight this off-season, and he looks like Troy Aikman out there.

He's still got to field his position better at third, and still needs to show more consistent power and aggressiveness at the plate, and he knows that. But if his off-season workouts are any indication of how dedicated he is to taking that next step, this may finally be his year.

I saw less than one hour of work Saturday afternoon before they packed things in to wrap up the first day of full squad minor league workouts, but in that time, between throws with Max, a few other things caught my eye as well:

1. Jorge Alfaro's BP session was the most inconsistent one I saw, but also full of wow. The 16-year-old catcher from Colombia is the definition of raw offensively (wish I'd taken a photo of the talk he and hitting instructor Luis Ortiz were having between turns at the plate—Alfaro wants it), but mature physically and extremely talented. I can't wait to see him show off his defensive tools, based on how the great Jason Parks described his work behind the plate.

2. Watching 23-year-old dirtdog Vin DiFazio take batting practice while 17-year-old wunderkind Jurickson Profar fielded fungoes at shortstop made me think of how different their paths have been, and how much I root for both of them. That's two players who want to be great, not an insignificant trait.

3. Absent from minor league camp were two other diametrically opposite players. One was outfielder Steve Murphy, who has retired. The 25-year-old was the Northwest League MVP in 2005 after being drafted by Texas in the 14th round that summer out of Kansas State, and by 2007 he was an everyday AA player. The former high school teammate of John Mayberry Jr. didn't come into pro ball with much fanfare, but had several years as a productive minor leaguer. The other was Emmanuel Solis, who signed at age 17 out of the Dominican Republic for more than $500,000 but never has produced. An experiment was underfoot last year to move the third baseman to the mound, but he's not on the camp roster as far as I can tell.

It had been three years since the Rangers had been rained out of a spring training game when they were washed out last week, and it had been three years since the club had twirled a Cactus League shutout before yesterday's blanking of the Indians. Brandon McCarthy pitched in the March 4, 2007 gem and in yesterday's as well. I didn't see any of the game, but McCarthy reportedly relied on a fastball with tremendous life to set three hitters down on strikes in his three innings of work (three hits, one walk), and Darren Oliver (one inning), Luis Mendoza (three innings), and Guillermo Moscoso (two innings) followed with six innings of one-hit ball.

Third baseman Matt Brown doubled off a lefty and tripled off a righty.

Chris Davis singled in three trips and sits at .522/.560/.739 with only four strikeouts in 23 at-bats.

Ian Kinsler will be held out of action for at least a week with a high right ankle sprain.

There's a little speculation brewing in local reports that Neftali Feliz is less than a lock to break camp with the big club, particularly if he doesn't begin to command his secondary stuff. If Feliz gets optioned, it won't so much be because of strong efforts from bubble candidates like Mendoza and Moscoso or flashes of awesomeness from newcomers Tanner Scheppers and Alexi Ogando, who are certainties to start the year on the farm—it will be strictly because of the state of Feliz's development and how to handle it best.

Mike Lowell is supposed to see game action for Boston tomorrow. Red Sox officials are praising his early work at first base.

Washington released Eddie Guardado.

Jason Botts is 1 for 12 in White Sox camp. Omar Vizquel is 2 for 15. A slimmed down Andruw Jones, on the other hand, is 5 for 14 (.357/.471/.500) with as many walks (three) as strikeouts, and two stolen bases in two tries.

The Pirates are reportedly not promising infielder Ramon Vazquez a job even though he's guaranteed $2 million. A trade is expected, and for obvious reasons the Rangers are being mentioned in Pittsburgh reports as a possible destination. Keep an eye on this one.

Jayson Stark's Grapefruit League travels produced a list of the hardest throwers he's seen in Florida this month, topped by Stephen Strasburg and Daniel Bard, each of whom touched 98, and six others who hit 97—including Tampa Bay's Joaquin Benoit. (Interestingly, at least four Rangers pitchers I can think of off the top of my head would have made that list had Stark made it over to Arizona the last couple weeks.)

Benoit told reporters, on the subject of new Rays teammate Hank Blalock: "I'll tell you what. If he's healthy, he's gonna be unbelievable. He swings hard at everything, and he's *not the kind of guy that swings hard and misses*."

Hmm.

Blalock on why he chose Tampa Bay: "I didn't have any other choice. That's why I'm here."

Nice touch: Texas got minor league infielder Travis Adair into a game last week as a "Just In Case" against Seattle—whose pitching coach is his Dad, Rick Adair. Travis worked a walk in a ninth-inning pinch-hit appearance.

Colorado signed righthander Rick Bauer and lefthander Scott Rice to minor league deals.

The Laredo Broncos of the independent United League released outfielder Juan Senreiso. The Long Island Ducks of the independent Atlantic League signed righthander Joselo Diaz. The Windy City Thunderbolts of the independent Frontier League signed first baseman-outfielder J.T. Restko to a contract extension.

Full day of baseball ahead. Catch you tomorrow.

March 15, 2010: From Surprise, AZ

I'm sure the fact that 17 players and coaches were gathered as Tanner Scheppers threw his side early Sunday morning was mere happenstance, but it seemed sort of fitting anyway.

The fascinating thing about this camp is how much buzz Scheppers and Alexi Ogando and Michael Kirkman, for instance, are getting as pitchers who could make impacts this season, when at this time last year one wasn't yet Rangers property, another seemed sentenced to never becoming a Rangers reality, and the third wasn't really on the map.

A year ago the camp buzz, properly so, was about Neftali Feliz and Derek Holland, two AA blue-chippers for whom places were being held by veterans whose time in Texas was likely temporary at best. Feliz and Holland were in big league camp on non-roster invites but kept around until the buses left Surprise for Arlington. Even though neither was deemed ready for major league work, everyone knew it was a matter of time, and that both would show up in September, if not forcing their way to Texas sooner.

The difference in 2010 is that there aren't really any placeholders who figure to make this staff. In fact, despite having stretches last summer when they were indispensable to a contending Rangers club, Feliz and Holland are not locks to come out of camp with jobs themselves, and not because of a Kris Benson or Jason Jennings who has the club's momentary confidence. The staff is deeper now than it was a year ago, and younger, both in the rotation and the bullpen. It's simply tougher to win a job than it used to be.

I remember hating that Boston could get away with optioning Clay Buchholz in 2008, less than a year after he'd thrown a big league no-hitter. Texas is getting there. If you had to snapshot the rotation battle right now, Holland would probably settle in as the seventh starter (though his Sunday effort probably keeps him in the hunt), and Feliz is all but out of the race to get the ball every fifth day. But then you get a comment like this one today from *Baseball America*'s Jim Callis:

I'm stingy when it comes to anointing prospects as potential No. 1 starters. I want to see one dynamic pitch, at least one plus pitch to go with plus command and plus makeup—and even then I err on the side of caution. That's why there are only six pitchers [on BA's *Top 100 Prospects list] whom I would stamp as having legitimate* No. *1 starter potential: Stephen Strasburg (No. 2), Brian Matusz (No. 5),* ***Neftali Feliz (No. 9), Martin Perez (No. 17),*** *Tyler Matzek (No. 23) and Jacob Turner (No. 26).*

Feliz has major league experience—major league *success*—and can't come close yet to cracking this rotation. As for Perez, in a year he'll be where Scheppers and Ogando and Kirkman are today, probably earning lots of ink dedicated to a timetable that stands to shrink with every Cactus League outing. Along with Perez will be a couple other young arms as unforeseeable now as Scheppers and Ogando and Kirkman were a year ago. The phrases "waves of talent" and "prospect pipeline" get used a lot with this organization. It's no longer a mission statement, a promise. It's a reality now.

It's sort of the same thing that's going on at first base. Chris Davis is having one of the best camps in baseball, Justin Smoak is getting real close (the missile he hit to the deepest part of the park yesterday for a left-center field, warning-track double came off Diamondbacks lefthander prospect Tom Layne, who allowed one home run in 97 innings last year), and then there's Mitch Moreland, who every time I see him seems to barrel the ball with video game consistency. Productive pre-arbitration bats aren't quite as in demand as high-end young pitching, but there's a definite market for them. And Texas is deep there.

Where the Rangers are not deep (though it's not as critical as on the mound or at first base) is at utility infielder, a role that's wide open right now. Joaquin Arias showed me again on Sunday morning that he's a back fields All-Star, but I still don't sense a tremendous amount of confidence from the manager in what he can do when the games count. Ray Olmedo has hit a little in camp (though he struck out in three of four hitless trips yesterday, lining out to right field his other time up), but is a career .228/.276/.293 hitter. Esteban German can do lots of things with the bat but has eight games at shortstop in eight big league seasons. Hernan Iribarren isn't a shortstop, either, and I still see Marcus Lemon as strictly a second baseman.

The idea of Ramon Vazquez coming back is something I could get behind.

Charlie Hough in the 1980s. R.A. Dickey in the '00s. Who's the latest Ranger to wield the knuckleball?

Photographer Ginger Newberg preserved the evidence: http://trsullivan.mlblogs.com/archives/2010/03/which_rangers_pitcher_is_this.html

There are few better days at the ballpark than 65 degrees and sunny, a spot on the berm, snow cones for the kids, and a half hour with Don Welke.

Josh Hamilton went deep and doubled in his first two at-bats yesterday, fulfilling a promise to his daughter Julia on what was her ninth birthday, but I was as happy with his third at-bat, in which he took four straight pitches, the first three for balls, before flying out. Vladimir Guerrero, who has probably taken more pitches in camp than he's taken against Texas in his entire career, watched ball one sail by before crushing a missile to center on the next pitch, a double that shot off his bat like it was jai alai.

The numbers were OK, but Frankie Francisco didn't look great in the ninth inning of the home game yesterday. Ben Snyder and Chris Ray weren't at their sharpest, either.

Engel Beltre entered the game late and had a solid at-bat in the eighth, singling the other way.

New Rangers reliever candidate Edwar Ramirez may be skinnier than Arias.

Since I was at the split-squad game in Surprise, I didn't see the "one inch from a disaster" moment for Kirkman in Glendale. The lefthander took a one-hop Reed Johnson comebacker off his left ear (the ball shot into right field for a double) in the seventh inning, knocking him to the ground. Kirkman was on his feet before the play ended, but the Rangers lifted him from the game. Everything seems to be OK.

Jarrod Saltalamacchia played for the first time in six days, reportedly throwing well and contributing a double.

Another 2 for 3 day from Chris Davis, raising two of his three numbers (.538/.571/.731).

Answer: Veteran sluggers Vlad Guerrero and Paul Konerko, 2009 rookies Randy Ruiz and Kyle Blanks, and Rangers third base coach Dave Anderson.

Question: Who has Darren O'Day drilled with a pitch since joining the Rangers?

When O'Day accidentally plunked Anderson during a pitchers' fielding practice drill yesterday morning, it was rip-roaring-hilarious to everyone on the field other than Anderson, who proceeded to fungo-rifle a one-hop screamer to O'Day on the next pitch, nearly handcuffing the sidewinder.

Warner Madrigal will have an MRI today due to continued soreness in his throwing forearm.

Eric Hurley, already on the 60-day disabled list as he rehabs from shoulder surgery, will miss 7-10 days of camp work due to surgery to repair a broken bone in his non-throwing wrist.

TCU lefthander Matt Purke threw a complete game on Saturday, allowing one run on four hits and no walks, fanning eight Texas Tech hitters.

Ted Price will be Rangers-Podcasting out here this week, with a video stream that can be found at http://www.ustream.tv/channel/rangers-podcast-in-arlington. I think if you head there now, you can set up a "follow" so you're alerted when new content is posted.

The Rangers, according to local reports, could make a first round of cuts today, shipping some players to minor league camp as regulars and key roster candidates (both pitchers and position players) start to command more playing time. Minor league games begin on Thursday.

But minor league workouts are now in full swing, and I'm headed that way this morning. More farm observations on the way tomorrow.

March 16, 2010: From Surprise, AZ

At some point each March I write about the sensory overload that the back fields will hit you with between the eyes, as four diamonds are buzzing with activity simultaneously, while four or five pitchers are busy throwing sides just a hundred feet away. You just can't see everything you want to see, and each year lately there's more you're sick about missing.

The scene Monday morning around the Eagle's Nest on the back fields was ridiculous. With minor league camp just a few days old and games not set to get underway until Thursday, pitchers have been getting their work in by warming up in four-barrel bullpen mode and then taking the hill on one of the four fields, pitching to hitters in what are called "tracking sessions," simulated pitcher-to-hitter confrontations where the bats stay on shoulders. Part of the objective is to get hitters used to seeing pitches for a few days; the other is for pitchers to get their early work in with more than just a catcher on the other end.

The Rangers had half of the minor league pitchers in camp throw tracking on Monday, close to 40 arms that moved swiftly in groups of four, first alongside each other in the bullpen and then each to one of the four fields fanning out from the Eagle's Nest, with motorized efficiency. This was "Group II" on Monday, and I'd be shocked if there are more than a couple organizations in baseball with as deep a stable of pitching prospects as yesterday's *half* of the Rangers' mound inventory that got their work in. Martin Perez threw yesterday morning. As did Michael Main. Blake Beavan and Wilfredo Boscan. Joe Wieland, Kennil Gomez, Corey Young. Braden Tullis, Richard Bleier, Richard Alvarez, Edwin Escobar, Matt Thompson. Robbie Erlin and Chad Bell and Tanner Roark, Beau Jones and Randol Rojas and Nick McBride. To name a few.

Maybe the most celebrated onetime two-way player among the Rangers' pitching prospects is Main, who had teams interested in drafting him in 2007's first round as a center fielder. Certainly the least heralded of the players Texas has converted from the field to the mound is 21-year-old Tim Steggall, who is four months older than Main but has yet to play a professional inning. Three years after Main was the Rangers' second first-round pick, the unimposing Steggall is in camp as an undrafted free agent signed toward the end of the 2009 season after a career as an infielder for the University of Puget Sound, Central Arizona Junior College, and UTA. Nobody drafted the .255-hitting shortstop. But Texas scout Jay Eddings liked the arm.

Main and Steggall got loose alongside each other as part of one of the first foursomes. Once they moved to the fields, Main to the southwest diamond and Steggall to the northwest, I headed straight for Main's field to see how he looked (he remains a favorite, even though he has yet to put together that breakout season I've been hoping for), but found myself darting a glance over at Steggall's field several times. Main didn't have his top command but looked physically strong (key for him) and had his fastball life back. Steggall didn't strike the same figure, nor should he have. He's a project without much projection, but there's some pop in that arm, and while any anticipation of what he might do pales substantially in comparison to what Main might do in 2010, he's an intriguing story nonetheless, a guy fighting to prove a scout and an organization right as he tries to make himself a prospect in a system as heavy on pitching prospects and as light on soldiers as it's ever been.

Watching Martin Perez pitch, no matter the nature of the drill, is an exercise in astronomy. As for this scene:

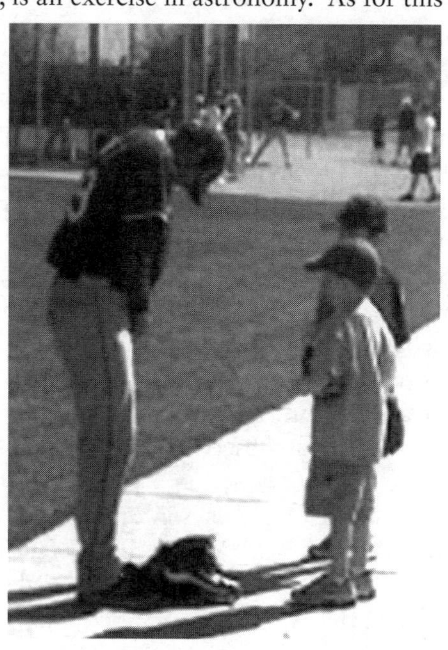

It isn't going to last much longer. Perez can still blend into a crowd. For now.

As Perez was warming up, 100 feet away Alvarez (whose comparisons to Perez are as unfair as Perez's to Johan Santana) looked like he'd put on a few pounds since last summer and was sitting a tick or two higher on his fastball.

Boscan is definitely bigger. Good bigger. Still love watching that guy pitch.

Ever sat around a table in a quiet, methodical, business-like meeting at work, come up with a reasonably good idea before the group, and everyone unexpectedly started hollering and laughing in celebration? Your good idea would have been the equivalent of a Thompson curve ball.

I don't know how much bigger the 5-foot, something-inch righthander Rojas (the 2009 Dominican Summer League Co-Pitcher of the Year: 8-0, 0.80, 48/6 K/BB in 67.1 innings) is going to be, but the 19-year-old Venezuelan was impressive in his tracking session. Rojas may be more polish than projection, but there's something there.

Among the hitters who stood in against Rojas was fellow 5-foot, something-inch, 160-pounder Teodoro "Cafe" Martinez, an interesting center field prospect whose father, Carlos Martinez, was just as skinny but played in the big leagues at 6'5". Have to wonder if Cafe, who turns 18 today, isn't finished growing.

Neil Ramirez didn't throw yesterday, but his name is coming up a lot this week. In a positive way.

Observations on three lefthanders: (1) Erlin may not be generating as much buzz as a guy like Ramirez, but I'm not sure he shouldn't be. The Robbie Ross comps are practically inevitable given his size and handedness, and it wouldn't surprise me at all if Erlin were to flourish in his first full season (2010) the way Ross did in his (2009). (2) It's unfair of me to keep saying I wish lefthander Escobar were three inches taller. (Hey, I wish Julio Borbon threw better, too.) There's a real good chance I'm wrong about Escobar. (3) Bell isn't the kind of pitcher who will dazzle in a bullpen or tracking session, but he's impressive. Deep assortment, good size with maybe a little projection, mound savvy.

Jason Parks has been posting his own Surprise scouting reports on Rangers prospects at http://www.facebook.com/pages/Baseball-Time-in-Arlington/273254723463?ref=ts. Always worth checking out what Professor Parks has to say. These aren't your average fan observations, or even your above-average fan observations. These are scouting reports.

This is one of the bigger days in camp as far as roster battles are concerned. C.J. Wilson and Neftali Feliz are each slated to go four innings against the Cubs as they try to hold onto their shots at a rotation spot. On the to-do list for Wilson: greater first-pitch strike efficiency. On Feliz's: better command of his secondary offerings.

I didn't see Rich Harden's effort last night, but it sounded like a mixed bag, better late than early in his 3.2-inning, 80-pitch (50-strike) effort. The Harden ERA is now 9.72, but he and Ron Washington sound less concerned with the results than the upticks in velocity, pitch counts, arm strength, and consistency.

X-rays on Josh Hamilton's left wrist (after he'd been drilled by Giants starter Madison Bumgarner) came back negative. He'll likely be held out of action a couple days.

Ben Sheets allowed 10 runs (nine earned) in Oakland's game against Cincinnati yesterday, getting chased without recording an out. His spring ERA is now 31.15 (15 earned runs in 4.1 innings).

Texas decided not to make a first round of reassignments yesterday, as had been speculated in several local reports. Other teams are a couple days into widespread options, and the Rangers should follow suit later this week.

Among the Braves' first cuts: reliever Steve Marek, optioned for the second straight March to Atlanta's AAA club. He was half of what the Braves got for Mark Teixeira, along with Casey Kotchman, one year and two days after they'd shipped Elvis Andrus, Feliz, Matt Harrison, Jarrod Saltalamacchia, and Beau Jones to Texas for Teixeira and Ron Mahay.

Arizona signed Kris Benson to a minor league contract. The Dodgers reassigned Eric Gagné to minor league camp. Milwaukee did the same with A.J. Murray, and the Mets did so with R.A. Dickey.

The Sioux City Explorers of the independent American Association released outfielder Anthony Webster.

I believe the tracking sessions give way to live BP on the back fields this morning. Should have more hitter observations for you tomorrow.

March 17, 2010: From Surprise, AZ

I stared down the barrel of the gun. Looked into the eye of the beast. Pitched to Joe Mauer.

I took Grand Avenue. Willingly.

The details are unimportant. I knew better, but a late change in Tuesday afternoon plans and a quick look at directions to Mesa for Cubs-Rangers led me to believe I could outsmart The Grand and force it, once and for all, to do my bidding.

I got to the game an hour late.

(To be fair, the sold-out crowd of more than 13,000 in a stadium and parking lot not set up to handle much more than that factored in. But The Grand won. Again.)

I walked in just as the game's two pivotal at-bats took place. Neftali Feliz was evidently sharp in innings one and two and to start off inning three, taking care of the Cubs the first time through their order—two strikeouts in a one-hit first, two strikeouts in a one-hit second, and an infield pop-out and fly to left to quietly start the third.

But then the top of the order came back up: single, double, and the two at-bats I arrived to see—a two-run Xavier Nady double and, after Marlon Byrd was down 0-2, he worked the count full before shooting a hard single through the box, driving home the third run of the inning and staking Chicago to a 3-0 lead that would hold up in a 4-1 Cubs win. Feliz was slated to go four innings, but his trouble the second time through the lineup ended his day after three.

This team expects to win this year, and Feliz simply isn't ready for the responsibility of giving the club six or seven strong, every fifth day. Not yet. That's OK—there are other candidates making strong cases to round out the rotation, and Feliz may still develop into a lockdown rotation horse. But he's not there yet.

As for C.J. Wilson, his unlikely candidacy for the starting five gains momentum. After Omar Beltre pitched the fourth (interesting; missed low from time to time, but had several Cubs hitters guessing wrong in a scoreless frame that included two strikeouts), Wilson came on for the fifth, with a plan for him to log four innings of his own. Pitch counts have long been an issue for the lefthander, even in his late-relief assignments, and first-pitch strikes have been a problem in camp.

Wilson met the challenge. He faced 15 batters, starting 12 off with strikes (including the final nine he faced). His first inning of work, in fact, went from uh-oh to dazzling quickly—after starting leadoff hitter Ryan Theriot off with three pitches out of the zone, he came back to strike Theriot out looking and, overall, fire seven strikes in eight pitches to retire Chicago in order. In his second frame, nine strikes and five balls. In his third, seven strikes and one ball, locking up the opportunity after just 33 total pitches to go out for a fourth inning of work. He needed 14 pitches in that inning, but did a good job wiggling out of a mess he created after Tyler Colvin singled sharply to center on a full count and Nady clubbed a ground-rule double to right center on the next pitch. Faced with runners at second and third and nobody out, Wilson got a grounder to third and two grounders to second to strand the runners, end the inning, and complete his day.

In his four innings of work (47 pitches, 32 for strikes), Wilson gave up one run (a no-doubt Jeff Baker homer in the seventh) on three hits, no walks, and five strikeouts—all looking. His pace seemed good, he mixed a sharp breaking ball with a fastball that he located well, and he did a good job working both sides of the plate. But the big thing may have been pitch one: those 12 out of 15 first-pitch strikes followed an effort his last time out when he was just 4 of 12.

Wilson's biggest disappointment of the day might have been that the Cubs opted to use the DH in the game, stripping from him a long-awaited opportunity to hit.

Interesting top of the fifth: Justin Smoak and Taylor Teagarden each worked the count full and forced Cubs pitcher Esmailin Caridad to throw six pitches, but given their minor league track records, that wasn't so surprising. But then Joaquin Arias worked a seven-pitch walk, which on some nights is as many pitches as he'll see in four at-bats combined.

I still just don't see Arias (who proceeded to get caught stealing) winning the utility infield job, and my guess is that he'll be traded rather than exposed to waivers.

Josh Hamilton's bruised left hand is better, but he had a tooth infection yesterday.

Ian Kinsler could miss another full week with his right ankle sprain but is expected to be ready for Opening Day.

Warner Madrigal's MRI showed no structural damage, and he'll try to work back from his forearm tightness in hopes of getting back on the mound before the end of camp.

Eric Hurley looked like a quarterback getting in his pregame warmup tosses yesterday morning, as a nearby coach was hauling in the return throws from the catcher during Hurley's bullpen session (a concession to Hurley's broken left wrist).

A few notes from live BP on the minor league side Tuesday morning:

Lefthander Glenn Swanson is now throwing from a Venafro-esque low slot.

Righthander Danny Gutierrez's power curve wasn't quite as nasty as Matt Thompson's the day before, but it's a true swing-and-miss pitch.

Righthander Wilmer Font had trouble getting on top of his curve, but the 19-year-old looks physically more and more like a big league pitcher every time I see him. Hunch: He gets traded in July. Sold high.

Another hunch: While Font is considered anywhere from the fourth-best pitching prospect in the Rangers system to the seventh-best in most reputable rankings, this time next year righthander Neil Ramirez will be in that same tier.

Lefthander Robbie Ross is far from imposing physically but always seems to be in command on the mound. Love his future.

I went to a tryout for the Reds in Georgetown, Texas in the spring of 1990. One stage that day was a BP set-up where pitchers and hitters each toed in, one at a time, facing each other for one series of pitches before stepping out for the next pair. I figured out with about a dozen hitters ahead of me that I was going to miss Austin McCallum lefty Robbie Beckett (who would be San Diego's first-round pick a couple months later) by one hitter. A left-handed hitter, I think I lost three pounds in those 15 minutes hoping no hitter would duck out ahead of me, forcing me to step in against Beckett, a huge kid with huge velocity and huge unawareness of where his pitches would land (he'd walk about a batter per inning in more than 860 pro innings of work).

I thought about that experience yesterday for the first time in many years, as left-handed hitters Jacob Kaase and Tommy Mendonca both got buzzed up and in by filthy but erratic southpaw Geuris Grullon during back-to-back BP turns.

I finally saw something out of Jurickson Profar yesterday that I wasn't crazy about: an Alfonso Soriano look to his right-handed cuts. (But Profar is half Soriano's age. He'll get straightened out.)

Mike Lowell is seeing action for Boston at first base (he has one hit and a strikeout in four trips over two appearances) but "is not moving well," according to scouts who talked to ESPN's Gordon Edes. (Edes then pointed out that Lowell has never run well.) The Marlins are said to have shown some interest in bringing the veteran back to Florida.

Kevin Millwood got a back-fields Orioles intrasquad assignment this time and was a little better: three runs on four hits over five innings (88 pitches).

Interesting: Washington released controversial 25-year-old outfielder Elijah Dukes. Not even a designation for assignment?

Houston got infielder Jose Vallejo through waivers and outrighted him to AAA Round Rock.

Kansas City optioned catcher Manny Pina to its AA club. It will be Pina's third run at the Texas League.

Righthander Derrick Turnbow ended his comeback attempt with Florida due to shoulder pain.

Righthanders Sidney Ponson and Jake Dittler signed with the Long Island Ducks of the independent Atlantic League.

On the punch list for today and tomorrow: Hoping to see Alexi Ogando, Miguel Velazquez, Vlad Guerrero, Michael Main, and Tommy Mendonca at work.

And no more of The Grand.

March 17, 2010: From Surprise, AZ

The Rangers have optioned righthanders Omar Poveda (out for the season) and Omar Beltre and lefthander Zach Phillips to Frisco, and have assigned the following non-roster players to minor league camp: lefthanders Kasey Kiker and Clay Rapada, catcher Emerson Frostad, and infielder Marcus Lemon. No surprises in the bunch (while not surprising, it's interesting that the club wants to see some more of righthander Alexi Ogando before sending him out on option).

March 18, 2010: From Surprise, AZ

I swear this is the truth.

I printed an old newspaper article about Miguel Velazquez last week, preparing to write his story while here. I'd seen him at Instructs in September but not at full strength. He's not only among the most promising position player prospects in the system. He's also among the organization's most fascinating stories.

I realized Tuesday night that my week was nearing its end and I still hadn't seen much of Velazquez (number three on my "32 Things") in action. He was a top priority Wednesday morning.

I tracked number 98 down as he stepped in as one of righty Tim Steggall's live BP foes. Velazquez saw six pitches, and let four go by. I had my super-corny hook: This would be a story about a player with enough restraint, enough discretion—now—to be different from the kid once sentenced to three years' probation in Puerto Rico for an incident in which his brother shot a man who'd tried to kill their sister, to let borderline pitches go by during a brief batting practice session that wasn't going to last long.

Then the day changed.

The story was no longer about a 22-year-old kid in the process of overcoming a kind of adversity few in this game are faced with, of proving to the organization that he's worth believing in, of putting his past in the past and moving forward with the desire to be something better, to eliminate doubts, to win in this game.

Wednesday would instead be about a man nearly three times older, facing those exact challenges.

Note to the nearly 100 new subscribers in the last 24 hours: If you want details on Ron Washington's transgression, a failed MLB drug test that turned up positive for cocaine, evidently between June 8 (when his contract was extended through 2010) and July 14 (when the All-Star Game was played) (likely during the West Coast road trip the final week before the Break, based on one local column last night), I'm not your guy. Just about every beat writer in town was at the press conference at which Washington delivered an emotional, contrite statement and took questions until there weren't any more, as were at least three or four national baseball reporters. You can get the facts, the timeline, and the baseball implications from them.

Also in the room, filling each of the 50 or 70 chairs that weren't occupied by the dozen or so writers, and lining the back and side walls of the room, were just about every one of Washington's players and plenty others who are auditioning to be. His coaching staff. A number from the baseball operations department. Washington's wife, Gerry. Nolan Ryan. And Jon Daniels.

It was an impressive show of support by the players in particular, all in street clothes and all there by choice, not asked by Washington or the front office or anyone else to attend. They'd just learned the news moments earlier in the clubhouse, as the 57-year-old man addressed his club privately. They didn't need to be at the press briefing a few hundred yards away, having already heard from their manager everything they'd hear at the presser (if not more). A 40-man roster showed up to support him.

According to one local report, Michael Young spoke up during the emotional team meeting, after Washington had apologized and before another handful of teammates got up and spoke, saying: "I've got his back. Anybody who doesn't feel that way isn't a Texas Ranger."

Washington reportedly avoided league suspension by virtue of the fact that he went to MLB and confessed before his positive test results. He avoided dismissal as Rangers manager because, as he explained it, Ryan and Daniels declined his offer to resign. Not without considering it, they admitted.

"Just because someone in your family makes a mistake," Ryan said, "doesn't mean you stop loving them."

Daniels added that when Washington came to him and Ryan with the admission, they were shocked, angry, disappointed—like he expects Rangers fans might react to Wednesday's news—but then they decided to work through things with him. "We still believe in him," Daniels and Ryan each repeated several times to reporters. The man known as a coach who believes in and fights for the underdog is now more of one himself.

Man, I don't know what to think about all of this. It's a setback for the man and the organization, a potential distraction for the ballclub. Can it serve as a rallying point for the players? Yeah, I guess, maybe, but this is a club of guys who didn't need another rallying point.

Even if, taken at face value, yesterday's news doesn't impact Washington's immediate standing with the franchise, does it affect his future? How could it not? He said he hoped the Rangers will continue to allow him to lead the club. Ryan and Daniels have given him that opportunity by refusing last summer to accept his offer to step down. But going forward? It's not the reason his contract doesn't extend beyond 2010, but it's *a* reason, says team management. How his team deals with this development won't determine his fate in and of itself, but it's a factor.

This much I expect: There will be some in the media who will try and drive a wedge internally, suggesting Washington has lost his players and the ability to lead. Get ready for it. It's already afoot.

I thought T.R. Sullivan nailed this: "In this business, it's not whether you are right or wrong but it's how loudly you scream that counts. Rush Limbaugh and Ann Coulter set the standard on that score and all others have blindly followed. . . . Righteous indignation and a call for draconian measures [are] the obvious card to play in such matters."

Guess I'm guilty myself of bringing a writer's name into the discussion (aggravating the offense: I recommend reading Sullivan's entire piece — http://trsullivan.mlblogs.com/archives/2010/03/of_ron_washington_rush_limbaug.html) — but rest assured there will be plenty who will see to it themselves that their names are part of the talk show prattle and water cooler talk.

(Stated another way, by Evan Grant: "[T]ypical of today's media, the minute the story broke, we acted to try and make the story more juicy than it was. In the first 12 hours after the story broke, columnists were jumping all over one another to make the most provocative claim about the incident. Work in a charge of blackmail or hint at potential racism, and you are likely to draw more attention.")

Even if there's no truth to a wedge in the clubhouse or an extortion attempt or some other fraction of what's written, stories will beget stories and will grow into something bigger on the first trip into every city this season, and will drive local blog posts and radio segments as soon as the team has lost four of five, especially if that happens before the Cowboys report to camp.

And don't get me wrong: The media is not to blame for any of this. Washington is responsible for his incredible mistake and for creating a public relations mess and a point of embarrassment and humiliation, and it's hard to imagine that gets erased from the ledger as long as his fitness to continue at the helm of the team is evaluated, now, the next time the team finds itself in an extended skid, next winter. The men who preserved his job say they still believe in him, and I don't doubt that, but his bad decision, however out of character, has to have endangered that trust, even if it's intact at the moment.

Ron Washington has always been an advocate of the second chance, managing for an organization that believes in extending them—Josh Hamilton, Danny Gutierrez, Khalil Greene, Miguel Velazquez (whose story will have to wait for another day)—and now he gets one himself.

There's honor in that, and a chance at some level of redemption, I suppose, but this is a franchise that feels it's on the brink of something great, that's heading toward a new ownership group (one that includes Ryan) intent on strengthening the club's image, that had just about everything that really matters pointing in the right direction.

Though I thought things were handled by Washington and the organization as well as could possibly be expected, Wednesday was a disappointing day, and in an unforeseen way, it may be critical for Washington's club to get off to a strong start to the season to sustain the stability that the franchise has worked so hard to establish.

March 19, 2010: From Surprise, AZ

At 3:58 Thursday afternoon, on the batting practice field behind the Batting Practice Field, Vladimir Guerrero stepped in against Ron Washington to take his cuts in preparation for the night's game.

Thwack. Thwack. Thwack. Thwack.

Just 150 feet away, on the nearest of the four bullpen mounds, stood Alexi Ogando, stepping to the hill to get loose for entry into the B game that was a little more than halfway done.

Thwack. Thwack. Thwack. Thwack.

Today the 35-year-old slugger and the 26-year-old hurler from Dominican towns 60 miles apart have little in common other than the sound of bat on ball and ball on mitt, but that wasn't always the case.

The December 11, 2005 Newberg Report, days after that winter's Rule 5 Draft:

Outfielder Alexi Ogando, whom Texas acquired in the AAA phase of the draft out of Oakland's system, is fascinating. Not long ago, he was ranked right with and sometimes ahead of A's outfield prospect Javier Herrera, who went into the 2005 season as their number three prospect. But the player that some scouts have compared physically to ***a young Vladimir Guerrero*** *missed the 2005 season due to visa problems and there remains a risk that he won't be able to cure them for the 2006 season. Still, it's a terrific $12,000 risk for Texas to take. His power to all fields is judged to be major league average right now—despite the fact that the 22-year-old has yet to play above Short-Season A—and his right field arm is among the strongest in organized ball. The 6'5" outfielder hails from shortstop hotbed San Pedro de Macoris.*

The Rangers planned at the time of the draft to take Ogando and make a pitcher out of him. Bet they never envisioned that they'd have Guerrero in a Texas uniform before they could get Ogando to the States, but they're both here now, and both are going to make an impact on the big league club in 2010.

Between 2006 and 2009, Ogando—quarantined in his homeland and denied re-entry into the United States due to the visa-marriage scam he got caught up in, and even rumored at one time to be considered for sale to the Japanese leagues when Texas wasn't sure the immigration issue would ever get cleared up—put up absurd Dominican Summer League stats that were the pitching equivalent of the offensive numbers Guerrero terrorized the Rangers with over the same period. In 81 relief innings, featuring crazy command of a lively upper-90s fastball and a devastating slider, Ogando allowed 65 hits (.223 opponents' average), including just one home run, and issued only 10 unintentional walks, striking out 114. That's one walk per nine innings, and nearly 13 strikeouts per nine. Tack on 2.4 groundouts for every flyout (a ratio that actually sat at 10:1 in 2009). Sensational, despite the level of competition.

I'd seen Omar Beltre pitch years ago before he was lost to the same immigration snafu, but I'd never seen Ogando pitch, and there was a reason I had him near the top of my list of "32 Things" a week ago today:

2. Alexi Ogando. Omar Beltre, too. But Ogando has a better chance to make me come away from Surprise with the same feeling I got after seeing Ian Kinsler, Derek Holland, and [Tanner] Scheppers for the first time in camp.

As Ogando got loose, I paid little attention to the Guerrero BP session (though the systematic report was hard to ignore) or the difficult inning Edwar Ramirez was fighting through in the B game that Ogando was preparing to enter. I was watching the lanky righthander throw bullpen pitches.

He was standing on a remote mound in a remote part of a spring training complex in a remote town in Arizona. I can't begin to imagine how uniquely surreal that moment, because it was on United States soil, might have been for the 26-year-old, if he took a second to think about where he was and what he was doing as he finished his bullpen work and waited for the home half of the inning to wrap up.

The crowd for this informal Rangers-Brewers matchup, for which the scoreboard was never turned on and which featured at least two innings that rolled before three outs were recorded, featured lots of Texas and Milwaukee braintrust (including Brewers GM Doug Melvin and Assistant GM Gord Ash) and lots of media and lots of fans, many of whom had presumably carved out a plan to see Scheppers pitch. He was impressive if a little inconsistent in his inning and two-thirds—keeping the ball down, showing an impressive slider and curve, touching 97 with his fastball—but Ogando gave the surprising crowd an extra reward for being there.

He needed 10 pitches to retire Milwaukee in order. Nine were strikes. Three swings and misses (two on the slider, one for strike three), a couple called strikes (both on the slider), two fouls back, a fastball low and in, and a couple harmless flyouts to right field.

He's going to help this year. Scheppers will, too, and everyone is writing about that and making back field appointments to chronicle his ramp-up. You won't see many (any?) mainstream media writeups on Alexi Ogando this morning, even though he relieved in the same B game that Scheppers relieved in, but that's a mistake. They are both wildly part of the picture here, and soon, though neither has thrown so much as an official minor league pitch stateside.

There's a reason that Scheppers and Ogando remain in big league camp, while Beltre and Kasey Kiker and Zach Phillips and Clay Rapada have been reassigned to the minor league side. It's no knock on the latter four, who weren't going to make this club out of Surprise and are in need of innings that are becoming more scarce, but it says something about Scheppers and Ogando, who, like Neftali Feliz and Derek Holland a year ago, are being kept around big league coaches and teammates and games just a little bit longer, by design.

One last trip to the back fields this morning, and I'll dump some final spring training notes on you (as well as thoughts on the potential implications of the Tommy Hunter strained ribcage muscle and Matt Harrison performance last night) in the next report.

Stateside Alexi
Quietly making his case
For a short farm stay

March 19, 2010

Texas has reassigned non-roster corner hitters Justin Smoak, Mitch Moreland, and Chad Tracy to minor league camp.

March 21, 2010

Three predictions:

Matt Brown is Mike Simms (plus a little third base).

Max Ramirez is Jim Leyritz.

Ramon Vazquez will join the Jon Shave/Jim Mason/Bobby Jones/Nick Capra/Larry Biittner/Bill Ripken club.

(Not an unrelated note: Ray Olmedo has reportedly been reassigned to minor league camp.)

(Not a very significant note, though I'm choosing to point it out and I'm sure others will, too: Gordon Edes of ESPN Boston reports that the Rangers are scouting Mike Lowell today. The Marlins, Yankees, and Blue Jays have scouts in Red Sox camp, too.)

Let me suggest to you that if you didn't watch yesterday's Rangers-Dodgers game, Derek Holland's line will look worse to you than it should. Keep in mind that pitchers who work late in spring training games tend to have inferior defenses behind them.

So happy to be home from Arizona just in time for the start of spring, and snow. Ugh.

As for our week in Surprise, 32 Things I'm Glad I Saw:

1. A 15-minute glimpse of Alexi Ogando, warming in the pen and then throwing a 1-2-3 inning at a Brewers B squad, was plenty. I had him at number 39 in my Top 72 Prospects list in the Bound Edition, that low because he was still locked out of the United States, seemingly indefinitely, but even if his immigration issue had been cleared up before I went to print, I probably wouldn't have put him any higher than 15-20 in the system. Now? No question: he's a top 10 prospect.
2. Corner outfielder Miguel Velazquez. Had him at number 25 in the book, and the number two outfielder in the system, and the number four breakout candidate among hitters. Too low, in every case.
3. Right now, we can look back at 2007 as a watershed year developmentally for the organization, the year that Elvis Andrus, Neftali Feliz, Martin Perez, Julio Borbon, Derek Holland, Matt Harrison, Jarrod Saltalamacchia, David Murphy, Tommy Hunter, Mitch Moreland, Velazquez, Engel Beltre, Blake Beavan, Max Ramirez, Michael Main, Tomas Telis, Tim Smith, and Leury Garcia were brought into the system. Missing from that list is righthander Neil Ramirez, limited by injuries to just 110.1 innings in three seasons. He's about to jump onto the list, and probably not at the back of it.
4. Some pitchers' stuff plays up when they move from starter to reliever, where the doses are shorter and the adrenaline is higher and the third and fourth pitches can be left in the equipment bag. Getting a chance to watch C.J. Wilson go twice through a fairly representative Cubs lineup made me think he could be an anomaly, just as good if not better in a rotation role (*cf.*, Adam Wainwright, Scott Feldman, Ryan Dempster).
5. The impressive show of support by the players and coaches at Ron Washington's press conference was the one bright spot in an otherwise terrible day.
6. Julio Borbon's throwing stood out on the batting practice field, and not in a good way, but he made an outstanding peg to third in the Brewers game Thursday night. He's going to have to show it a lot more to get teams to think twice about going first-to-third on a single, but at least we know it's there.
7. If Harrison were not part of the same trade that brought Andrus and Feliz to Texas, or if he'd been drafted by the Rangers, there'd be a lot more buzz about the camp that the 24-year-old (younger than Ogando, Doug Mathis, Guillermo Moscoso, Warner Madrigal, Pedro Strop, Luis Mendoza, Moreland, Craig Gentry, Chad Tracy, and Max Ramirez) is having. Velocity's up and he's locating everything.
8. Not now and maybe not in 2010 at all, but lefthander Michael Kirkman has a chance to sneak up on everyone the same way.
9. I actually saw less of Vladimir Guerrero than I thought I would, because I was usually watching something else when he was doing his thing. But I did notice that his fan mob has displaced Josh Hamilton's and Nolan Ryan's from the top spot.
10. Guerrero, Hamilton, and Beltre taking pitches.
11. How did Mitch Moreland fall to the 17th round in 2007? That's a knock against 30 teams, not just 29. He barrels the ball as consistently as any prospect this system has produced since Ian Kinsler broke out six years ago.
12. The big league pitching staff, stronger than it's been in years, has more young core arms than it's had in years. The thought that not only Ogando but also Perez and Tanner Scheppers will factor in before long is pretty great.
13. The catching depth has disintegrated in the last year (regressions, trades, injuries), but even if it hadn't,

16-year-old Colombian Jorge Alfaro would probably sit atop the current crop. He's more raw in some areas than others, but he's a dazzling talent.

14. Among the things I'm really bummed about not seeing was Alfaro in dedicated defensive drills, and righthander Jake Brigham throwing a side or live BP or an inning of work. I had Brigham at number four on my pitcher breakout list in the book, and after what I heard this week, I'd probably move him higher than that.

15. Third baseman Tommy Mendonca has lots of work to do, but the foundation is there. His bat ceiling has been compared to Chris Davis, but there's more to the comparison than that: Mendonca has the ability to be a lockdown corner infielder that also hits like one. Tremendous defensive tools.

16. On Thursday morning I noticed Mendonca began his BP work by leaving the donut on his bat before shedding it later in the session. I asked the Rangers why. Seems it's calculated to tighten up a player's swing path and help him get the feel for the head of the bat, and is used from time to time with hitters who swing from the opposite side than they throw from (a left-handed-hitting, right-handed-throwing player like Mendonca often has a weaker top hand that an R-R or L-L player wouldn't have). Switch-hitter Leury Garcia is working with the donut some, too. It's a technique Edgar Martinez used to use, even though he was an R-R guy.

17. Esteban German is a great guy to have in AAA, ready in case someone gets hurt. But the role he's fighting to win is more about defense, and he's not dependable.

18. One thing I'm very glad I saw: Limby lefthander Geuris Grullon didn't hurt anybody.

19. It's a big year for Main and third baseman Johnny Whittleman. That's different from saying it *will* be a big year. It's time for those two. Main has to prove he can stay on the mound, and Whittleman has to prove he can field the position and take more advantage of his slug potential. Both are in very good shape. Time to produce.

20. I may be coming around on lefthander Edwin Escobar a bit. Would I have written Francisco Liriano off because I didn't like his frame? Rich Harden? (Caveat: I'm not making a Liriano or Harden comp.)

21. I still prefer Jurickson Profar, but the gap between him and Luis Sardinas is smaller for me than it was when I saw them in September. See the Gil-Aurilia/Cooper-Bagwell/Kotchman-Morales/etc. discussion in the Sardinas feature in the Bound Edition.

22. The best third-round picks Texas has made in the last 11 years are Hank Blalock and Taylor Teagarden. The latest, lefthander Robbie Erlin, has pitched only four professional innings, but is going to make the Rangers (particularly Butch Metzger, Kevin Bootay, and Ron Hopkins) look very good.

23. The best seventh-rounder over the same period? Probably Smith, unless you count unsigned righthander Virgil Vasquez (2000). My money's on righthander Matt Thompson replacing them. I'm super-excited about him. Strike-thrower with a knee-buckling curve.

24. Vin DiFazio is a baseball player.

25. Glad to have the chance to be around Wayne Kirby and Don Welke, of course.

26. Righthander Wilfredo Boscan (bigger in a good way) completely overmatched outfielder Cristian Santana (a not-so-good big) in a live BP session. Not sure which player it said more about.

27. Despite the first half of 2009, I might be more optimistic about Chris Davis right now than I was coming off his outstanding 2008 debut. Cleaner bat path, head is more still, and he's using the opposite field like he needs to. The statistics don't matter in March, but you can't dismiss the confidence factor that comes from numbers like the ones he's putting up.

28. I read a few stories earlier this month about the organization challenging Nelson Cruz to take on more of a leadership role. Maybe it was because I was looking for it, but it did seem like he was stepping forward more. He's a good example of a guy getting knocked down a bunch and never giving up.

29. The only thing that separates Brandon Boggs from David Murphy might be opportunity. Murphy didn't get it in Boston, and so far Boggs hasn't gotten it in Texas. I wouldn't bet against similar careers.

30. Davis, Moreland, Justin Smoak. Carlos Pena, Travis Hafner, Mark Teixeira. Worth discussing another time?

31. The last thing I saw in camp, on Friday morning: Whittleman, Beltre, and Velazquez taking BP on three different fields, at the same time. One guy who has been too selective, one guy who's not selective enough, one guy who just needs at-bats. Big beta on those guys, especially the first two.

32. This may not matter to the casual baseball fan, and may not ring true to some since I'm an admitted homer and come into all of this with an optimistic fan's perspective. But everywhere you turn on the south side of the Surprise complex, from the steady veterans to the high-ceiling rookies to the swarm of minor league arms, from the big league pitching coach and hitting coach to the former organizational soldier who now graduates from managing in the Dominican Summer League to doing the same in the Arizona Complex League, from the President and the General Manager to the guys running the scouting and development departments who you hope don't get hired away too soon, from Darren Oliver to Jorge Alfaro, there's so much this franchise has in place that backs up the consistent comments coming from all corners of the organization that it's time. Time to

shift focus from *Baseball America* awards to dethroning the Angels, time to get the real thing underway, time to expect to remain standing after 162. I love everything about spring training, including it coming to an end.

Fifteen sleeps.

March 22, 2010

According to Tom Haudricourt of the *Milwaukee Journal Sentinel* (and now several local reports), Texas has traded non-roster infielder Ray Olmedo to the Brewers for non-roster catcher Matt Treanor.

A defense-first veteran big leaguer, the 34-year-old Treanor (married to Olympic volleyball gold medalist Misty May) should make the Rangers' Opening Day roster in the event that Jarrod Saltalamacchia is not healthy for the start of the season. Treanor had an out clause with Milwaukee if not added to the 40-man roster by a certain date; it's unclear what that date was and whether the Rangers have added Treanor to the roster to prevent him from leaving for another job.

March 24, 2010

Under two weeks to go, and we now know, barring health setbacks, how the Rangers rotation will apparently shake out to start the season.

Against Toronto on April 5, 7, and 8: Rich Harden, C.J. Wilson, and Scott Feldman.

Against Seattle on April 9, 10, and 11: Matt Harrison, Colby Lewis, and Harden.

The Rangers reportedly said coming into camp that Wilson had to emerge as one of the club's best two starters to force his way into the rotation, but that's not why he pitches Game Two. The idea there was apparently to go right-left-right-left with the first four, mixing up looks.

One benefit of putting Harden atop the rotation rather than Feldman (who has had a better camp) is that Harden's second turn comes in Arlington (against Seattle) rather than in Cleveland, and his third turn comes in New York rather than in Boston.

So what, you ask? Harden against the Mariners lifetime: 5-2, 1.90, slash line of .186/.265/.257, 55 strikeouts and 19 walks in 52 innings. Solid. In Cleveland, he's been unhittable in a small, six-inning sample, but for whatever reason, he's walked an Indian per inning. Still, hard to ignore the effectiveness against Seattle and the idea of a strong effort on getaway day.

Harden in New York: 3.52 ERA, .268/.354/.411 slash, 12 strikeouts and seven walks in 15.1 innings.

Harden in Boston: 17.61 ERA, .355/.522/.839 slash, nine strikeouts and 13 walks in 7.2 innings. Ouch.

The other thing, of course, is Feldman was one of baseball's most effective road pitchers last year, going 12-4, 3.56 away from Arlington. Throwing him at the Indians in their yard, in what will be their second home game of the season (after Wilson pitches their home opener), is attractive.

As for the idea of going right-right with Lewis and Harden, two things: (1) it's impossible with an odd number of starters to alternate more than once through the rotation; and (2) they bring a significantly different type of stuff. Or are supposed to, at least.

The seven-man bullpen, then, should be manned by Frankie Francisco, Darren Oliver, Neftali Feliz, Darren O'Day (the inflammation around a bone in the back of his elbow is not thought to be serious), Dustin Nippert, and two of the following: righthanders Doug Mathis, Chris Ray, Brandon McCarthy, and Guillermo Moscoso, and lefthanders Derek Holland and Ben Snyder.

The guess here? Mathis and Ray get the gigs, and McCarthy and Holland get optioned (assuming the former clears—though his type of waivers is revocable and so if he's blocked from being optioned to Oklahoma City, he stays in Arlington and Mathis is probably asked to start a fourth tour with the RedHawks).

McCarthy and Holland are slated to get their final A game starts today and tomorrow (while Harrison and Lewis pitch in minor league games the same two days). Feliz had his finest outing of the spring on Monday, touching 97 and commanding his off-speed stuff in a three-inning B game appearance against Milwaukee. He'll work in relief the rest of the way in camp.

Lots of Rule 5 picks around the league have already been returned to their 2009 clubs, and it seems that Snyder is probably headed in that direction. If he were to clear league-wide waivers (which he must do before being offered back to San Francisco—if another teams claims him, he becomes its Rule 5 property all season, just as O'Day was with Texas last year when the Mets tried running him through waivers in April, four months after drafting him via Rule 5 from the Angels), the Rangers might attempt to work out a trade with the Giants, sending them another prospect for Snyder, who would then be eligible to be assigned to a minor league roster in the Rangers' system.

If Wilson is in fact viewed now as a starter, and Michael Kirkman is going to be developed further as a starter, the Rangers might consider Snyder as someone who, even if not ready, could fill a need foreseeably soon. Zach Phillips and Clay Rapada will presumably work in left-on-left relief on the farm, and though I doubt Kasey Kiker will be used that way in April, I still think the bullpen might be where he's headed professionally. Still, Snyder might be someone Texas tries to keep in the system if the club can get him through waivers, which seems likely (though agreeing on a trade with the Giants will be more difficult).

In my last report, discussing Wilson, I mentioned Feldman, Adam Wainwright, and Ryan Dempster as examples of pitchers who moved from significant relief roles to the rotation and fared well. Another obvious example that I overlooked, maybe more instructive than any of the others: Kenny Rogers, a high-octane southpaw reliever in his early big league years before becoming a dependable starter, seeing his walk rate dip and strikeout rate increase once he moved to the rotation.

Wilson admitted not having his best stuff on Monday, but after a shaky first inning (preoccupied with his upcoming first at-bat, maybe?) he allowed only two more hits in the second through fifth, retiring nine straight at one point. His changeup played up and he worked at a quicker tempo than the reliever who used to pace behind the mound and stretch his arms out and sweep the rubber with his glove between what seemed like every pitch.

You don't even have to ask him whether the fourth-inning, opposite-field double off Barry Zito, a kindred spirit who Wilson was once asked to help recruit to Texas, will be a lifelong pride point. The hit didn't count anywhere but in the armchair number three hitter's head.

Tommy Hunter's ribcage strain will evidently force him to the disabled list to start the season, and his ramp-up will presumably resume with a minor league rehab assignment in early- or mid-April. And Ron Washington was clear: this will be a meritocracy, not a situation where an injured player automatically gets his spot back once healthy. Hunter (who is conditioning again but not yet throwing) will have to earn his way back and unseat someone the Rangers believe doesn't give them as good a chance to win.

Ian Kinsler hit off a tee Monday and is about ready to resume batting practice and test his ankle around the bases. He's aiming for a Monday return to game action.

I think Josh Hamilton is supposed to be back in camp today, after flying to Dallas on Monday for some dental work.

Jarrod Saltalamacchia reported improvement in the muscle spasms in his upper back and neck but won't return to action today.

Warner Madrigal has begun throwing again, coming back from his latest bout of tightness in his right forearm.

Newly acquired catcher Matt Treanor has a March 30 out clause but isn't expected to exercise it if not on the 40-man roster by then.

According to one local report, 31-year-old journeyman infielder Nick Green, who had a run last year as Boston's starting shortstop, could be on the Rangers' radar as they continue to evaluate their options for the utility infielder role. He's in Dodgers camp on a non-roster invite and isn't a lock to make the Los Angeles club.

The Giants are reportedly shopping 27-year-old utility infielder Kevin Frandsen.

It's an old theme in this newsletter, but one thing that worries me about attempts to trade for a fringe big leaguer like Ramon Vazquez is that a team like Pittsburgh may try to hold Texas up for a prospect like Kiker or Miguel Velazquez, figuring that since they're tier two prospects for Texas (but might be virtually untouchable for another club), the prospect-heavy Rangers can afford to move them for a big league need. Surely Texas won't capitulate, but I can see it getting in the way of a deal.

Since being returned to minor league camp, Marcus Lemon has begun to see action in center field.

Another way to look at my recent comment that every team, even Texas, made a mistake by letting Mitch Moreland fall to the 17th round in 2007: Like Kinsler, taken in the same round four years earlier, credit the player for taking to instruction and making himself better, and credit the organization for one heck of a job seeing what the player could become and getting him there through development. It's not as if Moreland (Mississippi State) and Kinsler (Missouri) were underscouted, starring at prominent NCAA programs. They fell because teams perceived flaws. They thrived because of how they were developed by the Rangers.

Several of you asked why I didn't include Adrian Gonzalez when I wrote on Sunday: "[Chris] Davis, Moreland, Justin Smoak. Carlos Pena, Travis Hafner, Mark Teixeira. Worth discussing another time?" The reason is Gonzalez didn't join the Rangers system until after Pena and Hafner were gone.

The Rangers have released lefthander Glenn Swanson, righthanders John Slusarz and Chris Matlock, catcher Billy O'Conner, and infielders Mike Hollander and Denny Duron. Swanson, whose tremendous start to the 2007 season was curtailed by an elbow injury that led to Tommy John surgery, had been experimenting with a new sidearm slot in camp.

In addition to outfielder Steve Murphy, lefthander Cliff Springston and righthander Justin King and outfielder Aja Barto have retired.

Scott Lucas has dozens of sensational photos from spring training on his website.

Solid feature on Michael Young by Jon Paul Morosi of Fox Sports.

The White Sox released outfielder Jason Botts.

Detroit optioned righthander Armando Galarraga to AAA six days ago.

After assigning Eric Gagné to minor league camp last week, the Dodgers released the former closer at his request.

The Laredo Broncos of the independent United League released outfielder Juan Senreiso.

Victor Rojas is onto something: www.yakcy.com

Slightly off-topic: Best episode of "Lost"—ever?

Things started to line up just a little bit last night (fun fact: Nestor Carbonell, who plays Richard, is Rafael Palmeiro's cousin), though that's not to say that I have any idea what's going to happen in the nine remaining episodes, and that's just how I want it.

Different story with the Rangers rotation, which started lining up yesterday as well, but if it's all the same, I'd prefer that there aren't any more twists or turns in these final 11 spring training games.

March 24, 2010

The Rangers have reportedly optioned righthanders Edwar Ramirez and Pedro Strop and outfielder Brandon Boggs to Oklahoma City and lefthander Michael Kirkman to Frisco. The club has also reassigned non-roster righthanders Tanner Scheppers and Geoff Geary to minor league camp. No surprises.

Scheppers's April assignment is unknown but, according to a local report, the organization plans to limit him to approximately 100 innings this season. Expect his early outings to be limited—Texas doesn't like to shut pitchers down before season's end due to inning count, preferring to monitor innings every time out so that they'll be available late in the year, whether to contribute to a minor league playoff chase or, in the case of Scheppers and others like him, possibly a pennant race in Arlington.

March 24, 2010

According to Susan Slusser of the *San Francisco Chronicle*, Texas has traded righthander Edwar Ramirez to Oakland for non-roster infielder Gregorio Petit. The 25-year-old Petit was reassigned to minor league camp three days ago by the A's, with whom he'd spent his entire nine-year pro career.

Considered a defense-first infielder (and primarily a shortstop), the Venezuelan is a career .268/.322/.369 minor league hitter (.278/.304/.333 in 54 big league at-bats). He went 6-for-11 (.545/.667/.818 with four walks and two strikeouts) in camp for the A's before being reassigned.

Petit presumably enters the mix for the big league utility infield job.

The removal of Ramirez, purchased on March 9 from the Yankees, clears up a roster spot for the Rangers since he was on the club's 40-man roster.

March 24, 2010

The Rangers have officially announced the Ramirez-Petit trade and have also confirmed that infielder Hernan Iribarren has cleared waivers and been outrighted to Oklahoma City.

The removal of Ramirez and Iribarren from the 40-man roster puts the roster at 37 current members (not counting Alexi Ogando and Omar Beltre, who will need to be reinstated by the end of camp).

March 26, 2010

A .300 clip
Healthy for hitting safely
Not for the standings

Texas is 6-14-1 in Cactus League play. It's the American League's worst mark, and better than the Nationals by a mere game. With nine exhibitions left to play, the Rangers need to win five to avoid posting the worst spring training win-loss percentage in franchise history.

But here's the thing. If Texas does win five of nine going into the season, peeking just above the .349 win percentage they recorded in 1973, I think I'll be OK. Camp records don't mean a whole lot, but losing a lot is losing a lot, and I'd be able to ignore something as ugly as 11-18-1 as long as it included a decent enough 5-4 run to finish things out. Even a little momentum would be super-welcome over this last week and a half.

So would clean bills of health at second base and catcher and sidearm reliever. There's optimism that Ian Kinsler is about to shake off the high ankle sprain and get back on the field (Monday?), that Jarrod Saltalamacchia's pain-free batting practice yesterday could mean he will play today (DH'ing in a minor league game, leading off every inning) and tomorrow (catching in a Cactus League game), that Darren O'Day's elbow inflammation is nothing serious. But until they're playing regularly and without limitation (example: Josh Hamilton putting that early-in-camp shoulder bruise behind him), they'll still show up as bullet points at the end of the daily newspaper stories. Gotta have those three guys right in a week, especially Kinsler and O'Day.

What do we make of the awful exhibition record? Small sample size alert: Texas has won at least 87 games five times in the last 15 years. In three of those years the club was great in camp: 1996 (19-11 spring, 90 wins/playoffs); 1998 (21-10 spring, 88 wins/playoffs); and 2009 (21-14 spring, 87 wins). Once it was mediocre: 1999 (14-14-1 spring, a club-record 95 wins/playoffs). Once it was bad: 2004 (12-18 spring, 89 wins)—and that was a club that even the front office admitted played over its head during the regular season.

Another way to look at it: in those 15 years, the three times Texas has won at least 19 spring games each coincided with one of those seasons of at least 87 wins.

So maybe there's some correlation. It hasn't been a very good camp in terms of the results, and while health and repetitions and rhythm are more important than the team's Arizona record, it sure would be nice to see the club get on a little roll before flying back to Texas.

All that said, spring records depend not only on the 25 guys who will start the season introduced along the first base line, or the other veterans and young players in legitimate competition for those jobs, or the key prospects who are a year or two away. Seventy-two players have appeared in the Rangers' 21 games. A number of the players contributing to wins and losses won't show up at all in the regular season.

And again, on that health issue, I'll take the Rangers' 6-14-1 mark with a reasonable assurance that, other than Tommy Hunter, nobody being counted on to log significant innings in April will be limited physically over the Angels' 7-12 with Ervin Santana (elbow) and Scott Kazmir (shoulder) getting scratched from their most recent starts. But I'm interested in how the next week or so goes.

There are all kinds of reasons Texas absolutely has to get off to a good start this season, and the schedule arguably lines up pretty well. Seems putting together a good finish to March would be worthwhile.

A thought on the acquisition of infielder Gregorio Petit: While he may battle for the utility infield spot, his non-roster status is helpful. Ray Olmedo was deemed to be of less value to the club than veteran catcher Matt Treanor, and two days after Olmedo was shipped away, Petit was acquired. Why? Maybe because Texas doesn't expect it can get Joaquin Arias through waivers for an outright assignment to Oklahoma City. In other words, Arias makes the big club, or he ends up in another organization, leaving the RedHawks with Esteban German, Marcus Lemon, Hernan Iribarren, and now Petit to man the left three infield spots and be ready in case of injury.

I still don't see Arias (reliability) or German (shortstop defense) winning the final bench job. Ramon Vazquez? (We really wouldn't trade Luis Mendoza—who is out of options—for Vazquez, as one local reporter suggests? Really?) Augie Ojeda? Kevin Frandsen? Willie Bloomquist? Nick Green? Chin-lung Hu? Someone.

Oakland assistant GM David Forst told Susan Slusser of the *San Francisco Chronicle* that the Rangers called the A's about Petit as soon as he cleared waivers in early February. Petit was outrighted a week and a half before news broke that Khalil Greene would not report to camp with the Rangers. Even when Greene was here, the situation was no different with Arias. The odds of him returning to the RedHawks are slim.

Colby Lewis in a minor league start yesterday: 10 strikeouts and no walks in six innings, average of 14 pitches per frame.

Prediction: This is Frankie Francisco's final season in Texas. If he pitches well, maybe the club approaches him this summer with a two-year offer, but he'll want a three-year deal as he heads into free agency for the first time. The Rangers won't want to commit that long, given his relatively short track record closing games and the presence of Neftali Feliz, Chris Ray, Tanner Scheppers, and Alexi Ogando as conceivable candidates for the ninth inning (not to mention C.J. Wilson, under control through 2011, if the rotation thing falters), and they'll probably just take the compensatory first-round pick and let Francisco move on. And if he doesn't pitch particularly well, then of course the club probably cuts ties for a different reason.

Two trades that Jon Paul Morosi of Fox Sports thinks make sense: Mike Lowell coming to Texas after all (presumably still for Max Ramirez), and Brandon McCarthy to Washington (return unspecified). There are apparently concerns about Lowell's mobility in Red Sox camp, which could make Matt Brown's defensive issues less of a factor as the club assesses whether to deal for a right-handed corner infield bat, particularly Lowell.

According to ESPN's Tim Kurkjian, a line drive that Nelson Cruz recently hit over Colorado left fielder Ryan Spilborghs prompted these two comments:

Spilborghs: "It hit my glove and still hit the fence on the fly. If I had caught it, the force would have taken me through the fence."

Rockies manager Jim Tracy: It was "the hardest hit ball I've seen in 35 years in a major league uniform."

Some observations from ESPN's Keith Law, who spent time on the back fields this week in Surprise:

On Martin Perez, whom Law ranks as baseball's number eight prospect: "In his outing on Tuesday, Perez was 90-94, touching 96 on one pitch, dialing up for those 94s when he needed it. His changeup, ordinarily his best pitch, was inconsistent, and he overthrew the majority of them, leaving them straight and anywhere from 84-87 mph, although he did flash one plus changeup at 78 mph with good arm speed and outstanding late fade. His curve was slow at 73-75 mph but had good rotation and true two-plane break. The Rangers have been working with Perez this spring on his feel for pitching, getting him to leave the big velocity in his pocket for when he needs it and avoid overthrowing that good changeup. He repeats his delivery well and was aggressive in attacking hitters; the physical comparisons to Johan Santana stand up well. He's a special prospect but I think 2011 is the earliest you might expect to see him in the majors."

On righthander Matt Thompson: "[S]howed an above-average curveball in the upper 70s, but his 88-90 mph fastball was straight and largely up in the zone. So far he's shown plus control in pro ball—walking just 10 of the 307 batters he faced—but he gave up a lot of contact due to that fastball. He just turned 20 last month, so he has plenty of time to find ways to keep hitters from whacking his fastball. The curveball and control give him a pretty good shot to succeed in a relief role, since he might miss more bats with added velocity from working in shorter stints."

On catcher Jorge Alfaro and shortstop Luis Sardinas: "Alfaro caught two innings and showed a 70 arm, including an incredibly accurate throw to second to nail a hitter who had singled in a run and was trying to take second; Alfaro's throw hitting the shortstop's glove just ahead of the bag so that the hitter couldn't avoid the tag. Sardinas, a switch-hitter, took BP and hit left-handed but didn't play the field; he has great bat speed, but his swing is long, from his Sheffield-esque wag to a late bat wrap behind his head, and he was very late on three average fastballs in his first at bat."

Hope you saw the Rangers edition of "30 Clubs in 30 Days" last night on MLB Network. An hour of greatness. I'm sure it will replay several times over the next couple days.

Righthander Vicente Padilla gets the Opening Day nod for the Dodgers. Manager Joe Torre called it an arbitrary decision, one that lines lefthander Clayton Kershaw up for the club's home opener. Padilla has given up five runs (4.50 ERA) on 11 hits and a walk in 10 spring innings over three starts, fanning nine.

Minnesota signed lefthander Ron Mahay to a minor league deal.

The Yankees optioned outfielder Greg Golson.

The Lincoln Saltdogs of the independent American Association signed first baseman Phillip Hawke, and the Wichita Wingnuts of the same league signed righthander Brock Piper.

I should have done this already—I'm not going to redo my entire Top 72 Prospects list from the book, but here's a revised top 27 after my week in Surprise:

1. Martin Perez, LHP (number 3 in December)
2. Neftali Feliz, RHP (1)
3. Justin Smoak, 1B (2)
4. Tanner Scheppers, RHP (4)
5. Alexi Ogando, RHP (39)
6. Wilmer Font, RHP (5)
7. Jurickson Profar, SS (6)
8. Miguel Velazquez, OF (25)
9. Mitch Moreland, 1B-OF (11)
10. Michael Main, RHP (7)
11. Robbie Ross, LHP (9)
12. Engel Beltre, OF (10)
13. Jorge Alfaro, C (U/R)
14. Michael Kirkman, LHP (15)
15. Robbie Erlin, LHP (48)
16. Danny Gutierrez, RHP (8)
17. Kasey Kiker, LHP (14)
18. Luis Sardinas, SS (22)
19. Blake Beavan, RHP (12)
20. Jake Brigham, RHP (34)
21. Neil Ramirez, RHP (29)
22. Pedro Strop, RHP (13)
23. Wilfredo Boscan, RHP (16)
24. Max Ramirez, C (17)
25. Joe Wieland, RHP (18)
26. Tommy Mendonca, 3B (21)
27. Matt Thompson, RHP (44)

Though about 10 of those players have appeared in big league spring training games this month, nearly all of them are now in minor league camp, leaving behind a group that I think we'd all like to see win more than every third game as we're now down to an even 10 sleeps.

March 26, 2010

Ron Washington on Rich Harden, before the Rangers' new ace made his Friday start:

"What I've seen from Rich Harden is what I remember seeing in Oakland. He always got hit hard in spring. I'd like to see him step it up and give us something to hold onto. It's not about velocity, it's about placing the ball where you want to place it. But, I've seen Rich have some very bad springs and some very good seasons."

Washington was right about Harden for the most part. They were in A's camp together from 2003 through 2006, and in the first three of those four the righthander was pretty awful during spring training, posting a .309 opponents' batting average and composite 6.84 ERA (followed by regular season marks of .232 and 3.60)—though underneath his generally poor numbers in 2005 were 29 strikeouts and five walks in 21 innings.

But in 2006? Statistics don't always tell the whole story, and so I suppose Washington might have seen Harden get hit hard again, but if so, the hard hits were finding lots of gloves: the Cactus League managed only eight hits off Harden in 14 innings (.167) and two runs (1.29 ERA). He walked six and fanned 19.

Harden was just as dominant in the spring of 2007 (Washington's first spring with Texas)—limiting opponents to a .206 average and posting a 1.53 ERA as he punched out 29 and issued only four walks in 17.2 innings, but three weeks after camp broke, he was on the disabled list with a strained shoulder, only to come back in late June for another four appearances (6.2 total innings) before he was shut down for the year.

Maybe that helps explain why Harden now takes the approach of easing into form, ramping his velocity up gradually. Those 77 strikeouts (and just 15 walks) in 52.2 spring training innings in 2005, 2006, and 2007 were good looking, but at what cost? Harden's 2008 camp ERA was 4.76. It was 10.38 in 2009. It's 9.17 now (down from 11.25 after today's mediocre effort). But if lackluster March numbers mean it's more likely that Harden will be relatively healthy when it counts, fine.

As for Harden's Friday appearance, he sat in the upper 80s for two innings (as he has for much of the month) before flashing 93 and 94 the rest of the way. Encouraging.

For what it's worth, Harden's Opening Day opponent,

Toronto's Shawn Marcum, had pitched five innings in camp before starting yesterday against Tampa Bay, allowing no runs on one hit and one walk, fanning four. But yesterday? Nine runs on nine hits and two walks and a hit batsman in five frames.

I'd really prefer not to see a 9-8 game on April 5.

March 27, 2010

Texas has optioned lefthander Derek Holland, righthander Brandon McCarthy, and outfielder Craig Gentry to Oklahoma City and righthander Alexi Ogando to Frisco, and has assigned non-roster catcher Kevin Richardson to minor league camp. The McCarthy move presumably means the club got the veteran through revocable waivers, a formality but a prerequisite to the option given the length of time since his arrival in the big leagues.

The pitching moves all but cement the makeup of the Opening Day staff, with righthanders Doug Mathis and Willie Eyre reportedly locked up in a competition for the final bullpen spot (though one report suggests roster member Guillermo Moscoso has a shot at the job as well). Mathis is on the 40-man roster; Eyre is not. Bet on Mathis getting the nod, with Eyre and Moscoso options should Darren O'Day (bone bruise or inflammation in right elbow) be unable to go to start the season.

The fact that righthander Luis Mendoza remains in camp suggests the club may be trying now to trade him. Failing that, he'll be designated for assignment (if he hasn't quietly been already).

The roster stands at 38 members but will be at 40 once Ogando and Omar Beltre are reinstated from the restricted list at the end of camp. (Mendoza's removal will bring it back down to 39.)

The Rangers have also announced that, contrary to several local reports earlier this week, Scott Feldman will get the Opening Day start, rather than Rich Harden, who will pitch Game Two (followed by C.J. Wilson, Colby Lewis, and Matt Harrison).

March 27, 2010

The latest entrant in the Rangers' parade of utility infield candidates is 25-year-old Andres Blanco, formerly of the Royals and Cubs, with 349 big league at-bats (.252/.295/.324) to his credit. Texas has traded a player to be named later or cash to Chicago for the infielder.

Since Blanco (primarily a shortstop but with experience all over the infield) is on the roster and out of options, if he doesn't oust Joaquin Arias and the field to land a job on the bench over the next week, the Rangers will need to remove him from the roster as well, exposing him to league-wide waivers or moving him in another trade.

March 29, 2010

Well, your Opening Day starter appears to be ready to go.

Now *that's* a tuneup.

Sure, it's just one game, but when it's turned in by the guy whose next stroll to the mound will be when the games first count, there's a certain peace of mind it provides. We don't yet know if the second baseman will be ready to go on April 5, or if the right-on-right sidearm specialist will be, but it sure looks like the number one starter is. Scott Feldman needed only 89 pitches to complete seven scoreless, throwing another 20 pitches afterwards in the bullpen rather than on the mound just so that Chris Ray and Frankie Francisco could tune up themselves with an inning each.

Another player who seemed to deliver some peace of mind yesterday was infielder Andres Blanco, acquired Saturday from the Cubs for a player to be named later or cash (a deal to be consummated by July 1, by the way, according to MLB.com's Carrie Muskat—there's reportedly no pool of players to choose from; if the clubs can't agree on a player, the deal will be closed with cash). It's easier for a starting pitcher to make a statement in just one day in March, but Blanco came close himself, singling twice in four trips from the leadoff spot (he's now 8 for 13 [.615/.643/.692] between Cubs and Rangers camp) and, more importantly, making a dazzling 6-3 play in the hole from shortstop.

Ron Washington on the utility infield job before yesterday's game: "Because no one is trying to seize the opportunity, that makes it difficult. I'm looking to see who can play baseball. That means understanding what a situation is asking you do to and doing it. That's not asking much."

One of the nagging things about Joaquin Arias's game is that, despite his obvious tools, his body language rarely seems to suggest an opportunity-seizing sense of urgency, and as for that last part, playing to the situation, Arias seems to fall short of that, too. You see a guy playing for his big league life get caught stealing in a situation where he shouldn't have been running in the first place, for instance, and the immediate thought is that the manager isn't going to trust that guy enough to use him.

Trust plays a big part when it comes to the bench. Using a role player in the late innings often means the game is on the line. Using him to give a starter the occasional day off is by definition a downgrade in the lineup. You have to trust the player to hold things together. The Rangers have given Arias years of chances to earn that trust, and he has one week left to do so before he'll suit up in Arlington or hit the waiver wire.

At this point, it might be that the only way Arias wins a job is if Ian Kinsler has to start the season on the disabled list, in which case Texas would elect to go with two middle infielders rather than one plus a corner man like Matt Brown or Max Ramirez.

But even if that were the case, Arias may have trouble fending Gregorio Petit or Esteban German off for that second job. The frontrunner for the first, after just one day of work, seems to be Blanco. He turns 26 on April 11, and at the moment it sure looks like he'll be celebrating it on getaway day in Arlington.

April 11 is also the day that Kinsler and Darren O'Day would be eligible to come off the disabled list if that's where they're headed, as long as they don't appear in an exhibition game this week. If they do play this week, the 15-day DL assignment can't be backdated past the day they show up in a game.

Feldman will throw live batting practice on Wednesday (or Thursday, depending on which story is accurate), putting him in line for next Monday's Opening Day assignment.

The 27-year-old made the point that the Opening Day start is cool and all, but this is actually the first of his career (five years with some big league service) to begin the season anywhere in the Rangers rotation.

The man who will take the mound before Feldman: Roger Staubach, tabbed by the Rangers to throw out the ceremonial first pitch.

Jarrod Saltalamacchia (neck spasms) played five defensive innings in a minor league game yesterday and could play in the big league game today.

According to a local report, if Mike Lowell (now dealing with a bruised left knee) is no longer a consideration for an upgrade at the backup corner infield job (over Brown or Ramirez), other names that could fit are Kevin Millar, Wes Helms, Fernando Tatis, Geoff Blum, and Willie Bloomquist, but the final two probably make too much money (though each makes about half of the $3 million that Boston originally expected Texas to assume of Lowell's $12 million salary).

Jayson Stark of ESPN writes that the Rangers are "looking for a veteran starting pitcher. The question is, would they move [David] Murphy? He'd be a pretty good outfielder for a team looking for an extra outfielder." That doesn't make any sense. Any starter that Texas could get for Murphy would be a back-of-the-rotation type, and the Rangers aren't in need of one of those.

San Francisco signed righthander Matt Cain to a contract extension yesterday (maintaining his $4.25 million salary this year, bumping his $6.25 million club option in 2011 to $7 million, and tacking on $15 million in 2012, plus a $1 million signing bonus payable in 2011). That cooks my idea from three weeks ago ("that [Chris] Davis or [Justin] Smoak gets traded this July, maybe with Derek Holland or Matt Harrison, plus Wilmer Font or Engel Beltre, to the Giants for righthander Matt Cain . . . and right-handed corner bat Mark DeRosa (set to earn $12 million in 2010-2011"), to the delight of many of you.

So dial back to a few ideas I came up with back in February:

1. "If (when) Kansas City is 20 games out in mid-July, despite a second straight Cy Young-quality season from Greinke, I'd call the Royals and offer them Holland, Font, [Alexi] Ogando, [Mitch] Moreland, and Engel Beltre for [Zack] Greinke and a middle reliever or veteran bench piece (whichever makes more roster sense at that point)."
2. Or "Smoak, Font, and [Kasey] Kiker for Brandon Webb." (Remember, we're talking about July, so this assumes Webb is healthy.)
3. Or "[Omar] Poveda and Engel Beltre for (righthander) Chris Young, or—if the decision is made to move Feliz into the rotation—Harrison, Font, and Engel Beltre for Heath Bell, who is under control through 2011 (a year longer than Frankie Francisco is)." (Obviously Poveda is now out of the mix. Make it Joe Wieland.)

A fourth: Michael Kirkman, Ogando, Ramirez, and Moreland to Florida for Ricky Nolasco and left-handed reliever Renyel Pinto.

A fifth: if Josh Willingham remains a National at mid-season, Moreland and Kiker for the outfielder.

Boston released lefthander Brian Shouse.

A week from today, they count. Today, Matt Harrison takes the hill against Colorado, hoping to wrap up his excellent camp with as strong a statement effort as the one Scott Feldman turned in yesterday.

March 30, 2010

tune up (tōōn ŭp), verb

1. To adjust so as to put oneself in proper condition; to prepare for a specified activity
2. *Informal*: To maul; to work over; to deliver a righteous beating to

We talked yesterday about how Scott Feldman's Sunday effort was the epitome of the first kind of tune-up.

What Neftali Feliz did yesterday embodied the second.

With Texas nursing a 7-6 lead against Colorado, Feliz was called on to close things out for Texas in the ninth.

Batter one: 97, 98, 100 (according to MLB.com Gameday). Strikeout looking.

Batter two: 99, 99, 101, 81, 100. Strikeout swinging.

Batter three: 99, 80, 100, 100, 80, 100, 100. Strikeout swinging.

Some have written that three of those 100s were actually 101s. Regardless, of Feliz's 15 pitches, 11 were strikes. Said the 21-year-old after the game: "I was trying to guide the ball and be too fine when I was pitching as a starter. I just really had to get in that state of being a reliever.

"It was one of those days where I came out and knew I had that one inning and gave it my all."

Ron Washington on his expectations for Feliz: "That he doesn't take how good he is for granted. That he keeps the fire burning in his belly. That he realizes that when we put him in the game, we're putting him in for one purpose, to leave everything he has out there."

I don't know if Feliz is eventually going to be a lockdown starting pitcher in the big leagues, but efforts like Monday's—and quotes like the one he delivered minutes later—almost make it hard to resist the idea of turning the eighth inning, and maybe eventually the ninth, over to the young Dominican for a long, long time. Almost.

There's no TV or radio for today's game against Arizona. But even if there were, you wouldn't get a glimpse of Feliz back at work. He'll pitch on the back fields, in a minor league game.

The consecutive-day assignment is a key one. The Rangers had him pitch back to back just once in 2009—actually, it's the only time the righthander has done it in his five-year pro career—and the results were impressive: a scoreless, one-hit eighth against Round Rock on July 16 (10 pitches, six strikes, no walks or strikeouts) followed by a perfect eighth against the same club on July 17 (17 pitches, 11 strikes, no walks, two strikeouts). It was one of the final minor league tests for Feliz, who was in the big leagues just over two weeks later.

But dig a little beneath the surface and the red flag emerges.

After those two appearances in two days (his sixth and seventh straight scoreless efforts out of eight games as a reliever), he then got three days of rest and, while his strikeout rate certainly didn't suffer, his effectiveness did.

On July 21, he allowed only his second home run of the season, in a two-inning stint that featured four strikeouts.

Then, next pitching on July 25, he gave up two runs on three hits (including a triple) and two walks in two frames. He fanned five, but threw only 28 of his 44 pitches for strikes, and allowed two Nashville Sounds to steal safely.

Feliz settled down after that, firing scoreless innings against the Albuquerque Isotopes on July 28 and July 31, after which he was summoned to Texas, where he was untouchable and indescribable for five weeks before proving mortal (yet still dominant) over the season's final month.

Still, at no time in that two-month run through the American League did Feliz pitch on consecutive days. He'll do that today, because the Rangers will need him to in 2010—particularly with C.J. Wilson now in the rotation. The plan is for Feliz and Darren Oliver to hold down the eighth inning, to preserve leads for Frankie Francisco to close out in the ninth.

Keep an eye on how Feliz fares today—despite the lack of a broadcast, there will be no doubt be real-time Twitter accounts of his inning of back fields work and plenty of beat coverage in the papers—but also on what happens the next time he pitches, which may be once more this week in Arizona and possibly Saturday in Frisco, setting him up to be available in relief of Scott Feldman on Monday, when it all counts.

In a camp in which consistency of velocity has been an issue in a couple cases (Rich Harden's down, Matt Harrison's up), yesterday's Neftali Feliz Show—12 fastballs that averaged 99.4 on the gun—could be as big a development as any, particularly given the struggles he had early in camp, and especially if he bounces back with another solid outing today, and the rest of the week.

March 31, 2010

According to local reports, Texas has reassigned infielders Esteban German and Gregorio Petit to minor league camp, leaving Andres Blanco and Joaquin Arias with the big club for now. Chances are both survive final cuts in the event that Ian Kinsler starts the season on the disabled list, an apparent likelihood at this point. Texas also sent catcher Matt Treanor (who chose not to exercise his out clause) to Oklahoma City.

Right-handed bats Max Ramirez and Matt Brown continue to vie for the corner infielder bench spot, and Doug Mathis and Willie Eyre are competing for the final bullpen job.

In addition, Rule 5 lefthander Ben Snyder has cleared waivers, setting up one of two resolutions: (1) the Rangers succeed in persuading San Francisco to take prospect(s) in return for him (in which case he'd be assigned to a club in the Texas farm system) or (2) the Rangers sell him back to the Giants for $25,000.

April 2010

40-MAN ROSTER (41*)

Pitchers (25)

Omar Beltre, Scott Feldman, Neftali Feliz, Frankie Francisco, Rich Harden, Matt Harrison, Derek Holland, Tommy Hunter, Michael Kirkman, Colby Lewis, Warner Madrigal, Doug Mathis, Brandon McCarthy, Luis Mendoza, Guillermo Moscoso, Dustin Nippert, Darren O'Day, Alexi Ogando, Darren Oliver, Zach Phillips, Omar Poveda, Chris Ray, Ben Snyder, Pedro Strop, C.J. Wilson

Catchers (3)

Max Ramirez, Jarrod Saltalamacchia, Taylor Teagarden

Infielders (6)

Elvis Andrus, Joaquin Arias, Andres Blanco, Chris Davis, Ian Kinsler, Michael Young

Outfielders (7)

Brandon Boggs, Julio Borbon, Nelson Cruz, Craig Gentry, Vladimir Guerrero, Josh Hamilton, David Murphy

60-Day Disabled List (1)

Eric Hurley

** Per MLB rules, righthanders Beltre and Ogando were permitted to participate in spring training without counting against the 40-man roster.*

April 1, 2010: TROT COFFEY

- According to a number of reports, mostly coming out of Boston, the Rangers have been on hand in Red Sox camp this week, presumably to scout Mike Lowell, and while Lowell is moving better and should be able to avoid the disabled list to start the season, a deal with Texas is probably unlikely at this point (in spite of "accelerated" talks) unless Boston is willing to pay almost his entire $12 million salary for 2010
- Earlier this week, Jon Daniels ranked the likelihood of the club acquiring a right-handed-hitting first baseman in lieu of going with Matt Brown or Max Ramirez at 50-50 (Jim Reeves, ESPN Dallas)
- Texas's interest in corner infielder Ryan Garko, who lost a camp competition with Mike Sweeney for a spot on Seattle's bench, is not high (Jon Paul Morosi, Fox Sports)
- The reason the Mariners placed Garko on waivers was that his big league debut was more than three years ago, requiring Seattle to get him through waivers in order to option him (this is presumably the revocable brand of waivers that Texas needed to acquire in righthander Brandon McCarthy's case, though the Mariners probably wouldn't revoke) (Dave Cameron, USSMariner.com)
- According to multiple sources, Texas isn't all that interested in first baseman Kevin Millar, who has been released by the Cubs (and who has the same agent as Lowell, interestingly)
- Texas expressed interest in Boston infielder Jed Lowrie before he came down with mononucleosis and the Rangers acquired infielder Andres Blanco from the Cubs (Rob Bradford, WEEI)
- The Rangers also considered infielder Cristian Guzman, who lost the Nationals shortstop gig to Ian Desmond, before trading for Blanco (Ken Rosenthal, Fox Sports)
- The Rangers, despite having added Blanco, may still be talking to Arizona about deposed infielder Augie Ojeda, but the Diamondbacks aren't interested in righthander Luis Mendoza and continue to ask for too much in return (Rosenthal)
- Tampa Bay has until tomorrow to add Hank Blalock to the active roster, and he's making noise that if he doesn't beat out the more versatile Reid Brignac and make the club, he'll exercise the out clause in his non-roster deal rather than accept a minor league assignment (Marc Topkin, *St. Petersburg Times*)
- The apparent beneficiary if Boston does move Lowell (or place him on the DL) would be former Rangers farmhand Tug Hulett, who is hitting .289/.340/.533 in camp
- Former Newberg Report journaler Michael Schlact will blog for MLB this season—check it out at http://schlact.mlblogs.com/

Doug Mathis has reportedly won the final Rangers bullpen spot, Nelson Cruz will apparently hit in front of Chris Davis to start the season, and Surprise will be in the rearview mirror later today.

I wrote a few days ago, when Texas was 6-14-1 in Arizona, that "[c]amp records don't mean a whole lot, but losing a lot is losing a lot, and I'd be able to ignore something as ugly as 11-18-1 as long as it included a decent enough 5-4 run to finish things out. Even a little momentum would be super-welcome over this last week and a half."

The club is now 9-17-1, a miserable record but one that includes several stalwart pitching lines in the latest 3-3 run. It does feel like the Rangers have found just a little bit of momentum.

This spring, maybe more than any in franchise history, on the field and off, packing up and getting out of Surprise couldn't come quickly enough.

April 1, 2010

According to multiple Twitter reports, Texas has claimed right-handed-hitting first baseman Ryan Garko off waivers from Seattle.

The move likely means Garko will assume the bench job that non-roster corner infielder Matt Brown and optionable catcher-first baseman Max Ramirez were competing for.

April 1, 2010

The Rangers, having gotten Rule 5 lefthander Ben Snyder through waivers, have reached an agreement with San Francisco to allow them to keep the 24-year-old reliever. Texas has traded 17-year-old lefthander Edwin Escobar to the Giants for the right to retain Snyder in the minor leagues.

Here's what I wrote about Escobar in this year's Bound Edition, in which I'd ranked him as the system's number 43 prospect:

Pitching in the Arizona League at age 17, lefthander Edwin Escobar had an outstanding unveiling in 2009, giving up one run on five hits and four walks in eight innings over his first three appearances, fanning 10. Thereafter, first-inning troubles (.345 opponents' average, 8.25 ERA) would dog him, and he'd finish his debut season with a 2-5, 5.00 mark. But several aspects of his season, including a 3:1 strikeout-to-walk ratio (48 strikeouts and 16 walks in 45 innings), were impressive enough to land Escobar just outside the league's top 20 prospects list compiled by Baseball America.

A relative of Angels righthander Kelvim Escobar and Brewers shortstop Alcides Escobar, the young Venezuelan sits in the low 90s and may not project for much more, given his thick 6'1" build.

Two weeks ago, after seeing him again on the back fields, I wrote: "*I may be coming around on lefthander*

Edwin Escobar a bit. Would I have written Francisco Liriano off because I didn't like his frame? Rich Harden? (Caveat: I'm not making a Liriano or Harden comp.)" My reservations about him stem from the lack of projection in his stocky, six-foot-ish frame, but he'll pitch most of the 2010 season at age 18 and already touches the low 90s. Even if he doesn't project for much more, there's something there. He's a prospect.

But there are a couple dozen pitchers ahead of Escobar on the Rangers' prospect depth chart. This trade is a good example of the significance of having not only as many blue-chip prospects as any franchise in the game, but also as much depth as any system. Escobar may turn out to be a dependable big league starter in four or five years, or he may never reach AA, which is where Texas will send Snyder in hopes of further developing him as a left-on-left weapon for the bullpen.

We won't know for a few years whether this was a good trade, but we know this now: the Rangers' depth can be credited for making the deal palatable enough to get done.

April 2, 2010

Kansas City at Texas, tonight, Rangers Ballpark.
Kansas City at Texas, tomorrow, Dr Pepper Ballpark.
Toronto at Texas, Monday, Rangers Ballpark.
To borrow a phrase: It's time.

This Surprise ending
Couldn't come quickly enough
See you at the Yard

April 2, 2010

The Rangers have traded right-handed pitcher Luis Mendoza to Kansas City for cash considerations. He was out of options.

April 2, 2010

The Rangers have signed righthander Scott Feldman to a contract extension that guarantees, according to local reports, $13.325 million through 2012, and includes a 2013 option that would pay another $9.2 million (with a $600,000 buyout should the option not be exercised).

April 3, 2010

In each of C.J. Wilson's last two starts in Rangers Ballpark, he threw 61 pitches. In the first, he threw 35 strikes. In the second, he threw 34 strikes. Nearly identical. In those categories, at least. In the others?

IP	H	R	ER	BB	SO	HR	Flyouts	Groundouts
2.2	9	8	8	2	0	2	13	4
5.0	0	0	0	2	4	0	3	5

Those two starts were 1,701 days and worlds and worlds apart. As a relief pitcher, for all the positives Wilson brought to the mound, he averaged 17.6 pitches per inning last year, 18.9 the year before, 17.2 the year before that. Too many for any pitcher, totally unacceptable for someone wanting to start.

Last night: A dozen pitches per inning.

I wrote this on September 4 last year (and I don't have the motivation right now to recalculate to include the season's final month):

Wilson pitching on no days' rest in 2009 (16 appearances): 10.80 ERA, 5.4 walks per nine innings, slash line of .344/.417/.531.

On one day of rest (20 appearances) : 2.37 ERA, 6.2 walks per nine, .147/.310/.235.

Two days' rest (12 appearances): 0.66 ERA, 3.3 walks per nine, .250/.333/.354.

Three or more days' rest (12 appearances): 0.00 ERA, 0.6 walks per nine, .170/.185/.189 (one walk and one extra-base hit in 54 plate appearances).

It looks like Wilson is gonna dig pitching on four days of rest, huh?

That was a wow effort, completing a knockout camp for Wilson.

A little more than a month after that final Wilson home start of 2005, he entered the seventh inning of a 5-3 win over Felix Hernandez and Seattle, giving up a run and getting two outs in a game that featured two other rookie pitchers: starter Josh Rupe, who allowed two runs over five innings in what was his big league debut, and reliever Scott Feldman, who pitched a scoreless sixth—maintaining a perfect ERA six appearances into his career.

Imagine if you knew on September 16, 2005, watching that game, that five seasons later Rupe would be starting the year in AAA again, that Wilson would have become the pitcher that he's become, and that Feldman, the former 30th round pick who had Tommy John surgery months after being drafted and who had his arm slot changed almost as many times as his role, would be signing a contract on the eve of the season, guaranteeing nearly $14 million over the next three years, or more than $22.5 million over four. Almost impossible.

The first outward commitment that the organization showed in camp to Feldman, who went 17-8 for this club in 2009, came a week ago when it was announced that he, and not Rich Harden, would get the club's Opening Day start. The second came yesterday with the news of the contract, a team-friendly deal if he's anywhere near the pitcher over the life of the deal that he was last year but also one that sets Feldman up for life, even if he were to never replicate 2009. If the 27-year-old wins 35 games the next two years, don't be surprised to see the club to rip up the deal and offer a new, longer-term commitment.

The Rangers talked yesterday about Feldman's history as a strike-thrower and a winner, his versatility and his durability, but what they kept coming back to was that they had determined early in camp, with Kevin Millwood gone, that Feldman was the guy they believed could lead the staff going forward, not as much in the sense of getting the ball April 5 as in providing an example to Derek Holland and Tommy Hunter and a dozen others over the next few years. "He represents what we want to see in our pitchers," said Jon Daniels, who made a point of the fact that every time management had sat down for a similar press conference in recent years, locking up a homegrown product who had developed into a core player, it was a hitter sitting between the manager and general manager for the photo opportunities. Feldman is the first pitcher in years to occupy that seat, and he occupies a lot more than that now, if you listen closely to what the front office is saying.

Ryan Garko is a lifetime .381/.438/.429 hitter in Rangers Ballpark. And a .313/.392/.495 hitter against left-handed pitchers for his career. He strikes out only 50 times for every 400 big league plate appearances. Primarily a first baseman, he hasn't caught in the big leagues but came up as a catcher prospect (and in fact won the 2003 Johnny Bench Award as the NCAA's top catcher in his final season with Stanford), making him at least an emergency option behind the plate.

Basically, he's what Texas would love to see Max Ramirez turn into. And at $550,000, at only a slightly greater cost. There are incremental bonuses that start to kick in if Garko reaches 325 plate appearances. It's a longshot that he'll be needed that often.

So the Rangers now have Garko in Texas and Ramirez at AAA, neither of whom would be around presumably if the club had instead traded for Mike Lowell, who would have cost Texas $3 million, if not more.

Will Garko be the hitter that Lowell will be in 2010? Maybe not. But maybe. Will he be the clubhouse factor that Lowell would have been here? No. But he's a lot less expensive, allows Texas to give Ramirez everyday at-bats at Oklahoma City to try and resurrect his trade value, and it's not out of the question that at age 29 he provides Texas as much in the limited role he'll be asked to handle as the 36-year-old Lowell would have.

You might recall that Texas was apparently hot after Garko at last year's trade deadline. From last July 28's Newberg Report:

According to [Joel] Sherman [of the New York Post], the Rangers "were convinced [late yesterday] they were the front-runners to get Ryan Garko from the Indians" and "were surprised when he ended up going to the Giants instead."

By the way, Garko's wasn't the revocable type of waivers that Brandon McCarthy, for example, had to clear in order to be optioned. Seattle placed Garko on irrevocable waivers.

Texas sold righthander Luis Mendoza to Kansas City for an undisclosed amount. Probably not much, just a sum that allowed the Royals to secure Mendoza—who is just as out of options for them as he was for Texas—without having to sweat the waiver claim process. The 26-year-old is a perennial winter ball star whose considerable stuff hasn't translated to big league success—or even AAA success, really. He's Kansas City's enigma now.

The trade of Mendoza and outright of Ben Snyder brings the roster down to 38 players, but that doesn't include Alexi Ogando or Omar Beltre, who will need to be reinstated to the roster this weekend in order to effectuate their options to the farm. Joaquin Arias survives, but when Ian Kinsler returns, he's the expected casualty, not only from the active roster but the 40-man version as well, as he's also out of options. He'll probably pinch-run for Vladimir Guerrero late in a game or two until Kinsler is back, after which chances are he'll end up with another organization.

Some incidentals:

Watching Andres Blanco take infield is a treat.

The cover story in this week's *Dallas Observer* is an excellent feature on Chuck Greenberg. Read it. (And note this comment: "It's my job to get this franchise to operate like a big-market team. The resources are here, and it's our job to cultivate them. If we do that there's no reason we can't spend our money along the lines of, maybe not Boston and New York, but what they do in Anaheim and Philadelphia." The Angels and Phillies both had payrolls in the $113 million range last year, about $45 million more than Texas.)

ESPN's Buster Olney has two Rangers on his list of 10 players "who had great spring trainings": Wilson (number three) and Michael Young (number five), calling the latter "the Texas metronome."

ESPN's Keith Law projects 87 wins for Texas, enough to prevail in the American League West—but sees the Rangers losing to the Yankees in first round of the playoffs. (Would we take that in lieu of whatever's behind Door No. 2? Yeah, probably.)

Vladimir Guerrero told the Dominican newspaper *El Dia* that he thought when he reported to camp with Texas that it was possible that the Rangers would sign righthander Pedro Martinez.

Frisco's pitching staff will include Martin Perez, Tanner Scheppers, Ogando, and Blake Beavan, among others. The organization plans to have Ogando start and Scheppers relieve at the outset, though the thought is that they're being groomed for the opposite roles. Innings will be carefully monitored for both.

Baseball America ranks the Rangers' minor league talent second in baseball, next to Tampa Bay's. Oakland was 11th, Seattle 12th, the Angels 26th.

Positional rankings: According to *BA*, Justin Smoak is baseball's top first base prospect, Neftali Feliz and Scheppers check in at number two and number 10 among righthanded starters, Martin Perez is the number two left-handed starter (Robbie Ross (17) and Kasey Kiker (19) make the list as well), Jurickson Profar is number 13 at shortstop, and Mitch Moreland is the number 17 outfielder.

Texas released minor league righthanders Kelvin Arendell, Reinier Bermudez, Jared Hyatt, Jorge Quintero, Jae-Kuk Ryu, Jared Schrom, and Bobby Wilkins; lefthanders Keith Campbell and Winston Marquez; catcher John Otness; and outfielders Santo DeJesus (once known as Juan Polanco), Kyle Rhoad, and Tim Rodriguez.

Boston righthander Junichi Tazawa, whom the Red Sox signed after the 2008 season despite offering the 22-year-old less than Texas did, will miss the 2010 season due to Tommy John surgery.

Outfielders John Mayberry Jr. and Justin Maxwell failed to win jobs in Philadelphia and Washington, and both were optioned.

Pittsburgh traded righthander Virgil Vazquez, like Mayberry and Maxwell a former Rangers draft pick, to Tampa Bay, but he'll go to AAA as relief insurance, as will righthander Joaquin Benoit, who lost his competition with righty Mike Ekstrom for the Rays' final bullpen spot.

Hank Blalock was beaten out by Reid Brignac for the final job on Tampa Bay's bench. Will Blalock stick with his declaration that he's not interested in being a AAA player? He reportedly has until Sunday to accept his minor league assignment (according to the *St. Petersburg Times*), and has semi-retracted his Wednesday comments, saying he has no plans to retire. We'll know soon enough if he'll be Durham Bull teammates with Benoit.

Oakland reassigned righthander Jason Jennings to minor league camp. Cincinnati released righthander Kip Wells. Arizona outrighted Jose Marte.

Jon Daniels and his crew of pro scouts don't get enough credit for the trade on the eve of the 2008 season that sent Marte, a decent prospect at best, to the Diamondbacks for righthander Dustin Nippert, who was out of options.

Philadelphia released outfielder Brad Wilkerson. Kansas City released righthander John Bannister. The Angels released lefthander Daniel Haigwood. Washington released lefthander Mike Venafro.

Righthander Jamey Wright made the Cleveland staff.

The Fort Worth Cats of the independent American Association once again signed lefthander Joel Kirsten.

More importantly:

Elvis Andrus missed last night's exhibition and will miss today's due to inflammation on the outside of his left wrist, but he's expected to be ready for Monday's opener.

Nelson Cruz was scratched last night with a bruised right thumb he suffered in Thursday's game but should be in Monday's lineup—and he might play today.

And Darren O'Day was pronounced ready to go (assuming no residual discomfort today) after testing his right elbow bone bruise in a 26-pitch, simulated game effort yesterday.

The timetable on Ian Kinsler's return remains uncertain, but the other timetable, the one we've been talking about for a couple months (that have felt a lot longer), is quite clear:

Two sleeps.

April 4, 2010

The Rangers have made the following moves:

- Placed second baseman Ian Kinsler (high right ankle sprain) and righthanders Tommy Hunter (left oblique strain) and Warner Madrigal (right forearm soreness) on the 15-day disabled list, retroactive to March 26; each is eligible to be activated April 10
- Optioned righthander Guillermo Moscoso to Oklahoma City
- Reassigned righthander Willie Eyre, catchers Toby Hall and Matt Treanor, infielders Matt Brown, Esteban German, and Gregorio Petit, and outfielder Endy Chavez to minor league camp
- Reinstated righthanders Omar Beltre and Alexi Ogando to the 40-man roster, and optioned Beltre to Oklahoma City and Ogando to Frisco; the reinstatements bring the roster to a full 40 members

The Opening Day roster, therefore, is:

PITCHERS (12): Scott Feldman, Neftali Feliz, Frankie Francisco, Rich Harden, Matt Harrison, Colby Lewis, Doug Mathis, Dustin Nippert, Darren O'Day, Darren Oliver, Chris Ray, C.J. Wilson

CATCHERS (2): Jarrod Saltalamacchia, Taylor Teagarden

INFIELDERS (6): Elvis Andrus, Joaquin Arias, Andres Blanco, Chris Davis, Ryan Garko, Michael Young

OUTFIELDERS (5): Julio Borbon, Nelson Cruz, Vladimir Guerrero, Josh Hamilton, David Murphy

Righthander Eric Hurley (rehab from right shoulder surgery) is on the 60-day disabled list, effective today.

The club also released two righthanders from minor league camp: 26-year-old reliever Jumbo Diaz, who pitched in late relief for Frisco last year after six seasons in the Dodgers system, and 27-year-old Clayton Hamilton, who spent two years with the Rangers (Bakersfield, Frisco, Oklahoma City) after the club selected him from Pittsburgh in the AAA phase of the December 2007 Rule 5 Draft.

April 5, 2010

I could give you three reasons why the Rangers will win the American League West, and three why they won't.

I could give you three each on the Angels, too, and the Mariners. Maybe two and four on the A's.

We saw win totals predicted from all corners this weekend, locally and nationally, and I suppose that in at least some cases it was at an editor's request. The fans demand it, right? I guess.

Tell me in August whether you think the Cowboys are a 12-4 team, or headed toward 9-7. I get that. But why don't we talk much in October about whether the Mavs are a 48- or 56-win club? Or whether the Stars are poised for 95 points, or instead just 85?

In basketball and hockey, where they play five times as many games as in football, only the experts talk on the eve of the season about win or point totals. Are they a playoff team? Are they ready to lock down home court/ice? Do they have a chance to contend for a title? That's what we hear about. As it should be.

In baseball, they play 10 times as often as in football, double the number of games of their arena counterparts. But for some reason we get bogged down on whether this is the year we win 92 instead of 87.

Someone who confidently chooses one number over the other before the first W or L is recorded must have a handle on when and how well Ian Kinsler will come back from his high ankle sprain—and on whether he can avoid trying to do too much like he did last summer when others were out of the lineup, on what Vladimir Guerrero has left, on whether Rich Harden can flip the switch right away, on whether Ron Washington's situation will galvanize or distract or neither, on whether Josh Hamilton and Chris Davis will be able to lock 2008 back in, on Elvis Andrus and Nelson Cruz taking the next step, on how that seven-game swing through Boston and Detroit coming out of the Break will go, on what C.J. Wilson and Colby Lewis and Matt Harrison and Chris Ray will be, on the way Clint Hurdle's proposed approach will affect results, on how Julio Borbon will fare now that there's a book out there on him, on which three Mariners starters Texas will face days after the trade deadline, on whether Scott Feldman and Neftali Feliz can repeat, on the catchers, on what sorts of contributions we'll get from Tommy Hunter and Derek Holland and Brandon McCarthy and Alexi Ogando and Tanner Scheppers and Justin Smoak, on whether Guillermo Moscoso and Eric Hurley and Pedro Strop and Michael Kirkman and Omar Beltre will be needed and how they'll respond, on the odds of Darren O'Day and Darren Oliver staying steady, on how many days the regular players on this club will lose to the disabled list.

I don't expect this to be a 96-win club, or a 76-win club. But I think it's silly to argue whether it's an 85-win roster, rather than a squad poised to win 88 times.

The talk last September 13, when Texas won Game One of a twinbill against Seattle, 7-2, to improve to 80-61, was whether, despite dwindling playoff chances, the team could cross that elusive 90-win plateau by putting together a winning record over the final 21 games. Nobody saw a 7-14 collapse and 87 wins coming.

Yet, though there are eight times as many regular season games left to play today, writers are assertively picking the number 87 or 89 or 92 out of the air and asking players and officials to weigh in.

I have no idea what the Rangers' 2010 win total will, or should, be. I'm not sure if Texas will win its baseball game this afternoon. I do have a pretty good idea who will suit up for Texas and Toronto this week, though, and my focus is on Feldman-Shaun Marcum, Harden-Brian Tallet, and Wilson-Ricky Romero. Even then, coming out of this series with three wins, two, one, or none probably doesn't tell us much more about where this thing is headed than we believe we know today.

Minnesota started the 2009 season 4-7, the Angels 4-8. Both played past 162.

I won't guess what the Texas record will be in a week, let alone in six months, but I'm counting on this group to play hard and play smart and play well for three-and-a-half months, well enough to justify the addition of two impact players in July, maybe one of them in time for a huge July 22-29, seven-game set against the Angels and A's in Arlington, the other before a three-game series in Anaheim concludes on August 1.

No matter what the record is at that point, I won't hazard a guess as to what it will be two months later after the Mariners and Angels come into Rangers Ballpark for 156 through 162. And I certainly won't pretend I've got a bead on that final number today.

I'm more interested in whether Texas wins a game than what the final score is. The important thing, whether it was a pitchers' duel or a slugfest, a blowout or an extra-inning walkoff, is that we were better than the other guys on that day. Same with the season. As long as we're better than enough of the other guys to keep playing beyond October 3, it doesn't matter to me how many games we won, or how big a cushion we had in the standings.

Predictions are fun. So are video games, and turning double plays in your backyard (you're Bert Campaneris, he's Bump Wills).

I'm not suggesting we shouldn't close our eyes and imagine the electricity of a September in Arlington that's about more than just a football season that will end with the hosting of a Super Bowl. This is unquestionably a year about which the players are thinking that way, management is thinking that way, an ownership group on the doorstep is thinking that way, and for all those reasons we should feel even more emboldened thinking that way.

But I look at this like I would the onset of a basketball or hockey season. Don't ask me for an over-under on victories. Is this a playoff team? Will the Rangers do enough, starting today, to win more times than 10 other teams in the league? I don't know, but this is about to be a year where that's the question, not whether "progress" will be made. The answer is likely going to depend on how many of those real player questions get answered acceptably.

And on which of those three reasons to say yes, and three reasons to say no, will come to pass. No formula can help us there, and just as no formula could have predicted 17 wins last year for Feldman, or 54 RBI for Hamilton, or seven wins over the final 21, trying to figure out now how many of the 162 that lay in front of us will end with daps near the mound is probably a waste of energy.

I know this much: They're always fascinating, but this Rangers baseball season, with the engines set to start in a few hours, promises to be one that we're going to remember for a very long time.

Hopefully for the right reasons.

April 5, 2010

Three rambles from a guy who's wiped out, who's baseball-hoarse, who was tense for nearly three hours beginning with the moment Sgt. Dana Bowman parachuted from a helicopter seemingly too far south of the right field edge of the stadium, and who couldn't be happier that The Great Game is back:

1.

2. A free Bound Edition to the first person who correctly identifies the pitch in today's game that prompted me to write down: "There it is. We're going to win this game."

3. Hisssssss....

April 6, 2010

I'm giving myself the day off, too. I'm sports tired.

For now, check out a few things:

Scott Lucas has put together a strong organizational depth chart for the Rangers, top to bottom. Great resource.

On the Frisco staff you'll find righthander Ryan Tatusko, from whom I'll have a new Back Fields Diary entry later this morning.

Also from Scott you'll see that we've replaced the eight-prospect photo rotation on the front page of the website with action shots of eight new players who stand out in the system right now. Scott took most of the shots a few weeks ago in Surprise.

Also worth checking out on the website is a message that Chuck Morgan posted on the Newberg Report forum. It involves Rangers Ballpark, Bound Edition cover artist Drew Sheppard, and the Wave. And it might make you happy.

Speaking of the Bound Edition, I've now gotten 224 responses to last night's invitation to guess which pitch made me think suddenly that we were going to win yesterday's game.

Two got it right. Books will go out in today's mail to Shawn Redd and Lonnie Wilson.

It was the 0-1 pitch to Nelson Cruz in the seventh that he laid off. The same 80-mph Shawn Marcum change that we'd swung through probably a dozen times. From where I sat the pitch looked maybe two inches low, right over the plate, and Cruz patiently watched it go by for ball one. Served a little notice that maybe we weren't going to keep biting on that pitch.

It felt like a turning point (even if he hadn't homered three fastballs later). In my head, strange as it might be, I thought at that moment we were going to get the W.

Have a great two days. It won't be easy for me, either, but try to patiently wait for Rich Harden-Brian Tallet tomorrow night.

April 8, 2010

"It was just an odd night," said Rich Harden.

Yep.

Am I concerned about Harden, who seemed to have little more idea where his pitches were going than the Toronto hitters who went down on strikes for an extraordinary eight of their 11 outs while he was on the mound?

Yes.

But not as concerned as I am about Josh Hamilton, who looks exceptionally uncomfortable and completely out of sync at the plate.

The Rangers issued 10 walks last night, after spending March as one of baseball's stingiest staffs as far as bases on balls were concerned.

Granted, spring training statistics don't mean a whole heck of a lot (see: Vladimir Guerrero's homerless camp), but the hope is that the club's low walk totals in Arizona were far more indicative of what to expect from this staff than last night's location disaster.

And that Hamilton's .373 batting average and .610 slug in camp suggests he can be more reliable in 2010 than he was in 2009.

But he looks like he's overthinking things and guessing too much, and that makes him an easy mark at the plate, as we saw last year.

Hamilton may never look as locked in this season as Nelson Cruz has for a month, and that's OK. But he needs to look a whole lot better than the 2009 version of himself, and in this admittedly tiny sample size of Games One and Two, he clearly hasn't.

I'd like to see Julio Borbon drop a bunt to lead off the bottom of the first today. After taking a pitch.

Thank goodness Monday's game ended well.

Losses happen in baseball, but the real ugly losses are hard to take. Last night's was a big old can of bad ugly. I was hoping that "O Canada" and those plummeting temperatures might have put Harden in a good place after an uninspiring spring. The changeup was on for the most part, but that sort of scattered fastball command leads not only to gifted bases but also to lousy pitch counts and a tax on the bullpen, and while Harden is historically not one who regularly goes deep into games, there's nothing acceptable about a pitch count looking like a radar gun reading in the fourth inning. That certainly can't happen every fifth day.

And as lost as Hamilton looks, that can't continue to handicap the lineup every day, particularly in the three hole.

It was on odd night, as Harden said. If by that he meant "abnormal," I sure hope that turns out to be true. If there was anything normal about it, then uh-oh.

C.J. Wilson has the task of putting Texas in a position to win the opening series this afternoon. He'd probably like for you to stop by his new blog but I would also recommend you check out the YouTube video (and wiffle ball BP session) he filmed with the producers of "Lost."

The four full-season minor league affiliates open today. A full season of daily game recaps from the formidable Scott Lucas begins tomorrow morning.

And finally, sometime later this morning the first 2010 installment of my weekly MLB.com column will turn up on TexasRangers.com. (This week's: Ranking the top 10 right-handed starting pitchers in the Rangers farm system.) I'll toss you a heads-up when it's posted.

April 8, 2010

According to multiple local reports, catcher Jarrod Saltalamacchia is headed to the disabled list with upper back stiffness. His last baseball action was Monday's walkoff shot to the right center field alley—unless you count the celebration scrum and a strikeout looking (in which he never took the bat off his shoulder) as a pinch-hitter yesterday. Veteran catcher Matt Treanor will reportedly be purchased from Oklahoma City to back up Taylor Teagarden during Saltalamacchia's absence. Treanor's arrival will necessitate a 40-man roster move.

Also, Josh Hamilton will sit today, as will Chris Davis, against Toronto lefty Ricky Romero.

Finally, if you have ideas for Ballpark improvements over the next year, stop by this thread on the message board: http://forum.newbergreport.com/viewtopic.php?f=1&t=10765. There just might be some folks in high places keeping an eye on it.

April 8, 2010

According to local reports, the Rangers have designated righthander Warner Madrigal for assignment to make room on the 40-man roster for catcher Matt Treanor, whose contract was purchased from Oklahoma City to replace the injured Jarrod Saltalamacchia on the active roster.

Texas has 10 days to trade Madrigal, release him, or get him through outright waivers in order to assign his contract to a minor league club in the system.

April 8, 2010

The local media accounts that reported Texas had designated righthander Warner Madrigal for assignment to create roster space for catcher Matt Treanor have now been corrected: Madrigal has instead been transferred to the 60-day disabled list.

April 9, 2010

It makes me very sad that I had no confidence with Josh Hamilton—*Josh HAMILTON*—at the plate with a two-run deficit and a man on second with one out to go yesterday. You know I'm a glass-half-full guy, but with two outs in the ninth and Hamilton stepping in against Jason Frasor as the tying run, it felt as if we were seven runs down. His rollover bouncer to second barely registered with me.

I hate that.

Ron Washington, acknowledging that he gave Hamilton most of the day off Thursday because he's been "out of whack" and had "lost his rhythm," said the left fielder will be back in the lineup tonight against Seattle lefthander Jason Vargas, off of whom he's a career 1 for 5 with a strikeout.

Through three games, the Texas Rangers are hitting .168/.248/.316 as a team. Only Houston's offense is OPS'ing less.

Take Vladimir Guerrero (7 for 11 with a home run) out of the mix, and the club sits at .107/.194/.238 as a group.

Against Toronto hurlers Shaun Marcum, Scott Downs, Frasor, Brian Tallet, Kevin Gregg, Ricky Romero, and Casey Janssen. Not anything approaching a Roy Halladay in the bunch. The mid-'90s Braves they are not.

The good news? I got chills at times watching C.J. Wilson pitch. Think of all the frontline starting pitchers the Rangers have had in however long you want to go back. Since Nolan Ryan and Kevin Brown and Kenny Rogers, name all of them who were four for four in these categories: stuff, location, reserve, and moxie.

It was just one day—maybe a few days if you count spring training—but Wilson was an absolute four for four.

Could he be Rogers?

The only other time in the last three seasons that a Texas starter took a no-decision after throwing at least seven shutout innings was Kevin Millwood, who did so last April 12. Entrusted with a 4-0 lead after seven, the Rangers bullpen couldn't hold on, giving up six runs in the Detroit eighth.

All six runs were credited to Wilson.

He'll get the Tigers again two weekends from now (after starts in Cleveland and Boston). The way Wilson looked today, it won't surprise me if he's facing Detroit hitters in the eighth inning again.

Sure hope Ian Kinsler is back by that second homestand (Detroit/Chicago, April 23-29). His timetable is a bit of a moving target, and so far it's only moving in one direction.

This Jarrod Saltalamacchia story isn't over. It's now not only about his inability to get settled physically. When the manager is calling a young player out publicly for "put[ting] us in a bad situation" and "need[ing] to mature"—*"I'm not disappointed in him for being hurt—that happens; I'm disappointed in how he has handled it"*—and that young player plays a position at which maturity and dependability and team-first thinking are key, it doesn't bode well.

Before you assume that the signals Nelson Cruz is taking that next step could put him line for a long-term extension, realize that he'll be 30 years old at mid-season. For that reason and not necessarily any others, he'll be motivated to capitalize on what could conceivably be his only shot at multi-year security, but how many years will the Rangers be willing to go? He's under team control (via arbitration) for another three years after this one.

And on a related subject, a callback to something I wrote on March 26:

Prediction: This is Frankie Francisco's final season in Texas. If he pitches well, maybe the club approaches him this summer with a two-year offer, but he'll want a three-year deal as he heads into free agency for the first time. The Rangers won't want to commit that long, given his relatively short track record closing games and the presence of Neftali Feliz, Chris Ray, Tanner Scheppers, and Alexi Ogando as conceivable candidates for the ninth inning (not to mention C.J. Wilson, under control through 2011, if the rotation thing falters), and they'll probably just take the compensatory first-round pick and let Francisco move on. And if he doesn't pitch particularly well, then of course the club probably cuts ties for a different reason.

This is not a knee jerk after yesterday's ninth: Francisco is going to be somewhere else in 2011. Who closes here next year? If Feliz sustains even moderate command of his secondaries like he did yesterday, isn't he the most plausible answer? This isn't the time to be thinking about a ninth-inning transition. But tuck it away.

Derek Holland, Blake Beavan, Wilfredo Boscan, and Joe Wieland in the Rangers' four minor league openers last night: 2.35 ERA, 16 strikeouts and three walks in 23 innings, 1.5 groundout-to-flyout rate. Stay tuned for Scott Lucas's complete game recaps in your mailbox later today.

Baseball America tabs Frisco's rotation (featuring Beavan, Martin Perez, Scheppers [though he probably won't start at the outset], Ogando [though he'll eventually relieve], and Kasey Kiker) as the third prospect-i-est in the minor leagues.

Perez is the youngest player in the Texas League by six months. Outfielder Engel Beltre is third youngest, Beavan is sixth, and infielder-outfielder Marcus Lemon is eighth. Hickory infielder Leury Garcia is eighth youngest in the South Atlantic League.

BA suggested before the NCAA season that LSU righthander Anthony Ranaudo would be the first college pitcher drafted this June (that may change due to recent elbow issues). Yesterday *BA* named Mississippi lefthander Drew Pomeranz its Midseason College Player of the Year. Ranaudo (11th round) and Pomeranz (12th round) were chosen by the Rangers in the 2007 draft (which included Julio Borbon, Tommy Hunter, Beavan, Michael Main, Neil Ramirez, Mitch Moreland, and Tim Smith, to name a few) but opted not to sign.

Pittsburgh released infielder Ramon Vazquez. Mike Lamb earned a spot on the Marlins' bench. Hank Blalock accepted his assignment to Tampa Bay's AAA affiliate, the Durham Bulls (and reached safely four times in five plate appearances [two singles, intentional walk, E-3, flyout to left] as the club's third baseman and cleanup hitter in a 5-3 win over Norfolk last night). Jason Botts signed with the Camden Riversharks of the independent Atlantic League.

Blalock's Bulls debut was also righthander Joaquin Benoit's. Pitching the sixth and seventh, he recorded all six of his outs on strikes (mixing in a single and a walk).

So Toronto gets out of town with a series win (and very nearly a series sweep), making it 10 years out of the last 11 that the Rangers have lost the season's opening series (last year's sweep of Cleveland is the exception).

Newberg Report: Rangers' Top Ten Righties

Scheppers set to make Minor League debut as reliever

By Jamey Newberg / Special to MLB.com
April 8, 2010

This year's Newberg Report column for MLB.com will have an alternating theme, twice a month analyzing or commenting on some sort of development with the Rangers at either the big league or Minor League level, the other two times a month featuring a top 10 list from the club's farm system—but not a straight ranking of the organization's prospects, as with this column the last two years.

One week it might be the top 10 corner infield prospects. The next, maybe the top 10 power hitters. Or the top 10 Latin American signees. Or the top 10 pitches (not pitchers, but pitches) in the system.

We'll kick things off this week with a look at the top 10 Rangers prospects from the deepest group in the organization: right-handed starting pitchers. Eric Hurley and Omar Poveda were not considered since they are currently sidelined.

1. TANNER SCHEPPERS, Frisco

Boasting a power fastball-curve combo that led some to suggest his stuff was second only to Stephen Strasburg's in the 2009 draft, Scheppers will make his official Minor League debut in Double-A, working in relief for Frisco. Having thrown just 30 innings last season (19 in the independent leagues and 11 in the Arizona Fall League), the 23-year-old will work in carefully monitored stints, as the club would prefer to have him pitching late in the season rather than shut down early to keep his workload at a certain level. He sits 95-98 with his fastball and has perhaps the deadliest hard curve in the system, giving him two out pitches that could put him in Arlington by season's end, with the possibility of a Feliz-like opportunity to pitch in high-leverage situations in some of the season's most important games.

2. WILMER FONT, Hickory

Returning to Hickory, where he went 8-3, 3.49 in 24 starts and five relief appearance last year, Font will look to find more consistency in his delivery and his results in 2010. A physically mature 19-year-old, the 6'4", 240-lb. Venezuelan has more strikeouts than innings pitched in his three pro seasons but has issued one walk for every two innings. His stuff and his size and his youth could make him one of the more coveted players in the system as far as trade talks are concerned, once you get past the untouchable trio of Martin Perez, Justin Smoak, and Scheppers.

3. MICHAEL MAIN, Bakersfield

While Frisco right-hander Blake Beavan chewed up 163 innings in 2010, his fellow 2007 first-round draftee Main has thrown only 147.2 innings total in his three-year pro career. Limited by a rib injury in 2008 and a viral infection in 2009, the 21-year-old may have as much to prove in 2010 as any key prospect in the system. He works in the low 90s with a hard curve.

4. DANNY GUTIERREZ, Extended Spring

The 23-year-old Gutierrez, acquired from Kansas City in September for Double-A catcher Manny Pina and Double-A outfielder Tim Smith, commands a fastball and curve that each profiles a tick above Main's, but off-the-field issues and a history of shoulder concerns headlined his time in the Royals system. The start to his 2010 season will be delayed as a result of a 50-game suspension handed down by Major League Baseball in February after he tested positive for a prescribed ADHD medication that he failed to secure a Therapeutic Use Exemption for from the league.

5. BLAKE BEAVAN, Frisco

Beavan returns to Frisco and is expected to get the RoughRiders' Opening Day start tonight. The Irving native established himself as perhaps the system's top strike-thrower in 2009, issuing only 29 walks in 163 innings—including 13 in 15 Texas League starts—but his 90-mph fastball isn't missing Double-A bats, which will be an issue as he gets closer to pushing for major league consideration.

6. JAKE BRIGHAM, Bakersfield

The results were ugly for Brigham in 2009, as he posted a 2-11, 5.52 record with Hickory, but it was the Florida native's return year from Tommy John surgery, a season in which location commonly lags arm health. There are few breaking balls in the system with more upside than the 22-year-old's curve, and he appeared in camp to have regained command of his fastball, setting up what could be a significant breakthrough season despite assignment to the hitter-friendly California League.

7. WILFREDO BOSCAN, Bakersfield

What Boscan lacks in power, compared to most of the names on this list, he makes up for with mound savvy and an advanced approach. At age 20, he'll once again work as one of the youngest pitchers in his league as he moves up to Bakersfield. His objective in 2010 will be to sustain his effectiveness late into the season, something he was unable to do last year, when he maintained solid walk and strikeout rates but got more and more hittable as the South Atlantic League season progressed. Boscan features once of the finest changeups in the system.

8. JOE WIELAND, Hickory

Like Boscan, his Hickory teammate Wieland was strong in the first half last year but struggled late in the season. Built not unlike a young Nolan Ryan, who incidentally makes frequent mention of Wieland as a pitcher on his watch list, the 20-year-old issued only two walks per nine Crawdad innings in 2009, fanning eight hitters per nine. But he was too hittable, particularly the second and third time through the opposing lineup, and Texas will look to the Reno native to maintain his effectiveness later in games and in the season in 2010.

9. MATT THOMPSON, Hickory

Thompson joins Wieland, Font, and Ramirez in the Crawdads' rotation to begin the season, and it will be the Burleson native's first assignment to a full-season squad. The 2008 seventh-rounder locates both his fastball and one of the organization's strongest curves, and is a candidate to be one of the Rangers' real breakout pitchers in 2010.

10. NEIL RAMIREZ, Hickory

Ramirez returns to the Crawdads, for whom he won three games and lost six (4.75 ERA) in 2009, a season marred by command issues once he arrived from extended spring training in June. The 20-year-old has formidable life in his low-to-mid-90s fastball and power curve, and this would be his draft year had he gone to Georgia Tech rather than sign with Texas out of high school, but fellow first-rounders Tommy Hunter, Beavan, and even Main have progressed further. This will be a big year for Ramirez to establish himself as a legitimate prospect.

Enough of that. It's just a couple losses, it's just April, it's just a *game*. But is it fair to suggest, maybe a little pointedly, that It's Time?

Thursday Kinsler got
One more shot in the ankle:
A shot in the arm?

April 10, 2010

Uh-oh.

April 11, 2010

According to at least one local beat writer's Twitter post, Ron Washington plans to go to Neftali Feliz to close out and save today's game, if necessary. Washington calls the situation "temporary," according to the post, adding that Frankie Francisco will eventually return to the role.

April 11, 2010

Apologies for going nearly dark the past couple days. I wasn't giving you guys the Milton Bradley Salute. I was away at a Y Guides campout with Max.

After the kids had finally gone to bed late last night and the dads sat around the campfire, the talk swung around at one point to the Rangers. I try (with some hope of success) to save most of my corniness for this newsletter, where I can just delete the groans, which explains why I kept my mouth shut when, already exhausted into a trance and watching the (we're-leaving-in-the-morning-so-might-as-well-burn-through-the-rest-of-the-firewood) flames whip around and shoot sparks in every direction, my thoughts wandered (maybe because of the 1980s rock shuffle playing at the time on Gould's iPod) to that early-'80s Topps Firemen of the Year card that had the legendary Rollie Fingers and Dan Quisenberry on it—as well as the less established Tom Hume.

Closers are rarely called firemen any more, but there's still a Hume for every Fingers and Quisenberry, if not two or three Hume's for every ninth-inning guy you can count on year after year. It's a tough job, with perhaps a shorter life expectancy than NFL tailback.

Theo Epstein was seated right behind me on Opening Day 2006, with one member of his Red Sox front office circle next to him and another two or three about six or eight rows in front of us. Based on how old they all looked, I'm guessing that Jed Hoyer and Ben Cherington and Craig Shipley were among the Boston officials sitting in those two rows.

Boston stepped out to a 5-0 lead behind Curt Schilling and extended it to 7-2 with an eighth-inning Mike Lowell solo shot off Joaquin Benoit. Schilling's day was done and Terry Francona sent rookie Jonathan Papelbon to the mound for the bottom of the eighth, and the top of the Rangers order.

Keith Foulke wasn't quite a Fingers or Quisenberry but between 2000 and 2004 had been among the American League's most dependable closers, culminating with a dominating 2004 post-season performance that included one run allowed in 14 playoff innings and the final pitch of the season, as Foulke sealed the sweep by tossing a Edgar Renteria comebacker to first baseman Doug Mientkiewicz to give Boston its first title in 86 years.

Foulke struggled with a knee injury in 2005 and lost the closer's job in June, finishing with an ERA of 5.91.

Still, he came out of spring training in 2006 having regained the ninth-inning post, despite sporadic work in camp (four innings, two runs on four hits, three strikeouts). And on Opening Day, though it wasn't a save situation, he was entrusted with the ninth, after Papelbon, who'd gotten a three-start, 14-relief-appearance big league look in the final third of the 2005 season, had been sent out to get through the eighth.

Stepping in against Brad Wilkerson, Papelbon fired strike one (called), missed with one, then got a strike swinging, a foul ball, and a rollover groundout to second.

Next up, reigning American League batting champ Michael Young: called strike, ball, foul, swinging strikeout.

And then reigning American League total bases leader Mark Teixeira: called strike, swinging strike, ball, flyout to left.

From what I recall (and I was especially keyed in because Papelbon was on my Greater Texas Fantasy Baseball Association staff), it seems like the 25-year-old sat 95-97 and pounded the lower third throughout his 13-pitch frame (10 for strikes). What I remember with 100 percent certainty is that whoever it was sitting six rows down—let's say Cherington and Shipley—stood from their seats after Teixeira's fly settled harmlessly into Manny Ramirez's glove, turned completely around, smiled back at Epstein and (I'm guessing) Hoyer, and both started laughing. One of them mouthed, "WOW." I peeked back and saw the same smile frozen on Epstein's face.

(My own "WOW" came in the following morning's report, in which I wrote: "The two guys from yesterday's game who are going to have bigger years than anyone expects: Laynce Nix and the exceedingly dirty Jonathan Papelbon." One for two.)

After Boston went quietly in the top of the ninth, Foulke entered the non-save situation to close things out, and he made the game interesting, retiring Phil Nevin on a fly to left before surrendering a Hank Blalock single, a Kevin Mench double, a Nix sacrifice fly to deep center, and a Rod Barajas groundout to third to end the game.

After Texas won Game Two handily, 10-4, in Game Three the Rangers took a 1-0 lead two batters into their first (Wilkerson double, wild pitch, Young single).

Kameron Loe made it stand up until the seventh, when Ramirez walked and Trot Nixon homered. Josh Beckett worked seven, and in to pitch the eighth was not Papelbon, but Mike Timlin. Texas collected two hits in the inning, drew a walk, and advanced on a wild pitch, but could not score. Scott Feldman threw an eight-pitch ninth to keep the score at 2-1.

Then Papelbon, not Foulke, trotted in from the bullpen for the save. The rookie slammed things shut, needing just 11 pitches to strike Barajas out swinging, coax a Nix pop to shortstop, and set Wilkerson down swinging. I wasn't there that night but can only imagine the looks on the faces of Epstein & Associates, after they'd probably conferred with Francona between Monday evening and Wednesday afternoon to decide that Papelbon, who had worked only as a starter in Red Sox camp (leading the team with five starts and 21.1 innings) and hadn't pitched all that well (5.48 ERA, .333 opponents' average) (sound familiar?), was the better bet, right away, to save games than the established Foulke.

Foulke wouldn't save a game all year. Papelbon: 35 in 41 chances, 0.92 ERA, 75/13 K/BB ratio. He hasn't given up the job since.

The purpose of that story is not to suggest that Frankie Francisco, with fewer skins on the wall than Foulke had, is about to relinquish the closer's job permanently to Neftali Feliz, who is generally considered a better prospect than Papelbon was (and whose 31-inning debut in 2009 was more dominant than Papelbon's 34 innings in 2005).

The point is that Firemen of the Year are sometimes not the same the year after. A lockdown closer can become something other than that before long, and not that infrequently. You have to have Plan B in place, especially if you're a team like Boston who expects to win every year—or Texas, who absolutely expects to win in 2010.

Does Ron Washington's own situation factor in, on the theory that he might feel even more pressure to get his club off to a strong start than any of us could have appreciated a month ago? Don't know. But the Rangers, like the Red Sox, look at their 162-game schedule as a step toward post-season baseball, not toward 2011, and the weekend development following a second straight Francisco blown save and an evident plunge in velocity and location and body language—that Texas would lift the 30-year-old from the closer's position for now, elevating Feliz to the role and Darren Oliver to the eighth inning—is a move less than a week into the season that gets made by a team planning to win, and needing to fix not only the ninth inning but also the psyche of a veteran reliever who will be needed in 2010.

We can all appreciate, notwithstanding Sunday's offensive execution (love, love, love seeing all those balls put in play to the opposite field), that, anachronistically, this franchise has become one whose strength is in its starting pitchers. (Not only does the big league rotation have a 1.67 ERA through six games—best in baseball by more than half a run—but go all the way down through the four full-season farm clubs and the organization's starters have a 2.57 ERA in 21 starts, with 7.5 strikeouts per nine innings and just 2.4 walks per nine.)

But having a problem at closer can undo, in minutes, what a starting pitcher has done over a couple hours. The offense showed some signs this weekend that it might be finding its rhythm. There's no such confidence right now with the closer. The Rangers lost three games out of 80 last year when leading after eight innings. They've already lost three (out of five) such games this season.

While Texas may not have had a decent alternative to Mike Henneman in 1996, there are backup plans here now, starting with Feliz, and possibly including other young arms like Chris Ray, Tanner Scheppers, Alexi Ogando, and Omar Beltre (and less prototypical options like Oliver and Darren O'Day), all of whom figure in only because C.J. Wilson, to his credit, no longer does.

The problem is that, outside of Ray (three years and an elbow surgery ago), none of them has any real experience closing big league games, and no contender wants to experiment any more than necessary.

But this experiment became necessary after Saturday, and for now Francisco, pronounced physically healthy, will pitch in low-leverage situations, while Feliz will be asked, hopefully with some regularity, to pitch under more pressure than he's ever been asked to, at least until Francisco is deemed ready to reassume his role, or until Feliz proves not to be ready for this.

Unless Feliz proves he's more than ready for all of this.

Concerned that Feliz is being thrown into an unfamiliar fire? He does have two saves as a Ranger (a scoreless two-inning, one-hit, three-strikeout effort against Boston on August 15 and a perfect 2.1 innings with two strikeouts in Baltimore three weeks later), and a couple three-inning saves in the Gulf Coast League as an 18-year-old in the Braves system, less than two months into his stateside career.

Tongue in cheek? Maybe. But Papelbon had only one career save before 2006, a season in which he'd make the All-Star Team as a rookie closer for the Red Sox: a three-inning effort in AAA the year before, after he'd already debuted as a starter in the big leagues.

They were both starting pitcher prospects, very good starting pitcher prospects in fact (but coming off rough rotation auditions in camp), and there's been at least as much talk, if not more so, about Feliz eventually settling in as this team's closer as there ever was about Papelbon in Boston.

But Foulke had lost Boston's confidence in 2005 and was the less effective reliever *for one day* in 2006 before that club made a change, giving the ball to a key starting pitcher prospect that they thought could give them some bottled lightning. Is the same thing happening here, with Francisco having struggled since mid-August (9.00 ERA in 20 innings, .329/.389/.529) and contributing heavily to the difference between a record of 5-1 and 3-3 getting out of the gate this year?

Maybe the most fascinating part about the move to Feliz is that Texas, starting Monday, is in Cleveland for that team's home-opening series, then in New York for three, and in Boston for three after that. As if the pressure of being The Guy isn't enough for a 21-year-old who was in Low Class A two years ago, this road trip will probably present the most energetic if not hostile road atmosphere Texas will encounter all season. And he still hasn't thrown on consecutive days in the big leagues, and in fact has done it just once as a pro—once in mid-July with Oklahoma City last summer.

But that's the thing, I suppose. You see Francisco sitting 91-93, nailing the center of the strike zone when that's not what he wants to do, and exhibiting the kind of body language you never want to see out of the pitcher who jogs to the mound for those final three outs. Maybe the Cleveland-New York-Boston gauntlet is one that's not healthy for Francisco right now.

The Rangers may need Francisco away from the ninth inning right now, but they're probably going to need him in some important capacity for this season to turn out the way everyone in the organization believes it should. There's no telling whether this transition will last a few games or a few weeks or if Francisco, like Foulke with Boston four years ago, has nailed down his final save for the club, supplanted by a younger, more dominant, more reliable option.

It's probably too much to hope for Feliz to seize this role immediately and permanently the way Papelbon did in 2006, but Texas believes he gives the club a better chance to hold leads right now than Francisco does, and that Francisco's season stands a better chance of recovery if he can regain his confidence in a less critical role.

It's a gutsy move, but it had become clear this week that it would have been even gutsier, at the moment, to keep running Francisco out in the ninth inning of close games.

April 13, 2010

So much for depressurized situations to let Frankie Francisco get things straightened out.

And so much for velocity hovering between 91 and 93.

As Texas loaded the bases with nobody out in the top of the ninth, with the score knotted at 2-2, Ron Washington and Mike Maddux had both Francisco and Neftali Feliz getting loose, presumably warming the former up in case the game remained tied and getting the latter ready in case the Rangers scored and set up a save situation.

The Rangers managed not to score, and Francisco came on with no margin for error, entering a game tied in the ninth on the road. It was as high-pressure a situation as the two save opportunities he failed to convert before being stripped of his job.

Make no mistake: Francisco gave up two hard outs to start the ninth, and it took eight pitches for him to put Austin Kearns away on strikes (despite getting ahead 0-2) to end the inning. But the results were there, as were the six 95 mph readings and one that tripped the gun at 97. That's a good start. And the confidence that comes from a 1-2-3 ninth in front of a sold-out Opening Day crowd, extending the game and giving the 3-4-5 hitters a chance to come up and do their thing in the 10th, setting the stage for a nice win to kick off a big road trip—that's a good day for the unseated closer.

Jon Daniels has made some outstanding trades since taking over as general manager in October 2005—believe it or not, he's now the 12th-most tenured GM in baseball—and two of his better trade acquisitions highlighted a high-octane 10th inning: Nelson Cruz turning a Jamey Wright fastball around 375 feet with a man on (it's not easy to "break out" two seasons in a row), and Feliz coming on to slam things shut with at least six of his 18 pitches hitting triple digits (including one at a reported 102 mph).

It's premature to say whether Texas has its new closer, but that's a good start, and if you were going to draw it up, you'd want Feliz to get one under his belt before the New York-Boston swing.

A good win, the club's first two-game win streak, and a 4-3 record (yes, that should be 6-1) that sits closer to Oakland in first than Los Angeles and Seattle in third and fourth.

Rich Harden has a 2.79 ERA and is by far the most frustrating Rangers starter to watch over the first seven games. A new era in Rangers baseball, without a doubt.

Seven games, six quality starts.

Julio Borbon's throw and Taylor Teagarden's block of the plate to erase a thundering Travis Hafner in the sixth and keep the game tied couldn't have been any better. That's more than just a big out in a 2-2 game. It's an entry in an advance scout's notebook, and another one or two of those from Borbon and it might lead to a couple opposing runners being held up at third when they might not have been otherwise.

Joaquin Arias has 10 hits in the last four games. Always a player who tends to get his hits in crazy bunches, he's praised Clint Hurdle for helping him wait on the pitch and go the other way—which is something I'm sure we've all noticed as well with Cruz and Elvis Andrus and Josh Hamilton over the first week. It's something Michael Young has always done (and Andrus was adept at it as a rookie as well—as was Hamilton in 2008), but on the days when this offense has clicked, there's been a noticeable opposite-field approach throughout the lineup.

Arias's fate will be interesting. When Ian Kinsler returns, the utility infield roster spot is going to be a defense-first role. There's no question that Andres Blanco is the better defender, particularly making the throws from the left side of the infield. Neither Arias nor Blanco can be optioned at this point, and so there's a real risk that, whichever player Texas decides not to keep around when Kinsler returns (not an imminent move, as he's expected to go out on a brief rehab assignment first) could be lost to another organization.

Speaking of which, I really liked what I saw out of catcher Matt Treanor on Sunday and hope Texas can keep him in the organization whenever it is that Jarrod Saltalamacchia is ready to return. It was just one game, but aside from the two RBI singles he just looked like a veteran catcher out there with Scott Feldman, Doug Mathis, and Chris Ray.

Doug Melvin purchased Doug Mirabelli for next to nothing from the Giants at the end of spring training in 2001, and then traded the 30-year-old that June to Boston for Justin Duchscherer. Ray Olmedo for Treanor near the end of camp this year wasn't a huge trade, but it looks like a very good one, and not because we can expect Treanor to be flipped for a solid pitching prospect.

Three walks from Andrus on Monday. More of that, please.

You should read the interview that John Sickels did with Rangers Director of Professional Scouting Josh Boyd.

We won't find out today whether Feliz will be asked to pitch on consecutive days because we're instead being treated to the rare (and unwelcome) mid-series off-day. The bullpen should be fully rested, though not at all set up the way we thought it might be a month ago. C.J. Wilson gets the start instead of the eighth, Feliz gets the ninth instead of the seventh, and Francisco gets something other than the ninth.

The offense has sputtered, the late relief has prompted an early bullpen shakeup, and the defense has had a couple ugly moments. Yes, 4-3 could be 6-1 (though the first win and the last could have just as easily been losses), but the story of the first seven games of 2010 is that the Rangers' starting pitchers have an ERA of 1.85, which is now more than a full run better than the second-best rotation mark (Oakland, 2.94), have the second-lowest opponents' batting average (.217, higher only than Toronto's .216), and have the second-lowest opponents' OPS (.620, higher only than San Francisco's .604).

It all begins with starting pitching, and there's no question that this team would be off to an ugly win-loss if the rotation had even been league-average. Solid starts do more than keep the game in check and give the offense a chance. They keep the bullpen rested and allow the manager to avoid stretching relievers into higher pitch counts than he wants or pushing them into situations they're not equipped for, or at least not ready for.

As for whether Neftali Feliz is equipped for the ninth, at least for the time being while Frankie Francisco gets straightened out, that's a developing story. But it got off to a very good start.

April 14, 2010

The Rangers have announced that lefthander C.J. Wilson has been scratched from tonight's scheduled start in Cleveland, due to food poisoning. The club says Wilson's condition is better today than it was yesterday, but out of precaution righthander Colby Lewis will make tonight's start—on regular rest as a result of Tuesday's off-day—and Wilson could start tomorrow, though that decision hasn't been made yet.

April 14, 2010

Jhonny Peralta. Matt LaPorta.
Lou Marson. Michael Brantley.
Asdrubal Cabrera. Grady Sizemore.
Luis Valbuena. Marson again.
Brantley again.
Travis Hafner.

Colby Lewis struck out 10 for the first time in nearly seven years—unless you count a 13-punchout effort against the Yokohama BayStars two years ago.

Lewis's 10-strikeout game on August 15, 2003 came against the White Sox, whose leadoff hitter Roberto Alomar struck out looking in the first and again in the third, after which he was ejected.

Alomar's brother Sandy Jr. managed not to get tossed tonight. He's Cleveland's first base coach.

On that 2003 night, Lewis threw 119 pitches, 82 for strikes.

Tonight: 117 pitches, 74 for strikes.

Lewis's ERA after the 2003 gem was 7.57. After tonight's: 2.19.

I love watching a pitcher who can locate a two-plane breaking ball. There haven't been a lot of those in this franchise's last 20 years.

I love Kevin Millwood for Lewis, Rich Harden, and Chris Ray.

You already know how much I love opposite-field hitting, which we saw a lot of tonight.

I love early night game start times.

I love dependable backup catchers.

I love watching Neftali Feliz grow. Love you, too, John Schuerholz.

I had much love for Eddie Guardado, who was what he was, but not as much I have for Darren Oliver.

I love the small sample size. Remember when there were two hitters on this entire roster hitting their weight? Tonight's lineup had four players who finished the game at .414 or higher, a fifth at .346, a sixth at .308.

I love that this team has developed a bend-don't-break character.

And, man, I love Nelson Cruz.

And he doesn't really like pitchers.

Boomstick.

April 16, 2010

Texas dropped the ball
Blew what should have been a sweep
On to Yanks & Sox

You can spend 3,000 December words on an off-season move to add a middle relief candidate, holding forth like you have a bead on what it will mean for the bullpen, if not the pennant race.

And then your three most reliable defensive players make blunders in one catastrophic April inning, three plays that sit somewhere on the spectrum between unfortunate and inexcusable, taken together bordering on something like impossible, and you realize how unpredictable this game is, and how all the objective data in the world is suggestive at best, persuasive yet not controlling, and maybe even distracting at times from the organic nature of the game and its players and its plays.

This team could very well be 8-1 with baseball's best record—in fact, it has trailed only once after seven innings. But they make you play nine, and too often in the first 1/18th of the season (keep that part in mind) Texas hasn't closed the deal, on the mound or in the field, and instead the club heads into the New York-Boston swing at what can only be characterized as a disappointing 5-4. Better than the Angels, better than the Mariners, better than the Red Sox. But disappointing.

There's so much to be encouraged about—starting with the starting five, which is pitching with that swagger that the front office talked about trying to develop and capture back when Nolan Ryan arrived and Mike Maddux was hired. Nelson Cruz appears to be taking the next step, one that only a fraction of the few even capable of taking actually convert on. Vladimir Guerrero and Darren Oliver aren't yet acting their age. The Neftali Feliz chrysalis is splitting.

The problems of the first week and a half aren't the type that armchair GM's insist they can fix by whiteboarding the perfect trade, or by starting the clock on the all-important, imminent call-up. They're the type that call for better execution (and sometimes concentration) by players clearly capable of executing.

And maybe that's what's so frustrating. The resignation of seeing games get away because Chan Ho Park or Ben Broussard or Kris Benson or Andruw Jones isn't getting it done is a lot different from the gut punch of watching a core player we tend to take for granted fail to come through.

Half of the Rangers' outcomes have taken the sabermetrics right out of it, and that's ok with me. The data might tell us what we can *expect* when a starting pitcher reaches that third time through the lineup or what happens when Josh Hamilton can't lay off the first-pitch breaking ball out of the zone, but could never prepare us for Thursday's defensive eighth, or for the difference between a Frankie Francisco outing where the squared-up shots don't find gloves and one where they do, or for the potential impact that the latter could have on his confidence going forward.

Texas has won two straight series, one at home against a division contender and the other on the road, and of course you'd take that. It doesn't make the nature of the last three of the Rangers' four losses any easier to take, but it hammers home for me that trying to diagnose how you get to 5-4 can drive you crazy.

Instead, maybe the proper prescription is to enjoy this unprecedented run of Rangers starting pitching and hope that it continues into these next six against two of baseball's best, a stretch that should include C.J. Wilson twice, and that the shortstop will have learned something Thursday the way the new closer did on Opening Day.

April 17, 2010

A local beat reporter wrote a few days ago that while Rangers starters were averaging 103.1 pitches per outing, the highest total in the American League (and third highest in baseball), it was "*not to suggest the Rangers are overworking their starting pitchers. It's more the opposite. The Rangers are getting their starters to go longer and throw more pitches, though, they are getting a wholly more efficient performance since the club decided to push starters a little harder.*"

To support the point he notes that Texas was averaging 16.5 pitches per inning, in line with the American League average, evidence along with the pitch counts of how deep the club's starters were getting into games.

All of that was true.

What the story did not mention was that Rangers' starters were throwing 4.10 pitches per batter faced, the worst mark in baseball.

Since then, including today's Scott Feldman start, the mark has crept up to 4.15, still the highest in the league.

Newberg Report: Of Rix, Mauer, Teixeira
Rangers still collecting returns from 2007 trade

By Jamey Newberg / Special to MLB.com
April 15, 2010

Chris Rix is the only four-year starter at quarterback in Bobby Bowden's 34 seasons at Florida State.

I'm not trying to pass myself off as the other "Jamie" Newberg, who is a college football analyst. This really is a baseball point I'm hoping to make.

Rix's record-setting Seminoles run (2001-2004) probably happened only because Joe Mauer chose baseball over his scholarship to play quarterback at FSU.

Mauer was the 2001 Gatorade National Player of the Year in both baseball and football as a senior at Cretin-Derham Hall High School in St. Paul. He was all set to follow fellow CDH alum Chris Weinke—the 2000 Heisman Trophy winner—at Florida State (after Weinke had given minor league baseball a six-year try himself), but when his hometown Minnesota Twins took him with the first pick in the June 2001 amateur draft, he turned FSU down and embarked on a baseball career, motivated to follow in the footsteps of yet another CDH graduate, future Hall of Famer Paul Molitor, who had finished his playing career three years earlier in a Twins uniform.

Rix, incidentally, despite his college achievements, is not the most decorated alum of Los Angeles-area Bishop Amat High School's football program, which produced Pat Haden, Eric Bieniemy, and Brian Russell. Rix played baseball for Bishop Amat as well, but didn't make a career out of it like Michael Young, Dan Haren, and Mike Lamb did.

Back to baseball, and it's probably time to get to the Rangers angle.

Was it serendipity that the Twins chose first in 2001, in a Cavaliers-LeBron sort of way? Yeah, maybe, but even if they chose 2nd or 3rd or 4th in that draft, they still might have gotten him. Most considered Mark Prior and Mark Teixeira to be the better draft prospects, and Tampa Bay chose Dewon Brazelton third (rather than Teixeira) because of signability.

When Mauer signed his landmark eight-year, $184 million contract extension last month, I heard some local venom on local talk radio about Teixeira's refusal to stay in Texas while Mauer chose loyalty over cash (though that can be debated) by locking up long-term rather than selling himself to Boston or the Yankees next winter.

But really—given the chance to rewrite history, as a Rangers fan would you trade Elvis Andrus, Neftali Feliz, Matt Harrison, Jarrod Saltalamacchia and Beau Jones (all acquired from Atlanta for Teixeira), and Justin Smoak (drafted No. 11 in 2008) right now for Teixeira and Ethan Martin (drafted No. 15 in 2008)?

I get the praise for Joe Mauer. I really do, and I have much respect for the man. And I'm a Mark Teixeira fan.

But let's not go overboard on the turn of events that made Teixeira a Brave (and an Angel, and a Yankee) instead of a lifelong Ranger. This franchise is better off due to Teixeira's disinterest in sticking around.

That's not to suggest the starters haven't been very strong. They've been outstanding, and are the reason the team has won as many games as it has.

But what's happened the last two days in Yankee Stadium has driven home a statistical point that seems worth noting. New York is predictably making Texas pitchers work—Yankee hitters are extraordinarily patient and fundamentally sound. But they're not alone. Rangers' starters' opponents are working deeper counts than any other team's starters' opponents.

Meanwhile, Texas hitters see only 3.64 pitches per plate appearance. The only offense in baseball that sees fewer pitches per trip is San Francisco's.

When the gap begins to narrow between those two composite numbers, it's going to feel like we're another step closer to being where this team is capable of being.

ADDENDUM: Elaborating:

Pitches per Batter Faced, Highest, American League Starting Pitchers:

1. Rich Harden, TEX (4.51)
6. Colby Lewis, TEX (4.23)
8. Scott Feldman, TEX (4.20)
10. Matt Harrison, TEX (4.11)
45. C.J. Wilson, TEX (3.75)

Again, this isn't a hatchet job on the Rangers rotation, which I have as much confidence in as any bunch the club has put together in the last 20 years. Just something worth noting, maybe, particularly when laid against the what's going on with the Texas offense, which just isn't working counts.

By the way, Wilson is 22nd *lowest* in the league—impressive, and, given his history, surprising.

But not as surprising as the fact that the only hitter on the entire Texas roster (with the exception of Matt Treanor) seeing as many as four pitches per plate appearance is the last player any of us would have ever nominated for being the early king, on this team, of getting deep into pitch counts:

Joaquin Arias.

April 18, 2010

I don't know if Rich Harden is hurt, but if possible, today's line . . .

Pitchers	IP	H	R	ER	BB	SO	HR	PC-ST	ERA
R Harden	3.2	5	4	4	6	5	1	94-53	4.72

. . . was probably kind, even tossing in the two hit batsmen, compared to how off he looked. When he missed, either in the strike zone or out, he usually missed badly, without nearly enough stuff to overcome his mistakes.

Frankly, it would be a little reassuring if there was some sort of minor physical issue that might explain what's going on with Harden. As it stands, he's not giving his team a good enough chance to win. Three and a half baserunners per inning isn't going to cut it, whether he's guaranteed $7.5 million or making the league minimum.

Speaking of which, Derek Holland just threw an eight-pitch (six-strike) first in Memphis, keeping Oklahoma City and the Redbirds scoreless. Holland came into the game with this line through two AAA starts:

Pitchers	IP	H	R	ER	BB	SO	HR	PC-ST	ERA
D.Holland	13.2	10	1	1	1	9	1	180-119	0.66

Pacific Coast League lineups aren't Toronto, Cleveland, and New York, but if Harden is dealing with some sort of physical issue, there's an interesting alternative right now in a guy on the same pitching schedule.

April 18, 2010

Derek Holland has been relieved after six scoreless in Memphis, with Oklahoma City ahead, 3-0.

Don't read too much into that. Holland had thrown 93 pitches (57 for strikes), after throwing 82 and 98 in his first two starts. Could he have given the RedHawks another inning? Probably. Was he denied the seventh because he's going to pitching in Arlington in five days? No. If a decision had been made to get Holland up here in five or six days, and if the organization decided he needed to be lifted early from today's start to protect him and the club, he'd have been gone from today's start before getting through six.

In other words, don't read anything into Holland's Sunday afternoon other than the obvious: it's another tremendous effort for the 23-year-old, who now has an ERA of 0.46 in three RedHawks starts (19.2 innings, one run [a Mike Restovich solo home run in the season opener], 17 hits [.236 opponents' average], three walks, 15 strikeouts).

It's less meaningful than the fact that Josh Hamilton, as Eric Nadel pointed out on the broadcast, has one hit to right field this season, and just one other ball hit hard in that direction (the line drive that Mark Teixeira snared going up today).

But it's a good development, as have been the minor league starts that Brandon McCarthy and Michael Kirkman and Guillermo Moscoso and Omar Beltre and Justin Smoak and Max Ramirez and Matt Brown and Craig Gentry and Chad Tracy and Tanner Scheppers and Alexi Ogando have gotten off to.

There are several reasons that strong starts by those players can be huge, given their chances to help in the big leagues this year. One of those reasons, and the easiest to get our heads wrapped around, is the idea that players like Holland could make the Rangers better right away.

But let's not get ahead of ourselves, even though I wouldn't discourage you from getting fired up about what the lefthander is doing in an effort to force his way back into the big league picture.

April 20, 2010

There are 3,444 songs on my iPod.

It's a somewhat random mix, comprised mostly of music I cared about between 10 and 25 years ago, but also a little newer stuff, and a handful of embarrassing songs from the 1970s whose sole merit for me is that they evoke memories of being a happy kid, in spite of their lameness.

With the exception of a very small number of singles (primarily key one-hit wonders from the '70s and a few present-day mashups), which make up maybe one percent of the songs, my iPod is just a hand-held library of the CD's I own. The upside is that the track shuffle mode I've had it on since loading the thing up four months ago for my car has yet to play a song twice. The downside is occasionally I have to fight (or forward) through a lousy B side from an album I might have bought 20 years ago for one or two other songs.

This weekend I ran into an unusually disappointing stretch of songs while driving around, not to and from the first two Youth League machine pitch games of Max's life (he's only been asking about when that day would come for six months), both of which were rained out, but instead running a bunch of mundane errands: first an obscure Big Star song I don't think I'd ever heard and don't care to hear again . . . then a Pete Yorn thing from seven or eight years ago off an album that held my interest for maybe three days . . . the one song off "Document" that I never cared for . . . Soul Asylum (what was I thinking?). And another half dozen disappointments, one after another.

But it didn't make me want to unplug the thing and toss it aside. The iPod concept's whole is not only substantially greater than the sum of its parts; in some ways the whole is as great as it is not only despite some of those parts but because of them. When a couple duds give way to "Nightswimming," or Mary J. doing "One" with U2, or George Harrison's "Something," their awesomeness is even awesome-r.

It may not surprise you that slogging through that dismal sequence helped me remember that as bad as those three games in Yankee Stadium were, it could be worse. It was just three of 162. It was a team not hitting, running into a team not missing, in mid-April, and it will get better. Texas was 5-7 last year, too, and ended up having a pretty nice season.

It's baseball. And I'm not about to unplug it.

I could have saved myself (and you) a lot of time by skipping all that nonsense you just read and simply tossing out a baseball analogy about Texas getting to Boston just before the running of yesterday's Marathon. But I didn't, because if I'm gonna push a forced cliché on you, I'm going all out. Just one more thing to fight through.

If the run of "Exit Music," "Drain You," and "Otherside" I caught coming home last night was any indication, I feel a turnaround coming. I could have lied and said Boston's "Don't Look Back" came on, fittingly, but (1) there's no Boston on my iPod and (2) this isn't sabermetrics.

I'm taking them as they come, accepting them for what they are, and hoping for seven strong from Colby Lewis tonight, or six total bases out of Chris Davis, or a four-game win streak, any of which right now would feel like landing on "Sometimes You Can't Make It On Your Own" and "I'll Take the Rain" and "Pendulous Threads," back to back to back.

And if it doesn't work out that way, I'll survive, and patiently wait on a little rally.

April 22, 2010

Six straight losses, baseball's longest current skid, and Texas sits at 5-9.

In four seasons under Ron Washington, Texas is 22-34 in the first 14 games each year, a .393 win percentage. Extrapolated over a full season, that translates to 64-98.

In games 15 through 162, Washington's Rangers are 224-220, a .505 clip, translating to 82-80.

Cliché as it might be, April losses count just as much as August and September losses, and these four clubs have had massive trouble getting going each year.

Why is that?

Kansas City purchased the contract of righthander Josh Rupe. Seattle signed infielder Ramon Vazquez to a minor league deal. The Long Island Ducks of the independent Atlantic League signed righthander Rick Bauer. The Grand Prairie Airhogs of the independent American Association signed catcher Ben Petralli. The Sioux City Explorers of the same league traded lefthander Jared Locke to the Sussex Skyhawks of the independent Can-Am League to complete an earlier trade. The Can-Am League's Worcester Tornadoes signed righthander John Slusarz and outfielder-righthander Rick Asadoorian (who evidently now goes by "Eric").

LSU righthander Anthony Ranaudo faces Mississippi lefthander Drew Pomeranz tomorrow night. They're not only two of the top pitchers in the NCAA this year. Ranaudo (11th round) and Pomeranz (12th round) were chosen by the Rangers in the 2007 draft (which included Julio Borbon, Tommy Hunter, Blake Beavan, Michael Main, Neil Ramirez, Mitch Moreland, Tim Smith, and others) but opted not to sign.

You should have gotten an email at 7:30 this morning with a link to this week's Newberg Report/MLB.com column, ranking the Rangers' best draft picks in each of the first 10 rounds over the last 20 years.

That's all I've got in me today. Jarrod Saltalamacchia's rehab assignment is underway in Oklahoma City, Ian Kinsler and Tommy Hunter are about to get game action in at extended spring training in Surprise, the Rangers are considering sending a right-handed reliever out (Doug Mathis has options and thus is the likely victim) so they can add another lefthander to the bullpen (Clay Rapada, who would require a 40-man roster move, may be the leading candidate, but he did pitch last night for Oklahoma City), Nelson Cruz's tweaky hamstring shortened his second straight game and he won't be in tonight's lineup, Josh Hamilton's home run last night looked pretty good, Justin Smoak's good at baseball (last night's two doubles, notably, came off a lefthander), and I don't want to start getting numb to upsetting losses.

April 22, 2010

New: A victory for the Rangers' best starting pitcher (in fact, the first-ever of his career as a starter).

Old: Taking a lead in the game (something Texas has done in 14 of its 15 games this season).

New: The first save for Darren Oliver since he was a Rangers rookie in 1994.

Old: Andres Blanco's schneid.

New: The manager ignoring the late relief book.

Old: That wretched six-game skid.

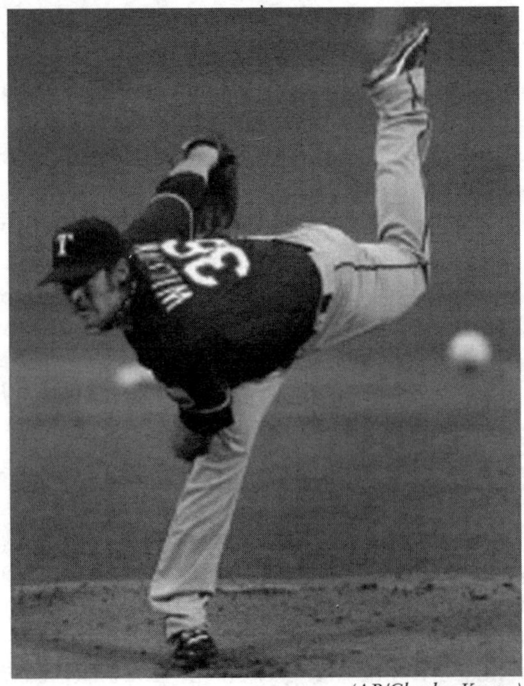

(AP/Charles Krupa)

Get this: Texas gets a shutout, throws first-pitch strikes to 22 of 33 Boston hitters, issues only two walks and allows zero extra-base hits, permits exactly one Sox hitter to reach second base (with two outs in the seventh inning, ending C.J. Wilson's night), and induces 17 groundouts and just six flyouts . . . but guess how many swinging strikes those 33 Red Sox hitters had?

Six.

Not a great number, but I'll take that six any day over the six that's now been erased from the "streak" column.

My baseball depression is so fickle.

April 22, 2010

It has been reported by T.R. Sullivan (MLB.com) and Jeff Wilson (*Fort Worth Star-Telegram*) and Anthony Andro (*Fort Worth Star-Telegram*) and Evan Grant (*Dallas Morning News*) on Twitter, as well as Kevin Goldstein of Baseball Prospectus and Jim Bowden of XM/Fox (also via Twitter), that the Rangers reportedly decided after tonight's game to option Chris Davis to Oklahoma City and purchase the contract of Justin Smoak.

A 40-man roster move will be necessary.

April 23, 2010

Max Scherzer's professional debut was on June 7, 2007, a year after he'd been drafted by the Diamondbacks. It came against the Bakersfield Blaze. He struck out eight in five innings. Two times, third baseman Chris Davis was the victim.

Scherzer has since been traded by Arizona to Detroit, and he gets the Tigers' start tonight, but he won't face Davis.

Instead, Scherzer, who was the 11th pick in the 2006 draft, will face off tonight against the 11th pick in the 2008 draft, Justin Smoak.

Davis was hitless again last night but had some positive moments, drawing one of the club's two walks and seeing a team-high 26 pitches, and making a key defensive play as he typically does, digging Michael Young's running throw in the seventh with two outs and two on. But he did strike out twice, giving him 17 in 15 games (48 at-bats), and he wasn't hitting the ball with much authority or producing any runs (one RBI).

Meanwhile, Smoak was putting together great at-bat after great at-bat for Oklahoma City, hitting .300/.470/.540 in 50 at-bats with 16 walks (second most in the minor leagues, next to Conner Crumbliss, a 23-year-old playing in Low Class A) and eight strikeouts, acceptable left-right splits (the biggest difference this year being that he's drawn 14 walks and fanned just twice from the left side), and solid (if not Davis-level) defense. He was lifted in the eighth inning of last night's game with the RedHawks ahead, 7-4, having fouled a ball off his foot in the seventh, but everything checked out after the game and he's headed to Texas, where the club will give him everyday work right away in hopes that he can sustain the zone he's in.

Newberg Report: Best Picks, Rounds 1-10

Ranking the top Rangers selections by round over 20 years

By Jamey Newberg / Special to MLB.com
April 22, 2010

My first Top 10 List from the Rangers' farm system this year was a fairly traditional one, ranking the top 10 right-handed Minor League starting pitchers in the organization. This week's will be a little more unconventional.

Texas has had a good run of amateur drafts recently, helping establish the franchise's farm system as one of the game's best. But even before the last several years the club came up big at some point on Day One of the draft most years, finding a player who proved he should have been drafted higher or turned out to be an example of tremendous player development once Texas got him into the system.

What follows are the best picks made by Texas in the last 20 years in each of the first 10 rounds of the draft.

ROUND 1: MARK TEIXEIRA, 2001
Say what you will about Tom Hicks and his tenure as Rangers owner, but he never shied away from paying well above slot when it came to the amateur draft, enabling Texas to stick with the "best player available" philosophy, or from dealing with Scott Boras. In Teixeira, the Georgia Tech All-American, the Rangers knew they'd have to do both when his expected bonus demands caused him to drop to the fifth slot in 2001's first round. It took a four-year, $9.5 million contract to land the switch-hitter, but that's one deal Texas never regretted stepping up to make.

ROUND 2: ROBBIE ROSS, 2008
For whatever reason, Texas has historically had extraordinary trouble in the second round. It wouldn't be a stretch to suggest the club hasn't produced a solid major leaguer in the round since Roger Pavlik in 1986, and even that year the better pick came a round later, when Dean Palmer was the choice. Three of the club's last four second-rounders have been third basemen (Johnny Whittleman [who now plays first base], Matt West, and Tommy Mendonca), and it's too soon to write them off as prospects, but none has scouts as excited as the other player: the 20-year-old Hickory lefthander Ross, who in two seasons is striking out more than a batter per inning against older competition, walking just one-fourth that total, and generating three times as many groundouts as flyouts.

ROUND 3: HANK BLALOCK, 1999
Blalock stands out as the best Rangers third-rounder since 1990 as it is, but for a while it looked like he could have been one of the great non-first-round picks in baseball in many years. In 2002, he was the consensus top hitting prospect in baseball, ahead of Teixeira and Josh Hamilton and everyone else. Thought then to be on his way to a career as a perennial batting title contender who would run into his share of home runs from the left side—a Joe Mauer-type hitter—he's instead a 29-year-old Triple-A player who's had trouble staying healthy and productive.

ROUND 4: KEVIN MENCH, 1999
Watch out for Hickory right-hander Joe Wieland in this slot, but for now the best Rangers fourth-rounder in 20 years is Mench, who followed Blalock in the club's 1999 draft crop and who arrived in Arlington just a week later than Blalock did. Mench hit almost half of his 89 career home runs in his first three seasons with the Rangers, and in his fifth he was traded—with Francisco Cordero and another promising Rangers fourth-rounder, Laynce Nix—to Milwaukee for two outfielders whose careers Mench would have liked to have had: Carlos Lee and Nelson Cruz.

ROUND 5: C.J. WILSON, 2001

It's hard to call a draft class headed by Teixeira a disappointing one, but Texas had no picks in the second or third rounds in 2001, forfeited for the signing of Alex Rodriguez and Mark Petkovsek, and failed to sign fourth-rounder Josh Baker, a Houston right-hander who opted to pitch for the University of Alabama. Wilson, coming off a 2-10, 6.87 season for Loyola Marymount when Texas used a fifth to take him, is the only player from that draft class other than Teixeira to sign with Texas and reach the big leagues, but he's unquestionably one of the great scouting and development successes of the last 10 years in this system.

ROUND 6: AARON HARANG, 1999

It didn't command the same level of attention that the 2010 Frisco rotation does, for example, but the 1999 Pulaski Rangers rotation, featuring Colby Lewis, Harang, Ryan Dittfurth, and Nick Regilio, had a lot of us pretty fired up, at least as fired up as you could be about a short-season pitching staff. Harang went 9-2, 2.30 for that club, then 13-5, 3.32 for High A Charlotte in 2000, and was traded that winter with Class A lefthander Ryan Cullen for infielder Randy Velarde, setting off a string of veteran acquisitions (Andres Galarraga, Ken Caminiti, Petkovsek) Texas made to surround Alex Rodriguez. Not Doug Melvin's finest month of work.

ROUND 7: MIKE LAMB, 1997

A solid left-handed bat who had a knack for hitting good pitching, Lamb is now in his 10th big league season, one heck of an accomplishment no matter what round a player was drafted in. None of the 29 other players taken in the seventh round in 1997 had one-tenth the career Lamb has had.

ROUND 8: NICK MASSET, 2000

The big right-hander had first-round projections before Tommy John surgery wiped out his high school senior season. Texas used an eighth-rounder on Masset anyway, and retained draft-and-follow rights when he broke ties with LSU and instead enrolled at St. Petersburg Junior College. After developing in the Rangers system and reaching the big leagues in 2006, he's been part of two big trades (accompanying John Danks in the five-player deal in December 2006 that sent Brandon McCarthy to Texas and moving from the White Sox to Cincinnati in a 2008 trade deadline deal for Ken Griffey Jr.) and established himself in 2009 as a dependable middle reliever, though his 2010 has gotten off to a shaky start.

ROUND 9: EDWIN ENCARNACION, 2000

Taken a round after Masset, Encarnacion was traded three days after he'd hit his Incaviglia Rule date, packaged to the Reds as a tack-on in the deal that sent outfielder Ruben Mateo to Cincinnati for right-hander Rob Bell. Encarnacion, as it turns out, has had the best career of the three. Interestingly, the Reds picked immediately before Texas in the 2000 draft, and in the ninth round could have taken Encarnacion themselves, opting instead for a right-hander out of Mount Pleasant named Bryan Edwards, who was Encarnacion's teammate with Low A Dayton in 2001 and has bounced between the minor leagues and indie ball since.

ROUND 10: RUSTY GREER, 1990

Maybe the best draft on this list. Thurman Clyde Greer came out of the diminutive University of Montevallo, which has never produced another big leaguer, and he just got better, hitting .282 in Double-A, .297 in Triple-A, and .305 in a nine-year Texas career. Greer was an indispensable part of the three late-'90s Rangers clubs that were still standing after 162 games, a leader by example and a winner. The 279th player chosen in the 1990 draft may very well be a top 10 player in Rangers history.

Still, despite Davis's struggles and Smoak's locked-in-ness, I'm guessing this move wouldn't have happened this soon had the Rangers offense as a whole been in better shape. Ian Kinsler's return is probably still a week away at best, and maybe there were just too many holes in the lineup right now for the organization not to reward Smoak and give him an opportunity to give the club a boost offensively.

People will start writing baseball obituaries for Davis right away, but let's not get carried away. Smoak could hit .188 for a month—which is not only exactly what Davis is hitting now but also exactly what Mark Teixeira hit in his first month in the big leagues (actually starting 0 for 16 before collecting his first base hit)—and end up yielding his spot back to Davis if the team is in contention and Davis refinds his stroke like he did with the RedHawks last summer. Or Vladimir Guerrero could land on the disabled list at some point, which could open a door for both Smoak and Davis to hold down spots in the lineup.

I'm a Davis believer, and I expect him to have a very productive major league career—with someone—but this development serves as an extra reminder of why you never draft for "need" in baseball.

When Texas chose Smoak on June 5, 2008, Davis was less than two weeks into his AAA promotion, having hit his way out of the Texas League with a monstrous .333/.376/.618 two months. There was every reason not to pop the 21-year-old Smoak with the 22-year-old Davis barreling in toward the first base job that Ben Broussard and Chris Shelton were attempting to hold down. The Rangers could have taken the second player on their board, Georgia high school righthander Ethan Martin, and avoided the possible Davis-Smoak conundrum.

(And they would have selected Martin had this war room conversation ended differently while Texas was on the clock:

Jon Daniels: *We like Smoak and Martin. Smoak's an impact college hitter who will come quickly, but it will take millions above slot to sign him. Martin's a two-way high school player who we like as a pitcher.*

Tom Hicks: *Who's the better player?*

Daniels: *We believe Smoak is.*

Hicks: *Take Smoak.*)

Based on the early returns, Martin (who was the next pitcher taken, going to the Dodgers four picks later) would have been a solid add, too.

But five weeks from now, when Smoak is 100 at-bats into his big league career, Martin will probably be pitching against the Rangers' High A club when Inland Empire hosts Bakersfield for a May 26-29 series. Had Texas gone after Martin rather than Smoak, because of Davis's presence, they'd have another high-ceiling arm in their loaded system, which wouldn't be problematic—but it wouldn't help the Rangers in their effort to figure out how to address this first base issue today.

The Rangers didn't shy away from drafting Teixeira just because they had another young third baseman, Hank Blalock, a player they expected to build around for a decade. When the Cowboys decide to take a player like Dez Bryant, they have a pretty good idea how he's going to fit because in football, as in basketball, you get drafted and you are expected to contribute. Now, in most cases. Not so in baseball.

Things change. On the day that Smoak signed with Texas, right up against his August 15 deadline to do so, Davis had a big league OPS of .856—and that was after a two-week slump brought it down from 1.018. The idea that the polished Smoak would get to Arlington 20 months later was surely less far-fetched at the time than the possibility that Davis would be optioned back to AAA in July 2009 and again in April 2010 (where he might see some time at third base, occasionally switching spots defensively with current RedHawks third baseman Matt Brown).

Things changed. And Texas was prepared.

Incidentally, Smoak will not be a free agent until after the 2016 season. Had he come up as few as four days ago, he would have earned a full year of big league service in 2010 (assuming he didn't return to the farm), setting things up for free agency after 2015 if not locked up long-term beforehand. This move speeds up Smoak's arbitration timetable by a year (he'll likely earn Super Two status after 2012, meaning he'll have four arbitration seasons rather than three), but that's a less significant issue than the free agency spectre.

The likely 40-man roster casualty would seem to be righthander Omar Poveda, who is out for the season and could be transferred to the 60-day disabled list to create the roster spot. The move would result in Poveda earning major league pay, which hasn't been the case until now, as he's been on option and thus earning the minor league side of his split contract.

I have more to say about the Smoak-Davis ramifications but not much time this morning. Still, it's not as if this is a story that will last for just one or two news cycles. This doesn't have to be a zero-sum game, and we may reach a point later this season at which the success of one of our young first basemen doesn't necessarily mean the other has failed. The objective right now is for Smoak to give the big league lineup a boost, and for Davis to get things back in order in Oklahoma City.

If both things happen, Texas will be in very good shape, one way or another.

But first things first. Treating Max Scherzer badly would be a good start.

Shakeup at first base
Not even after we Lost
Smoak Monster cometh

April 23, 2010

The Rangers are pushing Scott Feldman's start from tonight to tomorrow, due to a stomach virus he's had for a couple days. Rich Harden will make tonight's start, on regular rest, in Feldman's place.

Also, the club has officially purchased Justin Smoak and optioned Chris Davis, and as speculated, roster space for Smoak was created by the placement of Omar Poveda on the 60-day disabled list.

April 23, 2010

That's a really nice win on several levels, and yeah, gift horses and all, but your resident glass-half-full homer is still mildly baseball-cranky.

A little sophistry from the fine folks at Topps, on the back of Rich Harden's 2010 baseball card:

"Rich has winning stuff; all he needs is a little help from his friends. In the 51 career starts in which he's gotten at least four runs of support while he was in the game, his record is 39-0."

What Topps didn't point out was, aside from the 12 no-decisions Harden has had under those circumstances, how many times he left with his club behind, but so early in the game that his teammates had time to take him off the hook for a loss.

Harden tonight: 4.1 innings, two runs on six hits and four walks, five strikeouts, 62 strikes out of 99 pitches, two groundouts and five flyouts, left with a lead, but didn't stick around long enough for Texas to get its fourth run for the folks at Topps—not that he stuck around long enough to even qualify for a victory.

Derek Holland tonight, for Oklahoma City: 7.1 innings, three runs (one earned) on five hits and no walks, six strikeouts, 75 strikes out of 94 pitches, nine groundouts and five flyouts.

That's right: Holland (2-1, 0.67) needed fewer pitches to get through 7.1 than Harden (0-1, 4.58) needed to get through 4.1.

Holland has quality starts—bigtime quality starts—every time out this year. Harden has one. And the other three have been whatever the opposite of "quality" is.

I realize that AAA is not the big leagues, but there are some overall numbers here that I'm not in the mood to overlook.

Holland is averaging nearly seven innings per start. Harden, just over four.

Holland is averaging 13.6 pitches per inning. Harden, 21.9.

Another way to look at it: Harden has thrown more pitches (387) than Holland has (367), even though he's logged fewer than two-thirds as many innings (Harden: 17.2, Holland: 27.0).

And though Harden has thrown 20 more pitches than Holland, he's thrown 25 fewer strikes.

Harden: 18 walks and three hit batsmen in those 17.1 innings.

Holland: three walks and one hit batsman in his 27.0 innings.

The burden that Harden's putting on the bullpen every fifth day is going to catch up to this staff before long, even if his perfect Topps stat remains unblemished. The card company suggests all the righthander needs is a little help from his friends.

That's a two-way street.

April 24, 2010

The Tigers had to scratch their scheduled starter hours before gametime, with a bullpen whose tensile strength was already being put to the test asked to go nine innings on the road in a nearly sold-out game against the other team's number one starter. Each of the Rangers' three AL West division-mates had already lost.

That's a game you've got to win.

Texas backs its ace with four runs on seven hits and two walks through the first inning and two-thirds.

The remaining seven and a third against the Detroit pen: Zero runs on four hits and a walk.

Meanwhile, Scott Feldman (still fighting the effects of the stomach flu, maybe? hopefully?) gives up eight straight runs after being staked to that 4-0 lead, surrendering eight hits and four walks and a costly wild pitch in 3.2 innings. Feldman didn't have a start in 2009 as bad as either of these last two until his 18th start of the season—at home against Detroit.

That's a bad loss.

Three times in the last five games, Texas has squandered a four-run lead.

Five times in the last seven games, the Rangers starter has failed to go five innings.

Doug Mathis, bravo. No better a ball-to-strike efficiency tonight than Feldman, but he battled. He might find himself back on the shuttle, necessarily, but that was a solid effort.

Jeff Wilson of the *Fort Worth Star-Telegram* proposes that one way to address the lack of a second lefthander in the bullpen would be to option Mathis and call Derek Holland up, not to replace Rich Harden, but Matt Harrison, who would slide into relief. If that's in consideration, it would make more sense to get a reliever up here in Mathis's place until Holland could go on Wednesday. Harrison probably can't pitch tomorrow even though he threw only 75 pitches on Wednesday, because he likely threw a side yesterday or today.

Regardless, maybe Pedro Strop (seven straight scoreless outings, though he did pitch last night and tonight) or Guillermo Moscoso or Omar Beltre (four scoreless outings out of five) or Alexi Ogando or Zach Phillips, all of whom are on the roster (though all right-handed other than Phillips), or southpaw Clay Rapada, who isn't, could come up here in Mathis's place to hold things down in long relief until Holland's spot comes up Wednesday. If Wilson is onto something.

Through 17 games in 2009, Texas issued 73 walks and fanned 99, holding opponents to a .282 batting average and throwing 17.8 pitches per inning.

Through 17 games this year, Texas has issued 72 walks and fanned 123, holding opponents to a .251 batting average and throwing 17.8 pitches per inning.

Yet the Rangers were 8-9 through 17 last year, 7-10 right now.

Why?

The offense through the first 17 in 2009: .274/.331/.513, 105 runs, 35 home runs. This year: .240/.315/.366, 71 runs, 12 home runs.

How does Vladimir Guerrero factor into all that? Big Bad Vlad had a lifetime line of .394/.471/.705 in 193 at-bats as an opponent in Rangers Ballpark. Nobody expected him to be *that* ridiculous in a Rangers uniform, but you know what? In 31 home at-bats this year, he sits at .548/.576/.839.

Then again, he's at .194/.257/.226 in the same number of road at-bats.

Three bad moments for Taylor Teagarden defensively tonight. Seems pretty certain that once Jarrod Saltalamacchia proves on his Oklahoma City rehab assignment that he's ready, he and Teagarden will switch uniforms.

Saltalamacchia caught all nine innings and singled, walked, and hit an RBI sac fly in four trips for the RedHawks tonight. Also in that game was Chris Davis's first 2010 home run, a three-run blast to right field that extended Oklahoma City's eighth-inning lead to 8-3 (in a game the RedHawks eventually won, 8-7).

Ian Kinsler will rehab with Frisco Monday through Wednesday and could join the Rangers in Seattle on Friday. Tommy Hunter threw 19 pitches (13 strikes) in an extended spring training game today in Surprise.

Crummy loss tonight. Sometimes when I write about a game like this, it's therapeutic, cathartic, but tonight I'm stuck with the feeling you get when you lose a routine fly ball in the lights or the dusk or whatever it was.

April 25, 2010

Saturday was a rotten sports day. The day began with word that Max's soccer game and what we thought would finally be the first game of his baseball career (not counting T-ball) were rained out. Then Texas coughed up a really bad loss against Detroit.

I woke up this morning thinking maybe Sunday could redeem things. I had a chance to actually contribute in my softball doubleheader after I was such a waste the last time out. We were going to get Max's baseball game in today. And Colby Lewis had an opportunity to put Texas a game up in this four-game set with the Tigers. I doubted all of those things would come together, but even a little positive after Saturday's uselessness would be good enough.

And it all turned out better than I'd hoped for. That was a great baseball day.

Not much of that matters to you, but maybe this will:

Frisco righthander Tanner Scheppers in 2010: eight innings, three hits (3 for 29), one run (1.13 ERA), zero walks, 13 strikeouts.

Frisco righthander Alexi Ogando in 2010: 9.2 innings, two hits (2 for 31), one run (0.93 ERA), two walks, 14 strikeouts.

Scheppers's opponents' slash: .103/.103/.207. Eighty strikes out of 118 pitches.

Ogando's opponents' slash: .065/.121/.097. One hundred two strikes out of 142 pitches (in fact, identical 51/71 splits against right-handed hitters and left-handed hitters, the latter of whom are getting neutralized by a filthy change).

Sorry, Scott, for stealing your thunder. I'm leaving Michael Kirkman and The Chad Tracy Show to you.

Guess who in baseball has more strikeouts than Colby Lewis.

Here's the list:

Tim Lincecum.

He has four more punchouts than Lewis—in 3.1 more innings. The two righthanders basically have the same strikeout rate (10.7 per nine innings).

Lincecum was the 10th player chosen in the 2006 draft.

The 457th player taken in that draft (by the Phillies) was Florida high school outfielder Riley Cooper.

Cooper would later be the 754th player chosen in 2009, by the Rangers, out of the University of Florida. Texas offered to pay him $250,000 (well above slot) if he'd play minor league baseball. He agreed to at first, then reconsidered.

The 22-year-old was chosen by Philadelphia again this weekend, this time by the Eagles, with the 159th selection in the NFL draft.

If that fifth-round slot calls for something in the neighborhood of what it paid last year, Cooper is looking at about $180,000-$190,000 to sign with the Eagles, where I'm guessing he'd have to unseat Jason Avant or Hank Baskett in order to push for meaningful reps behind DeSean Jackson and Jeremy Maclin.

But enough about football, and, soon, enough about basketball, which is about to make the Great Game the Only Game in Town again. Baseball roped me back in today.

April 26, 2010

According to a local report, Oklahoma City righthander Brandon McCarthy has been placed on the seven-day DL with a stress fracture in his shoulder, the third time in four seasons he's been diagnosed with it. Rest is prescribed, and evidently only a brief deactivation is expected.

McCarthy had made four RedHawks starts—all quality starts of at least seven innings—and was limiting opponents to a .178 batting average, had issued five walks against 18 strikeouts (in a Pacific Coast League-leading 28.2 innings), and boasted a positive groundout-to-flyout rate.

April 26, 2010

Know what makes me baseball-sad?

That when Florida put 24-year-old Miguel Cabrera on the trade market in 2007, the type of hitter that's available at that age about once a decade, our farm system wasn't in the shape that the top of Detroit's was then, and that ours is now.

Sports timing drives me crazy.

April 27, 2010

The Rangers have placed outfielder Nelson Cruz on the disabled list with a strained right hamstring, recalling outfielder Craig Gentry from Oklahoma City to replace him on the active roster. Cruz is leading the American League in slug (.758) and OPS (1.177).

April 27, 2010

The Rangers have activated Jarrod Saltalamacchia and optioned BOTH Saltalamacchia and Taylor Teagarden to Oklahoma City, recalling Max Ramirez, who will presumably back up Matt Treanor and give Texas an extra right-handed bat now that Nelson Cruz is out for at least two weeks.

Fascinating.

April 28, 2010

One thing Matt Treanor couldn't have known when he agreed not to exercise his out clause on March 30, and one thing he evidently didn't know:

1. That he'd be this club's frontline catcher less than a month later.

2. That the Rangers don't hit Mark Buehrle.

3. Treanor was going to start Tuesday night whether the Rangers had shuffled their catcher corps or not, but hours after the announcement had been made that Texas had not only optioned Taylor Teagarden but also activated and optioned Jarrod Saltalamacchia, recalling Max Ramirez to serve as the backup behind the plate, Treanor responded by contributing the first extra-base hits by a Rangers catcher all season. His home run and double off Buehrle (11-3, 2.93 against the Rangers coming into Tuesday, the most dominant numbers he has against any opponent he's faced more than a few times) accounted for the first three Texas runs, staking C.J. Wilson to a lead that he and Dustin Nippert and Frankie Francisco would make stand up.

The Teagarden move wasn't surprising, given his colossal struggles making contact and his occasional defensive lapses, but the Saltalamacchia move was an eye-opener. Among the things Jon Daniels said about the move was that Texas didn't want Saltalamacchia worrying about when the club was going to activate him from his rehab assignment. The option requires at least a 10-day stay on the farm (barring an injury to someone else at the big league level), during which the Rangers expect Saltalamacchia to focus on playing every day, not on when he'd get the plane ticket.

Meanwhile, Teagarden goes from having an opportunity to play every day in Texas, in Saltalamacchia's absence, to backing him up in Oklahoma City. Evidently, if Saltalamacchia's option lasts more than 10 days, the club would consider moving Teagarden to Frisco so both could play most days.

Nelson Cruz's deactivation resulted in a recall for outfielder Craig Gentry as well, and he had a couple nice at-bats against Buehrle, but it also meant Ryan Garko was going to get a start on Tuesday, despite coming into the game 0 for 11 as a Ranger. Garko's .480 average in 25 career at-bats against Buehrle was second best in baseball among hitters with at least 20 at-bats against the veteran lefty, and his .552 on-base percentage was tops. Garko hit a key single in the sixth, his first hit for the club, moving Vladimir Guerrero to third and setting up a Justin Smoak sac fly that extended a 3-2 lead to 4-2.

So Oklahoma City now runs a club out there that might feature, on a given night, Saltalamacchia and Teagarden at catcher and DH, Chris Davis at first base, and Derek Holland on the mound, all on option and none on temporary rehab assignment cameos—and the season is just over three weeks old. It's a concrete indication, if we didn't believe what the front office was telling us over the winter and in camp, that the organization has placed on itself an expectation of winning in 2010. The meritocracy extends to the early changes at the top of the lineup and the back of the bullpen, and should put veterans like Matt Harrison and Rich Harden and Garko on notice that jobs secured before Opening Day aren't tenured.

The RedHawks host New Orleans tomorrow night after taking the day off today. Holland (2-1, 0.67, 21/3 K/BB in 27 innings, four quality starts out of four) gets the start, but the off-day skews the pitching schedule that he and Harden (0-1, 4.58, 20/18 K/BB in 17.2 innings, slated to face Chicago tonight) were on together. Holland and Harrison are a couple days apart now, and if Holland deals again Thursday and Harrison struggles in Seattle on Saturday, would it be a shock to see Holland not pitching to Saltalamacchia or Teagarden in Omaha next Tuesday, but instead held back to make Harrison's next start in

Texas against Omaha's parent club, the Royals, a week from tomorrow?

Could Francisco be closing games again by time Kansas City comes to town, after his clean ninth last night? Doubtful, at least not as the first option. Neftali Feliz had the night off, having pitched the previous two days, and Ron Washington said after the game that the closer's job is still his. We've already seen this month that that job, like Chris Davis's and Saltalamacchia's and Teagarden's and Julio Borbon's leadoff assignment, is subject to change if the organization thinks there's an option more likely to help the club win games now. But Feliz isn't in danger of ceding the job after Monday's poor effort (his first back-to-back day assignment), despite Francisco's good work last night.

Francisco in his last seven appearances: seven innings, one run on three singles and two walks (.130/.200/.130), three strikeouts. He's finding a good groove, and right now that's good news as far as the eighth inning is concerned.

The rest of the bullpen (Darren Oliver, Darren O'Day, Chris Ray, Nippert, Doug Mathis) is pitching reasonably effectively to very well, which should stave off Holland-esque promotion watches on young relievers like Tanner Scheppers, Alexi Ogando, and Omar Beltre, not to mention Pedro Strop.

But if a decision were made to move Harrison to the bullpen after his next start, it would make sense to get a reliever up here until Holland's start, possibly a lefthander like Clay Rapada or Zach Phillips.

For what it's worth, John Perrotto of Baseball Prospectus writes that the Rangers are considering moving Harden into long relief to get him straightened out, a possibility that will draw more local speculation if he struggles tonight in his faceoff against Jake Peavy, who like Harden has yet to log a 2010 victory. Perrotto's BP cohort Will Carroll weighs in to say he doesn't think Harden is hurt, but does wonder aloud if he'd thrive in a bullpen role at this point in his career the way it worked out for Kerry Wood.

Wilson's fourth straight quality start to kick off the season was the first such Rangers streak since 1993, when Kevin Brown (six straight) and Charlie Leibrandt (four) pulled off the feat.

I said it two weeks ago and I'm even more convinced now: Wilson is our ace. And a Kenny Rogers career isn't out of the question.

The great Joe Posnanski points out that Royals righthander Zack Greinke has a 2.11 ERA in his 46 starts since August 16, 2008—and that Kansas City's record in those games is 22-24.

Greinke makes $7.25 million this year and has a limited no-trade clause. He makes $13.5 million in 2011, and again in 2012, without any no-trade protection. The Royals can and will be in last place with or without him. Wouldn't it make sense for them to do with the 26-year-old what every reporter in the country insists San Diego will need to do with Adrian Gonzalez—move him to get three or four pieces to build with like Texas did with Mark Teixeira?

Or like Florida did in 2007 with Miguel Cabrera, as we discussed in Monday night's report?

Colorado optioned 27-year-old catcher Chris Iannetta yesterday, a fascinating move for a guy who came into his own offensively under Clint Hurdle and parlayed it into a multi-year contract this past winter. He was hitting just .133/.235/.333 out of the gate this season.

TCU freshman lefthander Matt Purke: 7-0, 3.81 in 10 starts and a relief appearance, with 69 strikeouts and 13 walks in 56.2 innings.

Kansas City designated righthander Luis Mendoza for assignment, after he'd surrendered 10 runs on 10 hits and three walks in four relief innings.

Boston recalled lefthander Fabio Castro for one game, and Baltimore purchased the contract of righthander Alfredo Simon. Oakland optioned righthander Edwar Ramirez to AAA.

Two middle infielders tied in rumors to Texas over the last couple months made the transaction wires yesterday: St. Louis signed Aaron Miles to a minor league deal, and Boston designated Kevin Frandsen for assignment.

The Rangers released outfielder Eric Fry and left-handed reliever Ryan Falcon.

The Windy City Thunderbolts of the independent Frontier League signed infielder Donnie Ecker.

I'm going to be very interested to see when and how often Ron Washington entrusts a start behind the plate to Max Ramirez, but for now the microscope is instead on Rich Harden, who might be pitching tonight to stall yet another major change for this club.

April 29, 2010

Rich Harden threw a scant 53 percent of his pitches for strikes, only 11 first-pitch strikes in 25 batters. He hasn't had a 1-2-3 inning in any of his last three starts. He now has more walks than strikeouts for the season, and nearly as many walks (23) as innings pitched (23.2). That's a rate of 8.75 walks per nine innings.

The major league single-season record is 8.22. Established by Yankees lefthander Tommy Byrne in 1949 and not surpassed since.

Harden's velocity was down another tick, and he managed to induce one swinging strike: Paul Konerko with two on and no outs in the sixth inning, his final inning of work.

One swinging strike.

But he got the win.

Neftali Feliz's velocity and fastball command weren't where they should be. He was hit hard. Twenty-two pitches, 59 percent for strikes. *Zero* swings and misses.

Newberg Report: Davis' Fate Uncertain

First baseman could make it back with Rangers or another team

By Jamey Newberg / Special to MLB.com
April 29, 2010

Shortly before Rangers first baseman Chris Davis got word last week that he was heading back to Triple-A for the third straight year, he said during an interview: "You talk about the struggles and the journey it takes to go through the Minor Leagues. Some guys spend seven or eight years in the Minor Leagues and finally get a chance to be in the big leagues. It's definitely a game of opportunity and a game of chance." Davis' charge is now to earn that next opportunity, that next chance.

A number of fans in Texas (and a reporter or two) have decided that this particular demotion could spell the end of Davis' Rangers run, particularly in light of the fact that his roster replacement was Justin Smoak. Last year when Davis was optioned, Hank Blalock stepped in at first base in what was clearly a placeholder role. Not the case with Smoak, who most believe may never go back to the minor leagues and is under club control longer than Davis is.

But it's obviously too soon to put Smoak on next year's All-Star Ballot, or campaign for his Rookie of the Year chances in 2010. The club has already demonstrated a number of times this month that lack of production will only be tolerated for so long, in a year in which the expectation is to contend for a playoff berth. If Smoak were to struggle for a month, he could be back in an Oklahoma City RedHawks uniform himself.

As for Davis, his Rangers fate could go in any number of directions. Jason Botts split the 2005 season between Oklahoma and Texas. Same thing in 2006. And in 2007. And again in 2008. The big switch-hitter regularly terrorized Triple-A pitching, but things never clicked in Arlington, he eventually cleared league-wide waivers, then got a deal in Japan, and returned this year to the States for a camp audition (with the White Sox) that didn't go well. He's playing independent league ball right now.

On the other hand, there's Nelson Cruz, who had a similar four-year split between Triple-A and the big leagues, cleared waivers himself, and finally put everything together in 2009.

And they don't always take that long. Take a look at what Adrian Gonzalez did with the RedHawks in 2004 and 2005, and what he did the same two years in Texas. One trade later, he found his stroke as a Padre and has settled in as one of baseball's most dangerous hitters.

Sometimes it takes more than one change of scenery or opportunity. The Rangers traded for Ryan Ludwick in 2002, but got no big league production out of him in two years split between Texas and Oklahoma. Texas dealt Ludwick to Cleveland, and in two-plus seasons on the Indians shuttle he failed to get untracked. Detroit signed him to a Minor League deal in 2006 and didn't even give him a big league look. St. Louis took a similar chance on the outfielder for the 2007 season and struck gold.

While he hasn't had his Ludwick breakthrough, Laynce Nix finally had a productive season in the big leagues last year with Cincinnati, after four years of bouncing between Triple-A and the big leagues with Texas and Milwaukee.

Is Davis sentenced to a Botts path at this point? Or is he a trade away from making the club regret moving him as much as Gonzalez has? I'd wager something in between, and I wouldn't rule out Ludwick or Cruz production eventually for the 24-year-old.

Smoak's arrival could mean that Davis's next real opportunity comes with a new team, like it did for Ludwick. But it could still happen here, too, as Texas knows firsthand from its patience with Cruz that sometimes it takes several chances before things click.

But he got the save.

Despite all the uh-oh developments that Texas has packed into these first three weeks of baseball, a win today by Scott Feldman over Gavin Floyd, who is struggling more than Feldman this season and who has fared terribly in Rangers Ballpark, would give the Rangers a series sweep and even the club's record at .500 for the season.

And that would make for a Happy 58th Birthday for Ron Washington, born three years after Byrne walked opponents at an unmatched rate, and yet went 15-7 for the World Champion Yanks.

April 30, 2010

Mavs out of the way
Rangers now the sole focus
Time to turn it on

Scott Feldman deserved better yesterday, and while Darren O'Day and Dustin Nippert aren't in danger of losing their jobs, the bullpen has been a problem, accounting for seven of the club's 12 losses (last year's relief corps lost 19 games all year) and a .461 slug. It's easy to point quickly to the absence of C.J. Wilson, but that's lazy, as Darren Oliver has been effective in Wilson's vacated role. The problems are elsewhere.

Neftali Feliz and Frankie Francisco have contributed most heavily to the troublesome bullpen numbers, and they're not going anywhere either, but it's fair to assume that, in the natural course of things, reinforcements will be needed in various relief roles over the remaining 140 games, and there are several young relievers on the farm—including three who weren't stateside in the system last year—pushing for whiteboard discussions at 1000 Ballpark Way.

There were fewer than 6,000 paid in Frisco last night for the RoughRiders' 1-0, 11-inning win over San Antonio (fans of both clubs probably had another Thursday evening sports appointment), but what happened in the top halves of the eighth and ninth was probably worth noting.

Alexi Ogando, after three "starts" (designed to keep the relief prospect's innings carefully managed), was shifted to the bullpen (perhaps to begin getting him used to the situations he'll be asked to handle, and maybe to get him more regular work than the rotation assignment allowed). And Tanner Scheppers worked on two days' rest for the first time and pitched one inning, having had his first five Frisco appearances spaced out further and logging two frames at a time. Again, this could be an effort to step up the grooming process.

Their work last night, the first game they pitched in together:

Ogando's seventh: perfect inning, groundout-flyout-groundout. Seven pitches, four strikes. Reportedly worked 95-96, mixing in his advanced slider.

Scheppers's eighth: perfect inning, strikeout looking-groundout-flyout. Thirteen pitches, nine strikes. Reports of 96-98 and dirtiness in his own power curve and change.

Ogando this season (holding opponents to 2 for 34, fanning 14 of 34 batters faced, .059/.111/.088):

DATE	IP	H	R	ER	BB	SO	HR	PITCHES	STRIKES
Apr 9	2.0	1	0	0	0	3	0	32	22
Apr 13	2.0	1	1	1	0	3	1	34	22
Apr 17	2.0	0	0	0	0	3	0	26	18
Apr 22	2.0	1	0	0	0	4	0	26	18
Apr 26	2.0	0	0	0	0	5	0	27	19
Apr 29	1.0	0	0	0	0	1	0	13	9
TOTALS	11.0	3	1	1	0	19	1	158	108

Scheppers (holding opponents to 3 for 38, punching out half of his batters faced, .079/.079/.158):

DATE	IP	H	R	ER	BB	SO	HR	PITCHES	STRIKES
Apr 10	2.2	0	0	0	1	3	0	39	25
Apr 19	3.0	1	1	1	0	3	0	44	34
Apr 25	4.0	1	0	0	1	8	0	59	43
Apr 29	1.0	0	0	0	0	0	0	7	4
TOTALS	10.2	2	1	1	2	14	0	149	106

Omar Beltre, working out of the Oklahoma City bullpen, is probably going to get some work tonight in relief of lefthander Michael Kirkman, hoping to finish off an impressive April (to date: 8.2 innings, two runs [2.08 ERA] on six hits [all singles] and five walks [.194/.297/.194], 12 strikeouts, eye-opening ratio of 10 groundouts to three flyouts). He's been pitching on two or three days' rest each time out.

Will Scheppers, Ogando, and Beltre be up this year? For various reasons (long-term shoulder risk for the former, age for the latter two), it might make sense to err on the side of pushing them a bit. It's too soon, but given the erratic start that the big club has had in the bullpen this month, it's hard not to keep one eye on what's happening with those three out of the gate.

The other benefit, of course, is that very few pitchers jump into big league games with the kind of success and reliability that Feliz provided last summer. Scheppers, Ogando, and Beltre are going to be counted on to help in 2011. It would make sense to get them used to the major leagues in 2010, and get the acclimation period out of the way.

The way those three are dealing, the acclimation period may belong to opposing hitters.

April 30, 2010

The Rangers have promoted righthander Tanner Scheppers from AA Frisco to AAA Oklahoma City. As discussed in this morning's Newberg Report, the Texas League had been no match for the 23-year-old, who had allowed one run on three hits and *zero walks* in 11 RoughRider relief innings, striking out 19.

April 30, 2010

The Rangers, as expected, have activated second baseman Ian Kinsler for tonight's series opener in Seattle. To clear a spot on the active roster, the club has placed infielder Joaquin Arias on the 15-day disabled list with a lower back strain.

May 2010

40-MAN ROSTER (40)

Pitchers (21)

Omar Beltre, Scott Feldman, Neftali Feliz, Frankie Francisco, Rich Harden, Matt Harrison, Derek Holland, Tommy Hunter, Michael Kirkman, Colby Lewis, Doug Mathis, Brandon McCarthy, Guillermo Moscoso, Dustin Nippert, Darren O'Day, Alexi Ogando, Darren Oliver, Zach Phillips, Chris Ray, Pedro Strop, C.J. Wilson

Catchers (4)

Max Ramirez, Jarrod Saltalamacchia, Taylor Teagarden, Matt Treanor

Infielders (8)

Elvis Andrus, Joaquin Arias, Andres Blanco, Chris Davis, Ryan Garko, Ian Kinsler, Justin Smoak, Michael Young

Outfielders (7)

Brandon Boggs, Julio Borbon, Nelson Cruz, Craig Gentry, Vladimir Guerrero, Josh Hamilton, David Murphy

60-Day Disabled List (3)

Eric Hurley, Warner Madrigal, Omar Poveda

May 1, 2010

There's so much to be said about that one. It's the type of game that, if this season goes beyond 162, will be talked about reverently, and repeatedly, for a long time. Epic.

But I've said my peace. If you follow me on Twitter (@NewbergReport), you were besieged with 496 words spread over 31 Tweets throughout Texas 2, Seattle 0.

I'm out of steam, partly because it's already May 1 as I type this, a reminder of how much I hate that we're still in the AL West, which means a lot more of you are probably reading this after a full night of sleep than right at the end of one of the more amazing baseball games, Rangers or not, in memory.

I lasted longer than Wash did tonight, but I'm gassed.

First, though, three final words.

Colby. Preston. Lewis.

May 2, 2010

If there are 10 true aces in the American League, Seattle has two of them. And the Rangers have put one of the more disappointing March's and April's in recent franchise history behind them by winning back-to-back matchups against Cliff Lee and Felix Hernandez on the road, tossing Colby Lewis and Matt Harrison (two pitchers thought a month ago to have mid-to-back-of-rotation ceilings) out there to counter.

The result: Texas, amazingly, is back to .500 (12-12).

And in second place in the AL West, half a game behind Oakland, with C.J. Wilson facing Doug Fister this afternoon, a battle between two of the bigger starting pitcher surprises in the league over the first month.

Whether or not Texas completes the Seattle sweep, it's a series win to start off May, and series wins are what you shoot for. As the club heads into the second month of the season, the idea will be to replicate what the Rangers did under Ron Washington in May 2008 (19-10) and May 2009 (20-9), not what they did in May 2007 (9-20).

May 2, 2010

Feliz Cumpleanos.

First place.

(Is it wrong for me to feel a little bit bad for Mariners fans? What a mess.)

May 3, 2010

Baseball America executive editor Jim Callis, in a crystal ball feature foretelling the 2013 season, writes this:

The Rangers should be in complete control in the AL West. With Martin Perez, Derek Holland, Tanner Scheppers and 2010 first-rounders Jesse Hahn [Virginia Tech] and Brandon Workman [University of Texas] in the rotation, plus Neftali Feliz closing games, they'll finally have enough pitching. Julio Borbon and Elvis Andrus will run wild at the top of the lineup and Justin Smoak will drive them in, so Texas won't have any problems scoring runs either.

The Callis article reflects a commonly accepted premise among those who write about such things nationally, a belief that the Rangers, with the ripening of its top-ranked farm system, are about to settle into a run of contention. The one thing I think Callis misses (other than the easy "finally have enough pitching" comment that continues to get thrown around by some) is that, by 2013, if not 2011, a two-sentence note detailing the strength of the Rangers club is going to include a couple very big names in uniform elsewhere right now.

The Rangers Baseball Express ownership group will be in place at some point, hopefully soon, and the Texas payroll will start to look a lot different. No doubt, much of the increase will come internally, as young players reach arbitration status and arbitration guys reach free agency (imagine where C.J. Wilson's contract is headed—the Rangers are likely to try extending him into his 2012 free agency season soon, but if he's even willing to do that, an extension beyond 2012 is probably not in the cards), but I'd be surprised if the Greenberg-Ryan group didn't take a Step Five approach with Jon Daniels and Thad Levine and add a couple impact players between now and then.

Hahn and Workman would be great, but Zack Greinke and Grady Sizemore? Better. Much better.

But we're getting way ahead of ourselves. It's a testament to the strange tendency of the Ron Washington Rangers—and the 2010 mediocrity of the AL West—that three weeks of ugly have given way, a month into the season, to a run of good baseball and a perch atop the division, as Texas gets set to face second-place Oakland for six of the next 10 (bisected by a four-game set at home against Kansas City that will feature a Friday matchup between Wilson and Greinke—with the basketball season over, the postgame fireworks show shouldn't be the sole reason that one ought to approach a sellout).

There will be talk the next few days about Washington managing against the Athletics, an organization that went to the playoffs five times in his 11 seasons on the coaching staff, but what I'm more interested in is Rich Harden pitching in Oakland tonight. In 49 career appearances (47 starts) in Oakland-Alameda County Coliseum, Harden is 18-9 with a 2.98 ERA, with 285 strikeouts (8.8 per nine innings) and 107 unintentional walks (3.3 per nine) in 293 innings, and a glittering .216/.293/.329 opponents' slash line.

All that work came in the green and gold. Tonight will be Harden's first time to step on that mound in the bottom of the inning.

In Colby Lewis's Friday night gem, he threw first-pitch strikes to 74 percent of the Mariners he faced.

According to ESPN, seven of his 10 strikeouts came on his slider, which he had complete command of all night, and Seattle was hitless in 12 at-bats when putting his fastball into play—dropping the league to a .169 average against his fastball. Breaking ball command is such a good thing.

Scott Lucas's daily farm reports are bringing you lots of encouraging news on Chris Davis and Jarrod Saltalamacchia lately, but you really ought to be paying close attention to what Bakersfield outfielder Engel Beltre and Hickory outfielder Miguel Velazquez are doing as well.

Taylor Teagarden caught for the RedHawks Saturday and DH'd yesterday. He struck out four times in seven hitless at-bats, drawing one walk.

From Vladimir Guerrero, according to Franklin Mirabal of *Impacto Deportivo*: "In Anaheim they treated me well, but in Texas I've found a lot of friendships, a lot of Latin players, and that [make] me happy here. Right now, I don't think about retiring."

Hank Blalock is hitting .343/.408/.433 for AAA Durham. He's not showing much power but he's getting on base, a tradeoff I'm sure we would have been happy with the last few years here. He's hoping to force a look in Tampa Bay the way Joaquin Benoit (one scoreless inning as a Ray since his 17-strikeout, three-walk effort in 9.2 Durham innings) did.

You should read the tremendous interview of Eric Nadel (who got an opportunity to call some of the nationally televised Rangers-Mariners game on Saturday) by Baseball Prospectus's David Laurila.

Seattle released outfielder Eric Byrnes, a move I'm glad didn't come three days earlier.

Dodgers righthander Vicente Padilla is on the disabled list with irritation of the radial nerve in his right forearm and should miss all of May. His ERA in four starts is 7.06.

Kansas City got righthander Luis Mendoza through waivers and outrighted him to AAA.

The Angels claimed infielder Kevin Frandsen off waivers from Boston and optioned him to AAA.

The Kalamazoo Kings of the independent Frontier League signed righthander Bobby Wilkins. The Yuma Scorpions of the independent Golden Baseball League signed outfielder Cody Nowlin.

Nowlin was the Rangers' second-round pick in 1998, nestled between first-rounder Carlos Pena and third-rounder Barry Zito, both of whom went on to star elsewhere. The next stop for both Pena and Zito was Oakland, which was the first stop for Rich Harden, and I would be grateful if he, like the other two, dished out a little disappointment to his former organization that he's now getting it done somewhere else.

May 3, 2010

Firsts on May 3:

1. Tommy Hunter made his 2010 debut, throwing three sharp innings (no runs on two singles and one walk, 26 of 38 pitches for strikes) in a start for Oklahoma City.
2. We saw a pair of concentric rainbows in the East sky around 7 p.m.
3. Justin Smoak blasted a big league home run from the right side.
4. A multi-hit game for Craig Gentry, who was key tonight.
5. Neftali Feliz recorded saves on back-to-back days.
6. And I enjoyed watching Rich Harden make a Rangers start.

I enjoyed watching that very much.

Command. Control. Velocity. *Efficiency.*

First-pitch strikes two-thirds of the time. Sixteen swinging strikes (which is 16 more than in his last start).

Harden looked like the guy who went 18-9, 2.98 lifetime as a home pitcher in Oakland-Alameda County Coliseum, not the one who'd been so difficult to watch as a Texas Ranger until tonight. Harden came into tonight's game with 23 walks in 23.2 innings. Tonight: zero walks in seven frames. Before tonight, he'd thrown 57 percent of his pitches for strikes. Tonight: 71 percent.

In fact, only two A's hitters worked a three-ball count off Harden all night. (Well, one: Daric Barton did it both times.)

To sum it up: In each of Harden's last five starts, including tonight's, he has faced between 23 and 25 hitters. In two of those games, he lasted 3.2 and 4.1 innings. Tonight, he logged 7.0.

Tremendous effort, any way you look at it. That's the guy Texas was excited to land in December.

Jon Daniels made a point before the game that, despite all the moves the Rangers have made over the season's first four weeks, many of which have been fairly drastic, the club has not had to make one roster move involving a pitcher. It's a stunning thing to say about a Rangers club.

Rich Harden made it emphatically clear tonight that he wasn't going to make a pitching move necessary.

May 5, 2010

Don't go jumping to conclusions, but I thought this was interesting.

Derek Holland was in control of a 3-2 lead over Omaha through five innings last night.

He'd scattered two runs on four hits, all singles. Punched out eight, the best strikeout rate he'd had in any of his six starts. Issued just one walk.

The two runs came on a bunt single and infield hit in the third inning (after which Holland struck out ex-big leaguers Alex Gordon and Scott Thorman to end the inning). The result: his ERA rose to 0.93, which is still the best mark in the 16-team Pacific Coast League. He's second in the league in strikeouts.

Holland's fourth inning was quiet (strikeout, strikeout, groundout to first base). So was his fifth (strikeout, popout to second base, single to center, strikeout).

He'd thrown 83 pitches, his lightest pitch count since throwing 82 in Oklahoma City's opener on April 8. A very solid 57 of those pitches went for strikes. He'd faced 20 Royals, the fewest opponents he's faced all season.

He'd coaxed five groundouts, just one flyout. But not really. The one "flyout" was that pop to second.

Yet his night was done.

I haven't seen that there was any rain, or a dust storm in Omaha, or a light standard that blew out. I don't think there was any sort of extended game delay that would have prompted the club not to send Holland out for the sixth. His RedHawks teammates didn't freeze him up in the dugout with a long top of the sixth, sending just four hitters up.

Was Holland pulled after five effective innings and 83 pitches in a 3-2 game to make sure fellow lefthander Clay Rapada (one inning), AAA-debuting righthander Tanner Scheppers (two innings), and closer Pedro Strop (one inning) could get a prescribed amount of work in? Doubtful, considering Holland's chances to help the big club would seem to be more of an immediate consideration than those of the other three.

Was he lifted because he was hurt? Haven't seen anything to lead me to believe so.

Was he being protected because he's going to be starting for Texas in five days? Surely not. Scott Feldman wouldn't be in danger of losing his rotation spot, even if he hadn't rounded back into form last night by retiring the final 12 A's he faced. And Feldman surely isn't injured. There's no way Texas would have sent him back out there for seven innings after he'd given up seven runs through four frames if there was a physical issue—and Holland's night was over well before Feldman was stretched to seven in the West Coast game.

Was Holland's assignment cut short because the Rangers want him ready to start on short rest this Saturday? No chance, not after the way Rich Harden pitched on Monday.

Is Holland about to be traded? Of course not.

There's obviously an explanation, surely something not worth the 450 words I've coughed up so far. Maybe Holland developed a blister. Maybe he was fighting the stomach flu. Maybe a circuit did blow on a bank of lights in Rosenblatt Stadium and delayed the game 45 minutes.

But in these days of over-analysis and, as T.R. Sullivan noted on the radio pregame show last night, too much focus on the minor leagues, yeah, I guess I went there.

Don't expect a Newberg Report news flash updating this non-story. But I did find it interesting.

May 7, 2010

Crazy: One month in,
No pitching moves yet, all year
I'm ready for one.

Disgusting win.

The best teams lose games, the Royals win games, but the bottom line is that even though you can't win 'em all, you can at least expect to play winning baseball. That, despite the W, was not winning baseball.

I'll take it, of course. I'm thrilled that Texas escaped with a victory, and did it with some great work off a sensational closer, regaining a tie for the division lead. But . . . geez.

I was at the game, which usually means a Twitter assault. The first tweet I posted: "Harrison deals over first two frames. Tomorrow's Newberg Report already written."

It may just be wishful thinking, but I'd decided two things before the game:

1. If Matt Harrison got bombed last night, it would be time for Derek Holland.
2. If Harrison pitched well early on, it would be time for Derek Holland, with Harrison giving the bullpen a boost.

What I didn't count on was not only the latter coming into play . . . but the bullpen, on the same night, also hammering home the need for a shot in the arm.

Harrison's first inning: 11 strikes, six balls, four up, three down.

Harrison's second: nine strikes, two balls, three up, three down.

(Then the tweet.)

Harrison's third: eight strikes, three balls, three up, three down.

By time Harrison trotted out for the fourth inning, he'd been staked to an 8-0 lead, and had thrown an economical 39 pitches, an extremely efficient 28 of them for strikes. He'd gone through the Royals order plus one, and was very good.

The baseball marching orders for "doing what the game asks you to do" (a frequent Wash-ism) were clear at that point. Given the situation that an early eight-run lead presents, you throw strikes (his 72 percent strike rate was matched by first-pitch strikes to seven of 10 batters through three innings), let the defense do its job, save the bullpen (at least the key guys), and get this one in the books.

Instead, in the fourth and fifth, Harrison faced a dozen hitters, started seven of them off with a 1-0 count, and gave up a home run, two singles, and three walks—including a five-pitch walk to number eight hitter Mitch Maier to start the fifth, followed by a four-pitch free pass

Newberg Report: Top Minor League Additions

Rangers show knack for acquiring young talent via deals

By Jamey Newberg / Special to MLB.com

May 6, 2010

One thing that the salary cap has virtually taken away from football and basketball is the good, old-fashioned trade, the one where a team in the hunt sends a couple of top prospects to a team looking to retool in exchange for an impact bat or arm.

The headlines always focus on the star player joining the contender, but the reason those trades get made every year is they often pay huge dividends for the "seller," assuming their scouts do a good job targeting the right young players. A quick look at the team the Rangers are fielding right now reveals that half the starting infield (Michael Young and Elvis Andrus), two of the four primary outfielders (Nelson Cruz and David Murphy), one of the club's catchers (Max Ramirez), and three key members of the pitching staff (Matt Harrison, Neftali Feliz, and Frankie Francisco) were acquired by Texas as Minor Leaguers with another franchise.

What follows is a ranking of the top 10 players in the Rangers system acquired from other organizations. Only players who haven't exhausted rookie status were considered.

1. ALEXI OGANDO, RHP, Frisco

Texas used a pick in the Minor League phase of the 2005 Rule 5 Draft to steal the 22-year-old Oakland farmhand, at the time an outfielder with a big arm and big power that caused some scouts to invoke Vladimir Guerrero comparisons. Ogando was already caught up in the marriage-visa scam when Texas invested the meager fee of $12,000 to take him off the A's hands, with a plan to immediately convert him to the mound. It took four years for the Rangers to clear the right-hander's legal issues and bring him stateside, but their patience is being rewarded. Now 26, Ogando is off to a remarkable start as a RoughRider, allowing two runs on four hits and four walks in 13.2 innings, setting 19 Texas Leaguers down on strikes with a power package featuring an upper-90s fastball and plus slider. There's a good chance he could make an impact in Arlington this year.

2. ENGEL BELTRE, OF, Bakersfield

Beltre was the third-most prominent of the three players the Rangers acquired from Boston for reliever Eric Gagné at the trade deadline in 2007, seemingly a tack-on in the deal that brought outfielder David Murphy and left-hander Kason Gabbard to Texas. But the Rangers knew Beltre well from his amateur days in the Dominican Republic, and they wouldn't have made the deal without the 17-year-old, who had all of 34 games played in the States at the time of the trade. Flashing all five primary tools, Beltre had an eye-opening 2008 season but a miserable 2009. There are signs that it's all starting to come together in 2010, keyed by a dramatic improvement in both his walk and strikeout rates.

3. DANNY GUTIERREZ, RHP, Extended Spring

Off-field issues in the Kansas City system are what prompted the Royals to trade Gutierrez to Texas last summer for outfielder Tim Smith and catcher Manny Pina, two Minor Leaguers with big league potential but nowhere near the upside that the 23-year-old right-hander has. The patience that Texas has had to draw upon with Ogando and Beltre is different from the kind they'll need to show with Gutierrez, who was suspended by Major League Baseball for 50 games after a positive test for a banned substance. He'll go back to flashing mid-90s velocity and one of the system's dirtiest hammer curves when he comes back, most likely in Frisco.

4. PEDRO STROP, RHP, Oklahoma City

Colorado tried to sneak Strop off the 40-man roster and quickly re-sign the injured right-hander to a Minor League contract in September 2008, but Texas pounced and signed him before the Rockies could get a deal done. A converted infielder who features a mid-90s fastball and plus slider, Strop improved every month on the farm in 2009, earning a late-season look in Texas. He's currently working in late relief for Oklahoma City, allowing two earned runs each in his first and last appearances of the season but none in the nine times he pitched in between.

5. MAX RAMIREZ, C, Texas

Ramirez has been traded in July twice, first by Atlanta to Cleveland for closer Bob Wickman in 2006 and then by the Indians to the Rangers in 2007, for outfielder Kenny Lofton. He was nearly traded a third time this winter, to Boston for corner infielder Mike Lowell, before Lowell's failed physical killed the deal. Texas was selling low at the time, as Ramirez was coming off a miserable 2009 that was nowhere near in line with the career .311/.410/.512 numbers he'd put up in his first five pro seasons. The potential to be a productive, versatile hitter remains, but Ramirez is now 25 and probably projects as a role player at best.

6. GUILLERMO MOSCOSO, RHP, Oklahoma City

Texas traded catcher Gerald Laird to Detroit for Moscoso and fellow right-hander Carlos Melo in December 2008. Though he had only six games of Double-A experience at the time and had never thrown as many as 91 innings in any of his four pro seasons, Moscoso earned a promotion from Frisco all the way to Texas in May and spent the rest of the season bouncing between Arlington and Oklahoma City. He maintained the same strikeout rate (7.7 per nine innings) at all three levels in 2009, limiting his walks, and he's been working out of the RedHawks' rotation this spring, sitting at 1-2, 4.30 through five starts, with his sixth assignment slated to come tonight.

7. BEN SNYDER, LHP, Frisco

Selected by Texas in December's Rule 5 Draft, Snyder struggled in camp, but Texas got him through waivers on April 1 and convinced San Francisco to forgo buying the left-hander back for half the $50,000 draft fee and instead take 17-year-old southpaw Edwin Escobar in return. The Rangers assigned Snyder to the Frisco bullpen and while he's struggled with his command (issuing 10 walks in 17.1 innings), he's been difficult to hit (.137 opponents' average) and just as tough on right-handed hitters as on the lefties that Texas envisions spotting him against if and when he works his way up to the big leagues. Snyder's RoughRider ERA is 1.04, and he's stranded all six baserunners he's inherited.

8. DAVID PAISANO, OF, Bakersfield

Like Beltre, Paisano was a player that Texas keyed on at the back of a significant trade, even though the club knew he was years away from entering the picture. Picked up from the White Sox in the 2006 trade that sent John Danks and Nick Masset (and Jake Rasner) to Chicago for Brandon McCarthy, Paisano is a standout defender who is starting to put things together at the plate. Playing primarily right field for the Blaze (capable of playing center field but ceding that position to Beltre), the 22-year-old is hitting .308/.365/.436 in the early going this year.

9. BEAU JONES, LHP, Extended Spring

The fifth of the five players acquired from Atlanta in the 2007 Mark Teixeira trade, Jones is being held back in Surprise right now to work through a minor arm injury. The 23-year-old was solid between Bakersfield and Frisco in 2009 (3.57 ERA, 83 strikeouts in 70.2 innings). He's been passed by several other young left-handed relief candidates (including Snyder and Zach Phillips), but he's still young enough to push his way onto the radar.

10. CARLOS MELO, RHP, Extended Spring

Coming over with Moscoso in the Laird trade with Detroit two winters ago, the 19-year-old struggled in the Arizona League last summer (7.09 ERA, half as many walks as innings pitched) and is likely slated for a return to the complex league when it gets going again in June. The 19-year-old hasn't yet harnessed his mid-90s velocity, but there's projection for more in his lanky, 6'3" frame, and if he begins to develop command, he could give the Rangers another interesting high-ceiling arm.

to number nine hitter Yuniesky Betancourt, who'd earned all of one base on balls all season (101 plate appearances).

Harrison's night was done, needing 95 pitches to get through five innings (those 39 pitches through three frames were followed by 56 in the next two), and awful work by Dustin Nippert on his 29th birthday forced Texas to use every member of the pen other than Darren Oliver and Doug Mathis. The club lost the lead before pulling things out in the dramatic eighth.

Can we blame Harrison's collapse on the 127 pitches he threw last time out? I suppose if you were to look solely at his final line—four runs on four hits and three walks in five innings—but how does that excuse his inability to get the job done after the first time through the Kansas City lineup? He admitted after the game to a bout of minor stiffness that cropped up in the third inning and again in the fifth. Whether that's an excuse or not, Harrison's effectiveness fell off a cliff against a bad team, allowing them to get back into a game they had no business being in, and it took a nearly full complement of relievers and a heroic late-inning comeback to nail down a win that should have been a gimme.

Let's face it: Assuming nobody gets hurt, the rotation is pretty simple to assess. Scott Feldman is not going to lose his job. Rich Harden has bought himself several more starts at the very least, after the gem he pitched Monday. C.J. Wilson and Colby Lewis have been two of the great pitching stories in the American League so far.

Meanwhile, Holland has an ERA of 0.93 in six AAA starts. He's striking out a batter per inning, walking less than one-fifth as many. He's commanding everything, including an improved slider. He's ready to get back up here. And Harrison's spot is the only logical one for Holland to claim.

But getting back to the original point: I'd like to see Harrison moved to relief, rather than the RedHawks. It probably means an option for Mathis, but right now the bullpen could probably use another lefthander, and the fact that Harrison can give the club two or three innings if needed gives him a chance to be used in a couple different ways.

Would Harrison's stuff play up coming out of the pen? Hard to say. There are some promising numbers: batters leading off an inning against Harrison this season are hitting .161/.278/.194. If used against key left-handed hitters on nights that Oliver is unavailable (or earlier in the game than the club wants to use the veteran), Harrison can be called on: lefties are hitting .200 off him this year.

But with runners on base, Harrison's opponents are hitting .306/.362/.532. And he needs to hold runners better.

On top of that, interestingly, before last night's effort, the first time Harrison had faced a hitter in a game in 2010, his opponents were hitting .350/.422/.475. The second time: .256/.341/.436. The third: .147/.194/.265. Those numbers suggest he gets stronger as he gets deeper into the game.

But not last night. And I'm ready for Holland.

Holland's regular day to pitch comes around on Sunday. Would you push Feldman back two days (the team is idle on Monday), after his 111-pitch effort on Tuesday that started so poorly but ended well? Probably not. Six days of rest is too much. Move Colby Lewis from Tuesday (which will already be after an extra day of rest) to Wednesday? Unlikely.

Harrison is slated to pitch again on Wednesday, at home against Oakland (unless the club skips his turn with Monday's off-day affording that opportunity, pitching Lewis on Tuesday but accelerating Wilson to Wednesday, keeping him on regular rest). To ask Holland to take the ball that day will mean he'll have had seven days of rest, after throwing only 83 pitches on Tuesday. It's not ideal, but is it a better option than sending Harrison out there again? I think so.

But the best option? Skip Harrison on Wednesday (chalk it up to the minor tendinitis, not serious enough for a disabled list stay), let him pitch in mop-up relief if needed (or DL him and bring a reliever up temporarily), and bring Holland up to make the start on Saturday the 15th in Toronto, so that Lewis doesn't have to pitch on short rest. Holland can make his next RedHawks start, this Sunday in Iowa, and then join the Rangers in time for the start in Toronto, with one extra day of rest.

Holland's worst start in the big leagues came against the Blue Jays, on August 31 (10 runs in three-plus innings). But with the improved command and breaking ball that he's shown in AAA, he's earned the chance to be recalled when the team needs him, rather than spotted against the right opponent.

Would I prefer it if Harrison had thrown a gem last night in front of Royals GM Dayton Moore, who is under contract with Kansas City through 2014 and was in Atlanta when the big lefthander had developed into one of the Braves' top prospects, teeing it up for me to suggest that Texas (assuming resolution of the ownership issue) could try to pry Zack Greinke free in July with an offer of something like Harrison, Wilmer Font, Alexi Ogando, and the Royals' choice of Mitch Moreland, Engel Beltre, or Miguel Velazquez? Of course.

But he didn't, and though I've been ready for a couple weeks to see Holland back in Texas, now I'm really ready.

A few more things:

1. Wilson faces Greinke tonight, but the marquee matchup shouldn't faze him. Wilson's opponents in 2010: C.C. Sabathia, Mark Buehrle, AL ERA leader Doug Fister, Ricky Romero (quality starts five times out of six, fourth in the league in strikeouts), and Clay Buchholz.

2. The Rangers have said Jarrod Saltalamacchia will not return to Texas today, when he's first eligible

to do so. He's hitting well (.367/.407/.633, 12-game hit streak) but is still dogged by throwing issues.

3. Yes, I'm concerned about Michael Young.

4. I sure do enjoy watching Vladimir Guerrero do what the games asks him to do.

5. Having Ian Kinsler back in the lineup (did you notice the difference in his front shoulder and his bat path last night?) and in the infield makes a huge difference. I'm eager to see what the offense can do on a consistent basis once Kinsler and Nelson Cruz are in the lineup together.

6. Julio Borbon's outs look bad. I'm not so sure Craig Gentry doesn't stick around once Cruz is activated next Wednesday, with Borbon going back to Oklahoma City for some needed work. It may be time to start paying attention to Endy Chavez's rehab progress.

7. Justin Smoak's nine-pitch at-bat in the third, culminating in the missile to right, was a thing of beauty.

8. Is Josh Hamilton going to settle in to be as streaky as Dean Palmer?

9. Admit it: It's getting difficult to imagine Neftali Feliz becoming a starting pitcher.

10. Tangentially related subject: Tanner Scheppers, who logged two innings in five of his six Frisco appearances (one run on three hits and zero walks, with 19 strikeouts in 11 innings) and in his first Oklahoma City appearance (one run on three hits and one walk, two strikeouts), is reportedly on a plan under which he'll soon be asked to pitch three innings a couple times a week, and then ramp up further to four innings a shot. The idea is to stretch Scheppers out gradually so that he's not only a bullpen candidate in Arlington later this season but also an option for the rotation should the need arise. My money? He'll be getting eighth-inning outs in August. Incidentally, both of the runs Scheppers has permitted this year have come on solo home runs. Those two pitches aren't the sole reason the club wants the 23-year-old to work on getting the ball down. When Texas League opponents managed to put the ball in play against him, he got twice as many outs in the air as on the ground.

11. The Yankees, having lost Curtis Granderson to the disabled list, recalled outfielder Greg Golson from AAA. Florida designated Mike Lamb for assignment. Seattle placed malcontent Milton Bradley on the restricted list.

12. If you're in the business of making custom baseball cards (say, for a Little League team), give me a shout.

13. The Rangers are hosting a "Mom's on the Mound" event on Saturday from 8:00 a.m. until noon at the Ballpark. Those attending (men are invited as well) will go through hitting, pitching, and fielding rotations on the field, get instruction from Rangers staff, and play a game. You'll also get to take photos with Nelson Cruz and Clint Hurdle. The cost is $79 and includes a ticket to that night's Rangers-Royals game. More details at texasrangers.com/women.

14. Finally, I'm excited to announce that I'm going to do a **live, in-game chat session on Wednesday, May 19, at FoxSportsSouthwest.com.** If it goes well, we may try it a few times per month. Hope you'll stop by to participate or just take the action in while we discuss the Rangers-Orioles game as it unfolds. More details as we get closer.

As it stands now, that would be Derek Holland's normal day to pitch for Oklahoma City—if the RedHawks weren't idle that day.

But I'm betting right now he'll be in uniform that night anyway, sitting near Mike Maddux in the home dugout and watching Baltimore's hitters in preparation for the following night's start, rather than getting settled in Portland at the end of a travel day.

May 7, 2010

As I sit at my desk eating my pregame meal, realizing that I'm looking more forward to being at tonight's game than any in memory that didn't fall on Opening Day or in a late-season pennant race, because I do loves me a great pitching matchup, I thought I'd reissue a report I sent out on September 11, 2009.

Have fun tonight.

* * *

I was not interested in an off-day. That was irritating.

I gave Steelers-Titans the chance to fill the void, but all it did was remind me that What We Play For was taking the day off.

I stared at the Venezuela 13, USA 9 World Cup box score, ignoring the final score and fixing my gaze on the Justin Smoak line—4 for 6, two home runs, two doubles, five RBI, two runs—but that helped for a minute or two, at best.

To distract myself last night, I tried not to think about this weekend set of three against the Mariners and instead turned my attention back to a topic that I hatched last summer: The idea of making Zack Greinke a Texas Ranger.

Piecing together a few things, chronologically:

June 20, 2008 Newberg Report:

Which team says no: [Jarrod] Saltalamacchia, Eric Hurley, John Mayberry Jr., and Warner Madrigal to Kansas City for Zack Greinke (who was then 6-4, 3.33 for the season, and 27-39, 4.40 for his career)?

August 27, 2008 Newberg Report:

Saltalamacchia...[Matt] Harrison or Hurley...Mayberry or [Nelson] Cruz...Joaquin Arias...and Zach Phillips or Carlos Pimentel or Miguel De Los Santos or Geuris Grullon or Julio Santana or Matt Nevarez...for Greinke and Ramon Ramirez. Are we talking?

October 6, 2008 Newberg Report:

Ken Rosenthal of FoxSports.com, in a note regarding the decision facing the Royals on whether to trade righthander Zack Greinke, reports that Texas "made a big offer for him before the July 31 non-waiver deadline." According to Rosenthal, Kansas City says it won't move Greinke unless overwhelmed.

January 27, 2009 Newberg Report, the day after Greinke signed a new multi-year deal with Kansas City:

The first two years of Zack Greinke's four-year, $38 million extension with the Royals apparently contain "very minor" no-trade protection, according to Ken Rosenthal of Fox Sports. As for 2011 and 2012, when the righthander is set to make $13.5 million annually, the no-trade clause apparently goes away, and one league executive told Rosenthal: "He's going to get traded in one of the thirteen-and-a-halfs, unless he wins a Cy Young Award before then. And he could."

August 31, 2009:

Kansas City exercises general manager Dayton Moore's option for 2011 and extends his contract through 2014.

September 5, 2009:

Greinke allows no Angels earned runs (one unearned) over eight innings, lowering his season ERA to 2.22. But he gets no decision as Los Angeles beats the Royals, 2-1. Greinke's win-loss record remains 13-8. The rest of the Royals staff: 42-77—a win percentage that would extrapolate to a 57-105 season.

September 6, 2009:

MLB.com's Victor Rojas on Twitter: "royals have lack of mlb talent/depth & some bad contracts too - it's time to seriously consider trading greinke for gaggle of players"

No sense in rehashing Greinke's worth. I've spent enough time on that the last 15 months. At age 25 he's younger than Brandon McCarthy and Doug Mathis, the same age as Guillermo Moscoso and Luis Mendoza, and for me he's as great a technician as any starting pitcher in the American League.

And now Moore has job security. Lots of it.

So would he follow Rojas's suggested blueprint, one not unlike the plan in Texas that started with the 2007 trade of Mark Teixeira, and move Greinke for a slew of players with whom he can accelerate things for the Royals, who have proven this season that they can hold down the AL Central cellar comfortably and hurtle toward 100 losses even with a Cy Young-caliber season out of Greinke?

It would stand to reason that Moore's contract extension, which will keep him on Kansas City's payroll two years after Greinke is almost certainly going to be on someone else's, makes a winter Greinke trade at least a little more likely than it might have been a month ago, even if it's still a longshot.

What would it take? No less than it would have taken to get Roy Halladay.

The strength of the Royals' horizon is on the infield corners (where Alex Gordon, Billy Butler, Mike Moustakas, and Eric Hosmer figure in, with one likely settling in at DH and another, perhaps Moustakas, moving to a corner outfield spot) and in the rotation, where behind Greinke are, among others, Luke Hochevar, prospects Mike Montgomery, Danny Duffy, and Chris Dwyer and, assuming he signs, Aaron Crow. Kansas City desperately needs help up the middle, which is what Texas keyed on in part with the Teixeira trade—picking off players developed in the Atlanta system while Moore was the Braves' director of player personnel and then assistant general manager.

Moore wouldn't need to rely on Royals area scout Rick Schroeder to recommend Derek Holland, a player Schroeder was partly responsible for Texas drafting when he held a similar position with the Rangers. Holland and Neftali Feliz will be the first players Moore would ask Texas for. Among Schroeder's other draft recommendations from his Rangers days were Frisco reliever Brennan Garr and Frisco infielder Renny Osuna, but neither would figure into a blockbuster deal (unless tacked on, as lefthander Julian Cordero was when Texas added the Class A southpaw to the Francisco Cordero-Laynce Nix-Kevin Mench package to get Carlos Lee and Nelson Cruz in 2006).

Royals manager Trey Hillman's time as Rangers director of player development and Royals minor league skipper Darryl Kennedy's time managing on the Texas farm were long enough ago that none of the players they had here would fit the profile of what Kansas City would be looking to add.

But that's an elementary way of looking at things, anyway. In today's game, teams' scouting coverage is such that organizations have a book on just about every player in every system. Yes, from time to time there's a Dr. Keith Meister-Darren O'Day history that can add a layer to the evaluation process, but deals don't turn on past connections.

Plus, with Kansas City sharing Surprise with Texas, and fielding AA and AAA teams that compete in the same leagues as Rangers affiliates, the Royals obviously have a convenient perch from which to keep tabs on young Rangers players. The Royals have recently picked up Tug Hulett, Travis Metcalf, John Bannister, Manny Pina, and Tim Smith from Texas, for instance.

But that doesn't mean Moore may not have a soft spot for a player like Saltalamacchia or Harrison, both of whose pro careers he was in charge of getting underway back in 2003. Shame they're both going to end the 2009 season at less than full health.

So here we go:

Let's say Texas had to give up (1) Kansas City's choice of righthander Tommy Hunter or lefthander Martin Perez; (2) righthander Wilmer Font; (3-4) Kansas City's choice of either outfielder Julio Borbon and hitter Max Ramirez—or outfielders Nelson Cruz and Engel Beltre; and (5) shortstop Leury Garcia to get Greinke and, say, reliever Juan Cruz (owed $3.25 million in 2010 and a $500,000 buyout in 2011). Tack on (6) Garr as well.

You in? Which team walks away?

We now return to our regularly scheduled Pennant Race, already in progress.

May 7, 2010

C.J. Wilson always did like pitching the ninth.

That's winning baseball.

May 7, 2010

Getting the final out:

Louis DeLuca/DMN

Getting the final out . . . and the first one:

Tony Gutierrez/AP

May 8, 2010

According to multiple sources, Derek Holland will be recalled to start this week against Oakland, probably Wednesday or Thursday. Matt Harrison is apparently headed for the disabled list with biceps tendinitis.

May 10, 2010

Where would this thing be without Vlad Guerrero, or C.J. Wilson?

Where would things be *with* Ian Kinsler and Nelson Cruz playing so much as one game together through the first five weeks?

There are other questions along the same lines, maybe not as central to 18-14 but just as rhetorical, but there are questions like those that every team can ask a fifth into the season, and there's little point in looking back.

There's not much point in looking back at Oakland (one game behind Texas), the Angels (4.5), or Seattle (5.5), either, other than to understand that there's something in reach here, and looking forward to these next three with the A's, with Big Bad Vlad hitting at home and C.J. pitching on Thursday, the same day that Kins and Cruz should be in the lineup together for the first time in 2010, is almost enough to forget about how lousy things started this season, again.

Off-days aren't as depressing as six-game skids in mid-April, but like most this one isn't welcome at all, and yet despite the extra day the A's head to town for three that won't allow them to get Dallas Braden back on the mound, possibly a good break in a season that feels like it hasn't had many.

But the bad breaks and the good ones are history, less important than the 130 games—if not more—that lie ahead, yet meaningful in the sense that they've set things up so that the rest matter, a lot.

These next three are pretty big, and heading into mid-May that's all you can ask for.

May 11, 2010

According to multiple media outlets, the Rangers have promoted right-handed reliever Alexi Ogando from Frisco to Oklahoma City. In his first stateside season as a pitcher, the 26-year-old has been dominant thus far, scattering two runs (1.15 ERA) on four hits (.078 opponents' average) and five walks in 15.2 innings, setting 21 down on strikes with a power package that includes a fastball that sits mid-90s and touches the upper 90s, a plus slider, and a solid changeup. His promotion from Frisco to the RedHawks bullpen follows Tanner Scheppers's by a week and a half.

I'd bet a bunch that OKC isn't going to be Ogando's or Scheppers's final stop this season.

May 12, 2010

Crummy defense, especially the plays unmade.

Bad execution and squandered opportunities.

Walking the hitter leading off the inning—a hitter whose offensive numbers barely register.

A really questionable bullpen-engineering decision.

I had a bunch I planned to write about today, but that loss took too much out of me. Not because it was a loss, which in some reasonable amount we as baseball fans have to accept, but because of how it was lost and should have been won, against a team it would have been very useful to put away for one night.

Derek Holland, hope you brought a heavy dose of that efficiency with you from Oklahoma City. A solid seven would be fantastic. Especially given what happened last night, when the bullpen threw as many pitches (104) as starter Colby Lewis, with every reliever being called upon other than Doug Mathis, who got loose himself.

In the one start Holland has made against the A's (August 4), he gave the team only 4.1 innings in a 6-0 loss (incidentally, at the hands of lefthander Gio Gonzalez, tonight's Oakland starter). Can't have that tonight.

There are lots of other things that distinguished Oakland 7, Texas 6 that we can't have tonight, either.

May 12, 2010

Not going to send a nighttime report out. Busted out 13 tweets during the game (if you want, you can check them out on Twitter—@newbergreport), but I will add three things:

1. The Angels' 4-3 loss to the Rays drops L.A. to 15-21, that club's worst 36-game record in 20 years.
2. Hideki Matsui: one year, $6 million, .226/.307/.371. Vladimir Guerrero: one year, $6.5 million, .336/.370/.544. Angels five games in back of Texas.
3. Thank you, Derek.

May 14, 2010

Way to go, Big Bad
Angels' loss is Rangers' gain
Keep on impalin'

Remember the pall cast over the Rangers fan base when the club elected to let Ivan Rodriguez move on, not even offering him arbitration, sending a message through the press that his unique skill set had begun to erode and he was never very good at working with young pitchers anyway, and the 31-year-old proceeded to instantly lead a Marlins club led by a young rotation to a World Series title? Remember the hurt?

Imagine how much worse it would have been if Pudge had jumped from Texas to Oakland and done it.

I'm not predicting a Rangers title in mid-May, but it has to be pretty crummy for Angels fans to see their perennial MVP candidate, Vladimir Guerrero, tuning the league up at a .328/.361/.527 rate (while his replacement, Hideki Matsui, sits at .226/.307/.371 under roughly the same contract) for a team they're chasing in the division. With no draft pick compensation to patch the wound since Los Angeles didn't offer him arbitration.

The Guerrero-Matsui swap for Los Angeles may not sink to the level of Steve Nash-Erick Dampier (another local roster shift with the club spinning its departing star's alleged signs of decline), but given the Angels' lousy start, and Guerrero's insanely awesome one, I bet it's a handy point of depression for the Los Angeles faithful.

I'm sure I had as much fun watching Josh Hamilton hit in 2008 as I do watching Guerrero now, but I wouldn't swear to it.

Incidentally: Hamilton through 34 games in his storybook 2008 season: .292/.346/.533. He'd struck out 20 times in 137 at-bats.

Guerrero, at the abovementioned .328/.361/.527 slash rate through 34 games played, has fanned 13 times in 131 at-bats.

With Texas having won yesterday's game, getting fantastic work out of C.J. Wilson and Frankie Francisco (17 strikes in 20 pitches, all four batters punched out) and Elvis Andrus (a big bag of awesomeness, though with the requisite once-a-game brainlock of a player who occasionally does act his age), I'm going to go ahead and question a decision, not because I want to rant and rave about its insanity, but rather to ask what I'm missing.

Bottom of the ninth. Game locked at 1-1.

David Murphy singles with one out.

Justin Smoak singles him to third base.

Max Ramirez and Julio Borbon are set to hit. A run ends it.

Ron Washington sends Craig Gentry out to run for Smoak.

I didn't understand the move and, really, despite hearing a couple attempts to reason it out, still don't.

Here's why:

1. The obvious: The Smoak/Gentry run doesn't matter. If Murphy scores, the game is over. If, say, Murphy is cut down at the plate on an infield grounder, putting Smoak on second and Ramirez at first with two outs, fine—put Gentry in for Smoak at that point if you want. I can see that.
2. If the idea is that Gentry is going to steal second base to take away the double play opportunity (which they obviously didn't plan, as Ramirez took three straight balls without Gentry moving), I'd argue that would have been bad managing. If he gets thrown out, you've eliminated the chance to win the game with a fly ball.

Newberg Report: Catching Cold

Once considered deep position, Texas short on backups

By Jamey Newberg / Special to MLB.com

May 13, 2010

Ten years ago, Texas had baseball's best, most durable catcher. During the time Ivan Rodriguez was behind the plate for the Rangers, the club ignored the position from a developmental standpoint, and that failure to build depth ended up biting them.

From 1992 until 2002, the Rodriguez years in Texas (prior to his 2009 cameo), the Rangers signed the following catchers from the top 10 rounds of the draft:

1992: Scot Sealy (10th round)
1993: none
1994: Kevin L. Brown (2nd)
1995: Juan B. Rivera (9th)
1996: none
1997: Jason Grabowski (2nd), Mike Lamb (7th)
1998: none
1999: Chris Jaile (4th)
2000: Scott Heard (1st)
2001: none
2002: none

Not counting Lamb's experimental cameo in 2002 (four appearances in Triple-A, three in Texas), the only player from those 11 drafts to get past Class A with the Rangers as a catcher was Brown. That's awful.

Outside of Cesar King, signed by Omar Minaya in 1994, the Rangers didn't do a very good job of supplementing the position internationally during that time, either.

Texas was able to trade Brown in March 1998 for reliever Tim Crabtree (a one-time catcher himself, incidentally). That trade alone should have driven home the point. You can never have too many catchers, even if you have the world's best at the big league level. Because he won't be there forever. And because catchers make very good trade ammunition.

The Rangers' failure to develop behind the plate during Rodriguez's tenure led to the following two unpleasant moments in franchise history:

Oct. 28, 2002: Ivan Rodriguez declares free agency

Dec. 6, 2002: Texas trades hitter Travis Hafner and right-hander Aaron Myette to Cleveland for catcher Einar Diaz and right-hander Ryan Drese

The day after then-Rangers (and former Indians) general manager John Hart made that deal with Cleveland, Texas did this:

Dec. 7, 2002: Texas declines to offer salary arbitration to Ivan Rodriguez

Leaving aside the issue of whether the Rangers should have kept Rodriguez, the absolute absence of internal fallback options led to a very bad trade.

Daniels, who had been with the Rangers since January 2002, saw all of that unfold. Beginning in 2004, during his tenure as assistant general manager and then general manager, the organization has drafted, among others, Taylor Teagarden (2005), Chad Tracy (2006), and Vin DiFazio (2009); signed international free agents Manny Pina (2004), Cristian Santana (2005), Leonel ("Macumba") De Los Santos (2006), Tomas Telis and Jose Felix (2007), and Jorge Alfaro (2010); and traded for Jarrod Saltalamacchia and Max Ramirez (2007).

The system overhaul at catcher prompted Daniels to say this going into camp into 2008: "Catching certainly is the strength of our organization. We'll just let it play out. ... Some people may look at it as a logjam or that we have decisions to make, but I look at it as you can't have enough of a good thing."

He didn't seem to be embellishing matters. The national media, praising the Rangers for having as much depth at the position as anyone in the game, had decided either Saltalamacchia or Teagarden was poised to settle in for a Pudge-length tenure with Texas, with the other traded for someone like Clay Buchholz or Justin Masterson or Daniel Bard or Michael Bowden. Ramirez, despite defensive issues, seemed to be developing into a Hafner-type hitter. Pina was drawing Pudge-like comparisons with his tools behind the plate. Gerald Laird was still around at the time but less than a year later would be shipped to Detroit to clear up some of the perceived logjam.

Today? Saltalamacchia is in Triple-A, having regular difficulty throwing the ball back to the pitcher. Teagarden, 2-for-41 with 26 strikeouts between Texas and Oklahoma City, has been demoted to Frisco to get regular playing time. Journeyman Matt Treanor, the second-oldest position player on the team, is getting an extended opportunity to start for the first time in his career. Ramirez is playing caddy but has seen his value drop considerably after a miserable 2009.

Not long after being singled out for its standout depth at catcher, Texas is being pinpointed in national columns as one of a few teams who could be in the market for a new in-season solution behind the plate.

This year's draft is less than four weeks away, and there's little doubt that Daniels and his crew have put together a board based strictly on talent, irrespective of position and without regard to where the organization may already seem exceptionally deep. You never know whether that depth will play out three or four years down the road, when a draft class begins to mature—or even a year later, as we've seen with this franchise at catcher. Drafting for need, or neglecting a position because you feel like you're in good shape, is asking for trouble. Taking the "best player available" seems like an easy guiding principle, and thankfully it's one that Daniels subscribes to.

It's too bad the regimes that were in place during Rodriguez's first run as a Ranger, at least at his position, apparently didn't buy into the same philosophy.

3. I'd have been surprised to see Washington put on a hit-and-run at any point in the Ramirez at-bat. It's not what the game asks you to do in that situation. Not with the walkoff run at third.

4. If the idea is that Gentry is swift enough to beat out the front end of a double play, that makes no sense to me, either. If the force play is going to be that close (again, assuming no hit-and-run), that probably means a slow-developing play, which means even if the A's get the force, they're never going to complete the pair, and the game ends as Murphy crosses the plate. Stated another way, if Oakland is able to double up Ramirez, it wouldn't matter whether Vince Coleman or Bengie Molina were the runner on base unless he was put in motion—and Texas was not going to put Gentry in motion.

It ended up not mattering much that Smoak was lost for the game (Ryan Garko popped out in the 11th but did make a nice 3-6 play in the top of the 10th), but it might have, and it sure would have been nice to keep Gentry's availability alive for a spot when his speed tool would have been truly usable.

Am I missing something?

Garko (3 for 33, all singles) is reportedly about to lose his roster spot to Joaquin Arias, a move that was signaled once the Rangers began to play Arias at first base during his rehab stint with Oklahoma City. Gentry is expected to be optioned back to AAA with Nelson Cruz returning, so I suppose the idea is that Arias gives Washington the pinch-runner that Gentry's departure was taking away from the bench.

It wouldn't have bothered me to see Gentry stick (so Hamilton wouldn't have to patrol center every day) and Borbon optioned. Getting Borbon right is a big key for this season. He drew only his second walk yesterday (113 plate appearances), an obviously unacceptable rate for any regular but obscenely so for a player whose game is predicated on reaching base and *then* doing damage. The only Rangers regular seeing fewer pitches per plate appearance than Borbon is Guerrero. Chris Davis had a better rate. So did Taylor Teagarden. And Arias. Last year's good-looking Borbon spray chart has given way this season to lots of lazy volleys to the left fielder.

I'm not out on Borbon. Far from it. But he's got to get right, and I'd have been OK if today's ticket to Oklahoma City were given to him rather than to Gentry.

As for Garko, he was a low-risk (low-salaried) add that didn't work out, one that wouldn't have been necessary had Mike Lowell passed his December physical and come to Texas for Ramirez. Ironically, the way Ramirez has been swinging the bat the last few days, he's been giving the Rangers the kind of occasional production from the right side that they were looking to Garko for.

Smoak's home run on Wednesday night was his fourth, which gave him the lead among American League rookies—even though he's been around for barely more than half his club's games.

The Rangers' home run barrage that night was just the fourth time in what is now 35 games that the club has gone deep more than once.

Last year's offense had 21 multi-homer games in its first 35.

Take it further: last year through 35 games, the Rangers were hitting .279/.335/.500, with 201 runs, 77 doubles, 62 home runs, 101 walks, and 288 strikeouts. This year: .259/.328/.394, 165 runs, 53 doubles, 32 home runs, 117 walks, and 244 strikeouts.

Texas isn't hitting as well and isn't slugging as much, though a better walk rate (and a lower strikeout rate that suggests, even if not conclusively, that a handful of deep-count pitches that might been flailed at last season are now being taken) has the club reaching base nearly as often.

And yet the records and positions in the standings between the two seasons through 35 games are about the same (21-14 and 1.5 games up in 2009, 20-15 and two games up now).

The biggest reason the dropoff in offense hasn't resulted in a dropoff overall is obvious: The pitching got a lot better last season. But it's taken another huge step forward this year.

Last year's team ERA through 35 games was 4.74. This year's is 3.57 (the starters are at 2.96 over the last 13 games, with nine quality starts). Opponents were hitting .262 last year, .242 this year. Walks are up slightly this year (119 to 137), but the increase is not as dramatic as team strikeouts (188 to 258). Home runs are down (43 to 36).

He doesn't get all the credit (plenty should go to ownership, the front office, coaches and scouts, and the pitchers themselves), but Mike Maddux has been a top 5 acquisition during the Jon Daniels regime.

I thought about Maddux as Ben Sheets, his prize pupil in their six years together in Milwaukee, and Wilson, his renovated ace, absolutely locked horns for more than six-and-a-half innings. Competitive instincts aside, Maddux had to be proud.

Wilson wasn't as efficient or as sharp as he was in Friday's complete game, but that just underscores what kind of pitcher he's become, limiting the A's to one run over seven innings of work despite not bringing his best stuff to the mound. That's seven straight quality starts for Wilson, a Rangers franchise record for the start of a season. He's also thrown 69.1 consecutive homerless innings at Rangers Ballpark, another club record. In fact, he's allowed only four extra-base hits (all doubles) all season.

Remember the guy who, eight months ago, you'd hiss at as soon as he trotted in from the bullpen and delivered ball one to a hitter crow-hopping out of the way of his first-pitch fastball? Today, if you squint your eyes and try to envision Game One on October 5, isn't Wilson the guy whose hand you want the ball in as soon as the Anthem ends?

By the way, if you're not catching Wilson's weekly radio segment with Ben & Skin on ESPN Radio (103.3 FM), Tuesday mornings at 11:40, you're doing it wrong.

And whether you're doing it right or wrong, you deserve to listen to Ben Rogers's Wilson intro a lot of times: http://songtwit.com/2u8

Wilson was called for a balk that didn't count in yesterday's fourth inning. It was nullified by the single Jake Fox hit to center on the pitch, a rule that I would have appreciated the home plate umpire in the 1987 Waxahachie Tournament knowing when he wiped off my two-run homer in the first inning of a game we ended up losing to Fort Worth Southwest, 5-0. He ruled "no pitch," called me back to the plate, sent our leadoff hitter Steve Whitlow from first base to second, and tossed our coach out of the game.

Lefthander Matt Harrison threw off flat ground Wednesday and reported no residual problems from the biceps tendinitis that forced him to the disabled list.

I'm a day early, but Happy 22nd Birthday to Hickory outfielder Miguel Velazquez, my favorite position player in the Rangers farm system right now. Velazquez (.331/.403/.583) has the highest OPS (.985) among all hitters suiting up for one of the 14 teams in the South Atlantic League.

After I'd seen Velazquez in camp this March, I wrote: *"Had him at number 25 in the book, and the number two outfielder in the system, and the number four breakout candidate among hitters. Too low, in every case."* I moved him from 25 to 8 when I re-ranked the system's prospects on March 26. If I did a new ranking today, I'd have him higher than that.

Oklahoma City lefthander Michael Kirkman was number five on *Baseball America*'s Hot Sheet last week.

The Rangers named their minor league award winners for the month of April: lefthander Derek Holland (Pitcher of the Month), first baseman/outfielder Chad Tracy (Player of the Month), catcher Jose Felix (Defender of the Month), and lefthander Zach Phillips (Relief Pitcher of the Month, a new award).

Bakersfield righthander Cody Eppley, age 24, has yet to allow a run in 18 relief innings this year, scattering nine hits (one double) and one walk while fanning 24. Of his

30 outs on balls put in play, 25 have come on the ground, only five in the air.

Hank Blalock (.349/.405/.505 for AAA Durham) has an out clause approaching sometime in the next week, and he reportedly intends to exercise it if Tampa Bay doesn't activate him by that time (or within 48 hours of his notice to opt out). Two interesting notes: (1) Blalock is destroying International League lefties (.500/.538/.833); and (2) in 26 games, he's DH'd twice and played defensively the other 24 times—all at third base. The Mariners and White Sox and A's are among the teams rumored to have some level of interest.

There are some rumors, both locally and nationally, that Texas might be a match with the struggling White Sox on catcher A.J. Pierzynski (who gains 10-and-5 rights on June 14, enabling him to veto any trade). Not sure I'm in love with that idea.

The Yankees recalled outfielder Greg Golson again. Kansas City designated righthander Josh Rupe for assignment. The Mets released pinch-hitter Frank Catalanotto.

Kansas City fired manager Trey Hillman and replaced him with Ned Yost, at least on an interim basis.

Iowa Cubs righthander Thomas Diamond has a 2.17 ERA in seven starts for the AAA club.

The Newark Bears of the independent Atlantic League signed righthander Hector Carrasco.

It was pointed out last night that only nine of the Rangers' next 53 games are against teams who now have winning records, an almost unbelievable number. That stretch, incidentally, ends with the All-Star Break, and if the ownership situation is resolved by then, imagine the mid-to-late-July possibilities for improving the roster if this club maintains its division lead, or at least has it in reach.

Texas got out of town yesterday afternoon with six wins out of seven on the homestand and 12 of 16 overall, boarding a plane for Canada right after a 12-inning survival that knocked the A's two games back. I'm not sure if Ben Rogers makes it a personal rule to write songs only for players who are regular guests on the Ben & Skin Show, but if he's willing to swing with authority at a pitch out of the zone, he's got three days—after which Los Angeles comes to Arlington—to put one together for former Angel Vladimir Guerrero, who never struck out a minotaur-like unicorn with the head of Barry Bonds but has surely done many things equally awesome with those bare hands, that nuclear-war-ravaged helmet, and all that Big Badness.

May 14, 2010

Well, the anticipated debut of a lineup basically at full strength for the first time in 2010 lived up to expectations, but what I'm going to remember most about the everyday players tonight was the look on so many of their faces, like Mark Clark's teammates most nights he pitched in 1999, a season when there was something to be won. I don't suppose I need to elaborate on that, or on the obvious point about the look on the face of the 2010 version of Mark Clark after he gave his manager no choice but to take the ball.

Either the players as a whole or the starting pitcher, but not both, looked as demoralized as I did tonight.

After the top of the second, I posted on Twitter: "Harden staked to 8-3 lead before going out for the 2nd, and there's no way he records a win." But *that's* not what I meant.

Tommy Hunter, May 3: three scoreless innings (38 pitches).

Tommy Hunter, May 8: four scoreless innings (54 pitches).

Tommy Hunter, tonight: five scoreless innings (58 pitches).

It's too soon.

But I'm pleased he's on Rich Harden's schedule.

Matt Harrison can't be activated until a week from tomorrow.

As for tomorrow, when Texas will need a reliever (two ideally, but not realistically) to get to Rogers Centre in time to put on Kason Gabbard's jersey?

Won't be Oklahoma City's Guillermo Moscoso, who threw 100 (scoreless) pitches two days ago.

Or RedHawks reliever Alexi Ogando, who threw 34 pitches yesterday. Or Pedro Strop, who threw 26 of his own in the same game.

RedHawks lefthander Michael Kirkman would be on short rest tomorrow, but maybe more to the point is that he issued seven walks in four innings on Tuesday.

Frisco lefthander Zach Phillips threw 37 pitches on May 10 and none since. The RoughRiders are in the seventh inning tonight, and he hasn't pitched. They're at home, not too far from DFW Airport.

After that, you venture off the 40-man roster.

And the only way to accomplish doing that is to take someone now on the 40 and either run him off the roster or plant him on the 60-day disabled list.

That's about the only measure I'm resisting suggesting with regard to the man who amazingly put this team in a position to lose an in-the-bag game tonight and has the club handicapped 15 hours from now.

May 15, 2010

Jumping off from (1) a discussion we had on the Ben & Skin Show yesterday, and (2) the sideshow we all watched last night:

Vladimir Guerrero's contract, which pays $5.5 million in 2010 (with another $900,000 in roster bonuses), contains a $9 million mutual option for 2011, with a $1 million buyout payable if either side declines the option.

Rich Harden's contract, which pays $6.5 million in 2010 (with another $2.5 million in what now appear to be mostly unattainable graduated workload incentives), contains an $11 million mutual option for 2011, with a $1 million buyout payable if either side declines.

Pretty clear where both of those deals are headed.

Unless new ownership helps get the hitter extended (two guaranteed, market-value years plus an option for a third?) during the season.

According to at least one local report, the Rangers have two pitchers from the 40-man roster on a morning flight to Toronto that connects through Detroit. The decision as to whether to activate one (for Doug Mathis, who would be optioned) or both (which would mean both Mathis and Craig Gentry would be optioned without Joaquin Arias being activated yet—Max Ramirez would serve as both the backup catcher and first baseman today) hasn't been announced.

As the two pitchers are reportedly on the roster, candidates include Oklahoma City righthanders Guillermo Moscoso, Pedro Strop, and Alexi Ogando, Oklahoma City lefthander Michael Kirkman, and Frisco lefthander Zach Phillips. (Oklahoma City righthanders Brandon McCarthy and Omar Beltre are on the disabled list.) Oklahoma City and Frisco were both home last night.

I'll blast the list again when the move(s) are announced.

May 15, 2010

The Rangers have recalled righthanders pitchers Guillermo Moscoso and Pedro Strop from Oklahoma City, optioning righthander Doug Mathis and outfielder Craig Gentry to the same club.

Though Moscoso threw 100 pitches on Wednesday, today would be his day to throw a side between starts, so presumably he'd be available to give the club two or three innings if needed. Strop threw 26 pitches two days ago, but he's pitched on one day of rest four times this season, and on consecutive days two other times.

May 16, 2010

Texas has activated right-side infielder Joaquin Arias from the disabled list, returning righthander Pedro Strop to Oklahoma City on option.

May 16, 2010

You know what Toronto did better than Texas the last three? What the game asked them to do.

The Jays executed better, made their pitches, capitalized on run-scoring opportunities, played with confidence. I don't know how much better they are than the Rangers, but this weekend they looked markedly better.

Today, the Rangers' first two hitters reached safely in the first. In the second. In the fifth. In the seventh, when the first three actually managed to get on base.

The results? Zero runs. One run (sacrifice fly). Zero runs. One run (ground ball double play).

Ugly.

If the idea was for Josh Hamilton to play 140 or 145 games this year, maybe a few more, as a concession to the importance of keeping him strong all season, with all due respect to the trouble he has against left-handed pitching, the days he sits should come from among the following:

May 26, 29
June 6, 13, 20, 26
July 11, 18
August 1, 8, 15, 18, 21, 22, 29
September 4, 5, 6, 12, 19, 25, 26, 29
October 3

All day starts.

Hamilton during the day in 2007: .195/.259/.364 with 18 strikeouts in 77 at-bats
2008: .250/.314/.467 with 42 strikeouts in 152 at-bats
2009: .259/.344/.420 with 22 strikeouts in 81 at-bats
2010: .206/.265/.333 with 17 strikeouts in 63 at-bats

All told, in the big leagues Hamilton is a .233/.302/.413 hitter during the day. He's Jason LaRue.

That's compared with .309/.372/.539 at night. He's Miguel Cabrera.

John Buck is no Miguel Cabrera (though at .276/.325/.610 he joins Cabrera in the American League top 10 in OPS), but I sure wish he felt in December that his opportunity to play in Texas would have been as good as in Toronto, where he took one year and $2 million to sign days after Kansas City non-tendered him. The Rangers wanted the 29-year-old.

Mark Gonzales of the *Chicago Tribune* writes this evening that Texas has inquired about White Sox catcher A.J. Pierzynski, a development that, if true, does not make me very happy. He's hitting .198/.254/.292, makes $6.7 million, and has always been described, for what it's worth, as less than a great teammate.

A struggling Scott Kazmir vs. Derek Holland tomorrow night, Jered Weaver vs. C.J. Wilson Tuesday night.

Texas (losers of three straight) holds a division lead over Los Angeles (winners of three straight) that, at its current 2.5 games, will stand up at the end of the two-game series, no matter how it goes. But it's mid-May, and while head-to-head matchups bring things to a relative boil (Yankees-Red Sox is sure to get as much attention as Celtics-Magic this week), stacking up wins (regardless of opponent) and finding a rhythm, both as a team and player to player, is probably more important than what the last column in the standings looks like.

Where Texas and Los Angeles fit in the standings right now is meaningful to the extent that neither team is lapping the other, and neither is burying itself out of any race. The real question, however, that must be asked is, over the next 124 games (one fewer for the Angels), can the Rangers win as many as (or at least within two of) Los Angeles?

One way to ensure you can grab a win while the other doesn't is to do it at the other's expense, and while I'm not feeling real good about the offense against the lefthander Kazmir and the solid Weaver, I'll take my chances with Holland and Wilson doing what the game asks them to do.

May 17, 2010

I was thinking about how that game was started and finished, impressively, by the two pitchers featured on the front cover of the 2009 Bound Edition and helped along by the routine awesomeness of their shortstop, featured on the back cover of that same book and on the front cover of the 2010 version, the shortstop who provided two hits and a walk tonight and made a wholly non-routine play seem almost routine to start the eighth.

(I'm working on getting the audio for Eric Nadel's call of Elvis's play, by the way. A Cooperstown play, and a Cooperstown call. I'll email it out once I get it.)

I was thinking about how the three players on the back cover of the 2010 book, Justin Smoak and Tanner Scheppers and Martin Perez, may very well key a win over the Angels this time next year, prompting me to send an email out like this one.

It's obvious and trite to point out that all those gaudy farm system rankings of the past few years are now regularly producing big league results, but the fruition of the standout work that this franchise has been doing in scouting and player development is no longer just a promise of things to come.

To celebrate Texas 4, Los Angeles 3, for this week only I'm discounting the purchase of the 2009 plus 2010 Bound Editions, which would normally cost $45 (Derek Holland's uniform number), to a mere $30 (Neftali Feliz's number).

As always, you can pay by credit card at www.PayPal.com (GJSneaker@sbcglobal.net account) or by sending a check or money order to:

Jamey Newberg
Vincent Lopez Serafino Jenevein, P.C.
1601 Elm Street, Suite 4100
Dallas, TX 75201

Nadel-Andrus audio to you shortly.

May 18, 2010

According to local reports, the Rangers have gotten first baseman Ryan Garko through waivers and have outrighted his contract to Oklahoma City. The maneuver opens up a spot on the club's 40-man roster.

May 18, 2010

As foreign as it is to my constitution to admit this, there are games about which a bunch of breakdown and analysis would really take away from the simplicity of a battle won, a scrap survived, a relentless one-run victory over the team that, whether the Rangers care to acknowledge it or not, is the one against whom wins mean the most.

Solid.

If you check out FOXSportsSouthwest.com right now, you'll see a banner under the lead with a reminder that tomorrow night, right when Texas-Baltimore gets underway and until the final pitch, we'll conduct a live chat. A strong showing could mean we'll try this at least once per homestand and once per road trip. If you're near a computer during Wednesday's game, make plans to join us for the chat, whether you want to participate in the Q&A or just take it all in.

Texas	22	18	—
Oakland	19	20	2.0 or 3.0 games back
Los Angeles	18	23	4.5
Seattle	14	24	6.5 or 7.5

May 20, 2010

I'm gonna beg off writing this morning, not to give a little phony weight to my common suggestion that I write three or four times per week, but instead because a complete Newberg Report might be full of big league game thoughts, emotional overreactions, trade ideas, minor league notes and prospect comp's, massive amounts of Tanner Scheppers talk, a couple Juan Moreno references, and so on—and all of that was packed into a lively in-game chat session at FOXSportsSouthwest.com last night.

If you had time to read a report this morning, you'll have time to read the transcript from last night's chat. I'm not sure how long the transcript will be up, but surely at least the morning.

Thanks to the more than 600 of you who stopped by. For obvious reasons, I could only get to a tenth of your questions at best, but it was a blast to do and we're already looking at dates for the next one. Thanks also to Ben Rebstock and Brian Smith for their help setting the chat up and moderating it, and to John Rhadigan and Emily Jones and Dana Larson and Josh & Tom for touting it all night.

One note buried in the chat: I'm looking tentatively at Sunday, July 25 for Newberg Report Night at the Ballpark this year. I still have to check that date with the organization and with our keynote guests. Stay tuned.

A couple quick things to share:

1. *Baseball America*'s initial mock first round has Texas drafting Middle Tennessee State righthander Bryce Brentz at number 15 overall (the Matt Purke comp pick) and Ball State righthander Kolbrin Vitek at number 22 in two and a half weeks. Other notable first-round projections: University of Mississippi lefthander Drew Pomeranz at number two, Woodlands High righthander Jameson Taillon at number three, UTA outfielder Michael Choice at number 11, University of Texas righthander Brandon Workman at number 14, and LSU righthander Anthony Ranaudo at number 20.

2. A free Bound Edition to the first two readers who correctly identify why Bartolo Colon is going to be referenced in one of the next few Newberg Reports.

3. With all the talk about how bad Josh Hamilton has been in day games—and he has—shouldn't we acknowledge that his no-doubter blast to center field last night and the should-have-been shot to left field two innings later both came in daylight? Those two shots will get filed under the "Night" split since it was a night game, but unless the analysis has something to do with Hamilton's circadian rhythms, if we're strictly talking about how he sees the ball in natural light as opposed to under the lights, then maybe his second- and fourth-inning crushes on Wednesday are good signs.

Finally, I submitted this week's MLB.com, ranking the top 10 secondary pitches in the Rangers' farm system, late last night. When it goes live sometime today, I'll send out a link.

May 21, 2010

NC-17
Graphic violence, bat and arm
Boomsticks 1 and 2

I was there for all 20 runs and all 35 hits, but my friends were right: The moment I won't forget from Texas 13, Baltimore 7 was the throw Nelson Cruz made to the plate in the fifth, on Adam Jones's flyout to right with nobody out, men on the corners, and what felt like a teetering 8-4 Texas lead. Scott Feldman escaped the inning without further damage and retired five of the next six, starting all but one of them with strike one, throwing 17 strikes out of 23 in that span, and ending his night on a positive note.

Luke Scott didn't run on Cruz. There was no assist. It goes into the books as an F-9, and nothing more. But it was majestic.

Cruz might have been a triple short of the cycle (or as Jim Knox put it, "one hit" short of the cycle), but defensively he was nothing short of awesome.

May 22, 2010

Five of the Rangers' last six wins have been by one run (and the other one was two nights ago, when the closer was brought in to nail down a 13-7 win). After starting the season 1-4 in one-run games, the club has won 9 of its last 11 decided by one.

Texas is now 18-7 at home. It's the best home record in baseball, and the best through 25 games in franchise history.

That includes seven straight in Arlington, and 11 of the last 12.

Overall, the Rangers have won 11 of 15, 17 of 24, and 20 of 29. That final number trails only Tampa Bay (by one game) in the American League.

Josh Hamilton's pivotal sacrifice bunt (yes, his own idea, not a bench call) was the first of his big league career.

And the third of his pro career. He had one in 1999 for the Princeton Devil Rays of the short-season Appalachian League, and another for the Bakersfield Blaze (then a Tampa Bay affiliate) in 2002. Elvis Andrus was 13 years old the last time Hamilton moved a runner by squaring around.

Tonight, Derek Holland (2-0) vs. Randy Wells (3-2). Tomorrow, C.J. Wilson (3-1) vs. Carlos Silva (5-0, lifetime ERA against Texas of 5.20 in 13 starts, and an .844 OPS—including 9.09 and 1.060 in seven Arlington starts). Packed houses expected for both.

The Angels are 5.5 back. Oakland 4.0, Seattle 8.5.

Happy.

May 23, 2010

Dustin Nippert faced five Cubs hitters Saturday. He started all five with ball one.

For the season, he's faced 115 batters. He's started 62 with ball one. That's 54 percent of Nippert's opponents that start off with a 1-0 count. The league as a whole gets behind 1-0 just 42 percent of the time.

Enough of that.

OK, OK, OK. I get it. You want to know whether Roy Oswalt will be a Texas Ranger.

Newberg Report: Top Ten Secondary Pitches

A ranking of Rangers prospects' best complementary offerings

By Jamey Newberg / Special to MLB.com

May 20, 2010

The Rangers have always managed to put big fastball pitchers on the mound, the type who blow up radar guns and seduce scouts and fans. From Nolan Ryan to Bobby Witt to Mitch Williams to Robb Nen, Texas has never lacked in the big heat category.

But what Ryan was able to do that made him so uniquely, enduringly successful (and that often gets overlooked) was offset his triple-digit velocity with command of a hammer curve and Bugs Bunny changeup that prevented big league hitters from sitting on the heat.

Since Ryan retired, the organization had years of poor results developing pitchers able not only to miss bats with the fastball but to locate a breaking ball or change, as well. We're seeing it now with C.J. Wilson and Colby Lewis and Derek Holland (and occasionally Neftali Feliz)—pitchers whose fastballs play up because of breaking balls that keep hitters honest at the least, if not completely off balance.

And there's a lot more of that coming.

What follows is one ranking of the top 10 secondary pitches (based primarily on future grades) among prospects in the Rangers farm system—several of which could show up in Arlington before long.

1. TANNER SCHEPPERS, RHP, Oklahoma City: Curveball

The scariest thing about the idea that Scheppers has the most devastating breaking ball in the Rangers' system is that, outside of Feliz, the 23-year-old probably has the most dominant fastball, as well. The upper-90s velocity and hammer curve make him an obvious late-inning relief candidate, but the fact that he also locates a slider and change have the Rangers hopeful that his ultimate future lies in the rotation.

2. MARTIN PEREZ, LHP, Frisco: Change-up

At age 19, Perez is faring well against much older Double-A competition (3.34 ERA, 31 strikeouts in 29.2 innings), due in large part to a tumbling change that has made him even more effective against right-handed hitters than against lefties. Perez arrived in pro ball at age 16, wielding a fastball that scouts believed in and a curve that showed immediate promise, but his development of the change under the Rangers' tutelage has elevated him into the top tier of pitching prospects in all of baseball.

3. MATT THOMPSON, RHP, Hickory: Curveball

Thompson struggled with the transition from high school to pro ball after signing as the Rangers' seventh-round Draft pick in 2008, but the Burleson and Arlington product has developed quickly into one of the organization's top strike-throwers. His out pitch is a knee-buckling power curve with two-plane break. The 20-year-old improved to 4-1, 2.70 last night with a standout effort, holding Kannapolis to two runs on six hits and one walk, setting eight down on strikes and getting nine groundouts (with just two outs in the air). For the year, Thompson has racked up 38 strikeouts and just nine walks.

4. MARTIN PEREZ, LHP, Frisco: Curveball

Unlike Feliz and unlike Scheppers, Perez is unquestionably a starting pitcher, based largely on the fact that he has the makings of three plus pitches. While the changeup may be the more effective of his secondary offerings at the moment, it was the advanced feel he showed for his late-breaking curve that made him one of the highest-paid international free agents Texas had ever signed when they paid the Venezuelan native $580,000 in 2007.

5. DANNY GUTIERREZ, RHP, Extended Spring Training: Curveball

A true 12-to-6 hammer that buries itself on hitters, Gutierrez's curve promises to miss big league bats as long as the 23-year-old can get himself back on the mound after the latest of several off-field issues, this time a 50-game league suspension after testing positive for an ADHD medication that he failed to get a therapeutic use exemption for. Gutierrez, acquired last summer from Kansas City, touches the mid-90s with his fastball, but it's the curve that sets him apart.

6. MICHAEL KIRKMAN, LHP, Oklahoma City: Slider

A two-year struggle with his mechanics threatened to end Kirkman's career before it ever got untracked, but the durable left-hander put things back together in 2008 and took a huge step forward in 2009, earning a spot on the 40-man roster after the season. The 23-year-old locates a sharp slider to go along with low-to-mid-90s velocity, completely neutralizing left-handed hitters (.140/.245/.163). Despite a rash of walks in his last two starts, Kirkman stands at 4-1, 2.68 in eight Triple-A starts, striking out nearly a batter per inning and holding opponents to a .195 batting average.

7. JAKE BRIGHAM, RHP, Bakersfield: Curveball

Featuring a mid-90s fastball/power curve package and bulldog intensity, Brigham profiles as a potential eighth-inning weapon, though he needs to develop more consistency. The curve is a true out pitch when he locates it, with knee-buckling 12-to-6 action.

8. ROBBIE ERLIN, LHP, Hickory: Curveball

Erlin threw five perfect innings in his first career start on Tuesday, striking out nine of the 15 batters he faced. For the season, his numbers look like typos—25.1 innings, 11 hits, four walks, 31 strikeouts—and his finest pitch is a sharp, two-plane curve. The 2009 third-rounder stands only six feet tall, but he's pitching as effectively as you could ever hope for out of a high school first-rounder and could move relatively quickly.

9. ALEXI OGANDO, RHP, Oklahoma City: Slider

Ogando's slider flashes plus potential though he gets inconsistent action on it. Refining the pitch might be the final step in the 26-year-old's apprenticeship. His upper-90s fastball and slider/change offerings were too much for the Texas League to handle (he posted a 1.15 ERA, .078 opponents' average, 21 strikeouts, and five walks in 15.2 innings for Frisco), and so far Triple-A hitters have managed only two singles and a double off him in four innings, striking out six times without drawing a walk. Chances are that we'll see Ogando in Arlington at some point this season, with the timetable dependent in part on the progress he makes with the breaking ball.

10. JOSH LUEKE, RHP, Hickory: Slider

The 25-year-old Lueke needs a promotion. In 17.2 South Atlantic League innings, he's scattered 12 hits and four unintentional walks while punching out a gaudy 33 hitters, many on a filthy slider that misses bats and induces ground balls at heavy rates when opponents manage to make contact. Lueke saw action at Bakersfield the last two seasons; it will be interesting to see whether Texas gives him a third run at Cal League hitters or if instead they challenge him with a two-level jump to Frisco to test his fastball-slider combination against more advanced hitters.

I haven't gotten this many emails on one subject since St. Patrick's Day's off-the-field news.

Would Texas want Roy Oswalt? Of course. At 32, he remains one of the most consistently effective starting pitchers in baseball.

Would Houston trade Oswalt? Maybe. On the heels of the righthander's announcement that he'd waive his full no-trade clause to "try[ ] to get back to the playoffs," and that he thinks a trade might be "a good thing for both [him and the team]," Astros GM Ed Wade has pointed out that his ace "has a no-trade clause, not a 'trade-me' clause," as a way of saying he's not going to be forced by the player into trading him. Still, you'd have to think that Oswalt's apparent assurance to Astros owner Drayton McLane that, if traded, he'd "love to come back and finish [his] career" in Houston theoretically makes the idea of springing him for a mini-foundation of young talent more palatable.

Would Oswalt agree to come to Texas? Evidently. He's apparently told friends and reporters that there are three teams for whom he'd waive the no-trade and accept a deal—Texas, Atlanta, and St. Louis—with some suggestion that the Dodgers and Red Sox might be on his list as well.

And don't discount the prospect for Oswalt of pitching for Nolan Ryan and his former Round Rock manager Jackie Moore and his former Round Rock pitching coach Mike Maddux, with a club that sits in pretty good position as far as the standings are concerned.

There. It's on a tee, right?

Absolutely not.

Here's why you shouldn't hold your breath:

1. OWNERSHIP: Continuing to hide behind my policy not to comment on a ~~mess~~ situation I really know nothing about (and not to rely on or report any of the high-spun position statements fired off by the creditors bloc), I'm not going to predict where this is headed or when it gets resolved, but it seems relatively clear that a club that will have to draft a little more carefully than it might have otherwise in a couple weeks is not going to be able to take on a pitcher owed a guaranteed $29 million over the next two years while ownership remains unsettled.

OK. A turn of the donkey wheel, and the ownership chaos has vanished. Time to stitch up an "Oswalt 44" jersey in Rangers red?

No.

2. THAT $29 MILLION: Yes, I expect Rangers Baseball Express to be ready to infuse a chunk into the payroll when it takes the ownership reins, whenever that time comes. Yes, it makes sense that a playoff-caliber starting pitcher would be targeted. Yes, Oswalt fits the description. But even if $2.5 million per month the rest of the way this season is tolerable, is spending $16 million on Oswalt in 2011 (really, $18 million, since there's a $2 million buyout to void another $16 million commitment in 2012) the smartest way to improve next year's club, given where its perceived strengths and holes will be?

3. YEAH, BUT SURELY HOUSTON WILL PUT SOME CASH IN THE DEAL: Or maybe not. Ken Rosenthal of Fox Sports says McLane won't do it. But let's say he changes his mind. Every chunk of cash the Astros are asked to chip in cranks up the level of young players and prospects Houston will demand in return. Case in point: It's arguable that the package Toronto got from Philadelphia in December in exchange for Roy Halladay—AA pitcher Kyle Drabek, Low A catcher Travis D'Arnaud, and AAA corner infielder Brett Wallace (via Oakland, who received minor league outfielder Michael Taylor from the Phillies)—wasn't as strong as the Derek Holland/Justin Smoak package the Jays reportedly sought from Texas in July, but a key reason that Toronto wouldn't take less from the Rangers is that they were likely (and necessarily) needing a greater subsidy from the Jays for a year and two months of Halladay than the $6 million that Toronto sent Philadelphia for the 2010 season. (Another way to look at this, however: It might be that Toronto was using the Rangers all along to leverage better trade offers from other clubs, knowing that Halladay would ultimately veto any trade to Texas. If that's true, it wouldn't have made sense for Toronto to ever back down from the Holland/Smoak demand.)

The point? The more cash Texas asks the Astros for, to reduce its commitment to Oswalt, the more it will take in players to get him.

4. TEXAS MAY BE AT A DISADVANTAGE: Each of the last two years (June 18, 2008 and July 10, 2009), I've written a report pondering whether the strength of the upper tier of the Rangers' pre-arbitration roster depth and farm system might lead other teams to try and hold Jon Daniels up in trade talks. It's still a concern. It's even more of an issue when it's Houston on the other end. McLane lost Ryan to the Rangers. He may be about to lose AAA Round Rock (and with it, conceptually, the Austin market) to the Rangers. Houston isn't competitive on the field right now. If McLane considers Texas competition off the field, and there have long been logical suggestions that he does, there's zero chance he's going to take the chance of trading Oswalt in-state without a strong pitch from Wade that the deal is set up as a slam dunk to favor the Astros long-term.

Along the same lines, though, St. Louis and Atlanta aren't exactly perfect matches, either. You'd expect McLane and Wade would bristle at the thought of Oswalt piching for the division-mate Cardinals for the next two years, a team that visits Houston nine or 10 times a season and that the Astros are obviously chasing. (Plus, their rotation is fairly well set right now.) As for the

Braves, the rotation is far from their biggest need, they'll probably have a tough time catching Philadelphia or the Wild Card, and loading up for yet another Mark Teixeira trade that doesn't pay off probably isn't the best idea.

5. BACK PROBLEMS: Big concern? Not if you're trying to win now, as Oswalt is pitching healthy and averaging seven innings over his last seven starts. He's pitched nine times this year. All nine games have been quality starts. But then we get back to that $29 million through 2011, and back problems usually don't get better. Still, if the history of injections for low back issues were the reddest flag, it probably wouldn't hold a deal up.

6. BAD MATCH: Aside from pitching, chances are Houston is most interested in middle infield help, an area where Texas is relatively thin. But rewind to the Halladay trade: Philadelphia got Oakland involved in order to get the Jays the first baseman they wanted in Wallace. There are creative ways to meet the other team's needs.

Let's assume the ownership impediment is lifted. Would you offer Houston a package of Holland, righthander Blake Beavan (who is quietly having a very good encore season at Frisco, and in fact fired eight scoreless innings [four hits, no walks, eight strikeouts] against Houston's Corpus Christi affiliate last weekend, after throwing two gems against the Hooks in four 2009 starts), right-handed reliever Alexi Ogando, and a top middle infield prospect picked up for Chris Davis or Engel Beltre from a third club?

Not me.

And Houston probably doesn't do it, either.

For all the reasons that Texas and Oswalt seem like a really good fit, and that it would make a ton of sense for Houston to accommodate his wish to go somewhere else for a year and a half before coming back to finish his career where it started, accelerating a desperately needed rebuilding process, this one appears to have a bunch of hurdles that may be too difficult to clear.

Oh, and the Bartolo Colon reference the other day? Two of the four players Colon was traded for eight years ago are higher on my trade-for list right now than Roy Oswalt.

May 24, 2010

The Rangers and the Greenberg-Ryan Group have announced a plan to complete the sale of the franchise, by way of a "prepackaged" Chapter 11 bankruptcy plan that would permit the club to maintain normal baseball and business operations. Under the plan, the sale would be completed by "mid-summer."

I haven't tried to analyze this situation in this space and won't begin to now. Here's the substance of the team's press release, issued minutes ago:

Arlington, TX, May 24, 2010—Texas Rangers Baseball Partners, the current owners of the Texas Rangers Baseball Club, and Rangers Baseball Express, the local investor group led by team president Nolan Ryan and Chuck Greenberg, today announced a plan to facilitate completion of the previously announced sale of the Club to the Greenberg-Ryan group. The sale of the Club and its lease of the Rangers Ballpark in Arlington, together with the separate sale of the land around the Ballpark, have an aggregate transaction value of approximately $575 million.

The Rangers sale will be accomplished through a voluntary, "prepackaged," court-supervised process under Chapter 11 of the U.S. Bankruptcy Code pursuant to a plan previously negotiated and agreed to by the current Rangers owners and the Greenberg-Ryan group. The prepackaged plan, which is supported by Major League Baseball, current Rangers ownership, and the Greenberg-Ryan group, provides sufficient sale proceeds for the Rangers creditors to recover 100 percent of the portion of HSG Sports Group's debt that is guaranteed by the Rangers and for all Rangers creditors to be paid in full.

Texas Rangers Baseball Partners has requested that a hearing be held in 45 days to confirm the proposed sale and plan of reorganization. The sale is expected to be completed by mid-summer, subject to court approval, which will then allow the franchise to exit the Chapter 11 process.

"This plan to complete the sale of the Texas Rangers serves the best interests of the team, its fans, MLB and all other parties involved," said Baseball Commissioner Allan H. (Bud) Selig. "This agreement assures an orderly process to expeditiously transfer Rangers ownership to the Greenberg-Ryan group, and it protects the franchise's baseball operations. Rangers fans can have confidence that their team has the resources it needs to compete. Clearly, this could not and would not have happened without Tom Hicks' leadership and hard work over a long period of time."

This process and sale are expected to have no impact on Rangers baseball operations. While the sale is being completed, the current owners will continue to have control of the Club. Motions have been filed with the court in order that:

- The Rangers will be able to operate within their existing budget to sign and acquire amateur, international and professional players
- Ticket prices remain the same and purchased tickets will continue to be honored
- The fan experience at Rangers Ballpark will be unchanged, with all current amenities and promotions continuing as usual
- All salaries will be paid
- Rangers vendors and suppliers will be paid in full

"Since 1998, our family has taken great pride and joy in our association with the Rangers," said Tom

Hicks, who will be Chairman Emeritus of the Rangers. "We are proud to play an active role in resolving the deadlock in this complex sale process. Rangers fans deserve management's full focus on baseball operations, and Nolan, Chuck and their colleagues will be outstanding stewards of the Rangers. We stand ready to support them in every way possible, and as huge fans we will continue to cheer the Rangers on to the ultimate goal of a World Series championship."

"Our goal is to move forward with our plan to create a long-term record of success and championships," said Nolan Ryan, who will continue to serve as Rangers president. "We will achieve that by being active in the player acquisition market as well as our ongoing commitment to develop players through one of the league's best farm systems."

"We are pleased to take this important step towards completion of our transaction," said Chuck Greenberg. "Tom Hicks has laid the groundwork for this sale in a manner that best addresses the interests of the Texas Rangers as well as all parties that have a stake in the team. His agreement to sell the land around the Ballpark in order to facilitate the sale of the Rangers is just one example of how he has been instrumental in achieving a result that is best for the franchise and its fans. For our group, the focus will be on rewarding Rangers fans with great performance on the field and memorable experiences in the stands and in the community."

"Nolan Ryan has a proven track record with MLB club owners and I am prepared to submit this to the owners promptly for their approval," said Selig. "Chuck Greenberg and this group of local investors are dedicated to building the franchise's value and continuing the team's contributions to the Dallas-Fort Worth community."

MLB has agreed to provide the Rangers with a new credit facility to ensure that the Club continues to meet all of its obligations while the sale is being completed.

In a separate transaction, Ballpark Real Estate, L.P., an independent investment vehicle controlled by Tom Hicks, whose family also controls HSG Sports Group and its subsidiary Texas Rangers Baseball Partners, entered into an agreement to sell or transfer to the Greenberg-Ryan group approximately 153 of the 195 acres around the Ballpark and Cowboys Stadium that is owned or controlled by Ballpark Real Estate or the Hicks family. Rangers Baseball Express required this land as a condition to its willingness to purchase the Texas Rangers. In return for the transferred land, Ballpark Real Estate will receive cash, notes, and an ownership position in Rangers Baseball Express.

HSG Sports Group and its other primary asset, the Dallas Stars hockey team, are not included in the filing.

The filing took place in the U.S. Bankruptcy Court for the Northern District of Texas in Fort Worth. The Rangers filed customary "First Day Motions" with the Court, which are intended to ensure that the process is seamless and has no adverse impact on the Club's operations, employees and suppliers.

May 25, 2010

Texas 8.

Kansas City 7.

A resounding salute to this man.

May 26, 2010

If you're an Angels fan, delete this email now, without reading further.

What is an OPS of .794?

1. It's a number that signifies a player whose on-base percentage plus slugging percentage totals .794. Looking solely at players with enough at-bats to be on pace to qualify for a batting title, there are 84 with 2010 OPS's higher than .794. Nearly three per team.
2. Among those with OPS's above .794: Placido Polanco, Gaby Sanchez, Martin Prado, Alberto Callaspo, David Freese, Andruw Jones, and Johnny Damon.
3. Yes. Johnny Damon.
4. Michael Young's OPS is .825.

The point of all this?

Vladimir Guerrero's OPS in 2009 was .794.

He was an Angels hitter who produced, by that measure, at a rate that Prado and Callaspo and Freese and Damon are producing at this year.

Los Angeles, seeing that, at age 34, Guerrero played only 100 games and OPS'd at that rate after an .886 in 2008 and 10 consecutive years before that over .934 or greater, let him go. Didn't even offer him arbitration to secure a compensatory pick.

Guerrero's OPS right now is .974. Only three hitters in the American League (Justin Morneau, Kevin Youkilis, and Miguel Cabrera) have higher marks.

The last season that Guerrero's OPS was this high was his MVP season of 2004.

Last year (albeit in only 383 at-bats), Guerrero hit 15 home runs and drove in 50.

This year, in fewer than half as many at-bats (176), he has 12 homers and 42 RBI.

His doubles rate hasn't changed much (16 last year, eight this season), but the RBI two-bagger he swatted down the left field line in the seventh inning last night to extend the Rangers' lead to 8-6, on a sinking mid-90s fastball a foot inside, bearing in on his back knee, was just silly. (Said Young after the game: "He has the best set of hands I've ever seen. He just kept his hands inside and hit it.")

Which raises one other Guerrero improvement from 2009: Last year his swing-and-miss percentage on pitches outside the strike zone was 27.6. This year, according to ESPN Stats & Info: 16.9 percent.

We're lucky to be able to watch that guy play baseball every day.

I've gotten lots of question marks about last night's postgame email. Pictured was former Rangers manager Doug Rader. The reason: He coined the term "Winning Ugly." That may have been the ugliest Rangers win I can remember. Bad plays, plays unmade, fundamentals blown.

Amazing stat, courtesy of the *Fort Worth Star-Telegram*'s Anthony Andro: Last night was the first time all season that Texas has homered more than once in a road game.

Rich Harden's inability to put .146-hitting Willie Bloomquist away in the sixth inning demonstrated how different a pitcher he's become.

Harden led all big league starting pitchers in strikeouts per nine innings in 2009. And in lowest opponents' percentage of contact made when swinging.

And yet Bloomquist, who strikes out every fourth at-bat, never swung and missed in an 11-pitch at-bat, fouling eight Harden deliveries off (one slider and eight fastballs) and watching two settle outside the strike zone. The final pitch—Harden's last of the night—was slammed to left field, over Josh Hamilton's head, for a two-run triple that cut a three-run Rangers lead to one and led to a game-tying suicide squeeze.

Harden threw lots of strikes last night (73 out of 104 pitches) but once again didn't get the job done. It's sort of obvious to say he's no longer the pitcher he used to be, but the Bloomquist at-bat alone typifies how different he is from just last year.

This is sort of silly: seven of the Rangers' last eight games have been decided by one run. Happily, Texas has won five of those seven, but there's going to be a residual effect from all these close games the Rangers have played in 2010 (without checking, I believe I heard they're tied with Cincinnati for most one-run decisions this year).

My MLB.com column tomorrow will focus on a growing problem that all these close contests, and the inability of Harden and several others to get deeper into games, could be bringing on, with the possible solution not as obvious as you might think.

May 28, 2010

Rangers in on Roy?
Just don't see it happening
Watch out for L.A. ...

Speaking of the Angels, there remains one confirmation I need to firm up, but we've tentatively targeted Sunday, July 25, for Newberg Report Night at Rangers Ballpark, when Texas tees it up against the Angels for the fourth of seven head-to-head battles in a huge 10-game span.

Maybe the ownership transfer will be complete by then. Maybe a new impact player or two will be in uniform. Maybe it will be as big a July game as we've had here in years.

Expect the usual stuff: late-afternoon Q&A sessions with a couple of the best baseball writers in the country and some of the top officials in the Rangers organization—less than a week before the trade deadline—plus a raffle and auction of baseball memorabilia to raise money for charity, and tickets for close to 300 of us to sit together at the game.

We hope to lock the date in soon. Stay tuned.

In the more immediate future, our second live, in-game chat session hosted by Fox Sports Southwest will be this Wednesday, June 2, when Texas visits the White Sox for a 7:10 game pitting 2-5 righthanders Scott Feldman and Gavin Floyd against each other.

Finally, while I'd continue to suggest that Roy Oswalt isn't likely to be a Texas Ranger by time we gather on July 25, there are two other righthanders who pitched yesterday that just might be.

At Oklahoma City, in Game One of a doubleheader against Seattle's AAA affiliate in Tacoma, 2007 supplemental first-rounder Tommy Hunter (making his fifth start of the season) held the Rainiers to one run on four hits and two walks in four innings (68 pitches), fanning five. Jon Daniels said in a chat session yesterday that Hunter is ready to go whenever the need in Arlington arises.

Relieving Hunter was 2009 supplemental first-rounder Tanner Scheppers, making his sixth RedHawks appearance after six Frisco games pitched.

First Scheppers inning: strikeout swinging, strikeout swinging, lineout to right field.

Second Scheppers inning: walk, strikeout swinging, shortstop error to put runners on first and third in what was a one-run game, strikeout swinging, strikeout swinging.

Third Scheppers inning: strikeout swinging, strikeout swinging, 3-1 putout to close out the 2-1 victory.

Seven strikeouts and zero hits in three innings.

Overall, in 13 AAA frames, Scheppers has scattered two runs (1.38 ERA) on eight hits (.174 opponents'

Newberg Report: Relief for the Rangers' Pen

Starters need to work deeper into games to spare relief corps

By Jamey Newberg / Special to MLB.com

May 27, 2010

The Rangers relief corps has been solid for the most part in 2010, posting the sixth-best ERA in the American League and holding hitters to a .252 average. It's been an integral part of a club that has now had at least a share of the American League West lead for three weeks.

But not without a potential cost. As the club approaches the one-third mark of the season, Texas has asked its bullpen to throw more innings than any other AL club, with four of its six starters to date (Scott Feldman, Rich Harden, Matt Harrison, and Derek Holland) averaging fewer than six innings per start. Amazingly, Rangers relievers are tied for first (Chris Ray), third (Neftali Feliz), and eighth (Frank Francisco, Darren Oliver, and Darren O'Day) in the league in games pitched in 2010. The durability is impressive. But the workload is worrisome.

Things got to the point on Wednesday that, even after an off-day on Monday and with another one scheduled today, Texas resorted to asking Holland to pitch the eighth inning of a two-run game, four days after his last start and four days before his next one, presumably to give the rest of the pen a little break.

Continuing to put the bullpen through its paces at this rate (especially with the Rangers' league-leading total of one-run decisions, which overtaxes the key high-leverage arms in particular) threatens the health and effectiveness of the crew as a whole.

It might seem as if this potential problem has an easy solution, given the Rangers' depth in relief candidates. Harrison is on the verge of being activated and assigned to a bullpen role. Right-hander Pedro Strop, who made a big league cameo last week without pitching, hasn't allowed a base hit in his last five AAA appearances, a span of 30 hitters who have managed one walk. For the season, Strop has scattered 13 hits (.188 opponents' average) and five walks in 18.2 innings, fanning 20 and coaxing three times as many groundouts as flyouts.

Righthander Alexi Ogando has a 1.52 ERA between Frisco and Oklahoma, setting 33 down on strikes in 23.2 innings while walking only five. Opponents are hitting just .120 off the 26-year-old. Left-hander Zach Phillips has yet to allow a run in 6.2 Oklahoma City innings, after permitting two scores in 14.2 Frisco frames. Combined, in 21.1 innings, he's punched out 26 hitters and issued only seven walks, holding opponents to a .181 batting average.

Harrison, Strop, Ogando, and Phillips are each on the 40-man roster, as are big league-experienced Doug Mathis and Tommy Hunter (whose return could be to the rotation, possibly freeing up a current starter to work in relief). So are right-handed reliever Omar Beltre and left-handed starter Michael Kirkman, pitching well for the RedHawks but needing to cut down on their walks.

Then there's non-roster candidate Tanner Scheppers, coming fast. And big league veterans Clay Rapada, Willie Eyre, Geoff Geary (currently on the disabled list), and Jailen Peguero, if needed. Further down the depth chart but showing promise are Frisco relievers Ben Snyder, Cody Eppley, Beau Jones, Josh Lueke, and Evan Reed.

A wealth of options, right? Yes, but the problem is creating space.

The Rangers bullpen presently consists of Feliz, Francisco, Oliver, O'Day, Ray, Dustin Nippert, and Guillermo Moscoso. Moscoso is likely to be optioned to make room tomorrow for Harrison. Barring injury, who are you going to remove to make room for Strop or Ogando or Scheppers or any of the others?

Obviously, Feliz and Francisco and Oliver and O'Day aren't going anywhere. Ray has quietly been solid.

Nippert is out of options. He can't be sent to the farm without clearing waivers—and having been outrighted before, even if he does clear waivers, he can refuse a Minor League assignment and take instant free agency.

Realistically, Nippert's the only reliever in this beleaguered bullpen in any danger of losing his job (unless Harrison struggles in his new role), but unless the Rangers are willing to let him pitch for another organization, it may take a barky oblique muscle or sprained metatarsal to remove him from the relief corps and make room for a fresh arm.

It's probably safe to bet that Strop and Ogando and Scheppers will each pitch for Texas at some point this season. But for now, the Rangers bullpen, while unquestionably overworked, is pitching well. Texas has been in almost all of its games, having lost only twice by more than four runs (back to back six-run losses in

Toronto two weeks ago). The bullpen has an AL-leading 12 wins, frequently shutting the opponent down while the offense has done its job late. Only one team in the league has a better strikeout rate than the Rangers' relief corps.

The answer to the dangerously high stress being put on the Texas bullpen is not to begin making plans for reinforcements, as promising as we think some of them may be, but instead to expect the starters to step up. With only 12 of the club's next 41 games heading into the All-Star Break scheduled against teams with winning records, the burden is on C.J. Wilson and Colby Lewis to continue pitching regularly into the seventh, and on Feldman and Harden and Holland to give the club more innings than they have been.

That's the relief that the Rangers bullpen needs.

average) and seven walks while setting 22 hitters down on strikes. In his 11 Frisco innings, he permitted one run (0.82 ERA) on three hits (.079 opponents' average) and zero walks while fanning 19.

Combined: An ERA of 1.13, a .131 opponents' batting average, seven walks and 41 strikeouts in 24 innings.

With one exception, Scheppers has pitched on three or four days of rest every time out this year, so he's likely going to get the holiday weekend off in New Orleans before he takes the mound again, probably when Oklahoma City returns home to host Memphis.

But at the rate things are going, both in Oklahoma City and in Arlington, where the starting pitchers continue to fail to get out of the sixth inning on average and the current long man is walking far too many batters, I once ask the question I first posed on Twitter on May 13:

Alternate spelling for "Nippert" before long : S-C-H-E-P-P-E-R-S?

May 29, 2010

Texas has activated lefthander Matt Harrison from the disabled list and optioned righthander Guillermo Moscoso to Oklahoma City.

Harrison, whose 32 big league appearances have all been starts, joins the bullpen.

May 29, 2010

I say what I'm about to say without a lot of conviction. I may reverse course in two days.

Even once my Google Reader ceases to cough up as many articles each day containing the word "lenders" as about the previous night's game, I don't think I want to see a trade for Roy Oswalt. Or Cliff Lee. Or Lance Berkman. Or Paul Konerko. Or anyone else who would cost even one player from among Derek Holland, Tanner Scheppers, Martin Perez, and Justin Smoak.

It's not time.

Not time to break that group up, that is.

It may still be time to nail down a playoff spot in 2010. Probably not with the roster as presently constituted, but I have faith in Jon Daniels and his staff and scouts—who, driven by inventive and often unconventional ways of thinking, brought us Scheppers and Vladimir Guerrero and Alexi Ogando and Colby Lewis and Pedro Strop and Robbie Erlin and Elvis Andrus and Neftali Feliz and Tommy Hunter and Darren O'Day and who wouldn't surprise me if they asked Chris Davis to give catcher a AAA shot—to improve the club this summer.

By that I mean something like last summer's Matt Nevarez and Jose Vallejo for Ivan Rodriguez. Ray Olmedo for Matt Treanor. Jose Marte for Dustin Nippert. Ricardo Rodriguez for Vicente Padilla. Joselo Diaz for Matt Stairs, and Jesse Chavez for Kip Wells.

The Daniels trade that pushes up against that line the closest without crossing it is probably Francisco Cordero, Laynce Nix, Kevin Mench, and Julian Cordero for Carlos Lee and Nelson Cruz.

Just not Holland and anything else for Oswalt.

Or Scheppers for Konerko.

Why? Because even if this club fulfills on its pledge that It's Time, this is a franchise whose window is opening, not closing. I'm all for getting aggressive in July, addressing a hole or two and sending a strong front office message to the clubhouse that we're all in, but Atlanta did that in 2007 when, on July 31, a general manager motivated by a window he'd already bought shutters for traded for Mark Teixeira, Ron Mahay, Octavio Dotel, and Royce Ring, without much ultimately to show for it.

The Braves are doing just fine now. But they'd be better with Andrus and Feliz.

There are too many holes on this Rangers roster to think that a number one starter or a number five hitter would catapult them from AL West contenders to challengers for the pennant. Back to the Braves three years ago. Going into its July 31 game against Houston, Atlanta had lost nine of 14 and was 4.5 games back in the NL East (as far back as the club had been all season) and 2.5 games back in the Wild Card chase. Julio Franco (.217/.327/.289) and Scott Thorman (.220/.262/.402) were sharing first base. Its bullpen was led by Bob Wickman and backed by Rafael Soriano and a nondescript collection of righthanders Oscar Villarreal, Peter Moylan, Tyler Yates, and Chad Paronto.

That club's holes were as obvious as the bottom third of the Rangers' lineup.

After the massive July 31 overhaul, Atlanta went 29-27 the rest of the way, finishing 5.0 games back in the division and 6.0 games (and three teams) back in the Wild Card standings. The Braves missed the playoffs for the second time in 13 years.

Teixeira turned into Casey Kotchman (who turned into Adam LaRoche, who left without an arbitration offer) and Steve Marek. Mahay turned into 2008 draft pick Brett Devall, a high school lefthander whose has fought elbow and forearm injuries since signing. Ten days after arriving, Dotel landed on the disabled list for six weeks with a shoulder strain. He left for the White Sox that winter, having given Atlanta 7.2 innings of work and zero parting compensation. Ring threw 27.1 largely ineffective innings for the Braves in 2007 and 2008 before being designated for assignment, clearing waivers, and leaving in the winter via minor league free agency.

John Schuerholz, having already decided 2007 would be his final season as Braves GM, made one last run at a pennant. It failed.

You think Braves fans were any less pumped about the idea of Teixeira "coming home" than some Rangers fans are at the prospect of landing Oswalt, who has reportedly included Texas as just one of three teams he'd waive his no-trade clause to join? Think the average Atlanta fan knew any more about Neftali Feliz then than the average Metroplex general columnist knows now about Matt Thompson, if not Martin Perez?

Ask a Braves fan now whether he'd want a July 31, 2007 do-over.

Two things make this July's trade deadline sticky for Texas. One is the club is obviously immobilized financially. But even when that gets cured, by the end of July or not, in order to address the various glaring problems the active roster has, and address them in such a way that the team becomes a legitimate threat in October, the top tier of the farm system will have to get ransacked. It's not a realistic plan.

Very good baseball teams tend to break in one inexperienced position player a year, maybe two if at different times. They might introduce a couple young pitchers into key roles each season. There are far more Justin Smoak's than Jason Heyward's. Young players usually struggle to keep up with the adjustments that the league makes against them, as the book develops.

Holland and Feliz were the two kid pitchers Texas planned to count on in 2010. But neither was thrust out of camp into a role he wasn't thought to be quite ready for (a luxury, you might say, this team has rarely created for itself on the pitching side).

The Rangers knew that the rotation, coming off a season in which it was more reliable than it had been in years, could be better. The club basically turned Kevin Millwood into Lewis and Rich Harden, and while the latter hasn't worked out to date, there's no second-guessing that exchange. C.J. Wilson was given an opportunity to start, an opportunity that was made possible in part by the targeting and signing of Darren Oliver away from the Angels. Depth (and Matt Harrison's spring) allowed Texas to give Holland some added minor league seasoning.

Texas also added Chris Ray in the Millwood deal, strengthening a bullpen that needed another power arm with late-inning experience and giving Feliz a safety net in case he wasn't ready to hold down the eighth inning. But early struggles by Frankie Francisco gave Feliz an opportunity to step into a bigger role, and so far the move looks like it was the right one. (Did you realize he has yet to allow a hit on the road this season? Opponents are 0 for 25, with two walks.)

On the offensive side of things, the one young player that Texas was expecting to count on was Julio Borbon, who was coming off an impressive 157-at-bat debut last summer (.312/.376/.414, 19 stolen bases in 23 tries), primarily in the leadoff spot. In camp, the main questions tended to revolve around his readiness to hold center field down. Not until the final three games of the 2009 season did Borbon start in center for Texas, having worked primarily in left field. He actually got 21 starts as the designated hitter, starting defensively only 17 times.

Given Borbon's minor league track record at the plate (.321/.362/.425 and .307/.367/.386 in his two seasons after signing late in 2007), even accounting for an expected regression in 2010, more people were concerned coming into this season about his ability to patrol center field and limit the extra base than about his chances to lock down the leadoff spot. His work in spring training (.326/.368/.427 in a team-leading 89 at-bats) did nothing to trigger concerns about his bat.

Then the regular season got going. Borbon's tremendous struggles at the plate (he's been helpless against lefthanders, he's not hitting at all on the road, he's drawn two walks in 139 plate appearances, he's hit an excessive amount of lazy flies to left, he's worked the count to 2-0 *just two times all year*) have been mitigated to an extent by Andrus's seizing of the leadoff spot, but in spite of Borbon's moderate progress of late, I'd still expect Endy Chavez's name to start showing up with more regularity in the notes columns in the next couple weeks.

But that's the nature of young players, and we must remember that Borbon reached the big leagues in his second full pro season. He's still learning, and good teams can live with that. What becomes problematic is when there are multiple players in that category.

Borbon, right now, is where Chris Davis and Jarrod Saltalamacchia were a year ago.

And that's leads us to the problem.

This whole thing, the entire outlook for this team, at least for 2010, would be in colossally better shape if first base and catcher had taken a different progression than they have.

Davis, coming off an impressive 2008 debut (.285/.331/.549 with 88 strikeouts in 295 at-bats) that was no less promising than Borbon's 2009 summer, regressed terribly in the first half last year (.202/.256/.415 with 114 strikeouts in 258 at-bats). But he refound himself over seven weeks in Oklahoma City (.327/.418/.521 with 39 strikeouts in 165 at-bats), and then put together a largely overlooked, resurgent finish over the final six weeks of the season with Texas (.308/.338/.496 with 36 strikeouts in 133 at-bats), suggesting he might have locked in the adjustments that had eluded him in the spring.

As late as this March, there was apparently internal debate as to whether Davis or Cruz should be the one hitting sixth behind Guerrero and Ian Kinsler. Davis hit .364/.395/.494 in spring training, and he was nowhere near the list of roster questions coming out of camp.

Saltalamacchia, after posting big league OPS's in the low .700's in 2007 and 2008 (at young ages for a starting big league catcher), was being counted on to take the next step in 2009. He did make obvious improvements defensively, but he didn't hit. In April, Saltalamacchia hit .276. In May, .241. In June, .239. In July, .204. In August and September before being shut down for good, .143. A winter of health setbacks followed, and the job behind the plate was thrown open in camp.

But Saltalamacchia got only 25 spring training at-bats due to upper back and neck issues, Taylor Teagarden struck out 21 times in 40 Cactus League at-bats, and the club made a late-March trade with the Brewers for journeyman Matt Treanor, who was expected to serve as AAA insurance until Toby Hall was physically ready.

Instead, Treanor has nearly three times as many big league at-bats this season as Saltalamacchia and Teagarden combined, and hasn't done a whole lot with them (.207/.295/.283). I'm a Matt Treanor fan, and would be more than happy if he were my number two catcher the next however-many years. But he's not an everyday player on a contender, at least not one with other holes offensively.

It would have been a lot better if Saltalamacchia had nailed down the job envisioned for him three years ago.

And if Davis had picked up where he left off in August and September and March, allowing Smoak to continue to punish AAA pitching.

If those two things—not slam dunks but also not longshot expectations coming into the season—hadn't become major problems, with what have proved to be inadequate solutions, then this team would have a much healthier lead on the division, and would be better able to fight through Borbon's struggles as long as he was showing some signs of improvement.

Instead, Smoak is proving not to be ready (Nolan Ryan has said the organization thinks 150 plate appearances is a fair trial period, and Smoak is at 126 and seemingly regressing in his command of the strike zone and pitch recognition, if not confidence). Treanor is what he is. And Borbon is a .243 base-reacher.

Collectively, those three are hitting .201/.270/.282.

And the 7-8-9 slots (thanks in part to Andrus's 11 solid games in the bottom third of the order) sit at .219/.289/.279.

I'm not in the mood to check to see if there's a team in baseball (National League included) with a blacker hole at the bottom of the lineup.

Or in the mood to imagine Tanner Scheppers relieving John Danks in the ninth, or Derek Holland as the Astros' ace by time Roy Oswalt returns to that club in 2012 to finish his career.

It might be Time. If that means Texas should offer up a couple second-tier prospects (some of whom could headline other franchise's systems) to improve the roster in July, I'm all for that and would be disappointed not to take that shot.

But these are not John Schuerholz's Braves. This is a team that's getting better with promise for a lot more, promise that's not too far off and in many cases that we're all able to see, as opposed to just reading about.

If this team can settle its financial position by winter (if not by August) and add a couple impact pieces, and then internally add a rookie pitcher or two to the core each year, and maybe one young hitter, then we're in serious business.

But adding Cliff Lee or Lance Berkman wouldn't do enough to change where this club is headed in 2010, at least not enough to stomach the loss of Holland, or Scheppers, or Perez, or Smoak, not given the number of immediate holes that need fixing.

Give me an opportunity to add Josh Willingham for Wilmer Font, David Murphy, and Miguel Velazquez, and I'm all over it, as long as the Nationals will cooperate.

Blake Beavan and Braden Tullis for Jake Westbrook? OK.

Chad Tracy for Mike Lowell and a bunch of cash? I'd do it.

But anything this summer that spoils my vision of Derek Holland and Martin Perez in the 2012 Rangers rotation, with Tanner Scheppers in the bullpen, and Neftali Feliz in one or the other, with Justin Smoak at first base and hitting third, and every key member of the club's current core still under control (with the exception of Vladimir

Guerrero and C.J. Wilson, whose situations I'd vote to be addressed as the first order of Greenberg-Ryan business), would upset my stomach.

At least for the next couple days.

May 30, 2010

The Rangers have placed Nelson Cruz on the disabled list due to a strained left hamstring—notably, not the same hamstring that he strained in April to force his initial disabled list stint. Right-handed-hitting outfielder Craig Gentry has been recalled and is with the club tonight.

May 30, 2010

I'm tired of feeling overmatched and outsavvied by good, not great, teams. I'd forgotten how much I really don't care for how that feels.

I'm tired of seeing number eight and nine hitters working walks against our guys, while our 3-4-5 hitters roll over or pop out, a lot.

I'm tired of watching other teams find ways to put together sustained rallies while we kill the chance of any by running into outs.

I'm tired of envying nearly every other offense I've seen this season.

I'd be interested if someone who has more time than I have could figure out where Texas ranks in the number of innings with, say, at least seven batters sent to the plate.

It would be OK with me not to see our guys signaling whatever that overhand claw thing is back to the dugout after a bases-empty single when we're down three runs in the ninth.

I find myself wondering how things might have been different if physical and mental health issues hadn't killed deals to make Mike Lowell and Khalil Greene members of the Rangers' bench.

Texas is now 8-15 on the road, and was hitting .237/.297/.336 away from Arlington going into tonight's game. The road offense is a big bag of Nyjer Morgan (if his slump continues another day or two, that is).

I'm thinking about all those things because I don't want to think about why Derek Holland couldn't feel the ball in his hand tonight.

Another lousy day off on Monday, after which Mark Buehrle and the White Sox host Rich Harden and the Rangers.

Harden against his 2010 opposition the first time through the lineup: a slash line of .197/.352/.338.

The second time through: .224/.344/.368.

The third time through: .415/.490/.634.

(Not surprisingly, no hitter has faced him a fourth time this year.)

That convictionless report I sent out yesterday is taking firmer hold.

May 31, 2010

It's with some amount of satisfaction that I realized this morning that the draft's a week away and I've barely written a thing about it. As demoralizing as the big club's last week has been, give me a season every time in which we grumble about every pinch-hitting decision and every bullpen move and the makeup of the bench, rather than spend weeks debating on what the club is going to do in rounds one and two because the games that count have been swallowed by a surge of indifference.

The beauty of surgically examining every moment of every game, even when it's an exercise in heartburn, is that the season has given us reason to agonize over every pitch, to care about what's happening. There have been years, some not long ago, when draft speculation began to leak into the Newberg Report before Mother's Day, rather than on Memorial Day. Not this year, I'm happy to say.

Tommy Hunter goes this afternoon for Oklahoma City, putting him line to make Saturday's start against Tampa Bay if Derek Holland isn't able to take the ball that night.

As for the draft, here's a few recent projections of what Texas might do at number 15 and number 22 in the first round a week from tonight:

Jim Callis, *Baseball America* (May 28): Bryce Brentz (OF, Middle Tennessee State) and Justin O'Conner (C, Cowan [In.] HS) (*previous mock, May 14: Brentz and Ball State second baseman Kolbrin Vitek*)

Keith Law, ESPN (May 24): Brandon Workman (RHP, University of Texas) and Kellin Deglan (C, Langley (British Columbia) HS)

Jonathan Mayo, MLB.com (May 26): Kaleb Cowart (3B/RHP, Cook County [Ga.] HS) (*mock stopped at number 20*)

MLB Fanhouse (May 31): Karsten Whitson (RHP, Chipley [Fla.] HS) and Cowart (*previous mock, May 26: Workman and Cowart*)

Obviously, with six names identified in seven guesses, there's little consensus at this point on where Texas goes with its first two picks next Monday night. Things ought to zero in as we get closer, but we should also keep in mind that the Rangers (like most teams) are bunkered down right now, not taking time to whisper to writers what their board looks like.

Next week's draft is important. They all are. The Rangers wouldn't be where they are today and going forward if they hadn't killed it in the draft the last few years.

But it's still secondary to the next six against the White Sox and Rays, thankfully.

May 31, 2010

According to multiple local sources, lefthander Derek Holland has been diagnosed by team physician Dr. Keith

Meister with mild inflammation of the left rotator cuff and will be shut down for three to five days before resuming a throwing program.

The plan appears to be to place Holland on the disabled list before Tuesday's game, activating reliever Pedro Strop until Saturday's home game against Tampa Bay, when righthander Tommy Hunter would replace Strop on the staff to make that night's start in Holland's spot.

Hunter started for Oklahoma City this afternoon, giving up five runs on 10 hits and three walks in five innings, fanning two. He threw 94 pitches, 57 for strikes.

June 2010

40-MAN ROSTER (39)

Pitchers (21)

Omar Beltre, Scott Feldman, Neftali Feliz, Frankie Francisco, Rich Harden, Matt Harrison, Derek Holland, Tommy Hunter, Michael Kirkman, Colby Lewis, Doug Mathis, Brandon McCarthy, Guillermo Moscoso, Dustin Nippert, Darren O'Day, Alexi Ogando, Darren Oliver, Zach Phillips, Chris Ray, Pedro Strop, C.J. Wilson

Catchers (4)

Max Ramirez, Jarrod Saltalamacchia, Taylor Teagarden, Matt Treanor

Infielders (7)

Elvis Andrus, Joaquin Arias, Andres Blanco, Chris Davis, Ian Kinsler, Justin Smoak, Michael Young

Outfielders (7)

Brandon Boggs, Julio Borbon, Nelson Cruz, Craig Gentry, Vladimir Guerrero, Josh Hamilton, David Murphy

60-Day Disabled List (3)

Eric Hurley, Warner Madrigal, Omar Poveda

June 1, 2010

Scott Lucas had an amazing note in his farm recaps this morning, pointing out that in two of the three innings Tanner Scheppers pitched for Oklahoma City on Monday, he didn't strike out a batter—after registering at least one strikeout *in each of his first 24 innings pitched as a pro.*

Thinking about that stat while watching Rich Harden pitch tonight, it prompted me to check his game logs this season: Including tonight's game, Harden has pitched in 57 different innings as a Ranger. If you toss out the seven walkless frames in his Oakland gem a month ago, Harden has issued a walk or drilled a batter in 30 out of 50 innings (including seven of 10 *first* innings).

Not quite as stunning as the Scheppers note, but still pretty remarkable (the nicest word I can come up with).

But set Harden aside for the moment. Here's something else you should know about Scheppers.

Steve Holley of Scout.com recently spoke to RedHawks pitching coach Terry Clark (as shared by Lone Star Dugout's Jason Cole), and Clark had this to say about Scheppers: "He'll be starting within a couple of weeks. He'll go four innings (in his first start) and then next month, he'll probably go to five. That's what we all look at him as—a starter down the road."

You might have keyed in on the fact that, since his promotion to AAA a month ago, Scheppers made five straight two-inning appearances and then went three innings each of his last two times out, all outings coming on three or four days' rest.

But dig at his game logs a little deeper, and you'll see these pitch counts, in order: 31, 40, 44, 26, 49, 55, and 62.

Scheppers is still just at 27 innings for the season, a program calculated by the Rangers to (1) exercise care after he threw just 30 innings in 2009 (19 independent league innings in the spring and 11 Arizona Fall League innings in the fall) and (2) conserve his innings early so that he'll be available to help Texas late in the season rather than be shut down with games still on the schedule.

Pay attention to those pitch counts. Scheppers has been working strictly in relief, but there's more than just that Clark quote to suggest where this is headed.

Back to the bigs. Texas had no more than two hits with runners in scoring position in each of its last eight games. But tonight? Six of them. And probably not from who you expected: Ian Kinsler had a couple, but the other four? Joaquin Arias, Matt Treanor, Craig Gentry, and Justin Smoak.

Jarrod Saltalamacchia left Sunday's Oklahoma City game early with lower back spasms, but he was back in action tonight, going 0 for 4 and seeing Memphis succeed in its one stolen base attempt.

Brandon McCarthy was scheduled to throw a bullpen session in Oklahoma City today. Once activated from the disabled list (stress fracture in shoulder blade), he's expected to work out of the RedHawks bullpen.

Ben Rogers has suggested on the Ben & Skin Show and on ESPN Dallas's website that Texas ought to seriously consider trading Vladimir Guerrero this summer. I'll let you read his column to check out his reasoning, but I'll say the only way I'd think about doing that would be if (1) we were 15 games out and (2) could Casey Blake someone's Carlos Santana. Otherwise, no chance.

Frisco righthander Blake Beavan's eight wins are tied for the most in the minor leagues and are second only to Rockies righthander Ubaldo Jimenez for most in pro ball. He's leading the Texas League in innings pitched (69.2) and WHIP (0.90). The 21-year-old has fanned 45 and walked only nine, and is holding opponents to a .210 batting average with almost identical left-right splits.

If you follow me on Twitter (www.twitter.com/newbergreport), you got more of my in-game, knee-jerk thoughts on Harden than you probably cared for (though here's one I didn't include: hey, he's now 41-0 lifetime when getting at least four runs of support while in the game!). For three hours of knee-jerk fun and Q&A, stop by www.FOXSportsSouthwest.com tomorrow night for our second live Newberg Report chat session. We'll get started shortly before the first pitch of Feldman-Floyd and roll all the way until the final pitch of the game.

Out first chat a couple weeks ago was a massive success, the folks at Fox tell me. Let's step it up even further Wednesday night.

June 4, 2010

Lefties killing us
And then Vlad gets some shut-eye
(Glad Rays light from left)

When you send your 4-5-6 hitters up against a bad team's number two reliever, down one run, it shouldn't feel hopeless. But with White Sox southpaw Matt Thornton on the mound and injuries to Vladimir Guerrero and Nelson Cruz resulting in Texas having Josh Hamilton (now .234/.300/.344 against lefthanders), David Murphy (.238/.256/.310), and Justin Smoak (.056/.146/.139) in those slots, and the bench without a legitimate right-handed-hitting threat, what followed (four-pitch strikeout, five-pitch strikeout, four-pitch groundout) seemed almost inevitable.

(Texas is reportedly among the teams that have contacted Boston recently about Mike Lowell, who has asked to be traded—and who was nearly sent to the Rangers for Max Ramirez in December.)

Tampa Bay is set to send righthanders Wade Davis, James Shields, and Matt Garza to the hill for this weekend's series in Arlington, and the Rays go with

Newberg Report: Ranking the Rangers' Drafts

By Jamey Newberg / Special to MLB.com

June 3, 2010

The Rangers, who head into Monday's First-Year Player Draft with four of the first 49 picks, are an enviable position of strength for an organization that already boasts one of the deepest farm systems in baseball. The only two clubs with as many picks in the first and supplemental first rounds are the Angels (five) and Blue Jays (four).

Draft position is one thing. Making the right calls is tricky, though—moreso in baseball than in the other major pro sports. The Angels had five early picks in 2009, too, and passed over right-hander Tanner Scheppers four times before Texas gladly called his name with its second pick. As much as the Angels liked high school lefthander Tyler Skaggs (taken at No. 40 overall) and college right-hander Garrett Richards (No. 42), they'd probably like the chance to rethink their decision to pass on Scheppers, who went at No. 44 to the Rangers.

In the past 10 years, the Rangers' best Draft was arguably the one in which they had less Draft power than all but one year in the decade. You've got to scout and develop well to make the Draft pay off.

What follows is a ranking of the Rangers' past 10 Drafts.

10. 2002: Grady Fuson's first Draft as Rangers scouting director was handicapped by the club's winter signings of Chan Ho Park, Juan Gonzalez, Todd Van Poppel, and Jay Powell, costing Texas its picks in the second through fifth rounds, and leaving Fuson and his crew with just one pick (10th overall) in the Draft's first 171 spots. Eventual first-rounders Khalil Greene, Joe Saunders, Scott Kazmir, Nick Swisher, Cole Hamels, James Loney, Denard Span, Jeremy Guthrie, Jeff Francouer, Joe Blanton, and Matt Cain were all still on the board when the Rangers were on the clock, but Fuson went safe and missed, taking Drew Meyer, a curious pick and major disappointment. The Rangers' next selection, sixth-round right-hander John Connally Barnett, showed early promise but didn't have the fire to play. Right-handers Kameron Loe (20th round) and Jesse Chavez (42nd), and left-hander Sam Narron (15) were solid picks, but didn't make up for the poor showing at the top of the class.

9. 2005: When Texas took John Mayberry Jr. at No. 19 in the first round, fellow college players like Jacoby Ellsbury (No. 23) and Matt Garza (No. 25), both speculated by some to be Ranger targets, were still on the board. The Rangers' next two picks, Johnny Whittleman and Taylor Teagarden, have regressed, and so did fifth-rounder Michael Kirkman before he exploded back onto the scene in '09. Doug Mathis (13th round) and German Duran (6) have gotten to the big leagues, and Matt Nevarez (10th) and Jake Rasner (7th) have helped complete trades for immediate help. But this Draft hasn't produced an impact player.

8. 2004: First-round right-handers Thomas Diamond and Eric Hurley, each considered at one time to be the top pitching prospect in the Texas system, have had their development staggered by arm problems, serving as a reminder that you can never add enough pitching. Hurley is getting back to full health after a lost '09, while Diamond is finally knocking on the door—though with the Cubs. Several role players have reached the big leagues (Brandon Boggs [4th round], Travis Metcalf [11th], Tug Hulett [14th), and fifth-rounder Mike Nickeas was flipped for another one (outfielder Victor Diaz). Outfielder Justin Maxwell (10th) and reliever Sam Demel (35th) didn't sign and now figure into the plans for Washington and Oakland, respectively.

7. 2000: Texas missed badly with its three first-rounders—high school catcher Scott Heard, unsigned college outfielder Tyrell Godwin, and college right-hander Chad Hawkins—but hit on right-hander Nick Masset (8th round), infielder Edwin Encarnacion (9th), outfielder Laynce Nix (4th), and left-hander A.J. Murray (19th). Second-rounder Jason Bourgeois (who, with Godwin was compensation for the loss of Aaron Sele to free agency) is with his sixth organization (his hometown Houston Astros) and is making a strong push for his third big league look.

6. 2009: We're less than a year out from the '09 draft, but already a number of pitchers taken by Texas look like they lasted too long on teams' Draft boards, most notably Scheppers (supplemental first, compensation for the loss of Milton Bradley), Robbie Erlin (3rd round), Braden Tullis (8th), and Chad Bell (14th). The failure to sign the club's top pick, high school left-hander Matt Purke, was obviously a massive disappointment. Texas can salvage things a bit with its compensation pick at No. 15 on Monday, but it won't be a talent with the immediate upside the TCU freshman has.

5. 2008: First baseman Justin Smoak fell to No. 11 due to perceived bonus demands that didn't faze the Rangers. Left-hander Robbie Ross has a real chance to give Texas its first true payoff in the second round since Roger Pavlik in 1986. Fellow pitchers Joe Wieland (4th round), Richard Bleier (6th), Matt Thompson (7th), and Corey Young (12th) have gotten off to very good pro starts, and relievers Trevor Hurley (22nd) and Cody Eppley (43rd) have emerged this season as prospects.

4. 2007: The firepower Texas had in the '07 draft is part of what inspired the decision to tear things down—starting with the Mark Teixeira trade—and build through scouting and development. The loss of Carlos Lee to free agency produced right-hander Blake Beavan and outfielder Julio Borbon. The loss of Mark DeRosa turned into right-hander Tommy Hunter. The loss of Gary Matthews Jr. produced right-handers Michael Main and Neil Ramirez. Texas also found corner hitter Mitch Moreland and right-handers Josh Lueke and Ryan Tatusko in the 16th thru 18th rounds. Outfielder Tim Smith (7th round) became a tradeable commodity and reliever Evan Reed (3rd) has a chance. Imagine if the Rangers had popped Rick Porcello in the first round (rather than Beavan or Main), if they hadn't signed Frank Catalanotto (which cost the club pick No. 16), or if they'd managed to sign Anthony Ranaudo (11th) and/or Drew Pomeranz (12th), both of whom are slated to be first-rounders Monday. It was a sensational job by Ron Hopkins and his crew at targeting top talent throughout this Draft.

3. 2006: Would Kyle Drabek have been a better pick at No. 12 overall than Kasey Kiker? It certainly looks that way now. It probably would have never come down to that reported choice if Clayton Kershaw (7th overall), Tim Lincecum (10th), or Max Scherzer (11th) fell to Texas. The Rangers did well in several later rounds, finding eventual big leaguers Derek Holland in the 25th round, Chris Davis in the fifth, Craig Gentry in the 10th, and Danny Ray Herrera (sent to the Reds in the Josh Hamilton-Edinson Volquez trade) in the 45th, plus Miguel Velazquez (one of the club's top position player prospects) in the 19th round and left-hander Michael Ballard in the 14th. A number of others have a chance as well, including Chad Tracy (3rd), Marcus Lemon (4th), Jake Brigham (6th), and Brennan Garr (9th). Left-hander Cory Luebke (22nd) got away—he was a San Diego supplemental first-rounder the next year and is now among the Padres' top pitching prospects.

2. 2003: Fuson's second Rangers Draft was far better than his first. The club's 2003 class has produced one All-Star (Ian Kinsler, 17th round) and two pitchers who have had stretches in which they were among the best in the American League (John Danks, 1st round; Scott Feldman, 30th round). Wes Littleton (4th) had a brief run of success. Vincent Sinisi (2nd) and John Hudgins (3rd) didn't live up to their college promise and were eventually traded to Fuson's Padres for journeyman outfielder Freddy Guzman. Emerson Frostad (13th) and Adam Fox (10th) played important, if underappreciated, roles as organizational soldiers at the upper levels. High school right-hander Brad Lincoln (28) didn't sign; three years later he was the fourth overall pick in the Draft, taken by the Pirates.

1. 2001: Tim Hallgren's lone Draft as Rangers scouting director (following Chuck McMichael and preceding Fuson) produced only one more big leaguer than "Bachelorette" contestants, but the two who have played in the Major Leagues were outstanding Draft picsk: Teixeira in the first round (fifth overall) and C.J. Wilson in the fifth round. (The club's second- and third-round picks were forfeited due to the signings of Alex Rodriguez and Mark Petkovsek.) Incidentally, 14th-round right-hander Chris Bradshaw was eliminated in Week 2 of Season 4 of the "Bachelorette"—according to Wikipedia.

only one lefty in the pen (the mediocre Randy Choate). That's good. But this lineup, just league-average even with Guerrero's and Cruz's production, is a lot easier to gameplan without those two. Guerrero is supposed to be good to go sometime this series. Hope he's seeing the ball well.

After these three with Tampa Bay, Seattle comes to town, sending southpaw Cliff Lee to the mound Monday night. Sometime in the first inning, as Lee faces the top of the Rangers' order, or minutes thereafter, Texas will be on the clock for the first of its four first- and supplemental first-round picks in this year's amateur draft. On Monday we ran down a bunch of mock drafts projecting what the Rangers will do with the 15th and 22nd picks, and since then there have been a few updated guesses:

Kevin Goldstein, Baseball Prospectus (June 3): Asher Wojchiechowski (RHP, The Citadel) and Justin O'Conner (C, Cowan [In.] HS)

Baseball America (June 3: not really a mock but instead the musings of various *BA* draft experts as to what they would do if in charge of the picks): Stetson Allie (RHP, St. Edward [Oh.] HS) (pick made by editor John Manuel) and Nick Castellanos (3B, Archbishop McCarthy [Fla.] HS) (pick made by assistant editor Conor Glassey) *(previous mocks: May 28/executive editor Jim Callis: Bryce Brentz (OF, Middle Tennessee State) and O'Conner; May 14/ Callis: Brentz and Ball State second baseman Kolbrin Vitek)*

Keith Law, ESPN (May 31): Kellin Deglan (C, R.E. Mountain Secondary School (British Columbia)) and Kaleb Cowart (3B/RHP, Cook County [Ga.] HS) *(previous mock, May 24: Brandon Workman (RHP, University of Texas) and Deglan)*

Jonathan Mayo, MLB.com (June 2): Workman and O'Conner *(previous mock, May 26: Cowart (mock stopped at number 20))*

Jon Heyman, *Sports Illustrated* (June 2): Yasmani Grandal (C, University of Miami) and Vitek

Jon Daniels said yesterday that most of the players Texas likes at the unprotected number 15 pick, based strictly on talent, are not signability risks. He also said that the Rangers are not limited to slot by MLB while the bankruptcy proceedings are pending. The club is bound instead by its draft budget, which contains flexibility to go over slot.

For Scott Lucas's sake, I hope Texas doesn't pop Wojchiechowski and Illinois high school righthander Mike Foltynewicz Monday night.

According to initial reports, Derek Holland doesn't have thoracic outlet syndrome.

The Rangers' 9-5 win in Chicago on Wednesday was the club's first road win without a save all year. Only twice have they won a road game by as much as a four-run margin. Crazy.

Updating an incredible stat that T.R. Sullivan ran out there earlier this week: number nine hitters are hitting .312 off Rangers pitching this season. No other spot in the lineup is hitting over .289 against Texas.

According to MLB Fangraphs, the best slider in baseball right now (in terms of "pitch value") belongs not to Carlos Marmol or Francisco Liriano or Clayton Kershaw, but to Rangers righthander Colby Lewis.

There were rumors that the Rays considered designating catcher Dioner Navarro for assignment once Kelly Shoppach was activated yesterday, but instead the club placed shortstop Jason Bartlett on the disabled list.

ESPN's Buster Olney speculates that once Arizona catcher Miguel Montero returns to action, the Diamondbacks could shop Chris Snyder, with Texas a possible match (a sentiment shared by Baseball Prospectus's John Perrotto).

Ken Rosenthal of Fox Sports suggests Cleveland's Russell Branyan would be a better trade fit for Texas than Chicago's Paul Konerko, should the club seek a stopgap first baseman. Maybe, but I'd prefer a right-handed hitter.

Oakland designated righthander Edwar Ramirez for assignment. The San Angelo Colts of the independent United League signed righthander Ezequiel Astacio. The Chico Outlaws of the independent Golden Baseball League signed lefthander Matt Perisho. The New Jersey Jackals of the independent Can-Am League traded infielder Enrique Cruz to the Southern Maryland Blue Crabs of the independent Atlantic League.

R.A. Dickey has a 2.84 ERA in three Mets starts. Kameron Loe has two scoreless appearances out of the Milwaukee bullpen. Casey Daigle has two scoreless appearances out of the Houston bullpen.

And Joaquin Benoit is up to 12 scoreless appearances out of the Rays pen. Eleven dominant innings: two hits, two walks, 15 strikeouts.

We'll probably see Benoit in a critical eighth-inning spot at some point this weekend.

I hope it's with Vladimir Guerrero at the plate.

June 5, 2010

In spite of a really frustrating sixth and seventh last night on the mound, the line score shows only a one for Tampa Bay in each of those two innings, and another night of big production out of the maligned Rangers bottom third (seven hits, including a home run, 2 for 2 with runners in scoring position, one walk, one strikeout, and Max Ramirez with the club's highest pitches per at-bat number for the night) helped push Texas to a solid win against a very good team, getting this series and homestand off to a good start.

I've seen most of Josh Hamilton's at-bats this year, and I can't believe this is true:

His slash line of .300/.348/.529 is remarkably close to his line of .304/.371/.530 in his storybook 2008 season, a year in which he finished seventh in the MVP vote.

And not terribly inferior to Vladimir Guerrero's .333/.364/.557.

It sure doesn't seem like it.

Somehow, even though Texas piled up 13 hits and two walks and two hit batsmen, Tampa Bay needed only 116 pitches to complete eight innings. (The Rangers threw 178 pitches over nine.)

Ian Kinsler saw nine pitches in four plate appearances.

Someone asked me during Wednesday night's in-game chat session who my favorite Rangers player was growing up. If I were a kid right now, there's no question who it would be, and even as a 41-year-old, I think I might be accepting that Elvis Andrus is, over all these years, my favorite Rangers player ever. And he's going to get better.

The Rangers will likely option reliever Pedro Strop to Oklahoma City before today's game, clearing a roster spot for righthander Tommy Hunter to make the start.

Texas activated righthander Warner Madrigal from the 60-day disabled list and optioned him to Frisco. The club's 40-man roster is once again full.

The Rangers also activated righthander Brandon McCarthy from the disabled list (stress fracture, shoulder) and will work him out of the RedHawks bullpen.

The Rangers traded AAA reliever Jailen Peguero to Houston for future considerations to thin the Oklahoma City bullpen herd.

Frisco lefthander Martin Perez was placed on the disabled list with a cracked fingernail.

Cleveland designated righthander Jamey Wright for assignment, and the Mets did the same with Gary Matthews Jr., whose departure from Texas three and a half years ago for the five-year, $50 million Angels contract he's still living off of awarded the Rangers two compensatory draft picks that they turned into Blake Beavan and Julio Borbon.

As far as this year's draft is concerned, here are a couple more updated projections on what Texas will do Monday night with its picks at number 15 and number 22:

Jim Callis, *Baseball America* (June 4): Asher Wojchiechowski (RHP, The Citadel) and Bryce Brentz (OF, Middle Tennessee State) (*previous mocks: June 3 [fellow* BA *experts John Manuel and Conor Glassey]: Stetson Allie [RHP, St. Edward (Oh.) HS] and Nick Castellanos [3B, Archbishop McCarthy (Fla.) HS]; May 28: Brentz and Justin O'Conner [C, Cowan (In.) HS]; May 14: Brentz and Kolbrin Vitek [2B, Ball State]*)

Keith Law, ESPN (June 4): Delino DeShields Jr. (CF, Woodward Academy [Ga.] HS) and Brandon Workman (RHP, University of Texas) (*previous mocks: May 31: Kellin Deglan [C, R.E. Mountain Secondary School (British Columbia)] and Kaleb Cowart [3B/RHP, Cook County (Ga.) HS]; May 24: Workman and Deglan*)

Here's the thing. Several super-respectable writers who do their homework have, in the last two or three weeks, pegged (alphabetically) Allie, Brentz, Castellanos, Cowart, Deglan, DeShields, University of Miami catcher Yasmani Grandal, O'Conner, Vitek, Florida high school righthander Karsten Whitson, Wojchiechowski, and Workman as their projected picks in the Rangers' two first-round slots.

The reason the projections are all over the place is twofold: (1) the Rangers are historically discreet about their draft intentions; and (2) the first half of the first round seems to be unusually hard to peg this year, throwing mocks into disarray. The Rangers certainly have the 12 players mentioned above whiteboarded in some order in their 1000 Ballpark Way war room, but when everything past the top overall pick is still unclear days before the draft, it's fairly crazy to expect writers to have a good bead on what will happen at 15 and 22.

Not all of those 12 players will be around when Texas picks at number 15, but some will, and the Rangers will be prepared to take whichever one is highest on their board. Four years ago, they knew Clayton Kershaw wouldn't be around when their pick at number 12 came up, but there were several other pitchers they knew would still be on the board.

I wrote this hours before that 2006 draft:

Baseball America's Jim Callis predicts this morning that [Tim] Lincecum, the small fireballer who many project as a dominating closer but who some insist will be able to start in the big leagues, will be the Texas pick. MLB's Jonathan Mayo speculates that it will be [Kyle] Drabek, who is the most talented pitcher in the draft by most accounts—and yet every story about him this spring hasn't gotten to paragraph two without mention of his makeup issues. CNN/SI's Bryan Smith thinks the Rangers will end up with [Max] Scherzer, whose stock has dropped, possibly because of shoulder concerns.

Lincecum went 10th. Scherzer went 11th. Drabek was still on the board (and would be until the 18th pick) when Texas chose Kasey Kiker at 12.

You can bet that Texas would be thrilled to end up with any number of the names that include Allie, Brentz, Castellanos, Cowart, Deglan, DeShields, Grandal (who now appears to be locked in at number four to Kansas City), O'Conner, Vitek, Whitson, Wojchiechowski, and Workman, and that the club probably has other names ranked higher who will be available at 15. The baseball draft is more difficult to project than the NFL or NBA versions, both because of a much larger pool and because drafted players don't go straight to the big leagues and thus are typically drafted less on perceived need than in football or basketball, and so it's not unusual for mock drafts from expert observers to differ greatly from one another, and for any one writer's projections to change routinely leading up to Draft Day.

Jim Callis's legendary 2005 mock draft was dead on for the first 18 picks before Texas chose John Mayberry Jr. (rather than Callis's pick, ASU outfielder Travis Buck) at number 19. Callis didn't have Mayberry going in his first 48 picks (covering the first round and supplemental first). Callis is very good.

When you see a guy like Callis changing his Rangers projection the way he has the past few weeks—Brentz and Vitek on May 14, Brentz and O'Conner on May 28, and Wojchiechowski and Brentz yesterday—you know there are lots of moving targets in this draft, at least outside the war rooms, that probably aren't done shifting around.

But in the meantime, there's Hunter-James Shields today and Rich Harden-Matt Garza tomorrow, two afternoon games pitting teams trying to protect one- and two-game division leads against each other. That's the bigger story, and the draft, as it should be, will just have to wait.

June 5, 2010

Not long ago, out of a discussion I had with a couple friends, one of whom is not irrationally dependent on sports the way I am, came this question: "Would you rather watch an intense, memorable 5-4 Rangers loss that ended in a way you'll never forget, or miss a mundane 6-2 Rangers win and hear about it on the news?"

The answer was easy for me—unquestionably the latter—yet tough for him to comprehend.

Today was a perfect example.

Max's Little League game started at the same time as Texas-Tampa Bay, and as a result we only caught the last two innings on TV. So I didn't see much of Tommy Hunter's 9-5-1-1-0-4, and only a fraction of his 117 pitches (76 strikes). And I'm totally fine with that.

Before landing in Texas, Tampa Bay was 21-6 on the road this season. The Rays had played nine road series, and lost only one (when they dropped two of three to Oakland a month ago, in a series that included Dallas Braden's perfect game). They're going to lose this one, too, needing to take tomorrow's series finale in order to stave off what would be just their second sweep of the season (having dropped three at home to Boston a week and a half ago).

Wins like today's—even if you didn't see it—are adrenaline boosts, games where the offense stepped up and so did the pitching, and where the starting pitcher saved the bullpen, not an insignificant fact in a day game after a night game, not to mention in heat that apparently registered at more than 110 degrees on the playing surface. Only Chris Ray (in the 7th or 8th and again in the 9th) and Neftali Feliz (in the 9th) even got out of their seats to get loose (which doesn't count Feliz's grab of Josh Hamilton's 11th home run, which despite three ensuing hitless at-bats lifted his slug to .537, which is higher than the .530 he put together in his memorable 2008 season). Hunter shot down any thought of having anyone come take the ball from him, needing just 10 pitches in the 7th, 10 more in the 8th, and 11 in the 9th (despite an error that extended the game by one extra hitter) to shut things down.

Tommy Hunter was *big* today. As was Max Ramirez, whose work behind the plate this afternoon—if not these five weeks—shouldn't be neglected. Can we start asking whether Ramirez (who is hitting .262/.360/.429) should be considered any more of a placeholder than Hunter, whose 2010 big league debut was just tremendous? I understand that Jarrod Saltalamacchia is probably back soon, and I'm in no mood to let Matt Treanor go, but at this point it sure seems that Ramirez's right-handed bat would do the bench a lot more good than having Joaquin Arias around. It's not as if Arias can do anything defensively that Andres Blanco and Ramirez can't do better.

That was a masterpiece today. Anytime a pitcher and catcher can execute like that and give the bullpen a day to kick back and watch, I'm happy—even if I didn't get the chance to do the same.

June 7, 2010

I realized yesterday that Matt Treanor and I have two things in common, neither of which has anything to do with volleyball, and neither of which I'd expect anyone to know, so don't even bother guessing. I'm dropping this into the book just as a shout-out to a very small number of people.

The next report will hold a much more useful place in the book, as tonight the 2010 Major League Baseball First-Year Player Draft gets underway. The league will conduct the first and supplemental first rounds tonight, televised on MLB Network, whose studio crew will include the great Peter Gammons (along with draft experts Jonathan Mayo and *Baseball America*'s **Jim Callis, plus John Hart, Harold Reynolds, and Greg Amsinger**).

Texas selects at 15 (the unprotected pick awarded as compensation for the club's failure to sign high school lefthander Matt Purke a year ago), 22 (its own pick), 45 (compensation for the loss of Marlon Byrd via free agency), and 49 (compensation for the loss of Ivan Rodriguez via free agency).

An unidentified NL general manager was surely speaking hyperbolically when he said to Gammons regarding the quality of the draft pool after catcher Bryce Harper, shortstop Manny Machado, and righthander Jameson Taillon: "After that, there's virtually no difference between the fourth and 44th picks." Don't turn the TV off before the Rangers' picks at 45 and 49. While the 2010 draft class may not be as deep as those of 2007 and 2009, Texas popped Tommy Hunter with the 54th pick three years ago, and Tanner Scheppers with the 44th pick last summer.

The news was better on Saturday for Hunter, who threw the game of his life in Arlington, than it was for Scheppers, who landed on the seven-day AAA disabled list with a minor left hamstring strain, but on Draft Day they're reminders that the supplemental first round, in a sport where the draft class includes both college and high school players, is critical.

The Rangers had the opportunity to take Hunter in 2007 because they couldn't keep Mark DeRosa the winter before, and to take Scheppers in 2009 because they'd let Milton Bradley find work elsewhere, taking differing degrees of risk offering salary arbitration to each. Good scouting and an aggressive front office plan factored in, and now those two 23-year-old righthanders are key parts of this club's future, while DeRosa is on his fourth team since leaving Texas, Bradley his second.

According to one local report, despite the constraints in place with the sale of the team in limbo as bankruptcy proceedings continue, the draft budget that the Rangers submitted to and had approved by the league over the winter has in it between $1 million and $2 million for the organization to use to pay over slot to its draft class if it so chooses. Because the pick at 15, as compensation for last year's non-signing of Purke, carries no 2011 compensation should it not convert this year, the likelihood is that the Texas may get more aggressive with a signability risk at 22 or 45 or 49.

If you're one of those relied on to forward Newberg Report email news flashes to friends, today's a good day to tell them to sign up for the reports themselves. We'll send flashes out tonight as the Rangers' first four picks are made. The estimate is that Texas will make its pick at 15 at about 7:30 Central, and at 22 at around 8:05. Once the first round ends, the picks in the supplemental first will be announced at one-minute intervals.

Rounds 2-30 will be conducted tomorrow, and rounds 31-50 will take place on Wednesday, both starting at 10:00 a.m. But the big impact stands to come tonight, when the Rangers' four picks will keep them busier than any organization other than the Angels (five) and Blue Jays (four).

As you're watching former 30th-rounder Scott Feldman take on former fourth-rounder Cliff Lee tonight, keep an eye on your email for news flashes and Twitter blasts (@NewbergReport and @scottrlucas) on each of the Rangers' Monday selections.

June 7, 2010

The historically on-target Jim Callis of *Baseball America* has introduced a new name at pick number 15, speculating this morning that Georgia high school outfielder Jake Skole could be the Rangers' first pick (15th overall) in tonight's draft. Skole is a Georgia Tech football commit, and there's a wrinkle there worth noting: I believe that his football scholarship would permit his drafting club to spread his signing bonus out over five years, which could be a plus in the Rangers' situation, particularly if it would take an over-slot offer to sign him.

Interestingly, Callis has University of Miami catcher Yasmani Grandal going not to Kansas City at number 4, reported by many this weekend as a prearranged deal, but to Tampa Bay at number 17. Grandal presumably fits somewhere on the Rangers' board.

Callis continues to peg Middle Tennessee State outfielder Bryce Brentz as the Rangers' pick at number 22.

June 7, 2010

If you were the Diamondbacks and had the first pick in each round of the 2005 draft, you could have taken these players, limited in hindsight solely to the players who eventually went in each of the first 20 rounds:

1. Ryan Braun
2. Yunel Escobar
3. Brett Gardner
4. Brian Matusz
5. Michael Kirkman
6. Doug Fister
7. Michael Brantley
8. Austin Jackson
9. Mark Wagner
10. Josh Outman
11. John Lannan
12. Matt Joyce
13. Josh Thole
14. Pedro Alvarez
15. Alex Hinshaw
16. Andrew Bailey
17. James Russell
18. Desmond Jennings
19. Ike Davis
20. Andrew Cashner

For good measure, you could have taken Tommy Hanson in the 22nd round, Tyler Flowers in the 33rd, Chris Davis in the 35th, a skinny college sophomore-eligible pitcher named Tim Lincecum in the 42nd, and a high school righthander (whom you might have envisioned as a catcher) named Buster Posey in the 50th and final round.

We're half an hour from go time, and among the experts there's almost as little certainty as to what Texas will do at 15 and 22 as there is in Round 42, when five years ago Cleveland chose Lincecum but didn't sign him, or Round 50, when the Angels used the draft's 1,496th pick on Posey but didn't lure him from his commitment to Florida State.

OK, maybe that's an exaggeration. But even in the latest mock drafts posted by seven different respectable outlets, some of which have been published in the last hour or two, I count 12 different players who have been pegged as going to Texas at 15 or 22. I can't remember a crazier, more unpredictable first round, at least outside the war rooms.

Stay tuned for instant news flashes from Scott Lucas tonight, once the Rangers announce their selections at picks 15, 22, 45, and 49.

June 8, 2010

You can look at the top of the Rangers' 2010 draft class in one of two ways.

You can fixate on the fact that the club's picks at 15, 22, 45, and 49 were ranked by *Baseball America*, two weeks ago, as (respectively) unranked, 51st, 126th, and 98th in the publication's assessment of the draft's top 200 prospects.

Or you can note that the Rangers' first three picks were each speculated at some point in the week leading up to the draft by either Jim Callis of *BA*, Jonathan Mayo of MLB.com, or Keith Law of ESPN to be the Rangers' first overall selection at 15, and that two of the players were considered to be riding the most helium on draft boards in the last couple weeks.

You can view the apparent fact that, according to several sources overnight, the Rangers were on the verge of coming to terms with their first two picks—at slot or lower—as a sign that (1) they were overdrafted strictly because of their signability, or (2) the Rangers have gotten off to a great start by locking down those two down, giving them some cost certainty as they head into the remaining 49 rounds without having dipped into the $1-2 million pad they have budgeted for going over slot throughout the draft class.

Is outfielder-defensive back Jake Skole the next Grady Sizemore? Or the next K.C. Herren?

Can Kellin Deglan buck the odds at the most difficult position to draft well at (as Peter Gammons wrote on Saturday: "The 35-year history of the Draft is lined with monumental mistakes selecting catchers")?

Is flamethrowing Florida righthander Luke Jackson the next Eric Hurley? Or the next Shane Funk?

With several high-profile pitchers still on the board, and Tommy Mendonca a year into his pro career, was the selection of Mike Olt a duplicative shot taken on a power/defense third baseman with hit tool questions, or a worthwhile effort to add another slug prospect to a system relatively thin in that area?

In the baseball draft, there are often more than just two sides to every coin, particularly before the players even get on a plane. This year that feels more true than usual, compared with recent drafts that had a Justin Smoak or Tanner Scheppers to wrap our arms around instantly, or even a signability decision like Rick Porcello or Matt Purke to get the talk shows fired up about. In spite of the Rangers' firepower (four of the first 49 picks) and handicap (budgetary issues reportedly handcuffing the club more than in recent drafts), most experts probably won't single Texas out—at least through the first and supplemental first rounds—on a short list of the winners or the losers around the league.

It's always wise to adopt a "time will tell" attitude on any baseball draft, but with the top of this Rangers class, it seems almost obligatory. Even without a Smoak or Porcello story to get in the way of a good Tony Romo golf segment on local radio this morning, any or all of the Rangers' four picks last night could end up factoring in heavily to the big picture—or all four could disappoint.

The Rangers' four Day One selections:

1 (*15th overall, pick awarded for failure to sign 2009 1st-rounder Matt Purke*). **JAKE SKOLE, OF, Blessed Trinity High School** (**Ga.**) (scout: Ryan Coe)

(*last year's first-round pick: Matt Purke; recent Rangers first-round picks include Justin Smoak, Blake Beavan, Michael Main, Kasey Kiker, Thomas Diamond, Mark Teixeira, John Danks, Carlos Pena; best number 15 pick in last 25 years: Chase Utley [Phillies, 2000]*)

Jake Skole, safety prospect.

In football, at least.

In baseball? Maybe not.

Georgia Tech wanted Skole as a defensive back, offering the First-Team All-State selection a full scholarship to play safety for the Ramblin' Wreck as well as an invitation to walk onto the baseball squad in the spring, where he'd be teammates with his brother Matt, an All-Conference third baseman who just completed his sophomore season at the school.

But was his selection by the Rangers last night a safe one? Judging by his placement (if at all) on the various mock drafts published the last few weeks, and by his reportedly imminent agreement to a signing bonus at or near slot, you might think so.

The Rangers deny it.

First-year scout Ryan Coe, who joined the Rangers in October after coaching at Kennesaw State University for 12 years (he had former Ranger Jason Jones in 1998-99), got to know the Skole family when Jake was 12 years old. There were scouts around the league in on Skole when the 2010 season began, but none probably had a book on the kid like Coe, who also coached him in summer camps.

Before Skole's high school senior season got underway, he was nowhere to be found in *BA*'s pre-season ranking of the top 100 high school draft prospects, or the top 20 outfielders. When he then tore ligaments in his ankle three games into the season, getting tangled up with the opposing first baseman as he was trying to beat out a bunt, he presumably fell off the radar for a lot of clubs, and certainly the industry publications. The injury cost Skole nearly two months of action and, combined with what was thought to be a solid commitment to the Georgia Tech football program, much play during most of the mock draft season.

But he returned in time for Blessed Trinity's two-week playoff run, and in six games he hit .452 with six home runs and 21 RBI. In what would be his final high school game, on May 24 in the Georgia Class AA semifinals, Skole went 2 for 3 off of Cook County High School righthander Kaleb Cowart, whose 97-mph fastball helped make him the Angels' top pick last night, 18th overall. Skole singled and doubled off Cowart, barreling the ball both times, and suddenly his name started showing up on mock drafts and in blog write-ups. If anything, it might have forced Texas to think of Skole with the 15th pick—assuming he lasted that long (*BA*'s Jim Callis wrote on Friday that Toronto at number 11 was "one of a few clubs in on [the] fast-rising" outfielder, and John Sickels suggested that Tampa Bay had strong interest at number 17)—rather than waiting to use a later pick on him.

But regardless of where Skole thought he might go before his late May high school heroics, he's apparently not inflating his price to the point at which negotiations could drag on into nervous territory (as the 15th pick, which was compensation for last year's unconverted Matt Purke selection, would leave Texas empty-handed and without any 2011 compensation if the club failed to get a deal done by August 16 [unless the pick were a college senior]). Skole has reportedly already called Georgia Tech football coach Paul Johnson to tell him he's not coming to school, and an agreement with the Rangers could come this week, putting Skole in line to be in uniform when the short-season leagues kick off later this month, assuming his ankle is ready to go.

The Rangers will administer a physical before finalizing any deal, but they're confident that the ankle is fine. Both sides are evidently prepared to agree to something in the range of a slotted signing bonus (which would presumably fall just short of $2 million). This won't be like the Yankees' negotiations five years ago with fellow two-sport Georgia Tech recruit Austin Jackson, who turned pro out of Denton Ryan High School for a reported $800,000, which was a record figure for an eighth-round pick.

Incidentally, Skole won't need to actually play college football for the five-year amortized bonus we discussed yesterday to be available. The league has to approve the five-year option for two-sport players, and apparently it's a near-certainty for players like Skole with demonstrable two-sport opportunities, even if they never play the second sport.

A left-handed hitter who stands 6'1", 188, Skole has shown raw power and good bat speed, though he's had difficulty with offspeed pitches. A tremendous athlete who has been timed at 3.79 to first and 6.54 in the 60, he's generally graded as a corner outfielder but the Rangers believe he can handle center field. The future power grade and plus arm belie the occasional Johnny Damon comps, and though he might not profile as complete a player as Grady Sizemore, that name does come up, and not just because of the defensive back background.

As Skole develops, a J.D. Drew type of ceiling might make more sense than a Damon upside, especially once the organization gets to work on his swing mechanics. (And on that point, don't be surprised or discouraged if Skole shows very little punch for a month or so. The Rangers typically allow a first-year player 75 or 100 at-bats before they start to modify his approach—unless he asks for help sooner. For reference, in past Newberg Reports there are well-documented stories about how the club handled Chris Davis and Tommy Mendonca in their draft years.)

Baseball Prospectus minor league expert Kevin Goldstein's comment moments after the pick was straightforward: "Skole is brilliant at 15. Tons of tools and signable at 15. Just fantastic."

The Rangers insist that while the signability factor is a plus, they chose Skole because he was at the top of their board when pick number 15 came up. Now, does that mean Zack Cox and Stetson Allie, for instance, weren't on the board at all given their anticipated bonus demands and the unprotected nature of the pick, or did Texas simply prefer Skole from a talent standpoint? We won't know that answer, just as we didn't for years regarding Minnesota's choice of local prep Joe Mauer over Mark Prior and Mark Teixeira at the top of the 2001 draft, a decision that was widely characterized then as a signability concession.

Does Skole, who fairly or not will be inextricably linked to Purke (just as Scheppers and Milton Bradley are connected), have Purke's upside? At this point, no scout would say yes to that question. But was Skole a signability pick?

The Rangers say he wasn't. But the willingness to sign quickly does mean we ought to start finding out about him right away, and that's something we can all look forward to.

1 (*22nd overall*). KELLIN DEGLAN, C, R.E. Mountain Secondary School (B.C., Canada) (scout: Gary McGraw)

(*best number 22 pick in last 25 years: Rafael Palmeiro [Cubs, 1985]*)

Just two years ago, Texas was thought to have more depth at catcher than it knew what to do with. Every national columnist was speculating as to which blue-chip pitching prospects around the league Texas would be able to choose from by trading one if not two or three of Gerald Laird, Jarrod Saltalamacchia, Taylor Teagarden, and Max Ramirez.

Daniels, rightfully so, said before the 2008 season: "Catching certainly is the strength of our organization. We'll just let it play out. . . . Some people may look at it as a logjam or that we have decisions to make, but I look at it as you can't have enough of a good thing."

Today, Laird is gone, Saltalamacchia and Teagarden are wearing AAA and AA uniforms, and Ramirez is in Texas, backing up a 34-year-old journeyman getting the first chance of his career to be a frontline backstop.

Catching is hard to develop. And risky to invest in. But the Rangers have seen as much of Kellin Deglan as any club, and they believe he has a chance to be a tremendous asset, both at the plate and behind it.

A product of a British Columbia high school that has no baseball program, Deglan (who turned 18 last week) played for the Langley Blaze of the wood bat British Columbia Premier Baseball League (which counts Rich Harden, Justin Morneau, and Ryan Dempster as alums) as well as Canada's junior national team, which traveled to the Dominican Summer League in May and faced clubs that included the Rangers' Dominican affiliate. His club also toured Arizona in March, passing through Surprise at one point. (Deglan also spent a week living and working out with Morneau this winter.)

Big at 6'2", 200 but considered athletic for the position, Deglan throws well and shows a feel for the game. He has good hands and quick feet, logging pop times at or just under two seconds. The left-handed hitter flashes plus power, and scouts believe he will compete with the bat, though as with most catchers, patience will be required. Those makeup and leadership buzzwords will pop up with Deglan, too, which of course is probably as important for catchers as any other position.

Deglan's commitment to Florida International is moot, as he has reportedly already agreed to a below-slot signing bonus of $1 million, pending a physical later this week.

The Rangers system now boasts catching prospects from Venezuela (Tomas Telis and Leonel De Los Santos), Mexico (Jose Felix), Australia (Guy Edmonds), New Jersey (Vin DiFazio), Colombia (Jorge Alfaro), and British Columbia (Deglan). (Prediction: Texas drafts Columbia University catcher Dean Forthun in the 50th round tomorrow. Not really.)

Would it have made more sense for Texas to roll the dice at number 22 on a riskier over-slot player like Cox or Allie or Anthony Ranaudo or Zach Lee, since a failure to come to terms with the player would have meant extra money to allocate to other picks (or July 2 international free agents) and an extra first-round pick next year, when presumably the budgetary constraints will be less onerous? Surely it was an option the front office discussed, which must mean they love what Deglan brings to the system and had no interest in forgoing the chance to add him to the fold just to strengthen other parts of the draft or the budget in Latin America.

Especially when he was willing to sign for less than slot, which will help with the rest of the draft and on July 2 without deferring the pick for 12 months and losing that year of development.

1-Supp *(45, pick awarded for loss of Marlon Byrd).* **LUKE JACKSON, RHP, Calvary Christian Academy HS (Fla.)** (scout: Juan Alvarez)

(last year's supplemental first-round pick: Tanner Scheppers; past Rangers supplemental first-round picks include Julio Borbon, Tommy Hunter, Neil Ramirez, Colby Lewis, Chad Hawkins; best number 45 pick in last 25 years: Gerald Laird [Athletics, 1998])

Like Skole, Luke Jackson was a late riser, figuring in last month as a possible third- or fourth-rounder before showing up yesterday as a "strong" possibility for the Rangers at 15 or 22 (both according to Law) or as Florida's choice at 23 (Callis). It's not clear how easy a sign he'll be, as he has a commitment to pitch for the University of Miami in the bag, though he has suggested he's motivated to turn pro.

Jackson, a prep soccer player who didn't play baseball year-round and who didn't take up pitching at all until the ninth grade, sat 91-94 with late life for scouts all spring, touching 96 late in the season (up from 87-91 a year ago). His arm action is clean and at 6'2", 180 scouts believe there's projection for more (and for workhorse durability), but inconsistency with his 12-to-6 curve and changeup kept him from sitting in the same pre-draft tier as fellow Florida prep pitchers Karsten Whitson and A.J. Cole—though Cole remains on the board this morning, while Texas made sure Jackson didn't get out of the supplemental first round.

The 18-year-old went 8-0, 0.90 with two saves in 10 starts (including three shutouts) and four relief appearances for Calvary Christian this spring. In 54.2 innings, he scattered 30 hits (.155 opponents' average) and 19 walks while setting 87 hitters down on strikes. He drilled seven hitters and yielded one home run. At the plate, Jackson hit .308/.396/.436 in 78 at-bats, going deep twice and driving in 22 runs. Interestingly, he also committed 12 errors (five on days he pitched).

There's objectively less pressure to convert on this pick since it came in the supplemental first round rather than the standard first, but the last two times Texas has had supplemental firsts, they've turned out to be the key picks from those drafts. Last year, Scheppers fronted the draft class (with first-rounder Matt Purke not signing). In 2007, two of the club's three supplemental firsts—Julio Borbon and Tommy Hunter—have paid off sooner than first-rounders Blake Beavan and Michael Main, predictably so given their relative stages of development when drafted.

Jackson won't fit into either category—he won't follow first-rounders who fail to sign and he's not clearly further along developmentally than the Rangers' top two picks—but there's no reason to assume the Rangers don't have hopes just as high for the one pitcher they took on Monday as for the other three players they selected.

1-Supp (*49, pick awarded for loss of Ivan Rodriguez*). **MIKE OLT, 3B, Univ. of Connecticut** (scout: Jay Heafner)

(*best number 49 pick in last 25 years: Carlos Beltran [Royals, 1995]*)

Tremendous raw power and premium defense at third base. Sound familiar?

The Rangers used a second-round pick last year (62nd overall) on Fresno State third baseman Tommy Mendonca, who profiles in much the same way that University of Connecticut third baseman Mike Olt does.

Olt comes to the Rangers having just set UConn's all-time home run record with 44—eclipsing the 43 that Jason Grabowski, the Rangers' second-round pick in 1997, hit for the Huskies—but it's his defense that *Baseball America* tabbed as third-best in the draft (at any position) and that Director of Amateur Scouting Kip Fagg wanted to talk about last night: "We feel like [Olt] is a premium defender at third base," said Fagg. "He profiles as a power bat, but his strength is big-time defense."

Texas has spent early picks on third basemen with some regularity the last few years, but Johnny Whittleman (second round, 2005) and Matt West (second round, 2007) and Mendonca have each had their share of struggles. In a system short on productive corner bats, Olt will get a chance to establish himself as a reliable defensive player whose bat will play at third.

Olt played shortstop as a freshman at Connecticut, hitting .318 with 13 home runs and setting a school record with 61 RBI. He was named the top prospect in the New England Collegiate League the following summer and then hit .301 (eight homers and 40 RBI) as a sophomore, missing a third of the season with ankle and wrist injuries. Healthier in 2010, Olt hit .318/.401/.659 with 23 home runs and reestablished the school's single-season RBI mark with 76.

The 21-year-old has good hands and feet, solid range, and a strong arm from third. There are holes in his right-handed swing—he struck out 54 times in 264 at-bats this season—but the bat speed is there, and scouts believe in his approach at the plate and coachability. It's been a long time since third base was so uniformly thin in the big leagues, and in Olt the Rangers see a player they obviously believe could give them an developmental asset, particularly if he can make more consistent contact and take advantage of his power potential while providing lockdown defense at third.

The second round kicks off at 11:00 this morning, with Texas picking 72nd overall. The club then picks at 103 in the third round, 136 in the fourth round, and every 30 picks thereafter. Today's proceedings will conclude with the 30th round, and the 31st through 50th rounds will take place tomorrow.

June 9, 2010

Coasting to a win like that has been nearly as rare this season for Texas as Draft Day—the Rangers have only five wins of at least five runs, including their last two victories—and while Texas 7, King Felix 1 probably won't even get as much local play as The Strasburg Debut, it showcased several really positive things:

1. Two of the finest free agents signings anywhere in the league this winter: Colby Lewis and Vladimir Guerrero.
2. The continuing coming into focus of Justin Smoak, at the plate and around the bag.
3. A game in which the manager was comfortably able to give Ian Kinsler and Michael Young some late rest.
4. The best shortstop in the American League.

Elvis Andrus, whose defense I'd take over any other shortstop in the league, whose offense I'd take over any other shortstop in the league, and whose future I'd take over almost any other player in the league, is not only younger than two of the five Rangers prospects who were named Low A South Atlantic League All-Stars this week (outfielder Miguel Velazquez and reliever Trevor Hurley, who were selected along with starters Robbie Ross, Robbie Erlin, and Matt Thompson), but also younger than five of the players the Rangers drafted yesterday.

Think about that.

He's also two years younger than Frisco left-handed reliever Beau Jones, who in 13.1 RoughRider innings has scattered six hits and one walk while striking out 19, coaxing more groundouts than flyouts.

The Mark Teixeira Trade would have been just fine if it produced Andrus alone. Getting Neftali Feliz as well makes it a landmark deal. Toss in Matt Harrison and Jarrod Saltalamacchia, Atlanta's top pitching prospect and top position player prospect at the time, neither of whom we really know about yet, and it's closing in on Herschel Walker Trade status.

If Jones—reportedly added to the deal at the last minute at Jon Daniels's insistence, given a bout of Harrison shoulder soreness following his AA start six days earlier—makes it to Arlington, giving Texas five big leaguers out of five, including Andrus and Feliz, the trade becomes even more extraordinary.

Maybe not 7-4-2-2-0-14 extraordinary, but any general manager would have drafted Stephen Strasburg if they had the number one pick last year. I'm not sure how many front offices would have been able to pull the Teixeira Trade off.

If the drafting on Monday of Jake Skole (first round) and on Tuesday of high school outfielder Jordan Akins (third round), both two-sport college commits, allows Texas to create even more of a budget surplus by amortizing their signing bonuses out over five years, and if some of that surplus can be used at trade deadline time, whether this team is out of bankruptcy by then or not, the chances are obviously better that this season will extend beyond 162 games that count.

It's going to take playoff baseball—winning playoff baseball—for the Mark Teixeira Trade to share ground with the Herschel Walker Trade.

But that's about all that separates them right now.

Last night's excellent Rangers win included contributions from several former first-round picks (Lewis, Smoak, Josh Hamilton, David Murphy, and Julio Borbon), but there was also a former 17th-rounder (Ian Kinsler) hitting third and an undrafted free agent (Darren O'Day) getting the final three outs.

Whether Texas found another Kinsler in yesterday's second through 30th rounds, or keeps another O'Day from sliding through the draft altogether in today's 31st through 50th, we won't know for a while.

And though we've said it before, as much as I dig the baseball draft, give me a year like this every time, when the draft is incidental to what's going on in Arlington. I'm excited about Skole and Kellin Deglan and Luke Jackson and Cody Buckel and Akins and Justin Grimm and Zack Osborne, not to mention Garrett Buechele (18th round) and the fascinating but likely unsignable Brian Ragira (30th round), who is expected to matriculate from Arlington Martin to Stanford, but my mind is now refocused on C.J. Wilson against Ian Snell, and Tommy Hunter against Ryan Rowland-Smith.

Big thanks to Scott Lucas for his outstanding, instant news flashes on each of the Rangers' first eight draft picks Monday and Tuesday, and to Eleanor Czajka for once again putting together a one-stop information store for the entire Texas draft class on her Minor Details blog, where you can find player profiles, scouting video, and industry evaluations on each of the Rangers' 2010 picks.

The draft concludes today, after which work on getting the majority of the club's 53 picks signed and ready for short-season game action gets underway.

But in the meantime, there are two more at home against Seattle, with the Angels and A's each within a game of the division lead and facing each other for two more themselves, after which Texas moves into a 15-game stretch against the National League (Milwaukee, Florida, Houston, Pittsburgh, Houston again), a real chance to fatten up against nothing but under-.500 clubs while the Angels get the Dodgers and Rockies and the A's get the Cardinals and Reds over the same two and a half weeks.

I'll be at the Ballpark these next two nights, watching a former fifth-rounder and former supplemental first-rounder take the mound to try and help nail down a series win over the Mariners, with an undrafted kid from Venezuela doing his thing, as he does most nights, at shortstop and atop the order, to make the Rangers' future, tonight and next year and four years from now, something worth investing in.

June 9, 2010

The Rangers have announced that they've agreed to terms with outfielder Jake Skole and catcher Kellin Deglan, their first two picks in this year's draft. Skole was taken with the 15th overall pick Monday night, Deglan with the 22nd pick.

Both have been assigned to the Arizona League squad, which begins play June 21.

June 10, 2010

Total wins by a margin of at least five runs out of the Rangers' first 29 victories: Three.

Total wins by a margin of at least five runs out of the Rangers' last three victories: Three.

Number of times in 2007 an opponent held Ichiro Suzuki to one hit over three consecutive games: Eleven. (Texas was one of them.)

Number of times in 2008 and 2009 combined an opponent held Ichiro Suzuki to one hit over three consecutive games: Three. (Texas was one of them.)

Number of times in 2010 an opponent has held Ichiro Suzuki to one hit over three consecutive games: One. (Monday, Tuesday, and last night.)

If the official scorer hadn't reversed his ruling and awarded Ichiro a fifth-inning double on what was originally ruled a Justin Smoak error, we'd be looking at the first time since April 2006 that one team held Ichiro hitless three straight days.

Texas has won 11 of 13 games in the red jerseys this year.

Derek Holland had to cut short his first bullpen session since left rotator cuff inflammation forced him to the disabled list. Yesterday's scheduled 30-pitch session yesterday lasted just 17 before he complained of a "minor pinch" in his shoulder.

Rangers third-round pick Jordan Akins, a toolsy outfielder from Union Grove High School in Georgia, told UCFSports.com that he has agreed to sign with Texas for $350,000, forgoing a football-baseball scholarship to the University of Central Florida. If the figure is accurate, it appears to be right at or maybe slightly over slot.

Texas took bench coach Jackie Moore's son, Johnathan Moore, in the 45th round yesterday. The Houston Baptist catcher hit .355 with six home runs and 51 RBI in 54 games this season.

The Rangers' 39th-round pick yesterday, University of Alabama-Birmingham righthander Ryan Woolley, was taken in the sixth round a year ago (by Atlanta) but didn't sign. The Rangers' fourth-round pick in 2007, outfielder Garrett Nash, was chosen yesterday by Arizona, also in the 39th round, 15 picks before Texas tabbed Woolley. Nash has been on a Mormon mission the past two years.

Matt Purke is the Louisville Slugger NCAA Freshman Pitcher of the Year. He's gone 13-0, 3.40 for TCU, fanning 122 and walking 27 in 95.1 innings. The Horned Frogs are in Austin for the NCAA Super Regionals tomorrow through Sunday. Anyone have local TV details?

On Monday, the Washington Nationals drafted Bryce Harper. On Tuesday, they got the greatest debut in the history of mankind from Stephen Strasburg. On Wednesday, they signed Jason Botts to a minor league contract. The 29-year-old, who was hitting .342/.444/.530 in 149 at-bats for the Camden Riversharks of the independent Atlantic League, joins AAA Syracuse, where his teammates will include Kevin Mench and where his hitting coach will be Jerry Browne.

Florida designated Mike Lamb for assignment to make room for outfield phenom Mike Stanton.

No MLB.com column this week. I'm still recovering from the draft.

Our next Fox Sports Southwest in-game chat will probably be June 30, when Texas visits the Angels.

You're 18 years old. In one day:

1. You get an authentic Rangers jersey with your name on it, number 1 or number 21.
2. You and your family get to hang out in a room with Nolan Ryan.
3. You get to meet a bunch of Rangers players and then watch them—from a suite behind home plate—explode offensively, pitch well, and play great defense. You dream of one day playing on that field, in a game like that.
4. You get interviewed by Jim Knox.
5. Your parting gift: Someone agrees to pay you seven figures.

Good day, eh?

June 11, 2010

Josh on tap no more
On and off and on and off
Whatever works, man

Here's the funny thing. When Josh Hamilton started the 2009 season, at the urging of Rudy Jaramillo, by ditching the toe-tap that he used throughout his storybook 2008 campaign, the experiment lasted a dozen games (.229/.283/.354). Readopting the toe-tap for the balance of the 2009 season, he hit a more respectable .274/.321/.438 the rest of the way.

In 2010, maintaining the toe-tap, Hamilton seemed to be going just fine through the end of May (.281/.335/.500). But Clint Hurdle then persuaded him to drop the toe-tap again, and since that time he's a .436/.450/.846 hitter in 39 at-bats.

In his three Rangers seasons, Hamilton is a .293/.352/.501 hitter in 1,104 toe-tappin' at-bats. He's a .322/.355/.575 hitter in 87 tapless at-bats.

It's pretty clear that the key for Hamilton is not whether he's tapping his toe, but instead that his head's right at the plate. Right now, he's as locked in as he's ever been as a Ranger, whereas the last time he went without the mechanism he's back to going without now, he struggled terribly. He seems like the type of player who can cripple himself by overthinking things. See it, hit it.

Max Faulkner/FWST

We all know Vladimir Guerrero was the all-time Rangers killer in Arlington. In 193 at-bats as a visiting player, he hit .394/.471/.705 in Rangers Ballpark.

This year he's hitting .381/.407/.669 at home.

What a monster.

Speaking of which, the Smoak Monster is hitting .400/.514/.667 in 30 June at-bats.

(I found this interesting: Smoak is up to .222/.339/.389 overall. Frequent comp Mark Teixeira is at .226/.341/.391.)

Meanwhile, Julio Borbon is 13 for his last 24 (.542/.538/.667), and like Smoak just about every one of his hits (and several of his outs) lately have been barreled.

But Ian Kinsler is hitting .192/.288/.231 in his last 52 at-bats (and that's with several fluky base hits among the 10 he's had). I'm not sure I can remember him looking this uncomfortable at the plate, mechanically.

Still, no team in baseball is hitting at anywhere near the level that Texas is in June. The club's .329 average is the only mark in the big leagues over .300 this month, and its .499 slug is percentage points higher than Boston's and far ahead of everyone else.

All other things equal, bullpens tend to come into play more often in National League parks, and Tommy Hunter, while not as sharp as he was Saturday when he went the distance against Tampa Bay, gave the club a solid six last night and set up an uncomplicated night for the relief crew. Darren Oliver (three strikeouts), Darren O'Day (one strikeout), and Frankie Francisco (one strikeout) were perfect over an inning each (throwing a first-pitch strike to all but one Mariner over that stretch), and the pen is relatively rested going into this stretch of nine NL games in 10 days, all on the road.

In fact, in the four-game series Texas just completed, O'Day is the only pitcher on the staff who pitched twice (one perfect inning on Tuesday and another on Thursday, 23 strikes out of 31 pitches). That's remarkable.

Hunter's effort was the rotation's third straight quality start, after Colby Lewis (one Seattle run) and C.J. Wilson (two runs) each delivered seven solid innings.

Hunter is going to have a long career starting big league baseball games.

Oliver since May 8: one earned run (0.59 ERA) on eight hits (.160 opponents' average) and four walks in 15.1 innings, with 22 strikeouts. He's fanned nine of the last 13 batters he's faced.

Francisco over the same stretch: three earned runs (1.98 ERA) on nine hits (.188 opponents' average) and three unintentional walks in 13.2 innings, with 23 strikeouts.

Ichiro in the four-game series against Texas: 1 for 15, and an official scorer's changed ruling away from a hitless trip.

But you were betting on Borbon getting five more hits in three games than Ichiro did in four in this series.

Ron Washington plans to play Guerrero in right field every other day in Milwaukee and Florida, giving him two starts in each of those three-game series. He hasn't revealed his plans for Guerrero's usage next weekend in Houston.

In 45 at-bats in Milwaukee's Miller Park, Guerrero is a .356/.431/.667 hitter. In Florida's Sun Life Stadium, his slash line is .305/.350/.515 in 167 at-bats.

It looks like Nelson Cruz (hamstring) won't be back Tuesday as planned. He felt some soreness behind his left knee running the bases yesterday, got a cortisone shot, and will head out on a rehab assignment, at the soonest, early next week.

Derek Holland, after cutting a scheduled 30-pitch side session short after 17 pitches on Wednesday, says he's fine and should throw again today.

Incidentally, when Oklahoma City righthander Tanner Scheppers makes his first start as a Rangers prospect on Sunday, his Albuquerque opposition will be Vicente Padilla, who made rehab starts for High A Inland Empire on June 3 and June 8. Los Angeles is expected to activate Padilla after Sunday's start.

Brandon McCarthy is back on the AAA disabled list with inflammation in his right shoulder.

Righthander Danny Gutierrez, having served out his 50-game banned substance suspension (after testing positive for a prescribed ADHD medication that he didn't secure a therapeutic use exemption for), made his 2010 debut in relief for Low A Hickory last night, giving up a run on a single, double, and two walks in an inning of work.

Bruce Levine of ESPN Chicago is at it again, suggesting that Texas has "serious interest" in White Sox catcher A.J. Pierzynski.

(Yeah, yeah, Pierzynski gains 10-and-5 rights on Sunday. Too much is being made of that. He already has some level of no-trade protection. And knowing he's not going to be asked back this winter by Chicago, as Tyler Flowers gets closer [despite a current month-long AAA slump], he has plenty of reason to accept a trade to a contender and try to rehabilitate his market value.)

(I still don't want him.)

Cleveland released righthander Jamey Wright.

Boosted by the just-completed 5-2 homestand, Texas has the best home record in the American League (23-11). On the road (10-16), however, only Seattle (8-20) and Baltimore (6-25) are worse.

But Milwaukee (10-17) is the worst home team in baseball, and Florida (17-15) and Houston (14-20) are in the back half as well.

Something's gotta give in these next nine, and with Texas clicking on all cylinders right now, this road trip is set up for the club to get that road W/L healthier and extend what is now a 1.5-game cushion on the Angels and two games on Oakland.

Important road swing on tap.

June 11, 2010

Billy Beane gets credited for the now-prevalent philosophy that you spend the first third of the season figuring out what you have, the middle third addressing gaps on your roster, and the final third getting into the fast lane and flooring it.

We're now more than a rotation turn past the one-third point, and I'd say we know what we have in our fifth starter right now. It's really too bad that Derek Holland isn't ready to return, and that Tanner Scheppers isn't yet an option.

The middle third mandate is tricky, given the club's financial constraints, but . . . well, I've said enough on this sore subject (especially if you've been following me on Twitter).

Would you trade Ivan Rodriguez, Jake Skole, and Luis Sardinas for Matt Purke and Matt Nevarez?

In a second.

I got my first look today at Purke, and was blown away.

Damn.

The amazing Nike World Cup commercial probably cost as much to produce as installing a brand new video board at Rangers Ballpark, but if there was any way to hire the folks that put that piece of awesome awesomeness together to do a Rangers spot or two—imagine a similar action sequence put together of Elvis going into the hole, or Vladimir turning on a fastball low and outside, or Neftali doing his thing—I'd pay the price of admission just to see the finished product up on the video board as Elvis or Vlad came up to bat, or as Neftali was summoned from the pen.

Saw this today, and it seems like 10 years since I've seen anything like it in Dallas:

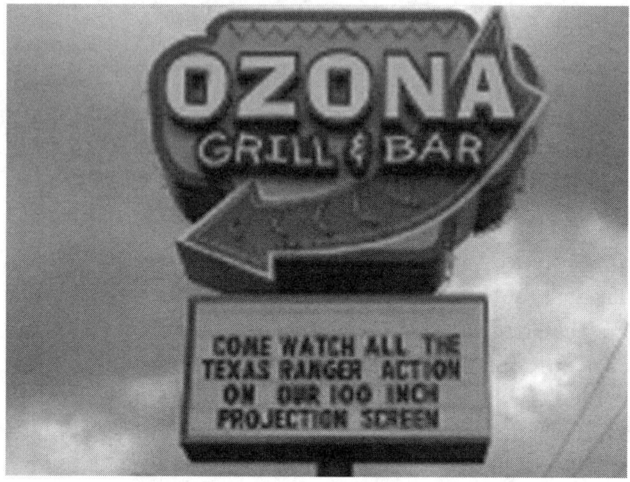

That sleeping giant is starting to rustle around a bit.

Last call for your minor league-related questions for my monthly column in the Rangers' July gameday program.

June 12, 2010

According to a Twitter post by ESPN's Enrique Rojas, the Rangers have right-handed reliever Alexi Ogando on a flight to join the team in Milwaukee. So as not to jinx things, I'm not going to speculate as to what the corresponding roster move might be.

I'll let you know when there's official word.

June 12, 2010

I promise objectivity with this report.

In 2003, one was on the fast track for Oakland, starting the season pitching in AA and moving quickly up to AAA before getting to the big leagues in the middle of the season. The other was A's property as well, a tools monster who flashed brilliance on the field but in whom Oakland didn't really know what they had. He was an outfielder known as Argenis Benitez.

Today, they're together again but now in Texas, and the roles have reversed. The latter is no longer an outfielder but instead a pitcher, no longer Argenis Benitez but instead Alexi Ogando, and he's the AA-to-AAA-to-Arlington fast-tracker, while Rich Harden, a rookie phenom in 2003, is someone that, despite all his obvious tools and occasional glimpses that there's still something there, is a complete mystery, at best.

Alexi Ogando has been recalled and will join the Rangers bullpen, after an odyssey to the big leagues unlike just about anyone else's, and Rich Harden has been removed from the rotation (with no announced replacement yet) and parked on the disabled list, victim of a left gluteal muscle strain.

My pledge of objectivity prohibits me from the obvious follow-up line.

June 14, 2010

It wasn't Colby Lewis's best start of the season, but close to it.

But his eight-pitch at-bat in the sixth inning, facing off against Milwaukee righthander Yovani Gallardo, was one of the great Rangers' at-bats of the season.

With Texas ahead, 2-1, Vladimir Guerrero singled and Josh Hamilton doubled to lead off the inning. Justin Smoak then struck out looking and Max Ramirez went down swinging, and Gallardo probably felt like he'd all but escaped, with punchless number eight hitter Andres Blanco and Lewis slated to hit. Brewers manager Ken Macha put Blanco on first, asking Gallardo to get Lewis out to end the inning.

Gallardo—top 10 in the National League in strikeouts (and ERA)—snapped off a curve that broke more than a foot to start the at-bat, and Lewis swung through it. Lewis then looked at a 94-mph fastball that missed a bit outside. Then he fouled off another sharp curve. And fouled off another 94-mph heater. And fouled off another curve. And watched a curve that Gallardo buried in the dirt. And fouled yet another 94-mph fastball.

And Lewis then did bad things to a curve that broke 12 inches but stayed inside, raking it just inside the bag at third base and down the line for a two-run single to give himself and his teammates a 4-1 lead.

Gallardo then struck Elvis Andrus out, just as he'd done with Smoak and Ramirez earlier in the inning.

C.J. Wilson faces Josh Johnson tomorrow night, and has immediately fallen far behind Lewis in the battle for starting pitcher bragging rights at the plate.

Alexi Ogando didn't pitch yesterday (why Frankie Francisco was called on to pitch the ninth inning of a 7-2 contest, in a day game after a night game in which he'd thrown 26 pitches, I'm not sure). But Tanner Scheppers did.

Ryan Aber of the *Daily Oklahoman* and Bob Hersom of OKCRedhawks.com shed some light on the Rangers' plan with Scheppers, who made his first minor league start yesterday and held Albuquerque scoreless on two hits (by ex-big leaguers Michael Restovich and Nick Green) and no walks in four innings, fanning a pair of Isotopes (ex-big leaguers Jay Gibbons and Restovich). Meanwhile, Oklahoma City spanked Vicente Padilla for six runs (four earned) in his 5.2 rehab innings.

Scheppers threw 55 pitches, 37 for strikes. Of his 40 fastballs, a number touched 99 mph, and he mixed in a good curve and inconsistent change. In blanking the Isotopes, he lowered his RedHawks ERA to 1.57 and his opponents' batting average to .188. In 23 AAA innings, he's walked 10 and punched out 29. The 23-year-old righty has now faced 28 straight hitters without a base on balls.

RedHawks pitching coach Terry Clark told Aber and Hersom that the organization's plan for Scheppers is to make three more starts at about four innings apiece (which would bring him to 46 innings between AA and AAA for the year). He'll then be shut down for a week (just as he was early this month), and make another four starts at five innings each, which would raise his total to 66 innings as of the last week or so of July.

At that point—assuming Scheppers hasn't first been summoned to the big league bullpen—Texas will be right up against the trade deadline, having blueprinted about 35 or 40 more 2010 innings for Scheppers. A majority, if not all, of those innings will probably come in the Texas bullpen. The plan is for Scheppers to help the Rangers in relief this year, and in a best case, in their rotation next year, when the organization believes he'll be ready to log 150-200 innings. The timing of all this is interesting, given that Texas might be weighing opportunities to trade for another power arm to stick in the bullpen for the stretch run—but they might have the right guy in AAA right now.

The big league focus is on this week's series in Florida and Houston, as it should be, but when you get looks at Ogando and Scheppers this summer, with Tommy Hunter and Neftali Feliz and Derek Holland ahead of them and Martin Perez and Blake Beavan and Pedro Strop behind them, it's going to be hard not to think about where this pitching staff is headed over the next couple years.

June 14, 2010: TROT COFFEY

- According to Ken Rosenthal of Fox Sports, who wrote on Friday that Boston was "actively talking" to Texas and Minnesota about Mike Lowell, the Rangers are exploring right-handed-hitting corner alternatives, including Arizona outfielder-first baseman Conor Jackson. Rosenthal notes, however, that, according to one source, "nothing is remotely close."

Incidentally, Jackson (.238/.326/.331 right now but an .800-OPS hitter in each of his first three full big league seasons, 2006-2008) was a player that the Rangers were reportedly interested in leading right up to the trade deadline in 2007, when Texas made the Mark Teixeira deal with Atlanta and the Diamondbacks were reportedly the runners-up.

June 14, 2010: TROT COFFEY

- Yes, there's a report from NBCSports.com's Craig Calcaterra this afternoon that Texas and Houston are "getting closer" to a trade involving righthander Roy Oswalt, and that the identity of the players who would be involved "is more or less agreed to," but that the deal is held up by that little matter of the $26 million or so that Oswalt is guaranteed through this year and next.
- No, I don't buy it.

June 14, 2010: TROT COFFEY

Actually, this is not really a COFFEY report. No grains of salt needed.

The Rangers have shot the Calcaterra/Oswalt story down.

No truth to it.

June 15, 2010

Just an awesome win.

C.J. Wilson (pitching off the same mound he made his big league debut on five years and five days ago) wasn't particularly sharp but minimized the potential damage, and kept his team in the game against baseball's hottest, if not best, pitcher.

Making his big league debut, Alexi Ogando could have been sharper as well, but there's plenty to love about his future, even if he is a couple months older than Hanley Ramirez.

But Matt Treanor, the Rangers' answer down to the club's final out against a right-handed closer because there's not a Conor Jackson or Mike Lowell or even a Brandon Boggs on the bench, stepped in against the team he had 723 of his 736 career at-bats for coming into 2010, two of which had produced triples, and crushed a two-run three-bagger on the first pitch he saw, a 94-mph fastball that he shot to deep, deep left center.

It was a great moment for Treanor, and for Neftali Feliz, who minutes later worked a quiet shutdown ninth after struggling mightily in his last effort, but we shouldn't overlook the great moment Julio Borbon had, also up with the club down to its final out, just prior to the Treanor shot. With two outs, the tying run on third, a virtual refusal to work a walk all season, Marlins closer Leo Nunez having thrown five strikes out of seven pitches—and having not issued a walk in his last 18 appearances, and the pressure of having the pitcher's spot and the thinnest of options off the bench behind him, the odds of Borbon slowing the game down and making Nunez throw strikes in that situation didn't even register.

But he drew his fourth walk of 2010, on five pitches, and made things happen with his feet, scoring easily behind Josh Hamilton on Treanor's shot one pitch later, rewarding Wilson with a no-decision and Ogando with a victory.

Sure would be great if some sort of switch has been flipped and Borbon starts to rack up a few walks, since to date he's been working free passes at about one-fifth the rate he did as a rookie last year.

Meanwhile, the Angels lost tonight, 7-1.

November 24, 2011, the six-year anniversary of the Marlins' trade that sent Josh Beckett, Mike Lowell, and Guillermo Mota to Boston for Ramirez, Anibal Sanchez, Jesus Delgado, and Harvey Garcia . . . instead of Beckett and Lowell (and maybe Mota) to Texas for Hank Blalock and John Danks (and maybe Joaquin Arias): Texas sends Martin Perez, Robbie Erlin, Luke Jackson, and Luis Sardinas to Florida for Josh Johnson and reliever Clay Hensley.

(Actually, no chance. Marlins VP Andy Silverman will threaten to jump off the roof of the new Miami Marlins Stadium if the club trades Johnson just as the team is about to open the new ballpark in 2012.)

(But I can dream.)

Johnson got 21 outs tonight, 20 of which were on strikes or on the ground. He's an extraordinary pitcher, and the Oklahoma native won't retire as a Marlin.

But he got a no-decision tonight, too. If something special happens this season, we'll remember this one.

OK, a few follow-up points about Newberg Report Night (July 25), based on your questions:

In the next couple days, I'll send confirmations to the many of you who have already signed up for the event.

For those choosing the $30 option (stadium seats), we will likely be in Sections 37 to 40 (lower bowl, first base side), somewhere in that area.

The suites will not be catered, though you are welcome to cater them at your own expense. You can also bring concessions up to the suites.

Yes, I will be sure you're sitting with the people you want to sit with, whether in the seats or suites.

Among the auction items will be a baseball signed by Michael Young, Josh Hamilton, Ian Kinsler, Scott Feldman, David Murphy, Justin Smoak, Derek Holland, Tommy Hunter, Craig Gentry, Brandon McCarthy, Chris Davis, and Rusty Greer (donated by Grant Schiller). Luther Davis of Davis Auctioneers, who helped us at the second Sherlock's event, is planning to join us for Newberg Report Night as well.

A couple people paid today and said they're surprising Dad with this as a Father's Day gift. Not a terrible idea.

We sold out last year in eight days, faster than ever before. We're going to beat that this year. In one day today, we're already 40 percent full. If you plan to come, don't wait too long to register.

June 16, 2010

Just like Ivan Rodriguez's final hit as a Ranger (the first time around at least), an opposite-field double that he rocketed to right center field, Michael Young's franchise record-tying and record-breaking hits were extremely fitting: a similar double to right center, pure opposite field genius befitting of both the Rangers' new all-time hit leader and the man who, on that list, he has displaced, followed by a shot up the middle that plated two runs, instrumental in a *victory*, the most appropriate part of all of this.

Young said after the 27th out that he's happy the record-breaking hit came in such a big spot in the game, so he wouldn't have to think about anything other than trying to push another couple runs across. (Which made me think of something I'd written four years ago.) And of course, nobody doubts the sincerity of his comment, or his final words to Nolan Ryan during the live TV interview that just finished: "Proud to be a Ranger."

Sorry to interrupt without having much to say. I'm proud that guy's a Ranger.

June 18, 2010

Little run, away
Game's biggest division lead
Now owned by Texas

It's been an excellent road trip. Facing two mediocre teams but matched up against good pitching more often than not, Texas has gone 5-1 so far on the trip, and now visits Houston for three, missing the Astros' top two starters (Roy Oswalt and Brett Myers), before returning home.

Got to keep taking care of business, not only this weekend but for these three weeks leading up to the All-Star Break, during which the Rangers face clubs with a losing record 19 times in 22 games, the lone exception being a three-game set in Anaheim June 29-July 1, against an Angels team that now sits 2.5 games back in the AL West.

The Rangers' final action before the Break is a July 8-11 series at home against Baltimore, intersected on the 9th by a bankruptcy court date in Fort Worth that,

Newberg Report: Beavan a Command King

Once billed as a K artist, righty cruising with new approach

By Jamey Newberg / Special to MLB.com

June 17, 2010

He was drafted as a big, brash, teen-aged Texas fireballer—in the mold of Nolan Ryan, Roger Clemens, Kerry Wood, and Josh Beckett—wielding high-90s velocity and a slider he was even more proud of. But he's turned into something quite different.

Blake Beavan may not be what he and even the Rangers thought three years ago that he'd be, but he's become one of the more likely candidates on the Texas farm to make it to the big leagues. And he's done so almost quietly, a word that was once the last you'd ever use to describe the Irving native.

Drafted in the first round in 2007, Beavan entered pro ball with huge stuff but a violent recoil in his overly upright delivery that the organization knew it was going to have to smooth out. Having signed too late in the 2007 season to contribute meaningfully to a farm club, Beavan got his career under way at Fall Instructional League, where work on his mechanics got under way.

There was some concern in the 6-foot-7 righty's first pro season that his modified delivery had robbed him of the plus velocity that helped make him the fourth high school pitcher drafted the previous summer, but few could argue with the results: making a team-leading 23 starts for low Class A Clinton in 2008, Beavan went 10-6, 2.37 as one of the Midwest League's youngest pitchers, issuing only 20 walks in 121.2 innings. The fact that he put that kind of season together not only against older competition but also while getting used to an overhauled mechanical approach made his rookie season even more encouraging.

In 2009, Texas gave Beavan a dozen starts for high Class A Bakersfield before promoting him to Double-A Frisco, where he went 4-4, 4.01 and issued a scant 13 walks—fewer than one per start—over 89.2 innings. The Texas League did hit .309 off him, though, and fanned only 34 times. The Rangers unsurprisingly sent him back to the RoughRiders for a repeat run at Double-A hitters when the 2010 season kicked off.

Despite it being his second year in the league, Beavan began the season as the circuit's fifth-youngest player. Two months in, he sits as one of its best pitchers. His eight wins are tied for the league lead, no pitcher has logged as many as his 83.2 innings or allowed fewer baserunners per nine innings than his 8.71. Beavan's 2.58 ERA is fifth-best in the league, his .222 opponents' average fourth-best, and only one pitcher has a stingier walk rate than his 1.18 per nine innings.

And while Beavan didn't miss nearly enough bats in his first run at Double-A hitters, this season he's seventh in the league in strikeouts, nearly doubling his rate from the year before.

The Rangers' Minor League Pitcher of the Month for May (he was the only pitcher in minor league baseball to notch six May victories), Beavan is showing an uptick in velocity (sitting 91-93 after working closer to 90 last year), improvement with the bite and depth to his slider, and, as always, command of it all.

Beavan is an exquisite strike-thrower, a durable workhorse who isn't tripping radar guns the way he did at Irving High School, but he's making huge progress. Had he gone to the University of Oklahoma instead of signing out of high school, 2010 would have been his Draft year, and he'd probably be negotiating his signing bonus right now, awaiting his pro debut. Instead, he's a Texas League All-Star, working on a streak of seven straight quality starts, and isn't far from being a Triple-A pitcher, if not a candidate for spot-start consideration in Texas.

Innings-eaters don't show up atop prospect lists or in trade rumors as often as velocity monsters, but they're extremely valuable. Beavan may not have Beckett's or Wood's stuff, he may not be as electric as Martin Perez or Tanner Scheppers, but he might have Tommy Hunter's moxie and durability. And every team can use that.

A big league scout recently told Kevin Goldstein of Baseball Prospectus: "People only talk about what [Beavan] can't do, or how he isn't doing what they think he should. I don't care. He's going to throw 200 innings a year in the big leagues."

When he gets there, he won't look anything like the kid Texas used its first of five first-round picks on in 2007.

He'll look more like a pitcher.

depending on what happens this Tuesday, *could* set things up for the league's ownership to approve the sale of the Rangers to the Greenberg-Ryan group well in advance of the conventional trade deadline.

Texas will come out of the Break with 23 of 42 games on the road, including 19 games against the three best teams in the East and two best teams in the Central, and another 19 against West foes.

But if the sale goes through sometime during that crucial stretch, imagine the idea that the rotation or bullpen or bench could be given a significant boost before it ends.

Not that the arrival of Alexi Ogando (who gets a hit every time he comes up, and a win every time he pitches) might not end up being a bigger boost than some contenders are able to make during trade season. Or that Tanner Scheppers might not make even more of an impact this summer than Ogando.

(By the way, if you dare credit Jon Daniels for the plan to steal Ogando from Oakland nearly five years ago, to convert him from outfielder to pitcher, to stick with him through the immigration nightmare, and to help forge a solution for getting him back into the United States, he'll correct you and point out that A.J. Preller and Mike Daly were primarily responsible for all of it, with Thad Levine and Danilo Troncoso instrumental in clearing the legal restraints.)

Nelson Cruz, heading out on a three-game rehab stint today, and Derek Holland, who could embark on a rehab assignment next week, and Tommy Hunter, who says his hip flexor strain is fine, are getting closer to returning as well.

I'm not sure whether Nolan Ryan assumed the sale would have been completed or not when he predicted at the beginning of the season that this team would win 92 games.

It's presently on pace to go 93-69.

A reader emailed this to me last night: "I am currently sitting in the Buffalo Wild Wings in Arlington, full of people ready to watch the Lakers and Celtics. And when Elvis' bunt was thrown wild, a chant of 'Let's Go Rangers' broke out."

This is getting pretty good.

As you now know, early this week we sold out of spots for Newberg Report Night, in about 48 hours. Several of you asked about the possibility of attending the July 25 game with our group, even though admission to the pregame events in the Hall of Fame Theater is closed. We can do that.

If you're interested in sitting with the Newberg Report group that Sunday night against the Angels, in Sections 37-40 along the first base line (lower bowl), you can get a discounted game ticket for **$15** (half the price of the full event admission). If you want to watch with our group from a luxury suite, you can do so for **$100** (the same price as the event admission but still a huge discount off of what it would normally cost to sit in a suite).

And the majority of your cost would still go to our charities, which this year are the Hello Win Column Fund (which supports local families impacted by cancer) and a local women's shelter.

If you're interested in attending the game with us on the 25th, the way to sign up remains the same.

Based on how the schedule lines up until then, particularly over the next three weeks, that night's game against Los Angeles could be pretty huge.

June 19, 2010

There have been years, too many of them, when this morning I might have written an entire report about Jurickson Profar's pro debut and made a big deal out of the fact that the leadoff hitter (Ryan Strasborger) and three-hole hitter (Andrew Clark) in between whom he hit last night are each five years older, and that the big Tri-City righthander that Profar doubled off of (Mequite Poteet, McLennan CC, and Lamar University product Ricky Testa) is six years older than the shortstop from Curacao.

But this isn't the morning for that, and not the season for me to feel compelled to devote this space to the things that Scott Lucas expertly covers each day, as a way of distracting myself from an epidemic rash of bad big league pitching, poor execution offensively, or an outbreak of lousy baserunning or routinely booting the ball.

There have been seasons, recently, where once we got to June every report I sent out might have had notes, and not necessarily at the tail end, pointing out that Buck Showalter and Bobby Valentine are candidates for the Orioles job, or that the Dodgers released lefthander John Koronka, or that the Yuma Scorpions of the independent Golden League placed outfielder Masjid Khairy on irrevocable waivers.

Instead, I'm able to share with you that Texas has won six straight on the road, has nailed down 13 of 17 in June, owns a 2.5-game division lead on the Angels, and is clicking on just about all cylinders. That's a lot more fun to write about.

Did Frisco lefty Martin Perez get drilled last night? Yes. Eight runs (seven earned) in an inning and a third. Cause for alarm? Johan Santana, in his final full minor league season, had starts in which he allowed 8, 8, 6, 6, 6, and 6 runs. In his final month of that 1999 season, he made seven starts and one relief appearance, posting a 7.65 ERA.

And he was a year older than Perez.

And pitching two minor league levels lower than Perez.

Don't panic.

I'm not suggesting you should ignore what's happening on the farm, obviously. If these stories about Texas showing legitimate interest in Roy Oswalt (who was mentored by Nolan Ryan and played for manager Jackie Moore and pitching coach Mike Maddux in his own final minor league season) have some substance, keeping close tabs on what Blake Beavan and Beau Jones and Engel Beltre and Matt Thompson are doing would be smart. If the Rangers can get out of court in time to pursue the top tier of what the trade deadline has to offer, they're not going to trade Justin Smoak and Tommy Hunter and Alexi Ogando to get a deal done. There will be minor leaguers involved. Not by themselves. But they'll figure in.

It's always worthwhile to pay detailed attention to what's going on in Hickory. Some years it serves an extra purpose, as a distraction. Others, like this year, it provides context.

Supplemental first-rounder Mike Olt signed for slot yesterday, and pretty soon he'll settle in at third base for Spokane, situated 40 feet to Profar's right. I look forward to every word of Scott's reports every day, and in mid-June they get an extra boost when we can read about Randol Rojas and Miguel De Los Santos and Nick McBride and Guillermo Pimentel at Spokane, and Jake Skole and Kellin Deglan and Luis Sardinas and Juan Grullon with the Arizona League squad, whose season kicks off Monday night.

But it's all backstory right now, less notable than Scott Feldman's 2.89 ERA in his last three starts or Josh Hamilton's 1.354 OPS in June—or the fact that Vladimir Guerrero sits at .327/.397/.577 for the month and yet is being out-OPS'd by Julio Borbon (.423/.456/.615) over the same stretch. Hickory lefthanders Robbie Erlin and Robbie Ross are having spectacular seasons, but that's less important than what Darren Oliver is doing.

Perez and Tanner Scheppers each struggled last night, but right now I'm more concerned about Elvis Andrus's .143/.211/.143 slash line, with 10 strikeouts in 35 at-bats, since he put those ridiculous highlights in his hair a week and a half ago. I don't care about the hair. I care that his .304 average has dropped to .282 in those eight or nine days, and he's looking a little out of sync.

And I'm trying to figure out why Ian Kinsler, who has hit in eight straight (.379/.472/.448) with as many walks as strikeouts, still doesn't look right to me at the plate.

This season, thankfully, has given us plenty so far to celebrate and to worry about and to focus on, moving bankruptcy proceedings and the spring training story of the manager's 2009 off-field mistake somewhere away from the center of our attention.

I'm interested in Erlin's Hickory start this evening and in McBride's start in Spokane, in whether Michael Main can maintain this Bakersfield run he's on in Game One of the Blaze's Saturday twinbill, and in how Brandon McCarthy fares in his return to AAA action tonight, his first action in two weeks and first start in two months.

But none of it matters as much right now as Colby Lewis-Scuffy Moehler tonight, or C.J. Wilson-Felipe Paulino tomorrow.

Am I interested in how Profar fares tonight against 25-year-old Tri-City rehabber Josh Sullivan, who was in the minor leagues when Profar was starring in the Little League World Series at age 12? Of course. Am I eager to see whether catcher Jorge Alfaro shows up on the AZL roster when that club begins play Monday? Absolutely.

But for now, it's all about what's going on in Arlington, and that's what you want to be able to say heading toward mid-season, the All-Star Break, and what could be a very interesting trade deadline season.

June 19, 2010

June 20, 2010

I have an old Word document where I jot down ideas for my next report, or tuck them away for a report down the road.

I don't always get around to using all the notes. And I'm not very good about house-cleaning, looking them over and deleting the ones I'll never use. The document is now 108 pages.

In it are a bunch of notes on this year's July 2 international free agent class. Some thoughts I never got around to writing about this winter, regarding players the AL West teams added this off-season, and who they lost. A lot of stuff I've piled up about Rich Harden.

The oldest two notes in the document: (1) something I heard in 1999 about a chance Texas had to trade Ken Hill at the 1997 trade deadline to Cleveland for rookies Bartolo Colon and Damian Jackson; and (2) an Instant Message from Peter Gammons in 2001 that said: "Carlos

It would never sell to the Network TV suits. "Too hokey," they'd say, "viewers would never buy it," and then they'd opt instead for a pilot called "Extreme Extreme Makeover: Home Edition," where Kate Gosselin and Helio Castroneves build a duplex each week, using only the tools found in the Iron Chef's kitchen, Donald Trump's hair products, and Howie Mandel.

Pena's brothers Pedro and Omar are playing for Wareham and each had two hits Thursday."

(Guess I can cross the first one off now. The second one stays, as a reminder to me of how much better this game is because Peter Gammons loves it.)

One thing that's tucked in that document is something I wrote in April but, for whatever reason, I didn't find the right report to put it in:

Blue-chip prospect		Blue-chip prospect
Substance abuse suspension		Regression on the field
Traded, sold low	December 21, 2007	Traded, sold low
Sports Illustrated mid-season awards: Runner-up, AL MVP	July 2008	*Sports Illustrated* mid-season awards: Runner-up, NL Cy Young
2008 All-Star Game (first full MLB season)	July 15, 2008	2008 All-Star Game (first full MLB season)
Whoops (Deadspin: photos/bar)	Just before Spring Training 2009	Whoops (Deadspin: video/guns)
Disabled list—ribcage strain	May 2009	Disabled list stint—back spasms
Second DL stint—abdominal surgery	June 2, 2009	Second DL stint—right elbow surgery
Regression on the field	April 2010	Substance abuse suspension

I was about to delete it tonight but as I stared at that final "Regression on the field" note for Josh Hamilton, which I wrote in April but which now seems like 10 months ago, I thought I'd toss it in here.

The parallels between Hamilton and Edinson Volquez's careers since The Trade have been remarkable. Pay attention to what Volquez has been doing on his ahead-of-schedule rehab (eight scoreless innings, three hits, no walks, seven strikeouts in two appearances), and if his location is there, you can see where he might surprise some people in the second half and have as much impact for the Reds as any trade deadline pickup gives another contender.

But whatever Volquez manages to do in 2010, it seems unlikely that it would parallel what Hamilton has been doing for the last five weeks (.421/.445/.744 in 121 at-bats since May 18, with nine home runs and 29 RBI in 30 games) and seems poised to do for the season.

To put it in perspective: In his storybook 2008 season, Hamilton hit .304/.371/.530.

Right now, even including his pedestrian six-week start to the 2010 season, he sits at .337/.381/.600 for the year.

He'd have to hit .280/.363/.477 the rest of the way this year to end up, in the same number of at-bats, with his 2008 slash line.

And that could happen. There's no way Hamilton keeps this ridiculous run going and stays this locked in all year. He may see his numbers recede a bit, but then again may be Ian Kinsler will pick his production numbers up, and maybe Nelson Cruz's hamstrings are done barking for the year, and even if Julio Borbon cools off, Elvis Andrus should get to clicking again eventually.

This offense is so different when Hamilton is right.

Another note I may never use if I don't use it now: While Colby Lewis leads major league starting pitchers in opponents' batting average (.187, ahead of Ubaldo Jimenez's .189), Chris Ray—who for whatever reason I still find that I don't completely trust—is holding opponents to a .189 clip out of the Rangers pen.

Lewis's complete opposing slash line is .187/.267/.323. Ryan Raburn, in other words.

Ray's is .189/.286/.333. Raburn after maybe a 1 for 5 with a double and a walk.

Meanwhile, Kevin Millwood, the pitcher whose departure essentially made Lewis and Ray (and Rich

Harden) Rangers, won his first game of the season on Saturday, and sits at .296/.348/.486 for the year. The average hitter against Millwood this year is in Ryan Braun/Hanley Ramirez territory.

Buster Olney featured Michael Young in his Sunday column for ESPN, including this anecdote:

[R]ight near the trade deadline last season, Rangers GM Jon Daniels recalled the other day, he got a phone call from Young, who was in the clubhouse. Texas was thinking about making deals to augment the team for a run at the AL West title—but to do so, of course, the Rangers would've had to trade some of their young players.

"Hey, listen," Young told Daniels. "I just want you to know—do what you have to do, but don't do something just to appease us down here."

In other words: Young understood if the Rangers decided not to trade for someone like Roy Halladay.

"We like where you guys are headed," Young told Daniels. "We like the young players."

I think I'm at the point right now, seeing what Colby Lewis has become and what Josh Hamilton has re-become, and seeing that good-looking 3.5-game lead in the West with a day off tomorrow and the Pirates and Astros (who tonight designated for assignment three players who played against Texas today: righthander Casey Daigle, outfielder Cory Sullivan—who will be replaced by Jason Bourgeois—and catcher Kevin Cash, whose departure paves the way for Jason Castro, the Stanford catcher whom the Astros passed on Justin Smoak in order to draft in 2008) coming to town, and the club possibly three weeks away from an ownership transition, where I'm hopeful that if Young makes that same phone call to Daniels in a month, Daniels "does what he has to do," and goes and adds a Guy.

In other words, remember that Step Five we talked about a year and a month ago? Say it with me:

It's time.

June 22, 2010

OK, that whiteboard document I mentioned the other day is starting to pile up with things I need to write about, but I'm not going to do a full-length report today.

I have just one question to toss out there.

I've read a bunch of articles and heard a bunch of radio talk in the last week suggesting something like this:

It would take a lot in the way of young players and top prospects to trade for Cliff Lee—but not as much as it would take to get Roy Oswalt, since he's under contract for the 2011 season while Lee would just be a two-month rental.

Really?

Answer this: What would you pay Oswalt on the open market this winter? Let's say this was his free agent year, just like Lee. Assume (however unlikely) that Oswalt would want just a one-year deal for 2011. You're Texas—not the Yankees, not the Red Sox, not the Angels. What would he be worth?

Would you pay him $10 million to pitch here in 2011?

$16 million?

$18 million?

If, like me, you would not pay Roy Oswalt $18 million to pitch for Texas in 2011 if he were on the open market, then the second year remaining on Oswalt's current deal is a negative, not a positive.

Right?

If you wouldn't choose to pay Oswalt $18 million to pitch in 2011 ($16 million base plus $2 million buyout for the 2012 option), then you'd be better off trading for Lee and recouping the two first-round picks in next year's draft when (if?) he signed elsewhere this winter.

Two other things on that point:

1. Sure, you'd get draft pick compensation a year later on Oswalt, but right now Lee is a solid Type A free agent while Oswalt is a Type B—if Oswalt stays in that territory over the next year and a half of baseball (will he really get better?), then he's going to kick back a supplemental first when he leaves via free agency (purportedly to return to Houston), rather than the first-rounder plus supplemental first that Lee is sure to bring. So with Oswalt you'd get the compensation a year later—and probably a first-round pick less.
2. Lee is a better pitcher.

All that ignores another obvious point—that Lee makes $9 million in 2010, while Oswalt makes $15 million. That means Lee will earn $3 million over the final two months this season, and Oswalt $5 million.

That $2 million difference isn't all that significant—if you were getting an equal or better pitcher, that is, which I don't think Oswalt is.

Now, Houston may *ask* for more than Seattle will, especially from the Rangers (see my May 23 report for reasons why), but don't assume the Mariners will be any more reasonable in their demands, or that they should be. Won't Jack Z need to be extra sure that he doesn't lose a Cliff Lee trade with a team he's chasing inside the division? Won't there be more suitors for Lee—not only because he's a better pitcher but also because his lack of the no-trade card that Oswalt has widens the field?

And back to my primary point—isn't the fact that Lee is a "rental" a *plus*, when weighed against the $18 million you'd have to commit to Oswalt to be in your uniform in 2011?

I think Lee is going to cost more. Probably more than Texas ought to give up. It seems to me that all these stories and talk show segments suggesting the price for Oswalt will be higher than Seattle's price for Lee are wrong.

If, instead, I'm the one who's wrong about that, then I don't need to take Houston's calls—unless they want to talk about Blake Beavan or Alexi Ogando or Michael Kirkman plus a bat (Mitch Moreland?) for Brett Myers. If not, and if the price for Oswalt really is greater than it is for Lee, then I'm not sure why I wouldn't take the time I'd be spending on the phone with the Astros and dial up the Mariners instead.

June 22, 2010

Texas, at 42-28, has the second-best record in baseball, one game behind the Yankees.

The Rangers' nine-game win streak matches the Dodgers and Braves for the longest by any team in 2010.

It matches the second-longest win streak in the franchise's 39 seasons (there was a 14-game run in 1991).

The division lead on the Angels, who just defeated the Dodgers, remains 3.5 games—but five, significantly, in the loss column.

What would the AL West standings look like if Vladimir Guerrero and Darren Oliver were still Angels?

June 23, 2010

June 24, 2010

June 25, 2010

Streakin' in the park
This one goes to eleven
Lots of highlight gold

According to Baseball Prospectus, the Rangers this morning have an 87 percent chance of winning the American League West.

The more pertinent number is 17.

Texas plays the Angels 19 times in 2010, and though we're within 10 games of the season midpoint right now, 17 of those head-to-head battles still remain.

The first three of those follow this weekend's series, Texas hosting Houston and Los Angeles hosting the Rockies.

Granted, these 11 straight wins have come against four teams that aren't going anywhere this year, but good teams treat bad teams badly, and if the Rangers had managed to go so much as a healthy 7-4 over that stretch, they'd have only a precarious half-game lead over the Angels.

Instead, the lead is 4.5 games—six in the loss column—and this team is playing with a resolve right now that looks like it belongs to a winner.

There's 90 games left to play, and obviously there's plenty of time for Los Angeles to turn this race around.

But if Texas can find a way to win, say, 10 of those 17 remaining matchups against the Angels, then that would separate these two teams by nine losses irrespective of the rest of the schedule, and you don't need a Baseball Prospectus table to tell you what the odds of October baseball would look like in that case.

June 27, 2010

There are 88 games left on the regular season schedule.

If the Rangers, owners of the second-best record in Major League Baseball and one game short of catching the Yankees, play .500 ball the rest of the way, they will finish 89-73.

The club is on a 98- or 99-win pace, and even playing mediocre baseball from here on out shouldn't bounce Texas out of contention.

Having the wherewithal to add a key piece or two over the next five weeks, and getting it done without crossing the line into crazy, would move the needle forward even more in what has been one of the most electrifying Rangers seasons ever.

There's going to be one general manager watching Tommy Hunter face off against Roy Oswalt tonight in Arlington, envisioning the opposing starter wearing his club's uniform in the second half. And I'm not sure there won't be two GM's doing exactly that.

I'll be a guest on Dale Hansen's Sports Special tonight (Channel 8, 10:30 p.m.). But I won't blame you for not

Newberg Report: Top Ten Minor League Tools

Texas balances pitching prospects and position players

By Jamey Newberg / Special to MLB.com

June 24, 2010

One of the things that stands out in a review of the position players with the highest upsides in the Rangers' deep farm system is that most are at the lower levels of the organization. While the Rangers' pitching prospects are stacked in crowded waves from top to bottom, the system is not as flush in hitters.

But Texas is working to address the imbalance. Through trades and intensified efforts internationally, the club has added a number of raw, toolsy players in recent years, mostly up the middle, favoring them over productive amateurs who lack projectability.

What follows is not a ranking of the top 10 position player prospects in the Rangers farm system, but instead a ranking of the top 10 tools among those players being groomed to hit and play defense in the big leagues.

1. LEONEL DE LOS SANTOS, C, Hickory: ARM

The slightly built "Macumba" earns the rare "80" grade (20-80 scale) for his standout throwing arm behind the plate. There are major questions about the 20-year-old's bat (he sits at .163/.180/.194 for the Crawdads this season), but the Dominican's defensive skills alone could get him to the Major Leagues.

2. JURICKSON PROFAR, SS, Spokane: GLOVE

Truthfully, the Rangers believe the 17-year-old Profar's hit tool, run tool and arm could be very special, not to mention his makeup and game instincts. But, it's his glove at this point that stands out. Remember, this is a kid whom most interested clubs wanted to sign as a pitcher, given the low-90s velocity he flashed in his early teens. Yet, his ability to catch everything he can get to earns as much praise as anything else he does. Incidentally, Texas made the aggressive move to assign Profar to the Northwest League to start his career, and thus far he has hit safely in each of his five games against competition four years older.

3. LEURY GARCIA, SS, Hickory: ARM

Garcia's arm and run combination have naturally prompted some to nickname the Dominican 19-year-old "Furcalito." Parts of his game remain raw and inconsistent, but he's a threat on the bases (38 steals in 43 attempts in his first 65 Crawdads games) and has an absolute cannon from short that belies his skinny 5'3" frame.

4. JAKE SKOLE, CF, Arizona League: HIT

Like Profar, Skole is a player whose whole Texas judges to be greater than the sum of his parts. Though an ankle injury wiped out nearly all of his high school senior season and led some experts to believe he might fall out of the first round of the draft, the Rangers had seen enough of him over several years to believe that his hit, run, arm, and glove tools would all play up, and they didn't want to take the chance that another team might have taken him if they passed on him at the number 15 pick, hoping he'd fall to 22.

5. ENGEL BELTRE, CF, Bakersfield: GLOVE

A player whose ceiling was compared to Darryl Strawberry and Ken Griffey Jr. when he signed at age 16 with Boston, Beltre has tantalized the Rangers with his raw talent ever since coming over in the Eric Gagné trade, but it hasn't been until this year (.326/.374/.464) that his tools have translated into production. The 20-year-old can do it all, but his glove, arm, and run tool stand out at the moment.

6. JORGE ALFARO, C, Dominican Summer League: ARM

Signed for $1.3 million out of Colombia before the season, Alfaro possesses tremendous raw power and advanced tools behind the plate, including a 70 arm that's strong and accurate. He's years away but has as much upside as any catcher in the organization.

7. DAVID PAISANO, OF, Bakersfield: ARM

An add-on that Texas insisted on in the Danks-McCarthy trade with the White Sox in 2006, Paisano has the range to cover center field but owns a true right fielder's arm, perhaps the strongest in the system from the outfield. The 22-year-old from Venezuela has been inconsistent at the plate. Though he's hitting .299 in a second run at California League pitching, he's gone down on strikes every fifth at-bat.

8. JOSE FELIX, C, Bakersfield: GLOVE

Felix is having a phenomenal year controlling the running game. There have been 53 attempts to steal with the 21-year-old behind the plate—and 33 of those runners have been cut down. The Mexico native's 62 percent caught stealing rate not only leads the California League, it's the only rate in the league higher than 38 percent. Felix has hit a little in 2010 (.285/.331/.376) but it's his tools defensively that will carry him up the chain.

9. MIGUEL VELAZQUEZ, OF, Hickory: POWER

In a system relatively thin on power-hitting prospects, Velazquez stands out. The 22-year-old completed his first full season in 2009, hitting for average and power at Spokane, and he got off to a tremendous start with Hickory this spring. While his numbers have cooled a bit over the last month, the raw power potential is tremendous. The Puerto Rico native now has 23 home runs in 588 career at-bats, and he's barely scratched the surface in terms of converting tools into production.

10. MIKE OLT, 3B, Spokane, & CHRISTIAN VILLANUEVA, 3B, Arizona League: GLOVE

The 21-year-old Olt and the 19-year-old Villanueva have only 13 and 8 pro at-bats stateside, respectively, but the Rangers are expecting big things from both, not only at the plate but also at third base, where both are considered advanced defenders with 70 gloves. Olt, a supplemental first-round pick out of the University of Connecticut last month, and Villanueva, a free agent signed out of Mexico in 2008, are years away at best, but the Rangers believe they have the chance to help turn a position of relative weakness in the system into a strength.

Others considered for this list but who narrowly missed inclusion were shortstop Luis Sardinas (run, glove), outfielder Teodoro Martinez (run), outfielder Guillermo Pimentel (arm), outfielder Craig Gentry (run, glove), outfielder Mitch Moreland (hit), outfielder Jordan Akins (arm, power, run), and catcher Kellin Deglan (arm).

flipping over if Texas-Houston is still going on, as the Rangers try to move a little closer to a 100-victory pace with a win over a pitcher who would probably like to make about two dozen starts in this ballpark over the next year and a half.

June 27, 2010

I'm not going to take one Roy Oswalt effort in Rangers Ballpark and come to the conclusion that he should no longer be on the radar, but I'll refer back to what I wrote six days ago, and suggest that if it would take less to get Cliff Lee, as some writers continue to report, then I see no reason to prefer Oswalt.

I'll also refer to this morning's report and suggest that any team peddling a veteran starting pitcher to Texas over the next month ought to be asking for Tommy Hunter as part of the return. Every team can use a guy like that at or near the back of the rotation.

(Including Texas, of course, and I'm guessing the Rangers won't be willing to move a 2010 rotation piece to get another, even if it's presumably an upgrade.)

The Yankees trail the Dodgers, 6-3, in the ninth inning. If Los Angeles holds on, New York and Texas will share baseball's best record, at 46-29.

I'm on Dale Hansen's Sports Special on Channel 8 locally in a few minutes (10:30 Central). Joe Trahan hosts tonight.

June 28, 2010

The Rangers have announced that righthander Omar Beltre will be recalled to make Wednesday night's start in Anaheim. The move pushes C.J. Wilson back to Thursday's start, and Colby Lewis to Friday's series opener at home against the White Sox.

Beltre, who along with Alexi Ogando had been unable to reenter the United States for five years until that situation was resolved this off-season, has a 2.39 ERA for Oklahoma City. Shifted from the RedHawks' bullpen to the club's rotation a month ago, his ERA in five starts is 1.25 and he's held opponents to a .203 batting average over that span, fanning 24 in 21.2 innings. In 37.2 innings altogether this season, the 28-year-old has allowed just one home run and induced twice as many groundouts as flyouts.

June 29, 2010

Tanner Scheppers moved from the AAA bullpen into the rotation two weeks ago. Teammate Michael Kirkman has rediscovered his command. Frisco horse Blake Beavan is on a ridiculous roll, firing 10 straight quality starts (7-2, 1.80, five walks and 42 strikeouts in 70 innings). Derek Holland and Rich Harden are getting healthier.

But when Texas decided to use Monday's off-day not to skip the fifth starter but instead to give Colby Lewis two extra days of rest (something he was afforded on occasion in Japan), the club could have thrown Dustin Nippert back out there against the Angels (who have slapped a 6.40 ERA on him lifetime, including a 9.49 mark in Anaheim) and not looked to the farm or the disabled list at all.

But rather than worry about Nippert giving them a third straight three-inning start, killing the bullpen in a crucial series, Texas chose to reach down for another option. The club could have held Guillermo Moscoso or Doug Mathis out of their last AAA starts to have them ready to go in Anaheim, but didn't. Matt Harrison (1.50 ERA over his last five appearances, though averaging just 38 pitches) could have gotten the opportunity. The call could have gone to Scheppers or Kirkman or Beavan, but the Rangers didn't feel the time was right for them.

As recently as 20 weeks ago, nobody would have bet on Omar Beltre having a big league career.

But even 20 hours ago, nobody could have guessed that Beltre would be the Rangers' ninth starter in 2010. In spite of his advanced age and spot on the 40-man roster, he got only one appearance with the big club in spring training, a one-inning look in which he fanned a couple and allowed one baserunner, on a walk. Ogando, by comparison, got into five Cactus League games. Kirkman got more of a spring training look than Beltre. So did Zach Phillips. And Michael Ballard. And Richard Bleier.

Who knows what Beltre will do Wednesday night when he takes the ball in the bottom of the first? Here's what you can expect: command of a fastball-slider-split repertoire, lots of ground balls, and a pitcher who won't be overwhelmed by what, objectively speaking, ought to be an overwhelming experience.

You've heard plenty about the long odds that Alexi Ogando faced and overcame in getting to the big leagues after a five-year exile from the United States, but the 28-year-old Beltre served the same sentence, was always a more heralded prospect, and thus theoretically had more taken from him than his fellow Dominican. After a five-year span during which no sentence that included Ogando was without Beltre's name as well, the two will be teammates tomorrow, not in the Dominican Summer League or in Oklahoma City, but in Anaheim as members of the Texas Rangers pitching staff.

After its heyday in the previous decade, Texas made a relatively light impact in Latin America in the 1990s. In 2000, however, the franchise got opportunistic. Cincinnati had secured a verbal agreement from the 6'3", 190-lb. Beltre in the fall of 1999 to sign for a reported $300,000. But the Reds delayed papering the deal so that they could assign Beltre's signing bonus to the organization's 2000 budget. The administrative tactic backfired.

As his deal hung in limbo, Beltre amped his velocity up several miles per hour that winter, touching the mid-90s as an 18-year-old (believed at the time to be 17), and he walked away from the Cincinnati commitment. Texas outbid several other interested teams and landed the big righthander for what was reported to be $650,000 in March 2000.

Believing he was ready for the challenge, not only physically but mentally and emotionally as well, the Rangers promptly assigned Beltre to the short-season Gulf Coast League, where he posted a 3.54 ERA, a .238 opponents' average, and just 15 walks in 61 innings. League managers named him the circuit's 10th-best prospect.

In his second season, Beltre posted similar numbers for advanced rookie-level Pulaski (fronting a rotation that included C.J. Wilson) while nearly doubling his strikeout rate, leading the short-season Appalachian League with six wins. Turning just 20 at the end of that season, he had replaced the injured Jovanny Cedeno as the club's top long-term pitching hope.

But elbow surgery wiped Beltre's 2002 season out, and he spent the 2003 (Low A Clinton) and 2004 (High A Stockton) seasons working in middle relief. He was healthy again, but his place on the club's prospect depth charts was receding.

It then disappeared during the span between 2005 and this January, when he was denied a work visa for five years due to his involvement in a marriage fraud and human trafficking scam. In those five years he was limited to pitching in the Dominican Summer League—there was even talk that Texas considered selling him at one point to a Japanese club, as bleak as his prospects for reentry into the States appeared to be—and while he was ridiculously dominant in the DSL (1.33 ERA, 120 hits and 29 walks in 176.1 innings, 222 strikeouts, one home run), he was a man in his mid-20s pitching against kids in their late teens, at a time in his pitching life when he probably would have reached Arlington if not for the legal issues.

As you watch Beltre pitch and begin to get a feel for his approach, you won't be that far behind the Angels, who simply can't have scouted him as extensively as most prospects on the doorstep of the big leagues are typically scouted. He's only logged 37.2 innings this season, nine AAA relief appearances followed by a mid-May transfer into the Oklahoma City rotation (a stretch of five starts that also included one relief outing when he returned from a two-week shutdown early in June due to a ribcage muscle issue—he also had a short disabled list stint in May with an elbow strain). And if the Angels only saw him work out of the RedHawks' bullpen, they saw a different pitcher from the one who was asked to go through an opposing lineup more than once.

As a reliever this year, Beltre posted a 3.94 ERA and .300 opponents' average, walking six batters per nine innings and fanning 11 per nine.

As a starter: 1.25 ERA, .203 opponents' average, three walks per nine, 10 strikeouts per nine.

And in spite of the healthy strikeout rate, he's nonetheless averaged just 13 pitches per inning as a starting pitcher. He's not going to light up a radar gun the way Neftali Feliz and Ogando and Scheppers will, but when he's right he's chewing up innings by pounding the zone, particularly with that splitter that generates a groundball barrage, often early in the count. Beltre's pitch efficiency is exactly what Nippert (20 pitches per inning, including 26 per nine in his two starts) has not been able to provide this year.

In his last start, a five-inning effort against New Orleans, Beltre (working with Jarrod Saltalamacchia) held the Zephyrs to two singles and no walks in five scoreless innings, fanning six hitters in a lineup that included blue-chip Marlins prospects Cameron Maybin and Logan Morrison.

Tomorrow, six days later, he'll face a lineup that includes Bobby Abreu, Torii Hunter, and Howie Kendrick.

If Beltre can locate the way he did on Thursday (75 percent of his 56 pitches for strikes), against a lineup completely unfamiliar with him and without the benefit of much of a book on him, he'll have a shot to keep Texas in the game early. Will he make an immediate impact the way Ogando has, making himself as indispensable? Doubtful, but a decent showing would probably earn him a home start against Cleveland next week and perhaps another one against Baltimore before the club reaches the All-Star Break.

Is there a chance that this is a showcase move, that some team in seller's mode has indicated some level of interest in Beltre heading into July? Can't rule it out. But this is a pitcher who will be 29 before the end of the season, and for that reason it's unlikely that a team looking to get younger will key on him.

But there's another layer to that analysis. If Beltre fares well tomorrow, and over a run of several starts heading into the back half of July, could it make Texas a little more comfortable parting with another pitcher who might figure into the rotation picture soon? Sure. Behind Lewis and Wilson and Scott Feldman and Tommy Hunter is a pool of candidates that includes Holland and Harden, and Scheppers and Kirkman and Beavan, and Harrison and Moscoso and Mathis. Martin Perez isn't going to be a factor in 2010, but he's back on track in Frisco. There's some depth there. A solid showing from Beltre could conceivably make a guy like Beavan or Kirkman less difficult to part with.

Who goes to make room for Beltre (who is already on the 40-man roster)? Nippert could be designated for assignment or hidden on the disabled list, though presumably you'd want him around for the Beltre start in case a long man is needed. That role could be assumed by Harrison, however—or Harrison could be optioned to AAA to replace Beltre in the rotation and get stretched out again himself. Surely Ogando is no longer a candidate to be sent back to Oklahoma City. And while Chris Ray has had his issues and could have the leverage of his assignments lessened due to Ogando's presence, I doubt he'd be optioned.

I'd bet on Beltre replacing Nippert or Harrison, the latter of whom would not have to be exposed to league-wide waivers.

And another thought: If Harrison goes down to AAA and slides into Beltre's vacated rotation slot, it could facilitate his own showcase. Despite the variance in experience, Harrison is a full four years younger than Beltre. It would stand to reason that the 24-year-old lefthander (who has 32 big league starts but won't be eligible for arbitration until after the 2011 season) would be involved in July trade discussions. Teams have seen him in the big leagues this year, and he's been especially good in June (2.03 ERA in relief, .208 opponents' average). That's a good reason not to send him down, of course. But putting him on predictable display for scouts every fifth day in Oklahoma City could have a different benefit.

There has been and will continue to be much talk about Vladimir Guerrero's return to Anaheim this week, rightfully so. I continue to ponder what the AL West standings would look like right now if you took Guerrero and Darren Oliver off the Rangers roster and put them back in Los Angeles.

But Beltre's arrival in a major league ballpark is a pretty big story as well, given all that he's gone through. While Guerrero will be the most recognizable figure in Angel Stadium this week, no player will be less familiar than Beltre, and from a baseball standpoint the Rangers are hoping that works somewhat to their advantage.

There's the matter of Scott Feldman-Joel Pineiro to take care of first tonight, but as far as tomorrow night is concerned, make plans to stop by www.FOXSportsSouthwest.com for our third live Newberg Report in-game chat session of the season. I don't have a good feel for how long Omar Beltre will last, but we'll get the chat started before the game begins and go all the way until the final pitch.

June 30, 2010

One heck of a baseball game. The kind you can imagine these two teams playing over and over in their 16 remaining matchups this year, and for the next few years, at least. That's as intense as June baseball can get. The game of inches moments, the blown fundamentals, far too many runners left on base, questionable bunt decisions and bullpen management—it was a game that very easily could have gone the other way.

To get to this point, having built a division lead that will stand no matter what happens in this series, a lot was made of the soft interleague schedule that the Rangers tore through, winning 13 of 15. But the schedule is what it is, and you have to go out and win the games. Last year, Texas split the season series with Toronto, Kansas City, and Baltimore, and lost 11 of 19 to Oakland—four of the five worst teams in the American League. The Rangers finished the year in second place in the West, 10 games back. If they'd properly beaten up on those teams and gone, say, 31-14 instead of 21-24, they'd have finished with the same 97-win total that the Angels did.

And that's partly because Texas managed to go 11-8 against Los Angeles last year. If the Rangers can repeat that success against the Angels this season (they've won 2 of 3 so far), they'll win this division.

Texas is 20-6 in June.

The Angels are 18-8.

Neither team is going away.

Hopefully Omar Beltre is half as impressive tonight as Alexi Ogando was last night (perfect 12-pitch seventh, eight strikes).

We chat during tonight's game, at www.foxsportssouthwest.com, starting shortly before the 9:05 first pitch. See you then.

June 30, 2010

The Rangers need to make a player move in the next 30 minutes to clear a roster spot for Omar Beltre to make tonight's start, and while it seems that an option of Matt Harrison to AAA is the likely move, the player getting the most Rangers buzz right now is Giants catcher Bengie Molina, who several national and local outlets are reporting is the subject of "serious talks" between San Francisco and Texas. The 35-year-old former Angel, a defensively advanced catcher standing in the way of Buster Posey settling in behind the plate, is playing on a one-year, $4.5 million contract for the Giants.

While a Fox report filed by Jon Paul Morosi and Ken Rosenthal suggested that Chris Davis or Jarrod Saltalamacchia could be of interest to the Giants, in the last few minutes Morosi stated on Twitter that neither would be involved in a Molina deal. San Francisco simply doesn't have the kind of leverage with Molina to command that sort of return.

The original article, posted less than 60 minutes ago, suggests that a trade could go down within 24 hours.

Ready for tonight's live in-game chat session? Head over to www.FOXSportsSouthwest.com and click the "Live Chat with Jamey Newberg" banner under the header image.

Not sure if we'll know about the Molina deal tonight, but soon enough we'll know whether Harrison will be the roster casualty to make room for Beltre.

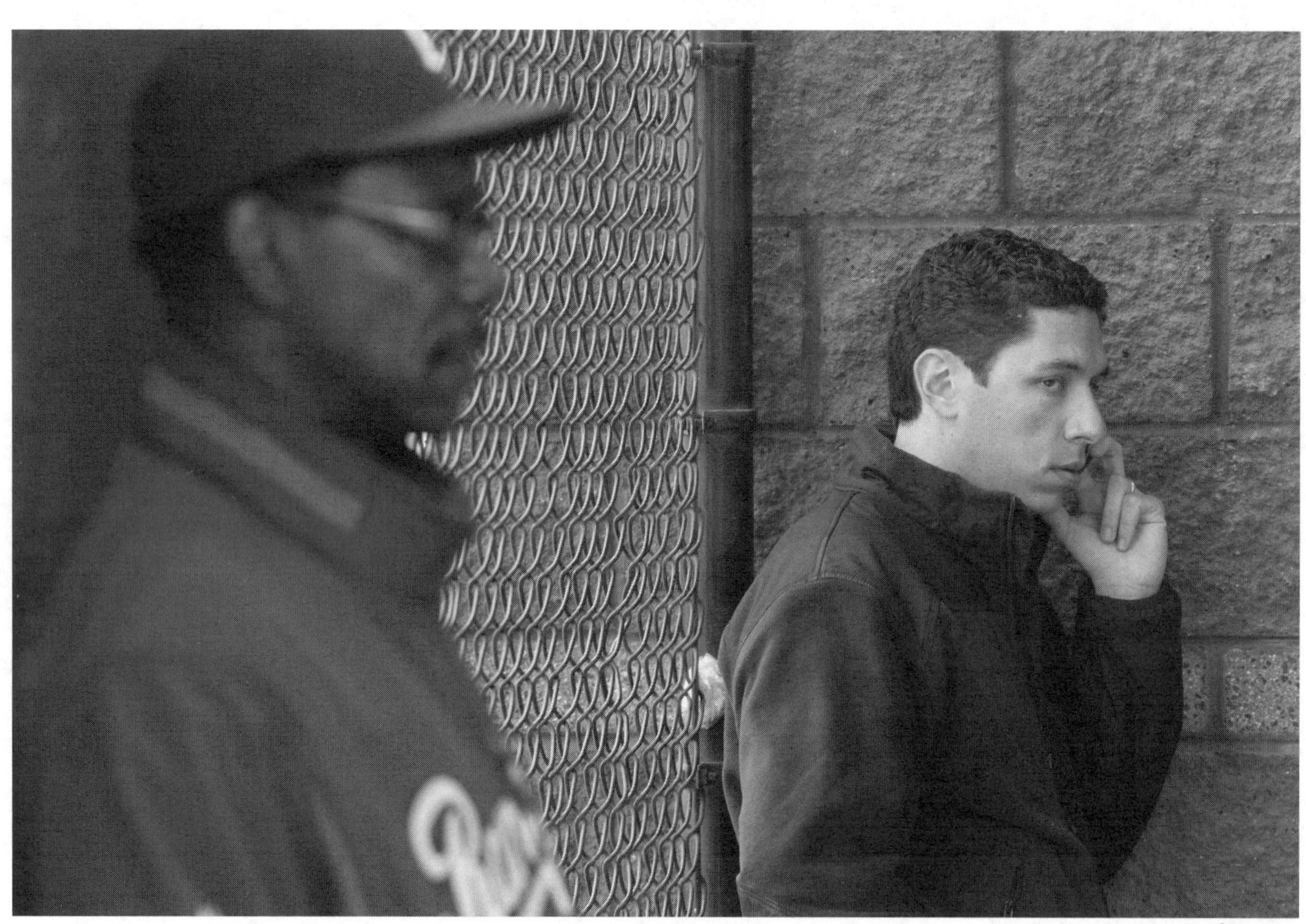

Brad Newton

JULY 2010

40-MAN ROSTER (39)

PITCHERS (21)

Omar Beltre, Scott Feldman, Neftali Feliz, Frankie Francisco, Rich Harden, Matt Harrison, Derek Holland, Tommy Hunter, Michael Kirkman, Colby Lewis, Doug Mathis, Brandon McCarthy, Guillermo Moscoso, Dustin Nippert, Darren O'Day, Alexi Ogando, Darren Oliver, Zach Phillips, Chris Ray, Pedro Strop, C.J. Wilson

CATCHERS (4)

Max Ramirez, Jarrod Saltalamacchia, Taylor Teagarden, Matt Treanor

INFIELDERS (7)

Elvis Andrus, Joaquin Arias, Andres Blanco, Chris Davis, Ian Kinsler, Justin Smoak, Michael Young

OUTFIELDERS (7)

Brandon Boggs, Julio Borbon, Nelson Cruz, Craig Gentry, Vladimir Guerrero, Josh Hamilton, David Murphy

60-DAY DISABLED LIST (3)

Eric Hurley, Warner Madrigal, Omar Poveda

July 1, 2010

Rich Harden, Scott Feldman, and Omar Beltre have made 30 starts this season, recording only eight wins. Their collective ERA is 5.59.

But they've started the three games during which we've done Fox Sports Southwest chats this season—and we're 3-0 in those games. (Thanks to the hundreds of you who participated.)

Beltre wasn't sharp last night—37 of his 85 pitches were balls, most everything was up, and he issued four walks (after walking only one in his last three AAA starts, throwing 70 percent of his pitches for strikes)—but there was plenty to like. His fastball has tons of life, his breaking ball is an out pitch, and only two of the five hits he gave up were hit hard—including the Erick Aybar home run he served up on the fourth big league pitch he threw. (It was only the second bomb Aybar has hit in 2010, and only the second Beltre has allowed this season.)

Beltre appeared nervous at times. He averaged over 21 pitches per inning (a dramatic difference from the 12.4 he averaged in those last three AAA starts), which resulted in a four-inning stint that didn't qualify for the win. But he set six hitters down on strikes, kept Texas in a game that it ultimately won, and you'd think he earned another start, probably when Cleveland visits Arlington next week.

When is a home run not as good as a triple? Never, unless you lack the three-bagger for the cycle and instead go deep for a second time and were hoping for some SportsCenter love. What Vladimir Guerrero did last night was better than a cycle, and couldn't have been more forceful.

Imagine you're an Angels fan. You go into this series 4.5 games behind Texas (six in the loss column), but confident that the division deficit is only temporary, especially after taking Game One in this series and, in Game Two, drawing a rookie making his big league debut after fewer than 40 innings above Class A. You get an early lead and knock the kid out after four innings, forcing Dustin Nippert into the game. You're feeling good, starting to imagine a sweep.

Then you see Guerrero, who had homered (and singled and added a sac fly) the night before in his first game in Anaheim as an ex-Angel, go 4 for 4 with two no-doubt home runs, a scorched double, and a single, driving in five of the Rangers' six runs.

It's easy to appreciate that win from a Rangers' fan's perspective, but think about how crummy a loss that had to be for an Angels fan. Like a Niners fan watching Deion Sanders or Charles Haley do his thing as a Cowboy, only Bigger and Badder.

Guerrero has stepped in against his former teammate Jered Weaver only three times (back on May 18 this year). He has a home run and a double in those three trips.

Weaver vs. C.J. Wilson tonight. The Rangers will say it's not all that big a game.

It's big.

Fox Sports reporter Jon Paul Morosi writes this morning that the player to be named later in the Bengie Molina trade, which is expected to be made official today, will be a Class A pitcher. ESPN's Buster Olney tweets that the player will be a "mid-tier prospect." That would theoretically include candidates like Wilfredo Boscan, Jake Brigham, Fabio Castillo, Michael Main (who has been promoted to Frisco), Carlos Pimentel, Neil Ramirez, Braden Tullis, and Corey Young. Do not fear a guy like Wilmer Font or Robbie Ross or Matt Thompson or Joe Wieland being part of this deal.

Morosi adds that the Giants will pay the remainder of Molina's $4.5 million salary, while Texas will be responsible for the balance of Chris Ray's $975,000 contract.

Olney suggests that the nature of the trade shows how Texas could accomplish a Cliff Lee trade even if the club is not out of bankruptcy: "They could include a contract of another player (Rich Harden?), and get some salary relief from SEA to even out the money—and in return, give SEA a strong package of prospects. A deal without adding $."

If that were the case, the type of prospects the Rangers would have to part with to convince Seattle to go in that direction rather than deal with another team would probably be massively prohibitive.

For what it's worth, Harden has an ERA of 0.86 in nine career Safeco Field appearances, with 46 strikeouts and 14 walks in 42 innings. He has held Mariners hitters to a silly .147/.226/.196 slash line in their home park.

According to Ken Rosenthal of Fox Sports, the Rangers had a scout on hand for Lee's last start. So did the Mets and Phillies. The Twins and Dodgers apparently did not.

According to a local report, Texas also scouted Cleveland righthander Fausto Carmona's last start.

We have had two sponsors step forward with regard to Newberg Report Night on July 25: the fine folks at OSAR Consulting (which creates the productivity solutions "Go-Work" and "GoWeb," to enhance your business, increase revenue, and reduce costs: http://www.osar.com/Services.aspx) and Leapfrog Executive Search (which offers "Retained Search for HR Leaders": www.lhre.net).

Among the prizes lined up so far for the charity auction and raffle:

- MLB baseball signed by Tommy Hunter
- MLB baseball signed by Tanner Scheppers
- MLB baseball signed by Derek Holland
- Rangers batting practice baseball signed by Rusty Greer
- Baseball signed by Michael Young, Josh Hamilton, Ian Kinsler, Scott Feldman, David Murphy, Justin Smoak,

Newberg Report: Buyers Beware

Trading for impact hitter not always risk worth taking

By Jamey Newberg / Special to MLB.com

July 1, 2010

Recently, ESPN baseball columnist Buster Olney, discussing the market for Prince Fielder, wrote that Scott Boras thinks he can get more for his client than the five-year, $125 million extension that Ryan Howard signed in April, and added:

"Whether that is true or not remains to be seen, but the fact that the agent is thinking that way won't help the Brewers market Fielder. Keep in mind, too, that perception of the Rangers' trade of Mark Teixeira in the middle of his fifth full year of service time—a good comparable to Fielder now—is now seen as a giant, overwhelming, one-side win for Texas. It's hard to imagine any team offering a package to the Brewers that is anything close to what the Rangers got for Teixeira."

The way that trade played out for Atlanta, not only in 2007 and in 2008 but also in 2009, it's hard to imagine a worse precedent for loading up to acquire a fifth-year hitter.

The Braves were in a tailspin in late July 2007, having lost nine of 14 and falling to a season-worst 4 1/2 games back in the National League East. But then-general manager John Schuerholz, who had privately decided that season would be the final of his 26 as a big league GM, wanted to take one last shot at a title and agreed to send catcher Jarrod Saltalamacchia and four Minor Leaguers to Texas for Teixeira and reliever Ron Mahay.

Looking at it from Schuerholz's perspective, the Braves would have Teixeira for both the 2007 and 2008 pennant races, and Matt Harrison was the only one of the four prospects (Elvis Andrus, Neftali Feliz, and Beau Jones were the others) who had any shot at all to show up during that same year and a half.

But Atlanta would go just 29-27 the rest of the way in 2007, missing the playoffs for only the second time in 13 years despite tremendous production from Teixeira (a .317 average and 1.020 OPS, with 17 home runs and 56 RBIs in 54 games). Sometimes the hill is too high to climb to expect one player to carry a team where it misguidedly thinks it belongs.

The Braves compounded things by making the decision, just before the non-waiver Trade Deadline the following year, to trade Teixeira to the Angels for Casey Kotchman and Minor League reliever Steve Marek. Atlanta was well out of the race, seven games below .500 and fourth in its division, and so it made sense to at least test Teixeira's market two months before he'd be able to leave via free agency.

But new Braves GM Frank Wren either heeded bad advice or found a shrinking market for a hitter who had the second-highest RBI total in baseball during his two half-seasons in Atlanta—but who couldn't get his team into a pennant race either year and who was thought to be a good bet to land in New York or Boston or Baltimore in the offseason. The difference between the five players that Texas got and the two that Atlanta flipped Teixeira for was staggering.

It got worse. Not only did Teixeira hit .358/.449/.632 for the Angels, who won 100 games and made the playoffs, but with the two compensatory Draft picks (for the loss of Teixeira to the Yankees) that more or less could have been Atlanta's, Los Angeles drafted high school outfielder Mike Trout (first round) and high school left-hander Tyler Skaggs (supplemental first) in June 2009.

Trout is probably one of the top 10 prospects in baseball right now, and Skaggs is having a breakout season as an 18-year-old in the full-season Midwest League.

Olney was correct in pointing out that the Rangers' trade of Teixeira to Atlanta in 2007 was a "giant, overwhelming, one-side win for Texas," but the Braves turned it into an even greater loss when they tried playing seller with Teixeira in 2008.

Teixeira produced as a Brave. That club is doing just fine right now. But those two trades went very badly for the Braves, and there's no telling where they'd be if they still had Andrus and Feliz, or even if they'd held onto Teixeira and taken the two first-round picks when he left for New York.

Prince Fielder isn't the player that Mark Teixeira is, but even if he were, implicit in Olney's observation is that giving up a loaded package of prospects for a hitter—even one as accomplished as Teixeira or Fielder—and even in exchange for a season and a half from the player just wouldn't be a very good bet.

Derek Holland, Tommy Hunter, Craig Gentry, Brandon McCarthy, Chris Davis, and Rusty Greer

- Autographed Yovanni Gallardo 8 x 10
- 2008 Newberg Report Bound Edition signed by Chris Davis, Doug Mathis, Blake Beavan, and Johnny Whittleman
- I'm not making this up (and couldn't): Sir Earl Toon from the group Kool and the Gang will call whoever the winner chooses and sing Happy Birthday to them over the phone

And these two needed to be set off from the rest:

Sports artist Pat Payton has donated one of 12 proofs of a print he has made of Nolan Ryan. I've seen the print. It's incredible. You can see it here: *http://www.PatrickPayton.com*

In addition, Payton has agreed to create a custom original piece of art for another winner—any player you choose. Payton's last original apparently went for over $5,000.

As always, we'll raffle off a bunch of the prizes and auction off a select few, including the two Payton pieces. Proceeds will go to the Hello Win Column Fund and to Genesis Women's Shelter.

More details as we get closer.

I think if I won the custom-made Payton piece, I'd have him do a rendition of Vladimir Guerrero the instant after last night's grand slam left his bat.

Unless Big Bad does something even more dramatic tonight.

July 1, 2010

According to *Baseball America* and multiple local reports, righthander Michael Main is the player to be named later in the Bengie Molina trade with San Francisco.

The 21-year-old Main, the second of the Rangers' five first-round picks in 2007 (drafted after Blake Beavan but before Julio Borbon, Tommy Hunter, and Neil Ramirez), went 5-3, 3.45 in 15 starts for High A Bakersfield this season. He'd been promoted to Frisco earlier this week but had yet to make his AA debut. If the report is true, Main accompanies righthander Chris Ray in the deal that will bring Molina to Texas.

Main (number one on my pitching breakout list last year, and number two on my list this year, behind Tanner Scheppers) came into the season with a career mark of 9-10, 4.39 in 37 starts and two relief appearances. While he's not on the top tier of the Rangers' pitching prospects, he is a prospect, seemingly fully healthy for the first time as a pro, and common sense would dictate that his inclusion was agreed upon only because San Francisco is adding cash to the trade so that it doesn't impact the Rangers' 2010 payroll.

July 2, 2010

If you're not crazy about Chris Ray and Michael Main for Bengie Molina, there's one way that we could have been sure it wouldn't have happened: If the Rangers were having a lousy season.

Or if Jarrod Saltalamacchia or Taylor Teagarden had taken a step forward, rather than both going backwards.

Or if the sale of the club had gone through by now.

Or if the Texas farm system wasn't as deep as it is.

Any one of those things would have killed this deal.

But instead, the Rangers started Thursday with the best record in baseball, a catching situation that reminded us this week it needed an upgrade, a financial strait jacket, and a heavy inventory of pitching prospects.

I never really trusted Ray, and particularly with Alexi Ogando's emergence and Tanner Scheppers getting close (and a chance for Pedro Strop to capitalize in between), I'm not sure we'll feel his loss at all. I don't love losing Main, though.

Was I too high on Main when I ranked him the Rangers' number six prospect going into 2008, his first full season? When I ranked him fourth going into 2009, and made him my number one pitching breakout candidate? When I ranked him seventh going into 2010, and number two on the breakout list?

Maybe.

Am I too low on Main when I suggest he'd be my number 18 Rangers prospect right now, 12th among pitchers?

Maybe.

There are two things I have no doubt about:

1. Main has a tremendous shot to pitch in the big leagues. He may not be Tim Hudson, as some initially thought he might be (or Bret Saberhagen, a comp I always liked better), but he has a decent chance to be solid.
2. There are at least half a dozen Rangers pitching prospects, and maybe 10 or 11, whom I would have moved Main before.

Yes, it's frustrating that the Rangers basically had to sell Main for $2 million in order to get a veteran rent-a-catcher they liked. But Jon Daniels is handcuffed with the club in bankruptcy court, and these aren't the days of Eric Hurley and Josh Rupe topping your pitching prospect depth chart, with a big league staff half full of guys who won't be around in two years.

The Rangers may have overpaid for Molina by including Main in the deal—and I'm in the camp that says they did—but given the inventory Texas has, I can understand (given the apparent inability to take on added salary) why this trade was made.

I say "inability," but maybe it was more like a "reluctance" to increase the payroll. We've heard in the last week or two that Texas does have room in the budget to add a contract of unknown size at the trade deadline, and if it took trading Main to preserve that for a bigger deal later this month (or even a big splash in the international free agent class, whose signing window opens today), then I'm OK with that.

Stated another way: If there's a deal out there to be made for a number one or two starter—who it is doesn't matter—and Texas can get it done for a package of players that's acceptable to you and me, if to close the deal the Rangers would have to add Main, you'd do that without looking back, wouldn't you?

But we now know this, even if we all suspected it beforehand: If Michael Main is the cost of $2 million in salary relief to get a player like Molina, the price tag in prospects to get someone like Cliff Lee along with a cash subsidy is one I don't even need to see. (Prominent Seattle blogger Dave Cameron agrees, tweeting yesterday: "Attn Mariners: Please trade Lee to Texas. Based on reported return for Molina, they will pay through the nose if M's pick up his salary.")

Main was consistently a back fields star in Surprise, in March and October, but he's had trouble staying healthy and has only 239 innings of work in four pro seasons, all in Class A or below. He's been good for the most part in 2010, posting a 3.45 ERA in 15 starts in the hitter-friendly California League. San Francisco will reportedly have the 21-year-old make his AA debut in the next few days, just as the Rangers were preparing to do.

But no matter how you tier things, Main is probably a pitcher whose departure can be survived. (Of course, the same was once said about Armando Galarraga.) In the wave that was working at Bakersfield, he was behind Wilmer Font and maybe Joe Wieland and Carlos Pimentel and Wilfredo Boscan and Jake Brigham (recently demoted to Hickory). At Frisco, he certainly would have been behind Martin Perez and Blake Beavan (and Daniel Gutierrez, once he works his way back to that level). A group at Hickory that includes Robbie Erlin and Robbie Ross and Matt Thompson is on the wave behind Main, but gaining on him and probably slotted ahead of him on the overall organizational whiteboard.

Among the 2011 Rule 5 class, while it's premature to handicap things, Perez and Beavan and Tomas Telis likely head a group that would have demanded roster protection ahead of Main. Plus, that doesn't include players from the 2010 group (Font, Pimentel, Boscan, Brigham, Gutierrez, Mitch Moreland, Engel Beltre, Kasey Kiker, Marcus Lemon, Miguel De Los Santos, others) who might be left off this winter but not lost, and then force their way into the roster picture in 2011.

And given Main's troubles with left-handed hitters (.285/.343/.506 this season with the Blaze), whether he'll continue to profile as a middle-of-the-rotation starter rather than a seventh- or eighth-inning reliever as he moves up the ladder could become an issue.

If Texas weren't squarely in contention, there would be no need to address catcher. But with about one-sixth of the club's remaining games coming against the Angels, you can't run Max Ramirez out there and allow Los Angeles to run at will, getting into scoring position and taking away the double play possibility at every chance. And you can't ask Matt Treanor (who's within a dozen games of a career-high workload) to catch every day, particularly in those seven games out of the season's final 14, head to head with the Angels.

And if the Rangers had been sold, maybe the trade would have been Ray for Molina, with no money changing hands and no prospect tacked onto the deal. Main is not Carlos Santana (and Molina is not Casey Blake), but it would have been nice not to have club finances impact the parameters of this trade.

Imagine what Daniels will be able to do with his roster once the financial handcuffs come off. The point of building a strong farm system, as we talk about here all the time, isn't just to develop young talent to groom for your roster—it's also to position yourself to make trades, whether it's to patch a roster hole, as with this deal, or to load up for an impact player.

It's going to be a great day when the ownership transfer is complete, and Daniels can use his tremendous farm system depth to acquire star players, instead of basically selling prospects to avoid taking on salary.

But dialing back to the present realities, the bottom line as I see it is this: Michael Main is a player, all things considered, that you can probably afford to give up.

It's just a shame, given current circumstances, that you had to.

Trading Molina
Main attraction for Giants:
Need cash? Prospect back

July 3, 2010

Tommy Hunter's first big league win came on his 23rd birthday, a 3-1 win in Rangers Ballpark over Tampa Bay.

Tommy Hunter's most recent big league win came on his 24rd birthday, a 3-1 win in Rangers Ballpark over Chicago.

There were lots of differences between the two wins. Hunter lasted only 5.1 innings in last year's, needing 90 pitches and throwing only 61 percent for strikes. More than half of the Texas lineup—Marlon Byrd, Andruw Jones, Hank Blalock, Jarrod Saltalamacchia, and Chris Davis—isn't even around any more.

Tonight, Hunter gave the Rangers seven-plus, throwing 72 percent of his 94 pitches for strikes, a tremendously efficient effort that included, for example, an 0-4 night by Jones that, despite accounting for two of Hunter's three strikeouts, amounted to only 11 Hunter pitches.

Hunter faced 29 White Sox tonight. He started off 25 with a first-pitch strike.

When I was on ESPN Radio yesterday, Ben Rogers asked me rank the top four young Rangers starting pitchers in terms of untouchability at trade time. I said Martin Perez would be the one I'd be least likely to part with, followed by Derek Holland, and then Tanner Scheppers, and finally Hunter—who is now 5-0, 1.98 for the season and has yet to allow more than two earned runs in any of his six starts.

But I finished the point by saying how much I love having Hunter on this staff.

You look at the current Rangers starting five, the rotation that's leading one of baseball's only three teams playing .600 baseball, and I would wager that Hunter is the most likely to be a Texas Ranger three years from now.

I'm still not sure why Joaquin Arias is still around but he did drive in a run and score another, both with John Danks on the mound, giving me an opportunity to shoehorn in the note that Arias and Danks were Stockton teammates in 2004, Frisco teammates in 2005, and Oklahoma teammates in 2006.

I'm more interested in sharing with you that Arias and Ultimate Journeyman Bruce Chen were Oklahoma teammates in 2007. Chen was perfect into the seventh tonight in Anaheim, earning the Royals' second straight win over the Angels, a game that just ended with Kansas City coming out on top, 4-2.

With the white-hot White Sox in Arlington, and the Angels hosting the hapless Royals, after these last two nights Los Angeles has given back the game it gained in the Rangers series. The division lead is back to 4.5 games.

Six in the loss column.

My work now turns to a report I've been meaning to write for about two weeks, one that I can't put off any longer (especially since I'm getting a dozen emails every day asking for it).

Back with that report in the morning. Or maybe Monday.

July 4, 2010

On Monday, Todd Kaufmann of BleacherReport.com ran a story on the Rangers and what Jon Daniels might do before the trade deadline. In it Kaufmann included the following, regarding a recent Twitter exchange I had with well-regarded Mariners blogger Dave Cameron:

For those of you who didn't see this before, Jamey Newberg of The Newberg Report was asked, via Twitter, by David Cameron of USSMariner.com what it would take to get a deal done to send [Cliff] Lee to Texas.

Newberg's response?

"Martin Perez (Double-A left-hander), Chris Davis, and a lesser prospect."

Timeout.

For those Ranger fans, or even Mariner fans, can you for even a second imagine the Mariners taking two minor leaguers and Chris Davis for Cliff Lee?

If I'm Seattle, I'm laughing Jon Daniels off the phone if he thinks that is all it's going to take for the Mariners to send Lee to the American League West leaders.

Sure, the Mariners got Lee from Philadelphia for just about nothing, but they're not going to take nothing to trade him.

One problem. He got it backwards.

Here's the actual exchange:

[me to Dave] *You're Jack Z, JD calls you. What do you realistically ask Texas for in exchange for Lee?*

[Dave to me] *Assuming I have to pick up all of the salary: Perez, Davis, + lesser guy.*

[Dave to me] *In my view, that's pretty close to what Mil gave up for Sabathia two years ago. Agree?*

[me to Dave] *I'd take Perez today over anyone MILW moved for C.C.*

Now while I might agree with Kaufmann that Perez, Davis, and a prospect won't be enough to land Lee (especially if Seattle has to pay for the final third of Lee's $9 million contract for 2010), it was Cameron's Mariners-centric proposal. Not mine.

And what did the Brewers give Cleveland for Sabathia in July 2008? First baseman Matt LaPorta, outfielder Michael Brantley, and righthander Rob Bryson, all minor leaguers, and big league lefthander Zach Jackson.

The Rangers drafted Smoak a month before the Sabathia trade. Their deadline to sign him was a month after the Sabathia trade. The day before that signing deadline, when the local papers were speculating that a deal might not get done—and that it might not be a terrible thing for Texas to walk away (and get an extra first-rounder in 2009) given the way Davis had exploded on the American League with what was then a .900 OPS—I wrote this:

I disagree.

There's no telling what players will be available at number 12 next June, but it's not likely any will have the upside of Smoak, who by all accounts should never have fallen to number 11 two months ago.

And here's the more critical point: Milwaukee got C.C. Sabathia last month because they had Matt LaPorta.

If he develops as expected, an already signing-bonused Smoak will be more valuable as a trade chip than having an extra pick at number 12 next summer would be.

So we now come full-circle (to the extent that a Twitter exchange between two bloggers registers), with one suggesting that the Sabathia trade could be a prototype for what Seattle might expect to get for Lee (who pitched with Sabathia on a 2008 Indians club that amazingly went only 81-81).

Two teams haven't gotten enough when trading Lee (Cleveland got Carlos Carrasco, Jason Knapp, Jason Donald, and Lou Marson from Philadelphia for the reigning AL CY Young Award winner last July, and the Phillies got J.C. Ramirez, Phillippe Aumont, and Tyson Gillies from the Mariners in December). Both packages were inferior to what the Indians got for Sabathia in 2008.

But Seattle will get more than a Sabathia package for Lee this month.

So what is Mariners GM Jack Zduriencik asking for?

Buster Olney of ESPN says "big bat potential . . . and two guys fit the description: Justin Smoak of TEX and Yonder Alonso of the Reds."

According to Ken Rosenthal of Fox Sports, Seattle wants "major league or major-league-ready hitters."

If you asked Bob Nightengale of *USA Today*, the Mariners "say they want hitters in return for Lee."

Charley Walters of the *St. Paul Pioneer Press*, who makes Texas "a slim favorite for Lee," says Seattle wants "lots of hitting prospects."

John Hickey of AOL Fanhouse gets very specific, suggesting the Mariners are targeting "outfielders and . . . left-handed starting pitchers" who project to provide an impact in 2012.

Gerry Fraley of the *Dallas Morning News* writes that Seattle "wants a young catcher in any deal" for Lee—but has no interest in Jarrod Saltalamacchia or Taylor Teagarden.

So here's what we know:

1. Lots of writers believe Seattle wants young impact hitters (and maybe left-handed pitching) in any deal for Lee.
2. Writers aren't always right.
3. A Mariners blogger I have a ton of respect for thinks a package of Martin Perez, Chris Davis, and a prospect might be enough.

So what would you offer for Lee, whose simply awesome 7-3, 2.45 season (78 strikeouts and five walks in 95.2 innings, three straight complete games and four out of five—with four of those five opponents leading their respective divisions) continues with a start that's underway right now in Detroit?

Obviously, the threshold question is whether the Rangers' sale has gone through. The Mariners aren't looking to move Lee just to shed a contract, but with Texas having sold Michael Main to the Giants for $2 million in salary relief this week, let's assume that to cover the $3 million that Lee will earn over the final two months that Texas has to toss in a prospect like Mitch Moreland, in exchange either for the cash or for Seattle's agreement to take Rich Harden in the deal to come close to offsetting the salary. (For what it's worth, which is probably not much, the Mariners were said to be interested in the British Columbia native Harden this winter.)

OK, here we go.

But before you assume that any trade for Lee, who would give this club a lockdown ace to help protect baseball's biggest division lead in the second half and to pitch Game 163, would allow Texas to recoup a couple first-round picks when he bolts for the Yankees this winter, hang on a second.

As of two weeks ago, Eddie Bajek's reverse-engineered Elias projections have Lee as a Type A player, which is no surprise, but at a projected 89.493 Elias number he's in the same neighborhood as Phillies outfielder Jayson Werth (85.125) and Rays outfielder Carl Crawford (83.000). So? New York is rumored to be targeting both outfielders this winter. If they end up outranking Lee and the Yankees sign one of them along with the lefthander, then they would surrender their first-round pick to Philadelphia or Tampa Bay, leaving their second-rounder for whichever team finished the 2010 season with Lee.

Certainly not a contingency that would, on its own, convince you not to pull the trigger on a Lee trade, but maybe worth tucking away.

Categories, if I'm Seattle:

CENTERPIECE PLAYERS: Martin Perez, Tanner Scheppers, Justin Smoak

NEXT TIER: Julio Borbon, Nelson Cruz, Derek Holland, Tommy Hunter, David Murphy, Alexi Ogando

AAA/AA-LEVEL HITTERS: Engel Beltre, Brandon Boggs, Chris Davis, Craig Gentry, Mitch Moreland, Max Ramirez, Jarrod Saltalamacchia, Taylor Teagarden, Chad Tracy

LOWER-LEVEL HITTERS: Jorge Alfaro, Teodoro Martinez, Guillermo Pimentel, Jurickson Profar, Luis Sardinas, Miguel Velazquez

AAA/AA-LEVEL PITCHERS: Blake Beavan, Omar Beltre, Cody Eppley, Daniel Gutierrez, Matt Harrison, Beau Jones, Kasey Kiker, Michael Kirkman, Josh Lueke, Brandon McCarthy, Guillermo Moscoso, Zach Phillips, Pedro Strop

LOWER-LEVEL PITCHERS: Richard Alvarez, Chad Bell (PTBNL), Wilfredo Boscan, Jake Brigham, Ovispo De Los Santos, Robbie Erlin, Wilmer Font, Trevor Hurley, Joseph Ortiz, David Perez, Carlos Pimentel, Neil Ramirez, Robbie Ross, Matt Thompson, Braden Tullis, Joe Wieland

AND: Rich Harden

This will be oversimplified (and probably overthought as well), but let's work on it this way. Let's say the proposed parameters for Lee are: one player from each of the first two tiers, and two more players coming from the remaining tiers.

The Rangers take Borbon, Cruz, and Hunter off the list, and move Ogando into the first tier. Profar is also off limits.

The Mariners immediately eliminate Saltalamacchia and Teagarden (I'm relying on Fraley's note here), and

Gutierrez and Kiker and McCarthy. They also drop Murphy, who doesn't really fit the 2012 profile.

(Cameron and fellow Mariners blogger Jeff Sullivan respectfully request that Zduriencik stay away from Guillermo Pimentel, the outfielder recently promoted from Spokane to Hickory, because it would just be too confusing.) (Not really.)

Several conversations down the line, the categories are whittled down to:

CENTERPIECE PLAYERS: Ogando, Perez, Scheppers, Smoak

NEXT TIER: Holland

AAA/AA-LEVEL HITTERS: E.Beltre, Davis, Gentry, Moreland, M.Ramirez

LOWER-LEVEL HITTERS: T.Martinez, Sardinas, Velazquez

AAA/AA-LEVEL PITCHERS: Beavan, O.Beltre, Harrison, Kirkman, Strop

LOWER-LEVEL PITCHERS: Bell (PTBNL), Boscan, O.De Los Santos, Erlin, Font, Ross, Thompson, Tullis, Wieland

AND: Harden

Holland was a favorite of Mariners pitching coach Rick Adair during his time as the Rangers minor league pitching coordinator. Adair told Mike Hindman in a 2008 *Dallas Morning News* interview, regarding the lefthander: "He's got tremendous baseball intelligence. . . . He's very consistent not only in his approach to pitching and his preparation, but in his delivery. Every pitch, every game, in every situation, he looks the same. He worked extremely hard. He's extremely competitive . . . . Every now and then, somebody just comes along . . . . [long pause] Actually, I've never seen somebody improve so much, so fast in my time coaching. How do you not get fired up about a guy like that?"

And let's not forget the game Holland threw against the Mariners on July 30 last year, with the rumors swirling that he might be on the verge of going to Toronto in a trade for Roy Halladay. One out short of a complete game. A fifth-inning single and a ninth-inning single. One walk, also in the ninth. Ten strikeouts.

I've changed my mind on Jon Daniels's behalf. Holland goes into the top tier (though he's no longer untouchable, and Tommy Hunter has a lot to do with that). Ogando goes back into tier two, but if taken it limits what the Mariners can have to round out the deal.

Zduriencik wants Smoak, Ogando, Beavan, and Engel Beltre, and Moreland added on if the Rangers need a $3 million subsidy or for Seattle to take on Harden.

Daniels offers Holland, Davis, Kirkman, and Engel Beltre. Moreland for Harden gets tacked on.

Zduriencik, though seduced by Holland's gem a year ago, insists on Smoak, because Minnesota is offering catcher Wilson Ramos and Tampa Bay is offering B.J. Upton to front their proposals. He tells Daniels that he'll put recently reacquired Russell Branyan in the deal so that the Rangers have an option at first base in case they don't want to entrust the spot to Davis for the pennant run. Branyan's left-handedness isn't ideal in that scenario, but he's a useful placeholder, and in any event, as far as 2010 is concerned, is going better than Smoak right now.

Zduriencik wants Erlin added to the deal in exchange for Branyan.

Daniels isn't willing to put Erlin in, but would put in Tullis, a pitcher the Mariners are familiar with from his amateur days and his work in the Northwest League last summer. And Moreland is out of the deal.

Zduriencik: Lee and Branyan for Smoak, Ogando, Engel Beltre, Beavan, Moreland, Erlin, and Harden.

Daniels: Lee and Branyan for Smoak, Ogando, Saltalamacchia, Tullis, and Harden.

Zduriencik says he can do better with another club. His compromise offer: Lee for Smoak and Holland. And Branyan for Tullis is fine.

I'm not sure I'd trade Smoak and Holland and Tullis for Lee and Branyan, even though the idea of adding Lee to this rotation makes the pennant run look a lot stronger, not to mention the odds of doing something in October, and even though there's a part of me that still believes Chris Davis (now .343/.390/.535 at Oklahoma City and actually hitting better against lefties than righties, though with 60 strikeouts in 245 at-bats) may figure it out, and even though I'm going to get two extra first-round picks (or maybe a first and a second) next June after Lee leaves for pinstripes. It would be different if I thought Lee was open to extending long-term here (like Roy Halladay did with Philadelphia last year). He's likely not.

But still, that's a deal I'd have to think about.

Before saying no.

And by the way, you can disregard this entire report. Everyone, from the papers to the blogs to the talk shows to water coolers, is just guessing.

July 4, 2010

A club-record-tying five Rangers are going to the All-Star Game. Josh Hamilton and Vladimir Guerrero will start, voted in by fans, and Elvis Andrus, Neftali Feliz, and Ian Kinsler were selected as reserves through a process of player voting and the input of AL All-Star manager Joe Girardi. Kinsler is an injury replacement for Dustin Pedroia, having finished second to Pedroia in the player vote.

Michael Young was named as one of five players eligible for the 34th and final spot on the American League roster. Online balloting (www.texasrangers.com or www.MLB.com) between today and Thursday afternoon will determine whether Young, Kevin Youkilis, Paul Konerko, Nick Swisher, or Delmon Young gets the nod.

The roster and the "final spot" candidates don't include Mark Teixeira, and if you'd suggested two years and 11 months ago that the 27-year-old Teixeira wouldn't be in the 2010 All-Star Game but the 18-year-old Andrus (playing at the time of The Trade in High Class A) and 19-year-old Feliz (pitching then in short-season ball) would be, you'd probably have nailed down the same level of credibility as the folks who decided today that Omar Infante belongs in Anaheim on the 13th but Joey Votto does not.

July 5, 2010

Thirty-five times this season, Scott Feldman has taken the mound immediately after the Rangers scored.

He's given up runs in 14 of those innings—25 runs overall, 24 earned.

Thirteen times, he's had an opportunity to execute a shutdown inning, which is the half-inning entrusted to a pitcher right after his team has take a lead in the game.

Nine times he's allowed runs—15 overall, 14 earned.

So Feldman's ERA in shutdown inning opportunities is 9.69.

Derek Holland's shoulder is fine, and his right knee is getting better. He'll throw long toss today, and is scheduled to throw live BP tomorrow.

Rich Harden threw a bullpen Thursday and again yesterday and is apparently throwing live BP today. He's raving about his mechanics and his fastball.

For what it's worth, last year Harden's ERA before the All-Star Break was 5.47. Afterwards it was 2.55.

Tanner Scheppers is apparently in the midst of his second planned one-week shutdown. He last started on June 28 and is slated to make four starts once he gets back on the hill, at five innings apiece.

Cliff Lee didn't throw his fourth straight complete game yesterday, but he did go eight strong (one run, nine hits, one walk, 11 strikeouts) in an 8-1 win over Central-leading Detroit.

Lee is on the same schedule as Feldman.

So is Dan Haren. And Brett Myers. And Fausto Carmona.

Presumably, at least two of Holland, Harden, and Scheppers can have upcoming minor league starts set up so that they will be, too.

July 7, 2010

It may not be as stunning a number as Juan Gonzalez's 101 RBI before the All-Star Break in 1998, but all things considered, the Rangers reaching 50 wins with four games still to play before the Break this year is pretty remarkable.

Only one other time in franchise history has Texas had 50 wins through 84 games—in 1996, the club's first playoff season.

With Tommy Hunter (5-0) set to go Thursday against Baltimore's Jeremy Guthrie (3-10), followed by Scott Feldman (5-8) against Brian Matusz (3-9), and Matt Harrison (1-1) and C.J. Wilson (7-4) slated to face two Orioles starters to be determined to round out the first half, Texas would seem to have a good chance to pack on another three wins to that total.

Three more hitless, scoreless innings for the bullpen tonight, and Alexi Ogando may have been the best of the three relievers Texas sent out there. He was given the toughest assignment, drawing Grebeck Nix and Carlos Santana among his three slated Indians, and he retired them in order, on 15 pitches, locating 11 for strikes, including three straight good-looking sliders to Nix, who had punished Texas fastballs all series.

Ogando became the first pitcher in 42 years to start his big league career with three straight relief wins, but don't expect many more from him this year, or in the foreseeable future. He's being entrusted regularly with leads now, and justifiably so.

Major league hitters are hitting an anemic .093 (4 for 43) off Ogando, including an 0 for 13 showing by left-handed hitters, against whom he's averaging just one ball per plate appearance. The only run he's permitted (not including three inherited runners) came on a Nix home run on Monday.

Justin Smoak is 3 for his last 33, with nine strikeouts in that span (and four walks). He was a .130 hitter over one week in April, a .187 hitter in May, and a .266 hitter in June, but back to .130 in July.

I'm all for patience with young players, and there have been a couple stretches in which Smoak has hit into some hard outs, but at what point do you decide (1) for the long term, he'd be better off working on necessary adjustments at Oklahoma City, where the pressure of a pennant race would be off, and (2) for the short term, Chris Davis (.355/.404/.559) would give Texas a better candidate to contribute offensively as the club nears a brutal Boston-Detroit-Angels stretch coming out of the Break?

Maybe I'm making too much of the fact that, after playing nothing but third base in 12 games since June 23, Davis slid back over to first base in Game Two of the RedHawks' twinbill tonight.

Could it be that Davis seeing time at first base for the first time in two weeks has something to do with multiple local stories tonight that trade talks between Texas and Seattle "appear to be heating up" regarding Cliff Lee, and that the Mariners are seeking a young impact bat—implicating Davis or perhaps even Smoak, whose departure would certainly make Davis a first baseman again as far as the Rangers' plans are concerned? (Seattle has also reportedly indicated interest in Ogando, Tanner Scheppers, Martin Perez, and Jarrod Saltalamacchia, though Texas is disinclined to make the three pitchers available.)

Sure seems that if Texas and Seattle do get together on a trade, Davis is going to be a big league first baseman again, either here or with the Mariners. And even if no deal goes down, Davis is pressing the issue.

The White Sox have just finished putting the Angels away once again. The division lead is now 5.5, seven in the loss column. If you are Texas and believe Chris Davis is not part of your plans, his trade value (whatever it is) will probably never again be higher. And Justin Smoak still has plenty of trade value, despite his rookie struggles.

Some may view it as an unfortunate by-product of playing winning baseball, but Step Five is here, and it seems, given the above, that Texas ought to seriously consider trading one of their two young first basemen in the next few weeks if there's a real opportunity to significantly improve the club elsewhere, likely in the rotation.

July 8, 2010

Just finished—White Sox 1, Angels 0. Five hits in the game, *combined*. Thank you, John Danks (9-2-0-0-0-7).

According to Jon Paul Morosi and Ken Rosenthal of Fox Sports, an unnamed GM "believes the Rangers have become the favorite to land Cliff Lee" from the Mariners.

July 9, 2010

Just a brutal day
For Texas Rangers baseball.
Nothing else to say.

July 9, 2010

Lots potentially going on.

Today would be a bad day not to be following me on Twitter (@newbergreport).

Even if you aren't yet a follower, click here for an idea of what might be developing, per various credible sources:

http://twitter.com/NewbergReport

July 9, 2010

Just because things have been kind of boring on the Rangers front lately, this just in:

According to several national reports from credible online and television outlets, Texas has reportedly traded first baseman Justin Smoak "plus three others" to Seattle for lefthander Cliff Lee and right-handed reliever Mark Lowe and some amount of cash.

A pair of local reports points out that Smoak is not in tonight's lineup and that Joaquin Arias is playing first base in his place. And that Lee, who was slated to start tonight for Seattle against New York, could start for Texas tomorrow.

As I wrote over the weekend, if those "three others" include Derek Holland or Martin Perez or Tanner Scheppers or Alexi Ogando, I'm not going to be very happy about this. My hope is that since those three were unidentified, none of those four arms are involved.

And if that's the case? This is starting to fire me up.

The Mariners-Yankees deal that many national outlets had characterized as being all but done this afternoon ("on the one-yard line") reportedly fell apart when Seattle decided it wasn't comfortable with the ankle injury that's currently sidelining AA second baseman David Adams, clearly the secondary New York prospect in the deal.

It stuns me that the two teams couldn't agree on a different second player (or have an extra prospect added to the deal, as Texas got Atlanta to do in 2007), considering the key player was not Adams, but catcher-first baseman Jesus Montero, and it was reportedly New York's agreement to part with Montero that convinced Seattle to call off talks with all other teams.

More when we know something official, including who all is in the whole deal, and much more in the next Newberg Report.

Wow.

July 9, 2010

According to at least one local report, righthander Blake Beavan is in the deal, and according to The Ticket, Frisco reliever Josh Lueke and second baseman-outfielder Matt Lawson are the other two. Seattle beat writer Larry Stone has the same three names.

If that's true—Justin Smoak, Beavan, Lueke, and Lawson for Cliff Lee and Mark Lowe and cash—I'm shocked. In a very good way.

July 9, 2010

What's the opposite of writer's block?

I have five leads in mind for tomorrow morning's Newberg Report.

No, six.

Eleven hours after I sent out the "just a brutal day" message, this one feels quite different.

OK, gotta go try and let the game come to me and settle on a lead. Check back with you in the morning.

July 10, 2010

The Rangers have officially announced that lefthander Cliff Lee will make his club debut tonight, facing Orioles call-up Chris Tillman in a game that will be preceded by an on-field ceremony honoring Michael Young as the franchise's all-time career hits leader, and that will be followed by a fireworks show that had been originally scheduled for last night before the rain delay resulted in a 1 a.m. finish.

The club is also offering tickets to a future game to all fans holding tickets to last night's game, due to the cancellation of the fireworks show.

And my very, very, very long July 10 Newberg Report is finished. I'm doing a quick edit right now and should have it out within an hour.

July 10, 2010: The Cliff Lee Trade

It will be popular to suggest that Jon Daniels has just made the opposite of his 2007 trade of Mark Teixeira to Atlanta, buying now as he sold then, but I'm thinking of another trade that Friday's acquisition of Cliff Lee reminds me of, in a 180-degree sort of way.

Daniels had been on the job a little more than a month when, days before Thanksgiving 2005, Florida traded big leaguers Josh Beckett, Mike Lowell, and Guillermo Mota for prospects Hanley Ramirez, Anibal Sanchez, Jesus Delgado, and Harvey Garcia. It was clear from a barrage of local and national media reports that, prior to the trade going down, Florida and Texas had been on the verge of closing a deal themselves, one that supposedly would have sent the same Marlins trio (though some reports omitted Mota) to Texas for Hank Blalock, John Danks, and possibly Joaquin Arias.

Because Daniels, the youngest general manager in baseball, had no trading track record, there were columns written denouncing the 28-year-old for failing to pull the trigger on the opportunity to land Beckett (the groundwork having reportedly been proposed by Florida owner Jeffrey Loria to Rangers owner Tom Hicks). Daniels himself has admitted he might have been too deliberate in his efforts to solicit input from multiple advisors within the organization.

But there has also been the notion that the player Florida wanted all along was Ramirez, and that a key reason Loria approached Hicks at the Owners' Meetings was to get him fired up about the idea of bringing the budding young ace Beckett home to Texas—which, the Marlins hoped, would be the leverage they needed to get Boston to agree to part with Ramirez. As talks progressed, stories emerged that a deal between Texas and Florida was expected to be finalized at any moment.

In stepped Boston, and Texas was boxed out.

That's the deal I thought about yesterday when I read this comment from Tyler Kepner in the *New York Times*:

[N]obody likes to feel used, and privately, that was the Yankees' prevailing sentiment on Friday, when the Seattle Mariners traded the All-Star left-hander Cliff Lee to the Texas Rangers for a four-player package headlined by Justin Smoak, a switch-hitting first baseman they had coveted for weeks.

Cliff Lee, Josh Beckett.

Justin Smoak, Hanley Ramirez.

Texas, Boston.

New York, Texas.

The Yankees, according to Kepner, felt "they were a pawn" as Seattle fielded offers for Lee, and nobody can accuse New York of being slow on any trigger. When the Rangers told Mariners GM Jack Zduriencik, evidently on Friday, that they'd put Smoak in the deal, he used the ankle injury to Yankees AA second baseman David Adams—unquestionably the secondary piece in the New York offer that was fronted by 20-year-old catcher Jesus Montero—as an excuse to back out of a deal that the entire national media had characterized as virtually done, one that apparently was agreed on pending the review of medicals. It took only two hours, according to Jeff Passan of Yahoo! Sports, for Texas to pounce in and close a deal.

(Said Passan of the "livid" Yankees: "This is how it feels. This, New York, is what it's like to be a baseball fan anywhere else in the country.")

(An "angered" Yankees official to Joel Sherman and George A. King III of the *New York Post*, regarding the "double-dealing" Mariners: "The Yankees do not do business that way. When we say something is a deal, it is a deal. . . . This is frustrating and disappointing.")

When Zduriencik told reporters Friday afternoon, after the announcement of the trade that sent Lee, reliever Mark Lowe, and $2.25 million to Texas for Smoak, righthanders Blake Beavan and Josh Lueke, and second baseman-outfielder Matt Lawson, that Smoak was one of four or five players he and his staff had pinpointed around the league as key trade targets, it became clear that even if Montero was on that list, Smoak was higher on it.

He was their Hanley Ramirez.

More evidence that that's what was going on here? Seattle held the number one trade asset in the league in Lee. The conventional trade deadline doesn't arrive for another three weeks. So why didn't the Mariners sit tight, letting demand build and desperation mount as July 31 approached?

As of yesterday, they could get Montero but not shortstop Eduardo Nunez (who they reportedly asked for in place of Adams [who hasn't played in seven weeks], after the Yankees initially agreed to substitute righthander Adam Warren for Adams).

They evidently couldn't get Mets first baseman Ike Davis.

Or Dodgers righthander Chad Billingsley or first baseman James Loney.

Or Tampa Bay outfielder Desmond Jennings.

Or Twins catcher Wilson Ramos plus outfielder Aaron Hicks, rather than Ramos plus righthander Kevin Slowey.

But what if one of those teams reconsidered later this month? Why did Zduriencik jump on July 9?

Because he got his number one man. He wanted Smoak. Texas agreed to move Smoak. Ballgame.

(Not that it was a widely popular decision. Several national writers have weighed in over the last 24 hours, suggesting that Montero should have been the Mariners' choice. Said Joe Sheehan, for example: "You're not going to win a Cliff Lee trade because Blake Beavan or David Adams works out; you're going to win it because you got a player who anchors a future contender or champion. Justin Smoak *may be* that player, but Jesus Montero *is* that player.")

It obviously benefits Texas a ton to get Lee now rather than at the deadline. These three weeks that remain in July should mean four or five extra Lee starts that might have otherwise gone to Matt Harrison, or perhaps Rich Harden or Derek Holland coming off of injury. And not just any four or five starts. Though Texas could adjust the rotation differently after next week's All-Star Break, Lee could face Baltimore tonight, then Boston on the road, Detroit on the road, the Angels at home, and the Angels on the road, all this month.

Put another way, a bad team that Texas desperately needs to punish tonight after brutal collapses the last two nights (by a bullpen that desperately needs a starter to go deep), followed by four very good teams.

I could lay out Lee's numbers against those clubs the last couple years, but what's the point? He's been brilliant against almost everyone.

Including in the biggest games. In five post-season starts last year with Philadelphia, Lee went 4-0, 1.56 (including the Phillies' two World Series wins), holding the Rockies, Dodgers, and Yankees to a .186/.219/.241 slash and fanning 33 while issuing six walks in 40.1 innings.

That total of six bases on balls in 40.1 playoff innings is the same number of free passes that Lee has given up in 103.2 innings this season. Pair them with his 89 strikeouts and you've got a pitcher averaging 14.83 strikeouts per walk, a ratio that has never been matched over a full season. (In fact, no qualifying pitcher since 1900 has exceeded 11 strikeouts per walk.) The next best rate in the big leagues this season? Roy Halladay's 6.61.

Lee has almost as many complete games (an American League-leading five) as walks (six) in 2010.

Diamondbacks righthander Edwin Jackson issued more walks (eight) in his June 25 no-hitter than Lee has issued this season.

Among American Leaguers with at least 10 plate appearances, who has the best career batting average against Lee? Ian Kinsler (9 for 20, .450).

Who has the worst? Erick Aybar (0 for 10, .000).

While we're at it, the Angels collectively against Lee, since 2008, have a .136 batting average, including .114 against his fastball, .077 when behind in the count, and .067 with two strikes.

That second of two starts Lee could make this month against the Angels won't be the first time he'll wear a Rangers lid in Angel Stadium. He'll be there Tuesday, earning the second All-Star Game nod of his career.

Lee is 8-3, 2.34 in 13 starts this season. He leads the league in ERA, and it's not a product of Safeco Field. The lefthander actually has slightly better numbers this year on the road (2.24 ERA, .223/.239/.321 slash) than in Seattle (2.47 ERA, .240/.243/.344 slash).

I'm not going to get into the Lee vs. Roy Oswalt debate, one that I never understood, but for many reasons, this trade made so much more sense to me than any deal for Oswalt would have. While I suppose there might have been an argument as to whether Oswalt or Colby Lewis, at this stage, would be a Game One starter in the playoffs, there's no question in Lee's case. He makes Lewis a very solid number two.

Is it really a foregone conclusion that Lee, an Arkansas native who still lives in Little Rock with his wife and two kids, will leave to sign with the Yankees this winter (which would give Texas (1) an extra supplemental first-round pick and (2) either a late first or possibly a late second or third as compensation)? That's a discussion for another time.

Deciding whether to pursue a pitcher of Lee's caliber was the easy part. Determining how much to give up—particularly given the reality that the offer would need to be padded a bit to cover for the cash necessarily coming back—was trickier.

Let's dial back to the report I wrote on Monday that focused on what I figured it might take to get Lee. I listed six categories—centerpiece players, a second tier, and four more groups: upper-level and lower-level pitchers and upper-level and lower-level hitters—and presumed it would take one player from each of the first two groups and then two more minor leaguers to complete the trade.

Specifically, I speculated:

1. Smoak or Holland or Martin Perez or Tanner Scheppers
2. Plus Alexi Ogando or Tommy Hunter or Julio Borbon or Nelson Cruz or David Murphy
3. Plus two more players from a list that might have included Beavan, Lueke, Omar Beltre, Michael Kirkman, Pedro Strop, Wilmer Font, Robbie Erlin, Robbie Ross, Joe Wieland, Chris Davis, Engel Beltre, and Miguel Velazquez

I concluded that report by guessing that, after a number of exchanges, the final Seattle proposal might be Lee for Smoak and Holland. And that I'd say no.

That Texas landed baseball's best left-handed pitcher, a proven big game warrior on a short list of the league's best pitchers, period, without giving up Perez or Scheppers or Holland or Hunter or Ogando is sort of stunning. I understand that Seattle was targeting a young hitter. But I'm still having trouble getting my head wrapped around a deal for a pitcher like this where you part with a young blue-chip position player but don't have to dip into what is a very deep top tier of your pitching prospect stable—and that's without even considering that you had to have the Mariners put cash into the deal, something other teams wouldn't have insisted on.

According to one media estimate, Lee and Lowe will earn $4.07 million the rest of 2010. The Mariners' subsidy means they will pay $2.25 million of it, Texas $1.82 million.

You tell me I just got Cliff Lee, early in July rather than late, and that Seattle is paying more than I am for him to wear my uniform, and I would fully expect someone like Beavan to be in the deal.

As the third piece. Not the second.

When I wrote about the Bengie Molina trade with San Francisco on July 2, I commented: "If Michael Main is the cost of $2 million in salary relief to get a player like Molina, the price tag in prospects to get someone like Cliff Lee along with a cash subsidy is one I don't even need to see."

To me, it would have made sense for a player like Beavan to be the cost of Cliff Lee cash, if Main was the cost of Bengie Molina cash. And if viewed that way, does that mean this deal would have been Smoak and Lueke and Lawson for Lee and Lowe if there were no cash component?

I sure would have hammered that angle home, just a week after the Main move, if I were Zduriencik. I've got to have Beavan (a Rick Adair favorite), but I need an upgrade on Michael Main as an added piece to the deal. If Seattle said righthander Joe Wieland needed to be in the deal, too, would Daniels really have said no, and missed the chance to add *Cliff Lee*?

Clearly, Zduriencik didn't find out.

Another way to view the Molina trade: By including Main, Daniels bought himself $2 million to use in a bigger deal. By getting Seattle to put $2.25 million in yesterday's deal, he still has that payroll cushion to use for yet another piece. A right-handed hitter as protection at first base? More on that later.

The Rangers' apparent restraint in this year's July 2 international free agent market preserved cash as well, as one local beat writer points out.

Sherman made an interesting point regarding the Commissioner's Office's green light on this trade, suggesting the added payroll not only still fits within the club's budget but could also be offset by a boost in attendance on nights Lee pitches. We're about to see what that looks like tonight. I don't know if the club keeps records on walk-up ticket sales, but isn't there a chance that tonight's will be the biggest in franchise history?

This is not to dogpile on Zduriencik. In the span of seven months he turned the underwhelming package of Phillippe Aumont, J.C. Ramirez, and Tyson Gillies (plus Lowe) into Smoak, Beavan, Lueke, and Lawson, with three brilliant months of Cliff Lee added in. Viewed solely on its face, that's a fantastic upgrade. And trading within the division? What does Seattle care if Lee pitches well for Texas for three months? The dilemma, if one exists, belongs to Texas, who has to envision facing Smoak and Beavan for at least the next six years.

The point is that there's no reason Seattle should have been reluctant to trade Lee to the Rangers just because they're division bunkmates. Just the opposite—long term, the Mariners stripped Texas of a couple players that they're now counting on to make core impacts.

Even if Smoak becomes Adrian Gonzalez, and even if Beavan becomes Brad Radke or Jeff Suppan, I can live with it. (Partly because in Smoak's case, Lee is not Adam Eaton.)

The idea of Holland or Perez or Scheppers (the latter two of whom are number 8 and number 25 on *Baseball America*'s mid-season Top 25 Prospects list, published yesterday) pitching near the front of the Mariners rotation (or closing games) for years to come is what made me most nervous.

Kevin Goldstein of Baseball Prospectus wrote earlier this week: "The Rangers line up for a trade with Seattle extremely well if Texas has the ability to make a deal due to their financial considerations, and if the Mariners are willing to trade within their division. Corner infielder Chris Davis is hitting .349/.397/.542 at Triple-A Oklahoma, and while he's struggled in the big leagues twice, his bat could be the long-term solution to Seattle's first base issue. Seattle would almost certainly ask for Martin Perez, one of, if not the top, left-handed pitching prospect in the game, and Texas is a pitching-rich system that could also dangle top lower-level arms like righties Wilmer Font and Robbie Erlin to help sweeten the pot."

That's the kind of trade—Perez, Davis, Font, and Erlin—that I expected Seattle to be able to make, with some team, though I hoped not with Texas. It would have been too much to give up, but closer to what I thought Lee's market probably was.

Beavan had taken one of the two or three biggest steps forward in the Rangers system this year. He's an innings-eater and a relentless pounder of the zone—which describes Lee as well—but the key difference between the two is that Beavan doesn't miss enough bats to project as a top-of-rotation starter (though he's improved somewhat in that aspect this season). Without the makings of a legitimate out pitch, Beavan can still be an extremely valuable constant in a good rotation—think Radke or Suppan or Hunter—but he doesn't have the ceiling of a Perez or Scheppers or Holland. Beavan's sturdy 10-5, 2.78 encore in 17 Frisco starts resulted in a promotion to AAA earlier this week, but he hadn't yet appeared with Oklahoma City when the trade went down.

The 6'7" righthander will apparently report to AA for the Mariners. There's been some talk that he could get a look in Seattle before the season ends (there were whispers about that in Texas as well), but it would kill a roster spot this winter since he doesn't need to be added to the 40-man roster until November 2011.

An interesting observation from Sheehan: "Beavan is actually a decent fit for the Mariners and Safeco Field, but exactly the wrong type of player for them to acquire. If the Mariners have shown us anything this year, it's that they can extract value for very little investment in their rotation. Doug Fister and Jason Vargas are middling guys who have put up good numbers thanks to a big park and a strong defense. The Mariners don't need to be wasting the trade value of a Cliff Lee on pitchers, because they can find pitchers. Beavan's place in this deal should have belonged to Engel Beltre or Jurickson Profar or some other high-upside offensive talent, because that's what they're struggling to develop. It's not that Beavan is bad, it's that they can make their own Beavan."

As for Lueke and Lawson, both have taken steps forward this year but were inventory in this system. Should the Rangers lose Lee this winter and recoup two first-round picks (or even a first and second or a first and third), well, put it this way: if draft picks were tradeable, Texas would certainly swap the 25-year-old Lueke (taken in the 16th round of the Beavan/Main/Borbon/Hunter draft) and the 24-year-old Lawson (14th round, same year) for the picks they stand to get for losing Lee.

Lueke, whose troublesome off-the-field story is one I don't feel like getting into, has been outstanding this year, posting a 2.11 relief ERA between Hickory and Frisco, fanning an eye-opening 62 batters and walking only 10 in 38.1 innings. He's a fastball-slider type who figures to factor in as a seventh-inning reliever if everything works out.

Lawson is an instinctive player and solid defender (primarily at second base, a little corner outfield) who has hit more and more as he's moved up the chain (.277/.371/.438 for Frisco this season). Ceiling? Maybe Joe Inglett. Tug Hulett. A role player.

As for Lowe, a 27-year-old with two years of club control after this season, he's a big righthander with a big arm who was effective last year (3.26 ERA in 75 relief appearances, 69 strikeouts and 29 walks in 80 innings, seven home runs) but whose 2010 season was cut short after a month due to a herniated disc in his lower back. He's recovering now from mid-June microdiscectomy surgery and is expected to miss the rest of the season, but there are suggestions that his rehabilitation is going well enough that he might be able to join the Rangers' bullpen in September.

It's key to note that this isn't an arm problem, and as hard as this relief corps has been worked, getting a fresh power arm down the stretch could be pretty useful. And Lowe (a UTA product) should figure in next year, perhaps to compete for the role that Chris Ray was brought in last winter to handle.

Though he may or may not pitch this year, Lowe's inclusion in the trade is sort of equivalent to Ron Mahay being tacked on in the Rangers' deal with Atlanta in 2007. That was the Mark Teixeira Trade, not the Teixeira/Mahay deal.

And this six-player deal, with all due respect to Blake Beavan, whose future I'd bet on more than Lowe's, is the Lee-for-Smoak trade.

Here's the thing about dealing Smoak, a player that I still believe in. Even if his career ends up looking more like Gonzalez's or Mark Teixeira's or Justin Morneau's than like Travis Lee's, it's massively easier to go find a first baseman than a frontline pitcher. Is Chris Davis that guy? Don't know. Mitch Moreland (.668 OPS in AAA in April, .824 in May, .880 in June, .885 so far in July)? Really don't know. (First things first: Will Moreland be moved back from right field to first base with Davis's promotion to Texas?)

But regardless of what happens with the ownership situation, at some point within the next year this club should be in a position to spend more on payroll, and there will be opportunities to go sign or trade for an everyday first baseman, if that becomes necessary.

Plugging holes in the rotation is a more complicated task, and Texas is in as good a position as any team in terms of developing young starters internally. The only place this trade really altered the Rangers' farm system depth was at first base. If I have to choose a position at which to suffer a setback in depth (and again, Davis and Moreland and perhaps Chad Tracy keep it from being an empty cupboard), I'll live with it at first base.

If Davis doesn't look in the next two weeks like he's figured things out, don't be surprised to see Texas grab a veteran before the trade deadline. Cubs first baseman-outfielder Xavier Nady's name has already been mentioned in a couple places.

For what it's worth, and for various reasons it may not be much, I do note that Davis was a more productive hitter in AA than Smoak (.319/.374/.644 for Davis vs. .328/.449/.481 for Smoak) and in AAA (.341/.407/.571 vs. .255/.386/.397), and has been in Texas as well (.253/.301/.474 vs. .209/.316/.353), though it must be pointed out that Davis's big league numbers have regressed each season since he arrived in 2008. If I had to bet on one's future, I'd probably still take Smoak, but his early work, particularly from the right side (not necessarily an advantage if you believe Davis's ability to hit AAA lefthanders has the chance to translate), suggests he's not the absolute lock for superstardom that most have predicted. His plate discipline and unusually low batting average on balls in play promise better things, but Seattle isn't hoping they got Lyle Overbay.

There's also the added benefit of getting Davis back in there defensively. Smoak made great strides with the glove the last two months, but he's not Davis's equal.

I'm pretty sure I'd take Montero ahead of either of them, even if he eventually has to move from catcher to first base. Given the choice between a 20-year-old whose ceiling might be Miguel Cabrera and a 23-year-old who could be Morneau, I'll take the younger guy, whether he's a catcher or not.

Opinions differ on Montero vs. Smoak. But we know where Seattle stands on that debate. And it wasn't just good fortune that had Texas in the position to do business with the Mariners yesterday.

I'm repeating myself, but drafting Smoak in 2008 set things up for a Matt LaPorta/C.C. Sabathia trade down the road. From the April 23 Newberg Report:

When Texas chose Smoak on June 5, 2008, Davis was less than two weeks into his AAA promotion, having hit his way out of the Texas League with a monstrous .333/.376/.618 two months. There was every reason not to pop the 21-year-old Smoak with the 22-year-old Davis barreling in toward the first base job that Ben Broussard and Chris Shelton were attempting to hold down. The Rangers could have taken the second player on their board, Georgia high school righthander Ethan Martin, and avoided the possible Davis-Smoak conundrum.

You never draft for need. You take the best player available. With ownership willing to spend what it would take to pay Smoak's expected signing bonus demands, Texas did take the best player available on Draft Day 2008.

And they had the best player available, at least in Seattle's eyes, again yesterday, enabling the execution of Step Five, for which It was Time.

As a result Texas now suits up the best big league pitcher available, the latest incredible development in what has been, and promises to continue to be, an extraordinary baseball season in Arlington.

July 10, 2010

So the worst team in baseball has come into Arlington and won three straight, and the gem tonight belonged not to Cliff Lee but to Chris Tillman, who was called up from AAA for the start after a previous 0-3, 8.40 run in four big league starts earlier this season.

Mariners GM Jack Zduriencik surely had an eye on this game, and while Lee didn't stand out (aside from contributing his typical complete-game effort), a Seattle trade that backfired badly on his predecessor Bill Bavasi was at the center of Orioles 6, Rangers 1.

On February 8, 2008, Bavasi traded Tillman and center fielder Adam Jones, probably the two stars of the game tonight, plus reliever George Sherrill (whom Baltimore flipped to the Dodgers last year for Josh Bell, another impressive young hitter) and reliever Kam Mickolio, all in exchange for Erik Bedard. It's turned out to be a hugely lopsided deal in Baltimore's favor, as Bedard missed half of 2008 due to shoulder surgery and half of 2009 with more shoulder issues, and has yet to come off his rehab work in 2010. Meanwhile, Jones and Tillman in particular are core players, and Bell could become that.

It's a reminder that trades that are anointed the minute they cross the wire take time to bear out. I can't wait for Lee's second half in Texas, and I'll survive his atypical effort tonight (just as I'm sure Mariners fans aren't jumping off the West Seattle Bridge even though Justin Smoak is 0 for 3 with three strikeouts so far against the Yankees tonight), especially considering his travel plans meant he didn't even arrive at the Ballpark until 5:00. But the epitaph on this trade hasn't been written yet.

Tomorrow's a new day, and I'd really appreciate Texas finishing the first half by avoiding a sweep at the hands of the Baltimore Freakin' Orioles, but as disappointing as tonight's loss was, all things considered, I'm still as pumped as ever about Cliff Lee and can't wait to baseball-decompress a bit Monday through Wednesday, and get geared up for a stretch run that I'm planning to never forget.

July 11, 2010

Baltimore 6 @ Texas 4.
Baltimore 7 @ Texas 6.
Baltimore 6 @ Texas 1.
Baltimore 4 @ Texas 1.
Gimme a Break.

July 14, 2010

Cliff Lee's drive-by appearance in the All-Star Game last night (one-pitch Martin Prado groundout, three-pitch Albert Pujols strikeout, two-pitch Ryan Howard groundout) didn't even really count as side work, but the way Texas has the rotation set up coming out of the Break, Lee will have a second opportunity to get some between-starts bullpen work in anyway. Rather than keep their new ace on regular rest by starting him in Boston on Thursday, the Rangers will have Tommy Hunter open the series and send Lee out against John Lackey on Saturday.

The starting five, accordingly, will go to work this way over the next 31 games (home games in all-caps):

Hunter:	bos	det	LAA	laa	oak	BOS	tb
Lewis:	bos	det	OAK	laa	oak	BOS	
Lee:	bos	LAA	OAK	sea	oak	BOS	
Wilson:	bos	LAA	OAK	sea	NYY	tb	
Feldman:	det	LAA	laa	sea	NYY	tb	

Clearly, Texas wanted Lee to kick off the home series against the Angels, who are hitting .136 against him since 2008.

Incidentally, a couple sources out of Boston last night reported that Clay Buchholz (strained hamstring) won't come off the disabled list to make Friday's start against Texas, but will instead make a minor league rehab start that night. Facing Lewis rather than Buchholz could be lefthander Felix Doubront. Tim Wakefield gets tomorrow's start against Hunter, and Jon Lester will go Sunday.

Buchholz has lots of company on the Red Sox disabled list: fellow All-Stars Dustin Pedroia and Victor Martinez, plus Josh Beckett, Jacoby Ellsbury, Jason Varitek, Mike Lowell, Manny Delcarmen, Jed Lowrie, Jeremy Hermida, and Junichi Tazawa. Adrian Beltre is day to day, and Mike Cameron is being used cautiously.

And yet Boston is 51-37, five games back in the AL East (behind the Yankees) and three out in the Wild Card hunt (behind the Rays). While I'm no Sox fan, that's the team that, year in and year out, I admire more than any in baseball.

I'm not trying to avoid feeling lousy about how Texas finished the first half, losing 7 of 10 against the White Sox, Indians, and Orioles, but imagine if you were the Angels. Before that 10-game stretch, you'd just taken two of three from the Rangers to carve the division gap down to 3.5 games. Stay close over those next 10, and coming out of the Break, when Texas would stare down the toughest part of its schedule, you'd make your move.

In fact, with the Royals, White Sox, and A's on your slate in that same 10-day stretch leading into the Break, maybe you could knock another game or two off that 3.5-game deficit before the first half ended.

If you knew then that the Rangers would drop those 7 of 10, you'd probably feel good about getting seriously close to catching them by time the league shut down for these three days.

Then what happens? You manage to win 2 of 10 yourselves, taking one of three from Kansas City and one of three from Oakland, sandwiched around a four-game sweep at Chicago's hands.

It's easy to say Texas could, and maybe should, be sitting with a lead of 6.5 or 8.5 games right now.

But the Angels probably feel like they should be a half-game out, if not a half-game up.

Last comment on that disgusting Orioles series: Texas came into it with the third-best runs-per-game average in baseball (5.25, behind only Boston and the Yankees), and Baltimore had the second-worst ERA in baseball (5.14, better only than Arizona).

The Rangers had baseball's ninth-best ERA (3.90). Baltimore was 27th in runs per game (3.58).

How did that happen?

STATS, Inc. doesn't quantify flatness.

One other thing about the All-Star Game:

Elvis? Come on, now.

(So the National League won its first All-Star Game since 1996. Think about what else last happened in 1996, about three months later.)

I would have lost this bet: Despite leading the American League in walks, C.J. Wilson has allowed three earned runs or fewer in eight straight starts. Doesn't seem like it.

Peter Gammons notes that Texas actually has three of the top 10 AL pitchers in "RSAA" (Runs Saved Above Average, a Lee Sinins creation that measures a pitcher's effectiveness by comparing runs allowed per nine innings to the league average and giving weight to total innings pitched): Lee is fifth, Wilson is eighth, and Colby Lewis is 10th.

Jon Heyman of *Sports Illustrated* issued his mid-season awards, naming Jon Daniels AL GM of the (Half) Year, Josh Hamilton runner-up for AL MVP, Lee runner-up for AL Cy Young, Neftali Feliz runner-up for AL Rookie of the (Half) Year, and Ron Washington third in AL Manager of the (Half) Year.

Would Lee be a Ranger today if the Indians had given him a no-trade clause back in 2006, when they signed him to the deal that, once his 2010 option was exercised (by Philadelphia), was worth $23 million over five years?

Having been traded three times in less than a year, Lee is going to make sure the mega-contract he lands this winter contains no-trade protection.

According to Nick Cafardo of the *Boston Globe*, Texas checked in on Cleveland righthander Fausto Carmona before trading for Lee.

We talked a few days ago about how Seattle targeted Justin Smoak as one of (and evidently atop the list of) several young hitters around the league they wanted in a Lee deal. In addition to Jesus Montero (Yankees), Ike Davis (Mets), and Desmond Jennings (Rays), who we discussed, Joel Sherman of the *New York Post* reports that Domonic Brown (Phillies), Gordon Beckham (White Sox), and Brett Lawrie (Brewers) were Mariners targets.

Daniels acknowledged in a radio interview that the Rangers-Mariners deal changed between Thursday night and Friday morning, and was then tweaked some on Friday once Jack Zduriencik made a concrete proposal. It's pretty clear that Smoak was off the table until Friday, and that once he was in the deal, it didn't take long for Texas and Seattle to get things done.

Daniels also said he wouldn't be surprised if Josh Lueke is in Seattle's bullpen by the end of the season.

Lueke could be a younger version of Mark Lowe, actually. (Though, interestingly, he's only a year younger than the three-year veteran, who will be a factor here in 2011 and 2012, if not this September.)

Tanner Scheppers sat 99 in his two-thirds of an inning at the Futures Game on Sunday, hitting 101 on the stadium gun once. I'm not sure it's the last time he'll pitch in Angel Stadium this month.

I'm betting on two more significant moves this month: a trade for a right-handed bat, and the promotion of Scheppers to give the bullpen a boost. (Of course, the returns of Derek Holland and Rich Harden will also impact the available bullpen options. Harden gave up one hit and one walk in 2.2 scoreless rehab innings for Oklahoma City on Sunday, fanning two; he threw 48 pitches, an uninspiring 28 for strikes, but it is the first time he'd competed in a month.) Daniels's July work isn't finished.

(To that point, there's less pressure now from a baseball operations standpoint for the bankruptcy process to play out before July 31. The Rangers didn't need payroll freedom to make the Lee trade—and really, if they didn't need Seattle to throw in $2.25 million, how much less do we think they would have had to put in the deal in terms of prospects . . . if Blake Beavan, Lueke, and Matt Lawson were downgraded significantly, would the Texas offer still have come out on top?—and they reportedly still have some budget room to add the bench bat they clearly still need.)

Baseball America ranked Scheppers's fastball as the best featured on Sunday.

Scheppers starts for Oklahoma City tomorrow. RedHawks pitching coach Terry Clark told the *Daily Oklahoman* a month ago that he'll be held to five innings per start. This gives Scheppers continued opportunities to work out of the stretch and refine his changeup.

Mitch Moreland remains in right field for the RedHawks (no move back in to first base yet), and is torching baseballs right now. After a solid .309/.412/.468 June (17 walks and 18 strikeouts in 94 at-bats), he sits at .349/.429/.721 in 43 July at-bats (six walks and five strikeouts).

After four games in Frisco (one at each outfield spot plus one at DH), Endy Chavez has been moved up to Oklahoma City.

In his first two starts for AA Richmond, Michael Main has allowed 10 runs (six earned) on seven hits and five walks in six innings, fanning two.

Beavan, Lueke, and Lawson have yet to debut for AA West Tenn in the Seattle system.

Chris Ray has pitched six times for the Giants, permitting one run on two hits and two walks in 6.2 innings, striking out five.

Matt Nevarez has a 4.79 ERA in 21 middle relief appearances for Houston's AA affiliate at Corpus Christi. Jose Vallejo is back from his off-season hand injury, and has a .162 average in his first 37 at-bats for the same club.

Jason Botts is hitting .471/.526/.824 in 34 July at-bats for AAA Syracuse in the Washington system. The Nationals have him splitting time between right field and first base. If Adam Dunn or Josh Willingham gets traded this month, could Botts get another big league shot?

Fox Sports Southwest produced a really good feature called "Spotlight: The Rangers' Minor League Gold Mine." I can't recommend it enough. Dana Larson interviews Jon Daniels, A.J. Preller, Josh Boyd, Don Welke, and others in the Rangers' scouting and player development departments, and it's as good a look into the inner workings of one of the real key aspects of the organization as I've seen. The 30-minute special re-airs on Saturday at 11:30 a.m., Monday at 10:00 p.m., and Tuesday at 5:00 p.m. Set your DVR's now.

Since being designated for assignment by Tampa Bay at the end of June, Hank Blalock hasn't surfaced anywhere else, as far as I can tell.

Gary Matthews Jr. is hitting .324/.352/.515 for Cincinnati's AAA squad in Louisville.

After Houston released infielder Drew Meyer from his AAA contract at the end of June (coinciding roughly with the arrival of Ramon Vazquez), the Angels added Meyer to their AAA roster.

Milwaukee released lefthander A.J. Murray. Boston designated lefthander Fabio Castro for assignment.

Matt Purke is *Baseball America*'s 2010 Freshman of the Year. Florida International outfielder Jabari Henry made *BA*'s All-Freshman second team.

The Kalamazoo Kings of the independent Frontier League released righthander Justin Miller. The Pittsfield Colonials of the independent Can-Am League released lefthander Matt White.

Does anyone have their kid playing fall baseball in the SVAA this year? Let me know.

Buck Showalter is reportedly about to be offered the Baltimore managerial job, and Bo Porter (whose one year in the Texas outfield preceded Showalter's arrival by two years) is a strong candidate to land the Marlins job this winter.

My MLB.com column this week: The Rangers' top 10 July trades of the last 10 years. Goes live tomorrow.

I know I'm supposed to care a little about last night's result, not so much because It Counts but because it could conceivably Count for the Rangers, but I just can't get worked up about it. I didn't need the momentary frustration of seeing Elvis give away an out right before Hamilton singled in what was then a one-run game, but overall I was just happy that Feliz didn't pitch and that no Rangers got dinged up.

And that Cliff Lee did what Cliff Lee do(es).

I'm ready for real games again, and while I'm not looking past Hunter-Wakefield or Lewis-Doubront, I stinkin' can't wait for Lee-Lackey on Saturday.

July 15, 2010

Since 2008, Texas has a 3-10 record in Boston.

And an 0-9 record in Detroit.

Time to see what this Rangers team is made of.

Newberg Report: Rangers' Top Ten July Trades

By Jamey Newberg / Special to MLB.com
July 15, 2010

The Rangers got the July trading season underway this year, striking with the Mariners on a deal whose 2010 impact may not be matched by any other trade that goes down before the non-waiver Trade Deadline arrives on the 31st.

It may be that Cliff Lee is the top player traded in the big leagues this season.

It may also be that Justin Smoak is the top prospect that changes teams.

July is a time for contenders to get stronger, and for teams out of the hunt to accelerate the process of rebuilding. Both types of teams can make a big impact if they trade well.

Texas has had big hits on both sides of the buyer-seller equation over the years. What follows is a ranking of the top 10 July trades Texas has made since its first playoff season of 1996.

10. July 31, 1996: Texas trades right-handers Mark Brandenburg and Kerry Lacy to the Boston Red Sox for left-hander Mike Stanton and outfielder Dwayne Hosey (player to be named, identified Nov. 4, 1996).

Stanton pitched for eight teams in 19 big league seasons, none of whom got fewer appearances from him than Texas. He was only marginally more effective than Brandenburg, whom he replaced in the Rangers' bullpen, but as a pitcher who had pitched in the playoffs four of the previous five seasons, he helped stabilize the club's relief crew over the final two months en route to its first postseason appearance. After appearing in three of four games against the Yankees in the playoffs, he joined New York as a free agent following the season.

9. July 17, 1998: Texas trades right-hander Todd Van Poppel and second baseman Warren Morris to the Pittsburgh Pirates for right-hander Esteban Loaiza.

In the midst of what would be the club's second playoff season in three years, Texas purchased Van Poppel's contract from Oklahoma City to join the rotation in late June. He made four starts and they didn't go particularly well, as he sat with an ERA of 8.84 after a three-inning effort on July 13. Texas called Pittsburgh about the relatively unknown Loaiza, who was in his second full big league season, and was able to grab him for the stretch run in exchange for Van Poppel and the college star Morris (who would finish third in the NL Rookie of the Year vote the following year), after the Pirates first asked for Class A left-hander Doug Davis. Loaiza had an enigmatic two-year run with Texas, eventually showing up later on this list as one of the great buy low, sell high examples in club history.

8. July 25, 1997: Texas trades third baseman Dean Palmer to the Kansas City Royals for center fielder Tom Goodwin.

With Palmer regressing and blue-chipper Fernando Tatis breaking through with an explosive .314/.390/.576 run at Double-A Tulsa, Texas GM Doug Melvin took the opportunity to move Palmer to Kansas City in an effort to upgrade the Rangers' center-field situation. Darryl Hamilton had departed the previous winter via free agency, Damon Buford was struggling to hold the spot down, and Ruben Mateo was still a couple years away. Goodwin came in and did his thing, not hitting much but tracking balls down in center and running himself into scoring position atop a lineup full of big bats. The following season might have been the best of Goodwin's 14 big league seasons, as he hit .290, reached base at a .378 clip, and scored 102 runs on what would be the Rangers' second playoff team.

7. July 31, 2007: Texas trades right-hander Eric Gagné and cash to the Boston Red Sox for left-hander Kason Gabbard and outfielders David Murphy and Engel Beltre.

The press considered Gabbard (4-0, 3.73 in seven Boston starts) the headliner in the package Texas received for Gagné, followed by Murphy, the former first-round pick out of Baylor who had yet to distinguish himself at any level, and then Beltre, who had all of 34 pro games to his credit stateside (and a .208 batting average in that small sample). But Texas reportedly prioritized the trio in the opposite order, with Rangers GM Jon Daniels telling Peter Gammons days after the trade, which nearly fell apart and would have resulted in Gagné going to Milwaukee: "When [Boston GM] Theo [Epstein] called and said he would put Beltre in the deal, it was down to the no-trade language and the paperwork." Gabbard made very little impact after the trade—not unlike Gagné in Boston—and while Murphy has exceeded most expectations, Beltre's breakthrough 2010 season suggests this No. 7 ranking may eventually be far too low.

6. July 1, 2003: Texas trades outfielder Carl Everett to the Chicago White Sox for three players to be named later: right-handers Frank Francisco and Josh Rupe and outfielder Anthony Webster (each identified July 25, 2003).

The White Sox and Rangers agreed on eight Minor League players from which Texas could choose two or three after nearly a month of intense scouting. The Rangers chose well, forgoing the most heralded of the eight - left-hander Corwin Malone—and selecting Francisco, an inconsistent starter who had slid through several Rule 5 Drafts, plus Rupe and Webster. (They eventually got a fourth of the eight, second baseman-outfielder Ruddy Yan, on a waiver claim a year and a half later.) Everett was never the same after the 2003 season, while Francisco made an immediate impact upon his arrival in Arlington in 2004 and has been a bullpen rock ever since.

5. July 11, 2003: Texas trades right-hander Ugueth Urbina to the Florida Marlins for first baseman Adrian Gonzalez, left-hander Ryan Snare, and outfielder Will Smith.

John Hart was quick to say that this was a Grady Fuson trade, and it was probably the best move Fuson engineered during his three-year tenure in Texas. Urbina was a classic rental player the minute he signed with Texas in December 2002, and he proved to be a tremendous pickup for the Marlins, posting a 1.41 ERA and saving four playoff games, including two in the World Series. It's too bad Texas didn't decide a year earlier than it did that Mark Teixeira was not going to be part of the long-term plans, as the Rangers traded Gonzalez badly in January 2006.

4. July 28, 2006: Texas trades right-hander Francisco Cordero, outfielders Kevin Mench and Laynce Nix, and left-hander Julian Cordero to the Milwaukee Brewers for outfielders Carlos Lee and Nelson Cruz.

Brewers GM Doug Melvin was familiar with Cordero, Mench, and Nix, all of whom had been acquired by Texas under his watch here, and for the second time in his career, he traded a premier power-hitting outfielder to get Cordero in particular—first Juan Gonzalez in 1999, and then Carlos Lee seven years later. While the key for Daniels was getting Lee—the club was just 1.5 games out of the division lead at the time—he came away with Cruz (who was Nix's age even though he'd amassed only five big league at-bats, compared with Nix's 816) and two compensatory Draft picks once Lee left for Houston after the season. With those two picks, Texas selected Blake Beavan, who helped land Cliff Lee last week, and Julio Borbon.

3. July 31, 1998: Texas trades left-hander Darren Oliver, Tatis, and outfielder Mark Little (player to be named, identified Aug. 9, 1998) to the St. Louis Cardinals for right-hander Todd Stottlemyre and shortstop Royce Clayton; Texas trades third baseman Jose Santos and right-hander Daniel DeYoung to the Florida Marlins for third baseman Todd Zeile.

Texas was one game behind the Angels when the trade deadline arrived in 1998. Oliver was struggling with a 6.53 ERA after two solid years in the Rangers' rotation. Kevin Elster's magic from two years earlier at shortstop had disappeared. Melvin saw a chance to upgrade the rotation and shortstop by hooking up with the Cardinals, who were out of the race. Tatis was the key to the deal for St. Louis, and Texas moved two second-tier prospects to Florida for Zeile to allow them to move Tatis in a pennant race without leaving a hole at third base. Stottlemyre would pitch one of the best games in Rangers playoff history in Game 1 against the Yankees that October, before leaving via free agency after the season.

2. July 19, 2000: Texas trades right-hander Esteban Loaiza to the Toronto Blue Jays for shortstop-second baseman Michael Young and right-hander Darwin Cubillan.

Toronto was within 1 1/2 games of the lead in their division but, giving the ball every fifth day to a young starter named Roy Halladay, decided it needed to replace Halladay's 11.05 ERA with a more dependable veteran. At the time, Michael Young (in Double-A at the time) may have been the least heralded of the Jays' middle-infield-prospect foursome that also included Felipe Lopez, Brent Abernathy, and Cesar Izturis, but he was the one the Rangers targeted in the deal. Loaiza lost more games than he won in three Toronto seasons before leaving via free agency.

1. July 31, 2007: Texas trades first baseman Mark Teixeira and left-hander Ron Mahay to the Atlanta Braves for shortstop Elvis Andrus, right-hander Neftali Feliz, left-hander Matt Harrison, catcher Jarrod Saltalamacchia, and left-hander Beau Jones.

This can't be vaulted to Herschel Walker Trade status until Texas wins something, but without question, Andrus and Feliz in particular are going to be key factors when the Rangers next play past 162. It took a commitment by the Rangers to retrench in wholesale fashion, not to mention an urge for Atlanta GM John Schuerholz to win one last time before stepping down from his post, but this is the standard against which Trade Deadline deals are now measured, and a rare decision by a club to sell an impact player two pennant races prior to free agency, rather than one. Texas had chances to acquire more recognizable names for Teixeira elsewhere, but elected to go for the higher risk, higher reward package the Braves were offering. The decision should pay off for years.

July 16, 2010

Boston massacre
(Umm, relatively speaking)
Good start to road test

July 17, 2010

The only thing less likely than Bengie Molina's cycle was the fact that he never had to slide.

Only slightly more likely than Molina's night was that, two games into the Boston series, Texas has already clinched a series split. Cliff Lee goes to the hill tonight to try and lock down a series win.

The magic number? The elusive number 67.

July 18, 2010

I heard Eric Nadel mention this during last night's game broadcast, so I assume it's out there through other outlets as well.

Apparently the Rangers intend to pitch Cliff Lee every fifth day, irrespective of club off-days, throughout the second half.

If true, take what I laid out a few days ago regarding Lee's next month of starts:

@Bos (last night), LAA, Oak, @Sea, @Oak, Bos

And replace it with this:

@Bos (last night), LAA, Oak, @LAA, @Oak, NYY

So an extra start against the Angels, and a Yankees game in place of a Red Sox game.

Whether this means extra rest for fellow starters, or an opportunity to skip a scuffling starter here and there, remains to be seen.

But having Lee pitch on regular rest, and more importantly at a greater frequency, is a good thing, especially considering he's obviously capable of giving this team nine innings at pitch counts that, from this rotation, typically leave about three or four innings for the bullpen to have to cover.

Ultimately, this probably means only one or two extra starts for Lee in the second half, but that in itself shouldn't be overlooked, nor should the ability this gives Texas to provide its other starters—and the bullpen—a little more rest going forward.

July 18, 2010

So you know what else this Cliff-Lee-every-fifth-day schedule means?

He's in line to pitch on Monday night, September 20, the opener of what could be a huge three-game set in Anaheim.

And on Thursday night, September 30, the first game of the season-ending, four-game series against the Angels in Rangers Ballpark.

And his next day to pitch would be Tuesday, October 5 . . . which ought to be when the playoffs kick off.

A week and a half ago, when the Yankees were thought to be on the doorstep of landing Lee, it was speculated that the club was also working on a counterpart deal that would have sent righthander Javier Vazquez elsewhere (Philadelphia for Jayson Werth?) because of New York's rotation depth. The Yankees already had C.C. Sabathia, Andy Pettitte, A.J. Burnett, Phil Hughes, and Vazquez, and someone was going to have to go to make room for Lee.

Think about what would have happened if Jon Daniels had waited another week and a half to close a deal with Seattle—or maybe more to the point, if Jack Zduriencik had been more patient. Pettitte strained a groin muscle today and is now out for more than a month, and Burnett cut his pitching hand slamming a clubhouse door shut yesterday.

Think Brian Cashman would have said no today, as he reportedly did when Cliff Lee was still a Mariner, to Zduriencik's ask of shortstop Eduardo Nunez along with catcher Jesus Montero? If you were a Mariners fan, would you want to know the answer to that question?

As a Rangers fan, of course, I'm glad we'll never know. Texas may have lost both Lee starts since his arrival, but I don't remember the last Rangers starter I had more confidence in.

Another thing: If New York now renews efforts to find a starting pitcher (Ted Lilly?), it could take up resources that might otherwise have been earmarked for a hitter like Ty Wigginton or Wes Helms that the Rangers are also after.

A few days ago I wrote about how crummy the Angels must have felt losing a game in the standings to Texas during a stretch in which the Rangers dropped 7 of 10.

How do you think they feel now, getting the sad-sack Mariners at home for four coming out of the Break, while the Rangers were off to Boston, where they've been terrible for two and a half seasons, for four games of their own—and not gaining any ground, as both Los Angeles and Texas won three times, each falling one extra-inning loss short of a sweep?

It's another almost impossible story line for Texas: the Rangers lose the Cliff Lee start in Fenway Park, and still win the series.

When the Angels come here for four on Thursday, they'll do so without Ranger-killer Scott Kazmir, who has landed on the disabled list with shoulder fatigue. But before that, Texas—now listed by Bodog as the third most likely World Series champion in baseball (behind the Yankees and Rays)—visits Detroit for three, a second straight appointment at a house of recent horrors for this club.

But the Rangers keep pointing out in 2010 that history may not be all that instructive this year.

July 19, 2010

I'm not sure in which extra inning I tweeted this, but I'll repeat it here:

"Well, we do deserve to lose this game, but life isn't always fair. Win it."

Plenty of blame to go around, and some props as well, but it all takes a back seat to the job that Matt Harrison did tonight in four scoreless frames.

Whatever the relief counterpart is to the Quality Start, Harrison delivered it. He wasn't perfect, wasn't overpowering, but that was a bigtime, bold effort, and as deserving of a victory by a reliever as they get.

As for Scott Feldman, I don't know. The movement was back in spurts but the location was once again terrible, and while the obvious alternatives aren't realistic options quite yet, maybe giving Harrison himself another chance to start five days from now against Los Angeles wouldn't be the worst idea. The Angels beat up on Feldman three weeks ago. They haven't seen Harrison since 2008, when he made one very good start (in his big league debut) and one very bad one against that team—but he's not the same pitcher now anyway.

It's at least got to be a discussion point.

With Los Angeles off today, Texas is now five games up, six in the loss column (and gets to shed the half-game factor for the first time in five weeks). The Angels have two in New York—Sean O'Sullivan's first start of the year, facing Phil Hughes, and then Joel Pineiro against Javier Vazquez—while Texas has two opportunities to win this series, first with Tommy Hunter against Armando Galarraga Tuesday night and then Colby Lewis against Max Scherzer on Wednesday.

And then Los Angeles is here for a very big four, including Newberg Report Night on Sunday, about which I'll send the latest details in the morning.

I'll say this about that very frustrating game. Not to excuse the mistakes and poor approaches and failed execution, but I can't remember too many Rangers teams that would have pulled a game like that out. And that, along with Harrison's effort, is a real positive that can be taken away from Texas 8, Detroit 6.

July 21, 2010

The entirety of last Thursday's report read:

Since 2008, Texas has a 3-10 record in Boston.

And an 0-9 record in Detroit.

Time to see what this Rangers team is made of.

Answer: Two series wins, and five wins in six games at the moment, the lone loss coming on a night when Cliff Lee gave up two runs on six hits and one walk (remember that it was intentional when his season walk numbers are referenced) in nine innings and was one out away from a victory.

Unbelievable.

But getting closer, each series, to believable.

A few quick things:

1. Tommy Hunter is now 7-0, the first Rangers starting pitcher to begin a season with that record.

a. Only twice in Hunter's starts did he not win. On June 16, he left in third with a strained hip flexor, having allowed one run (which actually didn't come across until he'd already exited). In fact, it's the only one of Hunter's nine appearances that wasn't a quality start (though Texas ended up winning the game). And on July 8, he went six-plus innings against Baltimore, leaving a 4-2 lead in the hands of the bullpen (one of Hunter's runners came across with Alexi Ogando on the mound).

b. Only twice in Hunter's nine starts has Josh Hamilton not homered: (1) on July 3, a 3-1 Rangers win over the White Sox in which no Texas hitter managed an extra-base hit off John Danks and three Chicago relievers; and (2) on July 15, a 7-2 Rangers win over Boston in which Hamilton doubled three times.

c. Almost as freaky: Since Hunter has joined the active roster, Hamilton has 13 home runs . . . seven coming in Hunter starts.

d. Hunter's next start: Newberg Report Night, this Sunday.

2. Two interesting AAA role changes in the last week: (1) righthander Tanner Scheppers has moved from the Oklahoma City rotation back to the bullpen and (2) hitter Mitch Moreland has moved from the outfield back to first base.

Said Assistant GM Thad Levine of the Scheppers transition: "With our current pitching depth and our goal for Tanner for innings pitched this year, we feel that he can make the most impact as bullpen depth for the major league team as we try to best position ourselves for playing meaningful games in September and beyond." Scheppers, who struggled in six RedHawks starts (5.84 ERA, .330 opponents' average, 19 strikeouts and eight walks in 24.2 innings), gave up two runs on three hits and a walk in two relief innings last night, fanning none. His arrival in Texas isn't imminent, but it's clearly in the plans.

Just don't expect it to be as soon as Newberg Report Night, like last year's surprise call-up of Neftali Feliz that was announced just as Jon Daniels completed his Q&A with us.

As for Moreland, who played his first 82 games of the season in left or right field, we speculated even before Chris Davis's return struggles that the trade of Justin Smoak could prompt a Moreland move back to first base. It has. In his five games since the transition, Moerland is hitting .294/.391/.471, right in line with his overall .286/.369/.475 slash. (Of course, Davis hit .354/.403/.555 in Oklahoma City this season.) Moreland's monthly OPS numbers: .668, .824, .880, .989. And since April, he has almost as many walks (38) as strikeouts (39).

Last night's solid Davis game notwithstanding, I expect another first baseman added to the roster in the next 10 days, but it won't be Moreland, a fellow left-handed hitter. The Rangers are going to get another right-handed bat in here, and it will be a veteran who can play first (Ty Wigginton, Mike Lowell, Jorge Cantu, Wes Helms, Xavier Nady). If Davis can build off last night's effort, he won't necessarily be replaced in the lineup, but he'll likely give up some meaningful at-bats.

Still, Moreland is on the radar.

3. *Baltimore Sun* reporter Jeff Zrebiec speculates that the Orioles could accept a middle infielder like Joaquin Arias or Leury Garcia or Luis Sardinas for Wigginton. I doubt the Rangers would make Sardinas available in a deal like that. Texas is also on the hunt for a left-handed reliever, according to Ed Price of AOL FanHouse.

4. An addition to the auction list for our event on Sunday: A visit to Chuck Morgan's control room and booth during that night's game.

5. Justin Smoak (.267/.267/.500) has struck out in nearly half his Seattle at-bats (14 of 30). Maybe more astounding: zero walks.

6. Josh Lueke has made two relief appearances for Seattle's AA West Tenn club: 3.1 scoreless innings, two hits, no walks, six strikeouts. Thirty of his 36 pitches have gone for strikes. Blake Beavan's first start for the same club: five runs on six hits and one walk in four innings, three strikeouts. Michael Main has a 7.84 ERA in three AA starts for the Giants, with seven walks and four strikeouts in 10.1 innings.

7. Jarrod Saltalamacchia has thrown out six of 51 would-be AAA base-stealers.

8. Dear Cowboys Fan: Save me a spot. I'm gonna be running late this year.

And feel free to stay a while.

July 21, 2010

NYY 10, LAAA 6.

See you tomorrow, Angels.

— ~~Cliff~~ Jamey

July 22, 2010

Sports.

July 23, 2010

Lee vs. Weaver
October intensity
Texas sets the tone

Newberg Report: Draft Preparation

Roster decisions made now will impact Rule 5 in offseason

By Jamey Newberg / Special to MLB.com

July 22, 2010

For fans of the Texas Rangers, the 2010 season has thankfully been one in which thoughts of what offseason decisions loom for the front office haven't even crept in. Handicapping who will be protected on the 40-man roster in November, and who will therefore be left exposed to the Rule 5 Draft in December, just doesn't matter as much as what could lay ahead for the Rangers in October.

But there is a reason to think about the Rule 5 Draft in July, given the depth of draft-eligible prospects about whom Texas has winter decisions to make. Chances are the Rangers aren't done trading this month, even after the acquisitions of Cliff Lee and Bengie Molina. Texas is still looking for a right-handed corner bat and possibly a lefty specialist reliever, and it's going to take prospects to get them—and if the club needs dollars thrown in to make the trades work, the prospects going the other way are going to be more significant than they would be otherwise.

Since Jon Daniels has taken over as general manager, Texas has averaged three or four Minor League additions to the roster each November. The analysis on who to add involves more than just ranking your players internally and picking off the top few names. It's also assessing the chances that the players in question are the type that could be drafted (which requires that they be kept in the big leagues for all of the next season), and the odds that they'd make their new club out of spring training.

Texas has evaluated well during the Daniels regime. The club has yet to lose a player in the Rule 5 Draft since he became General Manager after the 2005 season.

But it gets more interesting this winter, because of a larger number of legitimate roster-eligibles than usual. And with at least one more trade likely in the next week and a half, it may very well be this class of players that the Rangers are going to be asked to part with - and that, because of the competition for 40-man roster spots, the team may be willing to deal.

If the decisions had to be made today, it seems there would be three locks for addition to the roster: Triple-A Oklahoma City first baseman-outfielder Mitch Moreland, Double-A Frisco center fielder Engel Beltre, and high Class A Bakersfield right-hander Wilmer Font.

But after that, there are first baseman/outfielder Chad Tracy (Oklahoma City); left-handers Beau Jones and Kasey Kiker and Ben Snyder and right-hander Evan Reed (Frisco); right-handers Wilfredo Boscan and Carlos Pimentel and outfielder David Paisano (Bakersfield); and right-handers Daniel Gutierrez and Jake Brigham (low Class A Hickory), among others.

Right-hander Josh Lueke was a solid candidate, too, before he went to Seattle in the Lee trade.

Take Boscan, for example. Let's say you view the 20-year-old strike-thrower, on a tremendous roll the last month and a half, as a middle-of-the-rotation candidate in two years. And you see Tracy as a capable corner bat off the bench sometime in 2011. Certainly not core players you'd refuse to trade, and maybe longshots to earn roster spots this winter, but not the type you'd feel good about losing for $50,000 in the Draft. Is a package more than you'd want to give up for a two-month role player like Wes Helms? Probably. But if you thought one of them might be drafted away in December?

Is it worth adding a bullpen specialist like Will Ohman for a couple power arms like Brigham and Reed? Objectively, probably not. But if you're thinking about ways to get Robinson Cano or Carl Crawford out in October? And if you think you could lose Brigham or Reed in the Draft? Maybe you're willing to overpay a bit, given the circumstances.

Lueke was probably on that short list, along with Moreland, Beltre, and Font, of players Texas knew it would have to put on the roster this winter in order to keep them. Lueke's inclusion in the Lee trade with Seattle theoretically opens a spot for another prospect to protect, assuming Texas wants to devote four spots to players not quite ready to help.

But the list of credible candidates is longer than just a player or two, and for that reason it wouldn't be surprising to see the Rangers part with one or more of them before the end of the month, considering the real risk that they could be lost anyway four and a half months from now.

What an amazing, edgy, compelling baseball game. Great pitching, great defense, a crowd that sizzled for nine, as tied to their seats as the Rangers bullpen was most of the night. The fifth one-run margin in six Rangers-Angels games this year, and in this one, as much as any, it really felt like every pitch mattered. Intensely tense.

Texas has a six-game lead on the division now, for the first time since 1999, the club's last playoff season.

It's the first time since 2006 that the Angels have been as many as six games out of first. (And they're now only a game and a half up on Oakland.)

I didn't care for the decision to pinch-run Joaquin Arias for Vladimir Guerrero with one out in the eighth and found myself brooding in my seat for the next 10 minutes.

And then I realized how much I loved that it upset me that much.

Cliff Lee and Jered Weaver did what they do, but here's one key difference: in the third through sixth, Weaver threw 23, 19, 21, and 26 pitches. Lee never had an inning with as many pitches as any of those four Weaver frames.

As a result, Texas got Weaver out of the game after six. Granted, the Rangers did all their scoring while Weaver was on the mound, not pushing anything across against Francisco Rodriguez, but chasing Weaver by making him work was a solid gameplan, one that no Rangers opponent has been able to accomplish against Lee.

Weaver needed 118 pitches to get through six. Lee needed only 78 pitches over the same span, and he threw just 99 pitches as he came two outs short of going the distance.

And Lee threw nearly as many strikes (68 to Weaver's 72).

Five times he went to three balls on an Angels hitter. Overall, Lee threw eight pitches with a three-ball count—all for strikes, obviously.

He's as methodical as the pre-pitch routine he goes through behind the mound nine times a night.

Lee's streak of seven straight starts of at least eight innings is the longest in baseball since Cy Young Award winner Pat Hentgen did it for Toronto in 1996.

His streak of seven straight starts of at least eight innings and no more than one walk is the longest in baseball since Cy Young Award winner Greg Maddux did it for Atlanta in 1994.

Lee leads baseball in pitch-per-inning economy.

Ace.

Nelson Cruz's defense was pivotal in the 3-2 win, but how about the double he hit to center in the fourth? I'm not sure I've ever seen Torii Hunter pull up to play a carom off a wall that wasn't several stories high. Cruz hit that ball so hard that even Hunter didn't have time to get back on it. Few humans are capable of hitting line drives like Cruz can.

Good grief, Elvis Andrus is having an awful year on the bases. Worst I've ever seen.

The walkup crowd last night totaled a reported 8,600. The walkup in Lee's first home game was apparently over 14,000.

Texas drew just short of 40,000 last night. Shouldn't these next three all sell out?

Sunday's game, which rounds out Newberg Report Night, will evidently feature Angels rookie Trevor Bell, making his fifth career start and first in 2010, necessitated by yesterday's Los Angeles trade of Sean O'Sullivan (and minor league pitcher Will Smith) to Kansas City for third baseman Alberto Callaspo. Bell's big league ERA is 7.94, and his grandfather played Bozo the Clown for 24 years.

He'll face Tommy Hunter, who will attempt to improve to 8-0 for the season.

At the end of that game, Texas will be 3, 5, 7, or 9 games up on the Angels.

And there will have been three more nights of spontaneous, synchronized, passionate "Beat L.A." chants fired off by an electric, hungry home crowd whose sports brains are preoccupied with thoughts of Game 163, having been given no reason this summer to have this weekend's opening of a football camp in San Antonio circled on the calendar.

July 23, 2010

July 23, 2010

No Angels player reached second base.

Think about that.

What is C.J. Wilson right now? This team's number three? Number four?

No Angels player reached second base.

This team has the league leader in ERA (Cliff Lee) and the league leader in saves (Neftali Feliz), but it also has the league leader in walks.

And that man didn't walk anyone tonight.

Wilson also came into the game as nearly the least economical pitcher in the league, at 17.1 pitches per inning (Justin Masterson's 17.6 paces the AL).

Tonight: 13 per inning, which is better than what the league leader averages.

That league leader is Lee, who throws 13.3 pitches per inning, an obvious reason he's able to consistently go at least eight, which is what Wilson did tonight, for just the second time as a big leaguer.

We've all seen shots of Wilson attached to Lee's hip in the dugout on nights neither is pitching, just as Tommy Hunter was situated tonight. It's clear that Lee is rubbing off on Wilson and Hunter and the way they're approaching lineups, yet another reason that the Lee acquisition is such a huge thing, and will be for years to come, even if Lee is no longer around.

Wilson's effort tonight, while not a carbon copy of a typical Lee start, looked a lot more like vintage Lee than vintage Wilson. Only three strikeouts (none until the seventh), but only four baserunners. He was tremendous. Facing the team about whom he said, three weeks ago, following a 2-1 Los Angeles win that he took the loss in, "We're the better team, 100 percent—when we play up to our capabilities, it might not even be that close," he made his words stand up.

Said his manager afterwards: "I really believe C.J. came into his own tonight."

When Wilson blew Maicer Izturis away swinging to end the eighth and marched toward the dugout, the first player to slide across the dugout to meet him with a pat on the back side?

Cliff Lee.

He may not be here next year, but he's looking like a part of this team, even outside the lines.

As does Bengie Molina, whose fist pump after he squeezed the 27th out fired me up.

I don't love Molina. But I sure do like him.

Think about this: What if Andy Pettitte and Jason Varitek got hurt before Jon Daniels made his moves to get Lee and Molina this month, instead of days after those trades?

There are a number of good reasons to strike early on the July trade market if you're a contender. That's one of them.

The players on the current Angels roster are now 0 for 23 lifetime against Feliz, who has saved all five Rangers wins over the Angels this season. The sound of the crowd during his inning tonight, the deafening din that the announcers on TV and radio were both fighting through, would be my new ringtone if I could make that happen.

There have been more years than not when a late July report would probably have led off with the note that Derek Holland, trying to ramp up to rejoin the big league rotation, went three hitless, walkless, scoreless rehab innings tonight against a bunch of teenage Royals in Surprise, setting six down on strikes. It's a worthwhile note, particularly laid against the reality that Scott Feldman has to be approaching a point at which he's pitching for his rotation life.

But it's a footnote, not a lead.

The Channel 8 News sportscast led off tonight with the Cowboys camp kickoff party in San Antonio.

Screw that.

I love football, but not the way I love baseball, and right now the thing I love most about one that the other can never give me is that, after the awesome awesomeness of these last two nights, we get to do it all over again tomorrow night, and the night after that.

I love this game, and I love this team.

Especially when no Angels reach second base.

Perhaps the dream
Is dreaming us.
— "When the Angels Fall," Sting

July 24, 2010

Just a quick shot this morning.

Which is more mind-blowing?

That ESPN SportsCenter led off this morning with the Texas Rangers, even though at least one local sportscast (and I bet more) led off last night with the Cowboys' blue jeans party in San Antonio?

That Justin Smoak, who despite his offensive struggles drew 38 walks in 70 games with Texas, has played every inning of every Mariners game since The Trade and is up to 44 plate appearances with that club, but didn't draw his first Seattle walk until last night (in what was Josh Beckett's first big league inning in more than two months)?

Or that C.J. Wilson (104 pitches, 63 strikes) didn't register a strikeout last night until the seventh inning, when he set Bobby Abreu and Torii Hunter down on strikes, and then in the eighth, when he ended his own night by punching Maicer Izturis out on strikes . . . and that *those three strike three's were the only three swinging strikes he recorded all night?*

July 24, 2010

According to multiple local reports, Texas is placing catcher Matt Treanor on the disabled list with a strained right posterior cruciate ligament, recalling Frisco catcher Taylor Teagarden to replace him on the active roster.

Since going to down to AA after a month in Texas and a week in Oklahoma City, Teagarden has hit .281 in May, .250 in June, and .193 in July, striking out 75 times in 52 games. He was reportedly the choice over RedHawks receivers Jarrod Saltalamacchia and Max Ramirez because the club wanted the catcher most capable of controlling the running game in his role as Bengie Molina's backup, in Treanor's absence.

Giving this move some thought, it makes sense in that Molina is an obvious candidate to be pulled for a pinch-runner in close and late situations. In that case, you want your number two catcher to be able to enter the game in the eighth or ninth and make it less likely that the other team takes the double play away by running on you—no matter how trustworthy the catcher's bat might be, since that spot in the order is probably not very likely to come back around anyway.

July 24, 2010

There haven't been too many better pitching efforts against Texas than the ones Max Scherzer and Ervin Santana threw Wednesday and tonight. Command of a fastball-power slider combination is a pretty good recipe if you're trying to gameplan a way to suppress Rangers offense. Tip of the cap to Santana tonight, who hasn't always succeeded with his best stuff against Texas but really executed tonight.

According to at least one local report, Marlins corner infielder Jorge Cantu may have emerged as the Rangers' targeted right-handed bat as they zero in on one to add in the next week.

I'm more serious about this than I've ever been: I would love to hear that Chris Davis is going to spend the winter learning to play catcher.

We're going to move the Newberg Report Night raffle and auction from 4:45 up to 4:30 tomorrow, in the interest of time. Cash or checks only as far as raffle tickets and auction winnings are concerned.

Doors open at 3:00, and Kevin Goldstein will begin his Q&A at 3:30. Raffle and auction at 4:30, and Jon Daniels at 5:00. Come early and grab a seat; it's going to be a standing-room-only event.

(If you're part of the group that is attending only the game with us tomorrow, your tickets will be at Will Call no later than 3:00. For those attending the pregame portion, we'll have your game tickets for you when you arrive at the Hall of Fame lobby.)

We'll wrap up at 6:30 and join what could be a third straight sellout crowd as we try to improve 5-2 in the life of the event and as Tommy Hunter looks to go 8-0, matched up against Angels rookie Trevor Bell—another fastball-slider righthander.

Finally, whether you're attending tomorrow or not, you should watch these 27 seconds, courtesy of Baseball Prospectus's Will Carroll, who will miss our event for the first time, and Jenn Sterger, who might join us for one down the road:

http://vimeo.com/13613567

See you tomorrow.

July 27, 2010

Boston 6, Los Angeles 3.

The Rangers' division lead over the Angels is now 7.5 games, nine in the loss column. But that's not all.

The Angels (52-50) have actually slipped into third place, a hair behind Oakland (50-48), which is also 7.5 games back.

And Dan Haren made his Angels debut tonight in that loss to the Red Sox, getting knocked out in the fifth when he took a Kevin Youkilis line drive off his pitching forearm. Early diagnosis: Just a bruise.

Haren's next scheduled start is Sunday afternoon, against Cliff Lee, in Anaheim.

Haren's career against Texas: 3-5, 4.29 in 10 starts.

Lee's career against Los Angeles: 7-3, 3.07 in 10 starts. As we mentioned when The Trade was made, the Angels are hitting .136 as a team against Lee since 2008.

But first things first. Lee tonight at home, against Oakland lefthander Gio Gonzalez, in what has suddenly become the Rangers' fifth straight game against the second-place team in the division.

July 27, 2010

There are things that don't surprise you, but still blow you away, like a Josh Hamilton rocket shot that eludes the second baseman's horizontal reach by maybe two feet and turns into a standup triple, and like your generosity and the ability of Kevin Goldstein and Jon Daniels to hold an audience.

Last year we raised a little over $8,000 for the Hello Win Column Fund and the Wipe Out Kids Cancer Foundation at our annual in-season event, a record amount for us. But Sunday, the seventh time we've organized a Newberg Report Night at Rangers Ballpark, we raised more than $12,000 for HWC and Genesis Women's Shelter. You all are amazing. But not surprising.

This will be an ineffective attempt to paint a picture of what happened Sunday afternoon, for those of you who weren't among the 400-plus in attendance. But I'll try.

Last year, the day after our sixth Newberg Report Night, which took place two days after the conventional trade deadline, and three days after Derek Holland's 8.2-inning, 10-strikeout, two-hit gem against Seattle, I wrote a report that began this way:

A couple exchanges into Jon Daniels's 90 minutes of straight answers to a lot of excellent questions, one of you raised your hand and said, "First, I want to thank you for not trading the players we've heard you would have had to trade to get Roy Halladay."

The room erupted into a wild ovation that shook the walls.

JD smiled and said, before the fan who made the comment could get to his question: "I should do nothing more often. That was awesome."

Awesome as he said it was, this year he leaned over a couple minutes before his turn to take the microphone and said to me, as Luther Davis was wrapping up the auction: "Don't get up there and embarrass me."

It didn't matter what I said. My introduction lasted maybe 20 seconds, but I could have saved my energy and gone only with the final five words: "Ladies and gentlemen: Jon Daniels."

The 2009 ovation barely Richtered compared to what happened in that room when JD stepped to the podium Sunday.

His response once he was permitted to speak: "I'm still the guy who traded Adrian Gonzalez."

Daniels walked us through the Cliff Lee trade talks, which he said began while the Rangers were in Milwaukee June 11-13, and ended with a number of phone exchanges with Seattle GM Jack Zduriencik and high fives around the room three Fridays ago. He told us he expects Josh Lueke to be in the Seattle bullpen in September and for years to come, maybe eventually in the ninth inning. (To date: 6.1 AA West Tenn innings, no runs on three hits and zero walks, 12 strikeouts, 77 percent strikes.)

He reacted to the Angels' Dan Haren acquisition—the news of which broke during his Q&A—the same way he responded to the question about competing against teams with payrolls like the Yankees: We embrace the challenge. He said he expected Los Angeles to do something—which is part of why he wanted to act quickly this month, rather than be put in a position of having to react—and the Angels were last on his list of who he was hoping Haren would end up with, but it sounded as if he's more concerned about Haren the next three years than he is in 2010.

Is there a chance that Texas signs Lee long-term? The Rangers decided, and told Lee, that they won't even raise the subject during the season, out of fairness to the lefthander, who has been traded four times—three in the last 12 months—and has worked his whole career to get to this point, where he has some control over his future. JD's hope is that Texas has a good October run, which is the best possible recruiting tool there is, and if Lee likes his situation here, the club is obviously interested in talking to him about a new contract.

C.J. Wilson has been responsible for charting Lee's starts. Not by accident.

(Incidentally, I don't want to let this note get away: Ken Rosenthal of Fox Sports reported this morning that Texas has called Houston about Roy Oswalt *since* trading for Lee, though the clubs couldn't find a match.)

Asked about the recent stories that Texas didn't participate in Latin America this year because of financial constraints, Daniels pointed two things out: (1) while the club did make a decision this summer to reallocate some budget items toward the big club, given the real chance to get to October, the Rangers did make a significant international splash in January when they signed 16-year-old Colombian catcher Jorge Alfaro (for a reported $1.3 million); and (2) the organization didn't believe this year's Latin American class was a very strong one, relatively speaking.

Was Jake Skole a signability pick, as many (including Goldstein an hour earlier) have insisted? Daniels said there was nobody on the Rangers' board at pick number 15 whom they passed on because of money, and in fact there were only a few players higher on their Draft Day board than Skole at all.

Has the club decided not to look at Neftali Feliz as a starter down the road? Can't rule it out: See Wilson.

At Oklahoma City, Tanner Scheppers from the rotation to the bullpen and Mitch Moreland from the outfield to first base: Both moves were made with possible big league impact this summer in mind (though less likely with Moreland). Scheppers is one move we might see around August 1, when the club is going to be thinking about getting its 12 best arms in Texas, positioned for the stretch run.

One fan reminded Daniels that, two years ago at the same event, he pegged Tommy Hunter as a pitcher a little bit under the radar who shouldn't be, and then asked him to answer the same question this year. Daniels turned to Senior Director of Player Personnel and television star A.J. Preller and asked for his candidate. Preller tabbed Hickory lefthander Robbie Erlin, who Daniels noted is dominating the Low A South Atlantic League at age 19 (5-2, 1.67, 57 hits and 13 walks in 81 innings, 88 strikeouts) with terrific command, a mature approach, and an advanced ability to spin the ball.

Daniels asked Assistant GM Thad Levine to weigh in on one fan's request to name the single biggest surprise in the starting rotation. Levine's quick-twitch response: "Lewis, Wilson, and Hunter."

As for the idea that Josh Hamilton may not be back in 2011 because of club finances, Daniels suggested that's highly unlikely, and that Nolan Ryan's comment to that effect last week was merely an extreme possibility of what could happen if the club were to remain in bankruptcy much longer. (Daniels added that the club remaining in bankruptcy in the off-season would be more disruptive than it is right now.) If economic issues were to force the club to make any drastic cost-cutting personnel decisions, Daniels said, even contemplating a move to dispose of Hamilton (who has two arbitration seasons left) would be way down the list.

There wasn't a prospect in the Rangers system Kevin Goldstein wasn't asked about, and there wasn't one that he didn't have complete command of. Goldstein may not be as high on Elvis Andrus as the rest of us, and he may have missed, he readily admits, on Ian Kinsler (even though he saw him play repeatedly during his two-month, .402 run through the Midwest League in 2004), but nobody in Goldstein's business was strong on Feliz (who he now describes as "absolutely terrifying") before he was, and I don't think I've heard anyone as bullish on Engel Beltre as he is right now.

Beltre, a potential lockdown center fielder with 20-20 potential in Goldstein's view, is four years younger than Julio Borbon, but there's no question which of the two (who were acquired by Texas within a month of each other in the summer of 2007) Goldstein believes is the long-term answer here in center. (He also sees Martin Perez as a potential number one, but isn't alone there.)

Goldstein loves Jurickson Profar, largely because of unsolicited comments he heard from two scouts from other teams, days apart, about the way the 16-year-old stood at Fall Instructs last year.

But my favorite Goldstein comment, made well before Daniels, Levine, and Preller arrived, was when it was not the Rangers' farm system that he referred to as being loaded (still a top three system, he believes), but instead the Rangers front office, which he described as "scary smart." He emphasized how fortunate we should understand we are to have the people in charge of baseball decisions here that we do, and while I think we generally recognize that, it resonates even more when coming from someone with Goldstein's credibility who is so tuned into all 30 organizations.

Thanks to OSAR Consulting and Leapfrog Executive Search for sponsoring the event; to Pat Payton for donating his original artwork, which fetched two of the three highest bids in the auction; to Eleanor Czajka, Norma & George & Ryan Wolfson, Allen Cordrey, and Luther Davis for making the event click; to teammates Scott Lucas, Devin Pike, Marty Yawnick, and Ted Price for being there; and to the Rangers, foremost among them Rob Matwick, Paige Farragut, Paul Morrow, Chris Bielinski, Taunee Taylor, Heather King, Delia Willms, Chuck Morgan, and Sherry Flow; and to Cindy & Jeff Kuster and the Hello Win Column Fund and the folks at Genesis Women's Shelter, for doing what they do.

And, of course, to you all, for helping support HWC and Genesis and whoever else benefits from your generosity.

It's probably worth thanking Hamilton and Hunter and everyone else in uniform that night, for taking the Angels down for the third time in four nights. There was no surprise Feliz/backpack sighting, which highlighted last year's event, but there was more at stake on the field this year, almost 40,000 people in the building, and an electricity in the crowd that was unlike last year's, or any other in memory. I initially chose July 25 for the event because it was the only home Sunday that was anywhere near the trade deadline (always the most fascinating time to put Daniels behind a microphone), but it turned out to be an ideal day for other, bigger reasons, thanks to what this team is doing on the field.

Rob and Paige and I are working on trying to figure out a way to accommodate a bigger group next time, as this year's event sold out in 48 hours and probably could have doubled in size if we had the space.

July 27, 2010

According to multiple local reports, the Rangers have signed second-round pick Cody Buckel, a high school righthander out of Simi Valley, California, for a reported over-slot bonus of $590,000.

Supplemental first-rounder Luke Jackson, a high school righthander out of Florida, remains unsigned with three weeks to go before the deadline to reach terms.

July 28, 2010

Don't feel sorry for Cliff Lee. I don't think he's feeling sorry for himself.

Because what counts is the win, not the win-loss record.

Did he deserve a victory tonight? Obviously. Nine innings and no earned runs and five hits and zero walks and 13 strikeouts is what happens when you're eight years old and you rig your video game.

But Lee had to be that good, or else Texas probably loses that game in regulation.

Then again, if Ian Kinsler had covered second base in the sixth (and such a strange moment: neither Kinsler nor Elvis Andrus, who theoretically was charged with backing Kinsler up on any attempted steal, budged an inch), maybe Lee gets the shutout he earned.

On the other hand, if Nelson Cruz doesn't keep Kevin Kouzmanoff's shot to right in the park later in that inning, Texas would have been down 3-1 instead of tied at 1-1 and, even though everything would still have been unearned, it nonetheless would have been a home run off Lee at a very bad time. (As for Cruz: No kid even dares to dream of a game like that, short of post-season heroics. Right?)

But forget all the if's, and don't feel sorry for Lee.

Yeah, he's got one win in four Rangers starts. But he's gotten 27 outs in each of the three he didn't win, and 25 outs in the other one. You know how many batters Lee has walked in his 35.1 Texas innings? One.

And it was an *intentional* walk.

Don't feel sorry for Lee. He's been a mind-blowing addition, he's going to pitch in massively huge games for this team in September and October, and, no matter where free agency takes him this winter, he's going to get his money and he's going to get to pitch exactly where he wants to pitch for the next pile of years.

Tonight's 13 strikeouts were a career high for the 31-year-old. No Texas pitcher has had at least that many with no walks since Nolan Ryan punched out 15 over 10 walkless frames in a 13-inning, 1-0 win over the White Sox on August 17, 1990, when Lee was 11.

Lee is the first big league pitcher since Joe Niekro in 1982 to throw eight or more innings with two walks or fewer in eight straight starts.

Lee faced 32 Oakland hitters tonight. And threw 30 balls.

Less than a ball per hitter.

And I demand to know how many pitchers this year or over the last two or three or ten have had 88-*strike* games. Get back to me on that, please.

You shouldn't feel sorry for Lee when you see how happy he looked, standing at home plate, awaiting Cruz with his teammates as Boomstick circled the bases to send the A's off the field. Lee is no Todd Stottlemyre. There's some degree of fit here. Not sure yet how much. But there's something.

True, the Rangers have scored a total of seven runs while Lee has been the pitcher of record in his four starts, an embarrassing absence of run support. But don't feel sorry for him. Nobody discounts what he has meant to this team.

The next time Lee does his windmill/air toss/double ankle touch/rosin application/mound landscape/warmup pitch routine each inning, the next time he sprints off the field after the third out, the next time he talks his manager into leaving him in to finish the ninth, appreciate the extraordinariness of what you're seeing, particularly in that he's doing it with "Texas" sprawled across his jersey. Appreciate it; don't feel sorry for the man.

Nah, screw that.

I feel sorry for him, at least a little bit.

What a freakin' beast that guy is.

Texas	*59*	*41*	—
Oakland	*50*	*49*	*8.5*
Los Angeles	*52*	*51*	*8.5*

July 29, 2010: TROT COFFEY

First, real quick: The Rangers' Stretch Drive promotion closes at the end of the day tomorrow. You can reserve seats for the final 24 home games of the season, which includes five with the Yankees, three with the Red Sox, three with the A's, and the regular-season-ending four with the Angels—and guarantees you the option of purchasing the same seats for all playoff games. It also includes significant savings off gate prices. Basically, you get to be a season ticket holder now, just in time for the post-season.

More details are contained in the attached PDF and on texasrangers.com. You can also email Troy King at TKing@texasrangers.com with questions, or call 972-RANGERS.

- The Rangers were "inching closer to a first base acquisition" on Wednesday (Jim Bowden, MLB Network Radio/Fox Sports Radio)
- According to local reports and the identified national outlets, Texas is said to be in the mix, to one degree or another, for Prince Fielder (Jon Heyman, *Sports Illustrated*; Will Carroll, Baseball Prospectus), Adam Dunn (Jon Paul Morosi and Ken Rosenthal, Fox Sports), Jorge Cantu (Jayson Stark, ESPN; Rosenthal), Ty Wigginton (Rosenthal), Mike Lowell (Rob Bradford, WEEI, noting that Lowell is 11 for 22 with four doubles and four home runs in five rehab appearances over the last week), and Wes Helms
- We talked about the Fielder idea during a radio segment I did on 105.3 The Fan yesterday; I just don't think it makes sense to part with, say, Martin Perez or Tanner Scheppers, plus Chris Davis (who would be the 2010 version of the Nelson Cruz piece that was included when the same two teams made the Carlos Lee deal in 2006), plus an arm like Scott Feldman or Matt Harrison, plus another blue-chip prospect like Engel Beltre since the Rangers would need Milwaukee to dump a bunch of cash into the deal—if we're going to load up with a package that looks anything like that (and I do expect the Brewers to demand something along those lines since they'd be giving up a year and a half of Fielder), I'm going hard after Josh Johnson or Zack Greinke or someone like that rather than a hitter
- According to a local report, Texas refused to discuss Beltre with Seattle in the Cliff Lee trade talks
- I suspect it would take less to get Dunn than to get Fielder, but it's still probably a prohibitive demand (Washington reportedly asked either for second baseman Gordon Beckham straight up or a package including righthander Dan Hudson plus either catcher Tyler Flowers or outfielder Jordan Danks or third baseman Brent Morel from the White Sox); don't hold your breath
- Shoehorning this in: *Baseball America*'s Jim Callis issued a Prospect Dream Team earlier this week, including Perez in his starting rotation and making Scheppers his closer
- The Rangers haven't ruled out waiting until August to address first base (Rosenthal)
- According to a local report, Florida is interested in Frisco reliever Evan Reed as part of any Cantu trade
- The Marlins are "believed to be looking for [a] young" lefthander for Cantu (Rosenthal) (for Texas, Derek Holland and Perez and Robbie Erlin are obviously not up for discussion, which could put Harrison or Michael Kirkman or Robbie Ross in play, though I doubt Texas would move Harrison for a bench bat; Kasey Kiker likely has no trade value at the moment)
- The hangup between Texas and Florida on Cantu is that "the Marlins are balking at [taking on virtually all of the $2 million remaining on Cantu's 2010 contract] unless the Rangers are willing to dramatically upgrade the player return" (Stark)

- Nonetheless, "one [big league] source . . . believes that the Marlins, while still talking with other clubs, will get something done with Texas, as long as [the] Commissioner's Office signs off on [the] financials in the deal" (Gordon Edes, ESPN Boston)
- The same local report that mentioned Reed adds that "clubs are inquiring" about Bakersfield reliever Fabio Castillo (the Reed and Castillo notes illustrate the importance of the Rangers' prospect depth, as those two are probably on the third tier of the club's prospect inventory but are still drawing July interest)
- According to a local report, Texas has dispatched a scout to Washington to keep tabs on Josh Willingham and Cristian Guzman
- Various reports indicated that the Rangers were in on Derrek Lee, who wielded his 10/5 rights and declined a trade to the Angels on Wednesday
- The Angels may have "pulled back" from the trade market, deciding that, at 8.5 games back, the odds of extending their season past 162 don't justify gutting the farm system for a short-term fix (Rosenthal) (see Sosa/Alvarez/Fletcher for Baines/Manrique, which went down 21 years ago today) (yesterday afternoon's injury to scratched starter Joel Pineiro, who will miss 6-8 weeks with a strained oblique, surely sealed the Angels' decision) (I sorta wish they did give up a legitimate prospect or two for Derrek Lee)
- Los Angeles could even become a seller this weekend rather than a buyer, potentially listening to overtures for veterans like Bobby Abreu, Brian Fuentes, Hideki Matsui, and Maicer Izturis (Mike DiGiovanna, *Los Angeles Times*)
- Related note: Oakland righthander Ben Sheets is done for the year, needing flexor tendon surgery
- The second-worst part about the Angels' acquisition of Dan Haren, for me, is that the Yankees were said to be in on Haren, whose acquisition presumably would have taken them out of the Cliff Lee hunt this winter
- At least one local report suggests that there are clubs showing some level of interest in Scott Feldman and Rich Harden (also reported by Rosenthal)
- Texas maintained interest in Roy Oswalt, even after acquiring Cliff Lee (Rosenthal, Heyman), but this morning all indications are that the Astros and Phillies have agreed on players (reportedly including lefthander J.A. Happ, righthander Vance Worley, and maybe two more arms) and await only Oswalt's approval of the deal, which could include a decision on whether his 2012 option would be exercised now
- Sadly (if you're a Phillies fan), any package headed by Happ probably means Philadelphia will give up more for Oswalt than they got for Lee
- The Rangers asked Florida about righthander Chris Volstad but "were turned away" (Joe Capozzi, *Palm Beach Post*)
- The Red Sox, Yankees, and Tigers are interested in Oakland reliever Michael Wuertz, but Oakland, "barring [a] knockout offer," won't trade the right-handed slider specialist (Rosenthal) (I'd love to add Wuertz here, but not for what the A's would evidently want)
- Get this: When Texas recently approached Pittsburgh about reliever Joel Hanrahan, the Pirates, "according to a scout with direct knowledge of [the] teams' dealings," responded by asking for Neftali Feliz in return (Dejan Kovacevic, *Pittsburgh Post-Gazette*) (umm, wow)
- The $590,000 signing bonus that Texas gave this week to California high school righthander Cody Buckel, the club's second-round selection in June, was more than $80,000 over slot—the second-highest over-slot deal announced so far across the league (Callis; Kevin Goldstein, Baseball Prospectus) (Buckel, who is forgoing a commitment to Pepperdine, will report to the Arizona League)
- The Rangers have granted righthander Geoff Geary's request for his release
- The trade deadline arrives Saturday afternoon at 3:00 Central; stay tuned

July 29, 2010

Take this for what it's worth, as there's been no confirmation from the organization, but according to a local report, Texas will place second baseman Ian Kinsler on the 15-day disabled list today with a minor injury to his left leg, and will purchase the contract of Oklahoma City first baseman-outfielder Mitch Moreland. To make room for Moreland on the 40-man roster, according to the story, righthander Mark Lowe could be shifted to the 60-day disabled list.

The Kinsler injury isn't considered serious but the club reportedly wants to take this opportunity to get him right physically before the stretch run.

The article goes on to suggest that this development could vault Baltimore's Ty Wigginton over Florida's Jorge Cantu as a trade target over the next three days, as Wigginton is capable of playing not only on the infield corners but at second base as well.

Also, Tim Kurkjian said on ESPN SportsCenter this morning that he didn't expect the Brewers to trade Prince Fielder this week unless Texas were to bowl them over with an offer.

More as details develop.

July 29, 2010

Local reports now indicate that it's a strained left groin, rather than a left leg injury, that will force Ian Kinsler to the disabled list.

Also, Tampa Bay has apparently pulled righthander Jeremy Hellickson from his AAA start after three scoreless innings this morning. He's a deep blue chipper. If he's being pulled to preserve him for an imminent trade, it's going to be a big one.

Also, since we've had more than 120 new subscribers sign up in the last two hours, I'll resend this morning's TROT COFFEY around lunchtime. Apologies to the other 8,600 of you who will be receiving it for a second time.

July 29, 2010: TROT COFFEY

- According to Bob Nightengale of *USA Today* and Clark Spencer of the *Miami Herald*, Texas and Florida are "getting closer" on a deal involving Jorge Cantu, with the Marlins having agreed to pay "most, if not all, of the remainder of" the right-handed-hitting corner infielder's contract
- Baltimore is reportedly set to announce to hiring of Buck Showalter to manage the club

July 29, 2010: TROT COFFEY

- Philadelphia gets Roy Oswalt from Houston for lefthander J.A. Happ, outfielder Anthony Gose, and shortstop Jonathan Villar, and in a way the deal comes out smelling a little for both teams—the Phillies because they arguably gave up more to get Oswalt than they got for Cliff Lee over the winter, and the Astros because it's still not a slam dunk package, particularly considering they're throwing significant cash into the deal
- The Astros are apparently on the verge of flipping Gose to Toronto (Jayson Stark, ESPN)
- The Dan Haren trade (namely, the seemingly underwhelming return that Arizona got) sure appears to have hurt Houston, and any other teams looking to trade starting pitching; wonder if the Astros might have done better if they'd acted sooner
- Haren reported no problems with his bruised forearm after a bullpen session yesterday and is in line to start against Texas on Saturday (MLB Network crawl)
- As pointed out in a local report, another Rangers lefthander who could interest the Marlins in a Jorge Cantu trade is Frisco starter Richard Bleier; like Evan Reed and Fabio Castillo, Bleier is probably a tier three prospect in this system
- The Rangers and Brewers got "not very far at all" on trade talks for Prince Fielder (Ken Davidoff, *Newsday*)
- Although "these things are always fluid, . . . for now [the] Yankees are out" on Adam Dunn and are "checking into other alternatives" (Ken Rosenthal, Fox Sports)
- New York considered the Nationals' asking price too steep, along the lines of something they might have considered for a player like Cliff Lee but not one like Dunn; Tampa Bay has backed off of Dunn for the same reason, and the frontrunners now appear to be the Giants and White Sox (Joel Sherman, *New York Post*)
- The Yankees and Rays may, on the other hand, still be hovering on Dunn, even if they're not presently engaged in talks with the Nationals (Buster Olney, ESPN)
- The Rays are targeting Josh Willingham but, if unable to get him from Washington, may turn to Los Angeles for Bobby Abreu (Peter Gammons, MLB Network)
- The Rangers are "now involved in [the] second base market" after the Ian Kinsler injury, having already shown interest in Cristian Guzman over the past few weeks (Jon Paul Morosi, Fox Sports)
- That said, writes Morosi, the Rangers are among a few contenders who should stand pat at this point; Morosi adds: "It's almost time to print playoff tickets"
- Yes, as several of you have pointed out: Milwaukee is fielding interest in reliever Todd Coffey (Rosenthal)

July 29, 2010: TROT COFFEY

- While he says it's not a done deal, Ken Rosenthal of Fox Sports tweets as follows: "Marlins' return for [Jorge] Cantu will be Double A RHP Evan Reed & Double A RHP Omar Poveda, who is on DL recovering from TJ surgery" (I can definitely live with that, if true)
- Randy Galloway reports that Mitch Moreland will start for Texas at first base tonight
- Buster Olney of ESPN reports that the White Sox are saying that they're not in the mix for Adam Dunn

July 29, 2010: TROT COFFEY

- Joel Sherman of the *New York Post* reports that Florida will in fact trade Jorge Cantu, who is playing third base for Florida in the Marlins' ongoing game against San Francisco at the moment, with Florida paying $600,000 of the $2.1 million left on Cantu's 2010 contract; all indications seem to agree that the return would be righthanders Evan Reed and Omar Poveda
- Sherman also reports that Houston, who has apparently acquired first baseman Brett Wallace from Toronto for outfielder Anthony Gose (whom they'd picked up in the Roy Oswalt trade earlier today), could now move Lance Berkman (who has no-trade power) and move into a full-bore rebuilding phase; Ken Rosenthal of Fox Sports confirms that Berkman is now "in play"
- According to Jon Paul Morosi of Fox Sports, Texas has looked at Ryan Theriot, Joe Inglett, Craig Counsell, Cristian Guzman, and Kelly Johnson as potential second base protection for Ian Kinsler, who a local reporter notes has been dealing with his groin strain for a few days; Joaquin Arias gets the start at second tonight (incidentally, Cantu has played 218 big league games at second base, but none since two appearances in 2007)
- Again, don't overlook the first point above: Cantu has not been pulled from Florida's game against San Francisco; this is not a done deal . . . yet

July 29, 2010: TROT COFFEY

- Jorge Cantu has been lifted in the 8th inning of Florida's game against San Francisco, with Florida ahead, 5-0

July 30, 2010

Bengie, Cliff, Cantu
Busiest team in baseball
Bankruptcy be damned

The 2010 season has been the one in which I've written more than ever before, but at the same time have written less about the minor leagues than ever before. But that's where I want to focus today.

Dial back four years. Despite hovering between third and fourth place in the division, a few games behind first place Oakland, rookie GM Jon Daniels made three trade deadline deals in 2006, one major trade (Carlos Lee) and two smaller ones (Matt Stairs and Kip Wells). Ultimately, Texas played .500 baseball after the three deals, and finished the season in third place in the West, 13 games back.

The Rangers, owning a comfortable division lead this year, are taking no chances, having made three trades this month as well, again one of the blockbuster variety (Cliff Lee) and two that were smaller in scope (Bengie Molina and Jorge Cantu).

In each case, Texas would be right to expect a greater impact than it got from its 2006 counterpart.

The Rangers are in bankruptcy, a story that's filled a thousand column inches over the last two months. It is what it is. The team is playing its best baseball in years, if not ever, in spite of it. Where the team's financial condition and unclear ownership situation have had an impact is in the nature of the three trades the club has made in July, each necessitating the inclusion of cash from the other team to help fit the deals within a tight, immovable budget. So from that standpoint, Texas has had to part with greater prospects than it did in 2006, not only because the club acquired more significant players, but also because the cost of acquiring cash was added prospect consideration.

Nonetheless, the effect of these trades on the club's prospect depth may ultimately be only slightly greater than it was in 2006. I've tried to make the point over and over, and many others have as well: The benefit of building a strong farm system shows up not only in the arrival of young talent in Texas and resulting cost containment, but also in the development of ammunition to trade for veterans for the stretch run.

In 2006, Texas had what *Baseball America* tabbed as the number 16 farm system in baseball. That relative thinness on the farm meant that, in order to acquire Lee (and change-of-scenery 4-A outfielder Nelson Cruz), the Rangers had to part with young, affordable big league talent (Francisco Cordero, Kevin Mench, Laynce Nix), and to pick up an extra hitter and extra arm without giving up one of the club's few true prospects, they were limited to acquiring Stairs (for reliever Joselo Diaz) and Wells (for reliever Jesse Chavez).

Clearly, the group including Chris Ray, Michael Main, Justin Smoak, Josh Lueke, Blake Beavan, Matt Lawson, Omar Poveda, and Evan Reed, all traded away this month, is exponentially more valuable than what Texas gave up in 2006. But only Ray and Smoak came off the big league roster, each was replaceable (at least in terms of what they were contributing at the time), and the Rangers were able to make the three deals without touching their top minor league prospects (Martin Perez, Tanner Scheppers, Engel Beltre, Robbie Erlin, Wilmer Font, Mitch Moreland, Jurickson Profar, more).

We now learn that Daniels, while talking with Florida to get the Cantu deal done, was (according to Joe Frisaro of MLB.com) apparently "willing to part with [the club's] top three prospects, just to get the conversation rolling" about ace Josh Johnson, only to be told that Johnson was "unmovable."

Different situation, of course. A rotation headed by Lee and Johnson now, and Johnson for the next three seasons after this one, would have made it tolerable seeing Perez and Scheppers pitch for the Marlins, and Beltre patrol center field for that club. Johnson is the kind of player you load up for and don't look back.

But Daniels got Lee (controllable only for half a season plus the playoffs) for considerably less than that, and Molina and Cantu, too, obviously. Even considering the premium cost imposed to get cash thrown in.

How big a dent have these three trades put in the Texas system? Not much of one, if you ask Kevin Goldstein of Baseball Prospectus. Goldstein ranked the Texas system number two in baseball before the 2009 season and number two again before 2010 (when all of the eight players traded this month other than Ray were part of the crop), and he told us at our event Sunday that the system is still top three in the game. Yesterday's move of Poveda and Reed, whom Goldstein projects as middle relievers, certainly doesn't change that.

Could the 22-year-old Poveda and 24-year-old Reed develop in such a way that Florida can count this trade as a win? No question. What if Poveda, out for the year due to Tommy John surgery, regains his velocity (not a plus to begin with) and command (a key to his game) and his promising changeup plays up like Armando Galarraga's slider and he turns into a back-of-rotation starter Texas wishes it had back? What if Reed's mid-90s four-seamer carries him to Florida, he refines his slider, and, like Matt Capps or Kevin Gregg, one day earns a chance to save a small market team's games, or even short of that, turns into Jesse Chavez, the reliever who Texas traded for Wells and who would later get traded for Rafael Soriano, straight up?

It could happen. But the fact remains, even if both righthanders are decent bets to pitch in the big leagues, that both had a good amount of folks to pass in this system, which makes the trade sensible if for that reason alone. Whether Cantu (rather than another corner bench bat Texas had the opportunity to acquire) helps is something we have to trust Daniels and his pro scouts on, or not. But moving Poveda and Reed to get him is fine.

Think back a year to reliever Matt Nevarez and second baseman Jose Vallejo to Houston for Ivan Rodriguez. Same idea. Nevarez and Vallejo were outside the Rangers' top 30 prospects. Nevarez ended up ranked by *Baseball America* this winter as Houston's number 15 prospect. Poveda and Reed will rank higher with Florida than they did here.

Incidentally, the Marlins will need to reinstate Poveda to the 40-man roster after the season, and add Reed to the 40, unless they want to risk losing them in the Rule 5 Draft. Here, it's highly doubtful Reed would have been added, and Poveda was a candidate to be outrighted. In my column for MLB.com a week ago, I suggested that we could see Texas trade a couple draft-eligible prospects for a corner bat this week, especially given the deep Rule 5 Draft class the club has to make roster decisions on this winter. That's exactly what the Rangers did yesterday.

You can read any number of stories today about Cantu, so I won't dig too deep on what he brings. His 2010 season (.262/.310/.409) hasn't measured up to his 2008 (.277/.327/.481) or 2009 (.289/.345/.443) campaigns, when he drove in 195 runs with 45 homers, but he's still capable of driving in runs in bunches (he set a big league record with RBI in each his first 10 games this year) and fills a roster void here. While he's hitting lefties at an underwhelming .256/.296/.422 rate this season, he punished them in 2008 (.293/.359/.510) and 2009 (.322/.389/.503). He's not a great defender at either infield corner, but will be more dependable at first base than Joaquin Arias.

Cantu doesn't play second base any more—leading some to wonder whether Texas has yet another trade in the works with Ian Kinsler expected to miss more than the minimum 15 days due to his groin strain—but that's not what he'll be asked to do here. He'll figure in at first base with the newly recalled Moreland, and give Ron Washington something he hasn't had all season: a capable right-handed bat off the bench on nights that he doesn't start. (Small sample size alert: Cantu is a healthy .323/.400/.452 hitter in 35 career pinch-hitting plate appearances.)

Will Cantu (who projects to be a non-compensation free agent, for those of you wondering if the Rangers could have a chance to recoup a draft pick for him this winter; don't count on it) contribute any more than Stairs (.210/.273/.370) or Rodriguez (.245/.279/.388) did in their late-season runs with Texas? The Rangers (on the hook for about $1.5 million of the $2.1 million remaining on his 2010 contract) obviously hope so. But given the club's depth in minor league arms, assuming you like what the bat does for the 25-man roster, it's a trade that makes a lot of sense.

To make room for Cantu on the 40-man roster, righthander Brandon McCarthy was shifted to the 60-day disabled list. (Righthander Mark Lowe was moved to the 60-day DL earlier in the day to make room for Moreland.) To clear space on the active roster for Cantu, Texas optioned Chris Davis (.189/.267/.245 since his return three weeks ago) again. It's pretty clear (as I discussed in one of yesterday's TROT COFFEY's) that Davis is on the Nelson Cruz path (at best) and will likely get included in a trade this winter, needing that change of scenery that Cruz needed when the Brewers sent him to Texas in the 2006 Carlos Lee deal.

I'm guessing Davis was probably in play in the Rangers' recent talks with Houston about Roy Oswalt and with Milwaukee about Prince Fielder (efforts that, in both cases, were described by Jon Heyman of *Sports Illustrated* as "aggressive"). Houston ended up getting a young first baseman for Oswalt yesterday, flipping outfielder Anthony Gose (packaged from Philadelphia) to Toronto for Brett Wallace, as that club prepares for life after Lance Berkman, an eventuality that could arrive as soon as this weekend.

A thought: I wonder if a club shopping a versatile second baseman this weekend approaches Texas about Davis.

Moreland's time is now, and while his two singles and deep fly to center last night were a refreshing change from what we'd seen out of Davis this summer (and what Seattle has seen out of Justin Smoak, who sits at .159/.169/.270 with one walk and 23 strikeouts in 63 at-bats), he's a player who, despite exploding onto the scene the last two years, still needs to prove that he's a starting bat on a good big league club.

The 2007 17th-rounder, whom the Rangers experimented with on the mound after the 2008 season (he occasionally closed games at Mississippi State), was leading all of minor league baseball in hits in 2009 when he broke a bone in his foot with three weeks left in the season. He's short to the ball, barrels pitches with remarkable consistency, draws walks and doesn't strike out a lot, and is athletic enough to handle himself on an outfield corner (with plenty of arm, not surprising since he worked in the low 90s on the mound). A comp if it all comes together? Lyle Overbay is the one I keep coming back to.

Moreland, the Rangers' 2009 Tom Grieve Minor League Player of the Year, is a .313/.383/.509 hitter in four minor league seasons, and a .500/.500/.500 hitter for one big league night. Nice start.

Moreland's splits in 2010 are reasonably even, as are Cantu's. It's not clear how Washington will allocate time at first base between the two, and that may be something that Washington hasn't yet figured out himself.

But as Texas makes this road swing through Anaheim, Seattle, and Oakland over the next 10 days, before coming home to host New York and Boston, sitting at a season-high 18 games over .500 and having won 13 series out of 16, there's one thing that's unmistakable. Well, a few.

Jorge Cantu makes the first base situation and bench stronger. Bengie Molina has strengthened catcher considerably. Cliff Lee has overhauled every spot in the rotation, all by himself, and has changed the October outlook for this club.

And despite the fact that the Rangers had to dig even deeper in players than they should have had to in order to acquire all three, given the financial handcuffs on the organization that have yet to be removed, the impact that the Lee, Molina, and Cantu roster upgrades have had on the extraordinary depth this club has on the farm has been relatively minor, in a manner of speaking.

July 30, 2010

According to Bill Ladson of MLB.com and one local report, Texas has acquired middle infielder Cristian Guzman from the Nationals "for prospects."

Nothing has been confirmed, so hang tight before considering this a done deal.

More as this develops.

July 30, 2010

According to at least one local report, Frisco righthander and Newberg Report diarist Ryan Tatusko is going to Washington as part of the Cristian Guzman trade. The report suggests an unidentified second minor league pitcher is in the deal as well.

Tatusko has had a breakthrough season with the RoughRiders, going 9-2, 2.97 in 13 starts and 11 relief appearances, allowing just two home runs in 100 innings of work.

July 30, 2010

According to Bill Ladson of MLB.com, the second player going to Washington in the Cristian Guzman deal, along with Ryan Tatusko, is fellow Frisco righthander Tanner Roark. The 23-year old, taken in the 25th round in 2008, was 10-5, 4.20 in 17 starts and five relief appearances for the RoughRiders this season, and has a career mark of 24-12, 4.13.

Like Tatusko, Roark was probably a tier three prospect in this system—an achievement for the player as well as the scouting and development crew for a player drafted at that level—but will have a great opportunity with the Nationals to get to the big leagues.

July 30, 2010

Fascinating: according to a local report, Texas is testing the market to gauge interest in Scott Feldman and Rich Harden, the two pitchers who are candidates to make tomorrow night's start, hours after the non-waiver trade deadline passes.

According to the story, the Mets and possibly the Brewers could be interested. Still, surely a longshot.

July 31, 2010

So the latest add is second baseman (and former shortstop and putative outfielder) Cristian Guzman, a veteran brought in to hold the position down while Ian Kinsler mends. His arrival will surely result in the designation for assignment of either Joaquin Arias or Andres Blanco, with the other being on the hook for the same once Kinsler returns—though if the groin strain keeps Kinsler out until September 1, the club could get away with keeping the additional infielder since rosters can expand that month.

This plainly seems like an effort to boost dependability in the club's big league depth, a move that might not have been made if Kinsler were healthy, but might have been anyway just to protect against exactly what the club is faced with now. Guzman isn't even a guarantee to make the playoff roster if Blanco, a better defender, is still around, but the reason Texas traded for the 11-year veteran (who has played in three post-seasons) is to lessen the chances that Kinsler's extended absence keeps the club from getting to October in the first place.

Owed a little more than $2.5 million the rest of the season, Guzman will reportedly be paid about $2 million of that by Washington (according to ESPN's Buster Olney), which forced Texas to give up a couple third-tier prospects in Frisco righties Ryan Tatusko and Tanner Roark.

Neither Tatusko nor Roark was a top 30 prospect here, and may or may not show up near the end of such a Nationals list this winter. I had them at 72 and 58 in the Rangers system this past off-season, respectively, though Tatusko in particular has had a breakout season that probably vaulted him past Roark and into fringe prospect status, something he didn't have prior to 2010. In his last six Frisco starts, during the time of year when AA clubs hand out more scout credentials than any, Tatusko has gone 4-1, 1.34, averaging nearly seven innings a start. He's allowed only two home runs in 100 innings this season and has generated groundouts 1.67 times as often as flyouts.

He'll have a chance with Washington. It wouldn't be surprising, if he continues to fare well over the final month-plus of the minor league season, to see Tatusko added to the Nationals' 40-man roster this winter. That wouldn't have happened here.

I've asked Tatusko, who has written the Back Fields Diaries for the Newberg Report the last two seasons, if he wants to issue one final entry. I'll let you know what he says.

For the many of you who have written me, disappointed that Texas traded Tatusko, I'd suggest you ought to be happy. He'll have a better shot at a big league career now, something that was more of a longshot here, and he did an outstanding job of putting himself on the map and turning himself into an asset that helped make yesterday's trade deadline deal possible. This is good for his career.

Roark, who went 10-0, 2.70 for Bakersfield in 2009 (primarily in relief) and had a brief look in Frisco, returned to the RoughRiders this season and kept getting better, posting a 5.06 ERA out of the bullpen in April, a 4.43 ERA in the rotation through June, and a 3.51 ERA in six July starts (again, presumably with lots of scouts on hand). He has ordinary stuff, but tends to get results with it, and like Tatusko he'll have a much better shot of getting to the big leagues with his new club.

For what it's worth, in the Nationals front office are Jay Robertson (Special Assistant to the General Manager) and Doug Harris (Director of Player Development), both of whom were with the Rangers when Tatusko was drafted in 2007 and Roark was drafted in 2008.

And that's where I want to segue off and talk about scouting and player development for a second.

Back in 2007, when Jon Daniels and Thad Levine put a long-term plan in place for this organization, rooted in replenishing the farm system through trades and international signings and the draft, to get this team where it is now, the boldest and most prominent evidence that the plan was underway was obviously the Mark Teixeira trade that July. But dial back a month earlier.

You always go into a draft planning to kill it. Always. Texas had been aggressive with high-upside picks and overslot bonuses well before the five-step plan was hatched in 2007.

The common dictum is that if you get four or five big leaguers out of a single amateur draft, you've done well.

But take a look at what has happened with the Rangers' 2007 amateur draft (on following page). And behold its productivity.

Though Texas has been as busy as any club this month, due in large part to the development of the players it drafted in 2007, the Rangers may not be done.

The non-waiver trade deadline is a little more than three hours away. Stay tuned for TROT COFFEY's or news flashes as developments warrant.

July 31, 2010: TROT COFFEY

I don't know how I functioned as a baseball fan before MLB Network. Or Twitter.

Here's the latest, which pretty much sums things up right now:

- ESPN's Jayson Stark tweets: "We could have a fun hour coming up. One club says volume of calls is 'insane' right now. I've had 3 'gotta gos' in last 20 minutes!"
- *Newsday*'s Ken Davidoff tweets: "One official of club trying to get something done says it's 'very slow' [around the league] as we get to T-minus one hour"

  So there you have it.

  As far as Texas is concerned?
- MLB.com's T.R. Sullivan tweets: "Word right now is the Rangers are 'probably quiet' but may do something small before the Trade Deadline passes"
- Less than an hour to go.

July 31, 2010: TROT COFFEY

Yes, it's past 3:00, but there may be Rangers news yet to come:

- MLB.com's T.R. Sullivan tweets: "Rangers working on a Minor League deal as the deadline passes"

One thing to note: I'm fairly certain that if all the players involved are not on a 40-man roster, they need not clear waivers and thus can be traded now or tomorrow or any other time just as if the deal beat today's deadline.

On the other hand, if we're talking about any minor leaguers who *are* 40-man roster members being involved in the trade, the same rules apply just as if they were in the big leagues, and the trade will have had to beat the 3:00 deadline to avoid the necessity of waivers.

More as something develops.

July 31, 2010

The Rangers have announced that catcher Jarrod Saltalamacchia has in fact been traded to Boston, in exchange for righthander Roman Mendez, first baseman Chris McGuiness, a player to be named later, and cash considerations (reported by ESPN's Jayson Stark to be $350,000).

Mendez is a projectable 20-year-old from the Dominican Republic, toting a big fastball that's reportedly touched 97. He's pitched at two levels this year, including the short-season New York-Penn League, where he's fanned 35 and walked 19 in 33 innings. He'll join Short-Season A Spokane.

McGuiness, hitting .298/.416/.504 for Low A Greenville, will be promoted to High A Bakersfield by the Rangers. The 22-year-old was Boston's 13th-round pick out of The Citadel in 2009. He's hitting .337/.477/.566 in 83 July at-bats, with 20 walks and 18 strikeouts, so the decision to challenge him right away at a higher level seems reasonable.

Rd	Player	Pos	Age	From	Scout	Product
1	Blake Beavan	P	18	HS (TX)	Eddings	**Cliff Lee**
1	Michael Main	P/OF	18	HS (FL)	DeMutis	**Bengie Molina**
1	Julio Borbon	OF	21	Coll (TN)	Wood	**Rangers starter**
1	Neil Ramirez	P	18	HS (VA)	Ardolina	
1	Tommy Hunter	P	20	Coll (AL)	Wood	**Rangers starter**
2	Matt West	3B	18	HS (TX)	Taylor	
3	Evan Reed	P	21	Coll (CA)	Guggiana	**Jorge Cantu**
4	Garrett Nash	SS/OF	18	HS (UT)	Pratt	
5	John Gast	P	18	HS (FL)	DeMutis	*2010 sixth-rounder (St. Louis)*
6	Bobby Wilkins	P	17	HA (CA)	Flores	
7	Tim Smith	OF	21	Coll (AZ)	Pratt	**Daniel Gutierrez**
8	Jonathan Greene	C	21	Coll (NC)	Cuthbert	
9	Davis Stoneburner	INF	22	Coll (VA)	Ardolina	
10	Andrew Laughter	P	22	Coll (LA)	Taylor	
11	Anthony Ranaudo	P	17	HS (NJ)	Matsko	*2010 first-rounder (Boston, #39)*
12	Drew Pomeranz	P	18	HS (TN)	Wood	*2010 first-rounder (Cleveland, #5)*
13	Kyle O'Campo	P	18	HS (CA)	Flores	
14	Matt Lawson	2B	21	Coll (MO)	Smith	**Cliff Lee**
15	Hector Nelo	P	20	Coll (FL)	Alvarez	
16	Josh Lueke	P	22	Coll (KY)	Giegler	**Cliff Lee**
17	Mitch Moreland	1B/P	21	Coll (MS)	Wood	**Rangers starter**
18	Ryan Tatusko	P	22	Coll (IN)	Lee	**Cristian Guzman**
19	Kyle Murphy	OF	22	Coll (KS)	Smith	
20	Kenny Smith	2B	23	Coll (NC)	Cuthbert	
21	Erik Davis	P	20	Coll (CA)	Metzger	
22	Donnie Ecker	OF	21	Coll (ID)	McGraw	
23	Jake Kaase	SS	21	Coll (TX)	Taylor	
24	Chris Gradoville	C	22	Coll (NE)	Smith	
25	Andy Wilkins	3B/1B	18	HS (OK)	Eddings	*2010 fifth-rounder (White Sox)*
26	Kevin Keyes	OF	18	HS (TX)	Taylor	*2010 seventh-rounder (Washington)*
27	Drew Gray	C	21	Coll (MO)	Smith	
28	Mike Ortiz	1B	18	HS (FL)	Alvarez	
29	Ryan Falcon	P	22	Coll (NC)	Cuthbert	
30	Ben Henry	P	18	HS (SC)	Cuthbert	
31	Anton Maxwell	P	22	Coll (OR)	McGraw	
32	Gaspar Santiago	P	17	HS (PR)	Thon	
33	Jared Hyatt	P	23	Coll (GA)	Cuthbert	
34	Chase Hutchingson	P	18	HS (AR)	Eddings	
35	Jeff Schaus	OF	18	HS (FL)	Alvarez	
36	Brian Dupra	P	18	HS (NY)	Matsko	
37	Bryan Salsbury	P	17	HS (CA)	Flores	
38	Hunter Hill	P	18	HS (TX)	Eddings	
39	Tyler Fleming	P	21	Coll (KS)	Smith	
40	Sean Meehan	P	18	HS (WA)	McGraw	
41	Tom Edwards	1B	21	Coll (NJ)	Matsko	
42	Jason Sowers	1B	20	Coll (KS)	Smith	
43	Joey Rosas	P	20	Coll (AZ)	Pratt	
44	Kris Jiggitts	P	21	Coll (ME)	Smith	
45	Ryan Turner	P	22	Coll (GA)	Cuthbert	
46	Yoandy Barroso	OF	18	HS (FL)	Alvarez	
47	Ben Petralli	C	21	Coll (CA)	Metzger	
48	Dillon Baird	SS	19	Coll (AZ)	Pratt	
49	Brandon Hayes	OF	18	HS (OR)	McGraw	
50	Paul Zarlengo	1B	18	HS (IL)	Lee	

As for the player to be named, I wonder if it's someone Boston drafted last year but signed in August, since drafted players can't be traded until a full year after they sign.

The Sox are assigning Saltalamacchia to AAA Pawtucket. He was hitting .244/.326/.445 for Oklahoma City.

Saltalamacchia's departure creates a 40-man roster spot that infielder Cristian Guzman now fills. According to a local report, infielder Joaquin Arias heads to the disabled list (with a strained back muscle) to clear room on the active roster for Guzman.

Finally, according to Brian McTaggart of MLB.com, the only teams Lance Berkman would have waived his no-trade clause for, other than the Yankees, were Texas and St. Louis (and possibly San Diego and Tampa Bay).

More on the Saltalamacchia trade in the next Newberg Report.

August 2010

40-MAN ROSTER (40)

Pitchers (20)

Omar Beltre, Scott Feldman, Neftali Feliz, Frankie Francisco, Rich Harden, Matt Harrison, Derek Holland, Tommy Hunter, Michael Kirkman, Cliff Lee, Colby Lewis, Doug Mathis, Guillermo Moscoso, Dustin Nippert, Darren O'Day, Alexi Ogando, Darren Oliver, Zach Phillips, Pedro Strop, C.J. Wilson

Catchers (4)

Max Ramirez, Jarrod Saltalamacchia, Taylor Teagarden, Matt Treanor

Infielders (9)

Elvis Andrus, Joaquin Arias, Andres Blanco, Jorge Cantu, Chris Davis, Cristian Guzman, Ian Kinsler, Mitch Moreland, Michael Young

Outfielders (7)

Brandon Boggs, Julio Borbon, Nelson Cruz, Craig Gentry, Vladimir Guerrero, Josh Hamilton, David Murphy

60-Day Disabled List (3)

Eric Hurley, Mark Lowe, Brandon McCarthy

August 1, 2010

Seven innings, five hits, two walks, just three strikeouts. An economical 12.5 pitches per inning. First-pitch strikes to 21 of 29 batters. A tremendous 70 percent strike rate.

Sensational effort from Rich Harden. A great, great win, and yet another Cliff Lee-like performance from one of his new teammates.

For what it's worth, a reminder: last year Harden's ERA before the All-Star Break was 5.47. Afterwards it was 2.55.

Justin Smoak doubled and drove in a run yesterday. For AAA Tacoma. Seattle has optioned the first baseman, who had 10 hits and one walk (.159/.169/.270) and 23 strikeouts in 63 at-bats since coming over in the Lee trade.

Thomas Diamond will make his big league debut against Milwaukee on Tuesday, replacing the departed Ted Lilly in the Cubs' rotation. Diamond was 5-4, 3.16 for AAA Iowa, striking out 104 in 108.1 innings and holding the Pacific Coast League to a .218 batting average. (His worst effort of the year came against Oklahoma City two weeks ago, when he gave up eight RedHawks runs in four innings, including a two-run Jarrod Saltalamacchia triple.)

Before wrapping this mini-blast up and getting back to today's standard report—about Jon Daniels's third trade in three days and fifth in a month, different from the other four but genius in its own right—there's this, tweeted this morning by new Nationals AA righthander Ryan Tatukso:

There will be one last @NewbergReport article written and I am talking with @MLB to move my blog over there...stay tuned.

Lee vs. Jered Weaver this afternoon, as Texas goes for its 14th series win out of 17, which would knock the Angels back under .500, down to 10 games back and 11 in the loss column, and all but out of the race.

I should have today's full report out before first pitch.

August 1, 2010

Matthew Emmons, US Presswire

That moment was the first like it for Texas in 2010. And the last like it for Jarrod Saltalamacchia.

It happened on Opening Day, as Texas came back from getting no-hit into the seventh inning to walk off with a 5-4 win on Saltalamacchia's bases-loaded single off Toronto closer Jason Frasor.

He would pinch-hit for Taylor Teagarden in game two of the season, brought in to face Frasor with one out and one on in the bottom of the ninth, Texas down by three. Frasor got him that time, punching him out looking.

It would be Saltalamacchia's final appearance as a Ranger.

There have been very few baseball operations disappointments here since the five-step plan was implemented in the spring of 2007. Saltalamacchia ranks near the top of a short list.

But that's part of what makes yesterday's deadline trade of Saltalamacchia to Boston for three prospects (righthander Roman Mendez, first baseman Chris McGuiness, and a third to be named) plus $350,000 so fascinating for me.

On April 19, 1990, three days before that year's NFL Draft, Jimmy Johnson traded second- and third-round picks to San Francisco for defensive end Daniel Stubbs, running back Terrence Flagler, and picks in the third and 11th rounds. Johnson used the third-rounder he got in the deal to move up four spots in the first round to take Emmitt Smith, but it's the other part of the trade with the Niners I want to focus on.

Coming off a one-win season, the Cowboys had a pair of rookie quarterbacks in Troy Aikman and Steve Walsh, a promising second-year receiver in Michael Irvin, and a deep inventory of draft picks. Johnson knew that the draft ammunition was key to the big picture, and so when he essentially parted with a second-rounder to get Stubbs (who had become the University of Miami's all-time sacks leader under Johnson's watch) and Flagler (who had amassed only 145 yards rushing in three NFL seasons), he was making a pretty bold investment in those two.

Johnson released Flagler on September 2, 1990, one week before what would have been his first game as a Cowboy.

That may have been because the drafting of Smith made Flagler expendable, but Johnson still wanted a veteran tailback around, and on the day after Johnson released Flagler, he traded a 1991 second-rounder and fifth-rounder to Houston for Alonzo Highsmith, who had also starred for him in college at Miami.

Johnson released Highsmith one month into the 1991 season.

And he released Stubbs one month after that.

I remember thinking how easy it would have been for Johnson to hang onto Stubbs and Flagler and Highsmith for a couple more years (on what were then still thin, developing rosters), and how most general managers probably would have, if for no other reason than to ward off the talk show segments pointing out how much they'd given up to get those players and how little they'd gotten out of them before dumping them back onto the street.

But Johnson didn't give a damn about how it would look. All he cared about was whether they could help him win. I loved that about him.

Despite media reviews of the July 2007 Mark Teixeira trade suggesting that Saltalamacchia was the key to the deal (and a blogger or two making the same claim), the Rangers were quick to point out that this was not "Saltalamacchia plus four prospects" for Teixeira and Ron Mahay. We now know that Elvis Andrus, Neftali Feliz, Matt Harrison, and Beau Jones were all specifically targeted, and if Atlanta hadn't agreed to part with the minor leaguers in that deal, Texas might have moved Teixeira to Arizona or the Angels instead.

But Jon Daniels still had lots riding on Saltalamacchia, who was Atlanta's reigning number one prospect according to *Baseball America* (ahead of Andrus [2], Harrison [3], Jones [14], and Feliz [18]) and was viewed as the Rangers' long-term answer at catcher, eventually replacing incumbent Gerald Laird. Switch-hitter. Raw power, enough bat to be a candidate at first base. Athletic behind the plate, with a strong arm and quick feet. A hard worker. In the big leagues on his 22nd birthday, and in the eight weeks leading up to the trade, a .284/.333/.411 major league hitter. Six and a half years of control, at least. So much to like.

But what happened after that is well documented. The .745 OPS he put up in those two months with Atlanta became .721 in the final two months with Texas. Then .716 in 2008. And .661 in 2009.

And then five at-bats in 2010.

Saltalamacchia's time here was marked by a rash of injury issues, mostly tied to forearm soreness and numbness that led to thoracic outlet surgery late in 2009, and a lingering problem thereafter throwing the ball back to the pitcher, a struggle that may or may not have started out as a physical issue but that unquestionably became a mental one. At one point the Rangers reportedly set him up for daily work with the organization's performance enhancement staff.

And going back to that first series of the season, when he failed to disclose an upper back injury he'd sustained in the opener—leading Ron Washington (after the game two loss, in which Saltalamacchia never took the bat off his shoulder during his four-pitch, pinch-hit strikeout in the ninth) to tell reporters that the 24-year-old "put us in a bad situation" and "needs to mature," you have to assume that the young catcher lost some standing with the organization. Catchers need to be leaders, and setting an example is part of that.

An interesting comment yesterday from Boston GM Theo Epstein, regarding his new acquisition: "We feel like he's a classic guy with a high ceiling who needs a change of scenery. *He'd kind of been butting heads with the organization over there a little bit.*"

(And some interesting observations today from Bob Hersom of OKCRedhawks.com, who quotes Oklahoma City manager Bobby Jones as saying of Saltalamacchia: "He's different. I don't know how many friends he had in the clubhouse, but he was never disruptive and never a jerk. I mean, he's just in his own little world." Jones added, however, that Saltalamacchia worked his tail off in AAA.)

Most reports have suggested that Saltalamacchia had gotten past the yips while with Oklahoma City this spring, but after hitting early on (.377/.424/.623 in his first 14 games), he went cold, hitting .258/.290/.455 in May and .179/.291/.343 in June. Matt Treanor solidified the position in Texas once he replaced Saltalamacchia in April. Once Saltalamacchia was deemed healthy in April, and Taylor Teagarden was not hitting, Texas made the eye-opening move to option both to the farm, bringing Max Ramirez (a player they'd agreed to move over the winter to Boston for Mike Lowell and who never made much of a case in spring training for a roster spot) up from AAA to back Treanor up. Bengie Molina was acquired in July. When Treanor got hurt shortly after that, the recall went to Teagarden, not Saltalamacchia.

The thought four months ago that four players would see more time behind the plate for Texas this year than Saltalamacchia, when he's really only been shut down due to injury for a couple weeks, was probably as unlikely as his Opening Day battery mate, Scott Feldman, pitching himself out of the rotation. But at this point, to say the writing was on the wall as far as Saltalamacchia's place in the organization was concerned would be an understatement. Injuries, high expectations, centerpiece media treatment in a blockbuster trade. Whatever the reason, this was a player needing a fresh start.

A year and a half ago, when Jason Varitek was a free agent, rumors (mostly out of Boston) were rampant that the Red Sox wanted Saltalamacchia or Teagarden, and media speculation centered on one of Clay Buchholz, Daniel Bard, Justin Masterson, or Michael Bowden coming back. While the rumors were never substantiated by club sources, Epstein did tell reporters yesterday that Saltalamacchia "came with a really heavy price tag in the past." (Ken Rosenthal of Fox Sports tweeted yesterday that the Rangers' ask 18 months ago was in fact Buchholz, and several Boston beat reports suggest the same today.)

The Sox (whose catchers Varitek and Victor Martinez are both free agents this winter) took advantage of an opportunity to acquire Saltalamacchia at a time when he'd seemingly fallen out of favor with Texas. He'll report to AAA Pawtucket this week, but is a good bet to join the Red Sox when rosters expand in September, if not sooner (and will have only one option remaining after this season). Boston is banking on him figuring things out in his new environment.

Epstein's comment: "He's someone we *hope* we're buying low on right now, as he's battling a few different issues."

Epstein hopes so, having traded Engel Beltre (along with David Murphy and Kason Gabbard) to Texas for Eric Gagné, on the day that the Rangers had earlier picked Saltalamacchia up in the Teixeira deal. The Beltre acquisition three years ago had A.J. Preller stamped all over it, and so does yesterday's addition of Mendez.

Signed by Boston for a relatively modest $125,000 in July 2007 (weeks before the Saltalamacchia and Beltre trades), the Dominican righthander turned 20 just last week and is still filling his 6'4" frame out, suggesting that the mid-90s velocity he sits at now could project for more. He's touching 98 now—and reportedly registered triple digits at least once for Short-Season A Lowell this summer (the first pitcher in at least four years to do so)—and has a slider that some describe as an out pitch with plus potential. The changeup apparently needs work. If it doesn't come along, Mendez could project as a late-inning reliever. For now, he starts.

Pitching in the Dominican Summer League in 2008, Mendez fanned 46 and walked only 16 in 51 innings of work, scattering 43 hits and posting a 2.65 ERA. Pitching stateside in 2009, he dominated the Gulf Coast League, walking only eight in 49.2 innings and fanning 47, holding the league to a .184 batting average, and finishing with an ERA of 1.99. Only one player took Mendez deep all season (in his next-to-last inning of work), and in 10 starts and two relief appearances he allowed more than one run just two times. *Baseball America* named him the number 12 prospect in the league, and after the season tabbed him as Boston's number 23 prospect.

Boston challenged Mendez with a season-opening assignment to Low A Greenville in the South Atlantic League this spring, and the experiment didn't go particularly well. Facing hitters two and three years older, he made six starts, the final one of which came against Hickory on May 7. An Ed Koncel grand slam was among the four hits he gave up to the Rangers affiliate in two-plus innings, during which time he also issued a walk, threw a wild pitch, and drilled Cristian Santana and Matt West. Sitting with an 11.40 ERA and a .392 opponents' average (but 18 strikeouts in 15 innings), he was sent back to extended spring training and reassigned to Lowell once that club's season got underway in June.

In eight Spinners starts, Mendez went 2-3, 4.36, holding the New York-Penn League to a .240 average while fanning 35 and walking 19 in 33 innings. He'll make a lateral move, joining Short-Season A Spokane for that club's final month-plus of play.

Is Mendez the next Neftali Feliz? Don't count on it. There's a spectrum of explosive arms in this system that includes Tanner Scheppers and Wilmer Font and Pedro Strop on one end, and Carlos Melo on the other, and it's too early to plot where Mendez belongs. But that's an outstanding arm to add to a system relentlessly looking for more.

Keep in mind that of the 10 players Texas traded this month to add Cliff Lee, Mark Lowe, Molina, Jorge Cantu, and Cristian Guzman, eight were pitchers. You can never have enough good ones.

The addition of McGuiness is a little different from the prototype prospect targeted by Texas the last few years. Whenever the club has zeroed in on something other than pitchers, they've typically been up-the-middle players. McGuiness, Boston's 13th-round pick in 2009, is not that. But given Justin Smoak's departure and Chris Davis's struggles, adding a first baseman with upside to the system makes some sense.

McGuiness stands 6'1", 210. Hits and throws left-handed. Short to the ball. Hits for average but flashes some power as well. Knows the strike zone; walks a ton, strikes out sparingly. Solid if unspectacular defensively. Not much of a runner. Pitched some in college.

If all of that reminds you of Mitch Moreland, it's no accident. Nothing wrong with adding another Moreland to the ranks, if that's what McGuiness is.

The 22-year-old from James Island, South Carolina (half an hour from Smoak's Goose Creek hometown) hit .367/.525/.667 for The Citadel as a junior in 2009, leading the nation with 65 walks (against only 22 strikeouts in 207 at-bats) and finishing 12th in on-base percentage. After signing with Boston for $100,000, he hit .255/.374/.434 for Lowell last summer, drawing 36 walks while fanning 40 times in 196 at-bats.

This season, playing first base for Greenville, McGuiness hit .298/.416/.504 with 53 walks and 59 strikeouts in 282 at-bats, swatting 20 doubles and 12 home runs. He was third in the South Atlantic League in reaching base, and fourth in slugging. His season included a ridiculous .337/.477/.566 run in 25 July games, prompting Texas to decide he's ready for a new level. He's being promoted to High A Bakersfield.

Incidentally, McGuiness went 9 for 28 off Hickory pitching this summer, hitting three home runs (off Neil Ramirez, Joe Wieland, and Tyler Tufts) in seven games.

We don't yet know the identity of the player to be named later, or the nature of the designation. One possibility is that it's a player that Boston drafted last year but didn't sign until August, which means he wouldn't yet be eligible to be identified (per the Incaviglia Rule, which makes drafted players untradeable until 12 months after signing). I believe six 2009 Red Sox draftees signed last August: third baseman David Renfroe (round 3), righthander Madison Younginer (7), righthander Kendal Volz (9), first baseman Miles Head (26), righthander Eric Curtis (28), and lefthander Tim Webb (31). I don't see any way one of the first three are included, and the latter three don't seem to stand out.

Another possibility is that the player to be named hasn't been selected yet (meaning the Rangers have a specified pool of players to choose from within a certain amount of time), or that there's another reason procedurally that the two teams haven't announced the name.

The $350,000 that Boston put into the deal shouldn't be overlooked. Daniels told reporters yesterday that it will be earmarked to try and get another two or three of the club's 2010 draft picks signed before the August 16 deadline. Key among the club's unsigned picks are two hard-throwing righthanders—supplemental first-rounder Luke Jackson, who has a commitment to the University of Miami in the bag, and fifth-rounder Justin Grimm, who has one year of eligibility left at the University of Georgia—not to mention University of Oklahoma third baseman Garrett Buechele, the club's 18th-round pick.

If the cash component of the Saltalamacchia trade does enable Texas to lock up another two key draft picks, Daniels has pointed out that the trade will have effectively added five prospects to the system, capping off a month in which the club traded 10 young players away to get Lee, Molina, Cantu, Guzman, and Lowe.

Saltalamacchia may figure it all out and come into his own in Boston, and if that happens, so be it. I think we all had a good sense that, for whatever reason, it wasn't going to happen here, and it's encouraging to me that, much like Jimmy Johnson, Jon Daniels not only had that sense as well, but didn't let the past investment influence the current evaluation.

August 1, 2010

The Rangers are 2-3 in games that Cliff Lee has started.

When you've fallen two total outs short of going nine innings five times, and get a grand total of eight runs combined from your offense while in the game in those five starts, wins are going to be elusive.

But Texas has nonetheless managed to gain 3.5 games in the division since Lee's arrival, largely due to a 9-6 record in games in which he has *not* pitched.

A 9-6 record, to be sure, that's attributable in part to Lee himself.

August 1, 2010

From Peter Gammons in a piece he wrote today for MLB.com, titled "The Top 10 Deadline storylines," checking in at No. 1:

Meanwhile, here are the 10 most interesting storylines from the time leading up to 4 p.m. ET on July 31:

1. The emergence of the Texas Rangers as a major force in the American League. They awakened on Aug. 1 with the third-best record and the third-best run differential in the league, behind only the Yankees and Rays. General manager Jon Daniels has been so aggressive that he added Cliff Lee, Jorge Cantu, Cristian Guzman and Bengie Molina while the team was bankrupt and had built such a deep, talented organization that he could add four significant pieces and get cash from the Mariners, Marlins and Giants. If the next Rangers owner doesn't appreciate what Daniels has done, perhaps Barack Obama can make him overseer of the National Recovery Act. Remember, because of the Mark Teixeira trade with Atlanta, Daniels has the closer leading the league in saves and an All-Star shortstop. He traded for the player who is close to the best in the league (Josh Hamilton), signed the best DH (Vlad Guerrero) and since this time last year had the ingenuity to put together a rotation capable of winning the pennant with Lee, converted closer C.J. Wilson, Japanese import Colby Lewis and homegrown Tommy Hunter. Yes, Lee is first and Wilson fourth in the AL in Lee Sinins' Runs Saved Above Average.

Also, to help get your head wrapped around all the movement on the Rangers farm on the heels of this week's frenzied activity, you can count on Scott Lucas to sort it all out. Check Scott's website for a helpful, color-coded chart that looks like a wall at Sherwin Williams. A very well-organized wall at Sherwin Williams.

August 1, 2010

On days when I deliver at least three posts, I tend to get a few "unsubscribe" replies, so I go into this with eyes wide open as I churn out number five for the day.

Ken Rosenthal of Fox Sports just ran an interesting blog post, reporting that Boston and Texas discussed a deal before yesterday's deadline that would have sent Mike Lowell to Texas—and then onto the Yankees, with the Red Sox's full knowledge. No word on what the Rangers would have given Boston, or received from New York.

It's possible, of course, that the teams could revisit the idea this month since Lowell is sure to clear revocable waivers (given his contract), assuming the other players in the deal are off the teams' respective 40-man rosters, or were to clear waivers (or at least get to the recipient clubs through the waiver process) themselves.

And a final note, as I shamelessly get ahead of myself. Look at the Rangers' three playoff season rotations (at season's end) and what shapes up to be this year's. Which number one starter do you want? Number two? Three and four?

N.B.: (1) I've extrapolated the win-loss records of the 2010 starters over 162 games, which is a shot in the dark

YR	NO. 1 STARTER	NO. 2 STARTER	NO. 3 STARTER	NO. 4 STARTER
1996	Burkett (11-12, 4.24)	Hill (16-10, 3.63)	Oliver (14-6, 4.66)	Witt (16-12, 5.41)
1998	Stottlemyre (14-13, 3.74)	Helling (20-7, 4.41)	Sele (19-11, 4.23)	Burkett (9-13, 5.68)
1999	Sele (18-9, 4.79)	Helling (13-11, 4.84)	Loaiza (9-5, 4.56)	Burkett (9-8, 5.62)
2010	Lee (*14-8*, 2.51)	Lewis (*14-11*, 3.40)	Wilson (*15-8*, 3.11)	Hunter (*12-2*, 3.31)

as we're not quite to the two-thirds mark; and (2) Wilson figures as the number three starter right now but that spot could change, as could number four obviously, with a resurgent Rich Harden a certain post-season candidate if he's going well, not to mention Derek Holland.

I might just like the 2010 guy in every case.

Anyway, don't count on a sixth post tonight.

But if you're so inclined, mark your calendar for this Wednesday night, when we'll do another Fox Sports Southwest live in-game chat, with Wilson set to take on Mariners rookie David Pauley in Seattle.

August 2, 2010

Dear Texas Rangers Baseball Club Player on Your Off-Day,

If you watch the local news tonight, since you're off work, and notice that the lead story during sports is that the Cowboys quarterback seems to have bounced back from a dead arm scare brought about by a 17 for 35 effort in Saturday practice drills—*sigh of relief!*—and that said signal-caller has thrown 207 passes in camp so far (the fact that someone has been counting would be funny if not so sad), rest assured that making that the lead sports package was probably the decision of a producer or director beholden to ratings and not *news*, and not a reflection of what the 38,000-plus that are coming out to your workplace every night since the All-Star Break and the bullet Rangers viewership—a whole lot more loyal, interested, hungry fans than some seem to realize—really care about on August 2.

Don't worry: They'll probably get to a baseball package right after a daily update on ShoulderPadGate, as they run what they hope to be exclusive footage of the hobbled rookie receiver doing an about-face and begging the veteran disappointment whose job he's after to sign his ankle cast.

Hang in there.

And kick the Mariners' arses tomorrow.

Newberg Report Night photos (courtesy of Jeff Loy) of Jon Daniels, Kevin Goldstein, auctioneer Luther Davis, and Jamey Newberg, each answering a fan question about the spirited camp battle between rookie safeties Barry Church and Akwasi Owusu-Ansah

August 2, 2010

On August 13, 2008, a few weeks after his 18th birthday, Dominican Summer League Red Sox righthander Roman Mendez struck out seven Dominican Summer League Cubs in 4.2 innings. It was his high strikeout game after a couple six-punchout games a month earlier.

In 2009, Mendez fanned six one time, facing the Gulf Coast League Twins.

This year, the hard-throwing righty fanned six West Virginia Power hitters in one of six South Atlantic League starts.

Reassigned to Lowell in the New York-Penn League in mid-June, Mendez fanned half a dozen three different times in eight starts. But he never matched that elusive seven-spot he racked up two summers ago.

Having come over Saturday in the Jarrod Saltalamacchia trade, Mendez made his Spokane debut tonight.

Five innings. Three hits. One walk.

No runs.

And eight Salem-Keizer Volcanoes down on strikes.

Good night.

August 4, 2010

Going into last night's games, the worst team in the American League was Baltimore. Next worst was Seattle. Kansas City was tied with one other club (Cleveland) for the next-worst spot after that.

Last night those three teams beat the Rangers and the two teams chasing them.

Another Texas loss with several missed opportunities, though for some reason it didn't get under my skin like a loss normally does (maybe because nothing was lost in the division, which when you're ahead is a small positive).

But hopefully the team isn't dismissing it the way I am.

No, Mike Lowell cannot be the player to be named later in the Jarrod Saltalamacchia deal. Players to be named can't appear in the big leagues between the announcement of the trade and the completion of the deal.

Lowell came up big last night, in what was his first 2010 big league appearance since June.

Cubs righthander Thomas Diamond was pretty good, too, striking out 10 Brewers in his six-inning big league debut, giving up three runs on seven hits and three walks.

By the way, remember that rumored Boston-Texas-New York Lowell rumor from the weekend? According to Alex Speier of WEEI.com out of Boston, the deal would have sent Lowell to the Yankees, Saltalamacchia to the Red Sox, and prospects to the Rangers. But the Yankees apparently backed out late last week based on Lowell's medicals—and Lowell's no-trade clause included New York (his original team), though the deal never got to the point at which the veteran had to decide whether to waive it. Texas and Boston got together on Saturday without New York's involvement.

According to Kevin Goldstein of Baseball Prospectus, righthander Roman Mendez (who came over from Boston in the deal) touched 98 in his impressive Spokane debut on Monday.

Today's Cliff Lee stat: Texas has scored 10 runs in support of Lee in his five starts (eight while he's been in the game), spanning 48 innings.

In his two best seasons (his 2008 Cy Young campaign and this year), Texas has scored 10 runs *off* Lee in four starts, spanning 27.2 innings.

Righthander Evan Reed, sent along with righthander Omar Poveda to Florida for Jorge Cantu last week, left his AA Jacksonville debut on Saturday with tightness in his elbow.

Boston manager Terry Francona and Cleveland third base coach Steve Smith, who got into it last night at the tail end of the clubs' bench-clearing shove and shout, were on Buck Showalter's Rangers coaching staff together in 2002.

Philadelphia recalled outfielder John Mayberry Jr. (.258/.321/.410 for AAA Lehigh Valley) to replace the injured Ryan Howard on the Phillies' roster.

Thanks to photographers McCall Money and John Setzler, as well as webmaster Don Titus, for our Newberg Report website photo overhaul. Lots of new players featured on both the front page and the forum banner.

August 4 is notable in Texas Rangers history for being the day, 17 years ago, when Nolan Ryan put it to Robin Ventura. Today August 4 will go down in Rangers history as another landmark date, for another, very different reason.

Reminder: We chat again tonight. Our latest live in-game chat session at http://www.FOXSportsSouthwest.com/pages/chat will start a few minutes before the first pitch and roll until after the final pitch. See you then.

August 5, 2010

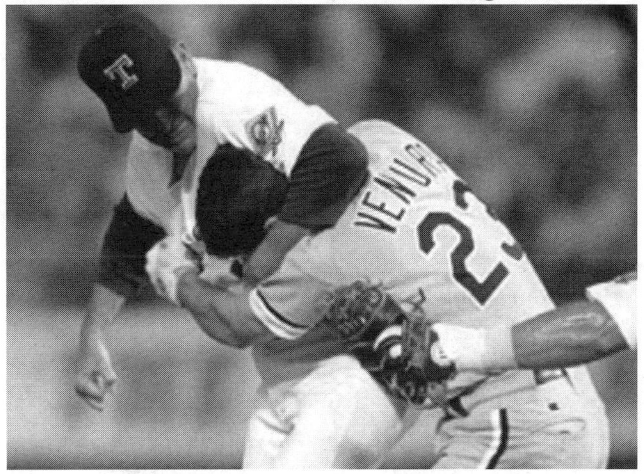

The second-most momentous August 4 in Texas Rangers franchise history.

	1	2	3	4	5	6	7	8	9	R	H	E
TEX	0	0	2	0	5	0	4	0	0	11	15	2
SEA	2	0	2	1	0	1	0	0	0	6	11	0

August 5, 2010

It took 15 months, and a 15-hour day in court. The keys are now being dusted off for the Nolan Ryan-Chuck Greenberg-Ray Davis-Bob Simpson group.

Someone ought to write a book about this season.

August 6, 2010

Run to the water
On a burning beach
And it brings me relief

We saw Crowded House, my girlfriend and I and two of our good friends, in Austin at The Backyard in April of 1994, the first year of Nolan Ryan's retirement from his playing days, the first month of The Ballpark in Arlington.

It was probably not very cool to be a fan of Crowded House back then, or for that matter to be a fan of the Texas Rangers, whose 23-year history was so sad that what was about to be their first-ever first-place season was pathetic in a way, as the club finished with a record of 52-62 that would be frozen by a work stoppage that killed the stretch run and the playoffs. On the night of the concert, the Rangers lost to Toronto, 13-3, one of five losses of 10 runs or more by Texas in just the first two months of the season.

It was a bad baseball team, one whose manager (Kevin Kennedy) got fired despite that division "win" that had eluded the 22 Rangers clubs that preceded it, the last five of which featured Ryan, who went 51-39, 3.43 with 10 strikeouts per nine innings over that span, all in his 40s. A proud five-year run with Texas ended without Ryan crossing the goal line into the playoffs. An extraordinary 27-year career ended in September 1993 with a torn elbow ligament, but not before a 98-mph fastball to Dave Magadan on the next pitch.

Whether Ryan would have pitched in the new ballpark the following year, we don't know. It was probably a disappointment for the warrior to go out the way he did, a man of iconic durability shut down by an injury, a ballplayer who didn't get back to the playoffs in this final run on the field.

I was in a room with Nolan Ryan yesterday, and six hours after that in another with Crowded House (again with those same two friends and my girlfriend, who I've now been married to for 13 years). Ryan looks a little different these days, as does Neil Finn, now sporting a McFeely moustache. But they both looked very happy on Thursday, happy to be at a microphone before a relatively small group, the latter because he's still able to do it, before his own private universe, however diminishing in size, the former because it was probably the last time he'd have to talk formally about what he was talking about, able now to focus fully on the business of getting a baseball team back to the playoffs.

When Finn brought his son on stage for a few songs last night, I'm guessing most of the 1,500 in the room (just about all of whom I probably deceived myself into thinking looked older than me) thought it was pretty cool. The segment of people living around here who cared enough about what Crowded House once was is a lot smaller than it was in Austin 16 years ago, and even then it was pretty small.

As small as what some in the mainstream media continue to assume makes up the core of Rangers baseball fans. They're wrong, of course. But just as it wasn't about record sales, or however it is that you quantify rock and roll coolness (an often opposite measure), it's not about whether the baseball team hangs more banners than the football team, or sells more advertising spots during the local news.

It's cooler to be a Rangers fan now that Nolan Ryan is part of things—and will stay that way—but he's not in this because of ego, or power, or money. He's in this because he's passionate about winning, like his new co-owners and this organization's baseball operations team and its players and its coaches.

And a quietly large core of baseball fans that's getting less quiet.

After last night's win over Felix Hernandez and Seattle, the 2010 Rangers season is exactly two-thirds over. Billy Beane, whose second-place team Texas visits for these next three, was supposedly the first to suggest that you spend the first third of the season evaluating your team and figuring out what you are, the middle third addressing needs, and the final third kicking into that next gear.

The new owners of the Texas Rangers, one of whom sat yesterday afternoon at a podium with a tie on and a huge smile on his face, had hoped to be in place by Opening Day, but instead they now head into this final third, like the rest of us, no longer having to distract ourselves with baseball games so as not to get worn down by court proceedings.

"Dreaming of glory/Miles above the mountains and plains/Free at last," Finn sang, hours after Ryan had talked about the last 15 months, a time during which he probably would have substituted a couple words other than "mountains" and "plains," but the President and soon-to-be Co-Owner of the Texas Rangers looked very ready for these two months ahead of him and us, and maybe another after that, free at last of a kind of battle that he never imagined having to fight and instead geared up to do the kind of battle true baseball fans are in this for.

Break it into thirds —
Assess it, and address it,
Now floor it: It's time.

August 6, 2010

Cliff Lee.

August 8, 2010

A few hours after Rich Harden gave it all back yesterday, Oklahoma City lefthander Derek Holland fired six scoreless innings in Salt Lake City (four hits, two walks, three strikeouts). His day was ended after 95 pitches, despite a comfortable 4-0 lead. (He'd thrown 60 and 87 pitches in his two previous starts, upon his return to AAA from his rehab stint in Arizona.)

Fellow Oklahoma City lefthander Michael Kirkman has five straight quality starts (4-0, 1.74, with 25 hits and 10 walks in 31 innings, and 30 strikeouts). He goes for the RedHawks today.

By virtue of two Texas off-days in the next five days, Harden's next scheduled start doesn't arrive until Saturday, the middle game of three against Boston in Arlington, with the Red Sox slated to send Jon Lester to the mound. Holland and Kirkman are both on the 40-man roster and would be able to go that night on extra rest (same with Omar Beltre, but he's been inconsistent lately at AAA).

Enough.

Given the division lead, I get the idea of giving Harden the ball one-fifth of the time to see if he can get himself straightened out in time for October. If he's right, he has playoff stuff (even if not playoff success: 1-3, 6.35, with more walks [10] than strikeouts [9] in 11.1 innings). But yesterday . . . .

Well, I've got nothing productive to say. And I don't want to be in a bad baseball mood, not with everything else that's going on. *Everything*.

So how about something else?

On April 25, 2007, the Indians staked C.C. Sabathia to a 6-0 lead, bouncing Rangers starter Vicente Padilla after four, but Texas clawed back. Michael Young doubled Kenny Lofton in with two outs in the ninth to tie the game, but after an intentional walk to Mark Teixeira, Matt Kata couldn't push another across. In the 11th, with Willie Eyre on the mound, Jhonny Peralta singled Victor Martinez home, giving the Indians an 8-7 win. Cleveland improved to 11-7. Texas dropped to 8-12.

The next day, Cleveland jumped on Kameron Loe for three runs in the first and never trailed. Texas outhit the Indians, 10-9 (including two Sammy Sosa home runs), but went 2 for 16 with runners in scoring position and lost the game, 9-4, getting swept for the second time in Ron Washington's first month as Rangers manager.

The day after that, April 27, Cliff Lee, coming off 14-, 18-, and 14-win campaigns for the Indians—his first three full big league seasons—made a rehab start for AA Akron, having started the season on the disabled list with an abdominal strain (an injury that had also cost him the first two months of his rookie season in 2003 and would cost him the first month of the 2010 season as well). He'd made a two-inning, scoreless start for High A Kinston on April 10. And then a four-inning, two-run effort for AAA Buffalo on April 21.

On April 27, 2007, Lee took the hill for Akron against the hated Reading Phillies. Working with catcher Tim Gradoville, who would play for Frisco in 2008, the 28-year-old fired five scoreless innings, scattering two hits and a walk while punching out seven. The Aeros came out on top, 5-1, as relievers Jake Dittler (who would also play for Frisco in 2008) and Jensen Lewis closed things out.

Lee returned to Cleveland after that start, and hung in the rotation through July, but after four bad starts in a row (the third of which came in Texas, as the Rangers slapped five runs on him in the first inning, on three doubles and three singles), he found himself back in AAA on July 27, along with outfielder Ben Francisco. Their two roster spots were taken by reliever Edward Mujica and Lofton, who was acquired that day from Texas for catcher Max Ramirez.

Lee pitched reasonably well for Buffalo for a month (1-3, 3.41), striking out at least a batter per inning in each of his seven starts (but walking multiple hitters each time out). He was brought back to Cleveland in September, but he worked strictly out of the bullpen, and not in key spots. His first three appearances were 10 days apart. All four of his appearances were Indians losses, with Lee entering at least three runs behind each time.

Cleveland won 96 games, taking the AL Central. But they didn't take Lee with them to the playoffs, leaving him off the post-season roster. The Indians downed the Yankees, three games to one, before dropping the dramatic ALCS to Boston, who came back from being down three games to one to win in seven.

And then in 2008, one year after having split the season between High A, AA, AAA, the Cleveland rotation, and the Cleveland bullpen, watching from home as his teammates battled New York and Boston in the playoffs, Lee went 22-3, 2.54, leading the league in wins and ERA and walks per nine and home run infrequency, and bagging the Cy Young with 94 percent of the vote.

I don't really have a point, other than: (1) to point out that, just three years ago, in what was Lee's sixth big league season, the man who reached 100 career wins on Friday in fewer decisions than any active big league pitcher other than Tim Hudson, Roy Oswalt, Johan Santana, Roy Halladay, and Andy Pettitte, and who hasn't walked a left-handed hitter in 2010, and whose 14:1 strikeout-to-walk ratio is the best in Major League Baseball in its 110 years of modern history, couldn't make his club's 11-man playoff staff; and (2) to avoid talking about Rich Harden's Saturday effort.

I feel better now.

August 9, 2010

Things I think:

1. Oakland has a starting five, and an August schedule, that ought to make every one of us think about the real possibility that Texas isn't going to coast to a playoff berth. You know what? Good.

Are the Rangers going to the playoffs? Yes. But the last thing this team needs (well, next to another injury setback) is to take the foot off the gas (think about how that's killed the Mavericks more than once going into the post-season), and I'm good if there's not a temptation—even a natural, subconscious impulse—to ease up for any more than maybe one final turn through the rotation going into Game One.

Sure would be nice to have that game in Arlington.

2. Nolan Ryan said last week that while Ron Washington is under contract only through 2010 but will be back next season, Jon Daniels has one more year on his deal, mirroring Ryan's own.

It's no longer necessary, even symbolically, for Daniels's contract to track Ryan's in length.

This is not meant to be a message to the ownership group, which I expect is already several steps ahead of this, but instead just a thing I think: Daniels needs to be extended, before the season ends, for a long time. Ryan is now a certainty to be around here for the long haul, and thank goodness for that. High on the list of this franchise's top assets are its general manager and lots of people who work here because of him.

It's time: To lock Jon Daniels up.

3. Oklahoma City lefthander Michael Kirkman fanned eight in 5.2 innings on Sunday, but walked four and served up two home runs. If the club doesn't want to give Derek Holland this Saturday's start against Boston, Rich Harden's spot could just be skipped and given to Colby Lewis, who—because of two intervening off-days—would still be going on an extra day of rest.

Harden (who threw more balls than strikes on Saturday) told reporters after the game that he "never got a feel for his release point," which is so frustrating to hear, and that he "know[s] what [he] need[s] to do to get back."

It's *August*.

4. Chris Davis has still played more third base at Oklahoma City than first base. And now he's the RedHawks' starting left fielder, seeing his first time in the outfield the last two days since his first minor league season (2006). Local reports suggest the Rangers are getting "much trade interest" in Davis, from Boston, among others.

Texas shouldn't trade him. Not now, at least. Because I think he has a good chance to follow the Nelson Cruz path and bloom late, in a new setting? (Carlos Pena and Russell Branyan have also been suggested.) I do still believe in Davis's future, but that's not why he shouldn't be traded now.

He won't clear revocable trade waivers this season, and that creates two problems: (1) Texas would have only one club to negotiate a trade with, and why limit your suitors? (2) Even if, say, Kansas City were the team that claimed Davis, there's no chance that someone like the disgruntled Zack Greinke reaches Texas on waivers (let alone the timing issue, which makes it difficult to have roster members on both sides of an August trade, unless really bad contracts are involved).

Save Davis for the winter, when the club should be in a position to make an impact trade for a starting pitcher or impact hitter and can capitalize on Davis's apparent popularity—if not with the team Texas is talking trade with, then with a third team that can fill a gap in the trade or in the Rangers' own system.

I still don't rule out the possibility that Davis figures it out here (even as a bench bat that can play at four corners) (and no, I'm not giving up on the catcher idea), but given the mounting number of failed big league chances, if he's drawing real interest then his greatest value may be in a deal.

5. Looks like Taylor Teagarden, in something of an upset, has not only gotten a chance to prove himself once again in Texas but is, at last, taking advantage of it. He doesn't need to keep up this power surge to be a solid number two catcher. He's starting to gain the confidence of his manager.

6. According to John Perrotto of Baseball Prospectus, the Dodgers are thinking about non-tendering catcher Russell Martin this winter to cut costs. Martin makes $5.05 million this year, and I believe he has two more arbitration seasons before he can opt for free agency. Hmmm.

7. I'm not seeing much of anything out of Cristian Guzman, who initially turned down the deadline trade to Texas before reconsidering. Not sure what he does better than Andres Blanco.

Wish we could have gotten in on Arizona's Kelly Johnson before the trade deadline. Can't imagine he'd slip through just about the entire league and get to Texas on waivers now to facilitate a trade.

Sure wish things had worked out with Khalil Greene this year.

Ian Kinsler's injury history and the organization's added flexibility financially are going to result in an upgrade at the utility infield spot next year. It's becoming a priority. Right?

8. Joe West is an irritating umpire to watch.

9. How confident are we that Vladimir Guerrero is going to bounce back? Since the beginning of July, he sits at .213/.278/.336 in 122 at-bats. Justin Smoak was more productive as a Ranger than Guerrero has been over July and August.

Let's say he pulls out of it a bit, but doesn't do anywhere near the level of damage he did in the first half (.319/.364/.554)? What do you offer him this winter to make sure he doesn't shop around? Tricky.

10. Smoak since his demotion to AAA Tacoma: .207/.314/.448. Josh Lueke (AA West Tenn and AAA

Tacoma): one run on seven hits and zero walks in 11.1 innings, 20 strikeouts. Blake Beavan (AA West Tenn and AAA Tacoma): four starts, 3-1, 4.50, 25 hits and two walks in 24 innings, 13 strikeouts. Matt Lawson (AA West Tenn): .363/.414/.525 in 80 at-bats. Chris Ray (San Francisco): 2.84 ERA with eight strikeouts and five walks in 12.2 innings. Michael Main (AA Richmond): 13.83 ERA with 21 hits, 14 walks, and seven strikeouts in 13.2 innings; hasn't pitched in 12 days. Evan Reed (AA Jacksonville): 1.2 scoreless innings in one appearance, left with tightness in his elbow. Omar Poveda: out for the season. Ryan Tatukso (AA Harrisburg): one start—one run on five hits and four walks in 4.2 innings, six strikeouts. Tanner Roark (AA Harrisburg): one start—three runs on seven hits and two walks in six innings, four strikeouts.

Roman Mendez made his second Spokane start yesterday, giving up four runs (all unearned) on seven hits (including two home runs) and one walk in 4.2 innings, fanning five. Seven groundouts, one flyout. Chris McGuiness sits at .261/.433/.304 for Bakersfield, with six walks and four strikeouts in 23 at-bats.

11. Yes, Tanner Scheppers has been solid most nights since returning to the bullpen for the RedHawks. But nowhere near as dominant as (40-man roster member) Pedro Strop, who since returning to AAA from Texas has put up these video game numbers: 8.2 innings, zero runs, four hits, zero walks, 16 strikeouts. Both are going to be here in September, but if one gets here before then, I'm not so sure it shouldn't be Strop.

12. I hope that Torii Hunter Jr.'s friends at Prosper High School aren't making fun of him because of where his Dad is playing. (Or not playing, while he serves his four-game suspension.)

13. Texas gets a bit of a break tomorrow, as A.J. Burnett was scratched yesterday with back spasms and will go for the Yankees in Arlington tomorrow night rather than Phil Hughes.

14. Several new prospects should enter the fold soon: The deadline to sign 2010 draftees is a week from today (two hard-throwing righthanders, supplemental first-rounder Luke Jackson and fifth-rounder Justin Grimm, are the key unsigned picks), and Daniels has suggested the Red Sox prospect to be named later in the Jarrod Saltalamacchia deal could be announced before long.

15. Sometime soon, when the club is on the road, we're going to have a game-watching Newberg Report event with Chuck Greenberg (who is "temporarily physiologically incapable of being elated"). We'll charge some sort of admission fee but it will all go to charity. Stay tuned for details.

16. There's been lots of talk, particularly since the All-Star Break, about how Texas was facing a really tough part of its schedule. Does anyone ever take the time to think about the idea that other teams are now at the point at which they have to say the same thing when Texas comes up on their schedule?

This sort of success is still taking some time to get used to.

And that's fine with me. Give me a battle over the next eight weeks rather than a whole lot of cruise control.

OK. Maybe seven.

August 10, 2010

Tweeting Texas 4, New York 3...

@newbergreport

Top of 1st inning: *Reminder to CJ: See how many pitches the Yanks took that inning? Channel your Cliffly and pound, pound, pound.*

Bottom of 1st inning: *I'm pretty much ok with that Andrus AB. Deep count, oppo approach.*

T3: *Terrible play by Cantu. (Saved by CJ.)*

T3: *Poundage. More, please.*

B3: *Bunting here makes less than zero sense, Cristian Guzman.*

B3: *If Guzman didn't start another game as a Ranger, I'd be fine with that. Rather have Freddy. Or Luis.*

B3: *Ha...used to get only the opposite. RT @ txtechgooner @NewbergReport u might be the most negative ranger fan there is. & mike rhyner exists.*

T4: *Brutal defensive inning. CJ now shoots for his second save of the night.*

T4: *This is Very Good CJ tonight, so far. Despite inconsistent zone from the AAA ump. Tremendous. #doingwork*

T4: *RT @jennifersterger @NewbergReport I concur. Mr. Wilson is as Yankees announcers love to say "effectively wild." That's code for a bad @$$*

T4: *Nick Swisher as Keanu Reeves. RT @jennifersterger @NewbergReport —so wait.. they have baseball in the matrix??*

B4: *Good grief I love this X-mo super slow motion stuff. Love it.*

T5: *Pretty elementary when CJ is commanding the curve like that, and locating his FB.*

T5: *Commanding the toss to 1B apparently another matter. F.*

T5: *That's a freakin' All-Star play by Molina. Very good throw. Extraordinary catch.*

B5: *RT @rangersfanwhit Are y'all joking? @ NewbergReport is extremely positive but if ppl don't produce they lose jobs. Baseball's no exception.*

T6: *This one has the feel of a Rangers-Yankees playoff game. #notallgood*

B6: *If only we had a 5th infielder nearly as good as our 4th outfielder.*

T7: *Ogando to Swisher & Thames: AO . . . K #swish #mt #crushingthezone*

B7: *RT @dwcook I love important baseball. So much.*

B8: *Ok. Go to Feliz in the 9th even if tied—off day yesterday and "off day" tomorrow.*

T9: *Jamey gets his wish, as Feliz is in. (via @aandro)*

B9: *The next Texas pitcher I want to see on the mound is Cliff Lee. End it.*

T10: *Credit Molina for staying with the slider with AO and Neffy as often as he has.*

T10: *All those high-octane innings and big K numbers... yet that last inning may have been one of Feliz's best ever. #5pitchesagainstheartoforder*

B10: *What did Murph *not* do tonight? What a game. What a Game.*

Two more things, non-Twitter variety:

• Seattle 2, Oakland 0. (Just ended.)

• Cliff Lee vs. Javier Vazquez on Wednesday, for the sweep.

August 11, 2010

The Rangers set an all-time record last night . . . that may last for one day.

Stated another way:

Fee fi fo fum.

Yankees-Rangers Sets All-Time Record TV Rating on FOX Sports Southwest

Tuesday night's Rangers 4-3 victory over the New York Yankees produced the team's all-time highest local television rating ever on FOX Sports Southwest, according to Nielsen Media Research. The game averaged an 8.0 household rating in Dallas-Fort Worth, shattering the team's previous record of 6.9 set on Sept. 16, 1998 vs. Anaheim. It also was the No. 1 rated program in the market on Tuesday.

An average of 204,000 Dallas-Fort Worth homes watched Tuesday's extra-inning victory that improved the Rangers' lead in the A.L. West to 8 ½ games over the Los Angeles Angels. The telecast peaked with an 11.0 rating (281,000 homes) from 10:00-10:15 p.m., and averaged a 10.7 rating (271,000 homes) from 10:00-10:30 p.m.

Since the All-Star break, Rangers games on FOX Sports Southwest are averaging a 5.4 rating, more than doubling the season's first-half 2.6 average. Tuesday night's record rating pushed the Rangers' season average to 3.3, a 23% improvement over last year at this point of the season.

— Ramon Alvarez, Fox Sports

August 11, 2010

If you and I work together, or if I run into you at a sandwich counter or gas station or grocery store tomorrow, or if you happen to have my email address, do not speak of that baseball game. I'm in no mood.

Losses scarred by bad plays are irritating, and I don't want to talk about this one. The bullpen had been asked to get a total of five outs in regulation in Cliff Lee's first six Rangers starts, but tonight they needed to get eight outs, which shouldn't have been all that problematic. But it took six relievers to do it, and 72 *pitches*, and they were far from the only culprits in this lousy loss, and I've already said more than I wanted to.

No report on Thursday, but I'm turning in a column for MLB.com tonight on August trades. It will show up on TexasRangers.com sometime Thursday morning, and I'll let you know when it's up.

August 12, 2010

It's never over 'til it's over, as we were reminded 12 hours ago, but according to several local reports, it's *over*.

In the last 30 minutes MLB owners conducted the necessary league vote on the sale of the Texas Rangers, and the Greenberg-Ryan-Simpson-Davis Group has been approved. Rangers Baseball Express now owns your baseball team.

Official word from the Commissioner's Office and the organization should come later this morning.

August 12, 2010

Great news: According to *Baseball America* and at least one local report, the Rangers and supplemental first-round pick Luke Jackson have agreed to a $1,557,000 signing bonus, which would be the fifth-highest bonus paid so far in this year's draft (despite the fact that Jackson was the 45th overall pick), exceeded only by four players chosen in the first 13 picks and in fact matching what Texas gave No. 15 overall selection Jake Skole. The bonus would be slightly more than twice Jackson's slot, keeping the Fort Lauderdale high school righthander from attending the University of Miami.

A local report indicates that Texas is also "pushing hard" to sign fifth-rounder Justin Grimm, a big righthander out of the University of Georgia, and that a possible deal could be awaiting clearance from the Commissioner's Office because it would also be over slot.

August 12, 2010

There are now local reports that *Baseball America*'s story from this afternoon that the Rangers and supplemental first-round pick Luke Jackson had agreed to terms is premature. There's apparently no deal yet, but instead merely confirmation from the organization that the highly touted Fort Lauderdale high school righthander was in town yesterday for a club physical.

It's obviously encouraging that Jackson was in for the physical, suggesting both the club and player are motivated to get a deal done by Monday's deadline, but it appears there's nothing done yet.

Newberg Report: Ten Biggest August Trades

July 31 deadline doesn't stop teams from trading

By Jamey Newberg / Special to MLB.com

August 12, 2010

While July 31 is commonly circled on baseball calendars as the annual Trade Deadline, to call it a deadline at all is misleading. Until that date, a player can be traded during the season with no real constraints. There are procedural hurdles to clear thereafter, but trades do get made in August every year, and sometimes they turn out to be impact deals.

After July 31, any player on a 40-man roster must first clear revocable waivers in order to be dealt (and if he does clear, he can be traded without limitation). Almost all players in baseball are run through August waivers, and if a player is claimed within two days of being placed on waivers, his existing club has a few choices.

Most commonly, the club revokes waivers, pulling the player back, and we probably never hear about it. But the club is also permitted to try and work out a trade with the team that made the prevailing claim (within two days of the time he would have cleared waivers). If no trade is engineered during that time, the window shuts and neither the claiming team nor any other may trade for the player. The player's existing club can also unilaterally stick the claiming team with the player and his contract, but that's not what we're here to discuss.

Carl Pavano was traded in August last year. So was Scott Kazmir. And Jim Thome and Aubrey Huff and Billy Wagner. There will be players traded this month, and as active as Jon Daniels has been this summer—before having the payroll flexibility he now arguably has—it wouldn't be surprising to see Texas make another move to fortify a roster it expects to take to the post-season for the first time since 1999.

What follows are the 10 biggest August trades of the last 20 Rangers seasons, ranked from worst to best:

10. Aug. 29, 1990: Texas trades designated hitter Harold Baines to the Oakland Athletics for right-handers Scott Chiamparino and Joe Bitker (both players to be named, identified Sept. 4, 1990).

The Baines tenure in Texas lasted a year and a month, an unfortunate turn of events that saw future All-Stars Wilson Alvarez and Sammy Sosa go away and two right-handers come back to contribute 112 career innings that made fewer headlines than the fistfight Chiamparino reportedly started after being victimized by a Rangers clubhouse prank. Tom Grieve, the Rangers' general manager at the time, has since admitted that the club—eight games out of first at the time of the 1989 deal to acquire Baines from the White Sox—had no business thinking it was in the race. The trade to get Baines is among the poorest in franchise history; the lackluster return Texas got when it flipped Baines a year later didn't help to rehabilitate it.

9. Aug. 19, 2002: Texas trades right-hander Ismael Valdez to the Seattle Mariners for left-hander Derrick Van Dusen and outfielder/second baseman Jermaine Clark.

If Jon Daniels, who was a first-year baseball operations assistant with Texas, and A.J. Preller, who was working with the Dodgers at the time, were calling the shots when the Valdez trade was made, the return probably would have looked different. There's no chance the current crew would have accepted a guy like Clark; instead, Texas would have targeted someone like 17-year-old left-hander Cesar Jimenez in exchange for a dependable back-of-rotation type like Valdez.

8. Aug. 27, 1999: Texas trades outfielder Adrian Myers (player to be named, identified Sept. 22, 1999) to the Seattle Mariners for left-hander Jeff Fassero.

Perhaps wary of depending too heavily on rookie Mike Venafro and journeyman Mike Munoz down the stretch, Texas wanted one more left-hander around going into the final month of the 1999 season. Fassero made very little impact. Though he was decent in three September spot starts, he allowed multiple runs in three of four relief appearances and pitched once in the playoffs, mopping up at the end of an 8-0 Game 1 loss to the Yankees. Myers was a fringy outfield prospect who ran a bit but never hit enough to make the final jump from Triple-A to the big leagues.

7. Aug. 25, 2008: Texas trades left-hander Eddie Guardado to the Minnesota Twins for right-hander Mark Hamburger.

The Rangers gave Guardado a chance to help his longtime teammates, who at the time were tied with the White Sox atop the AL Central and would end the season in the same position before losing a one-game tiebreaker to Chicago. Guardado would return to Texas in the winter for one final season with the club, his final in the league. Meanwhile, Hamburger has broken through a bit in 2010, fanning 49 in 45.2 Bakersfield innings while scattering 38 hits and 15 unintentional walks and earning a promotion to the Frisco bullpen at the end of July.

6. Aug. 18, 2009: Texas trades right-hander Matt Nevarez and infielder Jose Vallejo (player to be named, identified Aug. 20, 2009) to the Houston Astros for catcher Ivan Rodriguez.

More than just a token homecoming, Rodriguez was picked up in mid-August once Jarrod Saltalamacchia went on the disabled list with a shoulder problem and he was expected to back Taylor Teagarden up as Texas tried to stay in the race. But the Rangers legend hit .345/.394/.621 over his first eight games and settled in as the club's starter behind the plate over the final six weeks of the season. Nevarez and Vallejo were expendable, toolsy prospects who made sensible additions to a weak Astros system. They've had disappointing 2010 seasons, Nevarez because of colossal command issues and Vallejo because of a hand injury that nearly wiped out his entire season, while Rodriguez was able to land a two-year offseason deal with the Nationals that Texas was unwilling to match.

5. Aug. 30, 1991: Texas trades third baseman Steve Buechele to the Pittsburgh Pirates for right-handers Kurt Miller and Hector Fajardo (the latter a player to be named, identified Sept. 6, 1991).

Buechele had been a midseason callup in 1985, when Texas had an opportunity to move veteran Buddy Bell to Cincinnati for a promising young arm in Jeff Russell, and six years later the Rangers found themselves in a similar situation. With third-base prospect Dean Palmer deemed ready for the big leagues, Texas moved Buechele to Pittsburgh for two upside arms in Miller and Fajardo. It was the right time to get Palmer up to Texas and an inspired deal for both teams, as Buechele hit over .300 for the Pirates in the postseason and Texas was able to boost a system thin on pitching with a couple right-handers that unfortunately failed to reach their high ceilings.

4. Aug. 8, 1995: Texas trades right-hander Wilson Heredia (player to be named, identified Aug. 11, 1995) and outfielder Scott Podsednik (player to be named, identified Oct. 8, 1995) to the Florida Marlins for right-hander Bobby Witt.

Viewed perhaps as a minor deal when made, as Texas was a hopeless 11 games out of first and reaching for its former starter to address a black hole at the back of the club's rotation, Witt would bounce back from a five-win 1995 to tie for the team lead with 16 victories in 1996, the franchise's first-ever playoff season. Heredia pitched well down the stretch for Florida's Double-A squad in 1995 but missed the 1996 season due to injury and ended up back with the Rangers on a waiver claim that winter. Podsednik had yet to emerge from short-season ball after two Minor League seasons and in fact was left off Florida's secondary roster in 1997 and retrieved by Texas as well, via the Rule 5 Draft.

3. Aug. 31, 1992: Texas trades outfielder Ruben Sierra and right-handers Jeff Russell and Bobby Witt (and cash) to the Oakland Athletics for outfielder Jose Canseco.

It's easy to pan this deal in hindsight, given the circus moments that Canseco had in Texas in 1993, but he had one of his most productive seasons in 1994 when he helped open The Ballpark in Arlington with a 31-homer, 90-RBI season over just 111 games in the strike-shortened season, landing AL Comeback Player of the Year honors. Texas would move him that winter to Boston, for Otis Nixon and current Rangers Minor League hitting instructor Luis Ortiz. Sierra, perhaps the biggest surprise of the four players to have slid through waivers, was only 26 but would never again be the MVP candidate that he had been multiple times in Texas. Russell set Dennis Eckersley up that summer before signing that winter with Boston, and Witt had a mediocre run over two-plus seasons in Oakland before moving on to Florida.

2. Aug. 8, 1996: Texas trades right-handers Ryan Dempster and Rick Helling (the latter a player to be named, identified Sept. 3, 1996) to the Florida Marlins for right-hander John Burkett.

Texas held a two-game division lead and a history devoid of postseason play when Doug Melvin traded for Burkett for the second time, the first of which had been a disaster (when he sent prospects Rich Aurilia and Desi Wilson to the Giants in December 1994 but ended up losing Burkett to free agency before the 1995 season ever began). Dempster was producing results just one year out of high school, and Helling, though he'd struggled in three big league seasons, was leading the Pacific Coast League in ERA and in strikeouts, and had thrown a perfect game for Oklahoma City five days after the Burkett trade was announced (three weeks before the deal was completed). It was an excellent trade for the Marlins, and one Texas would never take back, as Burkett went 5-2, 4.06 down the stretch, winning Game 160, the day before the club clinched its first playoff berth, and then recording the only postseason win this franchise has ever had, a complete-game, 6-2 win in Game 1 of the AL Division Series in New York.

1. Aug. 12, 1997: Texas trades left-hander Ed Vosberg to the Florida Marlins for right-hander Rick Helling. Texas made the 1996 Burkett deal look even better a year later, when the Marlins sat in the Wild Card perch, three games ahead of the Mets, and had a rookie starter in Livan Hernandez whose Valenzuela-like explosion made Helling expendable, and felt they needed another left-on-left specialist in the bullpen despite the presence of southpaws Dennis Cook and Feliz Heredia. The Rangers had struck gold with Vosberg as a reclamation project whose first big league success came at age 32, and in 1997, well out of the race, they flipped the left-hander to Florida to get Helling back. The bulldog starter would win 20 games the next season—he's the last Rangers pitcher to do so—and was a key member of the Texas rotation from 1998 through 2001, the first two seasons of which marked the franchise's last two playoff appearances.

August 13, 2010

*Friday the Thirteenth:
Exorcise Yanks finale,
Massacre Boston*

And to further commemorate the spirit of the day: Here comes Chucky.

Yesterday morning, every Major League owner approved the sale of the Rangers to the investment group headed by Chuck Greenberg and Nolan Ryan and financially backboned by Bob Simpson and Ray Davis. It was a welcome moment of unanimity, and finality, completing a lengthy process that had so little of either.

Tonight's series opener against Boston will mark the first official game of the Rangers Baseball Express era, but before that Greenberg will announce various ballpark initiatives focused on improving the fan experience, improvements that he and the ownership group were probably ready to put in place Opening Day.

Fortunately, the atmosphere tonight and this weekend will feel in some ways like Opening Day, in other ways even better. The annual promise of a great season is still there nearly three-quarters of the way through, and for once the confidence is justified, not ridiculed. Attendance is spiking, viewership is breaking local records, and the buzz is swelling.

I'm sure the team is more resilient and more forgetful than I am, and was able to erase Wednesday night's mess from short-term memory on yesterday's day off. A lousy loss is still just a loss, and even the best teams in baseball lose more than a couple games a week, on average. I need to keep reminding myself that.

I looked back this morning on what I'd led off with on August 13 in past years of doing the Newberg Report:

- 1998: Julio Santana's impressive run of starts for Tampa Bay and a great Oklahoma start by current RedHawks pitching coach Terry Clark
- 1999: Promotions for Danny Kolb (Texas), Corey Lee (AAA), and Hank Woodman (AA)
- 2000: Gabe Kapler breaking the franchise hit streak record
- 2001: The awfulness of the (Rob) Bell Curve
- 2002: The Union's decision not to set a strike date
- 2003: A great Juan Dominguez start (in a game that Texas lost, dropping the club 20 games back in the West)
- 2004: Didn't write (Max was born the next day)
- 2005: Didn't write (but the day before: "What an awful baseball week. You go into Fenway Park and Yankee Stadium and score 26 runs in four games and lose every one of them," and a reminder that the front office had preached "managed expectations" over the winter)
- 2006: A recounting of the 1996 Dave Valle clubhouse story
- 2007 (two weeks after the trades of Mark Teixeira, Eric Gagné, and Kenny Lofton): A photo of John Danks, Chris Young, and Thomas Diamond from a 2005 Newberg Report event, and how whatever we might have envisioned then about the 2007 season turned out dead wrong
- 2008: A recap of one of the two or three greatest minor league games I'd ever seen pitched—a Derek Holland effort for Frisco that night with a line score that looks in retrospect like a Cliff Lee start (other than those Holland 97's that lit up the radar guns)
- 2009: How well the Rangers' number seven, eight, and 10 starters (Holland, Tommy Hunter, and Dustin Nippert) pitched in the previous three games

A lot of mid-August attempts to distract myself from what was going on with the big club. Not necessary this year.

It's pretty cool that whatever Rangers Baseball Express rolls out today won't be gimmicks to try and get people to think about coming out to the Ballpark, but instead improvements for those who are already filling the stadium and anyone else ready to jump on board for what should be a memorable stretch run.

Speaking of which, Jeff & Cindy Kuster, on behalf of the Hello Win Column Fund, are making available 128 tickets to upcoming Rangers games in a fundraising effort to help a local family that has been touched by a battle with cancer. They will use the money raised from the sale of these tickets, along with money raised at Newberg Night last month, to help single mother Maria

Aldana and her four children find a new home. Maria was diagnosed with breast cancer in November of 2008 and has been undergoing treatment. Her present home is in such poor shape that the costs to repair it would exceed the value of the home.

The Kusters are selling the tickets (face value $70) for $50 each, with the full amount going to the Hello Win Column Fund. All the seats are located in the Lexus Club Infield (Sections 222-230). Here are the available games:

Thursday, August 26 vs. Minnesota at 7:05 PM: 8 Tickets

Friday, August 27 vs. Oakland at 7:05 PM (Postgame Fireworks): 8 Tickets

Saturday, August 28 vs. Oakland at 7:05 PM (Mercy Me Pregame Concert): 48 tickets

Tuesday, September 14 vs. Detroit at 7:05 PM: 8 Tickets

Wednesday, September 15 vs. Detroit at 7:05 PM: 8 Tickets

Thursday, September 30 vs. LA Angels at 7:05 PM: 8 Tickets

Friday, October 1 vs. LA Angels at 7:05 PM (Postgame Fireworks): 24 Tickets

Saturday, October 2 vs. LA Angels at 7:05 PM: 8 Tickets

Sunday, October 3 vs. LA Angels at 2:05 PM: 8 Tickets

If you're interested, email Jeff at Jeff@hellowincolumn.com. Let him know what date and how many tickets you would like and he'll let you know whether the tickets are still available and details on how to pay.

In the meantime, Jarrod Saltalamacchia comes to town tonight as the latest member of the Darnell McDonald-Ryan Kalish-Daniel Nava Big Boston Debut Club, after doubling twice in four at-bats yesterday (he'd entered Wednesday's game as a late-inning defensive replacement). If he gets tonight's start, he'll catch Josh Beckett and face Hunter, who joined the Rangers organization two weeks before Saltalamacchia did back in July of 2007, a month of renewed hope for a franchise that's now turning hope into promise.

Tonight will be another symbolic moment in that process, as Greenberg and Ryan and Simpson and Davis take their seats as official owners of the team, seats in a building that will be almost fully occupied not because of anything happening off the field (in fact, despite it), but because of what this baseball team has proven these last four and a half months that it is, and just might be.

August 13, 2010

I haven't stopped laughing.

August 13, 2010

August 13, 2010

AP/Tony Gutierrez

Chuck Greenberg, nine hours ago:

"Every day of our lives, we can get a little better.... We need to reinvent ourselves regularly."

AP/Tony Gutierrez

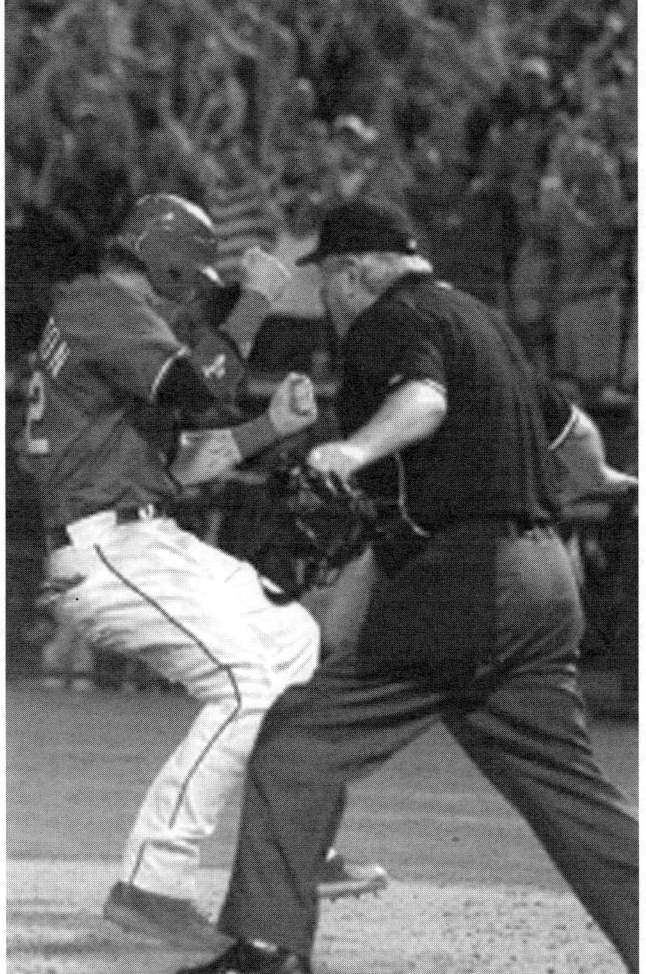

AP/Tony Gutierrez

August 14, 2010

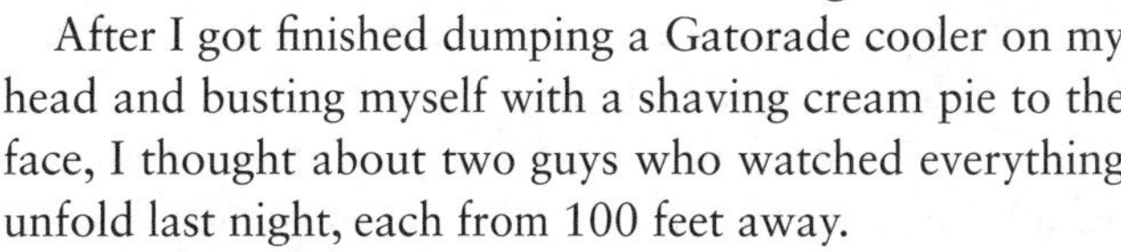

After I got finished dumping a Gatorade cooler on my head and busting myself with a shaving cream pie to the face, I thought about two guys who watched everything unfold last night, each from 100 feet away.

For the first time in more than four months, Jarrod Saltalamacchia was back in Rangers Ballpark, the place where his career was supposed to take off. He'd been a first-round draft pick out of high school. He'd gotten to the big leagues on his 22nd birthday, an almost inconceivably young age for a catcher. He was Atlanta's number one prospect for two straight years, ahead of Elvis Andrus and Neftali Feliz and Tommy Hansen and everyone else in the Braves system.

But he was blocked in Atlanta by Brian McCann, just a year older and already a two-time big league All-Star when the Braves decided to load up for a chance to trade for Mark Teixeira.

That was a perfect opportunity for Saltalamacchia. Texas needed a long-term answer at catcher, and targeted him as a major piece to one of the biggest trades the franchise had ever made. The stage was set.

But there were issues, both physical and mental, and ultimately he was blocked here, too, not so much by another player but by expectations that weren't met and setbacks that followed every instance of new hope.

Saltalamacchia was rescued again, in a way, by last month's trade to Boston, a deal that, in stark contrast to the one three years earlier, barely registered headlines outside the market he departed and the one he was

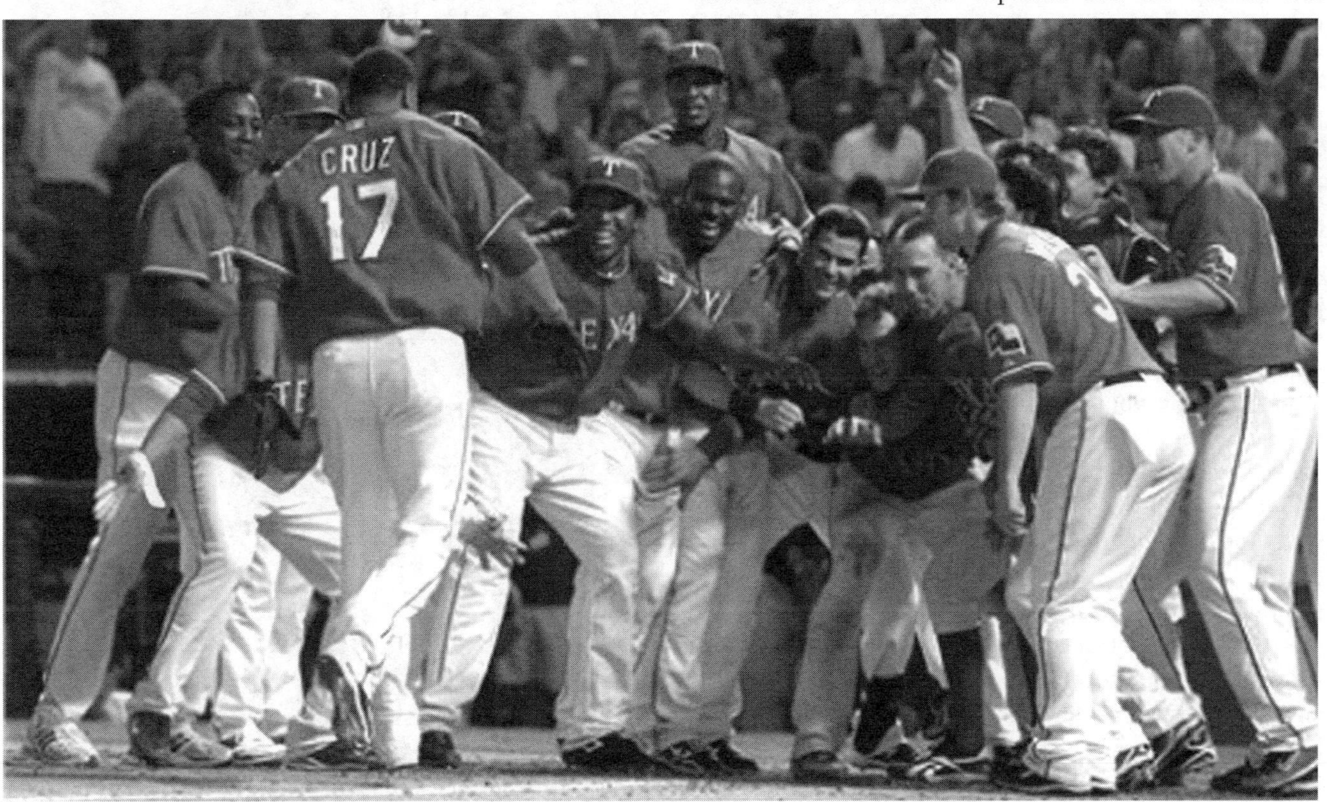

AP/Tony Gutierrez

headed to. The Red Sox had interest in Saltalamacchia for two years that we know of, and probably more. Looking for a candidate to step in after this season for at least one of Jason Varitek and Victor Martinez, both free agents this winter, Boston bought low on Saltalamacchia, trading three prospects to Texas, the two of whom that were named hardly more identifiable at the time to fans outside Boston than the still-unspecified player to be named later.

The Red Sox moved him laterally, from AAA Oklahoma City to AAA Pawtucket, recalling him this week when backup catcher Kevin Cash got hurt.

Saltalamacchia got his first Boston start under his belt on Thursday, going 2 for 4 with a pair of doubles against Toronto, scoring a run and gunning down one of two would-be basestealers in what was a devastating Red Sox collapse won by the Jays, 6-5, as they scored four runs in the ninth off Jonathan Papelbon and Daniel Bard and knocked Boston six games back in the AL East, four back in the Wild Card hunt.

So as it turned out, Saltalamacchia's second start of the season featured a walkoff in a game against Toronto—just like his only other start of 2010, when his shot laced up the right center field alley brought David Murphy home and helped Texas come back to defeat the Jays on Opening Day.

It was probably a pretty lousy plane ride to Texas for Saltalamacchia and his new teammates on Thursday, with Boston's roster decimated and its playoff chances eroding, coming off an epic disaster of a loss. This would be a huge series with the Rangers, a three-game set the Sox really needed to win.

Friday night the house was packed, just as it had been for Saltalamacchia's other 2010 start. And this, like April 5, would in a sense be another Opening Day for Rangers fans, with new ownership at long last in place.

Saltalamacchia, still carrying his blue Rangers bat bag, wouldn't start Friday night, but probably will tomorrow afternoon (if not tonight). The building will be packed again.

But last night he watched from the dugout, the other dugout, as his former teammate Josh Hamilton put together one of the great single-game performances any of us has ever seen and his former teammate Nelson Cruz boomstuck a Tim Wakefield floater, sending the ball into orbit and the Red Sox off the field, shuffling toward the trench where Saltalamacchia stood watching so many of his former teammates scrum on the field, just as they'd done when he ended Opening Day with that walkoff rifle to right center off Jays closer Jason Frasor.

It had to suck, watching that and hearing what was happening in the stadium, 47,000 strong. It's not hard to imagine him wondering why he wasn't part of the mob at the plate, part of the energy.

Standing at the plate, having bounced out of the other dugout, was Cliff Lee, and next to the Rangers' new owners, there's nobody in the stadium I was happier about getting the chance to experience that win firsthand. Not because Lee had undergone his own adversity a few years ago, coming off 46 wins in three seasons but failing to make Cleveland's playoff roster in 2007, the same year that Texas had hoped Saltalamacchia's arrival had solved a problem long-term. But because of the experience of the moment.

The run support for Lee has been lousy.

The heat is less than optimal.

The opportunities this winter for Lee, who was traded three times in less than 12 months, will be many, and for the first time he'll be able to decide where he pitches. For a long, long time.

But there's some magic here, something possibly special developing, a chance to do some great things over the next three months and next several years. We (Rangers ownership and management inclusive) all hope he wants to be part of that, an integral part of what's happening here, for many baseball seasons.

That's something I'm sure Jarrod Saltalamacchia wanted for himself as well, but last night only one of them got to celebrate a Rangers win at home plate.

I may never forget that game.

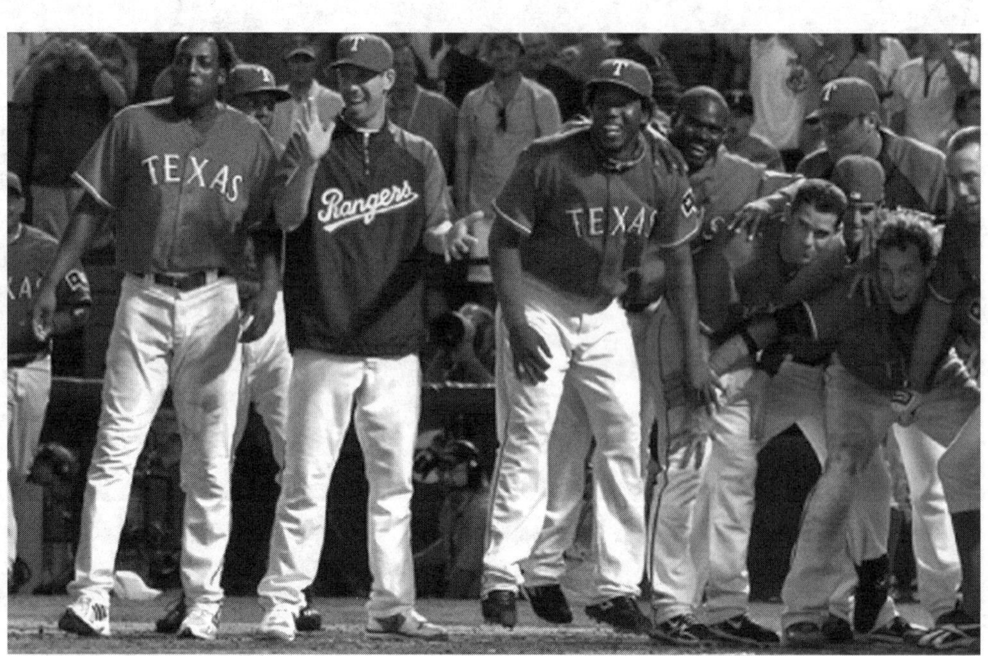

The Great Brad Newton

An update on the Lexus Club Infield tickets that Jeff & Cindy Kuster are selling at $50 each ($70 face value) to raise money through the Hello Win Column Fund, helping local families touched by a battle with cancer. There are now 44 tickets remaining from yesterday's 128. They are:

Saturday, August 28 vs. Oakland at 7:05 PM (includes Mercy Me Pregame Concert): 34 tickets remain (3 sets of 4 tickets, 1 set of 6 tickets, 2 sets of 8 tickets)

Wednesday, September 15 vs. Detroit at 7:05 PM: 6 Tickets

Thursday, September 30 vs. LA Angels at 7:05 PM: 4 Tickets

Also, reader Alan McNally is donating these five tickets to the Hello Win Column Fund:

Monday, August 23 vs. Minnesota at 7:05 PM: 5 tickets in Section 234 ($200 total; face value $225)

If you're interested in any of the above, email Jeff at Jeff@hellowincolumn.com.

Thanks again to those of you who have responded with "honor system" contributions to the Newberg Report this week. If you're still interested in participating, you can find details on the website. But again, this is voluntary and I don't want anyone to feel compelled to do it.

No Cliff Lee tonight, and probably no Jarrod Saltalamacchia, but we do get Colby Lewis vs. Jon Lester, and one of the great greatnesses of this sport is that, after a crushing loss like Wednesday's, you can wipe it away with a victory like last night's, and after that epic win, we get to do it all again tonight.

August 14, 2010

According to local media reports, the Rangers have acquired catcher Michael Thomas from Boston as the player to be named later in the Jarrod Saltalamacchia trade, joining righthander Roman Mendez and first baseman Chris McGuiness, both of whom were identified two weeks ago at the time of the deal. Boston's 12th-round pick in 2009 out of Southern University (and Marshall High School), Thomas will be converted to pitcher immediately, with the transition beginning right away in Surprise and extending into Fall Instructs.

The 21-year-old Thomas, whose 6'3", 215-pound frame fits a pitcher's profile, was hitting .156 for Low A Greenville this season, with 42 strikeouts in 90 at-bats. For some reason, he hadn't played since July 28. He'd signed with Boston on June 30 last year, so the 12-month Incaviglia Rule is not what prevented the two teams from identifying him before now.

Baseball America noted last spring that "[f]ew position players in the 2009 draft [could] match [his] raw arm strength, but the operative word in all phases of his game is 'raw.'" He'd thrown out 31 percent of South Atlantic Leaguers attempting to steal this season.

Notably, Rangers pro scout John Booher, who joined the organization in the off-season, was the area scout who followed and signed Thomas for the Red Sox last year. Rangers area scout Randy Taylor scouted Thomas in high school and believed in the arm as well.

There's Alexi Ogando on one end of the spectrum, and Johan Yan on the other, with Pedro Strop somewhere in between, but any time a player is converted from the field to the mound during his development, particularly in an instance like this where one organization targets a player in another in order to undertake the experiment, it's worth keeping an eye on.

Texas has also signed 32nd-rounder Steve McKinnon, a righthander from British Columbia, and continues to near apparent deals with supplemental first-rounder Luke Jackson and fifth-rounder Justin Grimm, two hard-throwing righthanders. The club also reportedly continues to negotiate with University of Missouri righthander Nick Tepesch, the club's 14th-rounder, in advance of Monday night's deadline to sign draft picks.

August 14, 2010

The Rangers have placed infielder Cristian Guzman on the 15-day disabled list with a right quadriceps strain, replacing him on the active roster by recalling righthander Pedro Strop.

August 15, 2010

Daisuke Matsuzaka has a 5.09 career ERA against Texas, which has hit a robust .311/.376/.578 off the righthander. The numbers swell to 9.00 and .350/.435/.850 in his one Rangers Ballpark start.

Yet today's lineup will be without Ian Kinsler, who is on the disabled list; Nelson Cruz, who isn't but is sidelined after tweaking his left hamstring last night (though there's a report this morning that Brandon Boggs will be recalled this morning [Craig Gentry broke his wrist in a collision with the outfield wall on Friday; surgery is set for Tuesday], likely for Pedro Strop, while the club monitors Cruz); and Vladimir Guerrero, who is expected (according to at least one local report) to get the day off.

Still, the club's most productive hitters against Matsuzaka have been Michael Young (7 for 11, including two doubles and a homer) and David Murphy (3 for 5 with a double).

C.J. Wilson against Boston lifetime: 1.50 ERA (including 0.68 in two starts), .152/.295/.190 in 24 innings.

Today's game is expected to be the hottest in Rangers Ballpark history. Both 29-year-olds are a bit better at night than during the day.

The Angels sit 7.5 games back, nine in the loss column. They send Dan Haren out to face Toronto's Ricky

Romero today, and after a day off tomorrow (which will take those pesky half-games out of the standings, barring rainouts, for about a week and a half), they travel to Boston, while Texas is in Tampa Bay. Los Angeles gets Clay Buchholz, old friend John Lackey, and Josh Beckett, while the Rangers draw David Price, Matt Garza, and James Shields.

It looks almost like playoff baseball this week.

I'll feel pretty good if this team wakes up Thursday in Baltimore with a seven-game lead on Los Angeles, who will travel to Minnesota after finishing up in Boston on Thursday.

Taking this afternoon's game would be a very good start.

August 15, 2010

Texas has placed righthander Rich Harden on the disabled list with right shoulder tendinitis, making room on the active roster for outfielder Brandon Boggs, who has been recalled.

Also, the Rangers announced the signing of 14th-round pick Nick Tepesch, a righthander out of the University of Missouri. The deadline to sign 2010 draftees is tomorrow night, with deals expected to be struck with supplemental first-rounder Luke Jackson and fifth-rounder Justin Grimm, both right-handed pitchers.

August 16, 2010

Outstanding win, one that belonged primarily to C.J. Wilson, Julio Borbon, and Taylor Teagarden, but for one little guy there was also this:

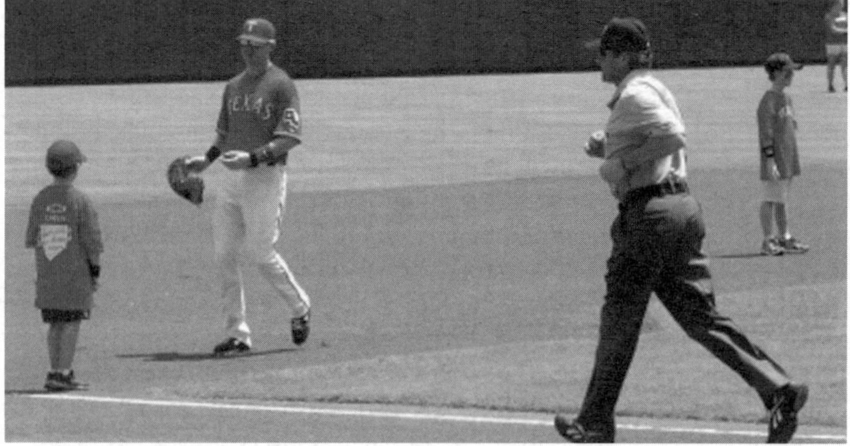

Ginger Newberg

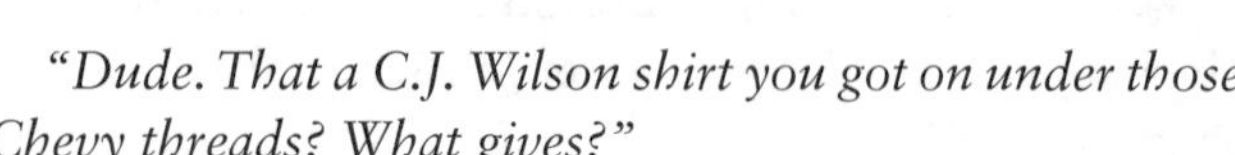

"Dude. That a C.J. Wilson shirt you got on under those Chevy threads? What gives?"

"Step off, Young. Show me something. Take one deep today. Something like that."

Brad Newton

AP/Tony Gutierrez

Sunday win, series win, Yankees-Red Sox homestand win. Birthday win.

August 16, 2010

Texas has placed outfielder Nelson Cruz on the 15-day disabled list, activating infielder Joaquin Arias from the DL.

Also, according to *Baseball America*, the Rangers have agreed to terms with Georgia righthander Justin Grimm, the club's fifth-round pick, for a reported bonus of $825,000 (in a $147,600 slot).

August 16, 2010

Texas has signed supplemental first-round pick Luke Jackson (for a reported $1.545 million bonus, according to local reports), having convinced the Florida high school righthander to forgo a scholarship to the University of Miami.

August 17, 2010

Ron Washington said before Monday's game that he planned to rest Elvis Andrus on Tuesday and get Joaquin Arias a start (at second base, with Andres Blanco getting the nod at shortstop).

Michael Young's neck injury notwithstanding, I'm going to be surprised at this point if that's still the plan.

If Josh Hamilton's game on Friday was one of the greatest in Rangers history, Arias's game last night—actually, his bottom of the eighth alone—pushes the needle on the other end of the spectrum.

I don't want to talk about what Arias did, and didn't do.

But Washington did.

After the game, in what I assume was a sanitized version of whatever he said to the team and probably even cleaned up compared to whatever he told the print media, Washington told Emily Jones, when asked on the Fox Sports Southwest telecast what message he had for the team: "Get your head outta your butt and let's play baseball."

Washington didn't name Arias when he said, "We just didn't support Cliff Lee.... He deserved a better fate than that," or when he offered that Lee should have been out of that inning in four batters. But he didn't need to name names, nor did Lee when he said, repeatedly, that it was just a "weird" "blur of an inning."

I was very interested in what Lee had to say, but he's an absolute professional and I didn't expect any harsh words. I saw all I needed to see, as we all did, when the cameras found him in the dugout a dozen times in the eighth and ninth after he'd been removed from the game. The look on his face was pure Don Draper, a stoic seethe that seemed to mask a mix of exasperation and resignation.

(From my Twitter barrage last night: "I refuse to mention the famous quote in Rangers history that the look on Cliff Lee's face is reminding me of right now.")

You know what? I hated that loss only because it was Lee's game. Otherwise it would have been a massively irritating loss that I would have gotten over as soon as I wrote about it. But the fact that it—once again—wasted a Lee gem, giving him, it seems, as I overreact, another five days to think about whether he wants his next five or six years to be with this team, makes me almost nauseous.

Yes, I know that Arias won't be here over any of the next five or six years. He won't be here in October, when it matters. He may not be here in September.

If he's not here tonight, I'm quite sure I'd be OK with that. Esteban German, fine. (It's not as if Arias is a great gloveman any more.) Hernan Iribarren or Gregorio Petit, sure. Alex Cora, said by Fox Sports's Ken Rosenthal to be on the Rangers' radar, come on down.

The man whose neck somehow retreats into his shoulders whether he's scampering around second for an uncontested triple or flailing back aimlessly on a catchable Texas Leaguer that isn't caught needs not be entrusted with another defensive assignment in a Rangers uniform. Arias is very fast (yet somehow still appears "unathletic"). He can do a couple things with the bat. But he's not a very good baseball player, and will certainly never be called a smart or instinctive one.

But that's not really the point.

I hate every single moment that makes me wonder whether Lee is a tick less likely to choose to be here after this season. He's not going to care whether Arias is among the 55 or 60 players in big league camp in March, but I would have been much happier if we'd gone into Tampa Bay and beaten David Price, with Lee shaking hands with Bengie Molina halfway between the mound and plate after delivering the game's final pitch.

Amazingly, that has happened one single time in his eight Rangers starts. Eight starts in which he, stunningly, has only two victories (and in which the team has just three).

And Texas has two straight really lousy losses in Lee starts.

I would have been very happy if that game had ended in a Rangers win. Lee would have been, too. I would like for Lee to be happy. I'd like that very much.

Monday was a good day for the Rangers on another front, as they officially came to terms with Florida high school righthander Luke Jackson (supplemental first round) and University of Missouri righthander Justin Grimm (fifth round) on the deadline to sign 2010 draft picks, a day after agreeing with University of Missouri righthander Nick Tepesch (14th round). All three should be key additions to a system that moved a number of pitching prospects in the last six weeks.

Jackson reportedly signed for $1.545 million, slightly more than double the recommended $764,100 bonus for the slot where he was drafted (and only slightly less than Texas paid first-rounder Jake Skole, taken 15th overall). Twelve first-round picks signed for less than Texas paid Jackson. Grimm reportedly got $825,000, more than five times his estimated $147,600 slot (and supplemental first-round money). Tepesch's $400,000 bonus was third-round money.

More cool news on the development front: The Rangers' Dominican Summer League squad (40-21) clinched a division title yesterday, defeating the Braves, 5-0, behind winter signee Victor Payano and two relievers. It was the 20th win in 22 games for the Rangers (including a run of 15 straight), and over those 22 games the club scored 119 runs and allowed only 37. The Rangers have now won the San Pedro Division title three straight years.

Director of International Scouting Mike Daly is in charge of the daily operations at the Rangers' Dominican Academy. First-year manager Kenny Holmberg skippers the DSL club, taking over for Jayce Tingler, who held the post the last two division-winning years before getting promoted to the Arizona League this season. Former Rangers farmhand Jose Jaimes, a rising coaching star, is in charge of a pitching staff whose 2.01 ERA is best among the 34 DSL clubs. The staff has more strikeouts (531) than innings pitched (529), a punchout total that is second most in the league, and 168 walks, which is second least.

Foremost among the DSL club's pitching prospects is probably righthander David Perez, who is 4-4, 1.41 in 13 starts, with 62 strikeouts and eight walks in 64 innings, a 2.38 groundout-to-flyout rate, a .202 opponents' batting average, and zero home runs allowed. Perez hasn't allowed a run in his last 33 innings, scattering 14 hits and two walks in that stretch while punching out 29.

Perez has pitched to Jorge Alfaro more often than any other catcher, and the 17-year-old has made huge strides behind the plate as the season has gone along, with the help of catching instructor Ryley Westman. Alfaro is probably the key position player prospect on the club, though 17-year-old shortstop Hanser Alberto (second in the league with a .358 average and a stunning 26.9 plate appearances for every strikeout—seven total strikeouts in 188 trips) is interesting.

Even the best players to emerge from the DSL program will take four or five years to get to Texas, at best—when Joaquin Arias is likely to be out of baseball, and Cliff Lee is on the back half of the megadeal he'll sign this winter.

I promise right now that I won't complain if Hanser Alberto throws to the wrong base late in a 2015 game, even if it costs Cliff Lee a win—as long as Lee is wearing Rangers red at the time.

I should have news in the next day or two on where and when we will stage our first game-watching Newberg Report event with Chuck Greenberg. It will happen sometime on the Rangers' next road trip.

August 17, 2010

Potentially not insignificant: Texas has signed veteran infielder Alex Cora to a minor league contract, assigning the 34-year-old to Oklahoma City—perhaps temporarily. Cora has experience at every infield position, primarily up the middle, and has played in 13 post-season games.

August 18, 2010

Monday night, August 30, Texas visits Kansas City. C.J. Wilson against either Kyle Davies or (if the Royals skip Bryan Bullington due to an intervening off-day) Sean O'Sullivan.

We'll have the large space at Sherlock's in Arlington (254 Lincoln Square Center, near Collins and I-30) for a game-watching party with Rangers managing partner Chuck Greenberg.

All TV's will be tuned to Rangers-Royals, and we'll have Chuck armed with a microphone to do Q&A with you all throughout the night.

Admission is free, but we encourage you to donate a few bucks (amount up to you) when you arrive. Every dollar donated will go straight to the Rangers Foundation to support local children in need.

I'll share more details as we get closer, but there's a chance it may be exactly that: Just a few hundred Rangers fans watching the ballgame together—only one of us will be an owner of the team.

Hope you can make it.

August 18, 2010

My commentary on today's Rangers activity:

Boston 7, Los Angeles 5.

(Well, actually 36, but I don't count Oakland.)

August 19, 2010: TROT COFFEY

- According to Troy E. Renck of the *Denver Post* and others, Colorado will release outfielder-first baseman Brad Hawpe today, having gotten him through revocable waivers earlier in the week. Renck notes that the Rangers are among the teams interested in signing Hawpe, and that there could be mutual interest from the Fort Worth native, whose Rockies career blossomed on Texas hitting coach Clint Hurdle's watch.

August 19, 2010

Four days ago, I wrote this:

The Angels sit 7.5 games back, nine in the loss column. . . . I'll feel pretty good if this team wakes up Thursday in Baltimore with a seven-game lead on Los Angeles, who will travel to Minnesota after finishing up in Boston on Thursday.

Since then, Texas has won just once (Sunday against Boston) before losing three straight (all in Tampa).

And yet the Rangers are eight games up, by virtue of the Angels going winless in the three games they've played in that time. Los Angeles has one more in Boston tonight, followed by three in Minnesota. Four games on the road, against contenders that need to win them.

Newberg Report: Manny Hurdles

A look at obstacles facing suitors for the Dodgers slugger

By Jamey Newberg / Special to MLB.com

August 19, 2010

Last week we discussed the Rangers' 10 biggest August trades of the last 20 years. Let's envision one that, if it were to come to pass, would probably shoot straight to the top of the list.

Imagine Manny Ramirez hitting behind Josh Hamilton.

It's a far-fetched idea, to be sure, but let's first look at how it would have to happen.

After the conventional July 31 Trade Deadline, any player on a 40-man roster must first clear revocable waivers in order to be dealt. If he clears, he can be traded without limitation. If he's claimed by one team, he can only be traded to that team—or pulled back and not traded at all (or his existing team can unilaterally stick the claiming team with the player's contract). If he's claimed by multiple teams, he can still only be traded (or unilaterally conveyed) to one team—the one with the worst win-loss record in the league the player plays in, or if no such team claims him, then the one with the worst win-loss record in the other league.

So for Texas to even have a shot at Ramirez, he'd have to go unclaimed by the 15 National League teams he doesn't play for, and then by every American League with a worse record than the Rangers. At the moment, that would mean 24 teams would have to pass on Ramirez for this discussion to even get to the next step.

Once a team puts a player on revocable waivers, the remaining teams have two days within which to place a claim. Once the waiver period closes, if the player is claimed then another two-day window opens, during which any trade has to be worked out. Because of these brief, finite periods of time, teams strategically time when to put certain players on revocable waivers in August. Some are run onto the wire early in August. Others later in the month.

In Ramirez's case, the Dodgers have been limited as to when they could place Ramirez on waivers, because players must be active in order to be run through. Ramirez, who has been on the disabled list since July 17 with a strained calf muscle, headed out on what should be a brief Minor League rehab assignment yesterday. Once he's deemed ready to go, he could return to Los Angeles and be activated—and placed on revocable waivers (though some reports suggest he could be placed on waivers while on rehab, as long as Los Angeles is able to certify that he's physically able to play).

So the first hurdle is that Los Angeles hasn't even been able to put the Ramirez tires out to kick yet. But there's a series of added hurdles to clear.

Whom can the Dodgers trade Ramirez to?

It would stand to reason that only teams legitimately in contention would have any interest in acquiring the slugger, or blocking another team's ability to do so. While we can't rule out the possibility that a National League team might be interested (San Francisco has been mentioned), it seems more likely that an American League club with postseason aspirations would entertain the idea of giving Ramirez at-bats down the stretch and into October without having to play him defensively every day. If he does get by all NL clubs on waivers, the American League clubs who could potentially benefit this summer from Ramirez with reasonable shots at the playoffs probably include—in order of claim priority as of today—Chicago, Texas, Boston, Minnesota, New York, and Tampa Bay.

As discussed above, if multiple AL clubs were to place claims, the one with the worst win-loss record would have the prevailing claim. Here's where it can be a little tricky: The standings are viewed for the purposes of claim priority as of the time the claim window closes, which is two days after the player is placed on waivers, not when the window opens. In other words, Los Angeles wouldn't necessarily be able to time the waiver request to steer Ramirez to the team it wants to deal with.

Who will want Ramirez?

If Ramirez does go unclaimed in the National League, the White Sox may very well make the prevailing claim. Recall that Chicago reportedly made a run at Ramirez on July 31 (after failing to get Washington to part with Adam Dunn) but got nowhere with its demand not only that it wouldn't give up any player of consequence but also that Los Angeles would have to cover all but $1 million of Ramirez's remaining salary.

Ramirez earns $20 million in 2010, the final year of a two-year, $45 million contract he signed in March 2009. Of the $20 million owed for 2010, only $5 million is actually payable this year, with the remaining $15 million deferred without interest ($3.33 million due in June 2011; $3.33 million due in June 2012; and $8.33 million due in June 2013). Deferred compensation would be prorated based on when the dollars are earned (not when payable), and so any team picking Ramirez up for what amounts to the final fifth of the season would be obligated to him for about $1 million over the remainder of the season, and about $3 million more spread out over the next three seasons (with the Dodgers on the hook for the rest of the deferred portion). But in the event of a trade, those allocations could be negotiable.

The point of the dollars discussion is that the money shouldn't be a major impediment. So if Chicago decided not to put in a claim, then Texas, Boston (surely only to block), Minnesota, New York, and Tampa Bay might find reasons not to do so themselves, but probably not fiscal ones. And again: If Ramirez were to go fully unclaimed, Los Angeles would be free to discuss a trade with any club.

Would Texas claim Ramirez?

Ramirez, who is hitting a robust .317/.409/.516 in 2010, could resuscitate what right now is a decimated, lifeless Rangers lineup. Bringing him aboard would be a bold statement by the new ownership group. A Ramirez-Hamilton-Nelson Cruz playoff outfield with Julio Borbon available to run and play defense late, and David Murphy on the bench, would be strong, notwithstanding the issues on defense you'd have playing either Ramirez or Vladimir Guerrero on a corner. (And what would you do on the road in the World Series?)

No matter what his off-the-field reputation is, the Texas clubhouse is probably one that could withstand the Ramirez baggage. And the dollars aren't prohibitive.

But there are still other hurdles.

If Ramirez were claimed, would the Dodgers trade him?

The Dodgers, 11 games back in the NL West and seven games (and four teams) back in the Wild Card hunt, are saying they're not ready to concede the season. They've added, not subtracted, in the last three weeks, bringing Ted Lilly, Octavio Dotel, Scott Podsednik, and Ryan Theriot aboard.

But they've played only one game more with Ramirez than without him in 2010, and if they've decided they don't want him back in 2012, they might decide they're just fine rolling now with Podsednik in left field and flip Ramirez for prospects.

What would the Dodgers expect in return?

A lot. Considering Ramirez will be a Type A free agent who will probably get at least a two-year deal somewhere if he decides to play next season, the Dodgers would likely offer him arbitration (unless the risk of him accepting the offer is one the club is simply unwilling to take) and recoup a supplemental first-round pick plus either a first- or second-round pick if he were to sign elsewhere. They'll expect a trade offer that beats the promise of two first-round picks, and won't trade him if they can't get it.

Would you trade Engel Beltre and Robbie Erlin for Ramirez? What about Tanner Scheppers and Miguel Velazquez? It might take more, but if it didn't, would that deal make you squirm—even knowing you'd be the team to get the two 2011 compensatory picks back if you didn't re-sign Ramirez yourself?

That's still not the final hurdle.

If the Dodgers would trade Ramirez, and the parameters are agreed to, would he consent to the trade?

Ramirez has a full no-trade clause. It doesn't mean Los Angeles can't go down the path we're describing (see what the Cubs did with Derrek Lee yesterday), but it does mean that if the Dodgers and another team come to an agreement on a deal, Ramirez can kill it unilaterally by refusing to give his consent.

But you'd think that the prospect of going to an American League club zeroing in on post-season play, and getting an opportunity to reassert his offensive value heading into winter free agency, would be enough to convince Ramirez to waive the no-trade protection and join a new club.

The possibility of Ramirez becoming a Ranger in the next 12 days is a huge longshot. A Ramirez trade of any sort is probably unlikely. Trades do happen every August, and sometimes big ones, but a series of procedural obstacles facing teams who want to sell and teams who want to buy after July 31 make it obvious why most impact deals tend to get done before August ever rolls around.

The fact that Texas is in a bit of a skid, not only in wins and losses but in rotation and lineup production, has been mitigated by the inability of the Angels to take any advantage of it whatsoever. If this AL West race is like an NBA game, where the team with the lead inevitably goes cold for a stretch, and just needs to find a way to get things straightened out and hold on, we ought to be thankful that the Angels (and yes, the A's) haven't made this any more interesting than they have.

There's still plenty of baseball to be played, and opportunities for this division lead to tighten up, but in a season where Texas has not only played really good baseball but also caught some breaks, this break—which continues to allow the club to rest some key players and get them well—has been a very good one.

August 20, 2010

Enough bad baseball.
Enough, man. Enough. Enough.
Enough bad baseball.

August 20, 2010

The Rangers have optioned lefthander Derek Holland to AAA Oklahoma City, recalling lefthander Michael Kirkman from the same club. The club also announced that righthander Rich Harden will come off the 15-day disabled list on Monday to make that night's start against Minnesota.

Presumably, Kirkman, who leads the Pacific Coast League in strikeouts and has the league's third-lowest ERA, will give Texas an extra bullpen arm until Monday, when he'd be the logical player to go out to make room for Harden.

August 21, 2010

HOW CAN THAT POSSIBLY BE THE SAME PITCHER WHO WAS 0-5, 12.05 AS A STARTER WHEN I MANAGED HIM?!??

That was exquisite pitching. C.J. Wilson had great stuff, located everything, exploited the outer edges of a big Jeff Nelson strike zone, struck out a career high 12 (with 10 strike threes down in the zone), got 36 called strikes. He went to 2-0 just one time (a sixth-inning Julio Lugo at-bat at a time when Lugo had Baltimore's only two hits), and only three times all night went to a three-ball count.

Twice this year Wilson has walked as few as last night's one. The first time was a zero-walk effort against the Angels four weeks ago, a night on which he registered only three strikeouts in eight innings. The second was in his last start—and the Rangers' last win—when he set eight Red Sox down on strikes and issued one walk in 7.2 frames.

Wilson's 12:1 ratio last night was Cliff Lee style, particularly after the third inning, when his pitches per inning dropped from 19.0 to 10.8. Wilson was perfect in the 4th through 8th, getting seven of his 15 outs on strikes, and five of those looking. He was drilling his spots all night, staying away from the wheelhouse.

When Wilson is locked in the way he was in that game, with stuff that's better than Lee's, that's unquestionably a guy who fits in a playoff rotation.

But the offense, once again held down, remains a concern.

If you're glancing at today's pitching matchup and thinking this is the day that the lineup wakes up a bit—and gives Lee some run support for a change—Brad Bergesen's 5.80 ERA is a little deceptive. Since July 31, Bergesen has a 2.22 ERA in four starts, holding opponents to a .206/.257/.392 slash. By way of comparison, Lee in the same stretch: 4.50 ERA and a .277/.298/.370 slash.

Dan Haren got torched by Minnesota last night, falling to 1-4 in six Angels starts, and Los Angeles gave back the game it had gained on Thursday, dipping again to eight games out. Oakland escaped with a win over Tampa Bay (with an eighth inning I wish I didn't see), to stay within seven.

The Rangers are cited as one of the teams interested in outfielder-first baseman Brad Hawpe, whom the Rockies are letting go, but various sources have also linked the Giants, Rays, Red Sox, White Sox, Twins, and Yankees to the 31-year-old. One issue: Hawpe isn't very good defensively. I'm open to the Manny Ramirez idea, but short of that kind of bat, I'm not sure how good an idea it would be to bring in another position player whose glove would be an issue, especially since Hawpe hasn't hit or reached base this season the way he had prior to 2010.

If the thought is that Hawpe could give the team more situational offense than Jorge Cantu, that's OK as long as third base is covered on the bench (and second base as well, because you can't just hope Andres Blanco won't be needed at both spots in a given game). Easier to plan for as of September 1, but that's still a week and a half away.

In that stretch, Texas will play 11 games. Cliff Lee's got three of those (Baltimore, Minnesota, Kansas City) and

C.J. Wilson's got another two (Minnesota and Kansas City). There's a three-game home set against the A's in there as well (next weekend), a series that could effectively bury Oakland's chances if the Rangers can hold ground until then.

But the bats have to do their part. Credit Wilson for carrying the offense last night, but over the next six weeks, the Rangers will need to find a way to start clicking across the board. Getting some key guys back from injury will help, but there's room for improvement all over the lineup.

August 23, 2010

According to at least one local report, the Rangers will activate righthander Rich Harden and catcher Matt Treanor today, placing righthander Scott Feldman on the disabled list (which means lefthander Michael Kirkman remains in the bullpen) and returning catcher Taylor Teagarden to Oklahoma City on option. Teagarden will surely return during September roster expansion.

August 23, 2010: Back to School Edition

How I Spent My Summer

Dear Miss Mulos,

April and May were OK, I guess. Was thinking by mid-May about having a great summer.

June rocked! It was awesome. Best June ever. (Went streaking!)

July was OK, nothing great. Got in a little vacation. Did some shopping. Had a bunch of new friends come over.

August hasn't been so great. Maybe thinking too much about September. (But did go to a live auction for the first time, which was . . . interesting.*)*

Back to business now. Recharged, focused, ready to do work, ready to roll. Expecting this to end up the best year yet . . . .

—T. R.

P.S. 32 is a magic number. </Schoolhouse Rock>

August 23, 2010

Twin Killing.

August 24, 2010

The Rangers have purchased the contract of veteran infielder Alex Cora from Oklahoma City, making room for the 34-year-old on both the active and 40-man rosters by designating infielder Joaquin Arias for assignment.

The Rangers have 10 days to trade, release, or outright Arias to the minor leagues.

August 24, 2010

What I wish for Jon Daniels on this date every year is a solid baseball win, a pennant race, and no more stories about him working somewhere else.

Minnesota	*72*	*54*	*L2*
Texas	*71*	*54*	*W3*

August 25, 2010

A few idle thoughts and notes:

1. Upon replacing Joaquin Arias on the roster with Alex Cora, Texas assistant general manager Thad Levine said: "The general thought going down the stretch is there is some value of having another guy who is playoff-tested and has a little more experience."

Cora's presence frees Ballplayer Andres Blanco up to play third base if needed. Jorge Cantu has no playoff experience (and no RBI, perhaps emasculating the handedness factor). Brad Hawpe has 51 post-season playoff appearances. Clint Hurdle saw all of them. Hawpe cleared waivers yesterday and is now a free agent.

Math.

2. Don't forget the game-watching party and Q&A with Chuck Greenberg at Sherlock's in Arlington on Monday. We'll get going at 6:00.

3. Colin Cowherd: Whatever. Jackwagon.

4. The Rangers, according to the *Los Angeles Times*, scouted Manny Ramirez on his Cal League rehab assignment last week and at Dodger Stadium over the weekend. Why haven't the Dodgers run Ramirez out on waivers yet? If he were to clear National League waivers, the White Sox are almost certainly the first team based on claim priority who would be interested. Texas is next. Has Los Angeles possibly been stalling in hopes that Chicago caught the Rangers in the standings, giving Texas

claim priority over the White Sox? That theory would make sense only if the Dodgers had reason to believe the Rangers would not only claim Ramirez, but would do so out of interest in the player (rather than just to block him from reaching the Rays, for instance) (and again, Texas has reportedly been scouting Ramirez), and only if the Dodgers knew what Texas was willing to offer in trade and they prefer it to whatever Chicago would offer.

With Texas winning three straight, the Sox are now three games behind the Rangers, so if the above had anything to do with the Dodgers' timing strategy, it's probably moot now.

5. The fact that Boston made the prevailing waiver claim on Johnny Damon means Texas passed. (Not sure how devastated the Sox are that Damon decided to stay in Detroit. I'm guessing the opportunity to block him from reaching Tampa Bay was a significant reason they made the claim, and they succeeded on that front.)

6. According to at least one local report, Houston and AA Corpus Christi have reupped on a four-year player development contract. No such deal yet between the Astros and the Ryan family's other minor league club, AAA Round Rock, and the story quoted Houston GM Ed Wade as saying that he's not optimistic the relationship will extend, and that Round Rock could end up affiliated with Texas (in place of Oklahoma City). Not a new story, but the first time I can recall an Astros official going on record.

7. One of Chuck Greenberg's minor league clubs, the State College Spikes of the New York-Penn League, will extend with the Pirates, according to *Baseball America* (not that there was any hint that Texas was thinking about leaving Spokane). No word yet on Greenberg's other club, the Myrtle Beach Pelicans, which are the Braves' High A (Carolina League) affiliate. The Rangers' PDC with High A Bakersfield expires this season, as does Atlanta's with Myrtle Beach.

Pittsburgh, by the way, assigned top picks Jameson Taillon and Stetson Allie to State College. The Pirates signed the righthanders for $6.5 million and $2.25 million this month, respectively.

8. The two largest bonuses given to college pitchers in this year's draft: Cleveland lefthander Drew Pomeranz ($2.65 million) and Boston righthander Anthony Ranaudo ($2.55 million). Texas drafted both pitchers out of high school in 2007.

9. *BA* reports that Texas, despite everything, spent the seventh-largest amount of draft bonus money ($8.4878 million) in the league this summer, and has been top 10 over the last three years even without reaching an agreement last summer with first-rounder Matt Purke.

10. Tommy Hunter beat Kevin Millwood on Sunday. Would you take Millwood's career (157 wins to date, an average of 13-11, 4.12 and 208 innings over a full season) for Hunter?

11. Mitch Moreland played a very good game last night. That's a solid ballplayer, who at worst is going to be this team's next version of David Murphy, with a slightly different versatility. But for now, can't Texas feel good about going to camp with him as the frontrunner at first base?

12. Boston released lefthander Kason Gabbard and infielder Tug Hulett.

13. The Rangers are on pace for how many wins? Say it with me, in your best Nolan Ryan tones: "92."

14. I haven't yet discussed the K-Rod Rules on playoff eligibility as they pertain to Tanner Scheppers because I'd be surprised at this point to see him in Texas at all this season. Back on August 14, Texas ran the righthander out to the mound on consecutive days for the first time. In that outing and the three since: five innings, seven runs (six earned), eight hits, nine walks, one hit batsman, two strikeouts, 56 percent strikes. He's a fantastic prospect. But he's struggling with his command right now.

Mark Lowe is a better bet to factor in.

15. Taylor Teagarden will surely be back in September, though. He impressed Ron Washington with his defense in this last run with the big club, and he started hitting a bit. For his career, Teagarden's March/April/May/June OPS is .469. In July, it's .670. In August, it's 820. In September/ October, it's .947.

16. Ian Kinsler, Nelson Cruz, Cristian Guzman, and Dustin Nippert could all go out on rehab assignments this week.

17. Jarrod Saltalamacchia was hospitalized (and DL'd by Boston) with a mystery leg infection. Doctors ruled MRSA out. That guy is cursed.

18. Cincinnati is thinking about moving Edinson Volquez to the bullpen.

19. The Dodgers signed righthander Geoff Geary to a AAA deal. The Grand Prairie Airhogs of the independent American Association traded catcher Ben Petralli to the Normal Cornbelters of the independent Frontier League for a player to be named.

20. C.J. Wilson (12-5, 3.02) against Brian Duensing (7-1, 1.92) tonight, maybe the league's two biggest surprise lefthanders this season. Each has won five straight decisions. Duensing's ERA over his last three starts is 1.48, while Wilson's is 1.25.

Even if the term "dog days" gets thrown around, late August games that matter are such greatness.

August 26, 2010

C.J. Wilson improved to 13-5, 3.02 last night, including 6-0, 2.29 in eight starts since the All-Star Break.

Texas is 20-6 in Wilson's starts this year, including 14 wins the last 16 times he's taken the hill.

He should get seven more starts in the regular season. Let's say he stays on this roll, maybe winning five, losing one, and getting a no-decision. Wouldn't an 18-6 record with an ERA in the three's put him in the top 10 for Cy Young consideration? Top five?

Wilson's next start comes Monday in Kansas City. He's pitched there three times in his career, all in relief, blanking the Royals on two hits and no walks in 2.2 innings, fanning three. He's slated to face righthander Kyle Davies, who has a 6.88 ERA in his last three starts and, in his one 2010 start against Texas, got slapped around for nine runs in four innings.

You can watch Monday's game with Chuck Greenberg, when we host our Newberg Report game-watching party at Sherlock's in Arlington that night. Doors open at 6:00, and we'll have every TV in the massive room set to the game. We'll also have a microphone in front of Chuck for Q&A that will start early and, one way or another, I expect will last throughout the game.

There's no cost to attend, but we'll have a voluntary admission (you decide how much, if you want to contribute anything) that will go straight to the Rangers Foundation, 100 percent, to support local children in need.

August 26, 2010: TROT COFFEY

- Tweeted this afternoon by Fox Sports reporter Jon Paul Morosi:

One rival exec describes #Rangers as "very active" lately. "They're trying to win the World Series," the exec says.

August 26, 2010: TROT COFFEY

- According to a local report posted in the last 10 minutes: "The Rangers are not interested in Brad Hawpe, who was let go by the Colorado Rockies last week and is a free agent. Hawpe is a left-handed hitter and the Rangers lineup is already loaded with left-handed hitters. A club official said the Rangers like the player but don't see him as a fit for their current needs."

August 27, 2010

Bewildering-Lee
Making his teammates better
But skidding himself

In other news:
Michael Kirkman.

August 27, 2010: TROT COFFEY

- According to Jon Heyman of *Sports Illustrated*, multiple teams placed claims on Manny Ramirez before the deadline that I believe passed at 12:30 Central time, which means Texas is almost a certainty not to acquire the Dodgers outfielder. The odds are that the White Sox are one of the teams that claimed Ramirez, and as they are below Texas in the American League standings, claim priority would not have gotten past Chicago and given the Rangers a chance at making the prevailing claim. There was some speculation that Ramirez, for various reasons, might have slid through waivers unclaimed, which would have given Los Angeles the ability to negotiate with any of the 29 teams on a trade, but if Heyman's report is true, Ramirez was in fact claimed, and if the White Sox aren't the team now on the clock through midday Tuesday to get together with the Dodgers on a deal, then it's probably a team in the National League or one with a worse AL record than Chicago.

August 27, 2010: TROT COFFEY

- The latest tweet from Jon Heyman of *Sports Illustrated*:

In continuing guessing game, I hear #rangers did not win claim. Neither did the couple teams behind them in picking order

August 27, 2010

11.5…9.5…7.5…~~5.5~~
What'll it be?

August 28, 2010

If the objective, or at least part of it, was for Texas to ensure that Manny Ramirez didn't replace Willie Aybar as Tampa Bay's designated hitter, then everything worked out. If the White Sox hadn't claimed Ramirez on revocable waivers yesterday, and no National League team did either, someone among Texas, Minnesota, and Boston would have had to place a claim to ensure that the Rays didn't get a chance.

The Rangers' reportedly placed a claim, but it didn't matter, because the White Sox had the first shot among those teams. So Ramirez will hit for the White Sox or Dodgers the rest of the way. Not the Rays.

If the objective, or at least part of it, was to add Ramirez to a roster that includes a rejuvenated Vladimir Guerrero and an imminently reappearing Nelson Cruz and a productive David Murphy (.316/.404/.539 in August), that's not happening.

But another plus could surface, if Los Angeles decides that it's either out of the race or, at 4.5 games and four teams back in the Wild Card chase, doing just fine with Scott Podsednik rather than Ramirez, and decides to trade him to the White Sox. From September 14 to September 26 there's a 12-game stretch in which the White Sox, sporting a lineup that would include Ramirez in place of Mark Kotsay or Andruw Jones, take on Minnesota (against whom Ramirez is a career .331/.389/.605 hitter) for three at home (.338/.448/.601), then after a set against Detroit go to Oakland for three on the road

(.319/.417/.534), and to the Angels for three on the road (.312/.396/.614).

Ramirez won't face Texas in 2010, but if he ends up in Chicago before Tuesday's deadline he'll face the three teams the Rangers care most about right now. And while I can't root for the White Sox, ever, simply because of the unbearable Hawk Harrelson, I'm a Manny Ramirez fan, and if he's wearing the black and white I can at least imagine his opportunity to do damage against the Twins on September 14-16 ending up as big for the Rangers—in spite of any metrics that diminish the significant of home field in the playoffs—as the fact that he won't be suiting up for the Rays . . . who the Rangers could face at home in Round One if they do catch the Twins again and hold them off (or on the road if they don't).

Quick update on Monday's game-watching gathering at Sherlock's in Arlington: Chuck Morgan will join Chuck Greenberg and us for the event, and Fox Sports Southwest is planning to record a couple video segments for "Rangers Insider." See you there.

August 28, 2010: TROT COFFEY

- According to Ken Rosenthal of Fox Sports, the Rangers are looking around for a fourth outfielder candidate (really a fifth outfielder, a role that Craig Gentry would have been counted on to fill had he not broken his wrist), and Dodgers right-handed hitter Reed Johnson is one possibility—any trade must be made by Tuesday in order for the player to be eligible for the post-season
- According to multiple local reports, Derek Holland is at Rangers Ballpark and would be recalled if the decision is made before gametime to place Frankie Francisco on the disabled list—the club had Francisco undergo an MRI on his right lat muscle this afternoon and is awaiting results

Required reading if you plan to be at the game-watching party and Chuck Greenberg Q&A at Sherlock's Monday night: the interview Grant Schiller did with Chuck a few days ago. You'll learn some things about him you didn't already know.

Finally, the Rangers have named Katie Crawford to the newly created position of "Fan Ambassador," a role in which she will be a direct liaison from Rangers fan base to the front office. You can send ideas and feedback and complaints to Katie at fanfeedback1@texasrangers.com.

August 28, 2010

The Rangers have placed righthander Frank Francisco on the 15-day disabled list with a strained right latissimus dorsi muscle, replacing him on the active roster by recalling lefthander Derek Holland from Oklahoma City.

August 30, 2010

Even spotted for the most part against lefthanders, Jorge Cantu hasn't done a thing since coming over to Texas, hitting an RBI-less .211/.262/.263 in 57 Rangers at-bats—and just .167/.242/.200 against lefties, with eight strikeouts in 30 at-bats. Southpaws have forced Cantu to hit into almost as many double plays (three) as he has hits against them (five), which doesn't include the twin-killing that ended yesterday's game since that one came off a righthander.

The Rangers, as pointed out by Anthony Andro of the *Fort Worth Star-Telegram*, are 3-8 in their last 11 games started by opposing lefthanders. That's not all Cantu's fault, but he's not helping. The Rangers are going to run into some among C.C. Sabathia, Andy Pettitte, David Price, Francisco Liriano, and Brian Duensing in October, not to mention Brian Fuentes, Boone Logan, Randy Choate, and maybe Jake McGee. Right now I can't imagine feeling better about Cantu than I would about Mitch Moreland stepping in against any of them.

Not that Moreland (.200/.250/.267) has blown lefties up himself. I just have no confidence in Cantu.

I didn't mind the trade to get him at the time, nor the one to get Cristian Guzman, because I'm good with the people running this team being aggressive instead of guarded and because the organization was dealing from strength in giving up Evan Reed and Omar Poveda and Ryan Tatukso and Tanner Roark to get them. But I'm up for some added aggressive and wouldn't be upset to see the club pick up another right-handed-hitting first baseman today or tomorrow, just to give someone else a look with October in mind. Getting Ian Kinsler and Nelson Cruz back will help against lefthanders, but there's a defined role for a right-handed bat that can play first base on this roster, and I'd be all for an upgrade over Cantu.

If we're to get that bat, no matter who it is, it might take another prospect or two, but it won't involve Michael Kirkman.

I say that not because the only team you could trade Kirkman to in the next couple days would be Baltimore.

I say that not because Kirkman can't be a player to be named later since he's in the big leagues.

I say that because, plain and simple, he's not going anywhere. For now.

But this winter, if Cliff Lee signs elsewhere and Texas decides to load up and trade for a veteran starter to head the rotation, you can make up a list of the players other clubs will ask about—Martin Perez, Tanner Scheppers, Alexi Ogando, Tommy Hunter, Derek Holland, Robbie Erlin . . . Julio Borbon, David Murphy, Moreland, Engel Beltre, Chris Davis, Jurickson Profar—and Kirkman fits on it. In the top half.

Texas drafted Kirkman in the fifth round in 2005, on the recommendation of second-year area scout Guy

Newberg Report: Short-Term Yield

How the players Texas traded in July have fared

By Jamey Newberg / Special to MLB.com

August 26, 2010

The impact that Cliff Lee, Bengie Molina, Jorge Cantu, and Cristian Guzman (and possibly Mark Lowe) have in Texas will be measured largely on what they do over the final third of the 2010 season and, the Rangers hope, in October.

In contrast, the young players that the Mariners, Giants, Marlins, and Nationals got in July from Texas in exchange for those veterans will be counted on to develop over a longer term, making what they do in a small sample size this summer relatively unimportant.

But that won't stop us from taking a look at what the 10 players Texas traded in July have done so far for their new organizations, ranked from the best debut to the least effective one. Again, this is not a big picture ranking of the 10 players—that assessment will take years—but instead a look at which of them have gotten off to the strongest starts since being traded.

1. Josh Lueke, RHP, Triple-A Tacoma: Until a shaky outing on Aug. 20, Lueke had been unconscious since joining the Mariners in the Lee trade. In six relief appearances for Double-A West Tenn, he struck out 14 and walked none in 7.1 scoreless innings, scattering four hits. In his first six games pitched for Triple-A Tacoma, he fanned 12 and issued one walk in 10.2 frames, allowing seven hits and just one earned run. He was tagged for three runs in an inning of work on Friday, but there's still a chance that he finishes the season in the big league bullpen, auditioning for a 2011 setup role.

2. Blake Beavan, RHP, Triple-A Tacoma: Beavan, who was on the verge of a promotion to Triple-A before Texas shipped him to Seattle, made three Double-A starts before the Mariners gave him his first look at Triple-A hitters. Three of his five Tacoma starts have been outstanding (2-0, 2.25, 13 strikeouts and three walks in 20 innings), while two others have been ugly (0-2, 13.09). He's very young for Triple-A, however, and now has 14 wins in what has been a breakout season.

3. Matt Lawson, 2B, Double-A West Tennessee: Lawson's breakout season with Frisco has held up since the Lee trade. After hitting .277 with an .809 OPS for the RoughRiders, the 24-year-old is hitting .328 with an .847 OPS for the Mariners' Double-A club. Lawson made six errors for Frisco, playing mostly second base with a little outfield mixed in. Playing strictly second base for the Diamond Jaxx (other than two shortstop appearances), he's committed just one error in 33 games—and it came in his first game following the trade.

4. Ryan Tatusko, RHP, Double-A Harrisburg: Tatukso has followed his 9-2, 2.97 breakout campaign with Frisco with a solid three-start debut in the Nationals system since coming over in the Guzman deal, going 1-1, 2.70 with 20 strikeouts and nine walks in 16.2 innings, holding Eastern Leaguers to a .210 batting average, and inducing twice as many groundouts as flyouts.

5. Tanner Roark, RHP, Double-A Harrisburg: Like Tatusko, Roark has been sensational since joining Washington, posting quality starts his first two times out and coming an out short of doing it again in his third start. In 17.2 innings, he's allowed four earned runs (2.04 ERA) on 14 hits (.212 opponents' average) and three walks, fanning 14, after he'd gone 10-5, 4.20 in 17 starts and five relief appearances for Frisco.

6. Justin Smoak, 1B, Triple-A Tacoma: After struggling terribly on his arrival in Seattle (.159 average with 23 strikeouts and one walk in 63 at-bats), Smoak was optioned to Triple-A Tacoma, where his first month looked like his early work in Texas: he's drawing walks and hitting for occasional power, but he's not hitting for average (.232). Smoak's potential is huge, but it's been a disappointing season, both before and since his inclusion in the Lee trade.

7. Chris Ray, RHP, San Francisco: After Ray held opponents to a .205 batting average as a Ranger, batters hit him at a .298 clip in his run with the Giants, which was halted in mid-August when he landed on the disabled list with a strain in the ribcage area. Sporting a 5.40 ERA for San Francisco, Ray's strikeouts remain frustratingly low for a short-dose reliever with power stuff.

8. Evan Reed, RHP, Double-A Jacksonville: The 24-year-old right-hander was having a terrific year in the

Rangers system (1.76 ERA, 36 strikeouts and 13 walks in 41 innings between Frisco and Oklahoma City, one home run) when he keyed the Cantu deal for Florida. He made only one relief appearance for the Suns, however, before complaining of elbow tightness and seeing his season end prematurely.

9. Michael Main, RHP, Double-A Richmond: Main was in the midst of a solid comeback season with Bakersfield, surpassing his career high in innings pitched by the first week of June and sitting at 5-3, 3.45 at the time of the Rangers' trade with San Francisco to get Molina. The Giants challenged Main with an immediate assignment to the Double-A Eastern League, and things did not go well. In five appearances (including four starts), Main logged only 13.2 innings, surrendering 26 runs (21 earned: 13.83 ERA) on 21 hits (.362 opponents' average) and 14 walks, fanning seven. He's been shut down since late July.

10. Omar Poveda, RHP, 60-Day Disabled List: The 22-year-old from Venezuela has missed the entire season after Tommy John elbow reconstruction surgery in March. The Marlins expect he'll be ready to go physically in Spring Training.

DeMutis, son-in-law of John Hart, who was presiding over what would be his final draft as Rangers GM. A quiet, humble kid out of Lake City, Florida, the 18-year-old Kirkman had drawn interest in high school from Florida State, Florida, Mississippi State, Miami, the University of Central Florida, South Florida, Virginia, and Boston College before settling instead on a commitment to his hometown community college. But he took slot money ($163,000) to sign with the Rangers even though *Baseball America*, for one, had projected him to go in the third round (ranked in Florida behind Andrew McCutchen and Ryan Braun and Chris Volstad but ahead of Jordan Schafer and Yunel Escobar and Josh Bell, not to mention Shane Funk, whom Texas drafted in round four), which would have called for at least double that amount.

Since that time, as perfectly chronicled last week by Mike Hindman, Kirkman's story has been as compelling as any in the Rangers system, swinging from promising to baseball-tragic to resurgent to dominant, all of it almost implausible, and he sits right now as a favorite to suit up in the playoffs for Texas.

After a dazzling debut summer in 2005 that began with an ugly five-start ERA of 6.06, followed by a five-start run at 2.50 and finally a four-start finish at 2.00 (58 strikeouts and 19 walks in 52.1 innings all told, zero home runs, a top six league finish in both ERA and strikeouts), an evil loss of command (impacted, doubtlessly, by elbow and hamstring injuries) crippled his 2006 and 2007 seasons (88 walks, 22 wild pitches, and eight hit batsmen in 74.2 innings) and, almost surprisingly, didn't cause the organization or the young man to move on. Texas had released Funk in spring training 2007, less than two years into his pro career. The club showed far more patience with Kirkman.

In 2008, Kirkman restored his confidence and his ability to locate, in some order, posting a 3.84 ERA in 16 starts and a relief appearance between Short-Season A Spokane and Low A Clinton, the latter of which was where his problems had begun in 2006. He walked 25 batters in 84.1 innings, fanning 67. The strikeout total was encouraging. But the walk numbers—fewer than three per nine innings—were eye-opening, considering where Kirkman had been the previous two years.

What happened in 2009 was remarkable. Led by minor league rehab pitching coordinator Keith Comstock—a former big league lefthander and fifth-round pick himself—under the oversight of pitching coordinator Danny Clark, the organization brought back some of the old elements in Kirkman's delivery and reintroduced the slider to his arsenal after ditching it before, and he exploded. Starting the season in the hitter-friendly California League, Kirkman made seven starts and one relief appearance for Bakersfield, never allowing more than three earned runs and sitting as the 10-team circuit's ERA leader (2.06) and strikeout leader (54 in 48 innings, with only 18 walks) late in May, when Texas promoted him to Frisco.

In 18 RoughRider starts, Kirkman went 5-7, 4.19, but he got markedly better as the summer wore on, firing quality starts six of his final seven times out (2-2, 2.51) and sitting 91-94, several miles per hour higher than he'd worked at the year before. When it came time to add players to the 40-man roster in November, Kirkman was unquestionably the Rangers' easiest call. *BA* ranked him as the Rangers' number 16 prospect over the winter. (I had him at number 15.)

Assigned to Oklahoma City to start the season, Kirkman was extraordinarily consistent, going 12-3, 3.00 in 22 starts without a monthly ERA over 3.75. Moved into the RedHawks' bullpen three weeks ago in an obvious effort to get him ready for big league work in that role, he pitched twice in relief before getting the call to the big leagues on August 20, in what was by all appearances going to be a short stay—giving the bullpen an extra arm between Holland's August 18 start and what would be Rich Harden's return from the disabled list on August 23.

But Scott Feldman's knee acted up on August 21, and Kirkman replaced him that afternoon, facing four Orioles and getting all of them out, three on strikes. When Feldman landed on the disabled list two days later, Kirkman's stay was extended, and he's been brilliant.

In four games pitched, he's scattered three singles (.136 opponents' average) and two walks in 6.1 scoreless innings, punching out seven. Four inherited runners have each failed to score. Among the hitters he's retired: Luke Scott, Ty Wigginton, Adam Jones, Jim Thome, Delmon Young, Jason Kubel, Michael Cuddyer (twice), Denard Span (twice), and Orlando Hudson (twice). Joe Mauer has two of the three hits off Kirkman, though one was an infield single, and he did get Mauer to ground out once. Jack Cust has the other hit.

That's right: While Kirkman was never viewed developmentally as a left-on-left specialist in the making (like Ben Snyder, for instance), he's shown, at least in an extremely small sample size (but also in AAA), that his varied repertoire can be effective against righthanders, who are 0 for 11 in the big leagues. He's a starting pitcher prospect who's getting a look in relief because that's where he can help right now, and possibly in October.

There have been 486 pitchers who have appeared in a Pacific Coast League game this season. None has more strikeouts than Kirkman's 130 (in 131 innings)—even though he's been out of the league for a week and a half. Only two have lower ERA's.

While scouts all over baseball surely had a book on Kirkman during his time at Oklahoma City (league coaches recently ranked his slider the best breaking pitch in the 16-team league in a *BA* survey), the evaluations might be getting new cover sheets after what's he's shown against the likes of Thome and Span and Scott and Young, each of whom the 23-year-old has set down on strikes. Scouts can learn plenty when you're doing it in AAA against Ruben Gotay and Kila Ha'aihue and Brock Bond, but there's an extra layer in the recommendation when you flash even a small sample of the fearlessness Kirkman has shown in his first shot against veteran hitters, in big spots, in important games.

There have been stories written this last week suggesting Kirkman has passed Holland in the pecking order here. Not sure that's fair to either of them. And this isn't Davis/Justin Smoak, or Jarrod Saltalamacchia/Taylor Teagarden, or Troy Aikman/Steve Walsh. There's room for both Kirkman and Holland, and different ways for each to factor in.

When the Rangers looked into Wigginton or Mike Lowell or Troy Glaus or Xavier Nady or Wes Helms over the last two months, and when they picked up Cantu, Jon Daniels was probably asked about Kirkman (the Marlins were "believed to be looking for [a] young [lefthander]" for Cantu, according to Ken Rosenthal of Fox Sports), but even if someone like Glaus or Lowell is on the table today and tomorrow, Kirkman is procedurally unavailable and wouldn't be up for discussion anyway.

It may be tougher for Texas to keep his name out of the mix this winter, though, if trying to revive talks about Josh Johnson or Zack Greinke or Ricky Nolasco, for instance.

But that's a wildly different situation from the one that involved adding Cantu and Guzman and Bengie Molina last month. It would make sense that the Marlins and Nationals and Giants—and probably the Mariners, too, in the Cliff Lee talks—asked Texas at some point about Kirkman, a AAA arm with an imperfect past on a crowded 40-man roster in a system boasting what most believe are bluer chips. A lefthander who looked in 2007 like he might have been done as a baseball player, just as Blake Beavan and Michael Main were being drafted in the first round with limitless ceilings and enthusiastic talk of timetables.

I'm all for the Rangers' aggressive contenders' approach (it's clear now that Manny Ramirez would be a Ranger today or tomorrow if Chicago hadn't placed a claim, as the Dodgers apparently are going to let the White Sox take his contract without insisting on players in return), but I'm also confident by virtue of the fact that Kirkman's still here that the club is just as aggressive now when it comes to hanging onto certain prospects.

And that when there's one like Michael Kirkman who has pushed his ceiling a little bit higher every year for the last three, getting better with the competition, he's not going to be flipped for a bench bat, even when it might have made the playoff push conceivably stronger, because one way or another he's the kind of arm the Rangers might be able to turn soon into a frontline big league starting pitcher.

August 30, 2010

Don't forget tonight's game-watching party at Sherlock's in Arlington (254 Lincoln Square Center, near Collins and I-30). Join Chuck Greenberg and Chuck Morgan as we watch C.J. Wilson take on the Royals in the same massive room we had for December's book release party.

Doors "open" at 6:00 (but feel free to arrive earlier). We'll do open-mic Q&A before the game and probably during it as well, depending on what feels right.

Emily Jones of Fox Sports Southwest is planning to be there to record a couple video segments for an upcoming episode of "Rangers Insider."

I'll have some 2010 Bound Editions on hand in case you're interested in buying a copy.

There's no admission fee but we encourage you to donate a few bucks (amount up to you) when you arrive. Every dollar donated will go straight to the Rangers Foundation to help support local children in need.

See you tonight.

August 30, 2010

The Rangers have activated outfielder Nelson Cruz from the 15-day disabled list, sending outfielder Brandon Boggs to Oklahoma City on option. The club also recalled outfielder Craig Gentry and placed him on the 15-day disabled list.

Word from the Rangers is that the club is considering whether to use Gentry as a pinch-runner down the stretch even though he'll be wearing a cast on his broken wrist. Placing Gentry on the big league DL also increases options as far as the playoff roster is concerned.

August 30, 2010

The Rangers have extended their Player Development Contracts with AA Frisco (through the 2014 season), Low A Hickory (through 2012) and Short-Season A Spokane (through 2012).

The omissions on that list of AAA Oklahoma City and High A Bakersfield are notable, given Nolan Ryan's ties to AAA Round Rock and Chuck Greenberg's ties to High A Myrtle Beach, two affiliates whose present PDC's (with Houston and Atlanta, respectively) expire at the end of this season as well.

August 30, 2010

At 6:00, when the game-watching party gets underway, the great Ted Price will start live-streaming the Q&A at http://dallassportsnetwork.tv/live/.

Ted will roll audio and video during the Q&A portions of tonight's event. (He won't show the game itself, of course.) He's also planning to archive it for later viewing.

August 31, 2010

Party like it's 1999 (or 1998 or 1996)?

If there's a Newberg Report event, the Rangers win.

Our record on Newberg Report Night, FSSW live in-game chats, and Chuck & Chuck Game-Watching Parties this season: 6-0.

Maybe we'll stage a Nickelback CD Demolition Night for Game One on October 5.

Thanks to Steve Richardson and his crew at Sherlock's for taking care of us, Eleanor Czajka and Norma Wolfson and the Rangers' Sean Decker for organizing your contributions to the Rangers Foundation, to Ted Price for live-streaming the event (archived footage should be up sometime this week at http://dallassportsnetwork.tv/live/), and to Emily Jones and Brady Tinker for coming out to record segments for Fox Sports Southwest "Rangers Insider" and "DFW Sports Beat." (I'll let you all know when the segments will air.)

But thanks mostly to Chuck Greenberg and Chuck Morgan, who were both in their wheelhouse all night, to C.J. Wilson and Andres Blanco, who were in theirs, and to the hundreds of you who came to the event. That was a good time.

We may try to do another one in September, schedules permitting.

August 31, 2010

According to at least one local report, the Rangers have acquired right-handed-hitting outfielder Jeff Francoeur from the Mets. It's expected that infielder Joaquin Arias, designated for assignment one week ago, would in fact be going to New York in the deal.

August 31, 2010

Texas has officially traded Joaquin Arias for Jeff Francouer, receiving cash in the deal from the Mets (reportedly so that Texas pays Francouer what it would have paid Arias the rest of the way), and has designated outfielder Brandon Boggs for assignment to make room on the 40-man roster for Francouer.

The Rangers have 10 days to trade Boggs, release him, or outright him to the minor leagues.

August 31, 2010

That one would have been almost embarrassing to win. Get lost, August.

SEPTEMBER 2010

40-MAN ROSTER (40)

PITCHERS (20)

Omar Beltre, Scott Feldman, Neftali Feliz, Frankie Francisco, Rich Harden, Matt Harrison, Derek Holland, Tommy Hunter, Michael Kirkman, Cliff Lee, Colby Lewis, Doug Mathis, Guillermo Moscoso, Dustin Nippert, Darren O'Day, Alexi Ogando, Darren Oliver, Zach Phillips, Pedro Strop, C.J. Wilson

CATCHERS (4)

Max Ramirez, Jarrod Saltalamacchia, Taylor Teagarden, Matt Treanor

INFIELDERS (9)

Elvis Andrus, Joaquin Arias, Andres Blanco, Jorge Cantu, Chris Davis, Cristian Guzman, Ian Kinsler, Mitch Moreland, Michael Young

OUTFIELDERS (7)

Julio Borbon, Nelson Cruz, Jeff Francouer, Craig Gentry, Vladimir Guerrero, Josh Hamilton, David Murphy

60-DAY DISABLED LIST (3)

Eric Hurley, Mark Lowe, Brandon McCarthy

September 1, 2010

September 1, 2010

There's a tendency to microanalyze every baseball trade, especially the good old-fashioned player-for-player swaps that you never see in football and that are rarely the point of NBA deals. It's what we do.

Joaquin Arias for Jeff Francoeur isn't that big a deal. It will get a bunch of attention because of who one of the players once was and what he was supposed to become, but while it adds something to the club without taking anything away (especially if Brandon Boggs slides through waivers and is outrighted), there's probably less chance of Francoeur having a major impact as a Ranger than there is of him leaving as lasting an impression in his time here as Kip Wells, or James Baldwin.

Following Francoeur's age 20 season for Class A Myrtle Beach, *Baseball America* named him the game's number 14 prospect. Matt Treanor and Andres Blanco had a combined total of one season in which they were among the top 14 prospects *for their own team*.

That's a large reason why the Texas trades for Treanor and Blanco, two more or less unremarkable National League journeymen who were picked up from Milwaukee (for infielder Ray Olmedo) and from the Cubs (for a player still to be named) in late March, right up against a different roster-finalizing deadline, got only relatively passing mention. They had little in their past to hang much of a story on, little was given up to get them, and little (at first) was expected of them.

All of that is true about Francoeur, other than the past promise. He was third in the Rookie of the Year vote at age 21—despite not arriving in the big leagues until July. He drove in 100 runs in each of his first two full seasons with the Braves, winning a Gold Glove in the second of those years. If you'd asked 100 baseball people then what Francoeur would be at age 26, even the most pessimistic would have never pegged him for a sub-.300 base-reacher and sub-.700 OPS'er who'd slide all the way through league-wide waivers en route to being traded to his third team, for an out-of-options infielder that had been designated for assignment and cleared waivers himself, to fill a bit role on a playoff contender that may not even lead to a post-season roster spot.

Treanor and Blanco weren't career disappointments, and thus weren't really news, when they were picked up in March. Francoeur has the *Baseball America* past, and the $5 million contract (which will be covered by the Mets while Texas pays for Arias, essentially), and that's what makes this trade different from, say, the addition two weeks ago of Alex Cora, who had been let go by the Mets himself.

Yet in a couple months, Francoeur will be a 26-year-old, in good health, non-tendered before getting through his arbitration years.

For now, as rosters expand with the arrival of September, Francoeur—who was reportedly picked up after efforts to get Boston's Mike Lowell or Colorado's Ryan Spilborghs or the Dodgers' Reed Johnson were denied, not to mention the trumped waiver claim on Manny Ramirez—will give the club some flexibility in a few ways.

He can make a run at giving Texas the right-handed bat off the bench that's been missing. (He's hitting .278/.355/.412 against lefthanders this season, after a .344/.356/.521 slash in 2009. And for what it's worth, though he's 2 for 12 in his career against C.C. Sabathia, he's 5 for 8 with a double and home run off of Andy Pettitte.)

He's still playable on an outfield corner (great arm, not much else).

Both of those things make it easier to sit (or pinch-hit for) Julio Borbon against tough lefthanders.

Down the stretch he's a guy who can help the Rangers give Josh Hamilton and his knee some extra down time and avoid having to play David Murphy every single day.

Basically, he's a fallback for an outfield in which every regular has issues (overall production or splittiness or health). And his presence on the bench gives the club more options to match up in key late-inning at-bats, especially with an expanded roster that's going to be heavy on extra defenders with not a lot of extra punch.

Plus, not that Jorge Cantu doesn't have his own future to play for, but Francoeur has something to prove, especially given his awful .190/.269/.305 second half and recent ill-advised playing time demands. He'll be a free agent this winter, probably needing a positive finish just to land a big league deal.

Francoeur has gone, in short order, from a Rookie of the Year phenom and established pre-arbitration middle-of-the-order threat to an underachieving player traded for Ryan Church to a role player traded, with cash that wasn't essential, for Joaquin Arias.

He's not a great player. The Rangers aren't expecting him to be. They're expecting him to be a minor upgrade in limited situations over some players, an option to lighten the September load on others. The whole time he'll try to make a case to be included in October, when rosters shrink back down to 25.

In other words, he's less important on this club than Treanor or Blanco. Even if the trade to get him, because of the time of year and the upside he was once thought to have, generates more ink.

September 1, 2010

Four Rangers have joined the club for tonight's finale in Kansas City, and one has departed.

Texas has activated second basemen Ian Kinsler and Cristian Guzman from the disabled list and recalled righthander Pedro Strop from Oklahoma City. Outfielder Jeff Francoeur has joined the team. None will start tonight. Kinsler will bat sixth on his return to the lineup on Friday.

Lefthander Cliff Lee was sent back to Arlington, where he received a trigger point injection in his lower back to relieve pain and inflammation. Lee's tentatively expected to make Monday's start against Toronto (which will come on one extra day of rest, which tomorrow's off-day is affording the whole rotation), dependent on how his regular side session goes this weekend in Minnesota.

There will be further roster expansion later this month, but for now the Rangers are trying to disrupt Oklahoma City's playoff push as little as possible. Righthanders Scott Feldman and Dustin Nippert are with the RedHawks on rehab assignments.

Ron Washington told reporters that he plans to start Francoeur in right field against lefthanders, ending the alignment that had Jorge Cantu at first base and Mitch Moreland in right. It will be interesting to see who starts at first base against lefties.

September 1, 2010

Ron Washington told Eric Nadel on the radio pregame show that Cliff Lee is slated to start in Toronto on Tuesday night, giving him two extra days of rest after last night's start in Kansas City. Tommy Hunter will go on Monday afternoon, on regular rest.

September 1, 2010

Welcome back, Nellie.

In spite of an ordinary 31-30 record since June 24, Texas leads the West tonight by 9.5 games—matching the largest lead it's had all year.

The Magic Number is 21.

This race is over.

But there's plenty of work to be done before October, primarily getting several players healthy and into much better grooves than they're in right now, and sorting out the best mix of 25.

This is pretty stinkin' fun.

P.S. Dial ahead three months. Michael Kirkman, Mitch Moreland, Tanner Scheppers, and Jurickson Profar for Billy Butler. Who says no?

(Answer: The Royals.)

(And the Rangers.)

September 2, 2010

Yankees 5, A's 0. Just finished.

The division lead is now 10 games, and the Magic Number is 20.

To celebrate, now through this Sunday I'll sell copies of the 2010 Bound Edition for $20 (a five-buck discount) and copies of any other Bound Edition (1999 through 2009) for $10 (a five-to-ten-buck discount). If you're interested, you can order through PayPal (the GJSneaker@sbcglobal.net account) or by sending a check or money order to:

Jamey Newberg
Vincent Lopez Serafino Jenevein, P.C.
Thanksgiving Tower
1601 Elm Street, Suite 4100
Dallas, TX 75201

Also, you can now watch about 35 minutes from Monday night's Q&A with Chuck Greenberg and Chuck Morgan at Sherlock's, in HD quality, at DallasSportsNetwork.tv. Thanks to Ted Price for recording the Q&A and loading it up.

Finally, a reminder: Much of tonight's edition of "Rangers Insider," which airs at 11:30 p.m. on Fox Sports Southwest, was recorded Monday at our event.

September 3, 2010

Labor Day Weekend
But there's much work to be done
Ready, set, ready

Just two more off-days, September 13 and 16, over these 31 days. The next one after that will be Monday, October 4, eve of the playoffs.

The only intrigue left on the Rangers' schedule is whether the clincher comes in Los Angeles or Oakland on the back end of the September 17-26 trip, or against Seattle or Los Angeles at home over the final seven. I'm not rooting for the Rangers' division lead to shrink over the next few weeks, but yeah, I am. I'd really like to see Texas come back from that last West Coast trip with a seven-game lead, at most.

An interesting, surprising note in the agate type yesterday: the Mets purchased catcher Mike Nickeas as part of the club's September roster expansion. The 27-year-old, traded by Texas to New York in 2006 for outfielder Victor Diaz, considered retiring last winter but

Newberg Report: The Expanding Horizon

Texas using September rules with short-term emphasis

By Jamey Newberg / Special to MLB.com

September 2, 2010

It's a bit of strange provision, that Rule 2(c)(2)(A), which allows clubs to expand the active roster from 25 players to as many 40-man roster members as they wish from Sept. 1 until the end of the regular season. A contending club could conceivably carry 15 or 16 pitchers or more for the most important games of the season, creating the ability to match up relievers all night long. And if the opponent has a 12-man bench? Buckle up for four-hour games where strategy is nothing like the other five months of the season.

But the rule is what it is, and by Sept. 1 most teams are no longer legitimately in a pennant race, giving them the opportunity to expand with young players they consider candidates to help the next season or ease players returning from injury back into action to get some reps before the season ends.

Prior to 2010, the Rangers were one of those teams every September during Jon Daniels' tenure as general manager, with the possible exception of last season, when the club was hanging on at the fringes of the race, sitting six games behind the Angels as the month began.

In 2006, with the club in third place and nine games back (10 in the Wild Card chase), Daniels used the expansion rules to get looks at Scott Feldman and John Rheinecker, who had been optioned to Triple-A a combined seven different times that year; Frank Francisco, who hadn't pitched in the big leagues since 2004 due to elbow surgery; and rookies Nick Masset and Joaquin Arias, both making their Major League debuts. It's customary to add a third catcher in September, and Texas did so by purchasing the contract of 31-year-old journeyman Miguel Ojeda. But he was the exception as the Rangers used that September to get advance looks at a handful of young players they were evaluating for 2007.

Texas was buried by September 2007, languishing in last place in the West, 19 games back at the end of August. The key move on Sept. 1 was the recall of Edinson Volquez, who was sent all the way back to Class A to start the season after a miserable eight-start debut in Texas in 2006. Volquez made his way back up to Texas with a tremendous summer that included a 14-2, 2.55 mark between Double-A and Triple-A, and he got the Sept. 1 start for Texas and remained in the rotation that whole month. Brought up for their big league debuts were pitchers Armando Galarraga, Luis Mendoza, A.J. Murray, and Bill White. Hank Blalock, Brandon McCarthy, and Travis Metcalf were reinstated from the disabled list. Journeyman outfielder Freddy Guzman got a brief look, as he'd gotten from Texas in the summer of 2006, and third catcher Guillermo Quiroz was purchased from Triple-A, as well.

The Rangers were in second place in the division on Sept. 1, 2008, but were well out of the race (17 games back, 13 in the Wild Card standings). Daniels used September to get additional looks at Taylor Teagarden, Max Ramirez, and German Duran, each of whom had debuted earlier in the season, and White and Metcalf, who were second-year rookies. Wes Littleton was recalled from the farm for ninth and final time as a Rangers reliever, while fellow right-hander Brian Gordon was purchased for his first and only big league bullpen look. Vicente Padilla also returned to the active roster from a hamstring injury, going 2-1, 3.18 in four late-September starts to finish the season with a 14-8, 4.74 mark.

Last year, with the Rangers in second place both in the division (six games back) and the Wild Card race (four games back), the nature of the Rangers' September call ups was clearly different. On the 1st and 2nd the club activated Eddie Guardado, Brandon McCarthy, Jarrod Saltalamacchia, and Esteban German off the disabled list (though Saltalamacchia's contributions would last only one game before he was shut down). Guillermo Moscoso and Warner Madrigal returned to deepen the bullpen, third catcher Kevin Richardson was purchased for the second time in three weeks, and Craig Gentry was summoned to give Ron Washington an extra runner and defensive replacement on the bench. Willie Eyre returned from his 10-day option to Triple-A on the 4th, and Andruw Jones came off the disabled list on the 8th.

Unlike the previous three Septembers, the additions Texas made in 2009 were obviously geared more toward building up for the stretch run than toward evaluating young players for the future. The emphasis on veteran reinforcements will be even more evident this month, but for different reasons as the Rangers protect a sizable lead.

On Wednesday, Texas activated Ian Kinsler and Cristian Guzman from the disabled list and recalled reliever Pedro Strop from Oklahoma City. Jeff Francoeur joined the club. And the club isn't done.

Feldman and Dustin Nippert are on rehab assignments with Oklahoma City and should be back before long. Teagarden is expected to rejoin the Rangers on Friday. Derek Holland returned over the weekend.

Texas, respectful of the RedHawks' stretch run, will probably summon further Triple-A reinforcements in waves, rather than raiding that club now. Doug Mathis and Omar Beltre are bullpen possibilities, as is left-handed reliever Zach Phillips. Ramirez could return. So could Mark Lowe, who came over from Seattle in the Cliff Lee trade, depending on how his rehab work in Surprise is going as he returns from back surgery.

The Rangers have considered the idea of activating Gentry from the disabled list despite his broken wrist, to take advantage of his run tool. Other pinch-running candidates include German and Willy Taveras, though each is off the 40-man roster and would force Texas to drop another player to make room.

Chris Davis, who has had a strong Triple-A season, is seeing time at third base, first base, and left field and could be brought back to give the club another late-inning defender and bat for the bench.

What we're not likely to see is, outside of Phillips, is a big league debut this month. Tanner Scheppers looked like a solid bet at midseason, but with an 8.33 ERA and .362 opponents' batting average in the second half, and a 77-inning workload after throwing only 30 innings between the independent leagues and Arizona Fall League in 2009, the odds are that his season will end once the RedHawks are done playing.

Plus, the auditions got rolling early this season. Alexi Ogando and Mitch Moreland and Michael Kirkman have already arrived and should all be on the roster in October, let alone September.

While the first few years of the Jon Daniels regime saw the Rangers taking advantage of the rules to look at future talent in September, in 2010 things are different. Texas is clearly using roster expansion with the short term in mind. The only thing that the club is evaluating is who can help this month and who deserves to play in October.

gave the game one more shot this season, hitting .276 between AA and AAA before getting Thursday's call-up, his first.

Just as interesting has been Seattle's decision to leave Justin Smoak—and Josh Lueke—in AAA rather than bring both up, as that organization should have nothing on the itinerary at this point other than evaluating players for 2011. The Mariners say they don't want to disrupt AAA Tacoma's season, and won't bring any players up from that club until its Pacific Coast League playoff run is completely over, which could be as late as September 21. The Rainiers are 1.5 games up in their division with four regular-season games to go.

Speaking of the Pacific Coast League, lefthander Michael Kirkman was named yesterday as the 16-team circuit's Pitcher of the Year, based on a vote of league managers, GM's, broadcasters, and media.

September 3, 2010

Yes, you all are right. There is that other bit of intrigue left, the chase for home field, as the Twins were taken to 13 innings last night and lost, 10-9 to Detroit, bringing Texas to within a game and a half of Minnesota as the two teams get set to play three big ones, starting tonight. Texas sends Derek Holland to the mound, with the Twins summoning AAA righthander Matt Fox, a 27-year-old who will be making his big league debut—as scheduled starter Nick Blackburn was pressed into service in the 13th inning last night (taking the loss as he was taken deep by Gerald Laird).

But I still want to clinch at home. What say we sweep these next three from the Twins, go 14-8 through that September 17-26 trip while Oakland goes, say, 17-5 . . . and Minnesota has a losing record over that stretch?

That would work for me.

September 3, 2010

The Rangers have announced the following moves:

- RHP Dustin Nippert reinstated from the 15-day disabled list
- C Taylor Teagarden recalled from Oklahoma City
- LHP Clay Rapada purchased from Oklahoma City
- RHP Omar Beltre recalled from Oklahoma City and placed on the 60-day disabled list with a right ankle sprain (making room on the 40-man roster for Rapada)
- OF Brandon Boggs outrighted to Oklahoma City after clearing waivers

September 3, 2010

According to at least one local report, the Rangers have signed righthander Mark Prior to a minor league contract for 2011. The 29-year-old ex-ace hasn't pitched in a major or minor league game since 2006. He'd last suited up for the Orange County Flyers of the independent Golden Baseball League.

Interesting.

September 3, 2010

The Rangers have announced that Prior will report to Oklahoma City, where he could pitch in relief right away. The RedHawks lead their division by two games with four to play.

In 11 innings with Orange County over the last month, Prior allowed one unearned run, fanning 22 while permitting five hits and walking five (.135/.250/.184).

That's a whole lot of strikeouts. (Flyers teammates Byung Hyun Kim and Cha-Seung Baek each struck out about a batter per inning this season.)

Prior is not expected to show up in Arlington this month.

Count on a Prior/Joe Mauer reference from Josh Lewin tonight . . . .

September 4, 2010

It's a go. Rangers Assistant GM Thad Levine will join us this Wednesday at the Dallas location of Sherlock's for our second game-watching party in nine days.

Details:

WHO: Thad Levine, Rangers Assistant General Manager

WHAT: Q&A session and Rangers-Blue Jays on every TV (Derek Holland is projected to start)

WHERE: Sherlock's Baker St. Pub (9100 N. Central Expressway, northeast corner of 75 and Park Lane)

WHEN: Wednesday, September 8, 2010; Q&A begins at 5:00 p.m., game time is 6:00 p.m.

COST: Free

Bring your A game for Thad. He's played a huge role in the architecture of this team alongside Jon Daniels, and putting a microphone in his hands is like throwing Josh Hamilton a fastball over the heart of the plate. It's gonna be a good time.

September 4, 2010

The team that lost four at home to the team with the worst record in Major League Baseball in July and yet bounced back after the All-Star Break to win five of seven in Boston and Detroit is now 0-11 in Minnesota, New York, and Tampa Bay in 2010, with one more shot at avoiding a winless season in those three teams' ballparks tomorrow (C.J. Wilson against Nick Blackburn) before playing again in one of those buildings a month from now, when the stakes are higher.

Hope the Rangers have got another, bigger bounceback in them. And I don't mean Sunday afternoon.

But as for tomorrow's effort to salvage something in this series, they'll evidently go to battle without Josh Hamilton, though precautionary postgame X-rays on his ribs have apparently come back negative. And probably without Elvis Andrus, who exited the game in the fourth inning with tightness in his right hamstring.

I understand that Oklahoma City, which lost today to Omaha, 2-0, still needs to win tomorrow or Monday to secure its playoff berth, and I understand the mindset behind giving the RedHawks a chance to see things through, but if it's all the same, I'd like to see runner Willy Taveras (who's only been with OKC for three weeks anyway) waiting for the big league team in Toronto before Monday's four-game series gets rolling.

If the 40-man roster is the issue, there's really no need for both Alex Cora and Cristian Guzman to be here now that Andres Blanco is back on the bench. One of them is fine. A player who does what Taveras can do stands a far greater chance to help Texas win a game these final four weeks (and possibly in October) than Cora or Guzman, and while I see the benefit of having one of them around, having both around at the expense of a real pinch-runner doesn't add up.

Injuries, if minor ones, to Hamilton and Andrus and Cliff Lee and Frankie Francisco. Colby Lewis in a bit of a rut these last couple starts. Julio Borbon's inexperience showing up in the outfield and on the bases. All of these things can be easily forgotten in a few weeks, but at the moment there's a bunch of sputtering going on, and while the division doesn't seem to be at risk, the importance of finding some momentum as a club feels a little further out of reach right now, as I allow myself to knee-jerk just a bit.

Concern is not the same thing as panic.

September 5, 2010

In a season full of you-gotta-be-kidding-me, Ron Washington apparently pulled a hamstring muscle during this afternoon's Twins Old Timers' Game in Target Field. He took himself out of the game defensively, though he did proceed to take his second at-bat after that (singling off Jack Morris after singling earlier off Bert Blyleven), exiting for a pinch-runner . . . and then reentered the game again, settling in defensively at second base after playing earlier in center field.

When Eric Nadel recorded his daily pregame spot with Washington, which aired seconds ago but was taped before the Old Timers' Game got underway, he finished the interview by saying: "Wash, take care of those hamstrings." Funny. Almost.

Not as amusing is word from Minneapolis that Josh Hamilton could miss a week, more or less, due to the bruised ribcage he suffered in yesterday's collision with the center field wall, an injury he said this morning makes him "feel like [he's] been in a car wreck."

Or reports that Elvis Andrus will miss two or three games with his own hamstring tightness. Cristian Guzman, not Andres Blanco (or Alex Cora), will get the start at shortstop against his former teammates this afternoon (after looking in his first stint with Texas last month like his own invitation to the Twins Old Timers' Game may not be far off). Guzman will also lead off.

C.J. Wilson is 11-4, 2.98 in 18 starts following a Rangers loss this season. In his last 12 such starts, Texas has won 11 times (including seven straight).

That righty Matt Fox, who virtually shut the Rangers offense down Friday night in his big league debut, permitting two runs over 5.2 innings? Minnesota designated him for assignment this morning, according to Joe Christensen of the *Minneapolis Star-Tribune*, to make room for pinch-runner and defensive sub Ben Revere.

Speaking of pinch-runners, Oklahoma City clinched a playoff berth last night (with Albuquerque's loss). Free Willy Taveras.

For what it's worth, the RedHawks game notes no longer list Scott Feldman as today's scheduled starter, instead denoting "TBA" for the afternoon assignment. Whether that's because Texas is holding Feldman back in case he's pegged to make Cliff Lee's Tuesday start (Lee was reportedly scratched from that start this morning, once and for all), or for some other reason, it might be interesting to see who takes the ball when that game begins at 4:05.

Mark Prior is supposed to make his Oklahoma City debut in relief at some point in that game.

Among the baseball things I'm most grateful for: That Oakland traded Carlos Gonzalez (and Huston Street and Greg Smith) to Colorado for Matt Holliday two years ago. Oakland's 2007 trade of Dan Haren and Connor Robertson to Arizona for Gonzalez, Brett Anderson, Chris Carter, Aaron Cunningham, Dana Eveland, and Smith was that club's Teixeira Trade, but moving CarGo a year later—who at age 24 is an MVP candidate—did the American League a huge favor.

According to Patrick Newman of NPB Tracker, the Rangers, Mets, and Rays were among the teams on hand to scout 24-year-old Japanese righthander Yu Darvish yesterday.

September 5, 2010

From the August 13, 2006 Newberg Report, about something that happened 10 years before that:

On Friday I went to the Alumni Legacy Luncheon, honoring the 1996 playoff team, and I wish the room held 50,000 rather than 500. Table number 33 was near the back of the room, but I'm certain we had the best seats in the house, because eight of us had a full hour and half with Dave Valle. I asked him if the story Rusty Greer told on the Ticket a couple weeks ago was true—the story about Valle calling a team meeting on August 9, 1996, telling Johnny Oates that he and his staff were not excused from the meeting, and neither were the trainers or the equipment guys or the bullpen catcher.

Coming off two losses in Detroit, which cut the Rangers' division lead over Seattle to two games, Valle told teammate Dennis Cook on the plane to Toronto that he felt like he needed to say something to the team but wasn't sure it was his place. "Cookie" told Valle, at the time a 12-year big league veteran with all of 62 at-bats in four months as Pudge's backup, that he'd earned the right to speak up.

Valle got in the face of every man in that clubhouse, the players and the trainers and the equipment guys and the bullpen catcher—and the manager—and challenged each of them: "Are you willing to do what it takes to win?"

Picture a second lieutenant lining up the troops, side by side, barking the same question, the same command, at each of them. Starting with the Senior General. "Are you willing to do what it takes to win?"

Johnny Oates, who had just granted Valle permission to hold the meeting and asked when the coaches should vacate the room, only to be told by Valle that nobody *was excused from the room, responded to his backup catcher: "Yes, sir."*

The Rangers reeled off seven straight wins. The division lead was extended to seven games, a season high (and without checking, probably a franchise high for the 25-year-old club).

Valle talked about the lead that subsequently almost disappeared, a nine-game cushion on September 11 that shrunk to one game on September 20 when Garret Anderson hit that two-run double that I'll never forget, that shot to left-center that turned a win into a loss in five seconds. Mark McLemore had given Texas a 5-4 lead in the top of the 10th. Mike Stanton got Jim Edmonds and Tim Salmon out to start the bottom of the inning, but then gave up singles to George Arias and Rex Hudler. And then Anderson almost cost me my life.

Valle said he was the most shocked person in the clubhouse when he saw his name in the starting nine the next day. Oates was notorious for his etched-in-granite lineups. Valle, as he put it himself, was like a backup quarterback, "getting to play every third Sunday." But with eight games to go and the team reeling, seemingly about to squander its chance at a first-ever playoff berth in cataclysmic fashion, Oates sat Pudge and put Valle in the lineup to catch John Burkett.

Valle homered to left off Jim Abbott in the seventh, highlighting a 2 for 4 night and a 7-1 Rangers win. It was the last of Valle's 77 lifetime home runs. And, in his words, maybe the biggest.

Texas would finish the year with six wins in those final eight games, and an invitation to the American League playoffs. The clincher came on September 27, a surreal 15-inning loss to the Angels that was dissected by a simple flip of the out-of-town scoreboard, late in the game, from "9" to "F," next to "SEA 1" that stood above "OAK 8." The Mariners were done, and the Rangers played on, losing the game that wouldn't end and then hugging each other on the field as fireworks went off forever and we all heard Holtzie's voice over the P.A. system, narrating the moment and failing to disguise that he was as overcome as any of us. I was in the stands until 2 a.m. that night.

Dave Valle said the best moment of his baseball career was when his boys were doused in champagne on September 27, 1996 (well, September 28), during a clubhouse celebration that didn't end until 5 a.m.

* * *

I don't know what's going to happen the next seven weeks, and neither do you and neither does Michael or Mark or Aki, or Buck or JD.

I can see Valle's finger in my face, asking if I'm willing to do what it takes to win.

I am. See you at the yard.

I've always hated the last two paragraphs of that report, because even on my own cheesiness scale it stands out as pathetic.

But in every season, every decent season at least, there's a moment when that Valle story is one I can't get out of my head, and right now it's there, and I need to go get something to eat to stop thinking about the last 30 minutes, and the last 10 games.

September 6, 2010

According to Ryan Aber of the *Daily Oklahoman*, infielder Esteban German is headed to join the Rangers in Toronto, giving Texas a legitimate pinch-runner. The 32-year-old, who played second base, third base, shortstop, center field, and left field for the RedHawks this season, stole 50 bases in 126 games, getting caught only seven times.

German is not on the 40-man roster, but since this move suggests that the idea of activating outfielder Craig Gentry at some point despite his broken wrist was ultimately dismissed, a move of Gentry to the 60-day disabled list could create the roster spot. On the other hand, there's no reason for Cristian Guzman and Alex Cora to both be here to back up Andres Blanco backing up the middle infielders and third baseman, and especially since German can play all over the infield, it would also make sense that he take either Guzman's or Cora's roster spot.

As for those "If the Rangers simply go .500 the rest of the way, Oakland would have to win 150,000 games and lose two to catch them" pronouncements, which I've now seen two dozen of the last few weeks, please stop. The second part sure paints a bright picture, but everyone seems to assume that the first part—that Texas can go on autopilot and win at least as many as it loses from here on out—is a given. Clearly, it's not.

Over the last 10 games, only one team in all of baseball has won fewer than the Rangers' three. The focus shouldn't be on what Oakland needs to do, but on what the Rangers need to do.

And that one team that's lost more than Texas has over the last 10? San Diego, whose seemingly insurmountable lead in the NL West has now shrunk to one game, with four weeks to go.

The Rangers need to start winning games. Can we just leave it at that?

September 6, 2010

The Rangers have purchased the contract of infielder Esteban German, designating infielder Alex Cora for assignment.

September 7, 2010

The American League West got off to a decent start this season. As the schedule approached mid-June, three of four teams were over .500.

But imagine if the standings looked like this in the middle of that month:

	W	L	W-L%	GB
OAK	34	29	.540	—
TEX	31	34	.477	4.0
LAA	25	38	.397	9.0
SEA	24	42	.364	11.5

Pretty ugly.

That's what has happened in this division since June 24 (when the Rangers' 11-game win streak came to an end).

Among the things I tweeted as yesterday's third inning was falling apart:

Right now it's hard to put a finger on how this team was able to do what it did in June. But thank goodness it did it.

Texas went 21-6 in June, a historically dominant month for this franchise. The rest of the season: two games under .500.

There's rain in the forecast here tomorrow, but not under the roof in Toronto, where the Rangers, after sending Scott Feldman out tonight against Shawn Marcum in a recurrence of the two clubs' Opening Day matchup, will give the ball tomorrow to Derek Holland, who will face "To Be Determined" for the second straight time out.

The last one didn't work out so well, when Holland was decent enough but Minnesota emergency starter Matt Fox shut the Rangers down before getting designated for assignment afterwards. Early word is that Jays lefthander

Marc Rzepcynski could go on short rest, after lasting just four innings Saturday against the Yankees (five runs on six hits and three walks and a hit batsman, 74 pitches overall).

On paper tomorrow's game looks like a better bet than tonight's, as Feldman returns from the disabled list and Marcum comes in on a streak of four straight quality starts (1-1, 1.93) against Oakland, Boston, Detroit, and Tampa Bay. The same Shawn Marcum who took a no-hitter into the seventh inning against Texas on Opening Day, only to see the Rangers bust open for five runs late to walk off with the first improbable win of the season.

When we gather tomorrow at Sherlock's/Dallas for our second game-watching party in a week and half, we'll raffle off three separate pairs of Lexus Club Level tickets to the September 27 game against Seattle. The significance of that one is that it's the Rangers' first home game after a 10-day trip to Seattle, Los Angeles, and Oakland—which means either that Texas will have clinched a playoff berth by then (making it the home crowd's first chance to celebrate that in 11 years), or that the game will be huge, with seven regular season games to go.

We'll have three winners (two tickets each). Raffle tickets will be $10 apiece at the door, with 100 percent going to the Rangers Foundation. We'll conduct the raffle at the end of the Thad Levine Q&A, which gets going at 5:00 p.m. and will be emceed by ESPN Radio's Ben Rogers and his close, personal homeboy Jeff "Skin" Wade.

September 7, 2010

Good grief.

September 7, 2010

When I was 20 years younger, after a bad exam or a frustrating Cowboys loss or an awful stretch of Rangers baseball I would grab my keys and head to the batting cages, hitting fastballs until I'd raised a couple blisters.

These days it's easier, just as therapeutic, more productive, and less self-flaggellating to go read with my kids.

Pick your catharsis. Grab a carton of Blue Bell. Pop in Season 5 of "The Shield." Blog, with the iPod set to random shuffle.

Get your mind off of this, because it's not good for you.

Then get your head right with ball again, and make plans to be at Sherlock's on Park Lane at Central Expressway on Wednesday.

Yes, because you can ask Assistant GM Thad Levine questions from 5:00 until the 6:00 first pitch (and maybe get some one-on-one time after that, too), but that's not the key reason.

Yeah, Rangers-Jays will be on every TV set for us all to watch together, and the event is free. But that's not what I'm getting at.

We'll raffle off two tickets behind the plate to this Sunday's Rangers-Yankees game and three separate pairs of Lexus Club Level tickets to the September 27 Rangers-Mariners game. Still not why I bring this up.

Here's why:

May 19, 2010: *Newberg Report/Fox Sports Southwest live in-game chat*—**Texas 4, Baltimore 3**

June 2, 2010: *Newberg Report/Fox Sports Southwest live in-game chat*—**Texas 9, Chicago 5**

June 30, 2010: *Newberg Report/Fox Sports Southwest live in-game chat*—**Texas 6, Los Angeles 4**

July 25, 2010: *Newberg Report Night at the Ballpark*—**Texas 6, Los Angeles 4**

August 4, 2010: *Newberg Report/Fox Sports Southwest live in-game chat*—**Texas 11, Seattle 6**

August 30, 2010: *Newberg Report Game-Watching Party v.1*—**Texas 3, Kansas City 0**

There was a walkoff win in that mix, a Rich Harden start, a Scott Feldman start (and a separate Feldman vulture win), an Omar Beltre start, an actual Rangers victory (a shutout, no less) in the last 10 days. Plenty of games that didn't look good on paper, but when we've had an event of any sort this season, we're 6-0.

It seems like there's no game these days that looks good on paper, but we're getting the band back together Wednesday night, and maybe that's enough. Call it a playoff beard. Hopping the baseline. Not talking to the pitcher putting up zeroes.

This man asks you: *"Are you willing to do what it takes to win?"*

Please make it out to Sherlock's on Wednesday. A pennant race may be depending on you.

Newberg Report: Rangers' Top Ten Prospects

Prospect depth should keep Texas among highest-ranked farms

By Jamey Newberg / Special to MLB.com

September 9. 2010

With the Minor League regular seasons having come to an end, with every Rangers affiliate but one making the playoffs, it's probably a decent time to take a snapshot of the players who might make up the list of the organization's top 10 prospects.

While the Texas system may not be ranked first or second by *Baseball America* like it was the past two offseasons, this is probably still a top-10 crop, even with all the prospects traded in July and the graduation of players like Neftali Feliz, Alexi Ogando, and Mitch Moreland to Arlington.

1. Martin Perez, LHP, Double-A Frisco: Perez started the season as the Texas League's youngest pitcher and got off to a strong start, but struggled with his command all year and finished with a 5-8, 5.96 record in 23 starts and one relief appearance. There's something to be gained, however, when a young prospect encounters adversity before getting to the big leagues, and Perez remains one of the top two or three Minor Leaguef left-handers in baseball.

2. Tanner Scheppers, RHP, Triple-A Oklahoma City: After a dominant pro debut through the season's first two months out of the Frisco and Oklahoma City bullpens, Scheppers had a month-long audition as a starter for the RedHawks at mid-season that didn't go particularly well. He returned to the RedHawks' bullpen and continued to strike out a batter per inning with upper-90s velocity and a hammer curve, reinforcing that his initial big league impact will likely come in relief, in 2011.

3. Jurickson Profar, SS, Short-Season Class A Spokane: The youngest player in the Northwest League - by seven months - wasn't overmatched by the aggressive assignment and will go into 2011 as one of baseball's top shortstop prospects. Just 17 years old, the former Little League World Series star from Curacao hit .250 as the Indians' everyday shortstop, with only 46 strikeouts in 252 at-bats, and 23 extra-base hits (third most on the team), against a league full of pitchers five years older.

4. Engel Beltre, OF, Double-A Frisco: Obtained from Boston along with David Murphy and Kason Gabbard for Eric Gagné in July 2007, Beltre hadn't turned his tantalizing tools into consistent production until this year. After hitting .331 with power for Class A Bakersfield, he was promoted to Frisco at the start of July and held his own all summer, though he faded late in the season, finishing at .254/.301/.337 in 181 RoughRider at-bats. Groomed as a leadoff hitter, Beltre has hit third and fifth most of the year, and he's a lockdown center fielder with a plus arm.

5. Robbie Erlin, LHP, Class A Hickory: Some experts said the only reason Erlin fell to the third round in the 2009 draft was that he stands under six feet tall. The 19-year-old proved in a league full of hitters three and four years older that he was underdrafted. Erlin posted a 2.12 ERA in 2010, the third-best mark of any starting pitcher in all of Minor League baseball. In 114.2 Crawdad innings, the southpaw fanned 125 and issued only 17 walks.

6. Michael Kirkman, LHP, Texas: A standout 13-3, 3.09 season for Oklahoma City vaulted Kirkman into the big league picture, as he was called on in August to reinforce the Texas bullpen. The 23-year-old was leading the Pacific Coast League in strikeouts at the time of the promotion, featuring a fastball that touched the mid-90s, a slider that PCL managers voted as the league's best, and an effective curve. His dominant numbers against left-handed hitters gave the Rangers confidence that he could succeed in relief, though his big league future could be as a starter. For now, he's a legitimate candidate for the playoff bullpen.

7. Wilmer Font, RHP, Class A Bakersfield: The youngest pitcher in the California League, Font made strides in 2010 before elbow issues cut his season short in July. The big right-hander was hittable for Low A Hickory in the spring but fanned 33 while walking only 13 in 29.2 innings, prompting a promotion to Bakersfield, where he held opponents to a .217 average and struck out 52 in 49 frames, though his poor walk totals had resurfaced before the midseason injury.

8. Robbie Ross, LHP, Double-A Frisco: Ross has made the same two-level split as Font in 2010, with tremendous results. The 5'11" southpaw posted a 12-11, 3.58 record between Hickory and Bakersfield, issuing only 37 walks while fanning 111 in 146 innings, coaxing a remarkable three times as many groundouts as flyouts, and surrendering only four home runs all year. He was rewarded with a promotion to Frisco for the Texas League playoffs.

9. Jake Skole, OF, Short-Season Class A Spokane: The Rangers' top Draft pick in 2010, Skole was challenged (after a brief run in the Arizona League) with an aggressive assignment to the Northwest League, where he was the circuit's third-youngest hitter. A tremendous athlete who would have played defensive back at Georgia Tech had he not signed, Skole played center field for Spokane and hit a respectable .254/.327/.348 in his first pro action.

10. Luis Sardinas, SS, Rookie-Level Arizona League: The 17-year-old from Venezuela was overshadowed by fellow shortstop Jurickson Profar when the two signed last July, but the slick-fielding Sardinas had an outstanding rookie season. He hit .311/.363/.350, getting a hit or walk in 22 of 26 games, holding down the number two hitter role on a club that went 31-24 and reached the AZL playoffs.

September 8, 2010

7-0.

September 10, 2010

Colby's last nine starts
Stuck on nine wins all that time
9-9-10: Win ten

Texas didn't blow Toronto out, but as Lewis spearheaded the split of the four-game series, the final time that the Jays had so much as the tying run at the plate in the 4-2 Rangers victory was with one out in the fifth, when Fred Lewis singled after a John Buck strikeout and was left stranded there as the Rangers righthander fanned both Travis Snider and Dewayne Wise to close out the frame.

So Texas is now 77-63, sitting 7.5 games up on Oakland, which was idle Thursday and kicks off a three-game set against Boston tonight.

Last year after 140 games, the Rangers were 79-61—but 5.5 games behind the Angels (and three behind Boston for the Wild Card spot). They were post-season longshots in the second week of September, even though they were within a game of a 92-win pace, something Nolan Ryan projected for the 2010 version, whose Magic Number is now 16 in spite of what's now just an 89-win pace.

And we know that last year's club didn't come close to that win total, running out of gas over the final three weeks (8-14) to finish with what was, in the end, a disappointing 87-75 record.

It would take that sort of collapse, and a 16-7 finish by the A's, for the two clubs to finish with a 162-game tie atop the division.

Not happening.

But thank goodness the rest of the AL West has been crummy this season.

How about seven wins in these next 11 (three games against the Yankees and two against the Tigers at home, followed by three in Seattle and three in Los Angeles) before Texas visits the A's for four? Starting tonight, when C.J. Wilson faces Javier Vazquez, against whom the game plan should be clear. Vazquez has averaged 19 pitches per inning the last month, a span in which his ERA is 6.53 and opponents' OPS is .929. Texas needs to work counts and get to the weak part of the New York pen early.

It's true that Wilson's last effort, Sunday in Minnesota, was one of his two worst all year, but it came after four straight quality starts, and he's been decent in two starts against New York this year (3.97 ERA), while the Rangers spanked Vazquez in their one 2010 matchup (six runs on eight hits and two walks in 4.1 innings).

Elvis Andrus is expected to return to the lineup tonight.

The best part of Vladimir Guerrero's box score last night: 3 for 4 with two runs scored. That .301/.345/.500 on the right side is a whole bunch of simple slashy goodness, too. But tucked toward the middle, in a game in which Rangers hitters saw a not-so-great 3.49 pitches per plate appearance, is the eight that Guerrero forced Toronto pitchers to throw him in four trips, including just five Shawn Hill pitches in his first three at-bats. The only player in baseball who sees fewer pitches per plate appearances than Guerrero's 3.17 is the awful Yuniesky Betancourt (3.13).

Of course, when you're 4 for 5 lifetime against Shawn Hill, which Guerrero happens to be, sporting a batting average that no other big league hitter can match against the 29-year-old, plate patience is probably an unnecessary bone to pick (and one that shows up lower on the list than Guerrero's baffling insistence on continuing to run wild on the bases).

Guerrero against Toronto this season: .541/.564/.784 in 37 at-bats. Don't be fooled by the edge his on-base percentage has on his batting average. Guerrero didn't work a walk against the Jays in 2010—he was drilled twice.

Darren O'Day has allowed four home runs this year. All came in his four appearances in Toronto's Rogers

Centre. Jose Bautista hit two of them, and Vernon Wells and Jose Molina chipped in with one apiece.

Mitch Moreland's .817 OPS is fourth highest on the Rangers, behind only Josh Hamilton, Nelson Cruz, and Guerrero.

(Yes, Chris Davis was pretty good his first summer, too, clocking in at .880. I'm not saying it's time to offer Moreland an eight-year contract. But he's had a very good rookie summer.)

There was a story written this week suggesting that Esteban German won't be eligible for the playoff roster since he wasn't brought up until after August 31. Simply not true. He's eligible, as a replacement, for instance, for Craig Gentry, who sits on the disabled list.

Hope you were able to catch Thad Levine's hour-long Q&A at the Sherlock's game-watching party on Wednesday night, whether in person or by tuning into Ted Price's live stream over the Web, but if you didn't, Ted should have the video uploaded soon. Lots of good stuff. I'll give you a heads-up when it's available.

I'd very much like to see left-on-left specialist Clay Rapada (10 batters faced, zero hits, one walk, three strikeouts, very little good contact) with this club when camp reopens in February. He fits.

Hope you've been following Scott Lucas's coverage of the minor league playoffs. A Rangers franchise-record six farm clubs out of seven reached the post-season. Win-loss records are never the priority as far as player development is concerned, but there is a certain value placed on prospects learning how to win, and given that this is a system that regularly pushes its players aggressively, making many of its clubs among the youngest in their leagues, and that has seen an extraordinary number of productive players traded away during the season, this has been a remarkable year on the farm.

Wait until you see in Scott's report today what Martin Perez did for Frisco last night.

Although nothing's official yet, the *Austin American-Statesman* speculates that the Rangers' expected AAA move from Oklahoma City to Round Rock won't result in the Astros assuming the RedHawks franchise. Instead, Houston is expected to take over the Nashville Sounds in place of Milwaukee, which would in turn move into Oklahoma City.

As Scott has detailed, Spokane outfielder Jared Hoying, the Rangers' 10th-round pick this summer out of the University of Toledo, was named the Northwest League MVP, on the strength of his .325/.378/.543 slash. The left-handed hitter added 20 stolen bases in 62 games. Spokane manager Tim Hulett is the league's Manager of the Year for the second time in three years.

The Rangers' Arizona Fall League (Surprise Rafters) contingent will include righthanders Adalberto Flores, Danny Gutierrez, and Eric Hurley, lefthander Tim Murphy, catcher Jose Felix, infielder Davis Stoneburner, and outfielders Engel Beltre and Joey Butler. Hickory pitching coach Brad Holman will serve in that same capacity for the Rafters. The AFL begins play on October 12.

Boston claimed Matt Fox off waivers, after Minnesota designated the righthander for assignment following his standout big league debut against Texas a week ago.

Jarrod Saltalamacchia has three hits in 10 Boston at-bats—and they're all doubles. He also has four walks, and no strikeouts. He's caught one of four runners attempting to steal.

The Rangers' highest unsigned pick in 2006, lefthander Kevin Angelle, was traded by the Wichita Wingnuts of the independent American Association to the York Revolution of the independent Atlantic League.

Playoff preview in Arlington this weekend? Texas and New York aren't at full strength, but since we're less than a month from playoff baseball, the undercurrent will be there, with three near-sellouts in store. Make no mistake: this series is sort of a big deal.

September 10, 2010

Lest you forget . . . .

Friday nights in Texas are *High School Football*, dammit.

So endeth this lesson.

September 11, 2010

C.J. Wilson's short night led Texas to use a franchise-record 11 pitchers, who combined to allow one run (on Pedro Strop's bases loaded walk in the sixth) over 10 innings.

Ron Washington summoned Matt Harrison, Strop, Alexi Ogando, Michael Kirkman, Dustin Nippert, Clay Rapada, Neftali Feliz, Darren O'Day, Darren Oliver, and

Scott Feldman, and he might have even slipped Gary Mielke, Rosman Garcia, Mike Bacsik Sr., Mike Bacsik Jr., DeWayne Vaughn, and the feared tag team of Dale Mohorcic and Cecilio Guante in there at some point.

If Tommy Hunter doesn't go deep tonight, maybe we'll see Duff Brumley, Eric Moody, Danilo Leon, and Tanyon Sturtze come to the rescue.

If those guys aren't available, Texas could summon Guillermo Moscoso and Zach Phillips from Oklahoma City, whose season and 28-year run as the Rangers' AAA affiliate came to an end last night. (More on that in Scott Lucas's report later today.) Doug Mathis is on the 40-man roster, too, but he started last night's playoff loss to Memphis.

Chris Davis is heavily rumored to be on his way back to Arlington as well. He pitched a bit at Navarro College, you know.

But really, only Strop and Oliver and Feldman and O'Day are probably in need of a night off.

If the audio file attachment of Eric Nadel's walkoff call didn't work for you last night, you can click the "Media/ Audio" link on the Newberg Report website and listen to it—and also to Cruz's extra-inning, walkoff blast against Boston on August 13 and a couple other things.

You can also go to the SportsNet New York website for an online appearance I did yesterday, helping host Ted Berg preview this series.

The Rangers probably won't catch Minnesota for home field, and the A's probably won't catch Texas for a post-season berth, but one thing that got lost a bit in last night's awesome awesomeness was that, with New York losing and Tampa Bay winning its own game in the ninth, the Rays have pulled to within a game and a half of the Yankees as those two clubs battle for home field and Wild Card, with the loser in that race likely hosting Texas when the playoffs get underway.

Hunter's job tonight is to eat innings. His teammates' job is to continue punishing A.J. Burnett, whose ERA is 8.10 in his last four starts.

Six Rangers have homered off of Burnett, though that includes Josh Hamilton, who's out indefinitely but was right in the middle of the home plate scrum last night, awaiting Cruz, whose three-run bomb off Burnett on June 2 last year was all that Texas could muster in what was a 12-3 loss to New York.

Burnett may not end up in New York's playoff rotation, and tomorrow's starter Dustin Moseley won't either, and as we've discussed this series in many ways shouldn't really be thought of as a playoff preview.

But there's a playoff atmosphere in Arlington this weekend, and if the Yankees can hold off the Rays over these next three weeks—and maybe even if they can't—tonight and tomorrow won't be the last time these two teams tee it up in Texas this year.

One thing that last night reinforced: I'm not going to sit here and predict we might have a new Senor Octubre, but Nelson Cruz sure likes bringing the Boomstick out when the moment is big.

September 11, 2010

Yes. I screwed up this morning and wrote that the loser of the battle between the Yankees and Rays for the AL East crown will host Texas in Game One of Round One of the playoffs. That's 100 percent wrong. The winner of that race hosts Texas, and the loser goes to Minnesota. (There's still a small chance that the loser will travel to Texas, if the Rangers manage to catch the Twins in win-loss record, but there's no chance that the Wild Card would host Texas.)

Sorry for the mistake. I was probably still intoxicated by my outstanding Cecilio Guante reference.

September 12, 2010

Tampa Bay drills Toronto, 13-1.

Mariano Rivera drills Jeff Francoeur, reenacting the Randy Johnson GEICO commercial. (Only with slightly less of a flesh wound.)

And just like that, as Texas reduces its Magic Number to 14, the Rays pull to within half a game of the Yankees and a possible first-round matchup with the Rangers. New York travels to Tampa after today's series finale in Arlington.

Francoeur is now 5 for 13 (.385/.400/.385) with one big hit-by-pitch and three RBI as a Ranger, which is two more than Jorge Cantu and Cristian Guzman have in a combined 121 Texas plate appearances.

Francoeur had been 1 for 1 lifetime against Rivera, with a single to center on June 28, 2006, his first full season in the big leagues, a year in which he hit 29 homers and drove in 103 runs at age 22, looking like he was embarking on a extraordinary career, one that would look nothing like a series of events that would see him traded unceremoniously for Joaquin Arias in an August 31 waivers trade four years later.

If you recorded the game, go back and look at what Ian Kinsler did with the first pitch he saw from Rivera, grounding it foul. Look at Kinsler's swing. Look at it.

Cliff Lee against Dustin Moseley (off of whom the Rangers have hit .347/.411/.520 in 24.2 innings) today, and New York will certainly give Rivera the day off.

If Lee, who says his back is better, returns to form this afternoon, Texas stands a real chance of sweeping New York in a series the Yankees needed, without Josh Hamilton. In a season full of mind-blowing moments, that would rank up there, even if not as high as the greatest closer of all time losing a game on a hit batsman.

September 12, 2010: Cliff Lee's Back.

That's all. Just had to corn things up with that headline. Couldn't help myself.

Volume three forthcoming.

September 12, 2010

We were reminded all weekend of Step One, as Mark Teixeira manned first base in the road grays, going 2 for 13 with no extra-base hits. He's a tremendous player, who made this team a lot better when he was moved.

We saw a whole lot of Step Two today, as Julio Borbon (added to the organization in June 2007) and Elvis Andrus (July 2007) and Neftali Feliz (July 2007) played up to the moment and looked like anything but second-year big leaguers in helping Texas complete an impressive sweep of baseball's best team.

And, of course, we saw today what Step Five was all about, as Cliff Lee carved up the team everyone expects him to join three months from now. Eight-plus innings from Lee, just two hits, and an uncharacteristic three walks—including to the first batter he faced and the last (Derek Jeter in each case). Just five strikeouts, but 14 groundouts and an efficient 109 pitches. Outstanding.

You and I made as many plays today as David Murphy did. Borbon and Nelson Cruz had a combined four touches: Two flyouts to right, Eduardo Nunez's single to center that broke up Lee's no-hitter in the sixth, and Jeter's RBI double to right center.

Nunez is the player the Yankees refused to part with in order to get Lee from the Mariners in July.

It was only the second time in Lee's 12 Texas starts that he delivered a strong effort and also got run support, and it now feels, just maybe, that we're about to see a string of those.

The last time Texas swept the Yankees at home was in 1996, a season in which the Rangers would eventually win Game One of the ALDS, in New York. The Rangers-Yankees karma since then has been lousy, but none of the players or coaches or baseball operations folks here now were here then (save Darren Oliver), and maybe this little three-game set did a tiny bit to minimize whatever stigma might still be attached, if there's actually any of that which exists other than with the fan base and media. (Then again, there's that 0 for 3 in New York this season.)

Up against Texas high school football Friday, college football Saturday, and NFL Sunday, the Rangers averaged nearly 46,000 per game for the series, the second-most ever for a three-game series in 39 seasons of baseball in Arlington. And now the Rangers get what amounts to two nights off. They can catch Dallas-Washington later this evening and some Monday Night Football tomorrow night, like the rest of us. Then it's back to work.

The Magic Number stands at 12, as Oakland just fell to Boston, 5-3. The A's kick off their series in Kansas City tomorrow afternoon, while Texas kicks back and waits for Detroit to arrive for a Tuesday-Wednesday two-gamer. The A's next travel to Minnesota, while Texas will be in Seattle for a series that Lee should close out on Sunday.

The Rangers won't seal a playoff spot that weekend, but they'll be a bunch closer to it by then, and the way Lee pitched today, they suddenly look a bunch more like a team that has a chance to do something big in the post-season.

September 14, 2010

The league has issued a one-game suspension for Ian Kinsler's actions in coming onto the field to join in the Friday night walkoff celebration following Nelson Cruz's home run. Dumb rule, but Kinsler should have never gotten himself thrown out in the first place.

He's appealing the suspension (at least for now) and is in tonight's starting lineup.

Josh Hamilton tried taking some cuts today but shut his session down after about 25 swings when he felt pain in his left ribcage. There's still no timetable for his return.

Frankie Francisco had an MRI today on his own ribcage strain but Dr. Keith Meister hasn't yet interpreted the results.

Taking advantage of this week's two off-days, the Rangers will move Cliff Lee's next start one day up to Saturday (which still gives him an extra day of rest), pushing Tommy Hunter back to Sunday, meaning he'll be going on seven days' rest.

The Round Rock Express have called a press conference for Thursday, during which it's been heavily speculated that the AAA club will announce a new affiliation with the Rangers.

Texas will open the 2011 season at home against Boston on Friday, April 1.

Derek Holland needs to start throwing more strikes.

September 14, 2010: Magic Number Update

September 15, 2010

I've been a little under the weather the last couple days, so I've reached out to our pal north of the border to pinch-hit today. You might remember this guy from a couple entries he shared with us in 2006.

But first, two quick things.

Huge thanks to Scott Lucas for his best year of daily reporting on the Rangers minor league system yet. I doubt we've seen his ceiling yet, though—instead of eight AAA games a season to report on in his backyard, he'll now get more than 70. Awesome work this year, man. Thanks.

The video of Thad Levine's Q&A with us at Sherlock's last week is now online at DallasSportsNetwork.tv, thanks to Ted Price. Among the highlights: a fascinating explanation of the process the club goes through when pursuing a trade, with a specific walk-through for us on the Cliff Lee deal, and some comments on how the organization views the catcher position in the short term.

(By the way, not only did that night's Game-Watching Party boost this season's Newberg Report event record to 7-0, it also broke the team's five-game skid and kicked off what is now a six-game win streak.)

OK. Behave for the sub.

THE NOUVEAU-BERGERON REPORT

The tragic number for the Jays is now down to four. It would be a waste of time talking about tonight's game in Baltimore or the weekend series in Boston. This isn't a bad team—we'd be in second place in the AL West—but there's plenty of work to be done if we're gonna make any noise the next few years in the East. Let's look at something two of the four teams who will be in the playoffs this year did in 2007 to help get them where they are now.

Texas traded Mark Teixeira (and Ron Mahay) to Atlanta at the July trade deadline that year, getting future cornerstones Elvis Andrus and Neftali Feliz, neither of whom had yet reached Class AA, plus rookie catcher Jarrod Saltalamacchia and lefthanders Matt Harrison (AA) and Beau Jones (Low A).

That November, Tampa Bay traded Rookie of the Year runner-up Delmon Young to Minnesota for young righthander Matt Garza and shortstop Jason Bartlett. (The Rays also gave up utility infielder Brendan Harris and minor league outfielder Jason Pridie, who the Twins had drafted via Rule 5 two years earlier but sold back to the Rays, and the Twins parted with relief prospect Eduardo Morlan.)

You think the Braves would like a do-over on that first one? General Manager John Schuerholz, about to vacate his post, got super-aggressive, trading for Teixeira, Mahay, Octavio Dotel, and Royce Ring on July 31, but ended up missing the playoffs for just the second time in 13 years. And the Braves haven't been to the post-season since.

They're two games out of first in the NL East right now. But how much better off would they be if they'd held onto Andrus and Feliz? Or moved those two in separate trades from each other and from Saltalamacchia, who lots of teams wanted, and Harrison, who was Atlanta's top pitching prospect coming into that season and second maybe only to Tommy Hanson at the time of the Rangers trade?

For one thing, if they'd kept Andrus they wouldn't have had to trade the player they felt made him expendable—the regressing Yunel Escobar—two months ago for middle-aged shortstop Alex Gonzalez. (As a Jays fan, I couldn't be happier that they did.)

Toronto has a unique surplus at a key position and an opportunity to get better because of it.

Tampa Bay had Carl Crawford and B.J. Upton in its outfield, Rocco Baldelli bouncing in and out of health, and Desmond Jennings coming when they decided in November 2007 to trade Young, who had some rumoured makeup issues, for a young starter with top-of-the-rotation potential. (They had Elijah Dukes, too, but he would be traded five days after Young was.)

When Atlanta traded Andrus in July 2007, the club had veteran shortstop Edgar Renteria locked up through 2009, and the 24-year-old Escobar two months into his rookie season, hitting .314/.358/.400.

The names aren't as glitzy, but the depth we have in catchers may be almost as strong as what the Rays had in the outfield and the Braves had at shortstop three years ago.

This year at AAA Las Vegas, we had J.P. Arencibia, MVP of the Pacific Coast League. At High A Dunedin, there was Travis d'Arnaud, ranked by Florida State League managers as the circuit's best defensive catcher. At Low A Lansing, A.J. Jimenez was ranked as the Midwest League's best defensive catcher. Some people think Short-Season A Auburn catcher Carlos Perez will be the best of the whole group.

It's the kind of strength behind the plate that the Rangers seemingly had two years ago . . . which illustrates the importance of not holding onto everyone too long.

At the end of the 2008 season, every newspaper in the Boston market and in North Texas, not to mention the ESPN and Fox folks among others, had Gerald Laird and Saltalamacchia and Taylor Teagarden and Max Ramirez lined up on one side, and Clay Buchholz and Justin Masterson and Michael Bowden and Daniel Bard and Nick Hagadone on the other, and constructed a thousand trade rumours. Who knows if the Rangers had any real opportunities to make a catcher-for-pitcher deal with the Red Sox that winter? But if they did, it's too bad for them that they didn't pounce.

And in short order, Texas has gone from catching-rich to completely unsure about the position going forward.

There's a lesson there.

And for Toronto, I think, an opportunity.

To draw a comparison, John Buck is probably our Laird. Nice player, but he's not the long-term answer, both because he's 30 years old and a free agent, and because Arencibia, the offense-first Saltalamacchia equivalent, is probably ready. While he's not as close to the big leagues, d'Arnaud is what Teagarden was in 2008, an agile defender who throws well and profiles as a regular despite less upside with the bat. There's not really a Ramirez equivalent in the Toronto system, just as there wasn't a Perez down below two years ago in the Rangers organization (though in retrospect maybe Jose Felix was that guy).

So if the idea is to take advantage of that depth now, rather than hope our guys' value builds even further, the question becomes whether to trade one of the catchers in a huge deal, like the Braves did with Andrus, or to move one in more of a value-for-value swap, like the Rays more or less did with Young.

The Jays system is average. There are high-end righthanders Kyle Drabek and Zach Stewart, plus a leadoff center field type in Anthony Gose, all of whom were acquired in trades, plus 2010 first-round righty Deck McGuire, Cuban shortstop Adeiny Hechavarria, and the catchers. Toronto needs to be building its young core, not loading up for one veteran player and mortgaging the top tier of the farm to do it.

So I like the Rays-Twins model better.

Which catcher do I trade? Depends on which one it takes to get the player we want, of course, but it seems that d'Arnaud should be the guy. Traded a year ago himself in what was Philadelphia's own Teixeira deal—Drabek, d'Arnaud, and Michael Taylor from the Phillies to the Jays for Roy Halladay (Taylor was flipped to Oakland for Brett Wallace, who was then sent to Houston in July for Gose, who had come from Philadelphia in the Roy Oswalt trade)—the 22-year-old was having a strong year at High A before a back injury cut his season short at the end of July. Would we be selling low since d'Arnaud finished the year hurt? Maybe so, but given the weak state of the position across the league, there could be a team willing to step up on him.

I don't move Arencibia. Let Buck sign elsewhere, and give J.P. the job. Keep Jose Molina around to back him up.

I'd rather not move Perez, and at age 19 with only short-season experience he's not going to key a deal yet anyway.

Jimenez isn't on the same tier as the others.

For me, Arencibia is the answer in Toronto right now, and we can be patient with Perez as he develops. If d'Arnaud isn't so devalued by the back injury that clubs are trying to steal him from us, it would make sense that he'd be the one to move.

Speaking of how the Rangers' catching depth turned upside down the past couple years, that's the team I want to deal with. They could use a long-term answer behind the plate. And they're loaded with trade pieces.

(Also speaking of Texas, you ought to read the outstanding article that good Canadian Jonah Keri published this week on pitching injuries, with its focus on what the Rangers are doing to build and protect their young arms. It's remarkable work.)

You know, it wouldn't surprise me to see the Rangers, who have used Matt Treanor, Bengie Molina, Teagarden, Ramirez, and Saltalamacchia this year, go after Buck this winter, just as they did last off-season. Maybe they go with Buck and Treanor, and keep Teagarden at AAA since he'll have one option left.

Felix will be at AA. Texas can pair him up with d'Arnaud and develop them together. Maybe that's the tandem in Arlington one day.

What do we target from the Rangers? What does Toronto need? In the short term, maybe a first baseman or DH (whichever spot Adam Lind doesn't fill) and some major bullpen help (several key guys are likely leaving this winter). Long term, the way this lineup strikes out, we could use some guys who reach base, and probably another outfielder to develop.

But you can't solve every need in one trade.

And you have to trade wisely. I don't even want to look back at what we did with Michael Young, Felipe Lopez, Cesar Izturis, and Brent Abernathy when we had all of them coming up as middle infield prospects. We traded all of them, and lost in every deal.

I want Tanner Scheppers or Alexi Ogando. Jason Frasor and Scott Downs are probably gone after this season, and who knows if we keep Kevin Gregg around? Either Scheppers or Ogando steps into the bullpen right away and eventually settles in as our Neftali Feliz.

I'd like Mitch Moreland, too, but I'm not sure the Rangers would move him unless they have a plans to bring in a big bat at first base this winter. David Murphy would be a great fit, but that's another player I'd have a hard time seeing the Rangers part with for a future piece, given their plans to contend again in 2011.

I like Pedro Strop, too. He hasn't done it in Texas, but neither did Robinson Tejeda.

And I love Engel Beltre, a five-tool center field talent who started to put things together this year.

Ramirez will be out of options and I like the bat, but if Arencibia settles in as the starter here, his backup needs to be a more dependable veteran. Again, Jose Molina is a perfect fit.

How about this: Travis d'Arnaud and John McDonald (yeah, he's 36, but he's under contract for $1.5 million next year and would give Texas a lockdown defender who can back up at every infield position, plus he's shown a little pop this season) for either Scheppers or Ogando, plus Chris Davis, who has an option left and needs a change of scenery?

Is that too much to ask Texas for? If it is, they're the kind of organization that would probably take a high-reward kid even if he's years away, maybe one from Latin

America. OK, give them 20-year-old Dominican righty Misual Diaz.

Or how about d'Arnaud and McDonald for Beltre and Strop?

Even though young catching is thin right now around the league, there are several teams with a surplus like we have. The Reds have Yasmani Grandal and Devin Mesoraco. The Nationals have Wilson Ramos and Derek Norris. The Rockies have Wilin Rosario, Jordan Pacheco, and Michael McKenry. The Yankees, behind Jesus Montero (man, Seattle screwed up on that Cliff Lee deal), have Austin Romine and Gary Sanchez. Cleveland has Lou Marson (who Philadelphia traded as part of its package for Lee a year ago) behind Carlos Santana.

The point is there are other teams out there with a high-end catcher prospect they can trade. I think the Jays need to jump on this before they find themselves like the Rangers did when they held onto their depth too long.

The Texas catching situation, with Buck and Treanor in the big leagues, Teagarden and Ramirez at AAA, and d'Arnaud and Felix at AA (with Jorge Alfaro and Kellin Deglan developing below, and maybe Vin DiFazio or Tomas Telis if his arm bounces back or Leonel De Los Santos if the bat comes around at all), would suddenly look pretty good again. And Scheppers or Ogando can be our Matt Garza—or we can bring in an upside position player like Beltre that fills a bigger developmental need than d'Arnaud does right now.

So: (1) d'Arnaud, McDonald, and Diaz for Scheppers or Ogando and Davis or (2) d'Arnaud and McDonald for Beltre and Strop. Who says no?

Thanks to my Jays buddies T.A. Seiber, Doron Barbalat (FrontOfficeFans.com), and Mick Doherty (Battersbox.ca) for talking this stuff through with me. Good day.

September 15, 2010: Magic Number Update

After tomorrow's day off, the next one will fall between Game 162 and the American League Division Series.

September 16, 2010

According to our own Scott Lucas, who is right now sitting in the press conference at which this announcement has just been made, the Round Rock Express have entered a four-year Player Development Contract with Texas, during which the Express will serve as the Rangers' AAA affiliate.

September 16, 2010

On the day that the Rangers announced a move of their AAA club from Oklahoma City to Round Rock, word comes this evening from the *Atlanta Journal-Constitution* that the Braves are moving their High A affiliation from the Myrtle Beach Pelicans of the Carolina League, where they'd been for 12 years, to the Lynchburg Hillcats of the same league.

The move, according to the story, is being made because it is expected that the Rangers will soon announce their own High A move from the Bakersfield Blaze of the California League to Myrtle Beach, a franchise that is owned by Chuck Greenberg. The *Myrtle Beach Sun News* reports, in fact, that Greenberg and Pelicans GM Scott Brown have called a press conference for 1:30 ET on Friday afternoon.

Stay tuned.

September 17, 2010

A's near-Royal flush
Was magically propitious
Crazy: Number's eight.

Texas hits the road for the next 10 games, a stretch during which the odds are that the playoff berth gets nailed down. Even the folks in creative for TBS agree that the Rangers are locks:

Thanks to Scott Gann and Katy Roffino for photographing those New York City billboards this week and

Newberg Report: 1990 89ers, Coach Station

Oklahoma City club featured over a dozen future coaches

By Jamey Newberg / Special to MLB.com

September 16, 2010

When the story is told of the final of the Oklahoma City franchise's 28 seasons as a Texas Rangers affiliate, the main characters will probably be Michael Kirkman and Mitch Moreland and Alexi Ogando, who starred on the way up; Chris Davis and Derek Holland and Pedro Strop, who made big contributions after coming back down; and Tanner Scheppers, whose first pro season ended just short of the big leagues. The RedHawks suited up 56 players in 2010, reaching the Pacific Coast League playoffs for the second time in three years.

The story of the Oklahoma City club that took the field at All Sports Stadium 20 years ago, when they were still called the 89ers, seemed far less compelling at the time, but in hindsight there was something staggering about that 1990 club, which posted a miserable 58-87 record, finishing 27.5 games back in the Western Division of the American Association.

Twenty-year-old Juan Gonzalez drove in 101 runs in just 128 games, coming off his big league debut the previous fall, but that wasn't the most remarkable thing about that club, nor was Dean Palmer's underwhelming Triple-A debut or the 14 losses that Mark Petkovsek managed to rack up or the roster spot devoted to right-hander Jeff Bronkey, the only former big leaguer born in Afghanistan.

On a club managed by Steve Smith - who would coach third base in Texas 12 years later—the roster was full of future coaches.

The 89ers' pitching staff wasn't very good, but in its bullpen were future big league pitching coaches Brad Arnsberg, Randy St. Claire, and Wayne Rosenthal, each of whom served in that role for the Marlins, which may or may not have anything to do with the fact that Oklahoma City was then owned by current Marlins owner Jeffrey Loria (Arnsberg, in fact, was also the pitching coach in Montreal when Loria owned the Expos).

Three of Oklahoma City's catchers went on to coaching careers: John Russell, who now manages the Pirates; Chad Kreuter, who was USC's head coach until last month; and Mike Berger, who was an 89ers player/coach from 1991 through 1993 and managed Low A Charleston in 1995 before embarking on what's now been a 15-year run as a pro scout.

Infielders Steve Buechele, Scott Coolbaugh, Gary Green, and Dave Engle all went on to manage in the minor leagues. So did outfielder Nick Capra, who is now the minor league field coordinator for the White Sox. Fellow outfielder Darryl Motley never managed, but he did serve as batting coach for the Kansas City T-Bones of the independent Northern League until this season.

And then there was the utility infielder on that Oklahoma City club, who at age 38 was a year older than the team's manager and who had the fourth-most at-bats of anyone on the roster, even though he hit only .238 and drew just five walks in what would be the final 364 plate appearances of his 20-year pro career.

He might have been the least productive player on a bad minor league team, but on a club with an extraordinary number of future managers and coaches, Ron Washington has since risen to a level in this game as a coach that none of the others can claim.

sharing them with us, and to TBS not only for putting Cliff Lee front and center but also resisting what had to be considerable pressure to go ahead and airbrush "Texas" out and put Lee in those birthright pinstripes. Impressive restraint.

When we recorded the latest edition of Rangers Podcast in Arlington last night, we wrapped up by predicting when Texas would actually clinch, and I went with a week from tomorrow, which I suppose is wishful thinking since that's a 3 p.m. game while the five games preceding it have 9 p.m. local starts.

The soonest that the Rangers can wrap this up, by winning out and Oakland continuing to lose, would be this Monday night, when Texas is in Anaheim and Oakland hosts Chicago.

Keep an eye on Wednesday, too. If, over the 10 games that Texas and Oakland play over the next five days, the Ranger wins plus A's losses total seven, the Rangers could actually clinch Wednesday afternoon, when the White Sox (Edwin Jackson) face Oakland (Brett Anderson) at 2:35 CT in the finale of that series, a game that should end well before C.J. Wilson faces the Angels' Dan Haren at 9:35 CT that night.

But if the division isn't wrapped up by that date, at least the Rangers and A's face off for the following four, making it more likely that Texas can clinch by squeezing the final out, rather than celebrating a scoreboard message. (That assumes that the A's can hold the Angels off from closing the 1.5-game gap between those teams beforehand.)

I'm sticking with next Saturday. If the Rangers and A's stay in rotation, Derek Holland will take the ball that day, facing off against Gio Gonzalez. Jeff Francoeur will have a key hit, cementing his place in Rangers history despite what could be the briefest of stints in the organization.

The 10-game lead that Texas has on Oakland at the moment matches the biggest divisional lead the club has ever held.

I got a couple dozen emails yesterday asking what happens to the players and coaches who suited up for Oklahoma City and for Round Rock in 2010. Easy: They follow their organizations. RedHawks players and coaches will remain Rangers assets, and will be in Surprise in February and March if not let go in the off-season. If reassigned to AAA, they will suit up for Round Rock in April.

I repeat that here for those of you in Northern California, South Carolina, or elsewhere who might wonder the same thing when the Rangers announce this afternoon that they have agreed to a player development contract with the High A Myrtle Beach Pelicans (a Chuck Greenberg franchise), ending a six-year run in Bakersfield.

Myrtle Beach is a four-hour drive from the Rangers' Low A affiliate in Hickory, North Carolina, a distance of 234 miles. I'm not sure how long the flight from Hickory to Bakersfield is, but the towns are nearly 2,400 miles apart. That's not the only reason this transition makes a lot of sense (the Carolina League also tends to be a better environment for developing pitching), but it's a much better situation logistically.

Incidentally, Milwaukee announced earlier this week that it's keeping its AAA club in Nashville, ending speculation that the Brewers would move into Oklahoma City, which would have left Nashville as the likely destination for the Astros now that their affiliation with Round Rock has ended. The Brewers' stay makes an arrangement between Houston and Oklahoma City a strong likelihood.

The MRI on Frankie Francisco's right side showed that his rib cage is healing. He should start throwing Monday.

Darren Oliver's $3.25 million option for 2011 vested when he made his 59th appearance Wednesday night. He's had a tremendous season (2.50 ERA, 63 strikeouts and 10 unintentional walks in 57.2 innings, .234/.286/.358 slash, 1.39 G/F), and would surely have been brought back even if the option had not locked in—though it should be pointed out that he was much sharper in the first half (1.36 ERA, .191 opponents' average) than he has been in the second half (5.00 ERA, .314 opponents' average). Don't expect as heavy a workload next spring.

One scout offered the following assessment of Nelson Cruz to Baseball Prospectus's John Perrotto: "He kind of gets overlooked in that lineup with Josh Hamilton and Michael Young and Vladdy Guerrero and Ian Kinsler, but he's a very dangerous hitter who has learned how to handle off-speed stuff. He's not a flashy guy but you can tell he likes hitting in big situations. That's why he's my pick to be the breakout star of the postseason."

Young was elected to the Arizona Fall League Hall of Fame, along with St. Louis righthander Chris Carpenter. Young played in the AFL in 2000, three months after Texas acquired him from Toronto. He was assigned to the Grand Canyon Rafters that fall along with Joaquin Benoit, Kevin Mench, Jason Romano, Spike Lundberg, and David Elder.

The Rangers' minor league award winners for August: Dominican Summer League righthander David Perez was Pitcher of the Month, Arizona League first baseman Jhonny Gomez was Player of the Month, Spokane third baseman Mike Olt was Defender of the Month, and Spokane righthander Ben Rowen was Reliever of the Month.

Baseball America named Hickory lefthander Robbie Erlin a second-teamer on its Minor League All-Star Team. Erlin's 2.12 ERA was third-lowest among all minor league starting pitchers in 2010.

Juan Gonzalez, age 40, will be teammates with Rangers outfield prospect Miguel Velazquez, age 22, on Puerto Rico's entry in the Pan Am Qualifier tournament.

We'll hit you up with an update once this afternoon's announcement out of Myrtle Beach has been made.

September 17, 2010

According to reports locally and out of Myrtle Beach, South Carolina, the Rangers announced at a press conference at BB&T Coastal Federal Field this afternoon that they have affiliated with the Myrtle Beach Pelicans on a four-year player development contract to serve as the organization's High A farm club. Chuck Greenberg, who owns the Pelicans, was in attendance at the press conference, along with Rangers GM Jon Daniels and Pelicans GM Scott Brown.

As part of the agreement, the Rangers will play an exhibition game in Myrtle Beach on Tuesday, March 29 (opponent to be determined), three days before the 2011 Major League season opens.

September 18, 2010: Magic Number Update

September 18, 2010: Magic Number Update

September 20, 2010

The Cowboys are such a polarizing, hot-button topic that any time I mention them, I get buried in email responses. That's never my intent, any more than when writing about my kids or my much-maligned taste in music, but it is what it is, and I'm sure this post won't be very well received, even though it's really about the Texas Rangers.

I'm a diehard Cowboys fan. My first love was baseball, at least as a participant, but my interest in sports as a fan was born with the Cowboys on TV (which in the mid-'70s was probably a more frequent occurrence than getting a televised Rangers game, as hard as that might be to comprehend today) and any number of family friends to spend an entire Sunday with. The game was the centerpiece. There was too much food before, during, and after. Street football at halftime. Culture shock as I saw emotional boundaries crossed by adults who normally didn't behave that way. All of it was super-cool.

Football isn't as near to my core as baseball is, as you might have gathered, but it's a pretty big deal to me.

And what the Cowboys gave me yesterday—and I've gotten this far with the football talk because I figure, since the Cowboys are who they are, that most of you probably either revel in this or commiserate—was one extra realization why I love my baseball team.

Among the things I tweeted during yesterday's football game was: "What's worse as diehard fan than knowing at fundamental level that your team chronically underachieves (whether on field or off)?" Seriously. We all know exactly why Dallas isn't as good as all the blathering pre-season build-up, and we know with just as much conviction that it won't be fixed.

It's demoralizing.

And yet another reason that to see what this baseball team has done over the last four seasons, choosing growing pains and building the right way as the only truly correct big-picture marketing plan, playing with a chip on its shoulder rather than a bar and grill talk show for every player, proving the naysayers wrong instead of right, is so rewarding.

It's September 20, and the Rangers' Magic Number is six. The Cowboys' is 14, on the wrong end. Some call it the tragic number.

This sort of reminds me, in a way, of how the Rangers' brief run of franchise relevance coincided with one of the darkest periods in Cowboys history. Dallas, coming off its three Lombardi trophies in four seasons when the Rangers kicked off their run of three division titles in four years, was not only bad but painful to watch over that 1996-99 span, averaging 8.5 wins and 7.5 losses under Barry Switzer and Chan Gailey with a roster that should have won more.

Texas had a real chance to put a bigger dent in the market share over the three years after that. While Dave Campo led Dallas to three straight five-win seasons, the Rangers finished in last place in the West those same years, despite having the best player in the world the final two of those.

If only the Rangers had built around Alex Rodriguez the way they should have.

Texas signed Rodriguez in December 2000, five months after the club had traded for Michael Young and six months before Mark Teixeira fell to the Rangers with the fifth pick in the 2001 draft. But the farm system was middle of the pack, a tremendous swarm of journeymen and once-were's were signed to play regular roles, Travis Hafner and Ryan Ludwick got no real chance here, and you don't want to peek at the 2000, 2001, or 2002 Baseball Reference pages to see what the pitching staffs looked like those years.

Rodriguez and Teixeira spent one season (2003) together before Rodriguez asked what he was in this for, and what should have been the emergence of a perennial contender was instead a failed bit.

Then there's Young, who was here before A-Rod arrived and who the veteran took under his wing but who still was presumably one of the "24 kids" Rodriguez couldn't bear to play alongside one more day.

Young has now played 1,496 big league games without so much as a playoff appearance, second in baseball only to Randy Winn's 1,700-plus.

The thing is, Winn has bounced around for five big league teams and has rarely been much more than part of anyone's supporting cast. It's different with Young. When Texas clinches its first playoff berth in 11 years, probably sometime this week, I'm going to be happiest for me. Next to that, I'll be happiest for Young.

My wife the rehabilitation counseling psychologist took the doctor's side yesterday when Jason Witten was on the delivering end of a one-sided, heated argument about his fitness to get back on the field, and while I'm cool with that, I loved the fire he showed. There aren't enough Witten's on that football team.

It wasn't until January 2010 that Witten had a playoff win in his career, which, regardless of whether the team deserved it over his eight seasons, was far too long for that player. Witten is the Cowboys' Young, whose own place on that bad list behind Randy Winn will be erased in a couple weeks.

The baseball team's Magic Number didn't move on Sunday, but it's just a matter of time before that hourglass is emptied, leaving the sole focus on getting Josh Hamilton and Frankie Francisco back in action and in rhythm, sorting out a small handful of unsettled spots on the playoff roster, and generally finding a way to take some general sense of momentum onto the plane that heads east for some of the baseball these guys all play for, and that we've all been waiting for, for years.

It sure beats waiting, for years, for the one thing from my football team that I'm reasonably sure I'm never going to see, and that would be far more upsetting if it weren't for the baseball team which, for plenty of reasons, I feel so much better about investing in emotionally.

September 20, 2010

I've been asked to sit on a panel tomorrow night at the *Dallas Morning News*'s "125th Anniversary Discussion Series" event at SMU, titled "Dallas Sports: Where we've been, where we're headed."

The panel includes:

- Brad Sham, Cowboys Play-by-Play Announcer
- Steve Orsini, SMU Athletic Director
- Tim Cowlishaw, SportsDay Columnist, *Dallas Morning News*
- And, undeservedly, me)

The topics of discussion will include:

- The development of North Texas's love affair with sports
- How local teams, national franchises, and rabid fans shape our culture
- The role of sports in education and entertainmen
- The road ahead: How sports will shape our future

Attendance is free of charge but you need to RSVP if you'd like to attend. The details:

When: Tuesday, September 21, 2010, 7-9 PM

Where: SMU Hughes Trigg Theater

3140 Dyer Street, Dallas, TX

How: Seating is limited. Reserve your space by going to www.dallasnews.com/125th

September 21, 2010

Last night doesn't mean a whole lot, especially when you separate the pitching lines of the guys who won't make the playoff staff from those who will, but there's still something about September games in Anaheim that irritate me.

Josh Hamilton spent more than five hours with Los Angeles-area back specialist Dr. Robert Watkins yesterday, undergoing a bone scan and other diagnostic tests, and is expected to return to Dr. Watkins today to discuss the results—and possibly get some sort of nerve-deadening shot, as last week's cortisone injection hasn't helped his ribcage soreness. The timing of his return is still unknown.

Frankie Francisco's Monday throwing session was delayed another day. He's expected to throw today.

Houston has affiliated with the Oklahoma City RedHawks.

Oakland refuses to move Saturday afternoon's start time, and as a result, due to Fox's national exclusivity and the network's decision not to make that day's game against the A's a national broadcast, the game is, for the moment, is the only one all season not scheduled to be televised. If the Magic Number is 1 or 2 going into that game . . . ho boy.

The Rangers have been working all angles with MLB, Fox, and Fox Sports Southwest for about a month to find a solution that would permit the game to be televised locally. Texas is hoping for a resolution by tomorrow.

Thanks for all your ideas last night for my final MLB.com Top 10 column of the season. I'm happy with the winning suggestion, but could have gone in a dozen different directions. Appreciate the feedback. The column will run on Thursday morning.

Reminder about tonight's "Dallas Sports: Where we've been, where we're headed" panel discussion, hosted by Tim Cowlishaw of the *Dallas Morning News*, at SMU Hughes Trigg Theater from 7:00-9:00 p.m. Seating is free but limited. Reserve your space by going to www.dallasnews.com/125th/ and clicking the "RSVP" link.

September 21, 2010

Evan Grant of the *Dallas Morning News* shares the following update from Jon Daniels on Josh Hamilton's condition:

"Josh saw Dr. Watkins this morning out here in CA. Dr. Watkins had given Josh a CT scan and a spec scan yesterday and another CT scan today. He diagnosed a small stable fracture in the 7th and 8th ribs, that previous tests (2 x-rays and an MRI) had not picked up. Dr. Watkins gave Josh an anti-inflammatory injection at the site of the discomfort, and an epidural nerve-block injection for pain management. It is typically 48-72 hours before it's known whether this treatment has the desired effect. Once the discomfort recedes to a point where Josh is comfortable, he can return to baseball activities."

September 22, 2010

I had a great time at SMU last night, hanging with Tim Cowlishaw and Brad Sham and Steve Orsini at the *Dallas Morning News* panel discussion and getting the chance to hear those three hold forth. Thanks to those of you who came out to the event.

One of the subjects that got Brad most fired up was the mindset of some fans that anything short of a league championship is a failure. The dialogue was launched in a Cowboys context, but Brad got around to suggesting that, even if the Rangers were to go three and out in the first round of the playoffs, if there's anyone who doesn't look at the 2010 season as a success, then the problem is not with the team but with that fan.

I came home and saw much of Colby Lewis's brilliant start in Anaheim, in a ballpark where his lifetime ERA had been 6.43 and his opponents' slash had been .393/.471/.679, and maybe it was because of what we talked about hours earlier at Hughes Trigg Theater, but my thoughts drifted to 1996, 1998, and 1999. Lewis put up a borderline dominant 7-4-2-2-2-10 line, relieved by Darren Oliver, whose Game Three effort in 1996—the first home playoff game in Rangers history—was not all that different from what Lewis did on Tuesday.

Was the 1996 Texas season a success, after the club won Game One in New York and then dropped the next two, with a key defensive play in each game none of us will ever forget, before taking and subsequently spitting up a 4-0 lead in Game Four to get eliminated?

Of course.

How about 1998 and 1999, when Texas managed to score a total of one run in each three-game sweep?

Sure. Disappointing, but it's not easy to play on after 162 in baseball, and the Rangers did so for the second and third times in four years. (Is a similar run of success on the horizon? Baseball Prospectus's Chase Gharrity thinks it just might be.)

Has this road trip been a success? No. The staff has a 2.85 ERA on this swing through Seattle and Anaheim, but the offense has averaged just 2.4 runs a game, and the record on the trip is 1-4. It looks disturbingly like those three playoff runs, when Texas posted an acceptable 3.48 ERA but scored only 1.8 runs per game, winning one of 10.

But this season has been a success, and will stay that way, as long as something impossible doesn't happen over these final 12.

Like we learned in 1996, 1998, and 1999, Texas is vulnerable to great pitching.

Know who else is?

Everyone.

It's not an excuse. But it's a September reminder of what baseball often looks like in October.

The Rangers have also had run-scoring stretches this year when it almost didn't matter who took the mound against them, but you certainly can't count on that in the playoffs, and if last night's game took place a couple weeks from now, we'd probably be talking for years about Nelson Cruz's decision to bunt in the seventh, much in the same way Dean Palmer's throw on that 12th-inning Game Two bunt and Kevin Elster's non-existent range in Game Three are as lasting 1996 memories, sadly, as Juan Gonzalez's epic symphony of destruction in that series.

Close, low-scoring baseball is typical in the post-season. From that standpoint the way this latest run of games has been playing out might be useful, an opportunity to get used to games in which a seventh-inning at-bat or second-inning play in center field could be as pivotal as a ninth-inning matchup against the other guys' closer with the game on the line.

You want to be healthy going into October, you want to have your rotation clicking and your bullpen steadied and your lineup riding a little momentum, but you also want to be playing smart baseball, not pressing, and not making terrible decisions or fundamental mistakes that could live forever if they were to happen in a best-of-five or best-of-seven.

It's been a remarkable month, as Texas, after winning on September 1, lost five in a row, then won seven straight, and since then has lost four of five. These wild swings are a little nerve-racking, especially with what's on the horizon.

As a result of this latest slide, the Rangers will head to Oakland after tonight's game with a Magic Number somewhere between four to six, with four to play against the A's.

It's going to be a big weekend.

Without Josh Hamilton, who is shooting to return to action sometime during next week's homestand that will close out the regular season. Or Frankie Francisco, who threw pain-free yesterday and might be on a similar timetable.

And without a blackout, it appears. No official announcement yet, but local reports indicate that the Rangers are nearing a resolution with MLB and Fox to get Saturday afternoon's game televised locally (possibly on KDFW/Channel 4). Today's the day by which the club has been hoping to get something done. I'll hit you up with any announcement when word gets out.

As for last night's event, I'm told that the SMU A/V folks will have it up on the Web sometime in the next few days. I'll send a link out when I get one.

The Magic Number better not still be six at that point.

September 22, 2010

According to at least one local report, Saturday's game in Oakland (3:10 CT start) will now be carried live in the DFW market on KDFW/Channel 4, with Josh Lewin and Tom Grieve on the call. No blackout.

The White Sox just scored a run in the top of the seventh to cut Oakland's lead to 2-1.

September 22, 2010: Magic Number Update

September 22, 2010: Magic Number Update

TIGERS
1965 ROOKIE STARS
JACKIE MOORE catcher
JOHN SULLIVAN catcher

September 23, 2010

Think back to the end of October, when we learned that the Rangers told C.J. Wilson a few weeks earlier that they might let him compete for a rotation spot in camp, but that in order to convince the club to move him out of his key set-up role in the bullpen, he needed not only to be one of the team's five best starters in Surprise, but in fact one of the two best. It almost seemed like an audition prescribed to fall short, a token opportunity extended to Wilson as a tip of the cap and maybe not much more.

Turns out he was the Rangers' best starter in March (3.24 ERA, 14 hits and eight walks in 25 innings, .167/.242/.298, 22 strikeouts, 33 groundouts/13 flyouts, under 10 pitches per inning). He not only won a spot in the rotation; he made the decision easy.

One of the shocking statistics of the 2010 season, one that's going to extend beyond 162, is this:

Texas is 15 games over .500 in Wilson's starts (23-8).

In everyone else's starts, Texas is two games over .500 (61-59).

Think about that.

Whether the true inspiration for the camp audition was Wilson's, or Nolan Ryan's, or Jon Daniels and his crew's, it was a tremendous decision and a huge challenge met, and while we all ask where this team would be without Josh Hamilton's performance or Neftali Feliz's emergence after Frankie Francisco coughed things up in the first week or Big Bad's first half or David Murphy's second half or Nelson Cruz's breakout or Colby Lewis's Comeback Player of the Decade bid or the steadiness of the Darren O's or the effectiveness of Tommy Hunter and Alexi Ogando or the staff-wide impact of the addition of Cliff Lee, imagine what 84-67 and a Magic Number of four with 11 games to go would look like if C.J. Wilson weren't in the starting rotation.

Fifteen games over when he gets the ball.

Two games over when he doesn't.

I have a ton of other notes to get to, but no time to do it today. I filed my final weekly MLB.com column of the season late last night and will blast the list when it's on www.TexasRangers.com at some point today. It's a ranking of the top 10 Rangers prospects of the last decade—without the benefit of hindsight. Ton of fun to write.

If we were to make a list of the top 10 moves Texas has made in 2010, the decision before spring training to give C.J. Wilson a chance to prove he could start, just to see what might be there, has to rank very close to the top.

September 24, 2010

Like Hamilton's ribs,
Offense is fractured right now
Needs an injection

Read the next three quotes from after last night's game, and then I have two points to make.

David Murphy: "You could draw conclusions that we're pressing or we're putting too much pressure on ourselves. I think it's just very bad timing."

Nelson Cruz: "We're trying too hard. We have to let things happen. We're trying to make things happen."

Elvis Andrus (who has just two hits in his last 28 at-bats—and they're both infield singles): "For me, I think I'm too aggressive. . . . Sometimes you try to force things when you don't need to."

OK, a couple things.

Number one.

When the 2010 schedule came out last September, I was encouraged:

But the thing I always look for first is where the Rangers open, and where they close, and for the first time since 1996, Texas will be in Arlington in both cases. The Blue Jays and Mariners visit for the first six games of the season (April 5-11), and the Mariners (three) and Angels (four) are here for the regular season's final seven games (September 27-October 3). I like that.

I didn't think about it then, but another fortunate thing about this schedule is that Texas is done with Oakland a week and a half before the first game of the playoffs. The same will be true in 2011, when the Rangers get Seattle home for three before finishing in Anaheim for three.

Now, there will be years when you want to tee it up with your primary competition to finish out 162, to make sure that you control your destiny (especially if you're the hunter, not the hunted). And that may work out perfectly next year, with those three against the Angels.

But as long as Dallas Braden, Brett Anderson, Trevor Cahill, and Gio Gonzalez aren't past their arbitration years, and maybe Tyson Ross too, I'd be just fine not seeing the A's in the last week of the regular season, as we're trying to secure a playoff spot—or trying to build a little offensive momentum going into the post-season.

Point number two.

With all that stuff about Rangers hitters trying too hard to make things happen, about putting too much

Newberg Report: Top Ten Prospects Of 2000s

Texas farm system produced many All-Stars during decade

By Jamey Newberg / Special to MLB.com

September 23, 2010

For the final Newberg Report Top 10 list of the season, we look back at the best Rangers prospects of the last decade, not in retrospect, but instead at the time they were coming up through the Texas system.

I went back and put together a list of the Rangers' top prospects from the winters going into the 2000-10 seasons, and then tried to determine which winter each player was at the pinnacle of his stature as a prospect. In coming up with the list, I did my best to summon up where my head was on each player at that time, without the benefit of hindsight. So as much as I'd like to switch Ruben Mateo and Adrian Gonzalez now, I'm playing fair.

So, here goes - the top 10 Rangers prospects of the past decade:

10. Ian Kinsler (going into 2005): The 496th pick in the 2003 First-Year Player Draft, Kinsler hit .402 in 59 games for Low A Clinton (with 30 doubles, which led all of professional baseball at the time) and .300 for Double-A Frisco in '04. Yet the club agreed, on July 30 of that season, as Texas sat half a game behind Oakland in the division, to trade the second-year pro—a shortstop blocked at the time by Michael Young, who had just slid over from second base when Alex Rodriguez was traded for Alfonso Soriano (and Joaquin Arias)—to Colorado, along with righthander Erik Thompson, for Larry Walker. Walker exercised his rights to veto the deal before accepting a trade to St. Louis only one week later. And even though Kinsler went into '05 without a clear path to Texas, a spot would be created when Soriano was traded after the season.

9. Carlos Pena (going into 2001): In Pena's second full season after being drafted 10th overall by Texas, he hit .299 with a .414 on-base percentage and .533 slugging percentage for Double-A Tulsa, raising his batting average 44 points from the previous season in High A, decreasing his strikeout total by 20 percent, and improving his walk total by 36 percent. ESPN named him the Minor League Player of the Year. But when '01 saw both the emergence of Hank Blalock and the drafting of Mark Teixeira, Pena was deemed expendable, even though he was just as productive that season at Triple-A and earned 62 big league at-bats. The Rangers traded Pena with Mike Venafro to Oakland for Gerald Laird, Ryan Ludwick, Jason Hart, and Mario Ramos in January '02, but he didn't put it all together until signing a Minor League deal with Tampa Bay—his fifth organization—in '07.

8. "Edison" Volquez (going into 2006): Edinson Volquez, known then as "Edison" (after previously being known as Julio Reyes), began the 2005 season as an anonymous member of the high Class A Bakersfield rotation but ended it in Texas, with as much hype as any Rangers starting pitcher prospect in years. In 140 combined innings across four levels, the 21-year-old struck out 139 batters and issued only 39 walks. He was named by league managers as the top pitching prospect in the California League and the No. 2 pitching prospect in the Texas League, appearing in the Futures Game and emerging as what appeared to be as sure a thing as young pitchers get. An uneven '06 and '07 led Texas to trade his unrealized potential to Cincinnati for Josh Hamilton.

7. Justin Smoak (going into 2010): After signing as the Rangers' first-round pick late in 2008, Smoak hit .304/.355/.518 in 56 at-bats for low Class A Clinton, and then .353/.468/.588 in 51 Arizona Fall League at-bats. In '09, he hit .296/.406/.630 in 27 big league Spring Training at-bats, and then .328/.449/.481 in 183 Frisco at-bats. Slowed by an oblique strain, the 22-year-old struggled after a mid-season promotion to Tiple-A Oklahoma City, but then slugged .818 with nine home runs in 55 at-bats for Team USA in the IBAF World Cup in September. Pegged by Baseball Prospectus Minor League guru Kevin Goldstein to have the upside of "a switch-hitting Justin Morneau," Smoak was called on by Texas less than three weeks into the '10 season, but was targeted by Seattle in July, enabling the Rangers to acquire left-hander Cliff Lee.

6. Martin Perez (going into 2010): The Johan Santana comparisons began to gather momentum in 2009, a season that began with the lefthander starting a combined no-hitter for Low A Hickory in his first appearance and ended in Double-A, where at age 18 he was the youngest player in the Texas League—by two years. After posting a 2.90 ERA over 114 2/3 innings between the two levels (199 strikeouts and 38 walks), Perez was ranked by *Baseball America* as the No. 17 prospect in baseball going into '10, paired with Baltimore's Brian Matusz as one of the top two Minor League left-handers in the game. His talent is so substantial that his struggles in '10 have done little to dampen enthusiasm about his future.

5. Ruben Mateo (going into 2000): When Mateo was summoned to the big leagues at age 21 in June 1999, he was hitting .342 for Triple-A Oklahoma, leading the Pacific Coast League with 58 RBIs (in 60 games) and with 50 runs, and one home run short of leading the league in that category as well, having gone deep 17 times. A center fielder with plus range and as deadly an arm as any right fielder in baseball, he was basically a Josh Hamilton-type of prospect. Even in his disappointing big league debut (.238 in 122 at-bats), more than half of his 29 hits went for extra bases. Unfortunately, Mateo's inability to stay healthy was another thing he shared with Hamilton, and his big league career produced only 876 at-bats, spread across four clubs.

4. Derek Holland (going into 2009): Even if Holland had been the first-overall pick in his Draft, rather than selection No. 747, what he did in his first full pro season would have been considered astonishing. Underneath the collective 14-2 record and 2.05 ERA he posted in '08 (including the Texas League playoffs) was a remarkable trend as the 21-year-old's competition got better. Holland held low Class A hitters to a .228 batting average. He held high Class A hitters to a .185 clip. After his promotion to Frisco, Double-A opponents hit .163 off him in the regular season, and then .141 in the playoffs. All told, including the postseason, Holland struck out 175 hitters and walked only 44 in 171 1/3 innings, induced more groundouts than flyouts, and surrendered only four home runs. He was young for the Texas League, where he made four regular season starts and three playoff starts, but gave up only three earned runs in those 46 2/3 innings.

3. Neftali Feliz (going into 2010): Feliz was really good in Triple-A in 2009, particularly once he was transitioned to the bullpen, but he was even better once he got to Texas late in the season. The 21-year-old struck out 8.7 Triple-A hitters per nine innings, but 11.3 per nine in the big leagues. He walked 3.5 per nine for Oklahoma City and 2.3 per nine for Texas. His Triple-A opposition hit .240/.318/.347—Major Leaguers hit a lifeless .124/.207/.210. Feliz started the season as the Pacific Coast League's youngest player, but in August had the best ERA (0.51) in the big leagues. He's the most exciting pitching prospect this franchise has ever produced.

2. Hank Blalock (going into 2002): At age 20, Blalock was leading the high Class A Florida State League in hitting (.380) and slugging (.557), was second in on-base percentage(.437), and was third in extra-base hits (27 in 63 games) when he was promoted in mid-June to Double-A Tulsa. He proceeded to hit for the cycle in his sixth Driller game ... and again in his eighth. After hitting .327/.413/.544 for Tulsa, Blalock was third in *Baseball America*'s voting for the Minor League Player of the Year, behind Josh Beckett and Adam Dunn. He proceeded to destroy Arizona Fall League pitching, hitting .344/.431/.713 and setting up what was an absolute lock to be a long, outstanding, productive career as a perennial batting title contender whose power would come. Today, still not 30, he hasn't resurfaced anywhere since being released by Tampa Bay in July—hard to comprehend.

1. Mark Teixeira (going into 2003): After protracted negotiations delayed the start of Teixeira's pro career until 2002, an elbow injury in Spring Training pushed his debut back to June, but the 2001 first-rounder didn't need much time to establish himself as the best prospect in the game. The switch-hitter put up near-identical lines for high Class A Charlotte (.320/.411/.593) and Double-A Tulsa (.316/.415/.591), going deep 19 times in 321 combined at-bats. He then punished Arizona Fall League pitching to the tune of .333/.437/.616 with seven home runs in 99 at-bats, and Baseball America named him the No. 1 prospect in baseball over the winter. They don't all work out the way they're supposed to. But this one did.

pressure on themselves, which of course reflects about a week of offensive offense, not just one game against the A's, how confident are we that this playoff-untested lineup will be able to heed their own self-help messages when everything's on the line—and the pressure reaches new levels—against New York or Tampa Bay?

September 24, 2010: Magic Number Update

So long, Angels.

September 25, 2010

Nine days ago, when Ted Price, Adam Morris, Ben & Skin, and I recorded the most recent episode of Rangers Podcast in Arlington, we were asked to predict when the Rangers would clinch. The Magic Number was eight at the time.

I said Saturday the 25th.

It's all teed up now.

Derek Holland has to know he's a longshot at this point to make the post-season roster, but at the same time he has a chance to contribute in a big way this afternoon. From one standpoint, when the clincher happens isn't all that important, but from another, the sooner it happens, the better. There are a couple bullpen arms and a hitter or two that could use some time off, with their playing time leading up to October 6 mapped out without worrying about game situations.

In one start against Oakland this year (his first 2010 big league appearance), Holland blanked the A's on five hits and a walk over six innings, fanning seven. He also faced them in relief once, yielding one run on three hits and three walks in 4.2 innings, setting two down on strikes. He ought to take some confidence to the mound today.

Last night, coming off three straight games without scoring an earned run—a first in franchise history—Texas racked up 18 hits, including seven in 15 trips with runners in scoring position, and managed to leave fewer runners on base than the A's did in what was a blowout win. One game doesn't equate to momentum, but on a night when all 10 Rangers who batted hit safely, some with serious authority and others whose flares found holes and others who did this:

Louis DeLuca/Dallas Morning News

. . . maybe it was the kind of game that helps unlock what has been a shackled offense.

A's lefthander Dallas Braden said before the game that, when he held Texas to one (infield) hit on Thursday, he used the Rangers' over-aggressiveness against them. Good message for the club to hear. It's one thing to nod your head when you hear it from your manager or hitting coach. It's another when the guy in the other uniform who absolutely shut you down tells you how he did it.

Here's another message. Friend of the Newberg Report Ken Davidoff writes, in a *Newsday* blog entry that doesn't have "Texas" or "Rangers" among its 600 words, that the Yankees and Rays will probably meet up again in the American League Championship Series, and that it "would be awesome."

Davidoff won't be the last one to write it. Bring it. This Rangers team is better as an underdog, with a chip on its shoulder.

Joaquin Arias as a Met: .200/.250/.200 in 15 at-bats. It's unfair to compare what he's done to what Jeff Francoeur has done as a Ranger (.379/.406/.517), because the Mets were essentially happy to give Francoeur away, but it's funny how that trade has produced exponentially greater results than the three non-Cliff Lee July deals in spite of the fact that Texas needed Francoeur to slide by a couple dozen teams on waivers (he actually cleared entirely) in order to acquire him on August 31, just in time to have him eligible for the post-season roster.

Another quiet acquisition, lefthander Clay Rapada (picked up for future considerations in December from Detroit and run through waivers and outrighted off the roster the same month), still hasn't allowed a hit as a Ranger. Nine September appearances—seven of them against teams with winning records, 19 batters faced, no hits.

Among those 19 batters: Robinson Cano twice, Curtis Granderson, Lance Berkman, Jim Thome.

The only way Rapada won't face any of them again this year will be if Texas draws Tampa Bay in Round One and doesn't advance.

Speaking of the post-season roster (which I'm not going to talk about in depth until after the Rangers clinch), Chris Davis is on it for me.

And starting.

Even against the Game One lefthander.

Davis's swing is quiet again, he's laying off pitches out of the zone, and he's possibly the best defender Texas has ever had at first base, right there with Mark Teixeira. He's more likely than Mitch Moreland or Jorge Cantu to save a run, and right now, the way he's going at the plate since returning from AAA (.444/.615/.889), he's the most likely of the three to produce one, too.

Davis's next stop after the playoffs: Dominican Winter League baseball.

Josh Hamilton said this week that he'd be open to a move to first base down the road. Right now that's the furthest thing from my mind.

And those notes I've been promising for almost a week now will still have to wait. Whenever we talk here about the minor leagues, or trade possibilities, or front office developments, it's still all about the big club and how those things factor in, and whenever we talk about the big club, it's simple: It's about getting to the 163rd game that counts, and seeing how much longer you can go after that.

Know what they're talking about in Los Angeles this morning?

2011.

In Boston?

Tom Brady.

It may not happen for the Rangers this afternoon, in the building where Ron Washington was raised as a coach, but it might, and more to the point, it can. Savor it. As the Angels and Red Sox can attest, games like today's in Oakland are never guaranteed. Texas may be entering a run of years when it will be thought of every spring as a contender, but things don't always work out.

There's nothing in sports like dogpiles and champagne. Today, when eight up with nine to go could become nine up with eight to go, is one of those days, in spite of the grind of the last six months and all the off-the-field commotion this team has fought through, that's positioned to be one we may remember for a long time.

Or it could fall short and let us down, setting up tomorrow, or the next day, for the payoff.

You never know, and that's part of what makes this game so rewarding when a season like 2010 all comes together.

September 25, 2010: Magic Number Update

September 25, 2010

We all have our histories with this team, some longer than others, with different levels of emotional investment and varying stations on the spectrum that ranges between belief and cynicism. But we're all together tonight, rewarded, and now we wait for what's next, and it feels damned good.

Right now I think about Josh Hamilton, without whom we're not here, and whose postgame experience and commitment happened to be somewhere else today, in some ways by choice, and I think about what all had to be going through his mind today, not that they were things that don't go through his mind every day.

I think about the manager, who last year made an unbelievable choice of his own, an awful mistake, the kind that even those who can forgive probably still can't fathom, and I think about the job he's done cultivating this team's personality and resolve.

I think about the general manager, who if Dennis Gilbert had bought this team last December would probably be GM'ing right now at 401 E. Jefferson Street in Phoenix or 12301 Roosevelt Avenue in Flushing. I think about what that must have felt like today, wearing the beer and champagne and looking on a frat-like celebration by a team that he was in charge of putting together, sometimes under extraordinary constraints.

I think about the team president, whose legendary career as a player included only one World Series appearance—when he was younger than Michael Kirkman—and just three other playoff appearances in 27 seasons, and whose excitement today would have been quite a bit different had the results gone the other way in the courtroom, a place I bet he had as much interest hanging out in as on an operating table. I think about what a bad result it would have been if he, and the general manager, were not around, or even if they were around but possibly not for long.

I think about the aging slugger whose last team thought he was closer to Cooperstown than to his prime, and who, rather than anything approaching done, was a huge part of what this team accomplished, as it plays on while his former club plays out the string.

I think about how I have absolutely no idea what goes through the head of someone like Alexi Ogando as he takes his rightful place spraying champagne and pulling on a cigar, months after wondering if he'd ever get the chance to play baseball in Surprise or Frisco, let alone Arlington.

I think about us.

I think about Eric Nadel and Chuck Morgan and Tom Grieve and John Blake and Jim Sundberg and Brad Newton, and how much they've given this organization for so many years, and deserve this.

I think about Josh Lewin, whose previous 13 seasons doing televised play-by-play (Cubs, Tigers, Rangers) never gave him the chance to call a game for his team like today's.

I think about Thad Levine, A.J. Preller, Scott Servais, and so many others whose fingerprints are all over this thing but who don't get enough credit. We'll miss them when they're gone.

I think about Carson Leslie.

I think about Nelson Cruz, whose past is nothing like Hamilton's, but who had lots of failed chances of his own and kept battling, and now rewards a team that showed plenty of patience in him and stands as good a chance as anyone else to be the team's key weapon in October. And about David Murphy, a 2010 hero in his role.

I think about Chuck Greenberg, who unquestionably comes in at a great time (not by accident) but whose strengths and energy and passion for the game are going to help make this great time great for a longer period than it might have been had someone else bought the team. He talked during the postgame celebration about how the game was sort of a microcosm of the season. I'm not so sure the 2010 season won't be a microcosm, at least on the field, of where the Greenberg-Ryan Group keeps this franchise for years.

Nonetheless, I think about Elvis Andrus and Neftali Feliz and Tommy Hunter and Julio Borbon, and hope they understand it doesn't always come together like this. Ask Nolan.

I think about Derek Holland, whose 2010 season will probably be highlighted by what he did today, as he may not travel east with the team a week from now.

I think about Darren Oliver and Colby Lewis coming back to where it all started, and contributing in such a big way.

I think about Matt Treanor and Andres Blanco, and who's more fortunate—them or us.

I think about Jorge Cantu, who broke a historically ugly RBI drought with what appeared to be a historically decisive one, and then when that wasn't enough, did it again two innings later.

I think about Cliff Lee, and what he's thinking about. And about how huge that trade was for this team, in so many ways.

I think about Tom Hicks.

I think about the career disappointment that the Mets couldn't wait to get rid of three and a half weeks ago, and who seems like he's been part of this thing for years.

I think about C.J. Wilson, and the extraordinary year he's had. I could make the argument that fewer pitchers should rank higher than Wilson in the AL MVP vote than in the AL Cy Young vote.

And, of course, I think about the veteran who bounced up and down like a kid as the ball began its downward arc toward his teammate in left field, the typically stoic ballplayer who leads because he's supposed to, not because he insists on it, the untoolsy infielder whose steadiness has him all over the Ranger record books but who also sat far too high on a list that he's a week away from coming off of forever, as his playoffless career will no longer be so.

I think the thing I'll remember most about Texas 4, Oakland 3 on September 25, 2010, even more so than Cantu's go-ahead single and stay-ahead homer or Andrus's baserunning heroics, will be the way Michael Young reacted to the moment that went from game-on-the-line to ballgame, and the way his teammates reacted after the scrum was over, every one of them lining up to pay tribute to him on the field, a sign of the kind of respect most of us have for him but to a greater degree, as he's set an example and set a tone for a group of players that have earned the right to play on.

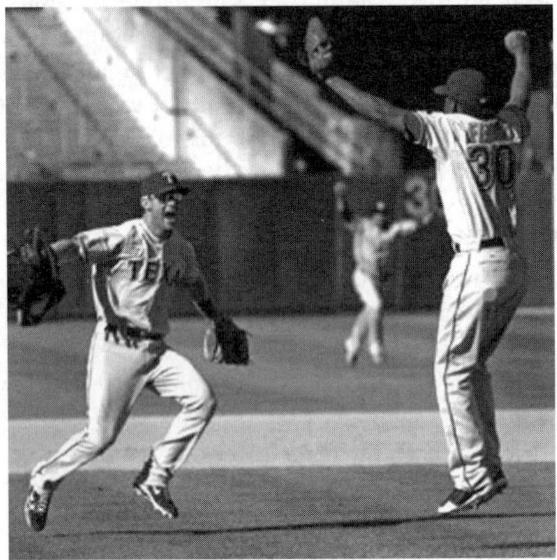

Louis DeLuca/Dallas Morning News

September 26, 2010

You know when the Rangers raised the flags honoring the 1996, 1998, and 1999 AL West championships?

In 1997, 1999, and 2000.

Know when they're going to raise the 2010 AL West Champs flag?

In less than 24 hours, just before the starters who have talked their way back into Monday's lineup take the field.

Nights like Monday night don't come around very often. Let's fill that building tomorrow.

September 29, 2010

The Rangers would have to win their final five to hit that 92-victory mark that Nolan Ryan projected in March, but the more important wins and losses this week will be staged in Toronto and Boston, and Tampa and Kansas City.

The Yankees, trailing the Rays in the East by half a game, are in Toronto for one more tonight, will be off tomorrow, and finish with three in Fenway. The Rays wrap up a home series against Baltimore tonight and visit the Royals for four to close the regular season out.

Whoever comes out on top in the East will host Texas in Round One of the playoffs, and the Yankees (94-64) have to win once more than the Rays (94-63), as Tampa Bay holds the tiebreaker over New York should they finish with an equal number of wins—making this effectively a 1.5-game lead—by virtue of having won 10 of the two clubs' 18 matchups this season. The Yankees not only have one fewer game left to do it in, they have the tougher opposition as well.

But at least one national reporter doesn't think the Yankees should sweat it the rest of this week, and in fact recommends that they fall short of the Rays.

In a story published last night, Jon Paul Morosi of Fox Sports suggests that Minnesota, and not Texas, should be viewed as the Yankees' "optimal first-round opponent," even though to draw the Twins would mean New York travels to open Round One rather than stays at home to host the Rangers.

Morosi talks about how New York has handled Minnesota's top three starters (not just this season but over their careers), how the Twins have struggled since clinching six games ago, and how the Yankees fared well in their one trip to Target Field this season, all of which could mean that, though "Yankees players wouldn't admit as much . . . , they have the psychological edge on Minnesota."

Morosi adds:

"By comparison, New York would have a much tougher time with the Rangers in a five-game series. Cliff Lee will start Game 1 for Texas, and Yankees fans would prefer to avoid the guy who was responsible for their team's only two losses in the World Series last year. Lefthander C.J. Wilson, slated to start Game 2, possesses the power stuff to handcuff New York."

It's cool with me if that's how this all shakes out. I've gone back and forth the last few weeks—preferring Tampa Bay at first, figuring that the Rays would represent a smaller psychological hurdle to deal with out of the gate, then thinking maybe the Yankees would be the better draw since they're probably more vulnerable to Texas in a best-of-five than in a best-of-seven—but on Sunday night I made up my mind.

Watching the late innings of New York's 10-inning, 4-3 win over Boston, I remembered how frustrating it can be watching Derek Jeter and Alex Rodriguez and Mark Teixeira and Robinson Cano get what seems like an extra strike to play with, while Yankees pitchers tend to get a wider zone. It's all perception and probably has little to no basis in fact, but it *feels* like New York gets the benefit of the margins on balls and strikes, and even if it's a mirage, it's one I don't feel like fighting through.

At least in the first round.

Ivan Nova is supposed to start for New York on Friday, followed by a pair of TBA's. Doesn't Sturdy Sergio Mitre deserve a fourth start this season? What did Dustin Moseley ever do to hurt you? Wouldn't Alex Rodriguez and Mark Teixeira benefit from an extra day or two off? Give Kevin Russo and Juan Miranda that extra look they've clearly both earned.

There are a few Round One roster decisions left to be made for Texas, and a huge season-ending series with the Angels if for no other reason than Josh Hamilton should be back on the field to test his physical readiness for the playoffs, but we don't yet know where the Rangers will be one week from today.

Go Red Sox.

As for the Rangers' playoff roster decisions, and a shoebox full of notes I've wanted to get to for about two weeks now, I've got to beg off for another day. The next couple reports will come from sunny Surprise, where I'm headed for a quick visit to Fall Instructional League. For the next few days, the focus will be on Jurickson Profar and Christian Villanueva, Jake Skole and Jorge Alfaro, Luke Jackson and David Perez, before we turn back next week to Cliff Lee and Josh Hamilton and Nelson Cruz.

And preferably David Price and Evan Longoria and Carl Crawford.

September 29, 2010

The Rangers have activated right-handed reliever Mark Lowe from the 60-day disabled list, moving righthander Guillermo Moscoso to the 60-day DL to make room on the roster. Lowe, acquired from Seattle along with Cliff Lee in July, will be in the Rangers' bullpen today.

This is, potentially, not an insignificant move. Lowe could make a case for inclusion on the Round One roster if he's effective, particularly with Frankie Francisco's availability for Round One highly doubtful at this point.

September 29, 2010

The Rich Harden era went out with a whimper today, as the righthander, pitching what amounted to a spot start as the club gets its playoff rotation lined up, went four-plus, throwing marginally more strikes than balls, and giving up four runs on six hits and three walks and one hit batsman (with two strikeouts) before giving the ball to Ron Washington one final time.

The bullpen trio of Derek Holland, Mark Lowe (making his Rangers debut against his former club), and Neftali Feliz threw five innings of one-run ball (four hits, one walk, eight strikeouts) as the offense scored the game's final five runs, the last one just about as improbable as you can imagine (aside from the truism that if Nelson Cruz is up with a chance to end the game, you might as well pack up your belongings), and taking Harden off the hook for the meaningless loss.

Harden's record as a Ranger: 5-5, 5.58 in 18 starts and two relief appearances.

But, hey, remember that note on the back of his 2010 Topps card? "Rich has winning stuff; all he needs is a little help from his friends. In the 51 career starts in which he's gotten at least four runs of support while he was in the game, his record is 39-0."

He's now 41-0 in those games!

Hey, nobody was more excited about Harden when he signed here. He seemed to be every bit as good a risk as Colby Lewis, and certainly brought more upside. His contributions were few (maybe a saber-type can quantify whether his impact was in fact negative, as he averaged under five innings a start and thus burdened the bullpen beyond reason), and in spite of it Texas is headed for territory that it hasn't seen in 11 years and that it figured Harden would lead them to, if the club was to get there at all.

I remember how pumped I was when I saw Harden and Mike Maddux walking together toward the bullpen mounds behind the batting practice field in Surprise six and a half months ago, with thoughts of 15 or 17 contract-year wins once Harden inevitably got those low March gun readings out of his system and was ramped up for the games that counted. Spring training will do that for you.

So will Fall Instructs, if you allow yourself to think in the long term. I baked at Rangers Ballpark this afternoon (it was so hot that I thought the game ended on a run-scoring strikeout), only to realize as I looked at the temperature readings that I'm headed for an extra 25 degrees of heat tomorrow. If I'm a little dizzied out there in Arizona, I might start to predict really big things for Hanser Alberto or Justin Grimm, though you know me well enough by now that I'd probably do that even in conditioned air.

Tampa lost today, and New York lost two minutes ago, so the Rays' lead is still half a game, and for all relevant purposes 1.5 games.

Catch you next from Surprise, with lots of thoughts on a good number of the five dozen young players getting their final work in for the year, plus plenty of discussion about what lies ahead for the older guys, whose season has a far less predictable end date than the crew at Instructs, or than Rich Harden's career as a Ranger.

October 2010

40-MAN ROSTER (40)

Pitchers (20)

Scott Feldman, Neftali Feliz, Frankie Francisco, Rich Harden, Matt Harrison, Derek Holland, Tommy Hunter, Michael Kirkman, Cliff Lee, Colby Lewis, Mark Lowe, Doug Mathis, Dustin Nippert, Darren O'Day, Alexi Ogando, Darren Oliver, Zach Phillips, Clay Rapada, Pedro Strop, C.J. Wilson

Catchers (4)

Bengie Molina, Max Ramirez, Taylor Teagarden, Matt Treanor

Infielders (9)

Elvis Andrus, Andres Blanco, Jorge Cantu, Chris Davis, Esteban German, Cristian Guzman, Ian Kinsler, Mitch Moreland, Michael Young

Outfielders (7)

Julio Borbon, Nelson Cruz, Jeff Francouer, Craig Gentry, Vladimir Guerrero, Josh Hamilton, David Murphy

60-Day Disabled List (4)

Omar Beltre, Eric Hurley, Brandon McCarthy, Guillermo Moscoso

October 1, 2010: From Surprise, AZ

My first trip out to Fall Instructional League was three years ago, a decision triggered by two factors:

a. A big league season that was limping to a last-place finish, 19 games back in the West; and

b. The explosion of high-end prospects the franchise had added since I'd been in Surprise that March for spring training

There was a third reason, related to the second: I didn't know how I was going to rank all those players added in the June draft and the July trading season and otherwise in that winter's Bound Edition Top 72, without getting the chance to see them, even if for just a few days.

Looking back at the roster of 45 that suited up in 2007 for Instructs—which primarily features only players from the lower (mostly short-season) levels of the farm system, plus a handful of upper-level players who need some extra work—you can see a crazy amount of impact on the 2010 playoff club.

Among those 45 were:

- Elvis Andrus
- Neftali Feliz
- Tommy Hunter
- Julio Borbon
- Mitch Moreland
- Derek Holland
- Max Ramirez
- Blake Beavan and Josh Lueke, who helped produce Cliff Lee
- Michael Main, who helped produce Bengie Molina
- Evan Reed, who helped produce Jorge Cantu

That's not to mention the Rangers' top pitching prospect at the moment, Martin Perez, or the club's top position player prospect, Engel Beltre, who were at their first Rangers camp as well.

The Rangers would probably admit that there may never be another fall crop like that one—for one thing, we hope never again to be that team that's selling off players like Mark Teixeira, Eric Gagné, and Kenny Lofton in July—but the point is that while the dozens of young players who are gathered here from leagues in Arizona, Washington, North Carolina, California, Texas, and the Dominican Republic for one final month of work amount to a footnote in a season like this one, spending a couple days on the back fields this time of year serves as a reminder of the importance of keeping the pipeline flowing.

Names like Luke Jackson and Luis Sardinas and Jake Skole may be more familiar than David Perez and Christian Villanueva and Jared Hoying, but there are prospects everywhere you turn out here, some of whom we've known about since the day they were drafted or signed internationally—and others who, like Holland and Ian Kinsler before them, will have opened eyes internally well before their numbers draw anyone's attention outside the organization.

By time I got from the airport to the complex on Thursday morning, most of the 67 players invited to 2010 Instructs were locked up in the late innings of a high-intensity Fungo Game, where everyone—including pitchers—took their turns at the plate, not stepping in against anyone on the mound but instead digging in with both a bat and a ball in hand. Jayce Tingler's squad won the game in dramatic fashion, in front of a crowd of maybe 12, as righthander Cody Buckel tripled and righthander Tanner Scheppers banged a walkoff sac fly to deep left center.

(The Scheppers swing, poorly phone-photographed by me:)

It was an off-day on the Instructional League schedule (those are necessary from time to time in 108-degree heat), setting the stage for the Fungo Game, but the Advanced Instructional League did play, as the Rangers-Royals squad traveled to Maryvale to take on the Brewers-Mariners team, in front of a crowd of 44.

While AIL lineups are a mix of players from the two clubs that share the roster, each day only one of the two clubs sends its pitchers, and yesterday was a Royals day. (I hear that Scheppers and camp star Fabio Castillo will pitch in today's AIL game, which might be enough for me to take that contest in rather than the standard IL contest.)

But I did get to see five Rangers prospects in action: third baseman Mike Olt, shortstop Leury Garcia, first baseman Jared Bolden, left fielder Josh Richmond, and designated hitter Vin DiFazio. The only one who distinguished himself in the chances he got was Garcia, who had a couple impressive at-bats and made a tough play on a ball slowed by a deflection off the pitcher's glove look easy.

You see these players over enough Marches and Septembers and you start to color in the picture, but for a fan like me to leap to any real conclusions on a minor leaguer in such limited looks would be foolish, considering that even the Rangers folks who watched John Danks every day as a farmhand and the Red Sox officials who watched David Murphy every day in the minor leagues underestimated what they had. Scouting isn't easy. And I'm no scout. I don't know what Garcia will become, but he sure is fun to watch, with that plus arm and plus-plus speed in that not-quite-5'10", 160-lb. frame, and while a lot more has to come together for the 19-year-old, the capacity is there for him to make it.

Garcia's not going to be Rafael Furcal despite the nickname, and a scout who really likes the player may lack the conviction to predict an Erick Aybar future, but Andres Blanco was a legitimate prospect once, well before his career was redefined as "journeyman," and if years from now Garcia solidifies a bench role for a contender, maybe even stepping things up in place of a key injured veteran for a few weeks, that would be OK, too. Blanco has a place in this game, and one day Garcia might as well.

While the big league team, which last night extended its division lead to a franchise-high 11 games as it tunes up for playoff baseball, is a bunch of grown men acting like kids with their claw-and-antlers bit that's led to a T-shirt craze, the organization is using T-shirts to try and help make men out of a bunch of kids in Surprise. The workout shirts in the above photo say the following on the back:

"I trust my teammates.
I trust myself."
— Michael Young, All-Time Texas Rangers Hit Leader

And the coaches' shirts:

The Ranger Way:
Attitude.
Discipline.
Teamwork.
Sacrifice.

The work being done out here by the organization isn't all about mechanics or technique.

Back home on Thursday, Neftali Feliz was busy setting a Major League record for saves by a rookie, nailing his ninth in nine tries against the Angels and 39th overall. Three years ago, he was at Fall Instructs, a 19-year-old with 81.1 career innings in three pro seasons, all at the short-season minor league level, making him less experienced than Andrew Doyle is right now. Is there another Feliz in this year's group? Doubtful, but read this:

[His] delivery has some moving parts and some wrist funk in the back, but there are no red flags and his arm is exceptionally loose and fast. His explosive fastball sits in the mid-90s and tops out at 98 mph. He also flashes a plus slider that reaches 87 mph, though it's inconsistent. His developing changeup also shows promise, giving him the makings of a three-pitch starter's repertoire. [He] has No. 1 starter upside if everything comes together for him, but his command is a work in progress, as he needs to do a better job repeating his arm slot and release point.

That's not a 2007 writeup on Feliz, but instead a September 2010 *Baseball America* writeup on righthander Roman Mendez, who was just named the number five prospect in the New York-Penn League based on the work he did this summer as a Boston farmhand, before coming to Texas in the July trade for Jarrod Saltalamacchia. Mendez is slated to throw a side today, and I can't wait to see it.

Meanwhile, the Rangers had six of the top 20 prospects in the Northwest League, as league managers recognized shortstop Jurickson Profar (number 1), Olt (4), lefthander Miguel De Los Santos (10), catcher Kellin Deglan (11), Skole (13), and Hoying (16) in *Baseball America*'s survey. *BA*'s Jim Callis calls Profar the fourth-best prospect in baseball among those who haven't yet played in a full-season minor league. Lefthanders Robbie Erlin (5) and Robbie Ross (15) were recognized in the South Atlantic League rankings, but they're not out here. Most full-season prospects are back home, recovering from the long season.

The focus right now, properly, is on Josh Hamilton's return to action tonight, Cliff Lee's outstanding tune-up effort last night, and whether the Rays will be able to hold the Yankees off this weekend after losing again last night. I don't ever mean to suggest, by all the attention I pay to what goes on in the minor leagues, that its significance is somehow greater than how it factors into making the big league team better, through scouting and player development and trades.

It's ultimately about what goes on in Arlington, but part of that involves what's going on right now in Surprise, as kids Michael Young has never heard of all wear a shirt stamped with his words, and all compete to one day get where Young and his teammates are, not only playing big league baseball but gearing up to extend things beyond 162.

It's Time in Texas
But Surprise development
Widens the window

October 2, 2010: From Surprise, AZ

It might shock a small few of you that from time to time I'll go overboard on a player. For every Elvis Andrus and Ian Kinsler and Derek Holland who's opened my eyes in

Surprise there's a Juan Moreno and a John Hudgins and a Johnny Lujan. You're advised to have the salt shaker handy when I get amped up about a prospect based on a small sample of firsthand, uninitiated observations.

With that said, there's a player out here who I was resigned a year ago to put on the second list but now has me thinking he might be back on track to fulfilling all the promise he arrived with. He's a player who slid quietly through last year's Rule 5 Draft, and was really never much of a candidate to be protected in the first place. That's probably about to change.

There could be any number of reasons that I was so high on Fabio Castillo when he signed out of the Dominican Republic in 2005. Maybe it was the monster bonus he landed as part of the Rangers' J2 class that summer (reported to be as much as $400,000). Maybe it was the general lack of high-end pitching prospects in the system once you got past Danks, Volquez, Diamond, and Hurley. Maybe it was what Castillo (along with Cristian Santana and Johan Yan) represented, a hopeful return to prominence in Latin America after years of relative irrelevance internationally, as A.J. Preller reeled in his first J2 crop since joining the organization.

My enthusiasm gained conviction with the 5.2-inning, one-single, zero-walk, 14-strikeout effort Castillo put up in his next-to-last start of the 2006 Dominican Summer League season, five months after I'd seen him in Surprise and said of the big righthander, who sported a prototype pitcher's build at age 17: "Castillo's what they look like."

Maybe so, but his productivity, like that of Santana (a catcher who is now a left fielder/DH) and Yan (a shortstop who is now a relief pitcher), wasn't measuring up. Castillo's ERA pushed up against 6.00 for Spokane in 2007 and sat at 6.75 as a starter for Clinton in 2008 (and 4.53 as a reliever), and while he was better out of the Hickory bullpen in 2009 (4.05, .269 opponents' average), he was a fourth-year pro pitching in middle relief in Low Class A and by then had been passed by what seemed like a thousand others in what had become a pitching-rich system.

Then came 2010. Assigned to the hitter-friendly California League out of spring training, Castillo allowed earned runs two times in his first 12 appearances (more than half of which lasted more than one inning), and he never really slowed down. In 36 Bakersfield relief appearances, he scattered 41 hits (two home runs) over 51.2 innings, good for a .219 opponents' average, the lowest of his career since that 2006 run through the DSL. Castillo fanned 65 and walked 26, posted a 1.92 ERA, permitted five of 19 inherited runners to score, and was 1.40 times more likely to coax a groundout than an out in the air.

His velocity was up to 94-97, he was commanding a nasty slider, his second-half ERA was 1.04 (.189 opponents' average, 2.31 G/F, no home runs), and late in August—in the midst of a stretch in which he hadn't allowed an earned run in 15 games (17 innings, nine hits [seven singles and two doubles], six walks, 26 strikeouts)—he was promoted to Frisco for a bigger challenge.

Castillo gave up a couple runs in his first AA relief appearance but put up scoreless efforts his next four times out (including two appearances in the Texas League playoffs). His stuff was creating a buzz that had been missing since his first couple years in the system. A buzz that might be the strongest of any pitcher in Surprise right now.

I went to the Advanced Instructional League game yesterday, knowing in advance that Castillo was slated to pitch the ninth. There were other reasons I was looking forward to that game—Tanner Sheppers, Miguel De Los Santos, and Ovispo De Los Santos were also pitching—but I was keyed up to see Castillo more than any of them.

Scheppers (15 strikes, five balls) sat 94-96 and had a very good curve in his inning of work—a real key for him—and both De Los Santos's were dirty though inconsistent. Hector Nelo (who didn't finish his inning due to some physical issue) and Trevor Hurley were impressive, as was center fielder Ryan Strasbourger, whose arm strength and run tool are drawing some Craig Gentry comparisons.

But the best position player I saw on Friday was Reds catcher Yasmani Grandal (impressive at the plate and behind it—Cincinnati has a good problem with Grandal and Devin Mesoraco coming, a problem I'd very much like to see Texas help alleviate).

So when I saw that Grandal was due to bat fourth in the top of the ninth inning, I was cool with it when Reds outfielder Denis Phipps singled sharply to left on the first pitch he saw from Castillo. I wanted to see a Castillo-Grandal matchup.

But then, after Cleveland shortstop Juan Diaz grounded out to second, moving Phipps to second base, Castillo (who sat 93-95 and touched 96) and catcher Vin DiFazio teamed up on a double play, as Reds second baseman Cody Puckett swung through 1-2 high heat and DiFazio cut Phipps down trying to steal third, leaving Grandal stranded on deck as the inning ended.

Castillo is what they look like again.

So are outfielder Jordan Akins, a physical prototype, and baby catcher Jorge Alfaro, both of whom stand out in drills and allow you to dream big about what they might be, and third baseman Christian Villanueva, who stands out in everything he does. The 19-year-old from Mexico (who hit .314/.365/.431 in his first season stateside) is remarkably smooth defensively, fundamentally sound, and has lightning quick hands at the plate that led one Rangers instructor to suggest he could develop along the same lines as countryman Vinny Castilla, whose power didn't arrive until he was a 27-year-old in his fifth big league season.

Between Villanueva and Mike Olt (also having a tremendous camp) and Tommy Mendonca, there's more playable depth out here at third base than there's been in years.

Righthanders Richard Alvarez and Roman Mendez threw bullpen sides alongside each other Friday morning. Alvarez looks stronger, and better, every time I see him. He's more polished than Mendez, whose raw stuff, if inconsistent, grabs your attention.

As pitching coordinator Danny Clark and about four others from the Rangers' crew of instructors worked with Mendez on some mechanical checkpoints, I couldn't help but think that the projectable 20-year-old, the new toy who came over in the Jarrod Saltalamacchia trade with Boston two months ago and thus is getting Rangers instruction for the first time, is Exhibit A of why those guys love their job and keep grinding it out anonymously, behind the scenes.

Righthander Luke Jackson, who probably would have been sitting in an Intro to Chemistry class at Miami on Friday morning if he hadn't decided in August to sign, followed Alvarez and Mendez in the bullpen. But he and Clark spent his 10 minutes with no catcher, and no baseball, working strictly on mechanics, specifically on balance points.

Thinking about college football this morning? Jake Skole probably is too, which is not to say he regrets deciding on pro baseball. Check out Spencer Fordin's feature on Skole for MLB.com.

One last morning of Instructs for me, then it's back to Texas, with full focus on playoff rosters and Game 1 and Game 4 matchups (the latter of which I have to believe depends on whether Texas is up 2-1 or down 1-2, despite reports) and why a former Rangers GM is a far more likely candidate in Queens than the current one and the welcome ice-cream-headache intensity of post-season baseball. For now, righthanders Justin Grimm and David Perez are among the young pitchers I expect to see in action today, and I'm looking forward to it.

But this has been a position player's camp, for the first time in years. And it's fair to say that the MVP of camp so far, if you talk to enough people with the organization, has been shortstop Luis Sardinas. Between Sardinas and Jurickson Profar, not to mention Leury Garcia and Hanser Alberto, the depth this franchise has at shortstop behind Andrus is going to create some excellent opportunities for the front office. Young shortstops with tools who play defense and contribute offensively help get deals for veteran pitching done.

I'd be going nuts, with conviction, about Profar's and Sardinas's future if it weren't for the cautionary tale of Fabio Castillo's development into a pitcher who, despite monster stuff and good health, went undrafted in December, as he should have.

Then again, Castillo's resurgence in the summer and fall of 2010 has been so encouraging that, because I am who I am, I might as well go ahead and start sweating whether Texas will be able to keep Profar and Sardinas from leaving via free agency in 2020, and worrying about the clubhouse impact when the two are running against each other in the Arlington mayor's race.

October 2, 2010

October 3, 2010: Magic Number Update

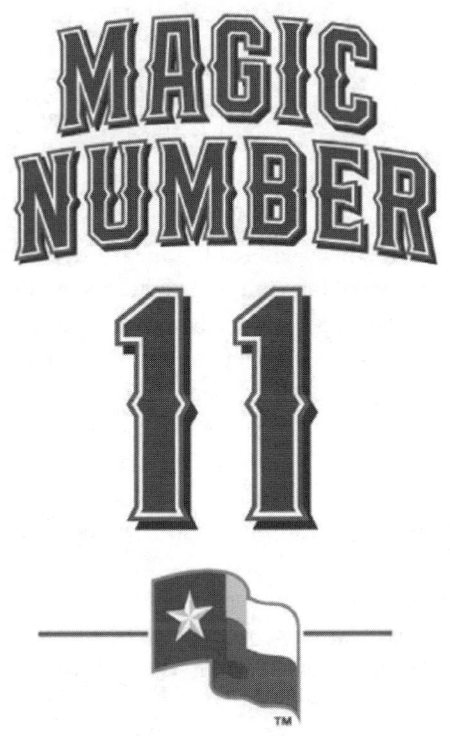

October 3, 2010

Dear Dan Haren:

You can watch the American League Division Series, with everyone else, on TBS.

Game times yet to be determined, but as for Texas-Tampa Bay, the dates are locked in and it's assumed to set up this way:

Game 1, @ Tampa Bay
Wednesday, Oct. 6, probably an afternoon start
Game 2, @ Tampa Bay
Thursday, Oct. 7, probably an afternoon start
Game 3, @ Texas
Saturday, Oct. 9, probably an afternoon start
Game 4, @ Texas (unless we sweep)
Sunday, Oct. 10, probably an afternoon start
Game 5, @ Tampa Bay (if necessary)
Tuesday, Oct. 12, time unknown

The American League Championship Series will get underway Friday, October 15.

The World Series starts Wednesday, October 27.

Bye, Dan.

October 3, 2010

The league has announced start times for the three Rangers-Rays games certain to be played:

Game 1, @ Tampa Bay
Wednesday, Oct. 6, 12:37 p.m. Central
Game 2, @ Tampa Bay
Thursday, Oct. 7, 1:37 p.m. Central
Game 3, @ Texas
Saturday, Oct. 9, 4:07 p.m. Central

Don Orsillo will have the TBS play-by-play, with Buck Martinez on color and Marc Fein reporting.

The Rangers have told righthanders Rich Harden, Pedro Strop, and Doug Mathis and infielder Cristian Guzman that they will not appear in the playoffs. Lefthander Matt Harrison and righthander Mark Lowe will head to Surprise, where they will continue to throw in preparation for candidacy for the ALCS roster.

That leaves 31 players who are traveling tomorrow to Tampa Bay, 25 of whom will make the ALDS roster. Mitch Moreland and Jorge Cantu are expected to make the team over Chris Davis, and Frankie Francisco is not a candidate for this series but could be ready if the Rangers advance.

Taylor Teagarden and Esteban German are likely to be left off the roster, as will two of the following five relievers: Scott Feldman, Dustin Nippert, Michael Kirkman, Derek Holland, and Clay Rapada.

October 4, 2010

Three years ago today, Cleveland set its ALDS roster, choosing 22-year-old rookie lefthander Aaron Laffey for the 11th and final spot on its pitching staff. He hadn't even been on the club's 40-man roster until August 4, but having gone 13-4, 2.88 between AA and AAA forced his way into the picture. He went 4-2, 4.56 in nine late-season Indians starts, initially lasting two starts before an option back to AAA and then returning on August 25 for the rest of the season.

Laffey was one of two Cleveland pitchers (along with fellow rookie Tom Mastny) not to appear in the club's three-games-to-one series win over the Yankees, as the Indians advanced to face Boston in the ALCS.

In Game 6 of the ALCS, with Mastny already having appeared in Games One, Two, and Five against Boston, Laffey made his first and only playoff appearance. The Red Sox (who had won Game 5 after Cleveland won three of the first four games) had jumped out to a 4-0 lead on Fausto Carmona in the first inning. Down 4-1 in the third, Carmona issued two walks and gave up a J.D. Drew RBI single to start the inning, and Rafael Perez was called on from the bullpen. He got Jason Varitek to fly out but proceeded to give up a single, double, walk, and single. With the score 10-1, in came Laffey.

The young lefty got out of the inning with no further damage and proceeded to fire three scoreless frames, marred only by a Mike Lowell single in the sixth.

Laffey made just that one post-season appearance for the Indians, a mop-up effort by any definition. When he was put on the club's playoff roster on October 4, 2007, it had been at the expense of Cliff Lee, whose 5-8, 6.29 record had followed seasons of 14, 18, and 14 wins out of the Cleveland rotation—the first three full big league seasons of Lee's career.

The next year, Lee went 22-3, 2.54, easily claiming the AL Cy Young by leading the league in wins, ERA, walk infrequency, and home run infrequency.

And now this man is the apparent reason that Lee, who went 4-0, 1.56 in five post-season starts last year, is on the Rangers' playoff roster, and slated to start Game One in Tampa Bay in two days:

Almost five years ago, on November 18, 2005, Tampa Bay outrighted outfielder Josh Hamilton, who had spent the previous three tumultuous seasons on the club's restricted list, as part of its effort to clear roster space to add righthander James Shields, catcher Shawn Riggans, and first baseman Wes Bankston (Plano's own) to the roster to make sure they weren't exposed to the Rule 5 Draft.

Hamilton came off the restricted list late in 2006, appearing in 15 games in July for the Hudson Valley Renegades (the next-to-last of which was a 6-4 loss to the State College Spikes, in that club's first season of existence, having been moved from Augusta, New Jersey by new owner Chuck Greenberg).

But that 50-at-bat resurfacing didn't convince the Devil Rays to do with Hamilton what they'd done with Shields, Riggans, and Bankston the winter before. Tampa Bay purchased the contracts of outfielder Elijah Dukes, righthander Mitch Talbot, and utility player Elliot Johnson in November 2006, protecting them from the Draft, but not of Hamilton, a decision that led the Reds to pay the Cubs to draft the 25-year-old in a prearranged deal on December 7, and that led Cincinnati to move him to Texas a year and two weeks later for Edinson Volquez and Danny Ray Herrera, and that will have led to Hamilton, a second-time MVP candidate, stepping up to the plate in the first inning on Wednesday, before Lee ever takes the mound.

There's not really a point to any of the above, other than an opportunity for me to work off some restless energy on an off-day between the games that count for 30 teams and the ones that only eight get to play.

I can say I remember what this was like 11 years ago, but I think I'd be lying.

October 5, 2010

David Price is a career 0-2, 7.45 pitcher in four starts against Texas.

Then again, the Rangers didn't win in three trips to Tropicana Field this year (and have lost 10 of 12 there), and overall were just a 19-25 team in 2010 day games.

But is that all about circadian rhythms, or natural daylight, the latter of which will be kept out by the dome?

Cliff Lee's stretch of four bad starts in a row in August started in Tampa Bay on the 16th of that month—the Joaquin Arias game that prompted the manager to tell reporters, after the game, that his message for his club was to "get your head outta your butt and let's play baseball."

Tampa Bay's starting pitchers other than Price since August 31 are 4-11, 5.85 in 23 starts. That includes 0-4, 7.59 from Game Two starter James Shields, over six games.

The Rays run wild, and the Rangers have difficulty suppressing the running game.

The Rays have been held to two hits or fewer seven times in 2010.

Will Neftali Feliz and Alexi Ogando stand up to the pressure?

Will Joaquin Benoit and Jake McGee?

Evan Longoria and David Murphy (who probably wouldn't start against Price anyway) may be good to go physically, but what about their rhythm?

Does any of the above matter?

When I go to the movie theater, I like the previews. They could show twice as many as they do and I'd be cool with that. But I'm tired of waiting for this series to start, tired of the previews.

I need Elvis Andrus to step in against David Price so I can stop thinking about all the reasons this series could go wrong, or go perfectly.

They don't play these games on paper, and in the case of some teams and some players they don't play them that often.

Somebody's going to have a Darren Oliver start. Somebody's going to make a Dean Palmer throw, or a Kevin Elster play unmade. Somebody might even put together a Juan Gonzalez series.

Someone could join the Billy Hatcher/Scott Brosius/Bucky Dent/Bill Mazeroski list by doing something in this best-of-five that will end up redefining his career.

I'm prepared to be fired up and devastated and anxious a lot, at times all of it in the same inning. Then again, I'm not. I don't think I'm really prepared for this at all. Antsy, maybe, but not prepared.

I'm not exactly sure what the next few days of Newberg Reports will look like, but my guess is that they'll look different. If you're not following me on Twitter (http://twitter.com//newbergreport), this might be a good time to start.

Back at you next from Sunny St. Pete.

October 6, 2010

That "get your head outta your butt and let's play baseball" game we talked about yesterday, the one that kicked off Cliff Lee's run of four ugly starts before he was temporarily shut down with back issues, was on August 16. Tampa Bay won, 6-4, scoring four runs in the eighth inning, an epic disaster of a frame in which Texas arguably gave the Rays as many as seven outs.

That was the Joaquin Arias game, though one thing I'd forgotten about it was that Arias didn't start, but instead was inserted defensively in the bottom of the seventh (after Mitch Moreland had hit for Andres Blanco in the top of the inning).

But more to the point, that game pitted Cliff Lee against David Price, and offers something possibly instructive as the two get set to tee it up again in a few hours.

Tampa Bay scored more runs, and had the same number of hits as the Rangers.

But through six innings, even though the Rays held a 2-0 lead at that point, Price had thrown 102 pitches, an average of 17 per inning. Lee had thrown just 66 (11 per inning).

A clearly fatigued Price threw seven more pitches in the top of the seventh, only one of which was a strike—a pitch that Bengie Molina doubled to deep left center ahead of a four-pitch walk by David Murphy that ended Price's day. Texas clawed back by scoring twice that inning and twice more in the eighth, giving Lee what seemed then like a safe two-run lead with six outs to go . . . before the Arias eighth.

Yes, Tampa Bay's bullpen is solid, and on a tear right now (finishing the season on a run of 32.2 innings without allowing an earned run). But the key to the Rays' post-season fortunes, and certainly to Game One, is David Price, and to wear him out the way Texas did on August 16 seems like a very good idea to try and gameplan again.

Much is made of the fact that C.J. Wilson leads the American League in walks allowed. But Price allowed the sixth-highest total in the league. The Rangers drew five walks off Price in that six-plus-inning effort two months ago, and if they can take as patient an approach this afternoon—despite the energy of the day—I like our chances.

I went back yesterday and read the report I wrote on July 4, the one in which I spent a crazy amount of time imagining what a conversation between Seattle and Texas about a trade for Lee might look like, what I thought it might ultimately take to get him, and whether I'd do it.

He was acquired for this series, and this game. He's fanned 25 Rays this year, and walked two. He's allowed four stolen bases all season, neutralizing the aspect of the game that Tampa Bay relies on so heavily to create runs. Yes, he's 0-3, 4.56 against the Rays in 2010, but let's dig a little bit on that.

On May 5, just Lee's second start of the season after returning from an abdominal strain, he gave up five runs (four earned) over eight innings, but he'd allowed only two runs going into the eighth, an inning that went this way: flyout to right, infield single, bunt single, looping single to short left center, lineout to shortstop followed by a throwing error by the shortstop, ending Lee's day. (Sound familiar?)

On May 16, Lee took a complete game loss, giving up two Tampa Bay runs (single scores in the seventh and eighth innings) on five hits and one walk, fanning 10.

And then there was the August 16 debacle.

Lee really hasn't been too bad against Tampa Bay this year, running into trouble only in the late innings, and even then as a frequent victim of crummy hits and poor defense.

His otherwordly 10.28 strikeout-to-walk rate this year includes a 12.50 mark against the Rays. Tampa Bay's .613 OPS trails eight other Lee opponents. Only three teams (Detroit, Oakland, Kansas City) struck out more frequently against Lee this year.

And again, Texas acquired Lee for October.

Last year, he started Game One of the NLDS for Philadelphia, getting a complete-game win over Colorado. He allowed one run on six hits and zero walks, fanning five (adding a single, sac bunt, and stolen base of his own for good measure).

In Game Four of that series (which was on regular rest), he gave up three runs (one earned) on five hits and three walks, striking out five Rockies.

In Game Three of the NLCS, he fired eight scoreless innings, scattering three Dodger singles and no walks while punching out 10.

In Game One of the World Series, Lee held the Yankees to one run—unearned—on six hits and zero walks in a complete-game win in Yankee Stadium, setting 10 hitters down on strikes. He came back in Game Five, with the Phillies facing elimination, and got another win, permitting five runs over seven-plus innings—but just two runs going into the eighth.

What were the experts saying before that Game One performance, after Lee had given up four New York runs on 16 hits and five walks in 12 innings (3.00 ERA) during the season? Bet they weren't anticipating 9-6-1-0-0-10.

Lee is a big game pitcher. A Game One pitcher.

It still shocks me that the Rangers got Lee—and more Seattle cash than they've had to pay Lee themselves—without giving up more. And, to a lesser degree, that Lee said yesterday: "I enjoy it here in Texas. It's been a good ride so far, and yeah, I could see myself being here in the future. . . . It looks like it's going to be a good team for years to come. And that's what I want to be a part of. I want to be a part of a winner."

It's not time to get ahead of ourselves and start thinking about whether Cliff Lee could be a Ranger for the next five or six years, but when he says things this week like, "Hopefully we do some damage here in the post-season, win the World Series, and that will make things a lot easier on me," it's hard not to be thinking about the long term at least a little bit.

Then again, what else is he going to say?

Man, I'm exhausted. Couldn't fall asleep last night. So I'm probably not thinking clearly in the first place. I need this game to start. I have no interest in overthinking this game anymore (but if you want some more analysis, and a really good breakdown, look no further than to our own Scott Lucas), and there's absolutely no good reason to be thinking long term right now.

Of course, that's what we've all been conditioned as Rangers fans to do. To think about the future. Because the present always had that "Just wait for where this team *will* be" undercurrent, so we could maintain our sanity.

That changed this year, and it changes in a big way today.

Price vs. Lee. An encore, in a sense, of that miserable August 16 game, But maybe with a different defense on the field, and hopefully a similar offensive approach, and the same pitcher, the consummate big game pitcher, healthy again, Texas could grab the opener of the series, stealing with it the home field advantage.

Game One is always important, but in this series it seems even more so than usual, given how much Texas relies on its ace, and how much the Rays depend on theirs.

Cue up the anthem. Please.

October 6, 2010

The Rangers have officially set their roster for the Rays series, with Dustin Nippert and Derek Holland claiming the final bullpen spots (over Scott Feldman, Michael Kirkman, and Clay Rapada), Mitch Moreland and Jorge Cantu earning the first base jobs (over Chris Davis), and Esteban German landing a runner spot at the expense of an extra arm. The Rangers will go with 10 pitchers this round.

The full roster:

RH Pitchers (6)
Neftali Feliz
Tommy Hunter
Colby Lewis
Dustin Nippert
Darren O'Day
Alexi Ogando

LH Pitchers (4)
Derek Holland
Cliff Lee
Darren Oliver
C.J. Wilson

Catchers (2)
Bengie Molina
Matt Treanor

Infielders (7)
Elvis Andrus
Andres Blanco
Jorge Cantu
Esteban German
Ian Kinsler
Mitch Moreland
Michael Young

Outfielders (6)
Julio Borbon
Nelson Cruz
Jeff Francoeur
Vladimir Guerrero
Josh Hamilton
David Murphy

October 7, 2010: ALDS Game One, Texas 5, Tampa Bay 1

It will go down, no matter what happens from here on out, as one of the most memorable, energizing, important games in Texas Rangers history, and in two ways it played out like I thought (hoped?) it might:

1. From Wednesday morning's report: "*[T]hat [August 16] game pitted Cliff Lee against David Price, and offers something possibly instructive as the two get set to tee it up again in a few hours. Tampa Bay scored more runs, and had the same number of hits as the Rangers. But through six innings, even though the Rays held a 2-0 lead at that point, Price had thrown 102 pitches, an average of 17 per inning. Lee had thrown just 66 (11 per inning). . . . [T]he key to the Rays' post-season fortunes, and certainly to Game One, is David Price, and to wear him out the way Texas did on August 16 seems like a very good idea to try and gameplan again. . . . [I]f [the Rangers] can take as patient an approach this afternoon—despite the energy of the day—I like our chances.*"

2. I tweeted this an hour before gametime, while watching batting practice: "*Got a hunch today. Frenchy.*"

Elvis Andrus grounded out to third to start the game, but it was an outstanding eight-pitch at-bat (six strikes) that signaled what was to come. Through four innings, Price was pounding the zone, firing 51 strikes and only 16 balls, but the sum total—67 pitches, or nearly 17 per inning—was exactly the kind of workload Texas needed to impose on the superstar lefthander.

Price didn't walk a batter, but Texas managed to spoil a ton of fastballs, and punished two 3-0 offerings, one that Nelson Cruz put on top of the restaurant in straightaway center field to push the Rangers' lead to 3-0, and another that Vladimir Guerrero doubled over center fielder B.J. Upton's head to score Josh Hamilton and give Texas a 5-0 cushion.

But dial back, and there was Francoeur, who attacked a first-pitch fastball from Price in the top of the second, blasting it off the center field fence for a double that opened the game's scoring.

This was no Juan Gonzalez solo outburst of offense. There were 10 hits from seven hitters, including three contributed by Bengie Molina, who homered and singled twice. There was no single star of the game offensively.

The star, of course, was Lee, who escaped a troublesome first (in which he matched Price's 24-pitch output), stranding three runners, and cruised for the most part after that, fanning 10 (six looking) without issuing a walk over seven innings. He threw a first-pitch strike to 21 of 27 Rays he faced, and went 2-0 on just one batter all day.

There have been seven post-season pitching performances of at least 10 strikeouts and no walks in baseball history.

Lee has the last three.

Yes, Tampa Bay barreled a good half dozen shots that were right at Texas outfielders—not necessarily bad Rays luck, as Gary Pettis had Cruz, Hamilton, and Francoeur positioned well—and Lee and Price had nearly identical lines in terms of innings pitched, pitches thrown, strikes thrown, absence of walks, and strikeouts. But the Rangers had nine hits off Price to Tampa Bay's five off Lee, and scored in four of the seven innings Price took the hill. Price had control but not command; Lee had both.

And with it, Lee gave Texas its first win in Tampa Bay this year, and erased his own winlessness against the Rays in 2010.

He's now 5-0, 1.52 in the post-season for his career. In five of six starts he's held a playoff offense to one earned run, or none. His 0.72 ERA in three Game One starts is the lowest in history among the 54 pitchers who have pitched at least three.

It was an uncharacteristic effort for Price, who only two other times all season had allowed as many as five runs, while it was exceedingly consistent with what Lee had done in the playoffs in 2009, with what he had done for the most part since joining Texas three months ago, and with the Game One vision the Rangers had when they traded for him.

Can't we agree that even if Justin Smoak goes on to have a Hall of Fame career, it's OK? Lee was brought here to pitch that game, and he did his job really, really well.

Man, I don't know exactly how I'm supposed to feel. Years of dashed Ranger hopes have me conditioned not to get too excited, I guess, a defense mechanism of sorts to guard against the mirage factor, but damn, in a three-hour period this team matched what it had accomplished in its first 38 years, winning a single playoff game. There were a few similarities to Texas 6, New York 2 from October 1, 1996, but some key differences as well, including having a guy on the mound who pitched not the game of his life (like John Burkett might have), but the game we've come to expect from him.

After Lee made the necessary adjustments once he got through the first inning, and when Guerrero's fifth-inning missile to the wall in center gave Texas a five-run lead, it felt absolutely insurmountable, and I'll go ahead and admit that, for the first time ever, I actually felt like throwing a claw down. (Though I didn't.)

(Which reminds me: check out the profile photo on Chuck Greenberg's Facebook.)

When I got to Tropicana Field (whose concourse made me think I was in Valley View Mall), I was surprised to see how loose and confident the Rangers looked in BP. Ron Washington apparently addressed his players briefly in a pregame meeting, and said "the heavy lifting is over and now's the time to have some fun." Washington's postgame comments were remarkably low-key, self-assured, and businesslike. I didn't expect this realization, but I think Washington is a manager perfectly suited to lead a team in October.

Much like his number one starter.

A few other observations:

Hamilton, Cruz, and David Murphy put on tremendous batting practice displays (in Hamilton's case not strictly clearing fences). Murphy looks ready to go, even though he'll apparently sit today's game out despite righthander James Shields getting the ball for the Rays.

None of Cruz's pinball-game BP shots were as majestic as his third-inning bomb, though.

Cruz continues to hit good pitching.

Price threw his fastball 80 percent of the time yesterday (higher than his 74 percent average during the season), even though Texas (.297) led the Major Leagues in hitting the fastball in 2010, per ESPN Stats & Information. The Rangers went 8 for 25 (.320) against the Price fastball in Game One.

Tampa Bay was uncharacteristically conservative on the bases in the first inning. Not sure it would have changed much if Jason Bartlett had been sent home on Evan Longoria's one-out single to left (and it's pretty clear he would have scored), but when Lee proceeded to punch Carlos Pena and Rocco Baldelli out, leaving Bartlett on third (and Longoria and Carl Crawford on first and second), it took some air out of the crowd, at least.

When Andrus grounded into a fielder's choice in the second inning (following Francoeur's run-scoring double and Molina's run-scoring single), ending up on first base as second baseman Sean Rodriguez flipped to the shortstop Bartlett to record out number two, I momentarily thought to myself that, if Michael Young were to follow with a double, Andrus might have actually been more likely to score from first base than Molina would have from second.

That said, I bet someone a quarter that Andrus was going to get picked off at some point in the game. He was completely confused by Price after reaching on that fielder's choice in the second, darting back to first two or three times on Price deliveries to the plate.

Jorge Cantu was wearing some sort of wrist brace on his glove hand and arm before the game. Whether or not that had something to do with how bad he looked against Price, striking out three times with bat speed that didn't have a chance, I'm not sure he's the club's best option at first base, regardless of who's pitching.

Washington worked with Cantu and Mitch Moreland on short-hop throws before the game, firing throws in the dirt from all points on the infield. It's probably something he did with Pena when they were in Oakland together, too, and Pena could have used the work yesterday. He struggled digging a couple low throws early in the game.

Washington said he didn't believe Neftali Feliz was nervous in the ninth, but instead was "overhyped," and just needed to settle down. After Feliz threw eight balls and four strikes to Pena and Dan Johnson to start the inning, Mike Maddux strode to the mound to calm his closer, and he proceeded to throw eight more pitches—all strikes—to close things down. Impressive. And maybe important, as there's a benefit to getting that first playoff experience out of the way for a young closer who will be counted on in bigger spots this post-season.

I find this sort of interesting: In save opportunities, Feliz posted a 2.18 ERA in 2010. In all other games (like yesterday's), his ERA was 3.54.

Home teams that have lost Game One of a Division Series have gone on to lose 20 of 28 series.

The last to win one of those was the Angels, who came back in 2005 to beat the Yankees in five games. The Los Angeles bench coach was Rays manager Joe Maddon.

Ben Zobrist, who homered, doubled, and barreled a lineout to right field against Lee on Wednesday, is 5 for 10 with a sac fly and sac bunt and three RBI against the veteran lefthander in 2010. (He also rifled a Feliz fastball to right for the first out in the ninth, with two runners on.) If Lee does sign with New York this winter, he and Zobrist (who is under Rays control through 2015) are going to see each other a whole lot for years to come.

By the way, Lee allowed no hits between Zobrist's double to lead off the second inning and Zobrist's seventh-inning homer.

I guess I understand the initial thought process behind giving Shields the ball today and Matt Garza the Game Three assignment in Texas (not that I agreed with it), but it now makes less sense with Tampa Bay in what has to be characterized as a must-win situation today. Shields, whose ERA is 7.59 since the start of September, leads the league in earned runs allowed, hits allowed, and home runs allowed. According to the Elias Sports Bureau, Shields has the seventh-highest ERA (5.18) of any pitcher to ever start Game Two of a playoff series.

Then again, Shields held Texas to two runs (one earned) on four hits and a walk over seven innings at Tropicana Field on August 18, after he'd blanked the Yankees on four hits and a walk (11 strikeouts) over 7.1 innings earlier in the month. Don't get overconfident. Those were two of his three best starts of the season, and they weren't that long ago.

Guerrero is a .394/.394/.636 career hitter against Shields, with just one strikeout in 33 at-bats. Julio Borbon, who gets today's start, is 4 for 9 with only one strikeout, and Andrus is 3 for 6 without striking out. Michael Young is 4 for 14 (.286) but two of the hits left the yard. Hamilton has one hit (a home run) in 10 trips against Shields, who was his teammate on the 2001 Low A Charleston Riverdogs.

Longoria, Pena, and Upton against C.J. Wilson?

A combined 16 lifetime at-bats.

Zero hits.

ESPN's Tim Kurkjian is touting Wilson as the best Number Two starter in the American League playoffs.

Great day for Jon Daniels and his crew, as July pickups Lee and Francoeur and Molina each came up big, as did winter acquisitions Guerrero and Darren Oliver.

I guess it wasn't a huge shock that the Rays left Dioner Navarro and Brad Hawpe off their ALDS roster, but while I admit I wasn't keeping up with their personnel decisions very closely, I was a little surprised that Jeremy Hellickson, Jake McGee, and Willie Aybar didn't make the cut.

Figures that Doc Halladay would basically make what Lee did an afterthought not only for Phillies fans cringing at what Lee did Wednesday afternoon, but also on MLB Network and ESPN. (Even the ruling on Greg Golson's catch in the ninth inning of Yankees-Twins is getting heavier rotation this morning nationally.) I know at least a couple DFW TV stations are out here. Hope they left Rangers-Rays enough time in the sportscast after breaking down the latest angle on the tip Dez Bryant left the Pappas Bros. wait staff.

Jason Collette of DockOfTheRays.com did a Q&A with me about the Rangers a couple days ago, if you want to check it out.

We'll get to the designation for assignment of Rich Harden (a non-story) to make room for enigmatic righthander Ryan Tucker, claimed off waivers from Florida, another time. It is, however, sort of ironic that on the day that Texas wins Game One of its first playoff series in more than a decade, the pitcher the club signed over the winter presumably to seize that role suffered the ultimate procedural indignity.

When Darren O'Day relieved Lee to start the Rays eighth, and he and Oliver retired the strength of Tampa Bay's order—Upton, Crawford, and Longoria—after John Jaso had singled to start the inning, the air-conditioned silence in the stadium was deafening. There's something surprisingly invigorating about being in a hostile sports environment whose hostility has been completely vaporized, and getting the chance to act like you've been there before—even though you haven't.

I got chills when Andrus stepped up to the plate for the game's first pitch. But I was very content as late as the eighth inning, with an almost uncomfortable awareness of something I wasn't sure I deserved.

The next assignment falls to Wilson, who's picked up a thing or two from Lee in the last three months, including an approach based on trust in your stuff (his is tougher to do anything with than Lee's) and an attack on the strike zone. That's exactly what Texas needs from Wilson today, as he attempts to give the team a 2-0 lead in a series headed afterwards to Arlington, where memorable, energizing, and important could await on a level this franchise has never had within reach.

October 8, 2010: ALDS Game Two, Texas 6, Tampa Bay 0

It was 2004, a season that qualified, on the scale of this franchise's moments of success, as storybook. The Buck Showalter Rangers won 89 games, fourth most in the club's history (more, in fact, than one of their playoff teams). Never mind the third-place finish—that was a gold star, considering Texas had finished fourth the previous four seasons (three with Alex Rodriguez). The Rangers were three games back when the season ended, having drawn to within two games a week and a half earlier, when David Dellucci's double past a laid-out Jermaine Dye completed an impossible comeback and a sweep of the A's.

Dellucci's walk-off liner to right instantly etched itself as one of the most famous plays in franchise history, earned the part-time outfielder a permanent place in Texas Rangers lore, and led to front office strategy sessions from which the "managed expectations" mantra emerged as a marketing message for 2005.

That season was Michael Young's first at shortstop, the second of his five straight years of 200 base hits, and the first of his six straight All-Star Game appearances, and in it he earned an eighth-place finish in the MVP vote. His highlight moments of the season were a 10th-inning, walkoff single in the Rangers' 16-15 win over Detroit (a game in which Texas trailed by 10 runs), and a 4 for 5 effort in the most important game of that season, including a pair of doubles, the second of which came ahead of Dellucci's Double.

It was also a huge year for another shortstop, 22-year-old Ian Kinsler, who in his first full pro season hit .402 for Low A Clinton and .300 for AA Frisco, earning a starting spot on *Baseball America*'s Minor League All-Star Team and the Rangers' Tom Grieve Minor League Player of the Year Award.

Had it not been for August 2003 Tommy John surgery, 23-year-old lefthander C.J. Wilson would have been Kinsler's RoughRider teammate that summer of 2004.

On Thursday, six years later, Young and Kinsler had the biggest hits of their lives, Wilson pitched the game of his life, and Dellucci and 2004 are no longer pet rocks that we as Rangers fans guard with our life.

I hope you'll find a way to forgive me if I don't have any idea how to handle this. I believed in this team, its players and coaches, its front office, and its future, and if pressed before the season I would have agreed that this could be the year for things to come together, for Step Five to arrive.

But even once the Magic Number hourglass ran out, I don't think in my most optimistic moments these last couple weeks that I allowed myself to imagine bringing two road wins home to kick off the playoffs. These couple days in St. Petersburg will stick a lot longer than the Dellucci double, surreal in so many ways, to the point at which I'm oddly content, rather than frenzied as I feel like I probably should be.

This is a damn good baseball team. With all kinds of winning intangibles outside the lines.

Yes: Young probably swung at the 3-2 Chad Qualls pitch before getting another life, destroying the next pitch 427 feet away to dead center to extend a 2-0 lead to 5-0. That was a bad break for the Rays. But (1) there was only one out, and though Randy Choate might have come in to face Josh Hamilton had Young fanned, and maybe three of the next four hitters wouldn't have singled under changed circumstances, it's not as if the check swing call would have ended the inning had it gone differently, and (2) that was a 2-0 game before the disputed call, in a game in which the Rays never did put a run on the board.

I'm not faulting Rays fans for being upset about the call. I would have been if that were my team trying desperately to stay in that game, and in this series. (Know what I'd like to see, at least in the playoffs? A camera positioned at each foul pole, to give us a vantage point similar to the corner umpires for calls like that. Let us see what the ump sees.)

But Young wasn't rung up, and all that meant was the at-bat continued. Young still had to do something with the pitch, and that he did, demonstratively. He would say, after the game, that he felt no different after his home run/single/three-RBI performance from the way he did after his 0 for 4 in Game One, because his team won each time, but make no mistake: That was the biggest hit of Michael Young's career, because it contributed in a big way to a huge win, and given when it happened and under what circumstances, it seemed to kill Tampa Bay's will (and composure).

Act like you've been there, and all that, but if it's all the same I'm going to say, despite the controversy of the moment, that that missile over the center field wall felt like not only a small piece of redemption for Young, who has had his struggles in the field and at the plate at times this year, but also a bear hug to fans like us who have hung with this team, in some cases, for a lifetime, even in the best years, of not quite getting it done.

Thankfully, no longer will we have to see an All-Star Game triple as the SportsCenter highlight of Young's career.

As for Kinsler, whose fourth-inning home run preceded Young's and whose RBI single later in the Young fifth were instrumental in the win as well, I have two words:

Bat path.

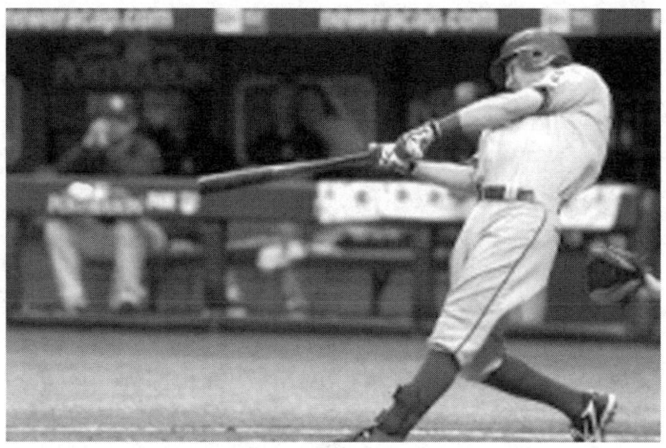

Man, I love *that* Ian Kinsler.

Then there's Wilson. Remember that stat from yesterday morning that I shared—that Evan Longoria, Carlos Pena, and B.J. Upton came into the game 0 for 16 lifetime against Wilson?

On Thursday, the entire Rays lineup was 2 for 22 (with two walks and a hit batsman) off the lefthander.

Wilson would say after the game that he picked some things up from Cliff Lee on how to attack the Tampa Bay lineup (and that he was inspired watching both Lee and Roy Halladay on Wednesday), adding that Lee is a better version of himself. Yesterday, Wilson was just about as good. The league's leader in bases on balls, he had terrific command of his four-seamer, slider, and cutter in particular, working in and out all day, changing speeds and keeping the Rays off balance, and in a noticeable departure from 2009, when things got a little sticky, he rose to the challenge rather than imploding.

The set-up reliever who talked the Rangers' decision-makers into a spring training chance to prove he could pitch every fifth day has done more than prove the decision right. He won't face the Rays again this series, and if Texas succeeds in closing this thing out and moving on, he should not only get the ball in Game One or Game Two against New York (at home) or Minnesota (on the road), but also give us all confidence that it will be a game the Rangers have a solid shot to win.

ESPN's Tim Kurkjian said before yesterday's game that Wilson's the best number two starter among the American League playoff teams, and Thursday he backed it up, in the biggest game of his life, with one of the best performances of his career, blanking Tampa Bay on two hits and two walks in 6.1 innings, fanning seven. Darren O'Day and Darren Oliver were masterful in relief, stranding the two Wilson runners left in scoring position—the only runners Texas allowed to get past first base all day—and not allowing a hit over the final 2.2 innings, nailing down Texas 6, Tampa Bay 0.

In that fluky 2004 season, Texas used 17 starting pitchers, getting the most starts out of 39-year-old Kenny Rogers, Ryan Drese, Chan Ho Park, R.A. Dickey, Joaquin Benoit, and John Wasdin. The latter four of them had ERA's between 5.46 and 6.78.

This year, the Rangers have started only 10 pitchers, and of course it's a dramatically better corps.

Michael Young still probably believed that 2004 team was capable of getting to the post-season, in spite of the pitching and even though Alex Rodriguez was no longer around. The way he's wired, until there's an "X" in the standings or the 27th out's been recorded or a check swing is ruled as strike three, he's still focused on getting it done. The All-Star Games and 200-hit seasons never meant much beyond the respect of his peers and his ability to stay on the field, all taking a backseat to winning. He talked yesterday about his teammates emptying the tank in Games One and Two, and how that's the plan Saturday as well.

Young never went into a season thinking Texas wasn't capable of being a playoff team, and certainly didn't manage his own expectations after those 89 wins in 2004. You know he didn't expect every season to end at 162 until 2010.

He wouldn't admit this either, not yet, but he and his team are accomplishing something special right now, something that has taken a long time for him, and for us, to be part of. I don't know where this is all headed, and there's still that conditioned reflex that's probably got most of us waiting for a bubble to burst, but I'm going to try hard to let this all sink in and understand what's happening here, as I fight through what's going to feel like a hundred hours before Colby Lewis throws pitch one tomorrow afternoon.

Emptying the tank
Leave it out there, bring it home
Win one more: Move on

October 9, 2010

"It's just [about] going right after those guys. Make them uncomfortable. Make them think about what they're doing, what they're going to swing at. Right now, they're real comfortable. They're just up there swinging and hitting the cover off the ball. So I've got to go in there and make them uncomfortable, make them do what I want them to do. It's a hard job, definitely a hard job, but somebody has got to do it. And I feel I'm the right man for the job right now."

So said Matt Garza, minutes after Texas 6, Tampa Bay 0 in Game Two.

"He's a tough competitor. He is a guy that will go out there and will do everything he can to get outs; he usually does. It's going to be very tough [Saturday] with him. But we have to maintain our composure and what we have to do, more than anything else, is take advantage of an opportunity if the door opens up. That's all you can do."

So said Ron Washington, about Garza.

Does that mean Elvis Andrus and Michael Young (the latter of whom is really the only Rangers hitter, along with Vladimir Guerrero, who has beaten up on Garza) need to be on guard when they dig in at the plate in the bottom of the first? Not necessarily.

Garza on September 2, the night before a start in Baltimore, where he'd been blasted for seven runs on 10 hits (including four home runs) in 6.1 innings six weeks earlier:

"I owe them a lot of payback for the type of outing I had last time against them. . . . I'm going to make them feel really uncomfortable in the box. So they know, this (stuff) doesn't happen, so don't get used to it. . . . I'm going to go in there, hair on fire, like I have been and go after them and say, 'Hey, you got me the first time, well I'm going to shove it down your throat this time.'"

Garza went on to beat the Orioles on September 3, yielding one run in 5.2 innings.

He didn't hit a batter. He just shut the Baltimore offense down.

The emotional Garza, who you might recall got into a heated argument on the mound with his catcher Dioner Navarro in a June 2008 start here, has extra motivation today. Rangers hitters have teed off in Games One and Two, slugging .479 as a team. Tampa Bay—baseball's best road team in 2010—faces elimination. And Garza's career ERA in Arlington, despite decent peripherals, is 6.04.

It's going to be a fascinating matchup, particularly early, when the late-afternoon sun could make Garza's and Colby Lewis's sharp breaking balls even more difficult to pick up.

The only Rays hitter who has faced Lewis since 2003 is Jason Bartlett, who struck out on three pitches when Lewis came in for Oakland in the eighth to mop up a 5-0 deficit to the Twins.

But if that unfamiliarity is an obstacle for Tampa Bay today, it may not be any more significant than the one the Rangers could face simply by virtue of having treated Garza badly in this ballpark before.

Wear red if you're headed to the Ballpark.

The televised postgame show will be on Channel 677 (Fox Sports Southwest's alternate signal) if you have DirecTV.

Have a great day.

October 10, 2010: ALDS Game Three, Tampa Bay 6, Texas 3

After I got home last night and made sure that Jason Bartlett didn't have something like 16 hits in 13 career at-bats off of Darren O'Day, I kept coming back to this:

I just don't understand why you bring Neftali Feliz in the game there, with the score tied in the eighth, using O'Day up for six pitches, leaving Dustin Nippert as the only available reliever (and if Cliff Lee and even C.J. Wilson really were bullpen considerations last night, that raises other questions).

That's it. That's not the sole reason Texas lost, but that's all I got this morning. My tank is emptied.

Today's sort of a big game.

P.S. *Bartlett was 3 for 5 lifetime against off O'Day. The smallness of the sample isn't the only issue there. There's also the fact that the three hits were a bunt single (when O'Day was an Angels rookie in 2008), a ground ball single past third baseman Robb Quinlan (also in 2008 with the Angels), and an infield single hit in August to Joaquin Arias, playing shortstop for the first time in the big leagues since 2006.*

October 10, 2010: ALDS Game Four, Tampa Bay 5, Texas 2

Nothin'.

October 11, 2010

It was the middle of the third. Tommy Hunter had thrown 33 strikes and just 13 balls to 12 Rays hitters through three innings, and though he'd given up a run, it came across on a terribly played pop-up to short right field.

Wade Davis, in only two innings at that point, had thrown 19 balls and 19 strikes.

And in spite of those numbers, the Rangers were the ones who looked dead offensively, the Rays the ones who looked loose.

Frankly, the ugly 19-19 ball/strike breakdown for Davis through two was deceptive, since several of the strikes were sliders well out of the zone that Rangers hitters flailed at. Davis should have been on the ropes. Instead, that's where he had his opposition.

You can safely bet that David Price won't throw 80 percent fastballs again tomorrow.

It may be cliché to say that the offense is pressing, that the team looks like it's playing not to lose rather than to win, but I don't know how else to describe it.

The Rangers' 2-3-4 hitters, Michael Young and Josh Hamilton and Vladimir Guerrero, were due up in the bottom of the seventh, with the score 5-2.

Seven pitches later, it was the top of the eighth.

The 5-6-7 hitters, Nelson Cruz and Ian Kinsler and David Murphy—who have been far more productive this series than the trio they follow—came up in the bottom of the eighth, with the score still 5-2.

Another seven pitches, and it was the top of the ninth.

We are *better than that*.

We need to forget the mistake pitches and bad swings and bungled plays in the field and go out Tuesday and turn the biggest game in Rangers history into the biggest win in Rangers history. More energy. More patience. More Cliff Lee.

You know what the Rangers are? Very good underdogs. That's what this team is. Its best players have been underdogs. Its manager, too. The franchise itself.

That doesn't necessarily mean they need to be uncomfortable as frontrunners, or unsure of how to handle it. But they do seem to thrive when they're backed into a corner.

And maybe that's OK, tomorrow. Texas is the underdog, not just because Game Five is on the road. Momentum has obviously swung to the Rays, whose lame duck left fielder, Carl Crawford, said *before* yesterday's game: "It feels like we're winning the series right now."

The Rangers need to develop a killer instinct. But for now, they've proven to be pretty good when they're not the popular pick, and that, combined with the fact that Cliff Lee is getting the ball, in the decisive game of a series in which the road team has won every game, is enough for me to start feeling pretty good about Tuesday night.

Just as the Rays overcame Games One and Two, Games Three and Four no longer matter. The opportunity to put the ball in the hands of exactly the right pitcher is here, and even if the circumstances have made Texas an underdog for tomorrow night's win-or-go-home ballgame, that's OK, and maybe just what this team needs.

October 11, 2010

I think I just got the good omen I've been looking for.

A law partner of mine just sent me the following email:

3 questions:
1. Are you going to Game 5?
2. Is Cliff Lee pitching?
3. Will Texas win?
My response:
N Y Y

There you go. NYY.

We win tomorrow night.

October 11, 2010

The Rangers have announced that they have signed a three-year contract extension with television analyst Tom Grieve, and that Josh Lewin, who has been the club's television play-by-play man for the last nine seasons, will not return.

October 12, 2010

I'm generally not a superstitious person, but I'm very sports-superstitious. I was as a player, I am as a fan. Given what's at stake tonight, I'm not messing around. This gets blown up into wallpaper today.

Tonight we experience something we've never experienced.

Tonight is what Steps One through Five were all about, starting with the trade of Mark Teixeira and the patience and untelevised grinding that followed. And why those 100 folks in untucked short sleeves and slacks lined up behind home plate before player introductions on Saturday are so important, even if the names and faces aren't as recognizable as the last player on the roster.

Tonight is the reason it was the right decision to draft Justin Smoak instead of Ethan Martin.

Tonight is the reason it will always be OK that Justin Smoak is now a Seattle Mariner, maybe for life.

Tonight is the reason we all invest the way we do.

Trust in Cliff.

October 12, 2010

A night of firsts, but two stand out for me:

1. The Texas Rangers have won a playoff series.
2. I'm absolutely speechless.

I will have more, but for the moment I'm going to continue to let the phone ring and the texts and emails pile up unanswered, and stop typing here in a second. I need to continue to do absolutely nothing but let this soak in.

Getty Images

October 13, 2010: ALDS Game Five, Texas 5, Tampa Bay 1

Every year the main section of my book has roughly 12 months of reports in it. I generally cut it off some time in October, when there's a natural break in the ongoing story.

Last year's book ended with an October 12, 2009 report, which concluded (before any marketing campaign had been launched) with these words: "*It's time to win.*"

One year later, to the day, this team won.

Not the big prize yet, of course. There are two more teams to beat, eight more games to win.

For some franchises, this wouldn't be quite as big a deal. For some, in fact, anything less than what happened last night might be considered a failure.

But for this team, what happened last night, with the entire baseball world having cleared the stage, had never happened before, and for a number of reasons it felt like it needed to. It's too early to call the season a success, but at the same time, no matter what happens going forward, that's what this season will be called once the final Texas Rangers game of 2010 has been played.

Nolan Ryan said in March he expected 92 wins. It took more than 162 games to get there, and if Texas had lost last night that's where the number would have been frozen. But Texas 5, Tampa Bay 1 was number 93 for the year, and this team plays on, with at least four more baseball games to go in 2010 and maybe as many as 14.

Group hug.

I haven't stopped smiling since about the sixth inning last night (when David Price missed the first base bag by the thickness of a *Sports Illustrated* cover and Vladimir Guerrero took advantage, scoring from second base). I haven't slept much. And I haven't allowed myself to think fully about the things I want to say in this space.

I'll get there, but bear with me. It will probably be tomorrow before I settle back into a writing frame of mind. Right now, no chance.

There's a lot more writing to go in what will be this year's version of the Bound Edition, and when in October the book will reach its natural end is impossible now to predict.

Especially since it might be in November.

October 13, 2010

Well, I've figured out tomorrow's lead.

In the meantime, if you see this guy, at the courthouse or at Twisted Root or at the next Scots-Purple Cobras fifth-grade football game (throw out the records), thank him.

You may not know my law partner Bob Jenevein personally, but he played a big role as far as I'm concerned in Texas 5, Tampa Bay 1 last night, at least for me. The great baseball fan that he is, he turned me around Monday morning into believing *we had this*.

Again, our email exchange:

Bob:
3 questions:
1. *Are you going to Game 5?*
2. *Is Cliff Lee pitching?*
3. *Will Texas win?*

Me:
N Y Y

That was my omen.

Now, if you'll excuse me, I'm headed down the hall to go pour a couple Shiner Bock's over Bob's head.

Back atcha tomorrow with a full-blown Newberg Report.

October 14, 2010: Essential Lee

There are images you never forget, a Nolan Ryan pitch that made history or a Rusty Greer catch that preserved a perfect game, a Pudge Rodriguez fist pump or Josh Hamilton double fist pump, an impossible Gary Matthews Jr. catch or improbable David Dellucci double.

Tuesday night's indelible image for me was Cliff Lee's march toward home plate as B.J. Upton lofted the first pitch he saw with two outs in the ninth, a simple yet striking walk toward battery mate Bengie Molina during which Lee never looked up or back, paid no attention to where Upton's pop-up was headed or where or when it might land, an understated set of steps that I'll never forget.

It started, as the ball shot straight up off Upton's bat, with Lee demonstratively clapping his left hand into his glove, then taking a slow, measured walk towards the plate, presumably never taking his eyes off his catcher the whole way even though we didn't get to see Lee's face in those 10 awesome steps.

We didn't see his face until well after we saw Lee leap into Molina's arms.

He never looked back. The baseball world watched the harmless flare settle into Elvis Andrus's mitt, ending the series, all but Cliff Lee, who wasn't even curious.

It was as if, just as most of his night had gone, he didn't need to see where the ball ended up, because his own visualization of the ball's path, start to finish, rang true with every pitch.

He was surgical all night long, with his four-seam fastball and his two-seam fastball and his cutter and his curve ball and his slider and his change, and for Lee there was no point in watching the 27th out get made. He knew exactly where the ball was going.

All night.

The man never looked back to see the biggest moment in Texas Rangers history.

He's so ridiculously cool.

He's Don Draper.

The local high school classes of 2029 are going to have an oddly large concentration of "Cliff's" in them.

Our next dog will be named Cliff Lee.

And he, or she, will startle all comers with a spectacular lack of wasted energy, an imposing subtlety, and an endless supply of cool.

His first time through the Rays lineup, Lee threw 28 pitches. Every one of them was a fastball, or a cutter. Every single one of them.

As the Rays order rolled and leadoff hitter Jason Bartlett stepped back in with one on and one out in the bottom of the third, and Texas ahead, 1-0, Lee, who knew in pregame warm-ups that the curve was going to be a reliable weapon for him in Game Five, and yet kept it in his back pocket through each Rays hitter's first look at him on the night, finally showed the big bender.

Lee had Bartlett down in the count, 1-2, and had thrown to first several times to keep Sean Rodriguez close, when he spun his first curve of the night, a pitch that stayed up and that Bartlett beat into the ground for an infield single to set up what would be Tampa Bay's lone run of the night (on Ben Zobrist's single to center). Lee escaped further trouble by getting Carl Crawford to roll back to the mound (and starting a 1-2-5 rundown to erase Bartlett from third) and Evan Longoria to bounce out to shortstop.

He never threw a second curve that inning.

But then the gameplan shifted. Texas took a 2-1 lead in the top of the fourth (when Nelson Cruz turned two mistakes into a run, first admiring a double off the center field wall that should have been a triple, and then inexplicably attempting to steal third with two outs [it's not as if David Price, who tends to work up in the zone, was prone to Brandon Webb a pitch or two into the dirt, which I suppose might have made the risk of getting thrown out worth the reward of moving from second to third] and coming home when Kelly Shoppach's throw toward third took off into left field), and Lee took a new plan to the mound.

After throwing just the one curve in his first 42 pitches over three innings, Lee would throw 18 of them over his remaining 78 pitches. And most of them were gorgeous. Or nasty. Depending on your perspective.

Lee would maintain the cut fastball, which was a tremendous pitch for him all night, but would show the Rays far fewer four- and two-seamers, actually throwing fewer over those final six innings than he did in the first three frames. From a strike efficiency standpoint, the curve was actually the least effective of Lee's six offerings (12 of 19 for strikes, or 63 percent), but several of them came in huge spots, and the threat of that pitch made everything else work. Of the 38 cutters Lee threw, a silly 33 of them were strikes (nine swinging, seven called, nine fouled, eight put into play), and very few were hit with any authority.

You've heard this many times by now: there have been eight playoff pitching performances in the history of the game of at least 10 strikeouts and no walks. Lee has now authored four of those masterpieces. Four other pitchers (Deacon Phillippe, Don Newcombe, Tom Seaver, and Sterling Hitchcock) did it one time each.

The great Dave Cameron of U.S.S. Mariner points this out:

Sandy Koufax pitched 57 playoff innings in his career, scattering 10 runs on 36 hits (two home runs) and 11 walks, striking out 61.

Cliff Lee has pitched 56.1 playoff innings in his career, scattering 12 runs on 38 hits (one home run) and six walks, striking out 54.

Lee tied an LDS record with 21 strikeouts (matching Kevin Brown's 1998 effort with San Diego), and his zero walks in 16 innings represented the first time a pitcher had thrown at least 15 walkless frames in such a series.

He put on an absolute clinic in Game 5. To say he located all night doesn't do his performance justice. The dude flat *painted*.

Three-fourths of Lee's pitches went for strikes, but very few pierced the zone—he annihilated the picture frame, with assassin's precision.

Meanwhile, the Rangers offense didn't so much punish Price as it pressured him, creating opportunities and capitalizing on them. I was too locked in watching the game, practically immobilized (outside of my Twitter barrage), and so the thought didn't occur to me until afterwards that the way the Rangers generated offense Tuesday night reminded me of the Super Bowl Saints, a team that probably had fans without a rooting interest thinking, "Man, I wish *my team* played baseball like that."

Yes, Cruz and Ian Kinsler did something no playoff teammates since Babe Ruth and Lou Gehrig had done in a playoff series of five games or less (hitting three home runs each, which Ruth and Gehrig did in 1928), but Game Five was more about audacity than brawn. The first three Texas runs, unbelievably, scored from second base without the ball ever leaving the infield—unless you count Shoppach's throw that sailed past Longoria into left field.

The last time a playoff run scored from second on an infield grounder was in 1970, when Orioles outfielder Paul Blair motored around in the eighth inning of Baltimore's World Series-ending Game Five against the Reds, as Cincinnati second baseman Tommy Helms tossed to reliever Ray Washburn covering first base on a Boog Powell grounder.

Forty years later, the Rangers did it twice, in the first (Andrus) and again in the sixth (Big Bad). And that doesn't count Cruz scoring from second on his crazed stolen base attempt, with two outs and Kinsler's hot bat at the plate.

It's almost funny: If you had to name the four Rangers with the biggest issues on the bases in 2010, it would probably be Andrus, Guerrero, Cruz, and the glacial Molina. They were the base-running stars in Game Five.

(It wasn't only Cruz's run that probably shouldn't have happened the way it did. Think about this: If Shoppach hadn't held onto a Hamilton foul tip on 2-1, Andrus's first-inning steal of second would have been nullified. Maybe he still would have stolen on the next pitch [which turned out to be a 2-2 ball], setting up Hamilton's run-scoring groundout to first. But maybe not.)

(And this: Price gets the primary blame for Guerrero's run, but Shoppach deserves some, too. If he wasn't out of position at the plate, Price's throw home almost surely cuts Guerrero down.)

The havoc that Texas created on the bases had to make the Yankees uncomfortable from their couches. New York can be run on, as the Rangers proved in 2010, stealing eight bases without being caught in the teams' eight matchups.

New York decided yesterday to flip Phil Hughes and Andy Pettitte in its rotation, setting up the following matchups: C.J. Wilson against C.C. Sabathia in Game One, Colby Lewis against Hughes in Game Two, Lee against Pettitte in Game Three, and Tommy Hunter against A.J. Burnett in Game Four.

The Yankees aren't modifying their playoff roster from their Division Series against the Twins, but the Rangers are. Pinch-runner Esteban German (who wasn't used against the Rays) will be dropped, replaced by an additional left-handed reliever. The bullpen, which was a bit shaky against Tampa Bay, needed the reinforcement, while David Murphy's proven health has made Julio Borbon a bench player, minimizing the potential need for an extra runner like German. Candidates for the southpaw spot include Clay Rapada, Matt Harrison, and Michael Kirkman.

Frankie Francisco, still not recovered from his rib cage injury, will not be added to the roster.

Ron Washington said that Jorge Cantu will likely be in the lineup at first base against Sabathia or Pettitte. He sat against Price on Tuesday after looking overmatched against him in Game One.

Lee's use on Tuesday meant he'll start Game Three instead of Game One, but a few thoughts there.

First, Texas was reluctant to use Lee on short rest in Game Four against Tampa Bay, which was at the time the biggest game in franchise history, so shouldn't we assume it would be unlikely for the club to have planned to use him on short rest in the ALCS? He wasn't going to pitch Games One, Four, and Seven.

Second, Game Three is the first game in Yankee Stadium—I sure don't mind Lee getting that assignment, no matter what happens in Arlington in the first two games.

Third, using Lee on short rest in any scenario would make it less likely we'd get nine innings out of him, and the way several of the relievers are going, you don't want to go into any game increasing the chances you'll need to depend on the bullpen.

Texas advanced without getting much of anything in the ALDS from who most would agree is its best player, Hamilton. Almost as stunning as the fact that Texas won the five-game series without winning a home playoff game is the idea that the Rangers move on without getting so much as an extra-base hit from Hamilton in the entire series.

But Texas has Cliff Lee, who the Yankees would have right now if they hadn't been so insistent on replacing injured minor league second baseman David Adams, alongside catcher Jesus Montero, with righthander Adam Warren instead of infielder Eduardo Nunez or righthander Ivan Nova in their trade talks with Seattle. Had that played out differently, the Rangers aren't in the ALCS right now. They probably would have reached the ALDS, but with a much different team, and not only at the top of the rotation.

Lee will start in New York on Monday and, if the series is still going, in Arlington a week from Saturday (or conceivably Friday). That feels really, really good.

There may be another indelible image or two to add to the bank, right around the corner.

October 15, 2010

While you wait another four hours for the first pitch, here's a TV spot, a blog appearance, and a photo to kill some time:

You can go to SNY.tv for an online segment I did with SportsNet New York yesterday, helping host Ted Berg preview the Rangers-Yankees series.

You go to bronxbaseballdaily.com to read a Q&A that I did with Rod Abruzzese of Bronx Baseball Daily, also previewing the series.

And you can enjoy this photo, taken by the great Brad Newton, showing Elvis Andrus hand Cliff Lee the baseball that he chose not to watch get caught for the final out of the Rangers-Rays series.

Have fun tonight.

October 15, 2010

Start spreading the news
Twelve hours until C.J. kicks
Rangers 4, Yanks 2

To answer your question:

Both.

Wishful thinking? Maybe. But that's what this is all about.

When I see Mark Teixeira step up in the top of the first and Alex Rodriguez in (hopefully) the second, in the back of my mind I'll have it tucked away that Tex is 0 for 5 lifetime against Wilson and that A-Rod is 1 for 13. But this is different now, and even those numbers feel like wishful thinking.

But if I'm going to toss those out, do I also toss out the fact that the Rangers suiting up for this series are 24 for 137 lifetime (.175) against C.C. Sabathia—and 12 for 99 (.121) if you don't count Michael Young's 12 for 38 (.316)?

I toss it all out, as well as the fact that my legs are almost numb right now, I figure because I probably haven't slept well in a week and a half. Because of this.

This I think I know: Over the next week and maybe for the rest of my life, I will harbor an irrational hatred for Nick Swisher, there will probably be a home plate ump or two whose name I'll remember forever, and not fondly, and there will be several moments and images that will push all other moments and images down in my mental sports scrapbook.

It will never be like this again.

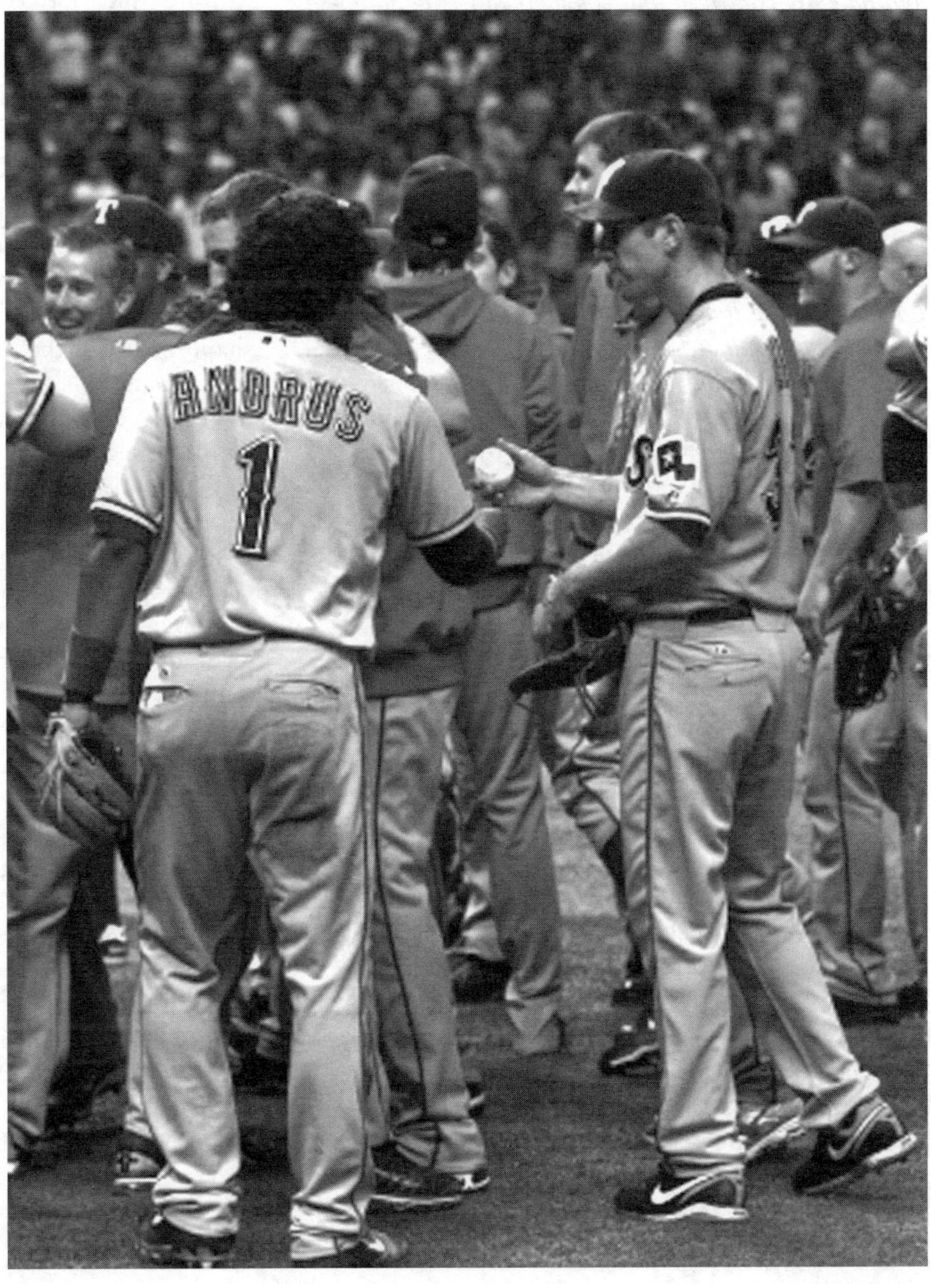

Texas could go on to win three World Series in a four-year span, and yet there will never again be a year like this one. Those of us who are Cowboys fans understand that.

There are lots of numbers in my head right now, streaks and trends and splits and precedent, and I'm going to make an effort, strenuous as it may be, to suppress all of them, and to do for myself whatever the equivalent is of Wilson looking over his left shoulder at the top of the right field foul pole, to center myself and block out the hype and the history and the punditry and the paranoia, and lock in on Wilson-Jeter, seeing it and every other battle in this best-of-seven not as a clash of numbers, but a series of exercises in pure sports combat.

Roger Angell said this: *"What I do know is that this belonging and caring is what our gamers are all about; this is what we come for. It is foolish and childish, on the face of it, to affiliate ourselves with anything so insignificant and patently contrived and commercially exploitative as a professional sports team, and the amused superiority and icy scorn that the non-fan directs at the sports nut (I know this look—I know it by heart) is understandable and almost unanswerable. Almost. What is left out of this calculation, it seems to me, is the business of caring—caring deeply and passionately, really* caring*—which is a capacity or an emotion that has almost gone out of our lives. And so it seems possible that we have come to a time when it no longer matters so much what the caring is about, how frail or foolish is the object of that concern, as long as the feeling itself can be saved. Naivete—the infantile and ignoble joy that sends a grown man or woman to dancing and shouting with joy in the middle of the night over the haphazardous flight of a distant ball—seems a small price to pay for such a gift."*

Enjoy this. Love it and hate it and lose sleep.

Enjoy this.

October 15, 2010

The Rangers have dropped both Dustin Nippert and Esteban German from the roster for the ALCS, replacing them with left-handed relievers Michael Kirkman and Clay Rapada.

October 16, 2010

Condolences, C.J.

Sorry about baseball.

October 16, 2010: ALCS Game One, New York 6, Texas 5

A good friend just sent this to me:

Here at the car dealership. . . . Have lived here 25 years. Never before have heard a bunch of people in DFW talking and arguing about last night's game. Could have sworn I was back home in Chicago! Whatever happens, the fact that this is occurring is great for the future of Ranger baseball. We're just as good as the Yankees and when we come back to Texas at 3-2, I hope you can find some joy in the fact that people in car dealerships all over DFW are arguing if Lee should start Game 6—with as much fervor as if they were talking about Wade getting fired.

Yep.

The crowd was fantastic last night. There was no hint of all those typical Rangers-Yankees crowds—typical even of the 1996-1998-1999 playoff series—that felt split down the middle. We need that again today. The team needs that again today.

Yes, the home field advantage is gone.

If it's an advantage at all. This franchise is winless in seven home playoff games, including three this month.

True, Phil Hughes has been ridiculous against Texas in his career, with 15.1 scoreless innings—all in Arlington—on just three hits (all doubles, by Josh Hamilton and Nelson Cruz and Taylor Teagarden) and four walks, with 13 strikeouts.

But remember that the Rangers on this roster were a collective .188-hitting bunch against C.C. Sabathia going into last night's game, when they went 6 for 17 (.353), slugged .588, and added four walks (.476 on-base).

Things felt pretty good when Texas not only reached safely with its first three hitters of the series but scored all three (only the second time in big league history that had happened). But the Rangers should have scored more in that inning.

Then New York reached safely seven straight times to start the eighth, off five pitchers, scoring five times. We miss Frankie.

Baserunners have stolen 51 bases in 54 tries against New York relievers in 2010, and that was apparently on Ian Kinsler's mind when he wasn't ready for Kerry Wood to throw over in the Rangers' eighth.

If Texas wins today, all the club needs is a win from either Cliff Lee or C.J. Wilson in Yankee Stadium to bring the series back to Arlington.

The Rangers need Colby Lewis to be big this afternoon. They need to shake last night off.

They also need us to shake last night off, which may take a little stepping up on our part, but that was a winner's atmosphere in the building on Friday, and more of that is needed.

This is a resilient team that has earned our resilience, and I'm in no mood to start talking about firing Wade yet. Win this one today, take at least one of three in New York, and bring this thing back home.

If you're one of those who thinks an electric crowd can factor in, I hope you'll be among the 50,000 out there in a few hours. We can do this.

October 17, 2010: ALCS Game Two, Texas 7, New York 2

Five-game series. The other guys own the home field advantage. Cliff Lee gets the ball first, and if the series goes long enough, he'll get it in the final game, too. In between, C.J. Wilson will start a game as well.

Sound familiar?

That's how it lined up for Texas against Tampa Bay, the American League's best team in 2010, and that's what we're faced with now against New York.

In that Rays series, Lee won his two starts and Wilson won his one, as the duo gave up a combined two runs on 13 hits and two walks in 22.1 innings, striking out 28. All three were on the road.

In the five games remaining in this series, one (tomorrow night's Lee start) will be on the road, as will Wilson's next scheduled start (Wednesday afternoon). Lee would come back around, if necessary, in Arlington, Saturday night, in a Game Seven.

I'll admit, after about an eight-hour day at Rangers Ballpark yesterday, that I haven't read much about Game Two, so forgive me if this has been discussed and knocked down already. But when I saw Tommy Hunter getting loose in the sixth inning yesterday, I began to wonder if the Rangers aren't thinking about going to Derek Holland (rather than Hunter) in Game Four on Tuesday—Holland has worked his way into a key spot in the bullpen but shouldn't be needed in relief of Lee tomorrow—or even Wilson.

The latter would be risky, as Wilson has never started a big league game on short rest, and he did throw 104 high-intensity pitches on Friday, but if the club believes he's conditioned physically and mentally to do it, imagine this: Wilson on short rest Tuesday, and possibly on short rest again on Saturday . . . which would mean Wilson (1, 4, 7) and Lee (3, 6) could start five of a possible seven games in this series.

Unlikely, but with Hunter warming in the sixth yesterday, you have to wonder what the plan is now for Game Four.

The big story in Game Two, of course, was the punishment the Rangers handed out to Phil Hughes, who had allowed three hits in 15.1 scoreless innings against Texas in his career, all in Arlington. The Rangers were .064/.154/.128 hitters against Hughes going into Saturday; if you limit it to the nine Rangers in yesterday's starting lineup, they had a collective .094/.147/.156 slash.

Yesterday? A cool .500/.565/1.000. Texas was 10 for 20 off Hughes, with seven of the 10 hits going for extra bases.

That included 5 for 11 (with four extra-base hits) in counts that got to two strikes. Texas had seven two-strike hits altogether on the day.

Meanwhile, Colby Lewis was strong out of the gate, needing just nine pitches (seven strikes) to finish the first ahead of the Rangers' havoc run in the bottom of the inning. It was a quick, efficient inning for Lewis, the kind that the dude in the black shirt a row back from me would have been proud of.

Lewis wiggled out of trouble in the second, though Robinson Cano (flyout to right), Nick Swisher (double to right), and Lance Berkman (lineout to right) all barreled up on him. Texas put up a four-hit, two-run second, and Lewis came back to strand a couple in the New York third, just as he'd done in the second.

Two more Texas runs in the third (on three doubles), and Lewis did what the game asked him to do, to steal a Wash-ism. He threw strikes in the fourth (eight strikes, four balls) and fifth (11 strikes, five balls—though that included a Curtis Granderson walk). When his command deserted him two outs into the sixth (10 strikes, including a Cano missile halfway up the home run porch, and nine balls), his day was done.

The lead at that point was five, and the bullpen was being entrusted not only with two inherited runners but the task of going 3.1 innings. After what happened Friday night, it wasn't exactly a comfort spot.

Clay Rapada, Alexi Ogando, Darren Oliver, Darren O'Day, and Neftali Feliz: 10 outs (four on strikes), no runs, one hit.

It wasn't the cleanest of bullpen efforts (80 pitches, just 47 strikes; four walks), but it was absolutely effective, and should be a terrific confidence boost for the beleaguered Red Bull crew. They get the day off today and possibly tomorrow in Lee's start, and should all be ready to go Tuesday.

A few other thoughts:

Is this the best couple weeks Elvis Andrus has had all year?

How many New York fans are dead certain that Derek Jeter's winter contract will be for four years, matching the length of time Andrus has before he can be a free agent?

Forget it, Yanks.

Ian Kinsler? Say it with me: Bat path.

Cano is an absolute beast. Love that guy.

(What if that trade six years ago had been Alex Rodriguez for Alfonso Soriano and Cano? Sigh.)

Texas walked seven Yankees. None scored.

One of the things Lewis said last night was that it felt like a regular season game yesterday. He admitted to being a little amped up against Tampa Bay, but was relaxed against New York.

I believe him. It's a uniqueness about this team's veterans and coaching staff.

The Rangers' 7-8-9 hitters (David Murphy, Bengie Molina, Mitch Moreland) yesterday: 5 for 10 with four RBI.

Moreland can play every remaining inning of the post-season, as far as I'm concerned. The only thing Jorge Cantu offers that Moreland doesn't is experience, and Moreland has proven, over and over, that he's not handicapped by his inexperience. At all.

By the way, I did my part yesterday. *Newsday*'s Ken Davidoff, who wrote one of the forewords for the 2008 Bound Edition, started his entry this way: "Let me start out by asserting that Jamey Newberg is the greatest guy I've never met."

Ten straight playoff losses against the Yankees was enough for me. I felt my small contribution toward the busting of that disgusting streak was to make sure I finally met the man face to face, after many years of emails and instant messages.

We met before the game. Streak busted.

Did the sweep against Minnesota result in too much rest for New York starters C.C. Sabathia and Hughes? Some of the Yankees suggested after Texas 7, New York 2 that it's possible.

Underlying tomorrow's Cliff Lee start: In the last 19 ALCS's that have started out locked up after two games, the team that took Game Three won the series 14 times.

But the intrigue for me goes beyond that, as we start to think about Game Four, and about the fact that Tommy Hunter was getting loose in a key spot in the game yesterday. The idea of C.J. Wilson and Lee pitching five games of a possible seven is a lot to digest, but confronted with the irritation of a day off during the greatest baseball time of my life, I'm having a tough time right now preventing my mind from jumping up and down a bit.

October 17, 2010

The dude in the black shirt was Greg Maddux.

October 18, 2010

The Rangers on the ALCS roster are a collective .308/.373/.462-hitting bunch against Andy Pettitte, which is sort of stunning. It's .327/.390/.497 if you include Vladimir Guerrero, Bengie Molina, and Jeff Francoeur's work in the post-season, where Pettitte has generally made his career mark.

Then again, the Yankees' collective .280/.329/.482 slash against Cliff Lee is equally hard to believe. Not surprisingly, the slash dips a bit (to .269/.314/.456) if you include the playoffs.

David Murphy has a 1.144 OPS in 12 plate appearances against Pettitte, but he'll likely start the game on the bench, ceding the start to the right-handed-hitting Francoeur and his team-leading 1.455 (11 plate appearances).

Lots of pinball numbers. But still feels like we're poised for a 2-1 game.

Enjoy this.

October 18, 2010

How *blank* are those two checks?

October 18, 2010: ALCS Game Three, Texas 8, New York 0

I have quite a lot to say (shocking, I know), but I'm sitting here, overlooking Times Square, with absolutely no chance at doing what we all just saw a fraction of the justice it deserves, at least not tonight.

I may never be able to do it justice. I'm that weak in the knees.

I'll spend some time at the airport tomorrow morning gathering my thoughts, but for now I'll say this: I sure hope what we saw tonight was a wedding.

There are lots of unforgettable numbers in Rangers history, and to that list we now add 8-2-0-0-1-13.

And, soon enough, we can hope, whatever stratospheric nine-figure number gets attached by one of tonight's two teams to the next five or six years of Cliff Lee's increasingly ridiculous legacy.

The greatest single-game performance in this franchise's 39 years, considering the circumstances and the stakes, is even crazier to digest when you realize the Yankees practically knew it was coming (read Monday's New York papers), and still had absolutely no answer, no usable gameplan, no chance.

It's sort of unbelievable—and at the same time exactly what everyone knew was going to happen.

October 19, 2010

8-0 is not the most common of baseball scores, particularly in games pitting two very good teams against each other, and so as I walked back to the subway station last night (er, this morning), addled by a deepening level of sleep deprivation that would, an hour later, somehow convince me to say something about a "wedding" in a slightly unhinged postgame Newberg Report, my thoughts wandered to the former trendy place-to-be-seen in the Quadrangle called 8.0.

On 8.0's menu was a kitchen sink explosion called "roadkill" (which I tested once myself, with what I remember to be not the greatest result).

That's what 8-0, Texas over NewYork, was last night. Baseball homicide, coldly perpetrated on enemy grounds.

Roadkill.

There's been a batch of sudden omens that I've latched onto this post-season, so I was feeling pretty good yesterday when I ran into these:

- An infant waiting at the airport gate repeating, over and over and over, the phrase "eeeh-TAH!!," which, half asleep, I heard as the child's attempt to exclaim, "It's Time"
- My cabbie from La Guardia wearing a Yankees cap but, when I tried to engage him in a little trash talk, admitting he didn't know the Yankees even had a game last night—or who they were supposed to play next
- The odd placement of a 20-year-old Toad the Wet Sprocket song that caught my ear in the Tampa airport two weeks ago . . . and another 20-year-old Toad the Wet Sprocket song heard yesterday afternoon when I arrived at the New York hotel

But when I settled into my seat, 10 minutes before game time, it hit me: Looking for omens is a waste of time on Cliff Lee Night in America. All you had to do is read Yankee quotes after Game Two and before Game Three to be very clear about where this was headed. It bordered on self-fulfilling prophecy.

The English language has its limits, or at least my grasp of it is a big bag of fail, as I'm out of words to try and describe what Lee is, or what he did last night. In a sport in which artistry wins games, not just Web Gems, what Lee did to the Yankees was the work of a transcendent artist. I can't ever remember a local athlete this consistently, and predictably, dominant.

Bullet points:

- Lee's 13 strikeouts last night matched a career high. He also recorded the highest swing-and-miss percentage of his season, getting Yankees hitters to whiff 29.8 percent of the time they swung.
- Those 13 strikeouts included six on fastballs, three on cutters (very cool that the Yankee Stadium scoreboard identifies pitches that specifically), three on curves, and one on a changeup.
- The Yankees swung nine times at Lee's change. Only once did they put the ball in play, an Alex Rodriguez groundout to shortstop.
- According to ESPN, the Yankees were 0 for 27 this year against Lee's cutter before Posada's sand wedge over Ian Kinsler's head to break up Lee's no-hitter in the fifth inning.
- Lee had at least one strikeout in every inning last night.
- Twenty-four outs. Thirteen on strikes. Think about that.
- New York was 0 for 3 with runners in scoring position—all coming in the sixth inning. Since the nightmare top of the eighth in Game One, Texas pitchers have held the Yankees to a 1-for-20 clip with RISP.
- The 30 strikeouts Lee piled up between post-season walks (dating back to 2009) is an all-time big league record.
- Lee's 1.26 career post-season ERA trails only Sandy Koufax and Christy Mathewson.
- New York has eight playoff wins and two playoff losses in New Yankee Stadium. Lee is responsible for both losses.
- Texas is the first team ever to record multiple shutouts on two hits or fewer in a single post-season.
- Lee is the first big league pitcher ever to strike out at least 10 batters three times in one post-season.

And, unless New York wins three straight, he's not done pitching. (And I'd suggest he may be back on the mound in Game Six if the Yankees win the next two, making Game Six an elimination game for Texas to stave off . . . and make sure there is a Game Seven to play.)

Stated another way, if Texas can win one of the next three, Cliff Lee is guaranteed a Game Seven start in Arlington—or a Game One start in Philadelphia or San Francisco.

(And by the way, this is as good a place as any: Don't think of this series as over yet. The Yankees are very, very good.)

Much was made of New York's successful ALDS gameplan against Twins righthander Carl Pavano, a strike-thrower on whom the Yankees pounced on early in the count to take count leverage away from him.

Asked about the team's planned approach against Lee, Mark Teixeira said: "We just can't be taking up there and waiting for our pitch, because it might not come. We might have to be more aggressive."

And then what happened? They go and let Lee get ahead last night. The first time through the Yankees lineup, Marcus Thames was the only hitter to swing at the first pitch. Was that smart? The apparent strategy to submit to Lee's will but try and get him out of the game earlier than usual seemed like an act of desperation, and possibly a foolish one, particularly coming from a team with that sort of ability to create offense. But, again, read the Yankee quotes leading up to Game Three, and you can't help but see the desperation, in what was then a tied series with New York having seized home field.

They don't tabulate GWRBI any more, but if they did, last night's game-winner would have been awarded to Josh Hamilton's shot five minutes into the game, as near in time to Kristin Chenoweth's anthem as to the first of Lee's windmill warmups behind the mound. Texas has scored in the first inning in each of this series' three games, twice on the strength of a Hamilton blast off an elite lefthander. Add in what was nearly a second home run and the missile he shot to left center past the rangy Brett Gardner to kick off the explosive ninth (also off a lefty, that time specialist Boone Logan), and it's safe to say that Hamilton is once again locked in—or at least needs to be pitched to as if he were.

Michael Young's impressive night—not only the three singles (two the other way) but also the 28 pitches he saw (including 17 in his first two-bats against Andy Pettitte)—bodes well, too. He's prone to staying hot for a couple weeks when he starts to consistently square up the opposite way, and this would be a real good two weeks during which to be locked in.

Elvis Andrus saw 27 pitches himself, and continues to have a breakthrough post-season, considering what was arguably a bit of a regression offensively in 2010.

Despite Pettitte's high pitch count (he needed 43 pitches to get through the Texas lineup one time), he was really good, of course. After Hamilton's homer in the first, the lefthander retired 19 of the next 21 (Young's second and third singles were the two at-bats that weren't outs), and no Ranger reached second base in that span.

But the battles that Andrus and Young and others engaged in with Pettitte helped end his night after seven, allowing Texas to get into the New York bullpen and turn a masterpiece duel into a pasting.

It's been written everywhere you look, but aside from that disastrous eighth on Friday night, this has been a series in which the Rangers have really had their way with New York, a team that disposed of the Twins in short order while Texas warred with Tampa Bay. Again, it's not over, but it's been a very impressive three games, almost flawless as playoff work goes.

Texas has now played eight playoff games. In seven of them, the road team has won. Bizarre.

The Rangers were winless in Tampa and New York during the regular season. They're now 4-0 in those two ballparks in the playoffs.

James Shields notwithstanding, the Rangers have beaten some of the best starting pitchers that the American League has to offer in the playoffs. David Price twice. Phil Hughes. Pettitte. And they punished C.C. Sabathia as well, even though they couldn't nail down a win that night.

This series is the 20th ALCS to start out at one win apiece. Of the previous 19, 14 have ultimately been won by the team that took Game Three. None of the five exceptions had Lee—though the last team that won Game Three to go up two games to one and still lost the ALCS (and in fact the only such team to do so since 1998) was the 2007 Indians, which had left Lee off the roster.

I went to Carnegie Deli for a pregame bite. There. I've done that now. No need for a return trip. (O-ver-RA-ted, clap, clap, clap-clap-clap.)

The energy in Section 226 (which may have shown up late on the TBS broadcast, no?) was fantastic. I don't know whether the "Let's go Rangers" chant was audible on the air, but it was *strong*. (And not particularly appreciated by the Yankees fans who hadn't fled for the exits by that point.) (The same Yankees fans who treated the pregame Rangers introductions not with boos, but with indifference, treating that time as the final few minutes of cocktail hour.)

Seeing what the Yankees do with their in-game presentation has me very excited about the potential we have once a new video board is put in place in Arlington. There's only one Chuck Morgan.

I know I've written about this three or four times now, but I still can't believe Cliff Lee is a Ranger—not so much in a "dream come true" sense, but instead shock at what the Yankees didn't do.

Why were the Yankees willing to trade blue-chip prospect Jesus Montero to Seattle three months ago, when they knew they would be the frontrunner to sign Lee this winter anyway? Because of last night, and this month. It wasn't to prevent Lee from getting cozy with some other new team; it was to make New York stronger this season. There's no other way to explain a willingness to part with Montero for those extra three months of work.

Which is why I just don't understand the decision not to add infielder Eduardo Nunez or righthander Ivan Nova to the deal to prevent the Mariners from reversing course and shipping Lee elsewhere.

Love it, just don't understand it.

Think there might be some Yankee players who don't understand it either?

Nunez and Nova have a *lot* to live up to now.

But for the moment, there's a greater burden on Teixeira, Alex Rodriguez, Nick Swisher, Curtis Granderson, and Jorge Posada, who are a collective 6 for 53 (.113) with 18 strikeouts and zero RBI in this series. Cliff Lee had a lot to do with that, but so did C.J. Wilson and Colby Lewis and a relief crew that, other than in one brutal inning, has done its job.

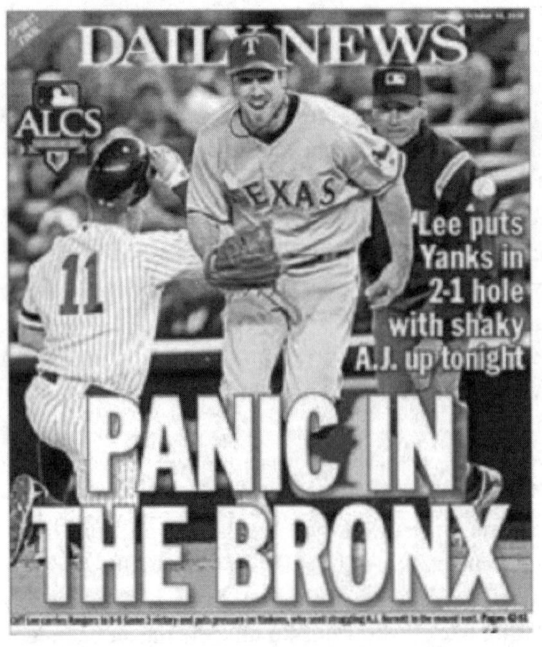
DAILY NEWS

ALCS

Lee puts Yanks in 2-1 hole with shaky A.J. up tonight

PANIC IN THE BRONX

As I send this report, I'm not yet back home from easily the greatest sports trip of my life, and possibly the best sports moment, and when I do land back on my couch I'm sure I'll still be delirious, not in the crazed sense but more just an out-of-sorts state, needing sleep but not expecting much for a while, yet oddly comforted by the rock-steady confidence that this inexperienced playoff team is showing, faring pretty damn well against the playoff-seasoned, pinstriped force that seems to have traded in its swagger as it talked itself into playing the underdog role.

October 20, 2010: ALCS Game Four, Texas 10, New York 3

The rosin on Cliff Lee's cap has a message for you:

The Texas Rangers are one win away from the World Series.

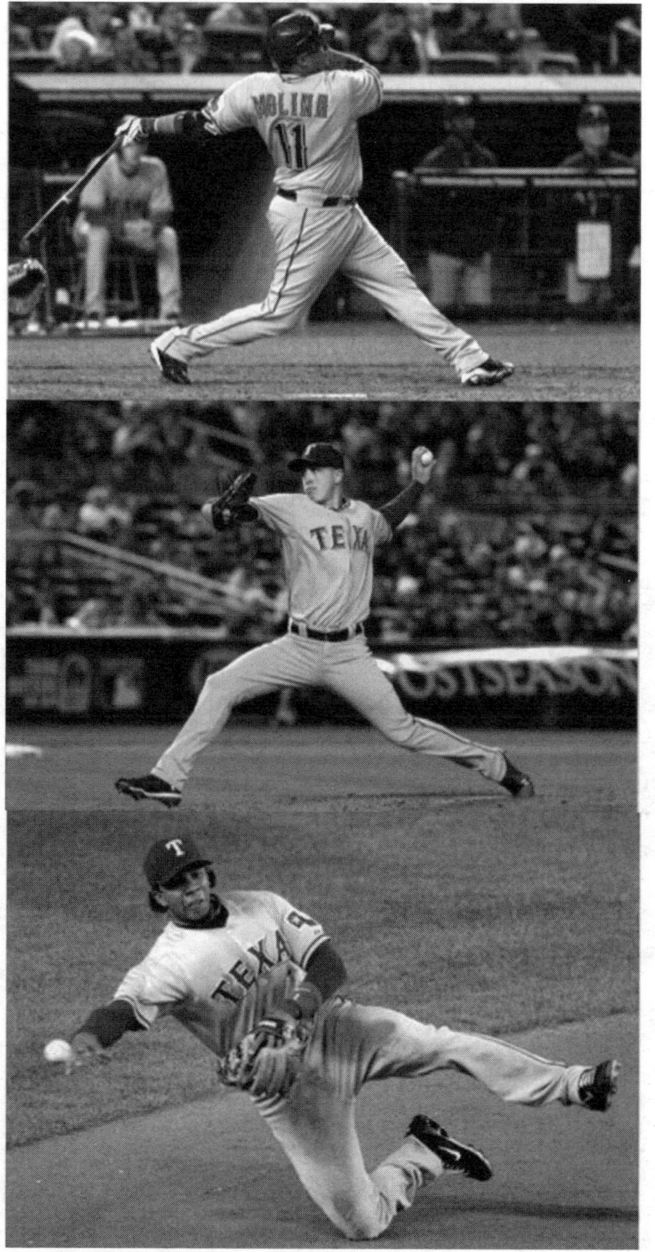

Acquired, with cash, for righthanders Chris Ray (who didn't make the Giants' NLDS or NLCS roster) and Michael Main.

Selected in the 25th round of the 2006 amateur draft, the final one in which draft-and-follow process was allowed, and signed 50 weeks later for fourth-round money.

Acquired, with Neftali Feliz and Matt Harrison and Jarrod Saltalamacchia and Beau Jones, for Mark Teixeira and Ron Mahay.

There are different heroes every night.

Including the man in the point collar. And a whole lot of people on his crew.

All those Eric Nadel audio clips I sent you from last night?

There ought to be lots more where those came from.

The Texas Rangers are one win away from the World Series.

October 20, 2010: ALCS Game Five: New York 7, Texas 2

As my buddy Darrell Cook so aptly said on Twitter:

The Rangers forced a Game Six.

That game had all kinds of junk in it, the kind that'll make you grumpy. C.J. Wilson had a really terrible day. The defense had a couple lousy moments. There was baserunning fail. An ominous, hold-your-breath injury.

And yet the offense battled all day, outhitting the Yankees and picking up at least two bases (hitting and/or running) in every inning until the eighth. Base hits from everyone but Vladimir Guerrero. No walks, but a healthy supply of baserunners. More than enough.

But what was nearly a complete absence of timely hitting paralyzed the Rangers' chances to make a real game of it. They created plenty of opportunities. Just didn't capitalize on them at all.

Since I haikued Rangers-in-six last week, it would be disingenuous of me to start brooding over where the team now finds itself, no matter how crummy a ballgame Texas just played. It's almost silly that it took six road playoff games for the Rangers to lose their first, and now they have two chances to close this thing out at home.

This team has earned a lot this season, including the right not to have us panic. The resiliency factor comes up a lot with these guys, particularly after the way they responded following two home losses to Tampa Bay and the Game One disaster against New York. I'm less worried about the Rangers' psyche than I am about the odds of beating up on Phil Hughes a second time, about Nelson Cruz being right even if he's able to play, about the Yankees getting Colby Lewis out of the game early again by working counts. Texas will be ready to go.

As far as Cruz goes, I might just be ready for an outfield of Josh Hamilton, Julio Borbon, and David Murphy on Friday, letting Cruz DH. Guerrero was really good yesterday, but that's been the exception this month.

As has been the game in which Texas has appeared overmatched. Just about nothing came together today, and I think we can all agree that that's easier to take than a loss like Game One's, when Texas was better all night with the exception of one nightmare half-inning, especially with a team like this one that has proven all year that it can bounce back from anything.

Two chances now to bounce back, in front of a packed Rangers Ballpark, but executing on that first chance sounds real good, and not just because it would keep Texas from having to face just its second elimination game this year.

While the idea of Cliff Lee in Game Seven would be more dramatic, more poetic, more epic, the Rangers have already given us more than their fair share of dramatic this season, and I'd sure appreciate it if we could wrap this thing up behind Colby Lewis in Game Six, setting Lee up instead for a brand new Game One, and Game Five after that.

October 21, 2010

You will recall the "*N Y Y*" omen I got a week and a half ago, the day before Game Five against Tampa Bay.

We may be in business, the day before Game Six against New York, as I just received this postcard (right) in the office mail.

Just as we said at the outset:

Rangers in six.

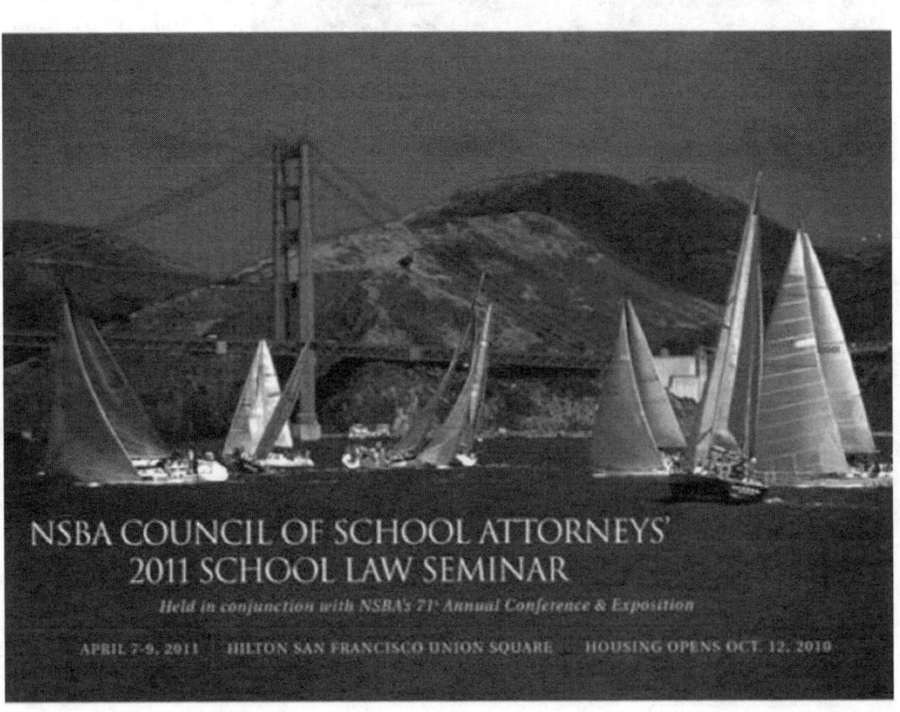

NSBA COUNCIL OF SCHOOL ATTORNEYS'
2011 SCHOOL LAW SEMINAR
Held in conjunction with NSBA's 71st Annual Conference & Exposition
APRIL 7-9, 2011
HILTON SAN FRANCISCO UNION SQUARE
HOUSING OPENS OCT. 12, 2010

October 22, 2010

ESPN's Buster Olney said on a national radio segment yesterday that he's never seen a baseball team more relaxed than Texas is right now, that the club seems able to shrug losses off like no team he's ever been around.

So there's today's dose of analysis. There's nothing left to say. It's all been said.

Friday Night Lights.
Rally Minka.

October 22, 2010

You know that scene in one of the Star Wars movies where Luke shuts his cockpit controls off and fires the kill shot to destroy the Death Star, relying just on instincts?

These two teams have played each other for a week now. Forty-four innings, 386 pitcher-hitter faceoffs, 1621 pitches. The front offices have done everything they can, and so have the advance scouts. There shouldn't be any tricks left, no alarms and no surprises.

Tonight, and maybe tomorrow, come down to two really good baseball teams, very familiar with each other, going at it in hand-to-hand combat, each looking for the kill shot. The next series that one of these two teams will get to play will have some novelty to it, but not this one, not anymore. This is raw, primal baseball, and I can't stand that Game Six doesn't start right this second.

Elimination
It's Time to end Yanks' season
Start spreading the noose

October 22, 2010

For those of you who emailed me or have been wondering about this: Yes, I know Minka Kelly is Derek Jeter's girlfriend. This morning's Rally Minka was not some random coincidence.

There's a reason for Rally Minka.

Check your September 10, 2010 "Newberg Report v.2." (I actually sent it out at 1:11 AM on September 11.)

And then check the box score from Texas-New York, September 10.

Incidentally, I have it on reliable authority that actor Brad Leland, who played Minka's dad on "Friday Night Lights," will be in the Ballpark tonight, among the 50,000 strong. He's a Rangers fan.

Five hours and 15 minutes.

October 22, 2010

Dear Subscriber Number 1, and Subscriber Number 9,748, and every Subscriber in between:

I love you.

October 22, 2010

Tonight's omen:

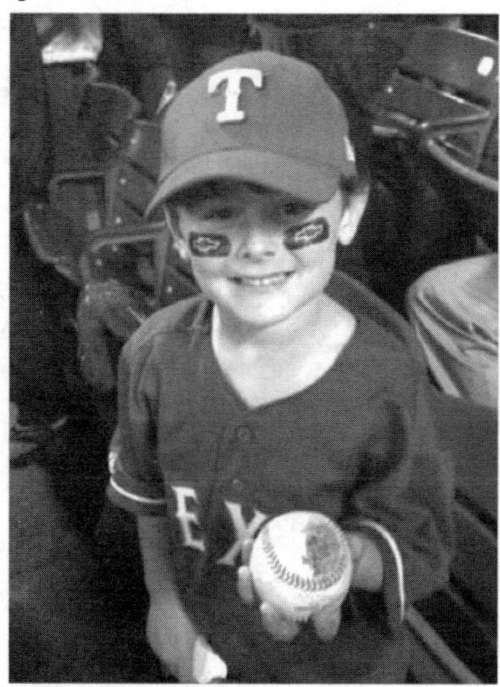

I'll explain another time. Soon. Maybe even tonight. Sleep is an unlikelihood.

For now, Rally Minka insists that this is the greatest Newberg Report email ever sent, because of the three audio files attached to it.

Don't mess with Rally Minka.

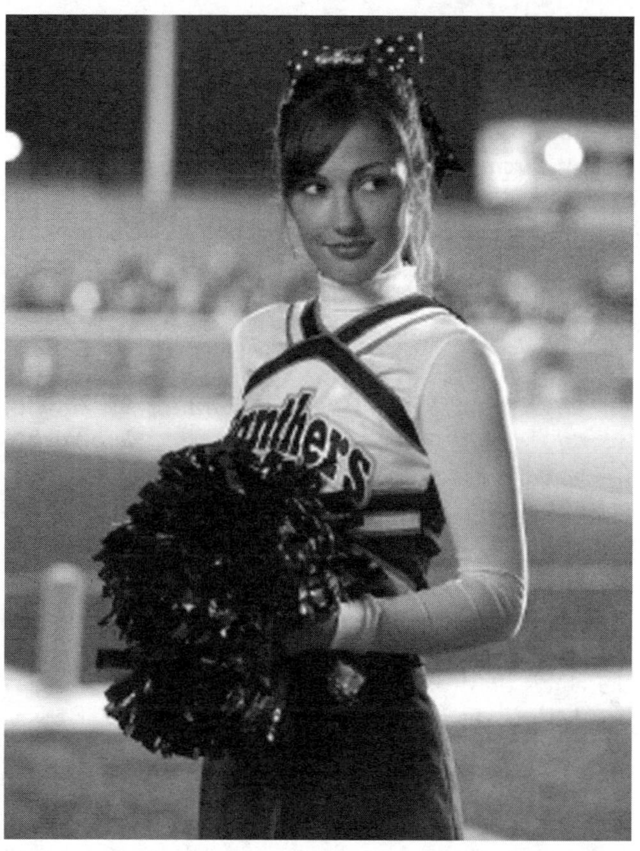

October 22, 2010

Step Six.

(More tomorrow. I think I'm finally a candidate for a little sleep.)

October 23, 2010

I just went out to pick up some celebration kolaches for the family and a *Dallas Morning News* that I'll probably never open. It's raining here this morning, very gray. The streets are quiet. Kinda sleepy.

More than half the people I ran into were wearing Rangers caps. I'm not joking. Four of them asked me, some total stranger in a just-woke-up ballcap of my own, some variant of: "How 'bout that game! Can you believe it?!?"

Stopping by a North Dallas donut shop and 7-Eleven is an admittedly super-small sample, but it feels like a baseball town right now, something that's been on my wish list since childhood, somewhere up there near a World Series in Arlington.

I haven't had nearly enough sleep, and it's not like I'm begging to be thinking any more clearly than I am right now, but the last 10 very cool minutes have me ready to write finally.

This will take a while, probably hours, and not consecutive ones, but I hope to have something out to you today at some point.

In the meantime, I have a favor to ask. My DVR behaved like a Phil Hughes pitch left up in Nelson Cruz's zone last night, and I sit here without a recording of the Game.

Three Bound Editions, any year, to the first person who can burn for me a DVD of the Game and the postgame trophy ceremony (and any other postgame celebration footage you were able to grab).

If three books isn't enough, I'm in a weak bargaining position. Exploit me.

Back atcha soon with a report on Texas 6, New York 1, World Series Drought 0.

October 23, 2010: ALCS Game Six: Texas 6, New York 1

Though for reasons that I'm sure will begin to become more clear before long, the late-'90s playoff run never felt like this one. Part of it was that this club's previous Mark Teixeira, slugger Juan Gonzalez, was reportedly not going to sign long-term for Larry Walker money ($75 million over six years), and at about this time in 1999, following the club's third playoff season out of four, the Rangers decided to explore the idea of trading Gonzalez. He was shipped to Detroit in November.

What followed in 2000 was a 71-win season, the club's worst in 12 years.

Texas then signed the best young player in baseball to the record-obliterating $252 million deal that was supposed to shoot the club right back into perennial relevance.

That contract was for ten years.

Starting in 2001.

And ending in 2010.

We can all make a list of a dozen reasons that last night's result was fitting. One that we'll all talk about well after his own date in Cooperstown is that the instant that Alex Rodriguez's 2010 season ended, the season that was supposed to conclude a landmark Rangers contract that would be the centerpiece of a World Series-contending roster, at that very instant Texas earned its first-ever World Series berth, not with him but against him and, in a way, in spite of him, as at least one of the "kids" he disparaged and deserted six years ago and many others who weren't around yet leaned forward, facing him, as were 50,000 of the millions who had once imagined big things with him in a Rangers uniform, and had been abandoned ourselves.

A-Rod was looking out at the team he couldn't bear to play with, and then with a 1-2 count he was just *looking*, as Kid Neftali followed 100-99-99 with a picturesque 83-mph slider, a buckler that broke 11 inches and once and for all broke the hearts of a thousand New York writers convinced that the Rangers were merely invited to the Yankees' progressive dinner that began in Minnesota and would continue in a National League park on Wednesday.

In a season that could never have been scripted—*never*—that last pitch, freezing Alex Rodriguez and sending this team to a place it had never been, a place that 10 years ago it had hoped with a pile of cash that A-Rod would help take them to, couldn't have been scripted any more perfectly.

Dial back to the eight innings before that moment, and to the year before A-Rod signed with Texas, and you find Colby Lewis. Drafted by the Rangers in the supplemental first round in 1999, Lewis was on a fast track to join a pretty good baseball team, and probably felt pretty good about the future of the franchise he was part of when A-Rod arrived after the 2000 season, when Lewis had just finished his first full pro season, in High Class A. The superstar shortstop was only four years older than Lewis, after all.

But it then fell apart for the A-Rod Rangers, who finished all three of his seasons here (2001-03) in last place in the division, getting Lewis's first 30 big league starts and a handful of relief appearances the last two of those seasons. His ERA over 161.1 innings was a bloated 7.08.

A-Rod was traded right before camp in 2004. Lewis lasted only a little bit longer, making three starts in April before being shut down with what was diagnosed as a torn rotator cuff. He was done as a Ranger. For six years, that is.

Alex Rodriguez wasn't supposed to be somewhere else in 2010, and Colby Lewis wasn't supposed to be back, pitching in a Rangers playoff rotation.

But they were, facing off over the last week six times, for the first time in their careers.

A-Rod went 1 for 6 against Lewis, one of the kids he ran away from six years ago.

Not that that matchup stood out in the six-game series for either Rodriguez (who hit .190 overall) or Lewis (who held New York to a composite .196 ALCS average, after holding Tampa Bay to a .118 clip in his one ALDS start against the Rays). But, given A-Rod's importance to the Yankees attack, and the history here, it sure was sweet, particularly as he got rung up by Feliz on the final pitch of the series, and New York's season.

When I predicted Rangers in six games a week ago, I didn't expect the Yankees to hit .201 or post a team ERA of 6.58. I didn't expect Texas to rack up more extra-base hits (24) or more stolen bases (9) in the series than any playoff opponent *ever had* against the Yankees, or score the second-most runs (38) of any New York playoff opponent—trailing only the 41 that Boston scored in the 2004 ALCS, a series that went seven games rather than six.

Texas, which hit .304 with an .890 OPS (the second highest ALCS OPS since the series went to the best-of-seven format 25 years ago) and pitched so well most of the time, dominated this series, plain and simple.

In that same October 15 report, I wrote: "*This I think I know: Over the next week and maybe for the rest of my life, I will harbor an irrational hatred for Nick Swisher, there will probably be a home plate ump or two whose name I'll remember forever, and not fondly, and there will be several moments and images that will push all other moments and images down in my mental sports scrapbook.*"

All of that is true, and there was that moment in the fifth inning last night when Swisher and home plate ump Brian Gorman threatened together to make Rangers history, as Gorman ruled no contact on a pitch that clearly hit Swisher, allowing Rodriguez to trot home on a wild pitch and tie the score, 1-1.

After Swisher grounded out on a 10-foot dribbler fielded by Lewis, Jorge Posada doubled to right, and that would have scored Rodriguez anyway, and maybe even Swisher—but in any event would have at least sent him to third with one out rather than two—but there's also the theory that the pitch sequence to Posada might have varied, and maybe he doesn't double at all. And even if Posada put the same pass on the ball, with Mitch Moreland holding Swisher on first, maybe he gloves the baseline-hugging shot that instead eluded him with the bases empty.

But two other things about the above.

First, that wasn't the key Swisher punk moment. There was an ESPN report on Thursday that, as reporters asked a few Yankees players for comment about Cliff Lee, Swisher fired off a tirade for all in the clubhouse to hear: "You guys are talking about Cliff Lee? Who cares? I can't wait to hit against his ass!"

April 16, buddy.

Second, last night's omen.

There was a little sense of dread that crept in on the blown hit-by-pitch call, as three balls had been barreled that inning (Rodriguez's double to the wall in left center, Lance Berkman's sacrifice fly to right center that might have gone out on other nights, and Posada's double to right), and there had been outs earlier in the game that New York had squared up on as well. Lewis had lost command in the sixth inning in Game Two, and with New York having tied the game in the fifth last night, and starting to hit the ball hard with regularity, the game didn't feel very good.

With Posada on second, and Derek Holland starting to get loose in the pen, the batter was Marcus Thames. On the third pitch, he fouled an inside Lewis fastball straight up, a mile high, and I knew I'd have a play on it from my seat. I can remember thinking the play needed to stay on my left shoulder, as our six-year-old Max sat to my right. The ball ended up hitting my hand and the hand of the gentleman to my left at the same time (I call pass interference), and a woman sitting behind us came up with the ball—and gave it to Max.

After that? Two more strikes to Thames, a foul tip and a swinging strike three.

After that? Texas erupted in the bottom of the inning for four two-out runs, blowing the game open and making it OK to start thinking about the words "World" and "Series" in earnest, to start to really believe that those "little town" blues were, once and for all, melting away.

After that? Eleven up, nine down over Lewis's next three innings, culminating with possibly the worst swing of Derek Jeter's career, before Feliz was summoned to slam it shut in the ninth.

Game-changer.

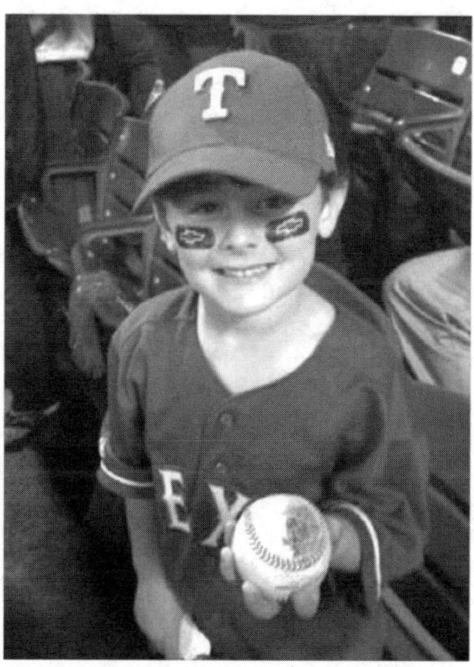

And a lot better than the omen I was really worried about—the dual cloudbursts just before and right at gametime, far too reminiscent of October 2, 1998, the lone home game of that year's ALDS sweep at the Yankees' hands. Texas blanked New York in eight of nine innings that night, but the four-spot the Yankees scored in the sixth off Aaron Sele made it feel like 40-0 (as the Rangers had scored just one run in the first two games combined), particularly when a three-hour sideways-rain delay followed New York's four-run inning by minutes.

Speaking of rain, can you imagine if Texas was pushed to a Game Seven tonight, and this lousy weather we had today ended up halting the game for such an extended period that Cliff Lee was forced out early due to inactivity?

Another what-if: Had Joe Girardi not flipped Andy Pettitte and Philip Hughes, lining Pettitte up to pitch Games Two and Six rather than Games Three (which he dealt in but lost to Lee) and Seven, would last night have gone differently?

As Max and I walked through the concourse an hour after the game ended, I heard someone singing, "Start spreading the noose." I smiled.

A little misleading, I guess. I was smiling for about two hours straight by that time, just as Max was as he fell asleep in the car on the way home, lullabied by a cacophony of celebratory car horns that sounded oh-so-sweet.

You must read what Peter Gammons wrote about the Texas Rangers today. You just have to do it.

Here's some other entertaining reading from the last week.

Filip Bondy (*New York Daily News*): "Ryan's no-hitters aside, this ALCS represents one of sports' great historical mismatches, 40 pennants versus zero. The Yanks should win this series just by throwing their pinstriped uniforms onto the field and reading from a few pages of The Baseball Encyclopedia. If only Bud Selig would agree to waive a few silly postseason rules, the Bombers might send their Scranton/Wilkes-Barre roster to Arlington for the first couple of games, make this a fair fight."

Neil Best (*Newsday*): "We have had four decades to get used to it, yet 'Texas Rangers' still doesn't sound quite right. It's a mixed marriage between a football state and a hockey nickname, one that has produced a reliably mediocre baseball franchise. Now, thanks mostly to a pitcher passing through on his way to the Bronx next season, the uninspiring Rangers are all that stand in the way of a World Series capable of distracting Football Nation."

Mike Greenberg (Mike & Mike Show, ESPN Radio), on Friday morning: "Even if you're a Rangers fan, you're hoping for a Game Seven with Cliff Lee."

Rob Neyer (*ESPN*): "I don't think the Rangers will let [Jon] Daniels get away. And it sure sounds like the Mets like Sandy Alderson. But if I grew up in Queens and somebody offered me a chance to escape Texas and run the New York Mets . . . ."

Good grief.

There's more, but leave those guys alone, especially the New York writers, in their time of mourning. Lay off. They're having to deal with the illicit taking of a birthright. Hold a good thought.

All those intentional walks to Josh Hamilton last night were the in-game equivalent of the Angels telling Vladimir Guerrero last winter that he couldn't get it done any more. Big Mad Vlad. Love it.

Mitch Moreland: A Starter Is Born.

Texas didn't clinch the West at home, and didn't win the ALDS at home, so nailing the ALCS down at home was extra-awesome, and I keep telling myself, with some amount of resignation but not too much, that it will never be the same again. At least not after the next week and a half.

The crowd last night was extraordinary. Really.

It's been written in several places the last couple days, but people are noticing a parallel between Cal Ripken's passing of the torch to Derek Jeter in 1996, and what might be happening now between Jeter and Elvis Andrus.

The Rangers/World Series commercial that Fox is running tonight gives me chills.

Speaking of tonight's game, I'm pulling for the Phillies but then I want the Giants tomorrow. I want this thing going seven, which of course sets Texas up better in terms of pitching matchups.

Too soon to focus on the World Series roster, especially before knowing the opponent, but is Jorge Cantu's spot in jeopardy?

Way too soon to think about the off-season, but what do you do with Nelson Cruz, who has three arbitration years coming up? Do you dare offer him a long-term deal that extends beyond that? Remember, despite his moderate service time, he's already 30.

Lee told Jon Paul Morosi of Fox Sports on Friday: "I love this situation I'm in. I love this team. I love my teammates. It's been a fun ride. It's been an unbelievable experience. . . . It's the closest to home I've ever played. This is great for my family, to be this close to home. . . . I would like to think there were a lot of Arkansans watching this game. Hopefully we can make them proud and bring home the World Series championship."

Not much need to add to that, is there?

Not now, at least.

Two months ago, Morosi tweeted this, as noted in a Newberg Report TROT COFFEY delivery: "One rival exec describes Rangers as 'very active' lately. 'They're trying to win the World Series,' the exec says." Whether Morosi's note was in reference to the Rangers' rumored pursuit of Manny Ramirez, who was conveyed to the White Sox two days later, or Jeff Francoeur, whom Texas acquired five days later, or something else the club was working on, the point was made.

This front office—and we must remember that John Hart brought Jon Daniels here, and Tom Hicks both entrusted a huge job to Daniels and brought in Nolan Ryan—is what Kevin Goldstein described to us at Newberg Report Night as "scary smart," and while I think this fan base is unusually cued into that, I hope we don't take it for granted. Just as Jimmy Johnson wouldn't have been as successful as he was without bringing Norv Turner, Dave Wannstedt, Butch Davis, Dave Campo, and Tony Wise aboard, Daniels will be the first to credit his directors and advisors and scouts, as he did on the trophy stage behind second base on Friday night.

Among the finest moves the Daniels crew has made, even if not as heralded as the Teixeira Trade or the Cliff Lee Trade or Volquez/Hamilton or the shift of C.J. Wilson to the rotation, was the almost unprecedented guarantee given to a Japanese export invited to return, a unique commitment to Colby Lewis, whose career arc, unlike

Alex Rodriguez's, has been marked not by landmark dollar amounts but by a pioneering scouting effort.

Scary smart has made this baseball team scary good when it's healthy and clicking, and right now Texas is both. I don't mind these few off-days before we get rolling again, facing off against Bengie Molina's former teammates or Cliff Lee's, but I can't wait to sit back and watch what's next, making me no different from you, millions of other Rangers fans, and Alex Rodriguez.

October 24, 2010

CHARLES WENZELBERG/NEW YORK POST

Nick Swisher

October 25, 2010

If you're a Rangers fan in the Bay Area and are going to Game One or Game Two, and happen to have an extra ticket in your group, and are trying to think of a Rangers blogger who might be fun to sell that ticket to, shoot me an email so I can try to make the burdensomeness of that decision go away.

I'm here to help, Fellow Rangers Fan.

October 26, 2010

Thirty minutes before kickoff of that game last night against the other Giants, this was the scene at a local Academy, where a massive Rangers display is all you see the minute you walk through the doors to the store:

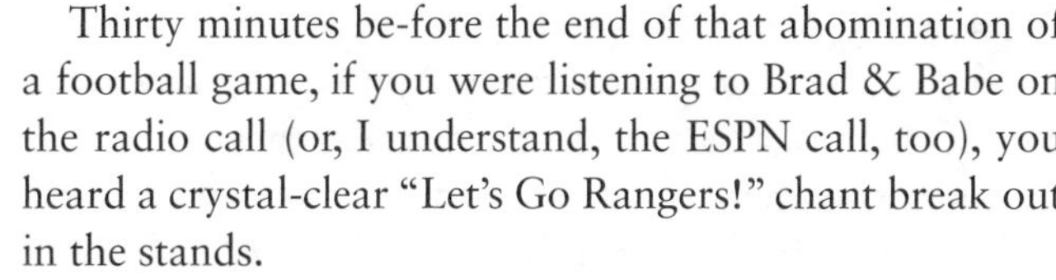

Thirty minutes be-fore the end of that abomination of a football game, if you were listening to Brad & Babe on the radio call (or, I understand, the ESPN call, too), you heard a crystal-clear "Let's Go Rangers!" chant break out in the stands.

Awesome.

Thirty minutes after the football game, you heard this week's barrage of excuses and weakness from the putative head coach, which only serves to reinforce how much I get fired up when I hear a Ron Washington press conference, an event of reliably (if sometimes recklessly) straight truth that, in the past month, for me, has elevated itself from "refreshing" to "galvanizing."

"We're here to whip their ass," said one of them yesterday.

"We're just not right on the right track," said the other recently. "It's just off kilter barely in those games that we've lost."

I think I now get it, far more than I ever did, as to why Ron Washington was the man for this job, and why Jon Daniels knew it.

That's one of the topics Ted Price, Adam Morris, and I explored last night as we recorded the latest edition of Rangers Podcast in Arlington. Ted should have the show uploaded sometime today. I'll give you a heads-up when that has happened.

One lowlight of the show was my lack of preparation for a lot of the World Series nuts and bolts that Ted wanted to discuss. My brain just isn't ready for what's about to happen.

There's already been a lot of very good writing and television about Rangers-Giants, and promises to be a ton more. Over the next seven or ten days the best baseball writers in the country turn their focus squarely on this team.

But I don't have it in me, not yet at least, to talk about roster decisions or lineup issues or how long I think this Series will go, and in whose hands the trophy gets raised.

I'm getting there, but last night during the podcast I was still struggling to get my baseball brain wrapped around Texas Rangers, San Francisco Giants, World Series.

Emotionally, I'm there, and have been since the Fifth Inning. But the part of me that's supposed to offer some sort of analysis, a fact or two to support a theory or to lay the foundation for a trend to keep an eye on, that part isn't ready to go to war. All of this is still a little too surreal.

Hopefully you've come not to expect much objectivity from me. But there will be some. There will. Soon enough I'll get buckled in and ready to roll, ready to bear down.

Listening to Wash helps.

So does the thought of Lincecum-Lee.

Wow.

Lincecum.

Lee.

I'm just about there.

October 27, 2010

The lead was 1-0, top of the seventh. Joey Votto swung at the first pitch of the inning, grounding out to Ian Kinsler.

Then Scott Rolen singled to center field. Matt Holliday singled to center field, too.

In came Matt Thornton, and he got Chris Young to pop out to first base. Thornton then got ahead of Marlon Byrd, and was one strike away from escaping the threat.

But Byrd battled back, and worked an eight-pitch base on balls.

With the bases loaded, up stepped Brian McCann. Thornton started him off with a strike, which McCann fouled off.

And then McCann laced a 98-mph fastball to right field, clearing the bases, with Byrd sliding in ahead of Kinsler's relay throw to the plate for the third run.

McCann's double gave his team a 3-1 lead that held up, breaking a 13-year National League All-Star Game losing streak.

And it's the reason I'm sitting here reviewing deposition transcripts in a hotel room in the Fisherman's Wharf district, rather than in my office in Dallas.

I've been writing about this team for more than 12 years now, and caring about it at an insane level for three times longer than that, and I need the assurance:

This is all going to start making sense in a little more than seven hours, at which point It will be Time.

The Texas Rangers, in seven games.

October 27, 2010

The Rangers have dropped left-handed reliever Clay Rapada from the World Series roster, adding right-handed reliever Mark Lowe in his place.

October 27, 2010

Control is not the same thing as command.

October 28, 2010: World Series Game One, San Francisco 11, Texas 7

From the early lead to the beatdown that followed, from the mistakes to the failure to capitalize on chances, last night's Giants win over the Rangers was similar in a number of ways to Monday's Giants win over the Cowboys.

But where Dallas plays with very little character, Texas has proven it has it in very deep supply, and that's why Wednesday's butt-whipping, while disappointing, doesn't bang my trust in this team.

The opener of the Yankees series, after the disastrous eighth, felt devastating. This one, a smackaround of the highest order, does not.

Cliff Lee was shockingly human. It crossed my mind that, given how unusually undominant he was, maybe he tweaked his back swinging the bat or sliding into third, but there's been no talk of that since the end of the game. He simply didn't have his breaking ball and got far too much of the plate too often, and San Francisco squared up a lot.

The unfortunate part is that Texas, despite squandering a huge opportunity to turn the first inning into something bigger, wasn't terrible against Tim Lincecum, but still couldn't come away with a win.

Eighteen runs (and 10 pitchers) in a game started by Lee and Lincecum just doesn't compute. I remember thinking, on our connection descent into Las Vegas at sunset on Tuesday evening, that the scene below looked like a pinball machine on tilt. That's what the Giants attack looked like last night. A couple bleeders down the right field line early, but lots of barreling up after that, particularly with two outs. I think I read that only one time all year did the Giants rack up that many extra-base hits. Nobody could have ever seen that coming, not in a game entrusted to Lee.

San Francisco did what Texas has done all post-season, jumping on opportunities, and the Rangers didn't do enough of that last night. And so, as a result, the Rangers need to win four out of six, but they're good enough to do it, and plenty resilient. Take Game Two behind C.J. Wilson, and Texas will have shifted home field advantage heading into Game Three in Texas on Saturday.

Because of the unusual sloppiness of Lee's start and the Rangers' defense last night, there's room for an argument that Texas let down a bit after the huge series win over the Yankees that got the club here. But we've come to know enough about this team that we need not worry that a bad loss could linger into the next game. The Rangers simply got their tails whipped, and that should have no bearing on Game Two, when the club can take advantage of its short memory, start with a clean slate as they did against the Yankees, and secure a two-game split to open this series.

October 28, 2010

According to multiple local and national reports, David Murphy will start in left field tonight, with Nelson Cruz sliding back over to right field and Vladimir Guerrero beginning the game on the bench.

October 28, 2010

Nothin'.
Nothin' in the morning, either.
Antlers in headlights.

October 29, 2010: World Series Game Two, San Francisco 9, Texas 0

OK, I'm fine now:
My team's in the World Series.
Just time to hold serve.

This Friday haiku thing is pretty stupid, and I knew it months ago. It was probably mid-season when I knew it had run its course (you were probably there long before that), but I wasn't about to cut it off, not during *this* season. Didn't want to jinx things. I'll give it up once 2010 is in the books. Not before that.

And I heard from *lots* of you last night, not commiserating but instead delivering the pep talk that in past years I've felt some sort of urge myself to deliver. Thank you for that.

I envy lots of things about this city I'm about to depart, heading back to Texas. There are things I envy about their amazing ballpark, too, but there's nothing that I envy more at this minute than the 2-0 lead the Giants now have over the Rangers. I think the Giants eighth surpassed the Mavs' fourth-quarter playoff meltdown against the Spurs years ago as the most deflating sports experience I've ever had, in a game that I still feel would have gone differently if Ian Kinsler's fifth-inning, 401-foot missile hadn't missed clearing the fence by a blister. Matt Cain (who I'd proposed trading Marlon Byrd, Eric Hurley, Omar Poveda, and Marcus Lemon for two years ago: bah) was brilliant, but C.J. Wilson was nearly as good, and if Texas had gotten that 1-0 lead . . . .

I'm hungry, real hungry. Sometimes that sucks, and it doesn't feel very good. But better, as a baseball fan, to be hungry on October 29 than dead.

I'll be in our House tomorrow, watching this team bounce back like it has a thousand times this year. It's the World Series, dammit, and 28 teams and the fans that care about them would trade places with us in a heartbeat.

Sorry for last night's postgame delivery, and for this silly haiku thing—but not really. I'm trying to keep up my end, to do what it takes to win, and the 5-7-5 every Friday was part of what got me back to the computer this morning, but less so than the dozens of emails I got from you all last night.

Let's go.

October 30, 2010

I wasn't really looking for an omen yet when I woke up at 5 a.m. on Friday, nor as I stood outside in the San Francisco dark and rain at 6 a.m. to grab a cab.

A taxi pulled up and I plopped into the back seat. Told the cabbie I needed to get to the airport. He turned his head back forward, and the front of his ballcap, which he was wearing backwards, swung around and stared me down.

We talked baseball for the next 20 minutes, and half of my mind that whole time was on 2004, as I stared at the Boston "B."

The Red Sox, before sweeping St. Louis in the World Series that year for their first title in 86 years, lost Game One of the ALCS to the Yankees, in New York. Ace Curt Schilling got drilled early, Boston managed to score some runs late, and the 10-7 Yankees win looked closer than it really was.

A lot like San Francisco 11, Texas 7 in Game One.

The Sox kept Game Two close but couldn't get anything going against Jon Lieber, failing to pick up their second base hit until the seventh inning. A close game that didn't feel that close. Final: New York 3, Boston 1.

Until the Rangers' eighth-inning bullpen disaster, a lot like the their Game Two loss to the Giants.

Boston had lost twice on the road to open the series. Lost Game Three at home, in fact, obliterated by a 19-8 score.

Won Game Four at home, in 12 innings.

Won Game Five at home, in 14 innings.

Won Game Six, back in Yankee Stadium.

Won Game Seven in Yankee Stadium.

I don't know if it's an omen, but it's recent history, and happens to be more than just precedent for a team to come back after dropping two post-season games on the road. Given where the Red Sox hadn't been in decades and looked like they weren't going to get once again, what they did in 2004 seemed even more impossible after falling down 0-2. More than just precedent. Maybe inspiration.

I got to the airport and boarded Flight 488 to Phoenix, where I'd connect on another flight to Dallas. Was the flight number a nod to number 48, Colby Lewis, going eight innings tonight? Or getting eight runs of support? Or Lewis and, somehow, Jorge Cantu (number 8) getting the most camera time at the end of a Rangers win?

Maybe the better omen is what Lewis (8-3-1-1-3-7) and Jonathan Sanchez (2-3-2-2-2-1) did in their respective teams' decisive LCS Game Sixes. Texas needs to be patient with the volatile Sanchez, who led the Major Leagues in walks in 2010 (doppelganger C.J. Wilson was second). And Lewis feels like the right guy to remind the Giants why they shouldn't be this confident at the plate.

A reader emailed me to report that a sports talk radio station in San Francisco was planning a parade on the air yesterday, convinced that when the Giants return home, it will be to celebrate, not to play baseball. Good. Very good.

Kevin Millar is part of MLB Network's studio show this morning, and I'm back to thinking about Boston in 2004.

The last time Colby Lewis pitched, some of you bristled at Minka Kelly's appearance in my gameday report, because, you said, no girlfriend of Derek Jeter should be counted on as a Rangers rally point. Nonsense. "Friday Night Lights," man.

She's now part of the cast of "Parenthood," which is set in San Francisco.

Fear the Rally Minka.

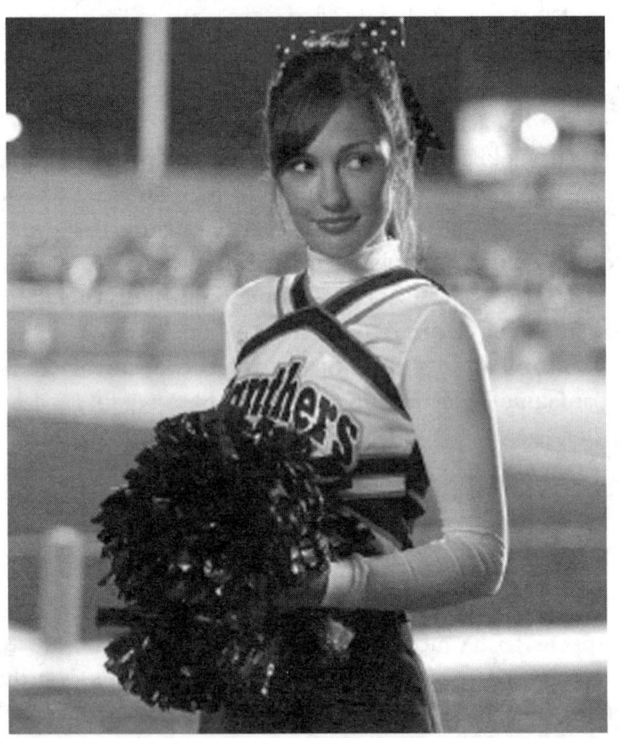

October 30, 2010: World Series Game Three, Texas 4, San Francisco 2

Three years ago he was the 530th player selected in the draft, in the 17th round.

Two years ago the Rangers experimented heavily with turning him into a pitcher, and in fact gave him the choice as to whether he wanted to make a wholesale career transition to the mound.

Four hours ago he had the greatest at-bat any Texas Rangers hitter has had in 2010.

Fastball up, ball one.

Curve upstairs, ball two.

Fastball inner half, destroyed into the upper deck in foul ground.

Fastball down and in, for called strike two.

Curve inside, fouled off.

Curve inside, fouled off.

Curve inside, fouled off.

Changeup down, fouled off.

And on the next 2-2 pitch, the ninth pitch of the at-bat, Mitch Moreland turned an 89-mph left-handed fastball around for a three-run, no-doubt bomb, a shot that won this game . . .

. . . in tandem with the man on the mound. The Rangers came into this post-season without a home playoff win in franchise history. They now have three.

All three belong to Colby Lewis.

Coming in each of the club's last three home playoff games.

After getting shafted in run support most of the season, Lewis hasn't needed much of it this month. Tack on his five innings of shutout ball in a no-decision against the Rays, and his post-season ERA now sits at 1.71, with a .176 opponents' average and 24 strikeouts in 26.1 innings.

While Moreland's at-bat was the greatest by a Ranger this year—and of course, a case can arguably be made that it was therefore the greatest in franchise history—Lewis may be the greatest off-season acquisition, all things considered, that any team in baseball made this past winter.

And if this thing ends up going seven, which lots of us predicted before the series got rolling, Colby Lewis will get the ball that Thursday night, presumably against Jonathan Sanchez.

On the omen subject, this morning I wrote this:

I got to the airport and boarded Flight 488 to Phoenix, where I'd connect on another flight to Dallas. Was the flight number a nod to number 48, Colby Lewis, going eight innings tonight? Or getting eight runs of support? Or Lewis and, somehow, Jorge Cantu (number 8) getting the most camera time at the end of a Rangers win?

He didn't go eight innings, but was basically one pitch away from doing it.

He didn't get eight runs of support, but he got eight hits, including a couple very big ones, and he made them stand up.

It wasn't Lewis and Cantu, but it *was* Lewis and the man who has made Cantu obsolete.

What a win.

Game Four Sunday night, Halloween.

I think we'll all be disappointed on level or another not to see some Rally Minka's in the crowd.

October 31, 2010

A few quick hits:

Colby Lewis started 26 of 30 Giants hitters off with strike one. Just tremendous.

The 22 Rangers hitters who faced Jonathan Sanchez—who led all Major League starting pitchers in opponents' batting average (.204) and was in the NL top 10 in strikeouts—swung and missed just three times.

That's as many swing-and-misses as Pat Burrell had in the first inning.

Nelson Cruz has 12 extra-base hits in the playoffs. That's the most by one player in one post-season in the history of Major League Baseball.

Alexi Ogando will be a huge factor tonight.

And Cliff Lee will make his final start of 2010 tomorrow night. Will it be his final start as a Texas Ranger?

Peter Gammons made a radio appearance on Boston's WEEI on Thursday:

As for the biggest name among the free agents—starting pitcher Cliff Lee—Gammons was short and to the point about his future.

"Cliff Lee is going to sign with Texas," Gammons said.

First things first, Big Game Hunter. Bring out that breaking ball, go as Colby Lewis for Halloween, and do your thing.

October 31, 2010: World Series Game Four, San Francisco 4, Texas 0

Cody Ross, Andres Torres, Aubrey Huff, Buster Posey, Edgar Renteria, Freddy Sanchez, Pat Burrell, Aaron Rowand, Travis Ishikawa, and Mike Fontenot.

Nelson Cruz, Ian Kinsler, Bengie Molina, Matt Moreland, Josh Hamilton, David Murphy, Elvis Andrus, Michael Young, and Matt Treanor.

And Matt Cain. And Cliff Lee.

All 21 of them have a higher OPS in the 2010 playoffs than Vladimir Guerrero.

I get that the manager trusts him. I get that he's a "cleanup hitter." I get that his teammates believe in and revere the guy, no matter what the numbers say.

I have no further comment. It's not as if he's lining into hard outs. What an awful, awful night for Big Bad, not exactly an aberration of late.

But that's not what I'm most disappointed about tonight, nor is it the loss of the Alexi Ogando to a strained oblique, though that sucked, nor is it the unfortunate lack of a putaway pitch in Tommy Hunter's arsenal (he didn't get spanked, but the barrage of spoiled two-strike pitches forced the bullpen into early action—the first pitch the Giants swung at and missed was Hunter's 72nd of the night).

Bottom line on that game is that Texas was flat shut down by a brilliant pitching performance. Tip of the cap to Mr. Bumgarner.

What disappointed me the most were some things that went on in the building tonight. I don't really want to elaborate right now.

Hey, I'm tired, too. The post-season can be draining, nerve-racking, tense. But c'mon.

Actually, I know this isn't the audience that should be directed to. It's the people who have enough disposable entertainment money to cross "World Series" off their bucket list, then play Solitaire on their cell phones starting in the second inning and leave the game in the seventh, sitting on their damn hands all the time in between. Those folks kept lots of you out of the ballpark tonight. They aren't on this mailing list and don't read Baseball Time in Arlington or Lone Star Ball.

But hey, they've now been to the *World Series*, man.

I don't know how we change the makeup of the 50,000-plus who will be in the stadium Monday night for Cliff Lee vs. Tim Lincecum. I wish I did.

But know this: It's the final game at Rangers Ballpark in Arlington in 2010, the greatest, most exciting season in franchise history.

We need to act like it.

ADDENDUM: I'm so badly not seeing straight about this that I called Mitch Moreland "Matt" in that last report, and left out that I'm sure that none of the 9,800 of you on this mailing list are either of the two people who barked at me tonight to "Sit down!"

It was by far the liveliest they got all night.

And I didn't sit down.

November 2010

40-MAN ROSTER (40)

Pitchers (20)

Scott Feldman, Neftali Feliz, Frankie Francisco, Rich Harden, Matt Harrison, Derek Holland, Tommy Hunter, Michael Kirkman, Cliff Lee, Colby Lewis, Mark Lowe, Doug Mathis, Dustin Nippert, Darren O'Day, Alexi Ogando, Darren Oliver, Zach Phillips, Clay Rapada, Pedro Strop, C.J. Wilson

Catchers (4)

Bengie Molina, Max Ramirez, Taylor Teagarden, Matt Treanor

Infielders (9)

Elvis Andrus, Andres Blanco, Jorge Cantu, Chris Davis, Esteban German, Cristian Guzman, Ian Kinsler, Mitch Moreland, Michael Young

Outfielders (7)

Julio Borbon, Nelson Cruz, Jeff Francouer, Craig Gentry, Vladimir Guerrero, Josh Hamilton, David Murphy

60-Day Disabled List (4)

Omar Beltre, Eric Hurley, Brandon McCarthy, Guillermo Moscoso

November 1, 2010

This comes from Chuck Greenberg.

This season has transcended expectations and transformed the psyche and hearts of legions of Rangers fans across Texas and throughout our country and beyond. At the core of the remarkable journey we have shared together is a ballclub and a community who collectively have consigned the conventional wisdom of the past to the dust bins of history, busting myths and charting a new course previously thought to be unattainable.

Can't pitch successfully in Rangers Ballpark. Wrong.

Can't compete successfully late in the season because the heat will break you down. Wrong.

Fans will lose interest when training camp opens. Wrong.

Fans won't come to Rangers Ballpark after the All Star break because it's too hot. Wrong.

Rangers can't win a playoff series. Wrong.

Rangers can't win a playoff game at home. Wrong.

Rangers can't beat the Yankees in the playoffs. Wrong.

Rangers can't get to the World Series. Wrong.

Rangers can't captivate the hearts and emotions of fans new and old deep into the fall. Wrong.

And on and on and on . . . .

I can't even begin to count the memorable moments we have shared this year thanks to a very special group of players with hearts and smiles as big as Texas, who always pull together, stand up for one another, and who have changed the sports landscape here in the Metroplex forever.

But here is a simple reality. Monday will be the last game played in Rangers Ballpark this year. We all owe it to ourselves, our players and each other, to celebrate with passion, enthusiasm and indefatigable belief from lineup cards to the final out, loud and proud.

The defining team of my young life was the 1979, "We are Family" Pittsburgh Pirates. I have often remarked how much this Rangers club reminds me of that team, with a confident but friendly swagger and an abundance of character and personality.

Now these two teams have something else in common. Both fell behind 3-1 in the World Series. Kent Tekulve, the great closer from the '79 Pirates, texted me after tonight's game to pass along this story. Before Game 5, Willie Stargell told his teammates:

"We are playing in front of the whole world. We may not win this thing, but before we go, let's show the world how the Pirates really play baseball."

The Pirates, playing against a team whose colors were black and orange, won Game 5. Then they returned to Baltimore and won Game 6. Then they won Game 7.

I know our players will show everyone how the Rangers play baseball tomorrow. As fans, let's do the same. We have one final opportunity this season to show the world what we have accomplished together and the passion we all hold for our players and our shared dreams.

The World Series is going back to San Francisco. And then there will be one final piece of conventional wisdom to prove wrong . . . .

Believe.

Chuck

(That last part was from me.)

November 1, 2010

I'm told by more than one of you that StubHub prices are falling for tonight's game.

Again: This is the final home game of the 2010 season. Cliff Lee is pitching.

It's the World Series.

This is an opportunity for us to amp the energy back up in our House tonight.

I'm invoking both Rally Minka and Dave Valle now, and suggesting that we can do our part tonight to send our team back to San Francisco, to push the resiliency envelope even further.

I know I don't need to say this to those of you who are on this mailing list, but man: Don't give up on 2010—not now.

November 1, 2010

According to at least one local report, the Rangers have deactivated righthander Alexi Ogando from the World Series roster due to a strained oblique muscle and have replaced him with righthander Dustin Nippert.

November 1, 2010: World Series Game Five, San Francisco 3, Texas 1

This one's gonna take a day or two to write. Bear with me. I love this team.

November 3, 2010

As I mentioned about a month ago, last year's Bound Edition ended, on page 322, before the release of any franchise marketing slogans for 2010, with the words: "It's time to win."

And that's what happened in 2010. Texas won.

There are 22 teams who have to go home after they play 162. Of the eight remaining teams, seven finish their season with a loss, with the one other team piling on each other in the middle of the field. There's only one team that gets to play on and then finish with a win, and if that's the definition of winning, nobody in baseball other than the San Francisco Giants won in 2010. But I will never define this Rangers season that way.

If you would have told me in March that the Major League season would end with Tim Lincecum facing off against Cliff Lee, I might have believed that.

But if you then added that the matchup would take place in Arlington—that one of those two pitchers would be Texas Rangers—(1) I would have doubted your mental stability and, (2) if convinced that you were on to something, I would have taken it in a second, regardless of whether the Rangers were the ones piling on, or watching the other guys pour out of the visitors' dugout like the rest of us and like the 28 teams whose season ended sometime in October.

Nolan Ryan said this three weeks ago: "Our goal is to get in the World Series and win the World Series, and if we fall short of that, we'll be disappointed. That's not to say we won't look back on the year and the postseason and feel good about what we accomplished, but we'll still feel like that we didn't finish what we wanted to do. So, if that were to happen, I think it would be motivation, obviously, to the organization and to the team itself to go to Spring Training next year with that goal in mind again."

And Jon Daniels said on a radio show this morning: "We didn't get it done. We need to get better. Let's figure it out."

Was Giants-in-Five disappointing? Absolutely. For a number of reasons.

But does that mean the Rangers didn't win in 2010? Absolutely not. They didn't Win, maybe, but they sure as hell won.

The final out of the season was recorded on our field. You gonna turn that down next year?

I sat in my seat for almost an hour after that final out Monday night, long after the friends I'd been at the game with had gone home. I didn't move. I watched San Francisco celebrate, I watched the Rangers in their dugout, some players leaning on the dugout rail, others slumped back on the bench, others gathering their equipment and shuffling off to the clubhouse.

I just watched. I have this habit, during games and immediately after the big ones, of honing in mentally on some things I want to write about. But I forced myself not to do that Monday night, as the grounds crew smoothed out the dirt around home plate for the last time this year. I tried to let it all sink in, and drain out. I felt eight months of mounting adrenaline receding, at last, leaving me exhausted.

The players talked in the Rays series about "emptying the tank," and that's how I felt Monday night, how I'm sure we all felt. The fuel that had carried me through 178 games that counted, 98 of them victories, was suddenly gone, even though hours earlier there seemed to be more than enough to carry me through another game, possibly two, as this resilient baseball team found itself once again in a corner.

And as I sat back, silent, still, watching the players in the road grays pull gray commemorative T-shirts over them, and replace their black and orange caps with those black commemorative lids that I wanted my team wearing when the final out of the final game was recorded, the tinny commotion of a hundred or two in the middle of the field started to get trampled by a chant coming from the fans who had stuck around. Right away, and again more than 30 minutes after the season had ended:

"*Let's Go, Rangers!*"

One last smile, and I got up from my seat one last time in 2010. I found myself surprisingly at peace.

It's never going to be like this again.

That's not to say this team is about to be broken up like the 1997 Marlins—or 2010 Rays—or that its core may have peaked like the 2006 Mavericks. But Texas could rattle off three World Series appearances in the next six years, and it will never feel like 2010. That's OK, but this is a season, however disappointing as the end was, we can't ever take for granted.

This was a year when the non-fan in the Metroplex became a casual fan. Casual became locked in. Locked in became hardcore. Hardcore became combustible.

Every one of us had ten times more people around us wanting to talk Rangers baseball these last few weeks. It's a proud time to be a Texas Rangers fan, because of what happened, and what's happening, both on and off the field.

This was the season that so many of you said to me in the last month that you wish you'd had with your Mom or Dad, and that your kids now will always have had with you.

Over the final five games, the Giants soundly beat Texas. They were the better team. This wasn't a World

Series that leaves us cursing an umpire or mourning a crushing error. The Rangers offense (which led baseball with a .276 team batting average this year) was flattened, hitting .190/.259/.288 for the Series—with much of that limited production coming in Game One, well after San Francisco already had that game in hand.

Texas hit .179 with runners in scoring position (while the Giants checked in at .405, capitalizing despite what was an overall .249 batting average—they collected 43 percent of their hits with two strikes and drove in 17 of their 29 runs with two outs). And the Rangers didn't create a lot of chances. They had one at-bat with a runner in scoring position in Games Four and Five combined—on Sunday, when Michael Young fanned to start the seventh, Josh Hamilton reached first on a Juan Uribe error, Vladimir Guerrero struck out, Nelson Cruz singled, and Ian Kinsler lined out to left field.

Not counting Cruz's home run late in the Series finale, the only two to reach third base in Games Four and Five were the two kids in the Steal-A-Base contest.

Guerrero's week was one big epic flail.

But he wasn't alone in his futility. Only ninth-place hitter Mitch Moreland hit over .250 (if you discount the 1-for-2 showings by Julio Borbon and Cliff Lee). Only Moreland reached base as much as a third of the time. Only Moreland slugged more than .450.

Texas scored five runs in the final four games of the Series.

But that's enough detail. The Giants were simply the better team over the last week. Are they the best team in baseball? The hardware and the *Sports Illustrated* commercials say yes. But they're a great example of what Ron Washington likes to say—that it's not a question, day to day, of who the best team is, but instead of which team plays the best baseball. That was San Francisco this week, hands down. I'd suggest the Giants aren't the best team in baseball, just as I'd concede that the Rangers weren't the best team in the American League over 2010—though they did play the best baseball in October, after earning the right to play in that month in the first place. And they did eliminate the two clubs that probably had the best claim to the "best team in baseball" label this year.

Considering the stack of adversity that Texas overcame in 2010, for this club to have been one of the final two standing defies reason.

The club's number one and number two starters were so ineffective that they not only lost their rotation spots but were left off the three playoff rosters, never even bubble candidates to make those squads.

The pitchers being counted to pick up the slack were a Japanese baseball export-import and a converted set-up man.

The starting catcher started one game.

The season-opening leadoff hitter and closer lost their jobs days into the season.

The five first basemen who appeared for Texas before Moreland arrived with two months left in the season hit a collective .199/.298/.310 for the year.

Kinsler missed a third of the season.

As did Cruz.

Hamilton missed less time than that, but at the worst time of the season, and even on his return was never close to 100 percent.

The deposed closer, who settled into the set-up role and was largely effective in it, missed the final five weeks of the season and the entire month of playoff games.

Elvis Andrus had an extra-base hit every 15.4 at-bats as a rookie in 2009. He had one every 32.7 at-bats in 2010.

Young made twice as many errors in 2010 as he did in 2009.

The targeted utility infielder (Khalil Greene) never showed up due to social anxiety disorder, leading to a parade featuring Gregorio Petit, Hernan Irribarren, Ray Olmedo, Esteban German, Arias, Cristian Guzman, Alex Cora, and, thankfully, Andres Blanco.

Cocaine. The manager.

Bankruptcy Court.

An inability to increase payroll through trade season.

But what Texas did in that trade season exemplified what this team did all year, in all phases. Backed up against a wall, handcuffed, dealing with roadblocks that no other team faced, Jon Daniels and his crew didn't resign themselves to a position of bystander and pulled off a July trade for the best available starting pitcher in the league, and acquired several other role players who helped in varying degrees.

Trade deadline deals pay off less often than you might think. The best mid-season pitching acquisitions over the last generation, based on immediate impact?

Rick Sutcliffe, Cubs, 1984.

Doyle Alexander, Tigers, 1987.

Larry Anderson, Red Sox, 1990.

David Cone, Blue Jays, 1992.

David Cone, Yankees, 1995.

Randy Johnson, Astros, 1998.

C.C. Sabathia, Brewers, 2008.

Cliff Lee, Phillies, 2009.

Cliff Lee, Rangers, 2010.

Pretty sure Texas was the only one of those nine teams whose expenditures were being controlled by Major League Baseball.

This front office is as resourceful as its players are resilient.

Lee lost twice in this World Series—his first two losses in 10 career post-season starts—but make no mistake: The Rangers would have made the playoffs without him, but wouldn't have won the pennant.

Was the Lee cutter that Edgar Renteria turned around Monday night for the decisive three-run home run the next-to-last pitch of Lee's career as a Texas Ranger? We don't know that yet. But we know Texas is going to fight for that not to happen.

Says Bob Simpson, one of the lead investors in the Greenberg-Ryan ownership group: "We're going to go after Cliff Lee—hard, and we have the financial firepower to do that. . . . And we'll do it within a model that's sustainable. The most important change for the Rangers is a model that's sustainable and not based on leverage or something that will jeopardize the long-term franchise. I don't know that it's ever had that before."

What did Lee—who misses his spots with his words about as often as with his pitches—have to say in the immediate aftermath of Monday night's season-ending loss?

"*We're* disappointed, but *we're* building something special here and *we* expect to be back here next year. . . . There's a lot to build on. *We* did a lot of firsts for this organization. *We* were the second-best team in the big leagues. *We* should be proud of that. *We're* going to use this as motivation and come in next year and try to do better."

Lots of first-person plural. Lots.

Then the qualifiers: "I like this team. It's a very fun team to play on. I expect this team to do some really good things next year. I don't know if I'm going to be a part of it or not. To be honest with you, I would love to be, but so many things can happen. You never know."

Go back to that day-of-trade press conference in July in Seattle, as Lee was getting set to face the Yankees—if he wasn't shipped to the visitors' clubhouse first—and you might recall what appeared to be disappointment, frustration, maybe even a little disillusionment over being convinced he was headed to New York only to be told he was going to Texas instead. Over the nearly four months since that time, Lee is either an extraordinary actor or a guy who has been won over by this organization and his teammates, and whose family might just view Texas as having a real edge on New York in both (1) proximity to their Arkansas home and (2) beer-throwing etiquette.

Said Lee just before the World Series: "I like it here. It's good for my family. There really couldn't be a better situation."

(For what it's worth, Joel Sherman of the *New York Post* writes this morning, while conceding that Lee "is everything [the Yankees] need," that they "are not motivated like they were with Sabathia," that they "are not as desperate now.")

This ownership group is used to going to war. This will be a different brand of battle, but it's going to be fascinating.

The success of 2010 wasn't only about Lee (which is of course a plus in terms of recruiting him to stay). Texas may have the best position player in baseball (notwithstanding his rough World Series). The best young closer. The best young shortstop. One of the best General Managers and baseball operations departments and ownership groups. One of the deepest farm systems.

And to the extent that we as fans can gauge this, one of the most effective managers in the game, if your measure is a man's ability to get the most out of his players and to set a tone of accountability, character, tenacity, and focus.

And, yes, resiliency and an aptitude for handling adversity.

The mental toughness of the manager and the third baseman define this team, and Cliff Lee appears to be right there with them. That's part of what gives me confidence that if the organization decides it can play ball with the Yankees in terms of the dollars it can offer Lee to stay here, the benefits will go far beyond what he can give the team every fifth day.

Said Young minutes after the final loss to the Giants: "Right now, this stings, obviously. To come so close to a world championship and fall short is a bitter pill to swallow.

"But we've established a different standard of expectations around here. We've built a great foundation. Now we know how good we can be and where we want to be."

Christina Kahrl of Baseball Prospectus wrote: "The present belongs to the Giants, but in the competitive dynamics of the present, it's easy to see how tomorrow more likely belongs to the Rangers."

You and I believed this time was coming, and very likely soon, but we'd have to admit that, even half a year ago, we didn't expect the World Series to arrive in Arlington before the Super Bowl. It's been an extraordinary year, one none of us will forget, one that came to an end Monday night and will be celebrated in the Rangers Ballpark parking lot tonight at 6:00. And the beauty of extending this season as long as Texas did is that, literally and otherwise, spring training is closer than it's ever been at season's end.

I don't know if there will ever be a more captivating, rewarding baseball season around here—I hope there is—and I know I wouldn't have enjoyed every minute of it as much without you guys. This baseball market has long been disparaged by the mainstream media, but we've always known what we are and what this could become.

And so, with this report, another book ends, this year's Bound Edition of the Newberg Report. But what it really is in the bigger picture is merely a chapter in a compelling story that's just getting started.

The great thing about this organization is that, coming off the disappointment of getting stomped on in its first-ever World Series appearance, this doesn't feel anything like a blown opportunity, a window that we allowed to slam shut on us.

No, the window here is just opening, opening wide, and given what the Texas Rangers accomplished in 2010, and with what this franchise has in place in every corner you look, there's a palpable confidence that, going into 2011 and well beyond that, with apologies to a spot-on and prophetic marketing campaign that will now be retired in favor of a new one, it is, unquestionably, still Time.

2010 Texas Rangers Draft

[**BOLD** denotes player signed by Rangers]

1. Jake Skole, OF, Blessed Trinity HS (GA) (scout: Coe)
1. Kellin Deglan, C, R.E. Mountain Secondary School (British Columbia) (McGraw)
1s. Luke Jackson, RHP, Calvary Christian Academy (FL) (Alvarez)
1s. Mike Olt, 3B, University of Connecticut (Heafner)
2. Cody Buckel, RHP, Royal HS (CA) (Guggiana)
3. Jordan Akins, OF, Union Grove HS (GA) (Coe)
4. Drew Robinson, SS, Silverado HS (NV) (Guggiana)
5. Justin Grimm, RHP, University of Georgia (Coe)
6. Brett Nicholas, C, University of Missouri (Smith)
7. Jimmy Reyes, LHP, Elon University (NC) (Kemp)
8. Jonathan Roof, SS, Michigan State University (Coryell)
9. Zach Osborne, RHP, University of Louisiana-Lafayette (Taylor)
10. Jared Hoying, OF, University of Toledo (OH) (Coryell)
11. Chris Hanna, LHP, Stratford HS (SC) (Kemp)
12. Josh Richmond, OF, University of Louisville (KY) (Lee)
13. Andrew Clark, 1B, University of Louisville (KY) (Lee)
14. Nick Tepesch, RHP, University of Missouri (Smith)
15. Ryan Rodebaugh, RHP, Kennesaw State University (GA) (Coe)
16. Ryan Strausborger, OF, Indiana State University (Lee)
17. Anthony Hasse, RHP, Cochise College (AZ) (Pratt)
18. Garrett Buechele, 3B, Oklahoma University (Eddings)
19. Brett Weibley, RHP, Kent State University (OH) (Coryell)
20. Sam Wilson, OF, Eldorado HS (NM) (Pratt)
21. Joe Van Meter, RHP, Virginia Commonwealth University (Matsko)
22. Ben Rowen, RHP, Virginia Tech University (Matsko)
23. Andrew Perez-Lobo, RHP, Christopher Columbus HS (FL) (Alvarez)
24. Jake Cole, RHP, Sahuaro HS (AZ) (Pratt)
25. Kendall Radcliffe, OF, Morgan Park HS (IL) (Lee)
26. Chase Johnson, RHP, Fallbrook HS (CA) (Flores)
27. Alexander Claudio, LHP, Isabel Flores HS (PR) (Thon)
28. John Kukuruda, RHP, East Nicolaus HS (CA) (Metzger)
29. Trae Davis, RHP, Mexia HS (TX) (Eddings)
30. Brian Ragira, OF, Arlington Martin HS (TX) (Eddings)
31. Justin Earls, LHP, University of Georgia (Coe)
32. Steve McKinnon, RHP, Cowichan Secondary School (British Columbia) (McGraw)
33. Matt Hill, LHP, Georgia Perimeter Junior College (Coe)
34. Kevin Rodland, SS, University of Nevada-Reno (Metzger)
35. John Lieske, RHP, Harlem HS (IL) (Lee)
36. Jason Kudlock, OF, Cal State Bakersfield (Guggiana)
37. John Pustay, OF, Pine Creek HS (CO) (Pratt)
38. Carson Vitale, C, Creighton University (NE) (Smith)
39. Ryan Woolley, RHP, University of Alabama-Birmingham (Wood)
40. Travis Meiners, OF, Dallas Baptist University (TX) (McAbee)
41. Colby Killian, RHP, Emporia State University (KS) (Smith)
42. Kevin Johnson, LHP, University of Cincinnati (OH) (Coryell)
43. Chris Roglen, OF, Rocky Mountain HS (CO) (Pratt)
44. Shawn Stuart, RHP, Merced Junior College (CA) (Metzger)
45. Johnathon Moore, C, Houston Baptist University (TX) (Fagg)
46. Daryl Norris, RHP, Fairhope HS (AL) (Wood)
47. Daniel Ward, RHP, Garfield Heights HS (OH) (Coryell)
48. Forrest Koumas, RHP, Lugoff-Elgin HS (SC) (Kemp)
49. Juan Gomes, C, Miami Southridge HS (FL) (Alvarez)
50. Trevor Teykl, RHP, Kempner HS (TX) (Taylor)

About the Author

12 About Jamey Newberg

THE LONGHORNS CRUSHED JAMEY'S DREAMS OF PLAYING BASEBALL PAST HIGH SCHOOL. TWICE.

Twitter
@NewbergReport

- ★ Jamey is a trial lawyer in the Dallas office of the law firm of Vincent Lopez Serafino Jenevein, P.C.
- ★ This is the 12th year that Jamey has published the Bound Edition of the Newberg Report.
- ★ The Newberg Report goes to over 10,000 email subscribers and has been featured in countless print and Web publications as well as on numerous local and satellite radio stations and television programs.

www.NewbergReport.com

Brad Newton